A FIRST LOOK AT COMMUNICATION THEORY

A FIRST LOOK AT
COMMUNICATION THEORY

SECOND EDITION

EM GRIFFIN
Wheaton College

McGRAW-HILL, INC.

New York St. Louis San Francisco Auckland Bogotá Caracas
Lisbon London Madrid Mexico City Milan Montreal New Delhi
San Juan Singapore Sydney Tokyo Toronto

This book is printed on acid-free paper.

A FIRST LOOK AT COMMUNICATION THEORY

This book is printed on acid-free paper.

Credits and Acknowledgments appear on pages 502–504, and on this page by reference.

67890 DOC/DOC 99876

ISBN 0-07-022796-9

This book was set in Palatino by Better Graphics, Inc.
The editors were Hilary Jackson and Jean Akers;
the designer was Rafael Hernandez;
the production supervisor was Louise Karam.
R. R. Donnelley & Sons Company was printer and binder.

Library of Congress Cataloging-in-Publication Data

Griffin, Emory A.
    A first look at communication theory / Em Griffin.—2d ed.
        p.   cm.
    Includes index.
    ISBN 0-07-022796-9
    1. Communication—Philosophy.   I. Title.
P90.G725   1994
302.2'01—dc20   93-14515

ABOUT THE AUTHOR

Em Griffin is Professor of Communication at Wheaton College in Illinois, where he has taught for the past twenty-three years and has been chosen Teacher of the Year. He received his bachelor's degree in political science from the University of Michigan, and his M.A. and Ph.D. in Communication from Northwestern University. His research interest centers on the development of close friendships.

Professor Griffin is the author of three applied communication books: The *Mind Changers* analyzes practical techniques of persuasion; *Getting Together* offers research-based suggestions for effective group leadership; and *Making Friends* describes the way that quality interpersonal communication can build close relationships. He also speaks and leads workshops on these topics in the United States, Singapore, and the Philippines. Professor Griffin's wife, Jean, is an artist. They have two adult children, Jim and Sharon.

CONTENTS

PREFACE FOR INSTRUCTORS

This text is for students who have no background in communication theory. It's designed for undergraduates enrolled in entry-level courses. In the past, many departments reserved systematic coverage of communication theory for a capstone course or senior seminar; communication theory texts were addressed to a sophisticated audience. Now the trend in the field is to offer a broad introduction to theory early in a student's program. *A First Look* is written for that beginning student.

The aim of the book is to present thirty-four specific theories in a way that makes them both interesting and understandable. By the time readers complete the book they should have a working knowledge of theories that explain a wide range of communication phenomena. Like most teachers, my ultimate goal is to help students pull together the various parts of the communication process into a unified whole. The first section helps students know how to spot a good theory, and the final section starts the process of synthesis by comparing and contrasting the theories according to the choices their authors have made. But before students can integrate the leading ideas in our field, they need to have a clear understanding of what the theories are. The bulk of the book provides that raw material.

Balance as a Guide in Theory Selection   The process of deciding which approaches to include has been both enjoyable and difficult. More than one-hundred professors submitted lists of theories that couldn't be left out. Not surprisingly, there was great disagreement. Some respondents requested theories that have historical significance for the field, others wanted students to focus on the latest developments. Many instructors urged a social science outlook, but others preferred a humanistic perspective. Most teachers emphasized their particular area of interest—interpersonal communication, rhetoric, organizational communication, linguistics, mass communication. I've tried to achieve a balance by selecting a wide range of theories that reflect the diversity of the discipline.

Some are classics. Twenty-five centuries ago Aristotle analyzed the effectiveness of a message by the speaker's logical, emotional, and ethical appeals.

Those categories continue to set the agenda for many public-speaking courses today. In the mid-twentieth century, Shannon and Weaver's model of information transmission popularized terms like channel capacity, information loss, feedback, and noise. These concepts shaped the next decades of communication inquiry. And just as a book about all-time baseball greats is incomplete if it omits controversial Ty Cobb, so it's foolish to consider theories of persuasion without discussing Festinger's theory of cognitive dissonance. At least half of the theories selected are proven candidates for a Communication Theory Hall of Fame.

It would be shortsighted, however, to limit the selection to the classics of communication. Some of the discipline's most creative approaches have only recently emerged. The amount of discussion over Petty and Cacioppo's elaboration likelihood model (ELM) indicates that it is becoming a standard in the field. Although less well known, Baxter's dialectical perspective is a powerful explanation of the ongoing tensions that threaten personal relationships.

Purists may be uneasy at the mention of theories not generated by communication scholars, but disciplinary boundaries are drawn for college catalogs, not for the pursuit of knowledge. Truth is truth whether discovered in a psychology laboratory, derived from sociological field observation, or culled from the creative mind of a rhetorical critic. The final selection was made on the basis of communication insight rather than solely on the academic background of the theorist.

Organizational Plan of the Book Each chapter introduces a single theory in about ten pages. Instructors who teach a three-hour semester course or a four-hour course offered in a quarter system can cover the material by assigning a chapter per class. I've found that most undergraduates think in terms of discrete packets of information, so the coverage-in-depth approach gives them a chance to focus their thoughts while reading a single assignment. This way students can gain a true understanding of important theories rather than acquire only a vague familiarity with a confusing jumble of related ideas. The one-chapter–one-theory arrangement also gives teachers the opportunity to drop theories or rearrange the order of presentation without damaging the fabric of the text.

The opening three chapters describe the function of theory, sketch the history of theory development in the field of speech communication, and suggest criteria for a good theory. I then present the thirty-four theories featured in the book. Each theory is discussed within the context of a communication topic: verbal messages, nonverbal messages, self-concept, motivation, perception, relationship development, relationship maintenance, influence, decision making, organizational communication, public rhetoric, media and culture, media effects, intercultural communication, gender and communication. These sections usually contain two or three theories. Each section has a brief introduction that outlines the crucial issues theorists address and places the subsequent chapters within that context. The placement of theories in familiar categories helps the student recognize that theories are answers to questions they've been asking all along.

Because all theory and practice have value implications, I've added a section on the ethics of communication. I also raise ethical questions throughout the text. The term *theory* when applied to ethics refers to normative principles of conduct, so an ethical theory must be judged on its assumptions, consequences, and internal consistency. Other disciplines may ignore these thorny issues, but to discuss communication as a process that is untouched by questions of good and bad, right and wrong, or virtue and vice would be to disregard an ongoing concern in our field.

Features of Each Chapter   Most people think in pictures. Students will have a rough time understanding a theory unless they apply its explanations and predictions to concrete situations. The typical chapter uses an extended example to illustrate the "truth" a theory proposes. Readers are encouraged to test different theorists' ideas by visualizing a first meeting of freshman roommates; trying to mend a broken relationship through a three-minute long-distance phone call; responding to conflict in a dysfunctional family; working in a Mom-and-Pop business that has been bought out by an impersonal, "bottom line" corporation; persuading a fearful airline passenger that flying is safe; raising funds to combat third-world hunger; considering the effects of heavy television viewing on violent behavior; and lying to avoid hurting a friend. I also use motion pictures such as *When Harry Met Sally* and *Children of a Lesser God* to illustrate the principles of the theories. The case study in each chapter follows the pedagogical principle of explaining what students don't yet know in terms of ideas and images already within their experience.

Some theories are tightly linked with a well-known piece of research. Festinger's $1.00/$20.00 cognitive dissonance experiment, Bandura's "Bobo doll" study of modeled aggression, and Janis's groupthink interpretation of the Bay of Pigs decision are three examples of theories closely tied to empirical data. When such an exemplar exists, I describe the research in detail so that students can learn and appreciate the benefits of grounding theory in systematic observation. Although the book is not intended to be a text on research procedures, readers of *A First Look* are exposed throughout to a variety of research designs and methods of data analysis.

I hope this book is merely a student's *first* look at communication theory. Most readers will encounter the names of Berger, Baxter, Burgoon, Pearce, Cronen, Watzlawick, Gudykunst, Fisher, Burke, Hall, and many others in subsequent studies. I therefore make a concerted effort to link theory and theorist. Since the works of the theorists selected have been extended or altered by subsequent research, major developments are catalogued in the later part of the chapter. But linking a particular theory with its originator promotes both recall and respect for a given scholar's effort.

The text of each chapter concludes with a section critiquing the theory. This represents a hard look at the ideas presented in light of the criteria for a good theory outlined in Chapter 3. I usually provide a brief summary of a theory's strengths—the author's ideas wouldn't have been included unless many in our field found them helpful and stimulating. But given the beginning student's natural acceptance of traditional wisdom, the critiques focus on the weaknesses, unanswered questions, and possible errors that still remain. I try to stimulate a "That makes sense, but . . ." response within the student.

I include a short list of thought questions after the text of each chapter. Labeled "Questions to Sharpen Your Focus," these probes encourage students to make connections between ideas in the chapter and also to apply the theory to their everyday communication experience. I find that the questions make a good starting point to stimulate class discussion. The words printed in italics also remind students of the key terms of a given theory.

Every chapter ends with a short list of readings entitled "A Second Look. . . ." The heading refers to resources for students who develop an interest in a theory and want to go further than a ten-page introduction allows. Each reference is annotated with a phrase that identifies its focus. Unlike typical endnotes, these books and articles are neither alphabetized nor sequentially placed to document every assertion in the text. The top item is the resource I recommend as the starting point for further study. Other bibliographic listings identify places to look for material on each of the major issues raised within the chapter. The format is designed to offer practical encouragement and guidance for further study without overwhelming the novice with multiple citations. The sources of quotations are listed in a Notes section placed at the end of the book.

I believe you and your students will get a good chuckle out of the cartoons that illustrate the text. But the decision to use cartoon art was based on more than mere enjoyment. Perceptive cartoonists are modern-day prophets. Their work often slips through mental barriers or attitudinal defenses that didactic prose can't penetrate. The cartoons displayed were selected from a pool of over 15,000 drawings. I was committed to using "Calvin and Hobbes," "The Far Side," "Cathy," and quality art from the pages of *The New Yorker* and *Punch* magazines. I use a cartoon only when I believe it illustrates a major point in the text without further comment or explanation.

While no author considers his or her style ponderous and dull, I believe I have presented the theories in a clear and lively fashion. Accuracy alone does not communicate. I've tried to remain faithful to the vocabulary that each theorist uses so that the student can consider the theory in the author's own terms, but I also translate technical language into more familiar words and terms. Students and reviewers cite readability and interest as particular strengths of the text. I'd encourage you to sample a chapter dealing with one of the more difficult theories so you can decide for yourself.

New Features of the Second Edition   Although I've retained the features that students appreciate in *A First Look at Communication Theory*—writing style, short chapters, extended examples, cartoons—I've made a number of changes in response to consistent requests from instructors who teach the communication theory course. The most obvious change is the addition of ten new theories:

1. I. A. Richards' meaning of meaning
2. Walter Fisher's narrative paradigm
3. Roland Barthes' semiotics
4. Judee Burgoon's nonverbal expectancy violations model
5. Charles Berger's uncertainty reduction theory
6. Leslie Baxter's dialectical perspective
7. William Gudykunst's anxiety/uncertainty management theory
8. Stella Ting-Toomey's face-negotiation theory
9. Deborah Tannen's genderlect styles
10. Cheris Kramarae's muted group therapy

Reviewers asked for expanded coverage in twentieth-century rhetoric, nonverbal communication, intercultural communication, and gender and communication. Eight of the ten theories I've added in this edition speak to these issues. Instructors in speech communication departments were also hopeful that I would add more theorists who work and write within our discipline. Seven of the ten theorists listed above are active communication scholars. Most of them spent hours with me on the phone or in person to help me make sure that I caught the substance and the flavor of their ideas.

I have updated the majority of the chapters that appeared in the first edition and rewritten paragraphs that students found confusing. Two chapters received major overhauls; Pearce and Cronen's coordinated management of meaning and McLuhan's technological determinism have been totally restructured.

From my standpoint, the most significant change in the book is the extensive discussion of scientific and humanistic scholarship that provides an integrative framework for the student. Chapter 1 (Talk about Theory) contrasts the epistemology, ontology, goals, and research methodology of the sciences and humanities. Chapter 2 (Talk about Communication) outlines the history of both academic approaches since the founding of speech communication departments. Chapter 3 (Weighing the Words) presents separate sets of criteria for evaluating scientific and humanistic theories. The final chapter of the book (Order Out of Chaos) revisits these issues and offers four options for dealing with the divisions in our discipline. The emphasis of the book continues to be on a comprehensive understanding of individual theories, but now students will have an easier time seeing relationships between the ideas of different theorists. The new "Questions to Sharpen Your Focus" feature also fosters integrative thinking.

Acknowledgments   I gratefully acknowledge the wisdom and counsel of the generous people who have helped me complete this project. I'm particularly thankful to Glenn Sparks at Purdue University for many years of advice and support for the entire project. Glenn helped develop the mass communication section. Linda Putnam at Texas A & M University graciously invested many hours so that I might gain an understanding of organizational communication. Her colleague Martin Medhurst provided a welcome perspective on rhetorical criticism. Larry Frey at Loyola University in Chicago was particularly helpful in developing the overview presented in the first three chapters. The unselfish assistance of these scholars gives fresh meaning to the term *collegiality*.

Many other communication professionals helped shape the final product. Bradford 'J' Hall (University of Wisconsin–Milwaukee) expanded my knowledge of intercultural communication, Diana Ivy (North Carolina State University) helped me understand major issues in gender and communication, Cliff Christians (University of Illinois) guided my investigation of ethical theory, while Ed Appel (Conestoga Valley High School) directed my study of Kenneth Burke. Al Goldberg (Denver University), Leland Griffin (Northwestern University), Bob Husband and Thomas Duncanson (University of Illinois), Sandy Alcorn (Dean of Social Work, Aurora University), and David Myers (Psychology, Hope College) offered critiques of individual chapters, as did my colleagues at Wheaton—Lynn Cooper, Mark Fackler, Myrna Grant, Ed Hollatz, and Gary Larson. Gary also invested many hours helping me create the index at the back of the book. Wheaton student Kate Dykstra first suggested using *When Harry Met Sally* to illustrate Deborah Tannen's genderlect theory. Ron Adler at Santa Barbara City College and Russ Proctor at Northern Kentucky University are the recognized leaders in our field in the use of feature films to illustrate communication principles, and they shared their expertise freely in helping me compile Appendix B.

A number of speech communication scholars reviewed the manuscript for McGraw-Hill's first edition of the text: Rusalyn H. Andrews, Blackburn College; Richard N. Armstrong, Wichita State University; Richard Bartone, William Patterson College; W. Steven Brooks, Northern Kentucky University; Randall Bytwerk, Calvin College; Stanley Deetz, Rutgers University; Kent G. Drummond, University of Wyoming; Samuel Edelman, California State University, Chico; Marjorie Fish, St. Cloud State University; Kenneth D. Frandsen, University of New Mexico; Susan Jarboe, Pennsylvania State University; Lenore Langsdorf, Southern Illinois University, Carbondale; Susan Mackay-Kallis, Villanova University; Charles Self, University of Alabama, Tuscaloosa; Richard L. Stovall, Southwest Missouri State University; Sharon Strover, University of Texas, Austin; Sari Thomas, Temple University; Carol Ann Valentine, Arizona State University; David Whillock, Texas Christian University; and Michelle Wolf, San Francisco State University. I'm grateful for their comments and questions, which invariably stimulated further research and a deeper understanding of communication theory. I particularly want to thank Thomas Socha of Old Dominion University and Charles Roberts of Eastern Tennessee State University for their line-by-line insights and extensive suggestions that went far beyond what any author has a right to expect. Charlie has continued his enthusiasm for the project and has created the excellent instructor's manual that goes with this text.

A number of communication theory instructors "field tested" the first edition of this book in their classrooms and then provided extensive reviews. Their comments had a significant impact on the choices I made for this edition and provided a humbling reminder that we are all beginners in the evolving field of communication theory. My thanks goes to George A. Borden, West Chester University; David Bullock, Walla Walla College; Jerry Butler, University of Arkansas, Little Rock; John S. Caputo, Gonzaga University; Leda Cooks, Ohio University; Robert T. Craig, University of Colorado, Boulder; Harold Drake, Millersville University; Roger L. Garrett, Central Washington University; Betsy Gordon, McKendree College; Ray Gozzi, Jr., Bradley University; Craig Johnson, George Fox College; Robert McPhee, University of Wisconsin, Milwaukee; Michael A. Netzley, Albion College; Richard Olsen, Radford University; James Rosene, University of South Alabama; Wallace V. Schmidt, Rollins College; David Schuelke, University of Minnesota; John Sherblom, University of Maine, Orono; Milt Thomas, St. Olaf College; Richard A. R. Watson, Chapman University; and Keith Williamson, Wichita State University.

I have been fortunate to have Hilary Jackson as my sponsoring editor at McGraw-Hill almost from the beginning of the project. Hilary shares my vision of a text accessible to the beginning student and continually encourages me to reach out to this reader. Her warm professionalism is a constant reminder of why I chose McGraw-Hill to publish the book. My editorial supervisor, Jean Akers, has proved unflappable as she has calmly transformed my manuscript, figures, cartoons, and notes into the book you are reading. Alice Jaggard did a superb job of copy editing, protecting me from inconsistencies of thought, grammar, and citations, but not changing my "voice" in the process. I am also thankful to my friend Bob Goldsborough, a features editor at *Advertising Age*, who worked through the original manuscript—just "for fun."

Without the help of my research assistant, Mary Michael, this revised edition would still be "in press." She ran computer searches, designed figures, looked up quotations, obtained permissions, and was uncanny at spotting fuzzy thinking that was masked by ambiguous pronouns or embedded in the passive voice. Mary is a superb writer and editor in her own right; when she signed off on a chapter I knew I could submit it with confidence.

Finally I want to recognize the continued understanding and loving encouragement of my wife, Jean. Her sense of humor throughout the project has served both of us well.

EM GRIFFIN

A FIRST LOOK AT
COMMUNICATION
THEORY

PART ONE

Overview

INTRODUCTION

INTRODUCTION

This is a book about theories—communication theories. After that statement you may already be stifling a yawn. Many college students, after all, regard all theory as obscure, dull, and irrelevant.

People outside the classroom are even less charitable. An aircraft mechanic once chided a professor: "You academic types are all alike. Your heads are crammed so full of theory you wouldn't know which end of a socket wrench to grab. Any plane you touched would crash and burn. All *Ph.D.* stands for is 'piled higher and deeper.' "

The mechanic may be right. It's ironic, however, that in order to criticize the study of theory, he used his own implicit theory of scholastic ineptness. Whether or not we recognize our ideas and assumptions as theories, we can't avoid using them in our daily lives.

The creators of theories examined in this book disagree with the mechanic's view of theory as being trivial and useless. Along with Kurt Lewin, one of the founders of modern social psychology, they believe that there's nothing as practical as a good theory. Perhaps an example from a theory you already know will back up this claim.

Theories Make Life Better. Consider the following situation. Jan is watching the late-night news on a local TV station and is anxious to hear the weather forecast. She's getting married the next day and has planned an outdoor garden reception. On the chance that it might rain, she has lined up a banquet room at a restaurant as a backup. But she must let the manager of the restaurant know by midnight whether or not she'll use the room. What's it to be? Inside or outside?

A smiling meteorologist tells her to expect a sunny day tomorrow with a high in the mid-eighties, but with a slight chance of thundershowers. Jan is encouraged, but over the years she has grown skeptical of anything the weather forecasters have to say. She thinks they should spend less time looking at their instruments and more time looking out the window. Yet at this point she wants more clues about the next day's weather, so she switches to the cable weather channel to listen to a more detailed weather report.

The cable channel's meteorologist points to a current weather map. The predominant feature on the map is a grey, saw-toothed crescent 200 miles to the northwest. The forecaster refers to it as a "fast-moving cold front backed by a high-pressure system." Jan is tempted to tune out the technical jargon, but with only an hour left to call in her decision to the restaurant manager, she listens intently to the meteorologist's explanation of the cold frontal weather system.

As the meteorologist continues the forecast for the following evening, Jan notes that the jagged line has passed over to the southeast. Having followed the words closely, she sighs with relief, cancels the banquet room, and tells her fiancé that any rain will be over by noon. It may be a bit breezy at the reception, with the temperature dropping into the seventies, but no one should get wet.

Jan made her decision solely on the basis of theory. There was no actual buzz saw ripping its way toward her hometown. The map was simply a model of the weather occurring over thousands of square miles. She placed her confidence in a well-tested theory regarding the movement of air. There's about a

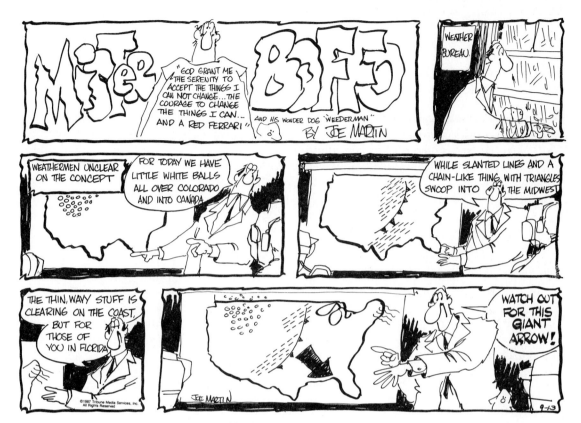

Reprinted by permission: Tribune Media Services.

90 percent chance she's made the right decision.

Only in this century have the weather-wise thought in terms of air masses with sharp leading edges. Before that, everyone had assumed that cold and warm air blended together like water from two faucets mixing in a basin. During World War I, a perceptive man named Vilhelm Bjerknes suggested that instead of merging, distinct masses of air collide like armies along a battlefront, with the weaker mass retreating before the greater force. At that moment, weather forecasting took a giant step toward becoming a science.

A working knowledge of cold fronts can ensure that Jan and her guests stay dry at the wedding reception. But let's face it, weather won't offer Jan much wisdom on how to de-

velop a solid relationship with her husband. However, a number of communication theories covered in this book could be helpful to Jan once the honeymoon is over.

For example, symbolic interaction theory describes how Jan's reaction to her husband will operate as a self-fulfilling prophecy that affects his self-image. When their family system is lopsided because of power struggles, the interactional view offers advice on how to reestablish the equilibrium by reframing the situation. Uncertainty reduction theory claims that the more Jan discovers about her spouse, the more comfortable she'll be with not knowing everything he thinks or does throughout the day. Dialectic theory highlights the ongoing tension the couple will feel trying to balance their twin desires for intimacy and independence. Finally, Deborah Tannen's theory of gender differences in communication style confirms that communication patterns in her marriage will be normal, if not entirely satisfying. (She hopes she's marrying a "big ear" who will listen sympathetically in times of trouble, but her husband may feel compelled to give advice on how to fix the problem.) We see, therefore, that air mass theory can help Jan have a good wedding; communication theory might help her have a better marriage.

A Guide to the Communication Scene. Theories are maps of reality. The truth they depict may be objective facts "out there" or subjective meanings inside our heads. Either way, we need to have theory to guide us through unfamiliar territory. In that sense, this book of theories is like a scenic atlas that pulls together thirty-four must-see locations. It's the kind of travel guide that presents a close-up view of each site. After using the atlas to visit a number of places, you might want to pursue a more in-depth study of a particular theory. But the first step is simply to see and appreciate the view.

This atlas of theories charts the key features of the communication process. The chapters in Part I introduce you to the nature and scope of the field. These chapters are like a satellite photo of the earth—they give you a panoramic view of the communication process.

Following the introductory chapters, we examine the actual turf. Each chapter presents a single theory to help you focus on individual theories one at a time.

The chapters are organized into six major parts: messages, intrapersonal communication, interpersonal communication, group and public communication, mass communication, and cultural communication. The part on messages is first because it deals with ver-

bal and nonverbal symbols—the raw material of communication. After that, theories are categorized according to the primary context in which they operate. Since theories are tentative answers to questions that occur to people as they mull over specific communication situations, it makes sense to group these theories according to the different communication settings that prompt the initial questions.

The part on intrapersonal communication concentrates on an individual's inner dialogue. Theories in the interpersonal cluster consider one-on-one interaction. The next collection of theories deals with face-to-face involvement in group and public settings. The mass communication part pulls together theories that explore the effects of electronic and print media. The final part focuses on culture, a communication context so pervasive that we often fail to realize its impact.

This organizational plan is like having six separately indexed file cabinets. Although there is no natural progression from one part to another, the plan provides a convenient way to classify and retrieve the thirty-four theories. The scheme also lends itself to a further division into common topical concerns. For example, the intrapersonal part splits into sections on self-concept, motivation, and perception. As with most file systems, there's a certain arbitrariness to the assignment of the theories, so be open to the possibility of cross-filing a theory under another part or section.

Since communication isn't a value-free activity, I've added a section on the ethics of communication. To deal with human intercourse as a mechanical process apart from values would be like discussing sex using ground rules that prohibit any reference to love. When applied to ethics, the term *theory* may mean something different than it does for the topics that go before, so I'll suggest special criteria for evaluating theories about communication ethics when we consider that topic.

The final chapter compares and contrasts theories according to their basic assumptions. Theories about communication share some common features, but there are also important distinctions that need to be acknowledged. Once you understand the theories, you'll be able to make connections and spot the differences.

Hints for Reading. The book usually introduces more than one theory within a topic area. For example, the section on verbal messages presents three quite distinct views of how words work. Don't assume that one has to be true and the others false. Rather, they all help explain communication behavior. Just as there is more than one effective way to deliver a speech, so every communication issue has multiple interpretations. Each may be legitimate.

You'll also find a consistent effort to link each theory with its author. It takes both wisdom and courage to successfully plant a theoretical flag. In a process similar to the childhood game king-of-the-hill, as soon as a theorist builds a theory of communication, critics try to pull it down. That's okay because truth is discerned by survival in the rough-and-tumble world of competitive ideas. But the survivors deserve to have their names associated with their creations.

There is a second reason for tying a theory to its author. Many of you will do further study in communication, and a mastery of names like Mead, Delia, Berger, Fisher, and Burke will allow you to enter into the dialogue without being at a disadvantage. Ignoring the names of theorists could prove to be false economy in the long run.

Don't discount the importance of the questions at the end of each chapter, either. They are there to help you sharpen your focus on key points of the theory. The questions can be answered by pulling together information from the text, and in some cases, from the text of your life. The italicized words highlight terms that you'll need to know in order to understand the theory.

I've included cartoons for your learning and pleasure. A cartoonist can illustrate a feature of the theory in a way more memorable than a few extra paragraphs. In addition to enjoying them, you can use the cartoons as minitests of comprehension. If you can't figure out why a particular cartoon appears where it does, consider the possibility that you don't completely understand the theory, and make a renewed effort to grasp the theorist's idea.

Some students are afraid to try. Like travelers whose eyes glaze over at the sight of a road map, they have a phobia about theories that seek to explain human behavior. I sympathize with their qualms and misgivings, but the theories in this book haven't dehydrated my life or made it more confusing. On the contrary, they add clarity and provide a sense of competence as I communicate with others. I hope they do that for you.

CHAPTER 1

Talk About Theory

I met Glenn Sparks and Marty Medhurst my first year as a teacher at Wheaton College. Glenn and Marty were friends who signed up for my undergraduate persuasion course. As students, both men were interested in the broadcast media. After graduating from Wheaton, both went on for master's degrees at Northern Illinois University. They each earned doctorates at separate universities, and both are now nationally recognized communication scholars. Glenn is on the faculty at Purdue University; Marty is at Texas A & M University.

Despite their similar backgrounds and interests, Glenn and Marty are radically different in their approaches to communication. Glenn calls himself a behavioral scientist, while Marty refers to himself as a rhetorician. Glenn's training was in empirical research; Marty was schooled in the humanities. Glenn does science; Marty does art.

Glenn and Marty represent two distinct perspectives within the field of communication theory. Ernest Bormann, a theorist at the University of Minnesota, refers to *communication theory* as an "umbrella term for all careful, systematic and self-conscious discussion and analysis of communication phenomena."[1] I like this definition because it's broad enough to include the different kinds of work that both Glenn and Marty do, and it also covers the diverse theories presented in this book.

To help you understand the theories ahead, you need to first grasp the crucial differences between the scientific and humanistic approaches to communication. As a way to introduce the distinctions, I asked Glenn and Marty to bring their scholarship to bear on a contemporary communication phenomenon—a television commercial.

SCIENCE OR ART: TWO LOOKS AT CINDY

Pepsi-Cola has long sought to position itself as the soft drink choice of young adults. In 1990 the company redesigned its Pepsi and Diet Pepsi cans to reinforce a youthful image. *Advertising Age* selected Pepsi's television spot heralding this change as one of the best commercials of 1991. I'll quote a portion of Bob Garfield's column in that publication to set the scene and then present Glenn's and Marty's separate perspectives on the ad.

SULTRY CINDY SAUNTERS INTO PEPSI'S PORTFOLIO
by Bob Garfield

Simultaneously smoldering and insouciant, she emerges from the gull-wing door of her Lamborghini Diablo like Venus on the half-shell. It is Cindy Crawford, the super-model, in a spot for Pepsi-Cola Co., and she has just pulled up to the Halfway Cafe.

We are way out in the country, at the crossroads of astonishing loveliness and transcendent sexuality. Watch her as she ambles sleekly across the dusty parking lot. . . .

Crawford is after the soda machine which she plugs to get a cold Pepsi, and commences refreshing herself. With her head rared back and her eyes closed, her simple act of sucking down a soft drink is an erotic tour de force. In the annals of TV-commercial cola chugging, this will remind no one of Mean Joe Greene.

The remoteness of the venue is part of the mystique, but nonetheless Crawford is not alone. There are witnesses to this scene: two 10-year-old boys, behind the cafe, just beyond a wood and chickenwire fence. Their attention is diverted as the car rumbles up, and they move close to get a better look at a thing of beauty. Their mouths are agape from the start.

By the time Crawford grabs the soft-drink can (emblazoned with Pepsi's new label graphics), they are pulled forward still more—as if by magnetism—and but for the music track, the '60s standard "Just One Look," you would surely hear them gasp.

Only after Crawford is done chugging can one of the kids finally summon words, a rhetorical question posed with palpable awe in his voice: "Is that a great new Pepsi can, or what?"

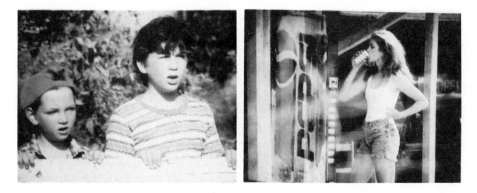

FIGURE 1.1
Two Boys and Cindy Pepsi-Cola Commercial

Then a cut back to Crawford and an arch voice-over: "Introducing a whole new way to look at Pepsi and Diet Pepsi." Then back again to the second boy and his concurring, innocent, prepubescent appreciation: "It's beautiful."[2]

Glenn: A Scientific Perspective

As a behavioral scientist, I want to understand the causes of human behavior. My first step is to come up with a theory that provides a compelling understanding of how television affects what people think, feel, and ultimately do. A good theory of media effects will accurately predict viewer response to a broad range of commercials and programs. Several scientific theories make accurate predictions about such media effects.

One such theory is that of classical conditioning, which relies upon the principle of paired association. You may remember from your psychology class that Pavlov's dogs salivated when an experimenter displayed a piece of meat and rang a bell at the same time. Soon the animals began to associate the food with the sound of the bell and started to lick their chops whenever they heard it ring—even in the absence of food.

The Cindy Crawford ad pairs the stimulus of a beautiful woman with the new style of Pepsi can. The theory of classical conditioning suggests that a male experiencing sexual attraction for the model on TV will connect these positive feelings with the sponsor's product. (Maybe he'll automatically start to drool when he sees the can on the shelf at his local 7-Eleven store.) By comparing measures of sexual arousal with subsequent purchases of Pepsi, researchers could gather evidence to support or reject the theory of classical conditioning.

The thirty-second commercial could also be used to test Dolf Zillmann's excitation transfer theory, which proposes that arousal of any kind can intensify the feelings that are experienced immediately afterwards. For example, the Crawford spot might be aired on the six o'clock evening news. According to excitation transfer theory, men who are "turned on" by the sexy model would respond to the following news story under the sway of this heightened emotion. Thus, a viewer's normal, positive feeling to a mildly encouraging account of Arab-Israeli relations now feels like the emotional high that might come from the outbreak of peace on earth. But that same stimulated viewer might also feel totally depressed when hearing an account of unemployment that would otherwise seem merely discouraging.

The important thing to note about these theoretical explanations is that the ad is only one small part of a more global testing endeavor. Scholars with a nonscientific orientation might produce rich descriptions and interpretations of this Pepsi commercial, or the social-political context in which it was produced. But the value of such an analysis may fade away when the ad is no longer shown. As a social scientist, I'd like to help discover general principles of human behavior that will continue to predict people's responses long after I've disappeared from the face of the earth.

Marty: A Humanistic Perspective

The creative department of Pepsi's advertising agency has made a number of conscious choices in producing the minidrama that unfolds at the Halfway Cafe. The set design, lighting, color, motion, dialogue, camera angle, editing, sound, and spatial relationships employed by the director invite us to participate in a common meaning. My task as a rhetorical critic is to discern Pepsi's seeming intent and to develop a compelling interpretation of the events displayed on the screen.

I see the Cindy Crawford commercial as a classic example of selling a product through the use of myth. Myths are ritualized patterns of story elements that recur throughout history. The narrative or mythos of this ad is the loss of innocence or coming of age.

The story begins with two naive boys engaged in youthful play. Their type of fooling around is the antithesis of the leering louts who ogle the Swedish Bikini Team in another beverage commercial. The boys move unself-consciously within a state of nature where birds sing, the dogwood blooms, and time seems to stand still. This idyllic pastoral scene is interrupted by the arrival of the breathtakingly beautiful Cindy Crawford—the ultimate woman of sophistication in her designer sunglasses and luxury technocar.

The sponsor's basic strategy is to associate the product with the object of desire. The colors of the can are reflected in the woman's blue shorts, white top, and red car. The camera caresses her body in the same way it plays over the soft drink container. The woman and her Pepsi are inseparable—she presses the can to her lips, hugs it to her breast.

As the woman consumes the drink, the boys consume her. Their eyes widen with their newly acquired forbidden knowledge. Just as Pepsi propels Cindy to her destination, so her secrets propel the boys to manhood. To be a man is to get close to the woman, which is to drink Pepsi. For the young-adult male target audience, drinking Pepsi is "going all the way."

I have tried to unmask the coming-of-age meaning that is offered by Pepsi-Cola. Other humanist critics might read the text in a different way. Feminist critics, for example, might focus on the voyeuristic nature of the ad, while Marxist critics might articulate the capitalistic strategy of desire that prompts people to want what they don't need. These multiple interpretations are evidence that human behavior is more complex than a simple cause-effect model would suggest. Scholars who claim they can predict viewer response ignore the fact that human beings have the capacity to choose their own meanings.

Although Glenn and Marty agree that the Pepsi commercial identifies the new look of its product with the stunning good looks of Cindy Crawford, their respective scientific and humanistic approaches to communication theory are obviously distinct in starting point, method, and conclusion. The separate world views of the arts and sciences reflect contrasting assumptions about ways of arriving at knowledge, the core of human nature, the very purpose of theory, and how to do research. The rest of this chapter sketches these differences.

WAYS OF KNOWING: DISCOVERING THE TRUTH VS. CREATING MULTIPLE REALITIES

How do we know what we know, if we know it at all? This is the central question addressed by a branch of philosophy known as *epistemology*. You may have been in school for a dozen plus years, read assignments, written papers, and taken tests without ever delving into the issue, What is truth? With or without in-depth study of the issue, however, we all inevitably make assumptions about the nature of knowledge.

Scientists assume that truth is singular. There's one reality "out there" waiting to be discovered through the five senses of sight, sound, touch, taste, and smell. Of course, no one person can know it all, but individual researchers pool their findings and build a collective body of knowledge about how the world operates. Scientists are confident that once certain principles or "truths" are discovered, they will continue to be recognized as truths down through the ages. They see good theories as mirrors of nature, as models of a reality that won't change until conditions change.

As a behavioral scientist, Glenn works hard to maintain his objectivity. He is a man with strong moral and spiritual convictions, but he doesn't want his values to distort human reality or confuse what *is* with what he thinks *ought to be*. He shares the academic commitment of Harvard sociologist George Homans to let the evidence speak for itself: "When nature, however stretched out on the rack, still has a chance to say 'no'—then the subject is science."[3]

Humanists, on the other hand, assume that people create their own multiple meanings. Reality is not a thing waiting to be found, but an interpretation of events which takes place in the mind of each individual, and that meaning varies according to the person, time, and place.

As a humanist, Marty believes that all meaning is subjective. We can never separate the knower from what is known. Marty is aware of his own ideology and consciously brings his values to bear upon the communication text under scrutiny. Rhetorical critics are successful when they convince others to share their interpretation of the way the text works.

HUMAN NATURE: DETERMINISM VS. FREE WILL

One of the great debates throughout history revolves around the question of human choice. Hard-line determinists claim that every move we make is the result of heredity ("biology is destiny") and environment ("pleasure stamps in, pain stamps out"). Free will purists insist that every human act is ultimately voluntary ("I am the master of my fate; I am the captain of my soul"[4]). Although few communication theorists are comfortable with either extreme,

most tend to cluster into one of these two camps. Scientists thus stress the forces that shape human behavior, while humanists focus on conscious choices made by individuals.

The difference between these two views of choice inevitably creeps into the language people use to explain their actions. Individuals who feel like puppets on strings say, "I *had* to . . . ," while people who feel that they pull their own strings say, "I *decided* to. . . ." The first group speaks in a passive voice: "I was distracted from studying by the argument at the next table." The second group speaks in an active voice: "I stopped studying to listen to the argument at the next table."

In the same way, the language of scholarship often reflects theorists' views of human nature. Behavioral scientists usually describe human conduct as occurring *because of* forces outside the individual's awareness. The explanation makes no appeal to mental processes or any kind of inner life, seeing behavior instead as a result of stimulus-response bonds.

In contrast, humanists tend to use phrases like *in order to* or *so that* since they attribute behavior to conscious intent. Their choice of words suggests that a person might decide to respond differently under an identical set of circumstances. For example, Marty would hold that an adolescent viewer could allow himself to be turned on by the sight of Cindy the first time he saw the Pepsi commercial but laugh at the two naive boys the second time around.

Human choice is therefore problematic for the behavioral scientist, because as individual freedom goes up, predictability of behavior goes down. Conversely, the roots of humanism are threatened by a highly restricted view of human freedom. In an impassioned plea, British author C. S. Lewis exposes the paradox of stripping away people's freedom and yet expecting them to exercise responsible choice:

> In a sort of ghastly simplicity we remove the organ and expect of them virtue
> and enterprise. We laugh at honor and are shocked to find traitors in our
> midst. We castrate and bid the geldings be fruitful.[5]

THE PURPOSE OF THEORY: UNIVERSAL LAWS
VS. RULES FOR INTERPRETATION

Even if Glenn and Marty could agree on the nature of knowledge and the extent of human autonomy, their words would still sound strange to each other because they use distinct vocabularies to accomplish different goals. As a behavioral scientist, Glenn is working to pin down universal laws of human behavior that cover a variety of situations. As a humanist, Marty is working to articulate the unique rules individuals use to interpret a novel event.

If these two scholars were engaged in fashion design rather than research design, Glenn would probably find or tailor a coat suitable for many occasions that covers everybody well—one size fits all. Marty might apply principles of fashion design to cut out a suit that makes a statement for a single client—a one-of-a-kind, custom creation. Glenn constructs and tests. Marty interprets and applies.

Theory testing is the basic activity of the behavioral scientist. Glenn starts with a hunch about how the world works, and then crafts a tightly worded hypothesis that temporarily commits him to a specific prediction. He can never completely "prove" that he has made the right gamble; he can only show in test after test that his behavioral bet pays off. Prediction and control are the name of the game.

The humanist explores the web of meaning which constitutes human existence. Marty isn't trying to prove theory. Instead, he uses theory to interpret the written, spoken, and nonverbal texts of people's lives. As knowledgeable human agents, people have reasons for the "truth" they create. These reasons are usually grounded in long-term tacit agreements with others about how a person ought to think, feel, or behave. The humanist scholar deciphers and frames the personal rules that shape the meaning individuals create. Interpretation and understanding are the goals of rhetorical critics.

RESEARCH METHODS: EXPERIMENTS, SURVEYS, TEXTUAL ANALYSIS, ETHNOGRAPHY

Whether the quest is for prediction and control, or for interpretation and understanding, scholars in pursuit of theory know that the task demands research. A leading textbook on research methods in our field is entitled *Investigating Communication: An Introduction to Research Methods.*[6] The authors distinguish four primary techniques for the study of communication. Experiments and survey research offer quantitative ways for the scientist to test theory. Textual analysis and ethnography provide qualitative tools that aid the humanist's search for meaning. I'll briefly describe the features of each method. After you read these brief sketches, take a look at Figure 1.2, which gives you some questions to ask as you read about a study of communication that uses one of these four methods.

1. Experiments

Working on the assumption that human behavior is not random, an experimenter tries to establish a cause-and-effect sequence by systematically manipulating a variable (called the independent variable) in a tightly controlled situation to see its effects on another variable (called a dependent variable). For example, Glenn suggested showing the Cindy Crawford commercial to a panel of men as a way to determine the effect of pairing a sexual stimulus with the soft drink product. For purposes of comparison, he could show a nonerotic Pepsi ad to a similar group. To make certain that he had successfully manipulated the independent variable of physiological arousal, he might use lab equipment to monitor sweaty palms and the heartbeat of each subject.

After the ads were shown, Glenn would then measure each group's expressed desire for Pepsi in the new can—on attitude scales, through taste tests, or by actual consumer behavior in the store. The theory of paired association gains added support if the turned-on viewers respond more favorably to the sponsor's product than do those exposed to the nonerotic ad.

2. Surveys

Using questionnaires or interviews, survey researchers rely on self-report data to discover what people think, feel, or intend to do. Before committing the Pepsi-Cola company to a multi-million-dollar changeover, the market research division of the company undoubtedly conducted a survey of consumer response to the new can design.

Survey methodology also helps scientists validate theory. For example, a researcher might question a representative sample of male shoppers who purchased six-packs of cola the week following the ad's introduction during the 1992 Super Bowl. A positive relationship between men's vivid recall of the ad and their report of an uncharacteristic choice of Pepsi over Coke would give credence to the paired association hypothesis of classical conditioning. Of course, there's no guarantee that their purchase wasn't affected by prime shelf display or discount pricing. It's difficult to prove cause-and-effect relationships from correlational data. Yet unlike a highly controlled laboratory experiment, a well-planned survey gives the social scientist a chance to get inside the heads of people in a "real-life" situation. There's less rigor than in an experiment, but more vigor.

3. Textual Analysis

The aim of textual research is to describe and interpret the characteristics of a message. You may have noticed from Marty's analysis of the Pepsi ad that the word *text* is not limited to written materials. Communication theorists use this term to refer to any intentional symbolic expression—verbal or nonverbal. Marty's critique is a contemporary example of the oldest tradition in communication research—the intensive study of a single message grounded in a humanistic perspective. Rhetorical criticism is the most common form of textual analysis.

A growing number of humanist scholars aren't content merely to interpret the intended meanings of a text. They want to expose and publicly resist some of these messages. These critical theorists—whether feminists, Marxists, or others with strong value commitments—seek to enlighten and emancipate people who may unknowingly get sucked into the "irresistible" meanings offered by those who control the channels of communication.

Lana Rakow, a feminist scholar in the Communication Department at the University of Wisconsin—Parkside, would have us consider the plight of women watching the Pepsi portrayal. Women can't escape the portrayal of Cindy Crawford as the erotic ideal—"the object of men's fetishistic gaze."

> The viewer must first produce . . . a sexist meaning before she can reject it. By then, it could be argued, it is too late. The viewer had to participate in the sexist meaning, even if against her will.[7]

For Rakow, and other critical theorists, advertising is the linchpin of oppression that needs to be resisted by those who are aware that television

EXPERIMENTAL RESEARCH

How precise are the *hypotheses*? Is each a clearly worded, simple, single cause-effect prediction?

Are the hypotheses *interesting* or are they self-evident?

Were subjects *randomly assigned* to the experimental groups? Did everyone studied in the experiment have an equal chance of being assigned to the different experimental conditions?

Was the *manipulation* of the independent variable "life-like" enough to allow the researcher to generalize the findings beyond the confines of this particular experiment?

Were *important extraneous variables* that may confound the findings controlled for? Might the findings be due to *other events* that occurred between the time subjects experienced the independent variable and when they were measured on the dependent variable?

SURVEY QUESTIONNAIRE AND INTERVIEW RESEARCH

Is there a *response bias* in the sample? Could there be differences between those who participated and those who did not? Was the *response rate* sufficient for the purposes of the research?

Was the *choice of a questionnaire or an interview* appropriate for answering the research questions posed?

Were the *questions worded* clearly and *leading* questions avoided?

Were respondents guaranteed *anonymity*?

Did the interviewers receive sufficient *training*? Did they *probe* effectively?

TEXTUAL ANALYSIS: RHETORICAL CRITICISM

Were the most *appropriate texts* selected for analysis?

Is the researcher sure that the texts selected are *complete* and *accurate*? What might be left out of these texts, and how might any omissions affect the results?

What type of *rhetorical criticism* was it: historical, Neo-Aristotelian, generic, feminist, metaphoric, narrative, dramatistic, fantasy theme analysis?

Did the critic produce a *compelling argument* about the meaning of the text?

In the final analysis, did the essay produce a *richer understanding of human persuasion*?

ETHNOGRAPHIC RESEARCH

What justified observation or interviews as the *appropriate methods* to use? Were the observations conducted *on-site*, where people are communicating *naturally*?

Did the observers *exhaustively record* all the communication behavior related to the research questions?

Are the findings described in *sufficiently rich and vivid detail* (a "thick description") so the reader may visualize the communication behavior observed and the context in which it occurred?

What assurances are provided that inferences are grounded in the data, not imposed or biased by the researcher's *a priori* assumptions?

Do the article's *findings* "put you in the respondents' shoes," so that you now have a better sense of how people in the group being studied act, think, speak and/or react to others?

FIGURE 1.2
Twenty Questions to Guide Evaluation of Four Research Methods (Selected from Frey, Botan, Friedman, and Kreps, *Interpreting Communication Research: A Case Study Approach.*)

imposes meaning on the viewer. This form of textual analysis isn't a detached and impartial enterprise; it is a powerful tool in the service of a reformist agenda.

4. Ethnography

In the 1990 Academy Award-winning film *Dances with Wolves,* Kevin Costner plays John Dunbar, a nineteenth-century Army lieutenant alone on the Dakota plains.[8] Amidst some anxiety and with great tentativeness, he sets out to understand the ways of the Sioux tribe that is camped a short distance away. He watches carefully, listens attentively, appreciates greatly, and slowly begins to participate in the tribal rituals. He also takes notes. That's ethnography!

Princeton anthropologist Clifford Geertz says that ethnography is "not an experimental science in search of law, but an interpretive (approach) in search of meaning."[9] As a sensitive observer of the human scene, Geertz is loath to impose *his* way of thinking onto a society's construction of reality. He wants his theory of communication grounded in the meanings that people within a culture share. Getting it right means seeing it from *their* point of view.

Most people have long regarded New York advertising as a world unto itself. A communication researcher could view the Pepsi commercial as an artifact of this particular subculture and seek to understand the web of meaning surrounding the creation of this and other television spots. An ethnographer would look for the Madison Avenue rites, ceremonies, rituals, myths, legends, stories, and folklore that reflect the shared meanings and values of the advertising industry. Perhaps Pepsi-Cola's agency, BBDO Worldwide, New York, would welcome an intern who is willing to assume a participant-observer role for a period of six months.

A LOOK AHEAD: SURVIVING AND THRIVING IN THE THEORETICAL TENSION

In this opening chapter I have tried to outline some important differences between scientific and humanistic views. While some communication theorists have a foot in both camps and their ideas don't fit neatly into one category or the other, the thirty-four theories featured in the book are split about evenly between the arts and sciences. A basic grasp of the distinctions will help you understand where a group of like-minded scholars are going and why they've chosen a particular path to get there.

You can't have read this far without realizing that a certain wariness exists between those who do science and those who do art. Glenn and Marty sometimes have trouble appreciating each other's scholarship. In their case, it's a creative tension that causes each man to expand his academic horizon.

In other instances, advocates of the two traditions have lobbed academic Scud missiles in each other's direction. Chapter 2 chronicles how this conflict has influenced the study of communication. This historical summary will help you understand why two professors in the same department may be a bit cautious in each other's presence.

Chapter 3 presents standards by which to judge the quality of scientific and humanistic theories. I think Glenn and Marty each perform their theoretical tasks in a quality way. Chapter 3 lays out criteria to evaluate both types so that you can make up your own mind.

QUESTIONS TO SHARPEN YOUR FOCUS

1. Compare Glenn Sparks' and Marty Medhurst's approaches to analyzing the Pepsi commercial. Which analysis makes the most sense to you? Why?

2. How do the *scientific* and *humanistic* approaches to the question, What is *truth*? differ? Which perspective is most satisfactory to you?

3. Think of the communication courses you've taken. What perspective undergirded the teaching? Was this due to the subject matter or the professor's orientation?

4. How do scientists and humanists differ in their views of *experiments, surveys, textual analysis,* and *ethnography* as research methods?

A SECOND LOOK

Recommended resource: Ernest Bormann, *Communication Theory*, Sheffield, Salem, Wisc., 1989, pp. 105–256.

Contemporary empirical study: Charles Berger and Steven Chaffee, *Handbook of Communication Science*, Sage, Newbury Park, Calif., 1987.

Contemporary rhetorical study: Sonja Foss, Karen Foss, and Robert Trapp, *Contemporary Perspectives on Rhetoric*, 2d ed., Waveland, Prospect Heights, Ill., 1991.

Attack on interpretive scholarship: Robert Bostrom and Lewis Donohew, "The Case for Empiricism: Clarifying Fundamental Issues in Communication Theory," *Communication Monographs*, Vol. 59, 1992, pp. 109–129.

Research methods: Lawrence R. Frey, Carl H. Botan, Paul G. Friedman, and Gary L. Kreps, *Investigating Communication: An Introduction to Research Methods*, Prentice-Hall, Englewood Cliffs, N.J., 1991.

Encyclopedia: International Encyclopedia of Communications, Vols. 1–4, Oxford University, New York, 1989.

Intermediate-level text: Stephen Littlejohn, *Theories of Human Communication*, 4th ed., Wadsworth, Belmont, Calif., 1992.

Intermediate-level text: Sarah Trenholm, *Human Communication Theory,* 2d ed., Prentice-Hall, Englewood Cliffs, N.J., 1991.

Intermediate-level text: Dominic Infante, Andrew Rancer, and Deanna Womack, *Building Communication Theory,* 2d ed., Waveland, Prospect Heights, Ill., 1993.

Introduction to the field: Frederick Williams, *The New Communications,* 3d ed., Wadsworth, Belmont, Calif., 1992.

Scientific scholarship: Glenn Sparks, "Understanding Emotional Reactions to a Suspenseful Movie: The Interaction Between Forewarning and Preferred Coping Style," *Communication Monographs,* Vol. 56, 1989, pp. 325–340.

Humanistic scholarship: Martin J. Medhurst, *"Hiroshima, Mon Amour:* From Iconography to Rhetoric," *Quarterly Journal of Speech,* Vol. 68, 1982, pp. 345–370.

CHAPTER 2

Talk About Communication

Communication is a hard term to define. Most definitions probably say more about the author than they do about the nature of communication.

Consider, for example, the different views of two theorists you will read about in the Verbal Messages section. Engineer Claude Shannon takes a scientific approach: "Communication is the transmission and reception of information."[1] Philosopher I. A. Richards worked from a humanistic perspective: "Communication is the generation of meaning."[2] Although not contradictory, neither definition speaks to the concerns that are voiced by the other theorist.

Because the field of communication embraces both scientific and humanistic views of the world, I choose to adopt a definition that doesn't favor one approach over the other. I like the definition given by Lawrence Frey, Carl Botan, Paul Friedman, and Gary Kreps in their research methods text. These writers define communication in a way that describes the essence of the process without being biased against any particular way of examining the subject:

> Communication is the management of messages for the purpose of creating meaning.[3]

This broad definition regards communication as an intentional activity, while not ruling out accidental outcomes. It gives equal weight to messages and meanings and opens the door for studying both content and relationships. The limits of the field are set sufficiently wide by this definition to include verbal and nonverbal symbols and to justify the study of intrapersonal communication—the internal messages we send to ourselves. In other words, the definition describes what communication scholars have really studied.

Folk wisdom suggests that we don't know who we are unless we know where we've been. We need to grasp a bit of our field's history before we can understand what the theorists in this book are trying to accomplish. The rest of this chapter provides that historical backdrop.

The first line of the song "Time," sung by the Alan Parsons Project, declares that "Time keeps flowing like a river."[4] Because a single river may contain many tributaries and more than one current, this stream-of-events metaphor captures nicely the history of communication theory and research. Chapter 1 focused on the twin currents of science and humanism. These diverse viewpoints surfaced in communication studies early in the 1900s, and the arts and sciences have ebbed and flowed within the discipline ever since.

All history is an interpretation of past events. I've identified seven significant historical periods of communication theory, research, and instruction during this century—a time in which the flow of communication study has swelled from a trickle to a flood. But don't be surprised when you see that the dates for the seven periods often overlap. Like the stages of a river's course, these periods are hard to separate.

THE EARLY YEARS (1900–1950): THE RISE OF RHETORIC

In the early 1900s, college speech teachers were members of English departments. Speech teachers stressed oral performance and were often looked down upon as "poor cousins" by those who studied and taught literature. In an attempt to gain respect and to carve out an academic discipline for themselves, a small group of speech teachers broke away from the National Council of Teachers of English in 1914 and formed the National Association of Academic Teachers of Public Speaking. (Even teachers of speech had a tough time pronouncing the acronym, NAATPS.) The name of the organization was later changed to the Speech Association of America (SAA). Although some speech teachers continued to occupy back offices in English departments, by 1935 more than 200 American college and university catalogues listed a separate department of speech.

The first issue of this new discipline's journal, the *Quarterly Journal of Public Speaking,* called for NAATPS members to have "a sufficiently scientific frame of mind,"[5] and a subsequent article stated that the main goal of the organization was to help members "undertake scientific investigation to discuss true answers to certain questions."[6] But for most speech professionals, this early tip of the hat to science seems to have been a concern for academic respectability within the university rather than a drive to discover laws of oral effectiveness. Other than the specialized study of speech disorders, such as stuttering and vocal strain, the scientific perspective didn't have a major impact on the field until after World War II.

During these early years, speech departments offered courses that gave practical advice to those trying to influence audiences through public address, oral interpretation of literature, radio announcing, drama, debate, and round-table discussion. Teachers drew on a body of wisdom from Greek and Roman times—the writings of Plato, Aristotle, Cicero, and Quintillion were the authoritative sources for instruction in public address.

As for scholarly research, a 1925 essay by Herbert Wichelns of Cornell University established rhetorical criticism as *the* appropriate theoretical activity of the field. He wrote that unlike the critical study of literature, the analysis of public address

> is not concerned with permanence, nor yet with beauty. It is concerned with effect. It regards a speech as a communication to a specific audience, and holds

its business to be the analysis and appreciation of the orator's method of imparting his ideas to his hearers.[7]

Wichelns' work established Aristotle's categories of logical, emotional, and ethical appeals as the standard way to evaluate persuasive discourse. This neo-Aristotelian method of speech criticism dominated the field for the next few decades. Rhetoric was an *art*, and for the majority of speech teachers, who had been schooled in the humanities, the scientific study of public address with its quantitative methodology seemed silly and trite. As for the rhetorical analysis of radio, film, or television, these media were dismissed as forms of entertainment which didn't have the importance of a formal political address or the public discussion of issues.

COMMUNICATION AND SOCIAL SCIENCE (1930–1960): MEDIA EFFECTS

Prior to World War II, few scholars referred to their work as "communication research." Those who did used the term to describe the scientific study of media effects, and they worked out of departments of sociology, psychology, political science, and journalism rather than within the field of speech. Rhetoricians had ignored the entertainment media, but many community leaders and parents wanted to know whether the new technologies of film, radio, and television were having a bad effect on their kids.

The Payne Fund, a charitable trust, sponsored the first concentrated effort to find out how the broadcast media influenced their mass audiences. This series of studies compared the moviegoing habits of children in the early 1930s with a host of variables that might show ill effects—lower grades in school, negative emotions, loss of prosocial attitudes, sleep loss, delinquency, declining popularity with friends, and many more. Were the movies a bad influence? Not surprisingly, the answer was, "It all depends. . . ."

Today we remember the Payne Fund studies not for their earthshaking results, but for their historical role in the field of communication research. The multiple measures and sophisticated analysis of this series of studies set the stage for the work of four men who came to be known as the "founding fathers" of communication research, even though all of them entered the communication discipline from other academic fields.

One of the founding fathers, political scientist Harold Lasswell, analyzed the content of propaganda to determine why it had a powerful effect upon those who heard it. He broke the communication process into five component parts: *Who* says *what* through *which channel*, to *whom*, with *what effect*. The apparent success of Nazi propaganda in the 1930s provided a context and a sense of urgency to his research.

Kurt Lewin was a social psychologist who had escaped Hitler's holocaust. His special concern for democracy led him to investigate ways for group members to make well-thought-out decisions and to lead discussions of issues.

Sociologist Paul Lazarsfeld founded the Bureau of Applied Social Research at Columbia University as a way of getting business and government funding. He would test his current theories by applying survey techniques to whatever marketing problem required an answer.

Finally, through his Yale attitude change studies, experimental psychologist Carl Hovland tested the persuasive effects of source credibility (believability in a speaker) and the order of arguments within a message.

The four founding fathers took a behavioral science approach to the effects of persuasive messages upon mass audiences. Their research was theory-driven, and they sought to be objective—not letting their personal values influence the conclusions they reached.

In a 1959 article entitled "The State of Communication Research," University of Chicago social scientist Bernard Bereleson declared that communication research was "withering away."[8] That was because each of the four famous researchers had retired, died, or abandoned communication research. Bereleson's assessment proved overly pessimistic because a number of younger members of the speech communication profession seized upon the scientific methodologies and findings of the founding fathers and developed their own research programs. Because of these social scientists, the discipline would never be the same.

THE EMPIRICAL REVOLUTION (1950–1970): THEORY IN A TEST TUBE

Speech departments in the 1950s continued to promote the ancient rhetorical wisdom that persuasive discourse was a matter of an ethical speaker using logical arguments—"the good man speaking well."[9] But younger faculty with training in the social sciences were no longer willing to accept this "truth" by faith. Armed with a scientific skepticism and new methods to assess attitudes, they put rhetorical principles to the test.

Aristotle, for example, wrote that *ethos* was a combination of a speaker's intelligence, character, and goodwill toward the audience. Empirically oriented speech researchers subsequently discovered that audience rankings of "communicator credibility" did indeed include factors of competence (intelligence) and trustworthiness (character).[10] But they found no evidence that audiences regarded goodwill or positive intentions as a trait separate from character.

Scholars interested in this kind of study adopted the media-effects term *communication research* to distinguish their work from the historical-critical textual analysis of rhetoricians. In 1950 a group of communication researchers founded what is now the International Communication Association (ICA) as a science-based professional organization to rival the SAA, which was grounded in the humanities. Traditional speech teachers of this era often accused communication researchers of succumbing to "the law of the hammer." This was a not-so-subtle dig at those who would pound away with newly acquired statistical tools no matter what the job required.

But irony did little to slow the radical transformation within the communication discipline. The change was undoubtedly speeded up by Shannon and Weaver's linear model of communication, which appeared at the beginning of this period (see Chapter 4). Frank Berlo, who wrote the leading communication textbook of the 1960s, reduced that model to four simple parts:[11]

Source-Message-Channel-Receiver

His SMCR model provided a common vocabulary and a standard way to view the communication process.

The empiricists continued to borrow their core ideas from other disciplines—especially social psychology. Indeed, seven of the thirty-four communication theories in this book come from that specialized branch of psychology. Their common methodology and unity of world view gave social scientists in the communication field a greater impact than their numbers alone would indicate. In 1969, the SAA changed its name to the Speech Communication Association (SCA). The term *communication* in the title was tacit evidence that the scientific approach now dominated the discipline. At the start of the 1960s few departments that taught speech had the word *communication* as part of their title. By the mid 1970s there were few that didn't.

THE TURBULENT SIXTIES (1960–1970): A LAUNCHING PAD FOR INTERPERSONAL COMMUNICATION

If time is like a river flowing through the field of communication, the decade of the 1960s was a ten-year stretch of white-water rapids. For America, it was the time of civil rights confrontations, urban riots, U.S. involvement in Vietnam, campus sit-ins, the coming of the Beatles, the hippie movement, the sexual revolution, the drug culture, and the assassinations of President John F. Kennedy, his brother Bobby, Martin Luther King, Jr., and Malcolm X. The unrest throughout the country was reflected in departments of speech and communication. Nowhere was the turbulence felt more than in the rocky transition from a focus on public address to a concentration on interpersonal communication.

In 1960, most members of the Speech Association of America still thought of speech as a platform art. Course titles in academic departments mirrored this mental image—Public Address, Oral Interpretation, Argumentation and Debate, Persuasion, History of American Public Address, and Classical Rhetoric. Even the study of small-group communication centered on discussion and decision making in the context of a structured meeting. Collegewide service courses were set up to improve message organization, reduce speech fright, and eliminate distracting *and ah*'s and *you know*'s from speakers' delivery.

For many professors and students, however, the niceties of formal public speaking seemed irrelevant in light of the raw struggle for power taking place on the streets outside the classroom. After all, who gave well-reasoned speeches any more? Who would listen? By 1970, most faculty regarded public address as outdated, and the shape of communication departments was radically altered. Consider the following evidence:

> At many schools, interpersonal communication replaced public speaking as the required course for all students. The curriculum centered on dyadic interactions that are characterized by a mutual awareness of the individuality of the others.

> Leading professors no longer taught public speaking courses. They focused instead on nonverbal communication, trust building, self-disclosure, conflict resolution, and other interpersonal issues. Behavioral scientists did the research, while humanists wrote the textbooks. Neither group seemed excited about public address.

> The encounter group movement had a strong influence on the way group courses were taught. Known also as "sensitivity training" or "humanistic psychology," the movement promoted an open and honest sharing of feelings between members and encouraged them to disregard social conventions that might inhibit gut-level expression.

> Persuasion became a dirty word. The prevailing do-your-own-thing attitude in society sanctioned an individualism that left little room for corporate responsibility or conscious attempts to change another person's behavior.

> The focus of communication ethics switched from telling the truth to loyalty to your communication partner. *What* was said became secondary to *how* it was said and to the way it *affected* others. Relationships were more important than message content.

> The popularity of concentrations within communication departments changed significantly. Interpersonal and media communication were hot. Oral interpretation, public address, and its history were not. Voice science and drama had a life of their own and often broke away and formed separate departments. Contrary to the expectation of empiricists who were riding high, however, rhetoric did not disappear. After decades of neo-Aristotelian sameness, new methods of rhetorical analysis emerged which guaranteed that rhetoric would not only survive, but thrive.

THE NEW RHETORICS (1965–1980)

A 1965 issue of the *Quarterly Journal of Speech* contained an article that used Aristotle's categories of *logos, pathos,* and *ethos* to analyze the relationship between message arguments and figures of speech in seventeenth- and eighteenth-century England.[12] This historical-critical study is remarkable today only as a typical example of speech scholarship from 1925 to 1965. Rhetoricians were apparently locked into a single method of analyzing a text. What had once been considered mainstream research was now in danger of being relegated to the backwaters of the discipline.

That same year, Edward Black's book *Rhetorical Criticism: A Study of Method* launched a rebellion against traditional rhetorical scholarship by advocating multiple approaches to analyzing speech events.[13] Douglas Ehninger was only one of many scholars who was quick to proclaim the demise of rhetorical orthodoxy:

> If Wichelns' landmark essay of 1925 gave neo-Aristoteleanism its birth, this
> book published exactly 40 years later may well deal the school its death blow.[14]

As it turned out, he was wrong. Aristotle's categories continue to offer a helpful way to analyze a message, the speaker who gives it, and the audience that hears it. (See Chapter 25.) Yet a host of new approaches came to prominence soon after Black's call for new rhetorics.

Observing the protest movements of the 1960s, rhetorical critics reached the same conclusion as behavioral scientists—that the impact of public marches and sit-ins had little to do with carefully crafted speeches or well-reasoned arguments. The sheer numbers of demonstrators and their militant behavior spoke louder than any phrase or figure of speech. Articles on "The Rhetoric of Black Power," "The Rhetoric of Confrontation," and other "rhetoric of . . ." studies began to appear in communication journals.[15]

Many humanists took offense at the nonartistic methods demonstrators used to capture the public's attention. There is nothing particularly subtle about a raised fist, a shouted obscenity, or the takeover of a public building. But if rhetoric was truly an effort "to discover all possible means of persuasion,"[16] scholars in the field decided they could no longer ignore the coercive techniques of social agitation and the way in which nonverbal behavior communicates.

The same logic applied to the influence of television, film, and popular music. Originally dismissed as "mere entertainment," the mass media were obviously shaping popular culture. English professor Marshall McLuhan captured public attention with his claim that the content of television was almost irrelevant (see Chapter 28). "The medium is the message," he announced, and thousands of students set out to investigate his assertion. Aristotle's rhetorical proofs of *logos, pathos,* and *ethos* seemed pale in comparison with the excitement of taking part in a media revolution.

Until the late 1970s, most U.S. speech communication professionals were unaware of European thinking on the connection between communication and culture. Although British, French, Italian, and German scholars might differ on details, most offered a Marxist analysis of the media's role in shaping societal values.

Known as "critical theorists," these humanistic philosophers and sociologists were especially critical of American empirical researchers who claimed to be doing objective science. Critical theorists scoffed at a media research establishment which professed to be neutral, but always ended up serving those who held political and economic power. By the end of this period, European critical theory had crossed the Atlantic and provided U.S. rhetoricians with fresh ammunition in their fight with social scientists.

THE HUNT FOR A UNIVERSAL MODEL (1970–1980)

While rhetoricians were diversifying in the 1970s, communication scientists were trying to consolidate. After two decades of empirical research, they could boast of scant new knowledge about the process of communication. Many suspected that the absence of a scientific breakthrough was due to the lack of a single grand theory that was needed to focus research efforts.

Each communication interest group had isolated and studied separate variables that members thought crucial to the process of communication. For example, public address researchers tried to find causes and cures for speech anxiety. Group dynamics investigators centered on traits and styles of leadership. Mass communication scholars focused on the effects of television violence. Persuasion researchers sought the different factors of source credibility, and the new area of interpersonal communication was all over the conceptual map with studies of self-disclosure, self-esteem, trust, nonverbal signals, conflict resolution, and much more. There was little discipline within the discipline.

In his book *The Structure of Scientific Revolutions*, philosopher of science Thomas Kuhn argues that a universal paradigm or model is the mark of a mature science.[17] Social scientists in communication departments were painfully aware that they hadn't achieved that status. Although successfully redefining the field as "communication" and assuming leadership in the newly titled departments, they still couldn't claim a unifying theory or approach that would guarantee academic respectability among their colleagues in departments of psychology or physics. So throughout the decade of the 1970s, empiricists pursued the dream of a universally accepted communication model.

Ultimately they failed, but it wasn't for lack of trying. At the same SAA-sponsored summit conference that prompted the change in the organization's name, communication scholars sought to define the central research focus of the discipline. They agreed that "spoken symbolic interaction" was their object of study, and calls for journal articles and convention papers over the next decade stressed a preference for message-oriented inquiry.

In an attempt to chart the factors that affect message creation and interpretation, textbook writers of the 1970s offered pictorial models of the communication process, each more complex than the one that came before. The various illustrations looked like Monopoly boards, cone-shaped springs, schematic drawings of electrical circuits, diagrams of football plays, family trees, furnace-thermostat feedback loops, splitting amoebas, Rubic cubes, ladders, hydraulic plumbing, and wheels within wheels. As intriguing as they were, no one model generated a consensus as *the* paradigm of the communication process.

The entire 1977 spring issue of *Communication Quarterly* featured a debate among advocates of three types of theory—laws, rules, and systems. From Chapter 1 you already know that *covering laws* are the goal of science and that *interpretive rules* are the product of a humanistic approach. An *open systems* approach doesn't fit neatly into either camp.

Systems theory refuses to treat any conversation as an isolated event. Theorists working with this model see a human communication system as a set of interdependent people who work together to adapt to a changing environment. Systems theorists differ from rules theorists in that they play down the role of individuals and concentrate on patterns of relationships within the entire system. They depart from a laws approach in that they regard the communication event as greater than the sum of its parts.

Debate as a cocurricular activity has a long and proud tradition of excellence in our field. Many public figures point to their collegiate debate training as superb preparation for critical analysis and thinking on their feet. But debaters rarely credit their opponents' arguments, and spectators are seldom swayed by what they hear. So it was with the theoretical debates of the 1970s. Champions of systems, rules, and laws took potshots at each other, while bystanders caught in the cross fire decided that no single way of viewing communication was so compelling that they should become a true believer and join the fray. Perhaps a single paradigm wasn't really necessary. Over time, the quest for a universal model of communication lost much of its steam.

FERMENT IN THE FIELD (1980–PRESENT)

The title for this section comes from a special 1983 issue of the *Journal of Communication* devoted to taking stock of the discipline. Thirty-five separate articles offered perspectives on the health of communication scholarship. Almost without exception, the authors described an academic profession working under great stress. Ten years later I see no reason to alter their judgment.

College and university communication departments are more numerous than ever before, and they often boast of more majors and greater class enrollments than any other department on campus. Sustained growth began in the 1970s with students flocking to courses in media and interpersonal communication. Growth has continued as a result of interest in organizational communication and the applied skills of leadership, consulting, negotiation, advertising, and public relations. At first glance, the runaway success of communication programs in the 1990s would seem to contradict reports of ongoing tension. Yet despite success at the registrar's desk, communication is still a divided discipline.

At the start of this historical overview, I compared communication scholarship in the twentieth century to a river with twin currents representing the arts and sciences. Figure 2.1 illustrates the stages and events that punctuate

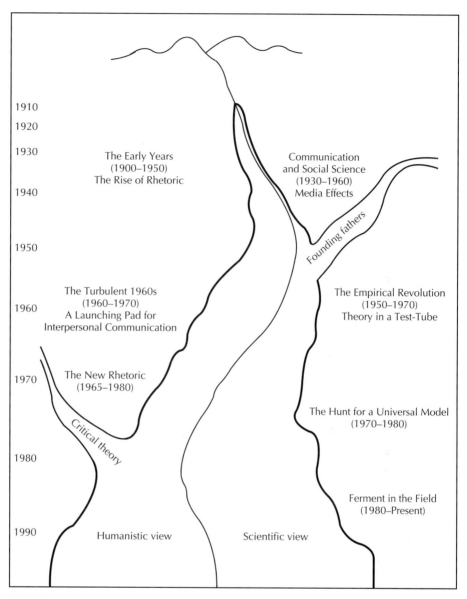

FIGURE 2.1
Communication Theory and Research—The Flow of History

that flow. Note that while the study of communication has swelled from a trickle to a broad river, the relative strength of scientific and humanistic inquiry has varied greatly from past to present. With the increase of critical and ethnographic analysis in the late decade, the two rival approaches of humanistic and scientific research are now roughly equal in the amount of interest they generate. But I've drawn the arts and sciences separate in this depiction of communication theory and research over the years, because that's the way it has actually been. The two currents of study have yet to mix. This estrangement between behavioral scientists and rhetoricians continues to be a chief cause for ferment in the field.

In 1992, the legislative council of the Speech Communication Association polled its membership for approval to change the organization's name to the American Communication Association. Fearing that their representatives were severing the association from its rhetorical roots, members rejected similar proposals in 1985 and 1989. This time 55 percent of the ballots approved dropping the term *speech,* but the vote fell far short of the necessary two-thirds majority. By now it's obvious that a name change won't close the communication gap that exists between scholars working from different perspectives. As the editors of the *Handbook of Rhetoric and Communication* are forced to conclude:

> In the present state of knowledge we cannot organize research and theory concerning rhetoric and communication within any single framework.[18]

Since communication research and rhetorical study differ so markedly and yet both hold an important place within our discipline, it's crucial for us to understand how to evaluate both kinds of theory. Applying the standards of science to rhetorical theory would be just as unfair as judging empirically grounded theory by artistic criteria. In Chapter 3, I will explore the basic ways you can identify good theory in each category. Surprisingly enough, you may discover several points of contact which give hope that the artistic and scientific currents within the field of communication sometimes flow downriver at the same pace, and may actually merge.

QUESTIONS TO SHARPEN YOUR FOCUS

1. At the start of the chapter *communication* was defined as "the management of messages for the purpose of creating meaning." How does this definition embrace the concerns of both the *arts* and *sciences*?

2. The title of the *Speech Communication Association* reflects many ongoing tensions within the discipline. Do you regard the word *speech* as an adjective or a noun? What difference does it make?

3. From your perspective, has there been a turning point in the history of the speech communication field that has special significance?

4. Think of yourself as rowing a boat on the river depicted in Figure 2.1. What part of the river would your interest in communication lead you to occupy?

A SECOND LOOK

Recommended resource: Thomas Benson (ed.), *Speech Communication in the 20th Century*, Southern Illinois University, Carbondale, 1985.

Early years: Robert Jeffrey, "History of the Speech Association of America 1912–1964," *Quarterly Journal of Speech*, Vol. 50, 1964, pp. 432–444.

Empirical roots: Jesse Delia, "Communication Research: A History," in *Handbook of Communication Science*, Charles Berger and Steven Chaffee (eds.), Sage, Newbury Park, Calif., 1987, pp. 20–98.

Interpersonal communication: Mark Knapp and Gerald Miller (eds.), "Introduction: Background and Current Trends in the Study of Interpersonal Communication," in *Handbook of Interpersonal Communication*, Sage, Beverly Hills, 1985, pp. 7–24.

Laws, rules, and systems: Communication Quarterly, Vol. 25, 1977, No. 1, entire Winter issue.

Ferment in the field: "Ferment in the Field," *Journal of Communication*, Vol. 33, No. 3, Summer 1983, entire issue.

Early years—a personal view: Loren Reid, *Speech Teacher: A Random Narrative*, Speech Communication Association, Annandale, Va., 1990.

Later years—a public view: "Communication 1940–1989," *Time (Retrospective)*, 1989, special issue available from Speech Communication Association, Annandale, Va.

CHAPTER 3

Weighing the Words

In Chapter 1 we looked at two distinct approaches to communication theory—humanistic and scientific. In Chapter 2, I traced the history of tension between rhetoricians and behavioral scientists in the field of speech communication. Both groups have trouble understanding and appreciating the value of each other's efforts. This workplace tug-of-war parallels the struggle between ranchers and growers in Rodgers and Hammerstein's Broadway musical, *Oklahoma!* One song calls for understanding and cooperation.

> The farmer and the cowman should be friends,
> Oh, the farmer and the cowman should be friends,
> > One man likes to push a plough,
> > The other likes to chase a cow,
> But that's no reason why they cain't be friends.[1]

The problem, of course, is that farmers and ranchers want to push a plough or chase a cow over the same piece of land. Daily disputes over fences, water, and government grants make friendship tough. The same can be said of the turf wars that are common between scientists and humanists. Differences in ways of knowing, views of human nature, goals of theory building, and methods of research seem to ensure tension and misunderstanding.

Friendly attitudes between the arts and sciences are particularly hard to come by when each group insists on applying its own standards of judgment to the work of the other group. As a first-time reader of communication theory, you could easily get sucked into making the same mistake. If you've had training in the scientific method and judge the value of every communication theory by whether or not it predicts human behavior, you'll automatically reject 50 percent of the theories presented in this book. On the other hand, if you've been steeped in the humanities and expect every theory to unmask the meaning of a text, you'll easily dismiss the other half.

Regardless of which approach you favor, not all scientific or humanistic communication theories are equally good. In each case, some are better than others. Like moviegoers watching one of Clint Eastwood's early westerns, you'll want a way to separate the good, the bad, and the ugly. Since I've included theories originating in both the arts and the sciences, you need to have two separate lenses through which to view their respective claims. This chapter offers that pair of bifocals. I hope by the time you finish you'll be on friendly terms with the separate criteria that behavioral scientists and rhetoricians use to weigh the work and words of their colleagues.

A TEST CASE: CARL ROGERS' EXISTENTIAL THEORY

Psychologist Carl Rogers developed a theory of therapeutic growth which is unusual in that it draws from both the humanities and the sciences. Although the focus of his existential theory is psychological health, it is also a theory of communication. Rogers believed that clients get better when a counselor's communication creates a safe environment. The dual roots of the theory and its emphasis on talking and listening make it useful as a way to illustrate two separate ways to evaluate communication theory.

The formal statement of Rogers' theory appeared in the encyclopedic text *Psychology: A Study of Science.* He postulated three necessary and sufficient conditions for client personality change in a therapeutic setting. If clients perceived a counselor's (1) congruence, (2) unconditional positive regard, and (3) empathic understanding, they could and would get better.

Congruence is the match or fit between an individual's inner feelings and outer display. The congruent counselor is genuine, real, integrated, whole, transparent. "In my relationship with persons," Rogers wrote, "I've found that it does not help, in the long run, to act as though I was something I was not."[2]

Unconditional positive regard is an attitude of acceptance that isn't contingent on performance. Rogers asked, "Can I let myself experience positive attitudes toward this other person—attitudes of warmth, caring, liking, interest, and respect?"[3] When the answer was "Yes," both he and his clients matured as human beings.

Empathic understanding is the caring skill of temporarily laying aside our views and values and of entering into another's world without prejudice. It is an active process of seeking to hear the other's thoughts, feelings, tones, and meanings as if they were our own.

Although the form, substance, and target audience of Rogers' work clearly establish his theory as a scientific venture, it was his humanistic commitment that shaped his counseling techniques. He assumed that given a positive interpersonal climate, people will be trustworthy, creative, constructive, and capable of releasing vast amounts of untapped human potential. He founded the Center for Studies of the Person in La Jolla, California, to explore and encourage this high view of human nature.

Like many humanists, Rogers doubted the presence of a universal truth "out there." He believed that the only reality we can know for sure is our own. "Neither the Bible nor the prophets—neither Freud nor research— neither the revelations of God nor man—can take precedence over my own direct experience."[4] This existential commitment—a belief in the uniqueness of human experience—placed Rogers in the forefront of humanistic psychology.

Now that you have a thumbnail sketch of the man and his message, let's take a look at the separate criteria that science and humanism use to judge the quality of Rogers' theory. We'll start with the wisdom of science.

WHAT MAKES A SCIENTIFIC THEORY GOOD?

Existential theory is credible because it fulfills what a leading text on social research methods calls the "twin objectives of scientific knowledge." The theory explains the past and present, and it predicts the future. Scientists of all kinds agree on three other criteria for a good theory as well—testability, simplicity, and usefulness. The rest of this section takes a closer look at these five requirements.

Scientific Standard 1: Explanation of the Data

A good scientific theory explains an event or behavior. It brings clarity to an otherwise jumbled situation; it draws order out of chaos. British philosopher Karl Popper writes that "Theories are nets cast to catch what we call the world."[5] Scientific philosopher Abraham Kaplan says that theory is a way of making sense out of a disturbing situation.[6]

Therapy is a disturbing situation. Clients usually avoid seeking professional help until the stress of their daily lives becomes unbearable. They enter the counseling relationship with a confusing mix of feelings—shame that they've lost control of their lives, relief that they can share their hidden secrets with another human being, hope that the "talk cure" will work, and anger at the high cost of treatment. The counselor may be overwhelmed by a torrent of words that recount old hurts, justify present actions, beg for understanding, and demand reassurance.

A good theory synthesizes the data, focuses our attention on what's crucial, and helps us ignore that which makes little difference. Rogers' theory organizes these verbal inputs into a coherent whole. His focus on the counselor-client relationship goes beyond raw data. It explains what's happening.

A good theory also explains why. When Willie Sutton was asked why he robbed banks, the Depression-era bandit replied, "Cuz that's where they keep the money." It's a great line, but as a theory of motivation, it lacks explanatory power. There's nothing in the words that casts light on the internal processes or environmental forces that led Sutton to crack a safe while others tried to crack the stock market.

Existential theory explains the process as well as the result. Rogers claims that there's a reason why a warm therapeutic relationship helps people change. It's because human beings already possess the inner resources to heal themselves. What they need is a safe environment where they can listen to their own desires free from the expectations of others. Most people really don't care how therapy works; they're content with the knowledge that hurting people get better when a counselor doesn't judge. In like manner, you can be a skillful public speaker without understanding *why* the audience likes what you say. But when you take a course in communication *theory*, you've lost your amateur status.

Scientific Standard 2: Prediction of Future Events

A good scientific theory predicts what will happen. On the basis of years of people-helping experience, Carl Rogers was willing to predict that a counselor's congruence, unconditional positive regard, and empathic understanding would lead to clients' psychological growth. His characteristics of a helping relationship would lose much of their power if they merely explained past counseling success without offering any clue to future effectiveness. Placing your bets ahead of time is the mark of good science.

The minimum requirement for scientific study is that phenomena are observable over time. Prediction is possible only when dealing with things we can see, hear, touch, smell, and taste again and again. As we notice things happening over and over in the same way, we begin to speak of universal laws. In the realm of the physical sciences, we are seldom embarrassed. Objects don't have a choice about how to behave.

The social sciences are another matter. While theories about human behavior often cast their predictions in cause-and-effect terms, a certain humility on the part of the theorist is advisable. Even the best theory may only be able to talk in terms of probability and tendencies—not absolute certainty.

Rogers' phrase "necessary and sufficient conditions" has the ring of certainty, yet he staunchly defended people's potential for novel response. Instead of insisting that genuineness, acceptance, and empathy would invariably lead to client health, he merely reported his own positive results and urged others to see whether their experience didn't bear out his prediction.

Scientific Standard 3: Hypotheses That Can Be Tested

A good scientific theory is testable. If a prediction is wrong, there ought to be a way to demonstrate the error. Some theories are so ambiguous that it's impossible to imagine conditions that would definitively disprove their claims. If there is no potential way to prove a theory false, then the assumption that it's true is mere guesswork. A boyhood example may help illustrate this point.

When I was 12 years old, I had a friend named Mike. We spent many hours shooting baskets in his driveway. The backboard was mounted on an old-fashioned, single-car garage where the double doors opened outward like the doors on a cabinet. In order to avoid crashing into them on a drive for a lay-up, we'd open the doors during play. But since the doors would only swing through a 90-degree arc, they extended about four feet onto the court along the baseline.

One day Mike announced that he'd developed a "never-miss" shot. He took the ball at the top of the free-throw circle, drove toward the basket, then cut to the right corner. When he got to the baseline, he took a fade-away jump shot, blindly arching the ball over the top of the big door. I was greatly impressed as the ball swished through the net. When he boasted that he never missed, I challenged him to do it again—which he did. But a third attempt was an air ball—it completely missed the rim.

Before I could make the kind of bratty comment junior high boys make, he quickly told me that the attempt had not been his never-miss shot. He claimed to have slipped as he cut to the right, and therefore jumped from the wrong place. Grabbing the ball, he drove behind the door and again launched a blind arching shot. Swish. *That*, he assured me, was his never-miss shot.

I knew something was wrong. I soon figured out that any missed attempt was, by definition, not the fabled never-miss shot. When the ball went in, however, Mike hearalded the success as added evidence of 100 percent accuracy. I now know that I could have called his bluff by removing the net from the basket so that he couldn't hear whether the shot went through. This would have forced him to declare from behind the door whether or not the attempt was of the never-miss variety. But as long as I played by his rules, there was no way to disprove his claim. Unfortunately, some theories are stated in a similar fashion. They are presented in a way that makes it impossible to prove them false. They shy away from the put-up-or-shut-up standard. They aren't testable.

Existential theory is vulnerable at this point. Although Rogers makes a bold claim about "necessary and sufficient conditions," how can we be sure a counselor meets those requirements? For example, it's hard to know when a therapist's words honestly reflect his or her inner feelings. And even if congruency could be measured, the concept of emotional growth is so murky that it would be impossible to show that it hadn't taken place. To most scientists, Rogers' existential theory looks like a never-miss shot.

There's a simple way to figure out whether a communication theory is capable of being refuted. Are scientific investigators actively trying to prove it wrong? A testable theory has heuristic value—it stimulates the curiosity of those with a flair for research. They itch to push it to the limit, much as a test pilot wants to wring out a new airplane. Carl Rogers' client-centered principles have generated many devotees, but it has received virtually no testing by empirical researchers.

Scientific Standard 4: Relative Simplicity

A good scientific theory is as simple as possible. A few decades ago a cartoonist by the name of Rube Goldberg made people laugh by sketching plans for complicated machines that performed simple tasks. His better mousetrap went through a sequence of fifteen mechanical steps which were triggered by turning a crank and ended with a bird cage dropping over a cheese-eating mouse.

Goldberg's designs were funny because the machines were so needlessly complex. That can happen with scientific explanations as well; it's easy to get caught up in the grandeur of a theoretical construction. "Why say it simply when you can say it elaborately?" Yet the rule of parsimony states that given two plausible explanations for the same event, we should accept the simpler version.

College professors often criticize others for offering simple solutions to complex questions. It's a jungle out there, and we're quick to pounce on those who reduce the world's complexity to a simplistic "Me Tarzan, you Jane." But every so often a few explorers will cut through the underbrush and clear a straight path to a truth, which they announce in simple, direct, concise terms. Take Rogers' conclusion, for example: Counselors are most effective when they are transparently real, are warmly accepting, and see the world through the client's eyes. The simplicity of Rogers' idea is a value of his theory.

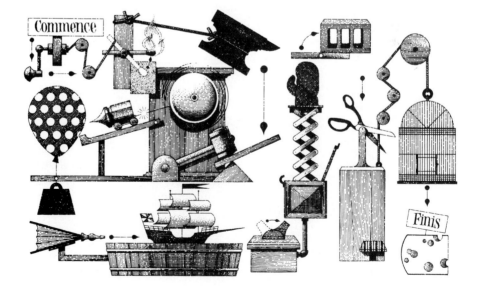

Scientific Standard 5: Practical Utility

A good scientific theory is useful. Since a fundamental goal of any science is increased control, scientific theories should offer practical help. Thousands of counselors, teachers, and other people-oriented professionals find Rogers' client-centered principles invaluable in their work. The insights of existential theory offer clients control of their lives as well. If clients are fortunate enough to benefit from the kind of helping relationship Rogers recommends, they should become more fully functioning people. If, on the other hand, their counselor is aloof, judgmental, or directive, the knowledge that these behaviors are counterproductive can free them up to seek help elsewhere.

In the introduction to this book I cited Lewin's claim that there is nothing as practical as a good theory. This final standard of utility suggests that scientific theories that aren't practical aren't good. As you read about theorists who work from a scientific perspective, let usefulness be a crucial test of each theory. If a theory offers helpful advice, act on it; if it offers no pragmatic insight for your life, discard it. There is one caution, however. Most of us can be a bit lazy or shortsighted. We have a tendency to consider as unimportant anything that's hard to grasp or can't be applied to our lives right now. Before dismissing a theory as irrelevant, make certain you understand it and consider how others have made use of its advice. I'll try to do my part by presenting each theory as clearly as possible and suggesting possible applications.

WHAT MAKES A HUMANISTIC THEORY GOOD?

Unlike scientists, humanists don't have a five-point, single set of criteria for evaluating their theories. But even though there is no universally approved model for artistically oriented theories, humanists repeatedly urge that theories should accomplish some or all of the following functions: create understanding, identify values, stimulate agreement, inspire aesthetic appreciation, and change society. The rest of the chapter examines these oft-mentioned ideals.

Humanistic Standard 1: New Understanding of People

Humanistic scholarship is good when it offers fresh insight into the human condition. Working out of a humanistic tradition, rhetorical critics seek to gain new understanding by analyzing the activity which they regard as uniquely human—symbolic interaction. Suppose, for example, that a scholar in the humanities wanted to study communication during times of war. He or she would start by selecting one or more *texts*—Lincoln's Gettysburg Address, Nazi propaganda during World War II, "Dear John" letters sent to soldiers in Vietnam, General Schwarzkopf's climactic Operation Desert Storm press briefing, or any other text that could shed light on wartime communication.

After verifying that the print or electronic record is what was really written or said, the critic would do a "close reading" of the text. This is a fine-tooth comb analysis of words, images, and ideas. The critic would also examine the historical *context* that influenced the creation and the audience's interpretation of the message.

When rhetorical theory is good, it will help the critic understand the text. The neo-Aristotelian classification of logical, emotional, and ethical appeals, for example, might help the critic figure out why people still memorize Lincoln's speech at Gettysburg. Or Clifford Geertz's interpretive approach could suggest that Norman Schwarzkopf's Desert Storm briefings were the product of a military culture that has its own rites, rituals, and myths. You'll read about these theories in the pages to come. If they help you make sense out of complex communication, then they fulfill the first humanistic standard for a good theory.

Some people fear that by relying on rhetorical theory we will read our preconceived ideas into the text rather than letting the words speak for themselves. They suggest there are times when we should "just say no" to theory. But University of Minnesota communication theorist Ernest Bormann notes that rhetorical theory works best when it suggests universal patterns of symbol-using: "A powerful explanatory structure is what makes a work of humanistic scholarship live on through time."[7]

Bormann's call for a powerful explanatory structure in humanistic theory might appear identical to the behavioral scientist's insistence that theory explains why people do what they do. But the two notions are different. Science wants an objective explanation; humanism desires subjective understanding. Klaus Krippendorff of the Annenberg School of Communication at the University of Pennsylvania urges us to recognize that we are both the cause and the consequence of what we observe. His *self-referential imperative* for building theory states: "Include yourself as a constituent of your own construction."[8]

Carl Rogers' existential theory more than meets the self-referential standard. For Rogers, congruence between a counselor's inner feelings and outward expression is crucial to self-understanding. And it is only through empathic listening that the counselor can have an understanding of the client's world. Rogers' claim that these communication skills create a safe atmosphere for interpersonal health in a variety of situations fulfills Bormann's desire for a powerful explanatory structure.

Humanistic Standard 2: Clarification of Values

A good humanistic theory brings people's values into the open. The theorist readily acknowledges his or her own ethical stance and actively seeks to unmask the ideology behind the message under scrutiny.

Not all humanists occupy the same moral ground, but there are core values which most of them share. For example, humanists usually place a high premium on individual liberty. Klaus Krippendorff wants to make sure that scholars' drive for personal freedom extends to the people they study. His *ethical imperative* directs the theorist to "Grant others that occur in your construction the same autonomy you practice constructing them."[9] When theorists follow this rule, monologue gives way to dialogue.

Many humanists value equality as highly as they do freedom. This commitment leads to a continual examination of the power relationships inherent in all communication. Critical theorists, in particular, insist that scholars can no longer remain ethically detached from the people they are studying or from the political and economic implications of their work. "There is no safe harbor in which researchers can avoid the power structure."[10]

Carl Rogers clearly states his value commitments. Even the casual reader quickly learns that "freedom of choice" is Rogers' highest ideal. He believes that people who are able to take responsibility for their actions can "be that self who one really is"—open, honest, feeling, warm, trusting, and so on. Most readers think Rogers' view of human nature is overly optimistic, but no one can knock existential theory for hiding its core values.

Humanistic Standard 3: A Community of Agreement

We can identify a good humanistic theory by the amount of support it generates within a community of like-minded scholars. Interpretation of meaning is subjective, but whether or not the humanist's case is reasonable is decided ultimately by others in the field. Their acceptance or rejection is an objective fact which helps verify or vilify the theorist's judgment.

John Stewart is the editor of *Bridges, Not Walls*—a collection of humanistic articles on interpersonal communication. As the book has progressed through five editions, Stewart's judgment to keep, drop, or add a new theoretical work was made possible by the fact that humanistic scholarship is "not a solitary enterprise carried out in a vacuum." It is, instead, "the effort of a community of scholars who routinely subject their findings to the scrutiny of editors, referees, and readers."[11]

A rhetorical theory can't meet the community of agreement standard unless it becomes the subject of widespread analysis. Sometimes rhetoricians address their critical arguments only to an audience of "true believers," who are already committed to the author's approach. David Zarefsky, the 1992 president of SCA, warns that rhetorical validity can be established only when a work is debated in the broad marketplace of ideas. For this rhetorical critic from Northwestern University, sound arguments differ from unsound ones in that

> sound arguments are addressed to the general audience of critical readers, not just to the adherents of a particular "school" or perspective. . . . They open their own reasoning processes to scrutiny.[12]

When it came to widespread scrutiny, Carl Rogers did it right. He presented the basics of his existential theory to all who would listen—

counselors, medical doctors, teachers, artists, and business leaders. More importantly, he debated his ideas publicly with leading thinkers from the rival psychoanalytic and behavioral schools of therapy. He obviously failed to convince everyone that his approach was best, but over the years many counselors agreed that showing congruence, unconditional positive regard, and empathic understanding were superb ideas.

Humanistic Standard 4: Aesthetic Appeal

A good humanistic theory is not just *about* art. It *is* art. Art looks at old material in a new way. The form of a communication theory can capture the imagination of a reader just as much as the content. According to University of Washington professor Barbara Warnick, a rhetorical critic can fill one or more of four roles—artist, analyst, audience, and advocate.[13] As an artist, the critic's job is to spark appreciation.

Carl Rogers was not particularly elegant in the way he expressed his ideas. He struggled to find a vocabulary that would adequately describe the fully functioning person who could emerge from the therapeutic process. Consider this somewhat awkward passage:

> This second observation is difficult to make, because we do not have good words for it. Clients seem to move toward more openly being a process, a fluidity, a changing.[14]

Rogers appears to fall short of the aesthetic standard that is the humanistic ideal. Yet thousands of readers found Rogers' personal reflections and narrative style far more captivating than the psycho-babble of other counseling approaches. Many readers were inspired to seek the aid of a client-centered therapist. It seems that the beauty of a humanistic theory is in the eye of the beholder.

Humanistic Standard 5: Reform of Society

A good humanistic theory generates change. Contrary to the notion that we can dismiss social philosophy as "mere rhetoric," the interpretive theorist is a reformer who can have an impact on society. Kenneth Gergen, a Swarthmore College social psychologist, states that theory has

> the capacity to challenge the guiding assumptions of the culture, to raise fundamental questions regarding contemporary social life, to foster reconsideration of that which is "taken for granted," and thereby to generate fresh alternatives for social action.[15]

Rogers' existential theory did just that! As a direct result of his influence, therapists came out from behind their couches and began to face their clients as well as their own feelings. Teachers backed off from traditional jug-in-mug lectures which stressed one-way transfer of information and started listening to the insights of their students. Bosses abandoned autocratic styles of leadership in favor of participatory management. And many men and women discovered that with little or no training they could enter into a nondirective helping relationship with a family member or friend. Rogers' ideas truly started a revolution.

BALANCING THE SCALE: SIMILAR WEIGHTS AND MEASURES

Figure 3.1 summarizes the standards that I suggest you use as you evaluate a communication theory. You'll find that I often refer to these requirements in the critique sections at the end of each chapter. As you might expect, the thirty-four theories presented in this book stack up rather well against these criteria. (Otherwise I wouldn't have picked them in the first place.) But constructing theory is difficult, and most theories have an Achilles heel that makes them vulnerable to criticism. All the theorists cited readily admit a need for fine tuning, and some even call for major overhauls.

Throughout this chapter I have urged using separate measures for weighing the merits of scientific and humanistic theories. A side-by-side comparison of the two lists in Figure 3.1 suggests that the standards used by humanists and scientists may not be as different as first thought. Consider the parallels at each of the five points:

1. *Explanation* tries to answer the question, Why? So does *understanding*.
2. *Prediction* and *value clarification* both look to the future. The first suggests what *will* happen; the second what *ought to* happen.
3. *Testing hypotheses* is a way of achieving a *community of agreement*.
4. For many students of theory, *simplicity* has *aesthetic appeal*.
5. A theory that actually *reforms* part of the world is certainly very *practical*.

Perhaps within the field of communication "the scientists and the rhetors should be friends." At least they can respect the thoughts of scholars in the

Scientific Theory	Humanistic Theory
Explanation of data	Understanding of people
Prediction of future	Clarification of values
Testable hypotheses	Community of agreement
Relative simplicity	Aesthetic appeal
Practical utility	Reform of society

FIGURE 3.1
Summary of Criteria for Evaluating Communication Theory

other camp. The final chapter revisits the possibility of linking behavioral and rhetorical ideas, but now we turn to a one-by-one description of individual communication theories. We'll start with verbal messages—theories of how words work.

QUESTIONS TO SHARPEN YOUR FOCUS

1. Carl Rogers' *existential theory* has both scientific and humanistic roots. Does it seem to be a better scientific or humanistic theory? Why?

2. How can we call a scientific theory good if it is *capable of being proved wrong*?

3. How can we decide if a humanistic theory provides a *reasonable interpretation*?

4. Any theory involves some trade-offs. No theory can meet every standard of quality equally well. Of the ten criteria discussed, which is most important to you?

A SECOND LOOK

Scientific approach: Steven H. Chaffee and Charles R. Berger, "What Communication Scientists Do," in *Handbook of Communication Science,* Charles R. Berger and Steven H. Chaffee (eds.), Sage, Newbury Park, Calif., 1987, pp. 99–122.

Scientific critique: Stephen W. Littlejohn, *Theories of Human Communication,* 4th ed., Wadsworth, Belmont, Calif., 1992, pp. 21–38.

Humanistic approach: Thomas B. Farrell, "Beyond Science: Humanities Contributions to Communication Theory," in *Handbook of Communication Science,* Charles R. Berger and Steven H. Chaffee (eds.), Sage, Newbury Park, Calif., 1987, pp. 123–139.

Humanistic critique: Klaus Krippendorff, "On the Ethics of Constructing Communication, in *Rethinking Communication,* Vol. 1, Brenda Dervin, Lawrence Grossberg, Barbara O'Keefe, and Ellen Wartella (eds.), Sage, Newbury Park, 1989, pp. 66–96.

Existential theory: Carl Rogers, "A Theory of Therapy, Personality and Interpersonal Relationships, as Developed in the Client-centered Framework," in *Psychology: A Study of Science,* Vol. 3, *Formulation of the Person and the Social Context,* S. Koch (ed.), McGraw-Hill, New York, 1959, pp. 184–256.

Rogerian principles applied: Carl Rogers, *On Becoming a Person,* Houghton Mifflin, Boston, 1961.

PART TWO

Messages

VERBAL MESSAGES

Most words have no logical connection with the ideas they represent. The link between the black blobs on the page that spell *s-u-n* and the fiery ball in the sky is merely a convention among English-speaking people.

The term *sun* may be arbitrary, but the mere existence of a word to designate the solar furnace influences the way we view our world. Ignoring a heavenly body which so obviously dominates the sky sounds impossible, but University of Chicago linguist Edward Sapir and his student Benjamin Lee Whorf believed that if we didn't have a word to describe the sun, we probably wouldn't see it. The Sapir-Whorf hypothesis of linguistic relativity states that the structure of a culture's language shapes what people think and do.[1] "The 'real world' is to a large extent unconsciously built upon the language habits of the group."[2] Their theory of linguistic relativity counters the assumptions that all languages are similar and that words merely act as neutral vehicles to carry meaning.

Consider the second-person singular pronoun that English speakers use to address another person. No matter what the relationship, Americans use the word *you*. German speakers are forced to label the relationship as either formal (*Sie*) or familiar (*du*). They even have a ceremony (*Bruderschaft*) to cele-

brate a shift in relationship from *Sie* to *du*. Japanese vocabulary compels a speaker to recognize many more relational distinctions. The language offers ten alternatives—all translated "you" in English—but only one term is proper depending on the gender, age, and status of the speaker. Most observers would conclude that English, German, and Japanese vocabularies reflect the differences in formality among native speakers, but the Sapir-Whorf hypothesis suggests that it works the other way around. Language structures our perception of reality.

The study of verbal messages is usually divided into three disciplines: syntactics, semantics, and pragmatics. As applied to verbal messages, *syntactics* investigates the relationship between words. The most highly developed syntactic theory comes from MIT linguist Noam Chomsky.[3] Contrary to the hypothesis of Sapir and Whorf, Chomsky's generative grammar claims that the human capacity for language is innate rather than learned. He lists a series of rules that transform the deep sentence structure within us since birth into the novel sentences we now speak. Because of the theory's technical complexity and low impact on the broader field of communication, I won't devote a chapter to generative grammar. Instead, Chapter 4 will

CALVIN AND HOBBES © 1986 WATTERSON. Dist. by Universal Press Syndicate. Reprinted with permission. All rights reserved.

present Shannon and Weaver's information theory, a model of message transmission that's included in most communication texts.

Semantics has to do with the relationship between a word and its referent. The study of semantics asks the question, What does the word mean? Two kinds of meaning reside in the person who uses a word. Denotation is the direction in which the word points. Connotation is the texture or emotional tone (affect) that goes with it.

Many communication scholars regard the ability to communicate with words as the essence of being human. For example, Polish-born Count Alfred Korzybski believed that language offers people the opportunity to pass on the accumulated experience of the past.[4] We can tell our sons and daughters which snakes are poisonous, how to grow food, and the best way to find a job. Since language has a high value for survival, Korzybski saw a moral imperative for human beings to speak with precision and clarity. We ought to do it well. According to Korzybski, we don't.

He and his followers in the "general semantics" movement picture us spinning enormous webs of words and then getting caught in our own symbolic nets.[5] It's not that we're careless, irresponsible, or mean. Rather, the very structure of language leads us astray. As the fox in Antoine de Saint-Exupéry's *The Little Prince* warns, "Words are the source of misunderstandings."[6] Not only do we possess a unique capability to communicate with symbols, we're also the only creatures who can talk ourselves into trouble. Korzybski's solution for this semantic mess was the scientific use of language devoid of affective overtones.

Writing before Korzybski, British rhetorician I. A. Richards conducted a similar study of linguistic misunderstanding. Both teachers concluded that people get into trouble when they assume words have an exact meaning, but Richards' analysis of the semantic problem is more sophisticated than Korzybski's, and the remedies he offers are less simplistic. Chapter 5 describes Richards' inquiry into the meaning of meaning.

Pragmatics focuses on the effect of the message—the relationship of words to behavior. Chapter 6 describes Pearce and Cronen's activity-based theory of the coordinated management of meaning (CMM). Like Korzybski and Richards, they believe that communication is the central activity of human existence. CMM suggests that all of us use communication to make sense of our interaction with others, to mesh our actions with the behavior of others, and to remind ourselves that there is more to life than the immediate moment. Pearce and Cronen refer to these linguistic functions as coherence, coordination, and mystery.

As you read the next three chapters, you might find it helpful to think of the game of Password as a model of all verbal messages. Password is a communication game in which players try to get their partner to think of a specific word by offering a series of one-word clues—synonyms, adjectives, or any other terms that might trigger the correct response.

The syntactic theory of Shannon and Weaver is like a Password instruction book that lays out the system of rules and procedures that govern the play. Richards' semantic theory offers insight on how partners might interpret the verbal clues they hear. When I offer the clues *street* and *dirt*, will my teammate respond with the word I have in mind (*road*) or with something else (*lane*)? The pragmatic theory of Pearce and Cronen explores the relationship between the words that are said and how players act toward each other. When my partner responds to my clever clues with a far-out answer (*rural*), will I roll my eyes, sigh in exasperation, and vow never to play again? Despite their diversity, all three theories can help us better understand the word game in which we all are players—the game of language.

Information Theory
of Claude Shannon & Warren Weaver

In the late 1940s, a Bell Telephone Company research scientist by the name of Claude Shannon developed a mathematical theory of signal transmission. As you might expect from a telephone engineer, his goal was to get maximum line capacity with minimum distortion

Shannon showed little interest in the semantic meaning of a message or its pragmatic effect on the listener. Like manufacturers of state-of-the-art compact disc players, he wasn't concerned whether the channel carried Beethoven, the Beatles, or The Boss. He didn't care whether the listener preferred the beat of rock or the counterpoint of Bach. His theory merely aimed at solving the technical problems of high-fidelity transfer of sound.

TECHNICAL SOLUTIONS TO SOCIAL PROBLEMS

In the wake of scientific discoveries spawned by World War II, Americans were optimistic that all social problems could be recast into mechanical terms susceptible to engineering solutions. Shannon was somewhat wary about the wholesale application of his mathematical equations to the semantic and pragmatic issues of interpersonal communication. But his hesitation was not shared by Warren Weaver, an executive with the Rockefeller Foundation and the Sloan-Kettering Institute on Cancer Research, and a consultant to a number of private scientific foundations. Shannon's published theory was paired with an interpretive essay by Weaver that presented information theory as "exceedingly general in its scope, fundamental in the problems it treats, and of classic simplicity and power in the results it reaches."[1] The essay suggested that whatever the communication problem, reducing information loss was the solution.

Most people working in the field of human communication had trouble following the mathematics of Shannon's theory, but Weaver's translation and commentary were easy to understand. Since the discipline was ripe for a model of communication and information theory was there to fill the need, its source-channel-receiver diagram quickly became the standard description of what happens when one person talks to another. Many of the terms we use today originated with Shannon and Weaver—*message fidelity, multiple channels, information loss, source credibility,* and *feedback.*

Because Shannon's theory explores the electronic transmission of messages, it might seem appropriate to discuss it in the context of mass media theories. But his twenty-three theorems focus on syntax, the relationship between words. Research since the theory's introduction contributes mainly to the field of applied linguistics. For these reasons, I include information theory in the section on messages.

A LINEAR MODEL OF COMMUNICATION

Since Bell Laboratories paid the bill for Shannon's research, it seems only fair to use a telephone example to explain his model, which is shown in Figure 4.1. Imagine you have a summer job at a camp located far from civilization. A few weeks' absence from a special person of the opposite sex has given you a strong desire to "reach out and touch someone." Finances, work schedule, and a line of others wanting to use the only pay phone available limit you to a three-minute long-distance call.

Shannon would see you as the information source. You speak your message into the telephone mouthpiece, which transmits a signal through the telephone-wire channel. The received signal picks up static noise along the way, and this altered signal is reconverted to sound by the receiver in the earpiece at the destination end of the line. Information loss occurs every step of the way so that the message received differs from the one you sent.

During his lifetime, Weaver applied the model to the interpersonal features of conversation. Your brain is the information source, your voice the transmitter. Noise could include a hoarse throat from yelling at the campers, background chatter of those waiting to use the phone, or the distraction of mosquitoes drawing blood. The received signal may be diminished by an ear that's been overexposed to hard rock, and, as will be discussed in the section

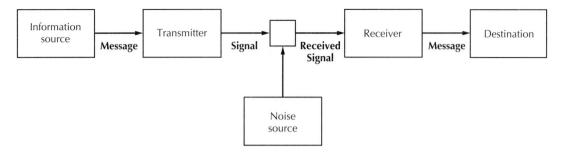

FIGURE 4.1
Shannon and Weaver's Model of Communication (Adapted from Shannon and Weaver, *The Mathematical Theory of Communication.*)

on perception, your friend is quite capable of altering the message as it moves from ear to brain.

Shannon concentrates on the technical center of his model. (Will the phone system work sufficiently well so that you can get your message across?) Weaver focused on the source-destination relationship. (What's going on between the two of you?) But all information theorists share a common goal of maximizing the amount of information the system can carry.

Information: The Reduction of Uncertainty

Shannon crafted a technical theory, so it's not surprising he has a technical definition for the term *information* that varies from how we would normally use the word. He doesn't equate information with the idea of meaning. ("The semantic aspects of communication are irrelevant to the engineering aspects."[2]) The lyrics of the nonsense song "Mairzy Doats" may contain as much information as the lyrics of Handel's *Messiah*. As Shannon uses the term, *information* refers to the opportunity to reduce uncertainty. He believes that information is the opposite of entropy.

"I wish you would make up your mind, Mr. Dickens. Was it the best of times or was it the worst of times? It could scarcely have been both."

Drawing by Handelsman; © 1987 The New Yorker Magazine, Inc.

Shannon borrowed the idea of entropy from the second law of thermodynamics, which states that the universe is winding down from an organized state to chaos, moving from predictability to uncertainty. Entropy is randomness. He applies the idea to communication by measuring the freedom of choice the information source has in selecting a message to send. The more freedom the sender has, the less predictable the message, and the more surprised the person on the other end will be.

Picture yourself making that long-distance call but this time in response to a blistering letter from your friend of the opposite sex who has heard that you're having a summer fling with a co-worker. The letter is clear: "Call me and just say yes it's true, or no it's not—nothing more!" The artificial limitation on your freedom of choice obviously means you won't require the three-minute channel capacity of the telephone line. But since your wavering friend has only an even chance of predicting your either-or answer, that one bit of information will reduce his or her uncertainty by 50 percent. As a matter of fact, that's how the theory defines a *bit* (taken from *binary digit*) of information. It's communication that can cut entropy in half. Let's play out the scene a few bits further.

Reducing Entropy Bit by Bit

At the beginning of the telephone conversation, you truthfully acknowledge romantic feelings for someone else. Your former friend breaks the rule stated in the letter and demands to know which one of the potential sixteen staff workers is the object of your affection. The conversation could literally narrow down the alternatives bit by bit.

> FRIEND: Is this new relationship with someone on the sports staff or the kitchen crew?
> YOU: Sports staff. [Cut in half to eight.]
> FRIEND: Which cabin does this special someone live in, Sequoia or Cherokee?
> YOU: Sequoia. [Cut in half to four.]
> FRIEND: First-year staff or an old-timer?
> YOU: First year. [Cut in half to two.]
> FRIEND: The redhead or the blond?
> YOU: The blond. [All uncertainty gone.]

Removing all uncertainty took four bits of information. Of course, it would have been less cumbersome simply to say the name in the first place, but either way four bits of entropy were eliminated.

If this conversation really happened, and if you truly cared about the person on the other end of the line, you would try to squeeze every bit of innovative explanation for your conduct into the three-minute period. That's what Shannon and Weaver mean by *information*. As they use the term, it "relates not so much to what you *do* say, as to what you *could* say."[3] Their focus on message possibilities inspired a touch of doggerel from University of Colorado professor Don Darnell:

> What one does is only one
> Of several things he might have done.
> One must know the things rejected
> To appreciate the one selected.[4]

A good connection for three minutes provides lots of opportunity to draw on a wide repertoire of messages. If lack of imagination or situational constraints limit you to a few predictable clichés such as "only good friends" or "doesn't mean a thing to me," Shannon, Weaver, and probably your ex-friend will regard your efforts as uninformative and redundant.

There are many fine things that can be said over a communication channel that don't qualify as information. Perhaps your phone call wasn't crisis motivated, but was merely a way to announce "I just called to say I love you." If the person on the other end had no doubt that you cared in the first place, the call is a warm ritual rather than information. If the destination party already knows what's coming, or the source isn't free to choose the message sent, information is zero.

Noise vs. Information

Noise is the enemy of information. For Shannon and Weaver, noise is more than an irritating sound or static on the line. It is anything added to the signal that's not intended by the source. Usually that kind of interference is an unintended by-product of the situation. In nonelectrical channels, noise can be smudged newsprint, *ah-um-er* vocal filler, or visual movement that distracts the listener. There is a ground-floor seminar room at my college that overlooks a grassy knoll. The first warm day in May brings out a flock of sunbathers to soak up the rays. No teacher can begin to compete with the view; the room is too noisy.

Noise may be intentional. For many years, the government of the former Soviet Union jammed the Voice of America broadcasts so that its citizens wouldn't hear news from the west. Hecklers try to drown out the words of a speaker in order to prevent the audience from considering an opposing viewpoint. We can even generate white noise to mask more disruptive sounds. That's the purpose of Muzak. Yet whether accidental or planned, noise cuts the information-carrying capacity of the channel between the transmitter and receiver. Shannon describes the relationship with a simple equation:

$$\text{Channel Capacity} = \text{Information} + \text{Noise}[5]$$

Every channel has a fixed upper limit on the information it can carry. Even if you resort to a fast-talking monologue in a no-noise environment, your three-minute telephone call restricts you to using a maximum of 600 words. But conditions are far from ideal. The noise on the line and the static in the mind of your jealous listener guarantee that many of your words won't be heard. You will need to devote a portion of the channel capacity to repeating key ideas that might otherwise be lost.

The way to offset noise is through increased redundancy. Shannon and Weaver regard communication as the applied science of maintaining an optimal balance between predictability and uncertainty. Without a great amount of repetition, reiteration, and restatement, a noisy channel is quickly overloaded. Yet too much redundancy is inefficient. Needless duplication diminishes our chance to make novel statements, and our initially avid audience may become bored and inattentive.

LEARNING THROUGH FEEDBACK

Shannon and Weaver's model is deficient in that it represents communication as a one-way flow of information. While the recent increase of voice mail and telephone answering machines may make unidirectional communication seem like the wave of the future, you would be wise to seek a response early in your three-minute phone call. On the basis of the feedback you receive, you can then encode the kind of audience-adapted message that speech teachers regard as the mark of effective communication.

Working independently from the Bell Lab program, MIT scientist Norbert Wiener conceived of human attempts to control entropy through feedback as exactly parallel to what happens in communication machines. During World War II he developed an antiaircraft firing system that would adjust future trajectory by reinstating results of past performance. Feedback is a way to introduce learning into the system, something ignored by Shannon and Weaver.

Wiener didn't fit the traditional role of a detached scientist. He considered confusion as a personal affront and was fond of quoting Einstein's comment that "God may be subtle, but not plain mean."[6] Wiener was convinced that humans could use thinking machines (we call them computers) to combat chaos. To designate the field of artificial intelligence, he coined the term *cybernetics*, a transliteration of the Greek word for "steersman" or "governor." He was one of the first to see computers as offering great promise to the human race, but he also feared they would be used by those in power to control people rather than things. His brief book, *The Human Use of Human Beings*, presents the essential concepts of information theory while adding thoughts on feedback and ethics.

Wiener noted that feedback systems need to be dampened slightly so that they aren't overly sensitive. One interpretation of the psychotic's plight is that of a hypervigilant person constantly trying to adjust to the conflicting expectations of everyone else. The implication for verbal feedback is that we should monitor the effect of our words, but not be tyrannized if the response we get falls short of our expectation.

NARROW APPLICATIONS OF INFORMATION THEORY

There is no question about the validity of the Bell Lab mathematical model of signal transmission. AT&T's phone system is one of the modern wonders of technology. Shannon's theory has also fostered modest advances in the study of the redundancy inherent in language, an issue of syntax.

Journalist Wilson Taylor developed a cloze procedure which deletes every nth word from the written text. Try filling in the blanks that replace every seventh word in the following passage from a Nero Wolfe mystery novel:

I had time to get a _____ of orchid-germination records entered into _____ PC before Fred came back to _____ brownstone at four-fifteen. The timing _____ he wouldn't run into Wolfe, who _____ was well into his playtime in _____ plant rooms. Fred looked almost as _____ as he had earlier. "What does _____ think, Archie?" the accused asked as _____ dropped into one of the yellow _____.[7]

Since everyday English is about 50 percent redundant, you were probably able to predict about five of the correct words. Here are the answers so that you can check: *batch—the—the—ensured—already—the—frazzled—he—he—chairs.* This is a highly readable passage. It would be much harder to supply the missing words from the context if the text were a portion of Shannon's technical treatise. There are times, however, when we will gladly trade readability for concentrated information. Classified ads omit filler words and many vowels from the message in order to convey more data for the dollar. The advertiser assumes the reader will have sufficient knowledge and motivation to wade through a highly concentrated stream of information.

Darnell used the same type of missing word test, but his "clozentropy" technique analyzed individuals rather than language in general. He found the fill-in-the-blanks procedure a reliable exam for competency in English as a second language, and he also used it as a way to spot potential group nonconformists by identifying those whose responses differed from everyone else's.

As interesting as the syntactical application of information theory may be, it's a far cry from the communication cure-all that Weaver proclaimed over forty years ago. A few applied researchers have tried to build on Shannon and Weaver's concept of reducing entropy. For example, Charles Berger's uncertainty reduction theory is a rare attempt to extend Shannon's ideas to face-to-face interaction (see Chapter 14). Berger believes that the desire to reduce uncertainty explains much of what goes on when people are in the initial getting-to-know-you phase of a relationship. But for those who applaud Weaver's attempt to frame information theory as an umbrella to cover syntactics, semantics, and pragmatics, the overall results must seem disappointing.

For those who regard Shannon's equations as technical models of signal transmission, Weaver's extension into questions of meaning and effectiveness must seem distasteful.

CRITIQUE: IS TRANSMISSION OF INFORMATION OVERRATED?

Shannon and Weaver's theory has great historical significance. Their model touched off an ongoing search for other physical representations of communication. Had they not conducted their ground-breaking work, this book might never have been written.

The theory's diagram of information transmission appears in almost every communication textbook. Over the years, millions of students have been exposed to the one-way flowchart that makes information seem like a commodity that is packaged, picked up by UPS, then carried through noisy city streets, delivered to its destination, and finally unwrapped relatively intact. Almost all the other theories I'll present in the book work to correct this linear conception of communication. Equating information transmission with communication, however, is an idea that dies hard.

Psychologist Janet Beavin Bavelas questions whether reducing uncertainty is always an appropriate communication goal. Along with three of her students at the University of Victoria, she examined numerous cases of equivocal communication that comes from being put on the spot in no-win situations. All of us have found ourselves forced to comment on a recommended movie, book, play, or concert which we thought was rotten. Bavelas thinks that the strategic ambiguity of a remark like "Interesting!" is superior to a straightforward response. My favorite example of equivocal communication is the schizophrenic patient who sent his mother a Mother's Day card which read, "For someone who has been like a mother to me."[8] Bavelas writes:

> Equivocation is not the deliberately deceitful "dirty old man" of communication. It is subtle, often commendable, and entirely understandable, if only the observer will expand his or her analysis to include the communication situation. When seen in context, not making sense does make sense.[9]

Information theory appears to ignore the human factor in human communication. When applied to interpersonal communication, Shannon and Weaver's model reduces people at the destination end to unfeeling bowling pins who have no say in whether they stand or fall. I doubt that the party on the other end of your long-distance phone conversation would feel that passive.

Social science literature on romantic jealousy also suggests the marginal usefulness of Shannon and Weaver's concept of information. When a couple manages to repair a damaged relationship, the result is usually due to third-party counseling, building self-esteem or encouraging assertiveness in the jealous partner, or a joint celebration and reconstruction of past times together. New interpretations are much more important than new information.

QUESTIONS TO SHARPEN YOUR FOCUS

1.   Shannon and Weaver use the term *information* in a highly specialized way. How do they define *information*?

2.   There are 512 pages in a book. If I tell you I am reading page 317, I have communicated 9 *bits* of information. Can you explain why?

3.   What are some examples of *noise* that you experienced as you read this chapter?

4.   Can you think of a recent phone call where your communication goal wasn't the *reduction of uncertainty*?

A SECOND LOOK

Recommended resource: Norbert Wiener, *The Human Use of Human Beings,* Avon, New York, 1967.

Comprehensive statement: Claude Shannon and Warren Weaver, *The Mathematical Theory of Communication,* University of Illinois, Urbana, 1949.

Introduction to concepts: Donald Darnell, "Information Theory: An Approach to Human Communication," in *Approaches to Human Communication,* Richard Budd and Brent Ruben (eds.), Spartan, New York, 1972, pp. 156–169.

Overview: Allan Broadhurst and Donald Darnell, "An Introduction to Cybernetics and Information Theory," *Quarterly Journal of Speech,* Vol. 51, 1965, pp. 442–453.

Advocates of broad theory: Seth Finn and Donald Roberts, "Source, Destination, and Entropy: Reassessing the Role of Information Theory in Communication Research," *Communication Research,* Vol. 11, 1984, pp. 453–476.

Advocate of narrow theory: David Ritchie, "Shannon and Weaver: Unraveling the Paradox of Information," *Communication Research,* Vol. 13, 1986, pp. 278–298.

Meaningful information: Robert Wright, "Information in Formation," in *Three Scientists and Their Gods: Looking for Meaning in an Age of Information,* Harper & Row, New York, 1988, pp. 79–110.

Cloze research: Wilson Taylor, " 'Cloze Procedure': A New Tool for Measuring Readability," *Journalism Quarterly,* Vol. 30, 1953, pp. 415–433.

Clozentropy: Donald Darnell, " 'Clozentropy': A Procedure for Testing English Language Proficiency of Foreign Students," *Speech Monographs,* Vol. 37, 1970, pp. 36–46.

Equivocal communication: Janet Beavin Bavelas, Alex Black, Nicole Chovil, and Jennifer Mullett, *Equivocal Communication,* Sage, Newbury Park, Calif., 1990.

Research on jealousy: Gregory L. White and Paul E. Mullen, *Jealousy: Theory, Research, and Clinical Strategies,* Guilford, New York, 1989.

CHAPTER 5

The Meaning of Meaning
of I. A. Richards

When I teach my seminar on intimate communication, I always save the last thirty minutes of class for discussing ideas that aren't covered in the reading assignment. Halfway through the semester a student named Brenda asked a personal question that sparked everyone's interest: "When a guy says, 'I love you,' but wants me to 'prove' my affection, how can I tell if it's really love?"

I was about to suggest to Brenda that a declaration of love paired with a demand that she "put out" physically sounded more like an expression of lust than one of love. But I caught myself and avoided the semantic trap that Cambridge University professor I. A. Richards labeled the "proper meaning superstition"—the mistaken belief that words have a precise definition. Instead, I responded to her question with one of my own: "What do you mean when you use the word *love*?"

If he were still alive, Richards might have smiled in approval at my response. For even though he was a poet, world-class mountain climber, literary critic, and the author of forty-nine books, Ivor Armstrong Richards was first and foremost a teacher. And the lesson he most wanted students to learn was that meanings don't reside in words; they reside in people.

THE NEW RHETORIC: A STUDY OF HOW WORDS WORK

Richards was a man born ahead of his time. When he was a young scholar in the early 1920s, communication education focused mainly on the study of rhetoric. And Richards made no secret of his disdain for the art of oratory. "So low has Rhetoric sunk that we would do better just to dismiss it to Limbo than to trouble ourselves with it."[1] He was impatient with rhetoric's exclusive focus on public persuasion, characterizing it as "sales-talk selling sales-talk."[2] As for the historical study of classical rhetoric, he once said that he "didn't think history ought to have happened" and therefore "didn't see why we should study it."[3]

Richards proposed a new rhetoric that would be the "study of misunderstanding and its remedies."[4] The old rhetoric had offered general rules for speakers who wanted to sway an audience. Richards thought it was more important to examine how much of a message we understand when we hear it. His new rhetoric focused on comprehension rather than persuasion.

Like Shannon and Weaver, who we looked at in Chapter 4, Richards believed that every conversation suffers from information loss. But instead of blaming channel noise for the leakage, Richards attributed the communication gap between source and destination to the nature of language itself. The goal of his new rhetoric was to put words under the microscope to see how they work. Since he regarded language as an extension of the human mind and sense organs, his study was rooted in the humanities rather than science.

WORDS AS SYMBOLS INTERPRETED IN CONTEXT

As is common in the field of semantics, Richards began his inquiry into the meaning of meaning by making a distinction between signs and symbols. A sign is something we experience, but at the same time the sign also refers to something else. Thunder is a sign of rain. A punch in the nose is a sign of anger. An arrow is a sign of whatever it points toward.

Words are also signs, but of a special kind. They are symbols. Unlike the examples cited above, most words have no natural connection with the things they describe. There's nothing in the sound of the word *kiss* or anything visual in the letters *h-u-g* that signifies an embrace. One could just as easily coin the term *snarf* or *clag* to symbolize a close encounter of the romantic kind.

Because words are arbitrary symbols, they have no inherent meaning. Like chameleons that take on the coloration of their environment, words, according to Richards, take on the meaning of the context in which a person encounters them. This suggests that "most words, as they pass from context to context, change their meanings."[5] Context is therefore the key to meaning.

All of us have had grammar teachers who drummed into us the importance of looking at context to understand an unfamiliar term. They convinced us that we can usually grasp the author's meaning by looking at the surrounding words in a sentence. But Richards used the term *context* to refer to much more than adjacent phrases. He defined context as the "cluster of events that occur together." This means that context is not just a sentence, or even the situation in which the word is spoken. Context is the whole field of experience that can be connected with an event—including thoughts of similar events. Let's examine Brenda's thought process as she used the word *love* to see how this works.

THINKING AS A SORTING OF EXPERIENCES

The immediate context of Brenda's question was a seminar discussion about a test designed to measure love within families. In the course of this discussion, Brenda began to make connections between the filial love of parents and her romantic relationship with the guy who said he loved her. When Brenda

"I have a pet at home."

"Oh, what kind of pet?"

"It is a dog."

"What kind of dog?"

"It is a St. Bernard."

"Grown up or a puppy?"

"It is full grown."

"What color is it?"

"It is brown and white."

"Why didn't you say you had a full-grown, brown and white St. Bernard as a pet in the first place?"

Reprinted with permission of Macmillan Publishing Company from *Communications: The Transfer of Meaning* by Don Fabun. Copyright © 1968, Kaiser Aluminum & Chemical Corporation.

asked about true love, I had just told the class that the scale's creator defined virtue as "love which is directed toward furthering the welfare of another."[6] Brenda obviously saw a contrast between this definition of love and her boyfriend's if-you-love-me-prove-it demand.

Richards described thinking as the process of sorting experience into various categories:

> A perception is never just an *it*; perception takes whatever it perceives as a thing of a certain sort. All thinking from the lowest to highest—whatever else it may be—is sorting.[7]

His use of the term *sorting* makes me think of arranging a deck of cards according to the four suits—spades, clubs, diamonds, hearts. It's as if Brenda's mind were a card table, and after shuffling all her life experiences she pulled out the memory cards of love for family and romantic passion because they both had red hearts on the corners.

Further discussion in class revealed that Brenda tapped additional contexts for her understanding of the word *love*. She pictured walking hand in hand on an empty beach, hugging a cuddly kitten, giving a blanket to a homeless man on the street, and watching her future husband change their yet-to-be-conceived baby's diaper. Is all this what the word *love* really means? It was for Brenda. That's why I. A. Richards insisted that no dictionary could define the meaning of a word. Meaning is personal. Words don't mean things; people do.

THE SEMANTIC TRIANGLE: PICTURING THE PROBLEM

Together with his British colleague, C. K. Ogden, Richards created his semantic triangle to show the indirect relationship between symbols and their supposed referents. Figure 5.1 illustrates the shaky link between the word *dog* and the actual hound that may consume the majority of your groceries.

The top of the triangle shows some thoughts that you might have when observing the Hush Puppy pictured at the lower right. Once you perceive the actual animal, thoughts of warmth and faithful friendship fill your mind. Since there is a direct or causal relationship between the referent and the reference, Richards connected the two with a solid line.

Your thoughts are also directly linked with the dog symbol at the lower left of the triangle. Given the way you sort through your perceptions, using the word dog to symbolize your thoughts is almost a foregone conclusion. Richards diagrammed this causal relationship with a solid line as well.

But the connection between the word dog and the actual animal is tenuous at best. Richards represented it with a dotted line. Two people could use that identical word to stand for completely different beasts. When you say *dog*, you might mean a slow-moving, gentle pet who is very fond of children. When I use the word, I might mean a carnivorous canine who bites anyone— and is very fond of children. (Note the slippery use of the term *fond* in this

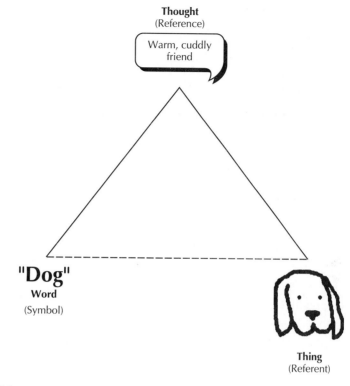

FIGURE 5.1
The Semantic Triangle (From Ogden and Richards, *The Meaning of Meaning.*)

example.) Unless we both understand that ambiguity is an inevitable condition of language, you and I are liable to carry on a conversation about dogs without ever realizing we aren't talking about the same thing.

Lest you think the identification of a word with its referent is a trivial problem, consider references to acquired immune deficiency syndrome. Just the word *AIDS* has a chilling effect on many who hear it. Ponder the plight of the manufacturer of a dietetic candy called "Ayds." Because the name of the candy sounds like the medical condition, sales fell 50 percent and the manufacturer was forced to change the name of the product.

Richards believed that his semantic triangle applies to all words—the descriptive terms of science, the emotive terms of poetry, and the vast majority of words that fall somewhere in between. But he didn't regard words as equal-opportunity puzzlers. He saw emotive language as the chief source of linguistic confusion. As Brenda and the rest of us in the intimacy seminar discovered, words like *love* can produce great misunderstanding. The greater the discrepancy in the life experiences of two people, the greater the probability that words meant to describe feelings and attitudes will create semantic chaos.

LINGUISTIC REMEDIES FOR MISUNDERSTANDING

Late in his career, I. A. Richards borrowed Shannon and Weaver's information theory model (see page 49) and altered it to show the necessity of common experience for the effective communication of meaning. Figure 5.2 shows his addition of comparison fields. The downward-pointing arrows stand for past comments made in specific situations. Clusters of arrows represent similar statements made in similar situations. The sum total of these "utterances in situations" forms the context that guides the speaker's selection of language or the listener's interpretation of those words.

According to Richards, two people in a conversation could fully understand what each other meant if they had a lifetime of identical experiences. Of course, that's not possible. Even identical twins have comparison fields that grow increasingly diverse as they grow older. But communication is best when both parties have a "long and varied acquaintanceship, close familiarity, lives whose circumstances have often corresponded, in short an exceptional fund of common experience."[8]

Since long-term interconnectedness is rare and not easy to attain, Richards suggested a variety of linguistic ways that people may create a greater region of shared experiences and thus avoid talking past each other. These

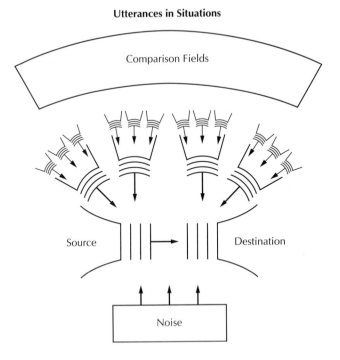

FIGURE 5.2
Utterances in Situations (From Richards, *Speculative Instruments*.)

include the use of definition, metaphor, feedforward, and Basic English. The rest of the chapter will examine these four remedies for misunderstanding.

1. Definition

Richards regarded definitions as symbol substitutions. They are words used in place of another word to explain the thought in a person's mind. Consistent with the links between words (symbols), thoughts (references), and things (referents) diagrammed in his semantic triangle, definitions, Richards reminded readers, always describe the ideas in our heads rather than the static reality of something "out there." Therefore, we should always begin a definition by saying, "When I use this word, I mean . . ." or something similar.

Definitions are like maps. They can guide us where we want to go only if we know where we are. We need a starting point—a place on the map where we can point and state with confidence, "I am here." Richards suggested a number of starting points that are liable to be within the comparison fields of our listeners. I'll again use the word *love* in a romantic context to illustrate some of these definitional routes. I've heard each of the following statements voiced by different people:

Symbolization   "That's what I mean by love." (Spoken while pointing at a couple exchanging their wedding vows.)

Similarity   "As I interpret the word, love is like a lifetime commitment."

Spatial relations   "I consider love to be sexual intercourse, nothing more, nothing less."

Temporal relations   "As I see it, individuals can love others only after they like themselves."

Causation   "I believe love inevitably leads to self-sacrifice."

Object of a mental state   "Love to me is desiring the best for another person."

Legal relations   "I judge a couple to be in a state of love when they have entered into a joint property agreement."

No one of these routes to understanding may provide an adequate way for Brenda to define what she means when she uses the word *love*. Richards recognized that some usage might require more than one starting point to adequately convey how a person interprets a word. But even with that option available, we shouldn't be surprised if Brenda and her boyfriend end up in different places when they speak of love. As Richards concluded:

> We ought to regard communication as a difficult matter, and close correspondence of reference for different thinkers as a comparatively rare event. It is never safe to assume that it has been secured unless both the starting-points and the routes of definition . . . are known.[9]

2. Metaphor

Richards introduced his discussion of metaphor with an attack on the idea that "an eye for resemblances" is a special gift belonging to poets alone.[10] He regarded language as naturally metaphoric, and considered it almost impossible to speak more than a few sentences without using a figure of speech. Metaphors aren't just "a happy extra trick with words." They are the very stuff of language. That's because we think in pictures.

Thinking is like sorting through a stack of mental photographs. We create a metaphor when we pull out two dissimilar pictures and put them together. In that sense, metaphors are two-for-one bargains. The composite image borrows characteristics from both of the original photographs but is itself a new thought. Richards described the process as a blending of diverse ideas:

> When we use a metaphor we have two thoughts of different things active together and supported by a single word, or phrase, whose meaning is a resultant of their interaction.[11]

We can see metaphorical thinking reflected in the language of love. For example:

love + flowers → seeds of love

love + calendar → seasons of love

love + illness → lovesick

love + youth → puppy love

love + fire → flames of love

love + gravity → falling in love

The first two metaphors on the right pick up on the developmental nature of love, the middle two capture its intensity, and the final pair suggest that love is almost impossible to control. Since these meanings might not be within the listener's experience of love, it's up to the speaker to create a secondhand reality through the use of metaphor. According to Richards, the process is often best when it's subtle:

> What is needed for the wholeness of an experience is not always naturally present, and metaphor supplies an excuse by which what is needed may be smuggled in.[12]

Richards doesn't offer step-by-step instructions on how to create powerful metaphors. Using one of his own metaphors, however, he does note that the discrepancy between the paired images is like the tension in a tightly drawn bow. The greater the apparent contradiction between the images, the faster the arrow or metaphor will fly when released. But if the metaphor isn't apt and misses the target, all that power is wasted. The listener has to be able to see the point of contact between the two images.

3. Feedforward

When Richards was 75 years old, the *Saturday Review* asked him to write an article for their "What I Have Learned" series. Instead of writing about the false assumption that words have inherent meaning, the importance of similar experience, or the function of metaphors, Richards chose the concept of "feedforward" as his most important insight.

We saw in the previous chapter on information theory that feedback is the effect of the receiver on the source. Feedforward works in the opposite direction. It is the anticipatory process of acting as our own first receiver so that we can pretest the impact of our words on an audience. If we don't like what we hear, we can always reframe the message to have a better effect.

As I write this chapter, I imagine myself reading my words sitting at a desk, sprawled on a bed, or riding on a bus. I picture a frown on my face while I try to sort out the difference between symbol, reference, and referent; a faraway look in my eyes as I remember a discussion about the meaning of love with a girl named Ann; a brief smile as I glance at the dog cartoon on page 59. I picture myself picking up a yellow marker to highlight the summary statement, "Words don't mean things; people do." I also say the words I've written out loud to hear how they sound. Do they make sense, or are they just paragraphs of gobbledegook?

The role-play process I've just described illustrates Richards' concept of feedforward. It's a humbling experience. I don't always like the response I imagine, so I stay at the word processor to see whether I can get it right. Feedback from students and instructors will soon let me know. But as with definition and metaphor—Richards' other remedies for misunderstanding—feedforward forces me to consider the experience of the other person.

According to Richards, communicators who avoid feedforward tend to be dogmatic. ("Don't confuse me with the facts; my mind's made up.") By contrast, those who try to anticipate the effect of their words are often more open-minded. They entertain doubts about whether or not they've made things clear and even question the rightness of their ideas. Richards applauded this tentative approach to truth. His commitment to feedforward is reflected in his book *Speculative Instruments*, which is listed in A Second Look at the end of the chapter. The title suggests an ongoing willingness to change what he says.

4. Basic English

While working together on their book *The Meaning of Meaning*, C. K. Ogden and I. A. Richards discussed their desire to develop a basic form of their mother tongue that would make teaching English as a second language simpler. They later selected 850 words that new speakers may quickly learn. Ogden and Richards had no doubt that any person who knows this group of words will be able to clearly discuss complex ideas.

Richards went to China for two years to field-test Basic English. He discovered that his belief in the system was right. Armed with these basic words and a working knowledge of the rules of language, a complete stranger to the English language was able to talk about almost anything.

Even though Harvard University gave Richards money to move forward with books, motion pictures, and other teaching helps, most English educators laughed at his attempt to make learning the language quick and simple. They thought it was a sad waste that this great man of arts and letters no longer seemed to care about beautiful prose. But Richards did not give up hope. As we saw from his picture of comparison fields, he was certain that common experience helped people make sense of what they were hearing. And common language produces common experience.

What is your reaction to Richards' design for language learning? Are 850 words enough to represent all the ideas and feelings in a person's mind? One thought for you before making your decision—every word that I have used in this discussion of Basic English has been taken from Richards' list. Note that the writing may be a bit rough and the word selection limited, but does a clear sense come through? Maybe Richards' idea is not so strange after all.

CRITIQUE: FINDING THE PROBLEM IS EASIER THAN FIXING IT

Despite the sheer volume of his writings and the scope of his enterprise, few modern-day semanticists, rhetoricians, or literary critics discuss the work of I. A. Richards. That's too bad. Richards was willing to plunge into the question of meaning—a semantic swamp that scares off most linguists and rhetoricians. His microscopic look at how words work provides the valuable insight that the symbols we use don't have a direct relationship with the things we want to describe.

Since *The Meaning of Meaning* first appeared in 1923, many scholars have independently reached similar conclusions. For example, Korzybski's theory of general semantics claims that words are attempts to map reality, but that a verbal map is not the territory, nor can it ever depict all of the territory.[13] Present-day postmodernist critics share Richards' distrust of history and contend that interpretation is the only reality we can communicate.[14] But I. A. Richards had these insights first.

Richards did a better job of explaining why misunderstanding occurs than he did in offering effective remedies to avoid the problem. His discussions of definition, metaphor, and feedforward are limited to a few chapters, and after introducing each topic, he failed to develop it further. As part of a theory of comprehension, he offered seven "speculative instruments" for probing the meaning of a word. But ironically, his theory of comprehension strikes me as incomprehensible, and I find his speculative instruments of no practical help when trying to understand what another person means. That's why I've omitted these instruments from this chapter.

Richards provoked a storm of protest over his teaching design for Basic English. Although he candidly admitted that part of his intent was to plant "mental and moral seed" within the illiterate peoples of the world, cultural imperialism was not what riled up his critics. They simply couldn't understand why a wordsmith of Richards' caliber would abandon a love for words that could express subtle nuances of thought. Perhaps the point is moot, because Basic English never caught on. But to me, Basic English is quite in line with Richards' primary assumption about verbal symbols. If words have no intrinsic meaning, it seems perfectly reasonable to express an idea by stringing together four or five common words instead of relying on a single esoteric term that could easily be misinterpreted.

So how can I. A. Richards' semantic theory benefit Brenda and her boyfriend? Because both of them bring different romantic experiences to their relationship, Richards' new rhetoric suggests that the couple will probably not reach agreement on a single meaning for the word *love*. But a knowledge of his main ideas would alert both parties to the fact that each of them interprets the word differently and would start them on a journey to discover how the other person is using the term. Even though they'll never completely succeed, the joint venture itself could draw them closer together.

QUESTIONS TO SHARPEN YOUR FOCUS

1. Richards claims that the *proper meaning superstition* is at the root of verbal misunderstanding. Using his *semantic triangle*, how would you explain this concept to a friend?

2. How does Richards' *new rhetoric* differ from the neo-Aristotelian rhetoric you read about in Chapter 2?

3. Can you think of a *metaphor* that would effectively communicate your concept of love to someone of the opposite sex?

4. What is the connection between Richards' concept of *comparison fields* and his hope for *Basic English*?

A SECOND LOOK

Recommended resource: I. A. Richards, *The Philosophy of Rhetoric*, Oxford University, London, 1936.

Overview of theory: Sonja Foss, Karen Foss, and Robert Trapp, *Contemporary Perspectives on Rhetoric*, 2d ed., Waveland Press, Prospect Heights, Ill., 1991, pp. 27–53.

Overview of theory: Daniel Fogarty, "I. A. Richards," in *Essays on the Rhetoric of the Western World*, Edward P. J. Corbett, James. L. Golden, and Goodwin F. Berquist (eds.), Kendall/Hunt, Dubuque, Iowa, 1990, pp. 304–320.

New rhetoric: Marie Hochmuth Nichols, "I. A. Richards and the 'New Rhetoric,'" *Quarterly Journal of Speech*, Vol. 44, 1958, pp. 1–16.

Semantic triangle: C. K. Ogden and I. A. Richards, *The Meaning of Meaning*, Harcourt, Brace & World, New York, 1946, pp. 1–23.

Metaphor: I. A. Richards, *The Philosophy of Rhetoric*, Oxford University, London, 1936, pp. 85–138.

Definition: C. K. Ogden and I. A. Richards, *The Meaning of Meaning*, Harcourt, Brace & World, New York, 1946, pp. 109–138.

Communication model: I. A. Richards, "Toward a Theory of Comprehending," in *Speculative Instruments*, University of Chicago, Chicago, 1955, pp. 17–38.

Feedforward: I. A. Richards, "The Secret of 'Feedforward,'" *Saturday Review*, February 3, 1968, pp. 14–17.

Basic English: I. A. Richards, *Basic English and Its Uses*, W. W. Norton, New York, 1943.

Collection of essays: Ann E. Berthoff (ed.), *Richards on Rhetoric*, Oxford University Press, New York, 1991.

CHAPTER 6

Coordinated Management of Meaning

of W. Barnett Pearce & Vernon Cronen

Imagine a group of musicians coming to a concert hall without a fixed idea of what composition they're going to play that evening. Because there is no conductor, no musical score, and no time to rehearse, they must improvise. The potential for interpersonal conflict and musical dissonance is great. Yet occasionally the individual members of this orchestra manage to coordinate their efforts and produce a piece of music that satisfies each performer. The predicament the musicians face is a metaphor of the problems people confront when they try to communicate with others. W. Barnett Pearce of Loyola University in Chicago and Vernon Cronen of the University of Massachusetts refer to the communication process as the "coordinated management of meaning."

Pearce and Cronen think that analyzing the notes the musicians play would be a sterile exercise compared with trying to figure out the process they'll use to determine what to play and how to play it. Although trained in the United States to be empirical scientists, these communication professors now reject the traditional western approach that sees communication as an exchange of ideas or judges its value on the basis of truth or falseness. They see communication as a "form of social action best studied as a process of creating and managing social reality rather than as a technique for describing objective reality."[1] In that sense, communication research is like standing backstage at the concert, watching the improvised performance. The researcher tries to decipher the personal rules that guide individual players as they blend or clash with the rest of the orchestra.

The coordinated management of meaning (CMM) theory assumes that as people try to make sense of their world, they act on the basis of the meanings they ascribe to events. The problem is that their individual interpretations may not coincide. Although not billed as a theory of dysfunctional communication, most of the examples Pearce and Cronen use to illustrate the princi-

FIGURE 6.1
Characters of *M*A*S*H* in the Early Years. *From left to right:* Frank Burns, Margaret Houlihan, "Hawkeye" Pierce, Henry Blake, "Trapper" McIntyre, Father Mulcahy, "Radar" O'Reilly, Corporal Klinger.

ples of CMM involve disagreements, disputes, or fights. They ascribe communication failure to the inability of parties to mesh their disparate interpretations. Pearce and Cronen note that coordination is difficult enough in one-on-one relationships (lovers, doctor-patient, lawyer-client), but even harder in the typical group situation, which requires a juggling act of multiple enmeshment.

I'll use the TV series *M*A*S*H* to illustrate the major principles of CMM. Not only did the show win ten straight annual Emmy awards as television's outstanding comedy series, but the fictional activities of the 4077th Mobile Army Surgical Hospital (MASH) unit on the Korean battlefield reflect the human values of CMM's creators. As one television reviewer wrote, "The villain was senseless violence, and the hero was the resiliency of the human spirit."[2] The scripted activities of "Hawkeye" Pierce, B. J. Hunnicutt, Charles Winchester, Frank Burns, Margaret "Hot Lips" Houlihan, Father Mulcahy, Colonel Potter, Klinger, and "Radar" O'Reilly support Pearce and Cronen's contention that "persons in conversation" constantly achieve coherence, coordinate actions, and experience mystery.

> The way communication works is grounded in three universal aspects of the human condition: persons interpret their environment and their experience; they interact with their fellows; and they remind themselves that there is more to life than the immediate moment. . . . These are not "options" in which per-

sons may or may not engage, or variables that may be present to some extent; rather, they are constitutive aspects of what it means to be human.[3]

The rest of the chapter will explore the CMM concepts of coherence, coordination, and mystery.

COHERENCE: HIERARCHY OF MEANINGS PROVIDE MULTIPLE FRAMES OF REFERENCE

Pearce and Cronen propose that an individual's meanings are organized hierarchically, as shown in Figure 6.2. Picturing the relationship as a series of boxes within boxes, they call it a "nestled hierarchy." Higher (larger) levels of meaning determine interpretations that are lower or deeper within the system. The authors don't insist that there are exactly six levels, and even the order can change. But Pearce and Cronen are committed to the concept that higher-level (larger) meanings provide a context for the lower (smaller) ones within.

Content.   In the final episode of *M*A*S*H*, Hawkeye says, "I can't say I've loved you all, but I've loved everyone I could." People who know the English language will have a rough idea of the referent for each word, but they won't know what to make of the sentence without a context. For Pearce

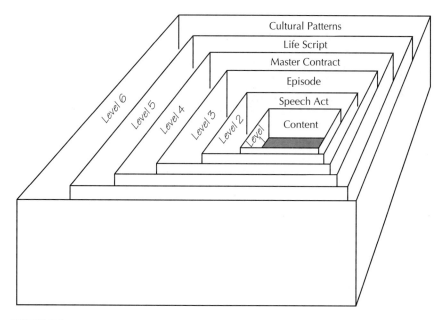

FIGURE 6.2
A Model of Hierarchically Organized Meanings (Adapted from Cronen and Pearce, "The Coordinated Management of Meaning: A Theory of Communication.")

and Cronen, questioning the validity of Hawkeye's words makes no sense. What we see and hear is neither true nor false; raw sensory data just are.

Speech Act. Hawkeye's statement came in the final episode of *M*A*S*H*, a two-and-one-half-hour special that portrayed the breakup of the Army surgical unit at the end of the Korean war. His words followed Major Margaret Houlihan's expression of love for her departing nurses. The usually hard-boiled head nurse professes, "I've loved you all," which triggers Hawkeye's rejoinder. His "I've loved everyone I could" comment draws laughter and sidelong glances from many of the nurses—including Margaret. This relational history is necessary to understand the meaning of Hawkeye's words. Just as punctuation gives a context for the printed word, the relationship embedded in a speech act dictates how the content is to be taken.

Episode. An episode is a communication routine that has definite boundaries and rules. Pearce and Cronen describe the sequence as "nounable." The label placed on an episode answers the question, What does he think he's doing? The answer in Hawkeye's case could be boasting of sexual prowess, disclosing a secret, telling a lie, cracking a joke, providing tension relief, or saying good-bye. The reaction of the nurses suggests that each of the last three options describes part of what was going on. From Hawkeye's point of view, it was a leave-them-laughing exit line. CMM theory regards the episodic level as the most important key to unlocking the meaning of an interaction.

Master Contract. Master contracts establish the relational boundaries between players. Even though there was a rough-and-tumble rivalry among the doctors in the unit, they showed a "we-they" solidarity when confronted by the bloodshed inflicted by the enemy or the stupidity perpetuated by their superiors sitting safely in Seoul. Every encounter shown on the screen can only be understood against a backdrop of a half-million fatalities in what seemed to the doctors a senseless war that was never officially declared by

Congress. With the exception of the gung-ho military attitude of Major Frank Burns (and Margaret in early episodes), members of the 4077th MASH unit embraced wide latitudes of deviant behavior. Hawkeye's womanizing, Klinger's transvestite dress, and Radar's attachment to a teddy bear were easily tolerated in light of the part each man played in overcoming a common adversary.

Life Script.   Pearce and Cronen describe life scripts as "clusters of episodes defined by the person as those in which s/he does or might participate." They avoid using the term *self-concept* because they fear it suggests a solitary fixed-in-stone view of self that doesn't capture the flow of activities which Hawkeye would call to mind if he said, "This is me." Every scene with Hawkeye shows that he has a life script that confronts tragedy with humor. His sarcasm holds insanity at arm's length.

Cultural Patterns.   Oriental audiences are puzzled by Hawkeye's irreverent individualism, but many Americans readily identify with his anti-authoritarian stance and sexual license. They find his freewheeling style so compelling because it represents what they would like to be. All dialogue in the television show is framed by even broader human concerns—fear of death, desire to be with loved ones, compassion for those who hurt, the urge for freedom, and so forth. Pearce and Cronen say that without these overarching human concerns, coherence would be impossible. As it is, they believe we still require a set of rules to coordinate our personal interpretations with those reached by someone else.

Rules for Meaning

The viewer of *M*A*S*H* is acutely aware that each doctor at the 4077th MASH has adopted a set of spoken and unspoken rules for making sense of the alternating boredom and horror of the war. For example, Hawkeye's activities show that he interprets events according to the following credo:

1. Medical competence excuses almost any other fault.
2. Military regulations are made to be broken.
3. Narrow-mindedness is the unforgivable sin.

Major Frank Burns violates all three of these guidelines. Burns is portrayed as an incompetent surgeon, a stickler for military discipline, and a hypocritical prude. No wonder Hawkeye interprets Burns' anticommunist remarks as episodes of lunacy rather than as words of a patriot.

Colonel Potter is more charitable. As a veteran Army officer who has "seen it all," the colonel's rules for meaning appear more flexible than Hawkeye's canons of judgment. Potter observes the same faults in Frank Burns that vex Hawkeye, but he merely regards Frank as "the head twerp" of the outfit. Despite their somewhat different interpretations, Hawkeye and the colonel share a similar need for coherence. Without rules to interpret the significance of others' words and deeds, neither man would be able to organize and sustain meaning.

CMM theory refers to sense-making guidelines as *"constitutive rules."* They link different levels of the hierarchy and determine meanings at lower levels. Constitutive rules offer coherence—a way to survive and even thrive in an interpersonal world that's often in disarray. When a new doctor, B. J. Hunnicutt, arrives on the scene, Hawkeye quickly fills him in on how to interpret the chaos he sees:

> The first thing you learn here, B.J., is that insanity is no worse than the common cold. You've heard of a military post? Ours is a compost. Only the wounded are new. The tedium is relieved only by the boredom. So pitch in, muddle through, pip-pip. Never mind the reason why, ours is but to do and not let 'em die.[4]

COORDINATION: NEGOTIATING THE RULES OF ACTIVITY

Hawkeye quickly came to appreciate B.J. because the new recruit "fit in" to the activities of the MASH unit. For Hawkeye, the essence of the frontline medicine was "meatball surgery," an emergency effort to stave off death until the patient could be stabilized. B.J. was able to adopt and adapt to the medical guidelines of Hawkeye and the other doctors:

1. Speed is more important than medical nicety.
2. No one pulls rank in the operating room.
3. Injured Americans don't have priority over Koreans.
4. Incoming wounded are subject to *triage*.

Pearce and Cronen refer to guides for appropriate action as *"regulative rules."* The rules answer the question, What should I do next? They build on the personalized meanings provided by constitutive rules and then direct sequences of interpersonal behavior. A formal statement of rule 4 would read as follows:

> The incoming wounded will be sorted into three groups according to their condition: (1) life-threatening, but survivable, injuries; (2) non-life-threatening injuries; (3) nonsurvivable mortal wounds. Injuries should be treated in that order.

For doctors at the 4077th MASH, it was a life-and-death rule.

When two or more people manage to coordinate their systems of constitutive and regulative rules, the result is like the smooth hum of meshing gears in a well-built auto transmission. But enmeshment doesn't always happen. In the case of Hawkeye and Frank Burns, their clusters of rules constantly clashed. For example, Burns breached Hawkeye's surgical priorities when he announced his intent to treat an American officer with a minor wound instead of first attending to a severely injured North Korean. The ensuing friction was typical of the conflict between Burns and Hawkeye featured on other episodes of *M*A*S*H*. Every interaction between the two men lurched forward amid much grinding of teeth and stripping of gears.

Hawkeye seemed to take delight in harassing or "baiting" Major Burns, while Frank relished the opportunity to report Hawkeye's misdeeds to superior officers. Viewers aren't shocked when the ongoing interpersonal battle turns far more bitter than the fight with the North Korean enemy. There is, however, a special kind of failed coordination depicted in *M*A*S*H* that's surprising because neither side wants the conflict to continue—yet it does. Pearce and Cronen call it an *unwanted repetitive pattern*.

Unwanted Repetitive Patterns

CMM focuses upon episodes of conflict that form unwanted repetitive patterns (URPs). These verbal fights recur over and over between two parties regardless of the topic or how pleasant each is with other people. Usually both parties have some knowledge of what's going on but seem powerless to break the cycle. They look back ruefully at the last unpleasant episode and mutter, "Darn, we did it again."

CMM's description of URPs fits the ongoing strife in *M*A*S*H* between Hawkeye and Dr. Charles Emerson Winchester III. Charles comes from an upper-crust Boston family, and unlike Hawkeye, who is somewhat of an uncultured slob, Winchester is fastidious about personal cleanliness and highbrow music. At various times he refers to Hawkeye as a "primitive," a "cretin," a "heathen," or a "barbarian." Hawkeye is no more complimentary in his references to Charles. The two men seem doomed to an endless pattern of verbal put-downs.

Pearce and Cronen don't regard URPs as the result of rotten personality or moral failing in either party. The theorists see, instead, the clash of two juxtaposed and incompatible sets of guidelines for behavior. They use the term *logical force* to describe the pressure that gamelike rules appear to exert upon both parties to act in a predetermined manner.

The *M*A*S*H* episode entitled "The Smell of Music" illustrates how people can get locked into unwanted repetitive patterns. Charles is offended by the body odor of B.J. and Hawkeye. They, in turn, are equally disgusted by the classical music he plays day and night on his French horn. "Make a deal with you, Winchester," B.J. suggests. "You knock off the horn, and we'll shower." Charles merely becomes more resolute: "Reek away, gentlemen. I shall continue to play as long as there is breath in my body and music in my soul."[5]

Pearce and Cronen list a number of factors that give URPs a destructive logical force. The viewer can see four of these forces at work in the seemingly childish behavior of each man in the conflict.

1. A strong link between an act and its antecedent. (Once both sides establish a causal connection between symphonic sounds and stench, it is difficult for either side to back down.)

2. A strong link between an act and a person's life script. (Charles is a snob; Hawkeye, a slob. Both men are proud of it.)

3. A narrow range of alternative acts. (The either-or choices of music or silence, showers or smell, don't leave much room for compromise.)

4. A weak link between an act and its consequences. (As long as Charles, B.J., and Hawkeye can remain stubborn without further repercussions, they have no incentive to change.)

Taken together, the logical force of these factors obligates Charles to reassert his right to play the horn and exerted an equal pressure upon Hawkeye and B.J. to continue their pungent protest. From within each man's system of regulative rules, holding firm makes sense. Neither side is able to step outside the destructive system. The standoff ends only when the rest of the unit resorts to washing down the offensive bodies of B.J. and Hawkeye with a high-pressure hose, and Margaret mangles the offending French horn by tossing it under the wheels of a passing jeep. The scene is great comedy but poor conflict resolution.

Conflict Within: Strange Loops

CMM is a theory which is continually evolving. Although early statements of the theory focused on coordination of meaning and activities between persons, recent versions have also analyzed a form of internal dialogue that occurs between the different levels of meaning within the individual. As was illustrated in Figure 6.2, higher-level meanings usually dictate interpretations lower down. Sometimes, however, lower meanings reflect back and alter the context in which they are enclosed. Pearce and Cronen call these reflected meanings "strange loops," and a *M*A*S*H* episode about Hawkeye's obsession with food calls to mind the vicious circle in which bulimics are caught. Hawkeye's fantasy of the perfect barbecue rib dinner led to some wacky antics on the show, but a bulimic's preoccupation with all kinds of food can manifest crazy-like behavior that is more dangerous than funny.

Bulimia is an eating disorder, more common in women than men. Like the compulsive overeater, the bulimic consumes vast quantities of food but, like the anorexic, also has a fashion model's obsession with being thin. The bulimic avoids gaining weight by vomiting before the food can be digested. Addiction counselors note that the secrecy of the binge-purge cycle has a devastating effect on self-esteem.

Figure 6.3 diagrams the strange loop in which a woman named Cathy and other bulimics are caught. Although her past experience offers no support for

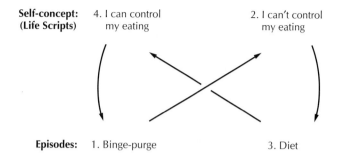

Self-concept: 4. I can control   2. I can't control
(Life Scripts)   my eating   my eating

Episodes: 1. Binge-purge   3. Diet

FIGURE 6.3
The Bulimic's Syndrome (Adapted from Branham and Pearce, "Between Text and Context: Toward a Rhetoric of Contextual Reconstruction.")

the myth, Cathy lives under the illusion that she can control her eating. Because of the addictive nature of the disease, sooner or later Cathy will have a binge-purge episode (1). The shame of feeling out of control reflects negatively on her self-esteem (2). Cathy vows to diet as a means of boosting her diminished image (3). Experiencing a measure of success, Cathy denies she has a problem and relies on willpower to control her eating (4), setting herself up for another lap around the strange loop.

Most addiction counselors think that Pearce and Cronen have described the bulimic's dilemma well. In fact, some therapists use CMM's strange-loop analysis as a tool to confront clients with the serious nature of their eating disorder. Unless the bulimic works to break the pattern, she'll be trapped on the racetrack of her own self-demolition derby. This schematic drawing can stimulate an "ah-hah" insight into the endless cycle of yo-yo dieting.

Although CMM is known as a *rules* theory, Pearce and Cronen don't use the term in a deterministic fashion. For CMM theorists, rules are not minilaws that dictate individual action, nor are they prescriptive tapes that play over and over in our heads. Rules are the regular gamelike patterns of activity that we can observe in others and in ourselves.

People caught up in unwanted repetitive patterns and strange loops may act in a way that seems written in stone. The explanations they offer for their behavior may be sprinkled with phrases like "I must . . . ," "I had to . . . ," "I could do no other. . . ." But even though people may feel they have no choice, CMM theory suggests that they usually do. Neither Hawkeye nor Frank Burns, Charles Winchester, nor B.J. are prisoners of the interpersonal rules systems of which they are a part. Pearce and Cronen celebrate human freedom, hope, novelty, and humor as the signs of a competent communicator who is able to achieve convergence with almost anyone.

MYSTERY: THE TIMES WHEN RULES DON'T WORK

CMM uses the term *mystery* as a reminder that there is more to life than the mere fact of daily existence. Pearce notes that "with a single exception, all societies of which records remain have told themselves stories that included descriptions of the mysterious."[6] The exception is our modern society that systematically debunks gods, ghosts, and giants. The authors of CMM believe that the attempt of rationalists and behaviorists to stick to the facts is a mistake and will ultimately fail. Pearce and Cronen applaud artists, poets, priests, children, science fiction writers, and anyone else who gives voice to what ultimately can't be said.

Perhaps because the characters can't ignore death (the great mystery of life), *M*A*S*H* episodes frequently acknowledge the unseen. For example, Winchester questions a dying soldier in an attempt to discover what's on "the other side." Radar O'Reilly validates his nickname with his uncanny ability to know when inbound choppers are on the way with wounded. And with literal sincerity, Colonel Potter refers to the presence of Chaplain Father Mulcahy as a "godsend."

Even when playing for laughs, the creators of *M*A*S*H* don't give easy answers to supernatural questions. B.J. asks Father Mulcahy to explain why the camp experienced a run of "bad luck" right after Colonel Potter ordered a Buddhist spirit post removed. The chaplain answers: "Bishop O'Hara at the seminary had a brilliant explanation for phenomena such as these. He said, 'That's the way the ball bounces.'" Consistent with these scenes from *M*A*S*H*, Pearce and Cronen emphasize that sometimes life moves beyond "mere factuality."

In his book *Communication and the Human Condition* Barnett Pearce pulls together the three concepts of coordination, coherence, and mystery by comparing communication to the process of drawing lines.

> For *coordination*, it is only necessary that those who interact with each other draw the lines at the same place—this allows them to "dance" with each other. For *coherence*, it is only necessary that there be some lines drawn somewhere— this allows us to tame the terrors of history and impose meaning and order on the world. But *mystery* is the reminder that such lines are ultimately arbitrary distortions. . . . Without such reminders, hard-eyed men and women forget that [a word] is the basis for coordination and coherence, not a map of "reality."[7]

CRITIQUE: WHAT DO THEY THINK THEY ARE DOING?

There's a professor at the college where I teach who gives one-question essay exams. Students are fond of characterizing their scope: "Describe how the universe works. Use examples." Pearce and Cronen's coordinated management of meaning reads like an answer to that question. CMM is an impressive macrotheory of human interaction, by far the most ambitious effort to spring from the ranks of speech communication scholars.

Pearce and Cronen have been responsive to criticism and continue to refine and recast their ideas. The theorists' recent integration of communication activities under the themes of coherence, convergence, and mystery offers a welcome counterpoint to reductionistic researchers who examine single factors like eye contact, language intensity, or source credibility. The authors' identification and analysis of nestled hierarchies, constitutive rules, logical forces, URPs, strange loops, and a host of other innovative creations could keep communication scholars busy for years to come.

Yet the very scope of the theory makes it difficult to pin down the central tenets of CMM. Vernon Cronen acknowledges the charge of critics that CMM is "a black hole in space" that sucks in almost every issue of human existence:

> CMM's creators keep dragging it into all sorts of issues that do not seem to be the proper place for communication scholars. I want to explain why this must be so with a very short story.[8]

Cronen then presents an enigmatic tale that leaves most readers unsure about the point he's trying to make. This isn't an isolated case. In terms of information theory (see Chapter 4), the literature of CMM contains many puzzling observations that fail to reduce uncertainty.

You'll recall that episodic meaning in CMM's nestled hierarchy responds to the question, What do they think they are doing? Pearce and Cronen's answer is rooted in the humanities rather than the social sciences, so any evaluation of CMM should be based on the interpretive criteria presented in Chapter 3. Undoubtedly, CMM's strength is the new understanding the theorists offer into the activities of "persons in conversation." This insight is offset by CMM's inability so far to create a community of agreement among communication scholars.

Viewers of *M*A*S*H* needed a few months to understand the complex character of Hawkeye Pierce. Once they began to grasp what he was about, the program's ratings soared. The same thing could happen for CMM. As soon as students of communication understand what Barnett Pearce and Vernon Cronen are doing, the theory could gain a wide and appreciative following.

QUESTIONS TO SHARPEN YOUR FOCUS

1. Given CMM's focus on *coherence, coordination,* and *mystery,* what type of research (*experiments, survey research, textual analysis,* or *ethnography*) is most appropriate?

2. Label five or more *episodes* in which you have been involved the last few days. Is there a common thread that runs through these episodes that can be explained by your *life script*?

3. Think of a time when you felt you simply *must act* in a certain way. To what extent can you see factors that increase *logical force* at work in the situation?

4. What hope do Pearce and Cronen offer to a person caught in a *strange loop* or an *unwanted repetitive pattern*?

A SECOND LOOK

Recommended resource: Vernon Cronen and W. Barnett Pearce, "The Coordinated Management of Meaning: A Theory of Communication," in *Human Communication Theory*, Frank E. X. Dance (ed.), Harper & Row, New York, 1982, pp. 61–89.

Original statement of theory: W. Barnett Pearce and Vernon Cronen, *Communication, Action, and Meaning: The Creation of Social Realities*, Praeger, New York, 1980.

Revision and extension: W. Barnett Pearce, *Communication and the Human Condition*, Southern Illinois University, Carbondale, 1989.

Unwanted repetitive patterns: Vernon Cronen, W. Barnett Pearce, and Lonna Snavely, "A Theory of Rule-Structure and Types of Episodes and a Study of Perceived Enmeshment in Undesired Repetitive Patterns ('URPs'), " in *Communication Yearbook 3*, Dan Nimmo (ed.), Transaction Books, New Brunswick, N.J., 1979, pp. 225–240.

Logical force: Vernon Cronen and W. Barnett Pearce, "Logical Force in Interpersonal Communication: A New Concept of the 'Necessity' in Social Behavior," *Communication*, Vol. 6, 1981, pp. 5–67.

Strange loops: Robert Branham and W. Barnett Pearce, "Between Text and Context: Toward a Rhetoric of Contextual Reconstruction," *Quarterly Journal of Speech*, Vol. 71, 1985, pp. 19–36.

Intercultural emphasis: Vernon E. Cronen, Victoria Chen, and W. Barnett Pearce, "Coordinated Management of Meaning: A Critical Theory," in *Theories in Intercultural Communication*, Young Yun Kim and William Gudykunst (eds.), Sage, Newbury Park, Calif., 1988, pp. 66–98.

Ethical implications: Vernon E. Cronen, "Coordinated Management of Meaning Theory and Postenlightenment Ethics," in *Conversation on Communication Ethics*, Karen Joy Greenberg (ed.), Ablex, Norwood, N.J., 1991, pp. 21–53.

Critique: David Brenders, "Fallacies in the Coordinated Management of Meaning: A Philosophy of Language Critique of the Hierarchical Organization of Coherent Conversation and Related Theory," *Quarterly Journal of Speech*, Vol. 73, 1987, pp. 329–348.

Comparative critique: Bradford 'J' Hall, "Theories of Culture and Communication," *Communication Theory*, Vol. 2, 1992, pp. 50–70.

Eating disorders: Judi Hollis, *Fat Is a Family Affair*, Haseldton, Center City, Minn., 1987.

M*A*S*H: Suzy Kalter, *The Complete Book of M*A*S*H*, Harry N. Abrams, Inc., New York, 1984.

NONVERBAL MESSAGES

When applied to communication, the term *nonverbal* is somewhat unfortunate. It sounds like leftovers—everything that remains after words are removed from a message. Despite the inadequacy of defining behavior by what it isn't, *nonverbal* is now the standard umbrella term in the field for a wide range of communication acts. The label covers such diverse phenomena as facial expression, posture, gesture, direction of eye gaze, tone of voice, touch, spacing, the systematic use of time, the clothes we wear, and all other human artifacts.

University of California psychologist Paul Ekman lists five separate functions of nonverbal signals.[1] Eye behavior provides a convenient way to illustrate the distinctions, but keep in mind that other nonverbal behaviors serve these functions as well.

1. Emblems. Certain eye movements are symbols that have specific verbal equivalents. A wink can say, ''I'm not serious.'' For example, a Good Samaritan helps a stranded motorist change a flat tire and then announces, ''That will be fifty dollars.'' Wink.

2. Illustrators. A downward gaze can visually portray a verbal description of depression. The observer gets a double dose of what it means to be downcast.

3. Regulators. Ocular cues control the flow of conversation. Eye contact means the channel is open. An averted gaze may signal an unwillingness to communicate.

4. Adapters. Rapid eye blinks increase when a person is under stress. The movement is an unconscious response that's part of the body's attempt to reduce anxiety.

5. Affect Display. Pupil dilation reveals increased emotional arousal. Other facial cues show whether that inner feeling is fear, surprise, or delight.

Try to identify the six different emotions displayed by the young American woman in Figure NM.1. (The answers are found at the end of this introduction.) Even if you are from a distant country, you're probably able to recognize each mood. Ekman and his colleague Wallace Friesen have compiled considerable evidence that basic facial expressions can be accurately interpreted across cultures.[2]

UCLA psychologist Albert Mehrabian suggests that interpersonal attitudes are picked up mainly through the nonverbal channel. His theory of implicit communication postulates three dimensions of emotional response—arousal, dominance, and attraction.[3] Changes in our facial expressions during a conversation are a good sign that we're interested in what someone else is saying. A stiff posture or body tension suggests that we consider the person we're with to be of higher status. The choice of a close interpersonal distance usually indicates that we like the other person.

Does it ever work the other way? Might attraction be the *result* of close proximity rather than its cause? Chapter 7 traces the development of Judee Burgoon's nonverbal expectancy violations model. Working from a behavioral science perspective, Burgoon tries to predict what will happen when a communicator converses at an inappropriate distance. Her model suggests that there are times when talking at a distance ''too close'' or ''too far'' may actually help a person achieve a communication goal.

Burgoon works within a behavioral science tradition that looks for universal principles to explain human gestures, facial

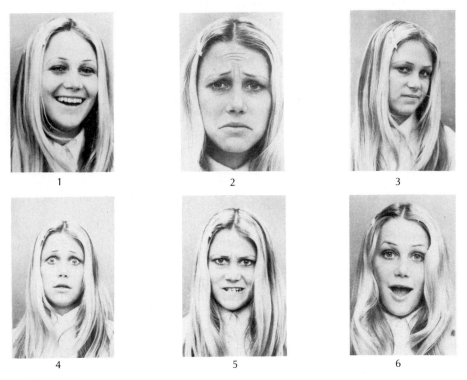

FIGURE NM.1
Identifying Mood from Facial Expression (From Leathers, *Successful Nonverbal Communications*.)

expressions, and other nonverbal variables. There is, however, an interpretive approach that is more in tune with the cultural relativism of the Sapir-Whorf hypothesis presented in the introduction to the Verbal Messages section. Anthropologist Ray Birdwhistell suggested that every culture has a language of gestures which has a vocabulary and grammar all its own.[4] The American *A-OK* symbol of thumb and forefinger forming a circle means "things are good." But a similar display in the Philippines can be a reference to money, and in Latin America it may be interpreted as an obscene gesture. Birdwhistell called his study "*kinesics*"; it was an attempt to establish a parallel between body language and the linguistic structure of verbal message systems.

French structuralist Roland Barthes also examined the forms in which signification takes place. He referred to himself as a "*semiologist*," one who systematically studies signs. Chapter 8 presents Barthes' semiotic theory, which seeks to break the code of nonverbal meaning. Film directors and critics note that the average film script is 50 percent shorter today than it was forty years ago, even though the length of the movie has stayed the same. Obviously, there are fewer words and more of something else. Barthes was interested in that something else—costumes, grooming, laughter, cars, houses, geographic location, music, lighting, and so on. He was less concerned with denotation (is the car a Mercedes or a Lexus?) than connotation (the feeling of unattainable luxury).

"That was unkind, darling. When their mouths turn up at the corners they want to be friends."
Used by permission of *the estate of* Michael ffolkes.

Barthes' concern for connotative meaning is consistent with the focus of most nonverbal theorists in the sciences and humanities. Both traditions stress that nonverbal messages have a powerful emotional impact. In the Relationship Maintenance section of this book you'll read about Paul Watzlawick's interactional view (see Chapter 15). He divides communication into two components—content and relationship—and agrees with Mehrabian that relationship is communicated primarily through nonverbal behavior. Most nonverbal signals act as relational punctuation that directs others how to interpret the content of the words. When there's a contradiction between what is said and how it's said, observers tend to credit the nonverbal signals. That's why many people say, "Seeing is believing."

[Facial expressions identification: 1. happiness 2. sadness 3. disgust 4. fear 5. anger 6. surprise]

CHAPTER 7

Nonverbal Expectancy Violations Model

of Judee Burgoon

One morning, years ago, I was walking back to my office puzzling over classroom conversations with four students. All four had made requests. Why, I wondered, had I readily agreed to two requests but had just as quickly turned down two others? Each of the four students spoke to me individually during the class break. Andre wanted my endorsement for a graduate scholarship, and Dawn invited me to eat lunch with her the next day. I said yes to both of them. Belinda asked me to help her on a term paper for a class with another professor, and Charlie encouraged me to play water polo with guys from his house that night. I said no to these requests.

Sitting down at my desk, I idly flipped through the pages of *Human Communication Research* (HCR). The year was 1978, and this relatively new behavioral science journal had arrived in the morning mail. I was still mulling over my uneven response to the students when my eyes zeroed in on an article entitled "A Communication Model of Personal Space Violations." "That's it," I blurted out to our surprised department secretary. I suddenly realized that in each case my reactions were influenced by the distance between me and the student.

I mentally pictured the four students making their requests—each from a distance that struck me as inappropriate in one way or another. Andre was literally in my face, less than a foot away. Belinda's two-foot interval invaded my personal space as well. Charlie stood about seven feet away—just outside the range I would have expected for a let's-get-together-and-have-some-fun-that-has-nothing-to-do-with-school type of conversation. Dawn offered her luncheon invitation from across the room. At the time, each of these moves seemed somewhat strange. Now I realized that all four students had violated my expectation of an appropriate conversational distance.

Consistent with my practice throughout this book, I've changed the names of these former students to protect their privacy. In this case I've made

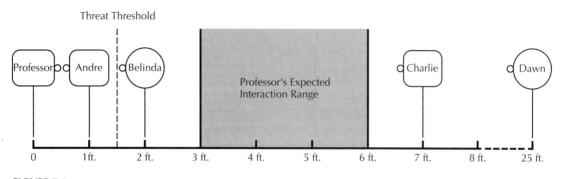

FIGURE 7.1
Nonverbal Expectancy Violations in a Classroom Setting

up names that start with the letters A, B, C, and D to represent the increasing distance between us when we spoke. (Andre was the closest; Dawn, the farthest away.) Figure 7.1 plots the intervals relative to my expectations.

Judee Burgoon, a young communication scholar teaching at the University of Florida, wrote the journal article that caused my outburst. The article was a follow-up piece on her nonverbal expectancy violations model that she initially introduced in HCR two years earlier. Since my own dissertation research focused on interpersonal distance, I knew firsthand how little social science theory existed to guide the study of nonverbal communication. I was therefore excited to see Burgoon offering a sophisticated theory of personal space. The fact that she was teaching in a communication department and published her work in a communication journal was all value added. I eagerly read Burgoon's description of her nonverbal expectancy violations model to see whether it could account for my mixed response to the various conversational distances chosen by the four students.

PERSONAL SPACE EXPECTATIONS: CONFORM OR DEVIATE?

Burgoon defined personal space as the "invisible, variable volume of space surrounding an individual that defines that individual's preferred distance from others."[1] She claimed that the size and shape of our personal space depends on our cultural norms and individual preferences, but it's always a compromise between the conflicting approach-avoidance needs that we as humans have for affiliation and privacy.

The idea of personal space wasn't original with Burgoon. In the 1960s, Illinois Institute of Technology anthropologist Edward Hall coined the term *proxemics* to refer to the study of people's use of space as a special elaboration of culture.[2] He entitled his book *The Hidden Dimension* because he was convinced that most spatial interpretation is outside our awareness. He claimed that Americans have four proxemic zones, which correspond to the four interpersonal distances selected by my students:

1. Intimate distance: 0 to 18 inches   (Andre)
2. Personal distance: 18 inches to 4 feet   (Belinda)
3. Social distance: 4 to 10 feet   (Charlie)
4. Public distance: 10 feet to infinity   (Dawn)

Hall's book was filled with examples of "ugly Americans" who were insensitive to the spacial customs of other cultures. Just as Pearce and Cronen regard successful communication as the coordinated management of meaning (see Chapter 6), so Hall strongly recommended that we learn to adjust our nonverbal behavior to conform to the communication rules of our partner. We shouldn't cross a distance boundary uninvited.

In his poem "Prologue: The Birth of Architecture," poet W. H. Auden echoes Hall's analysis and puts us on notice that we violate his personal space at our peril:

> Some thirty inches from my nose
> The frontier of my Person goes,
> And all the untilled air between
> Is private *pagus* or demesne.
> Stranger, unless with bedroom eyes
> I beckon you to fraternize,
> Beware of rudely crossing it:
> I have no gun, but I can spit.[3]

Burgoon's theory offers a counterpoint to Hall's and Auden's advice. She doesn't argue with the idea that people have definite expectations about how close others should come. In fact, she would explain Auden's thirty-inch rule as based on well-established American norms plus the poet's own idiosyncracies. But contrary to popular go-along-to-get-along wisdom, Burgoon's expectancy violations model suggests that there are times when it's best to break the rules. She believes that under some circumstances, violating social norms and personal expectations is "a superior strategy to conformity."[4]

Violations of Personal Space Are Arousing

Ordinarily, we don't even notice where a conversational partner is sitting or standing. We routinely space ourselves at what seems an appropriate distance and concentrate on the topic at hand. When I'm standing face-to-face with someone in a classroom, three to six feet seems normal. As long as the gap between the two of us falls within that range, the exact distance isn't an issue. But when another person takes up a position that is notably closer or farther than I had anticipated, something stirs within. Burgoon says that "deviations from expectations have arousal value."[5] The greater the discrepancy between our expectation and reality, the greater the stimulation. This hypothesized cause-and-effect relationship between proxemic violations and arousal is a pivotal assumption of her theory.

Cartoon by Peter Steiner. Reprinted with permission.

Burgoon defines the arousal caused by nonverbal expectancy violations as the "automatic orienting reflex that triggers alertness and attentiveness."[6] This isn't the heart-pounding, lip-biting, gut-wrenching reaction that precedes fight or flight. Rather, it's the standing-on-tiptoes, long-looking, holding-of-breath type of intensity that motivates a person to try to figure out what's happening.

Burgoon is not sure that this kind of arousal would register on a polygraph's measure of physiological changes, but she's convinced that it will break out into observable nonverbal cues. For example, she regards self-touching, forward body lean, tense posture, and frequent distance adjustments as signs of moderate arousal.

I don't honestly remember whether I displayed any of these cues when Andre and Belinda moved in close or Charlie and Dawn kept their distance. I do know that all four distance violations were striking enough that I began to search for hints on how to interpret these unexpected nonverbal behaviors. "What's going on here?" I wondered. The meaning of each student's proxemic behavior wasn't readily apparent in any of the situations, so I began to mentally review our relationships. According to Burgoon, that switch of attention from the message to the messenger is key to understanding the effects of nonverbal expectancy violations. The unusual interpersonal distance they chose forced me to reexamine how I felt about each one of them.

Is the Violator Rewarding or Punishing?

Burgoon's theory is the first of three you'll study that describes our human tendency to size up other people in terms of the potential rewards they have to offer. Social penetration theory and social exchange theory suggest that we live in an interpersonal economy in which we all "take stock" of the relational value of others we meet (see Chapters 13 and 16). The questions What can you do *for* me? and What can you do *to* me? often cross our minds. Burgoon is not a cynic, but she thinks the issue of reward potential moves from the background to the foreground when we are aroused by nonverbal expectancy violations. She uses the term *reward valence* to label the results of our audit of likely gains and losses.

The reward valence of a communicator is the sum of the positive and negative attributes that the person brings to the encounter plus the potential he or she has to reward or punish in the future. The resulting perception is usually a mix of good and bad and falls somewhere on a scale between those two poles. I'll illustrate communicator characteristics that Burgoon frequently mentions by describing one feature of each student that stood out to me as I thought about our relationship.

Andre was bright and hardworking, the best student in the class. Although writing recommendations are low on my list of fun things to do, I would bask in his reflected glory if he were accepted into a top graduate program.

Belinda had a razor-sharp mind and a tongue to match. Every comment she made seemed a verbal challenge that dripped with sarcasm.

Charlie was the classic goof-off, seldom in class, never prepared. I try to be evenhanded with everyone who signs up for my classes, but in Charlie's case I had to struggle not to take his casual attitude toward the course as a personal snub.

Dawn was a stunningly beautiful young woman. She had a warm smile and freely announced to others that I was her favorite teacher.

My views of Andre, Belinda, Charlie, and Dawn probably say more about me than they do about the four students. I'm not particularly proud of my stereotyped assessments, but apparently I have plenty of company in the criteria I used. Burgoon notes that the features which impressed me also weigh heavily with others when they compute a reward valence for someone who is violating their proxemic expectations. Status, ability, and good looks are standard "goodies" that enhance the other person's reward potential. The thrust of the conversation is even more important, however. Most of us value words that communicate acceptance, liking, appreciation, and trust. We're turned off by talk that conveys disinterest, disapproval, distrust, and rejection.

Why is the distance violator's power to reward or punish so crucial? Burgoon's answer is that "distance violations by themselves are highly ambiguous and require their victims to search the social context for other clues as to their meaning."[7] A violation embedded in a host of favorable signals takes on a positive cast. A breach of proxemic etiquette by a punishing communicator stiffens our resistance.

Violating Spatial Expectations: Plotting the Outcomes

Most communication theorists are quite specific about the type of outcome they predict. Some deal with interpersonal attraction, others with credibility, still others with persuasion. Burgoon believes that under certain circumstances, a distance too close or too far can affect all three areas. She obviously thinks interpersonal distance is a crucial nonverbal variable. One of her later experiments confirmed that proximity was more important than smiling, eye contact, touch, or forward body lean in achieving desirable outcomes.[8]

Burgoon's 1978 HCR article lists thirteen formal propositions concerning violations of personal space. One proposition states:

> The communication outcome of an interaction is a function of the reward value of the initiator, the direction of deviation from expectations, and the amount of deviation.[9]

Other propositions spell out specific detail. Figure 7.2 plots the projected rise and fall of good results for a punishing violator depending on the direction and extent of deviation. Figure 7.3 does the same for a rewarding violator. I'll walk you through the diagrams using the actions of Belinda and Charlie to illustrate the limited options available to a low-reward communicator, and then show the possibilities for favorable violation open to Andre and Dawn because they have high reward valence.

Belinda.   According to Burgoon's graph in Figure 7.2, Belinda made a mistake by unexpectedly moving into my personal space. Once inside my three-foot barrier, the closer she came, the more she called attention to our rocky relationship. Even if I was originally predisposed to help her on her outside project, her unwarranted proxemic intrusion would turn me against the idea. She would have done much better conforming to the normal professor-student spacing. The expectancy violations model rightly predicted my response.

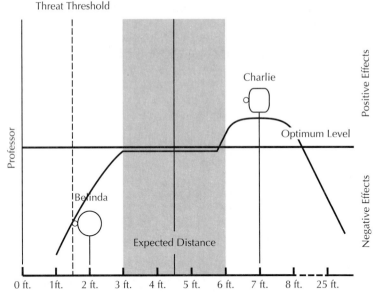

FIGURE 7.2
Predicted Effect When Violator of Expectation Is Perceived as Punishing (Based on
Burgoon and Jones, "Toward a Theory of Personal Space Expectations and Their
Violations.")

Charlie.   Burgoon states that "a punishing initiator will produce the
most positive communication outcome by observing expectations or deviating
slightly farther than expectations."[10] Even though Charlie was a nice guy, he
had "punishing power" in that he was living proof that I wasn't as good a
teacher as I wanted to be. Given that negative reward valence, he seemed to
do exactly what the model in Figure 7.2 recommends. He backed off to a place
just beyond what I would have normally expected. Burgoon doesn't present a
rationale for the small humplike zone in Figure 7.2 that offers Charlie the only
hope for positive effects, but according to the theory, Charlie did it right. (Do
you think I would have said yes to water polo if I had known the theory's
prediction *before* he asked me to play?) As it was, his withdrawn distance
reminded me of his nonpresence in class, and I ended up declining his
friendly offer. The theory missed on that prediction.

Andre.   As Figure 7.3 shows, it makes sense for a highly valued student
to take the risk of surprising the professor by coming closer than he or she
would expect. Since I greatly admired Andre, I would tend to interpret his
unanticipated nearness as a sign of mutual liking and respect. A well-
thought-out violation can achieve excellent results.

But Andre not only broke the rules, he smashed them. Twelve inches is
uncomfortably close when standing eyeball to eyeball. Burgoon defines the
threat threshold as "that distance at which an interactant experiences physical

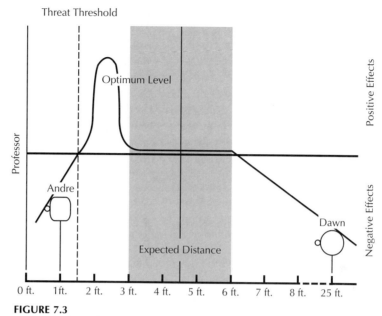
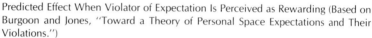

FIGURE 7.3

Predicted Effect When Violator of Expectation Is Perceived as Rewarding (Based on Burgoon and Jones, "Toward a Theory of Personal Space Expectations and Their Violations.")

and psychological discomfort by the presence of another."[11] That's exactly what I felt when Andre moved into my zone of intimacy. So according to the theory, his action should have hurt rather than helped his cause. But since I wrote the recommendation later that same day, Burgoon's original model again failed to predict real-life results.

Dawn. According to the expectancy violation model for rewarding communicators displayed in Figure 7.3, Dawn blew it. A close approach would have been a pleasant surprise, but her decision to talk from across the room guaranteed poor outcomes. The farther she backed off, the worse the effect would be. There's only one problem with this analysis; Dawn and I had lunch together in the student union the following day.

Obviously my 1978 attempt to apply Burgoon's model to conversational distance between students and at least one teacher was not encouraging. The theoretical scoreboard read:

Unpredicted random behavior: 3

Expectancy violations model: 1

But I observed that Burgoon's reported attempt to validate her ideas didn't fare much better. Her experimental study failed to support the model's dire predictions about extreme expectancy violations initiated by highly valued communicators—the very moves that had worked well for Andre and Dawn. By the end of the article, Burgoon hinted at the need to reconsider some of her theory's basic assumptions.

Of course, that was then; this is now. One of the reasons I chose to write about Burgoon's nonverbal expectancy violations model is that the current version is an excellent example of a theory that is continually being revised as a result of experimental disconfirmation. In science, failure can lead to success.

RETOOLING THE MODEL: FIFTEEN YEARS OF ADJUSTING DISTANCE EXPECTATIONS

Since that first empirical study, Judee Burgoon has put together an elaborate research program to test, revise, and extend her theory. Her career path has led from the University of Florida to Michigan State University, and then to the University of Arizona. At each school, Burgoon and graduate students under her guidance have probed and prodded different features of her model.

Burgoon's research started with a few trained assistants initiating space violations with strangers in a college communication laboratory. In order to check the model's value with older audiences in off-campus settings, she then sent scores of untrained volunteers into public locations—shopping malls, courthouses, bus stations. She also tested students who were good friends. After a dozen or more tests and resultant modifications, Burgoon's new and improved 1990s model is a dramatically altered version of the model introduced in the 1970s. When taken together, the five major changes listed below produce a violations theory that now accounts for my reactions to all four students back in 1978.

1. Application to Other Nonverbal Behaviors (and Beyond).   Burgoon no longer limits the scope of her violation model to proxemic behavior. Since most people have definite expectations about relational matters other than distance, she has applied her theory to touch, tone of voice, eye contact, and other forms of nonverbal communication. She recently suggested that patterns of response to violations of expectations are the same around the world. She's quick to acknowledge that what people expect varies from culture to culture, but she's convinced that the human way of processing violations is universal. Burgoon is also exploring the possibility that the model can cast light on how we respond to verbal messages that surprise us. For this reason she has now dropped the limiting term *nonverbal* from the title of her theory.

2. Realization That Some Behaviors Have Clear Meanings, Some Don't.   What is the message of a nonverbal violation? Although her early model didn't deal with this question, Burgoon now emphasizes that many nonverbal behaviors have socially recognized meanings. When the meaning is clear, our response is based on whether the act was an "upper" or a "downer" for us. In these cases, we care less about the valence of the person who acted unexpectedly.

Take eye contact, for example. Most of us expect that others will gaze at us about 60 to 70 percent of the time while we are talking. Burgoon's research shows that no matter who is doing the looking and listening, more eye contact would be better; less would be worse.

Proxemics are a different matter. "Distance violations by themselves are highly ambiguous and require their victims to search the social context for other clues as to their meaning."[12] That's when we look to the violator's reward valence for guidance. If the nonverbal message is clear, we won't need to bother. The surprising predictions of Burgoon's expectancy violations model come into play only when the meaning of the nonverbal behavior is uncertain.

3. Recognition That Nonrewarding Communicators Fare Best When They Conform to Others' Expectations. In her original model Burgoon advised the communicator who was held in low regard to choose an interpersonal distance slightly greater than others expected. She now drops this recommendation in favor of straight conformity. To extend the old adage, "When in Rome (and you aren't an honored guest), stand where the Romans expect you to stand." This revised conclusion explains why I was less sympathetic to Charlie's water polo invitation than I otherwise might have been. By extending the physical gap between us, he only served to remind me that our relationship was somewhat distant.

4. Elimination of the Threshold of Threat. Figures 7.1, 7.2, and 7.3 show a threshold of threat—a hypothetical point at which close violations of any kind turn sour. But in her research, Burgoon never found it. She discovered that close encounters of the surprising kind are welcome as long as the violator of expectations is viewed favorably. That explains why Andre's immediacy helped rather than hurt his bid for a grad school endorsement. Since the mid-1980s, Burgoon's reports on the nonverbal expectancy violations model make no mention of a threat threshold.

5. Awareness of the Surprising Potential of a Distance Too Far. Burgoon's very first experiment found that positively valenced communicators who kept their distance achieved their goals better than those who set up normal conversational spacing. Her next two studies supported this unanticipated finding. At first she assumed that proxemic aloofness contributed to higher status. But that speculation didn't pan out. She later concluded that arousal was the key factor:

> A distance violation that is of sufficient magnitude to arouse a person should cause its victim to search the context for explanations, since the behavior's meaning by itself should be somewhat ambiguous.[13]

There's no guarantee that the search for explanations will produce a satisfying answer for the unexpected void, but in Dawn's case, the valued rule-breaker became even more valued. The warmth of her smile, a steady gaze, and the genuineness of her invitation to eat lunch together took the sting out of impersonal space.

Given these major changes in her nonverbal expectancy violations model, what are Burgoon's recommendations? How close should you approach or how far should you hang back? Her advice today is quite simple. If you fear you come across as a person who is unattractive and has little to offer, stifle your deviant tendencies and do your best to conform to spatial expectations. If, on the other hand, you believe that your partner regards you as nice to be near, take the risk of sitting or standing at an interpersonal distance that could be a pleasant surprise. Burgoon is convinced that for rewarding relationships, a distance either too close or too far is better than spacing that's "just right."

CRITIQUE: WORK IN PROGRESS

I have a friend who fixes my all-terrain cycle whenever I bend it or break it. "What do you think?" I ask Bill. "Can it be repaired?" His response is always the same: "Man made it! Man can fix it!"

Judee Burgoon shows the same resolve as she seeks to patch up and redesign an expectancy violations model that has never worked quite as well in practice as its theoretical blueprint says it should. Every empirical test she runs seems to yield mixed results. For example, her latest version continues to predict that moving in too close or moving back too far away are superior proxemic strategies for a highly rewarding violator. The relationship could be graphed on the distance line of Figure 7.3 as a slowly curving large U—the best results occurring at either end of the proxemic scale. This is a fascinating counterintuitive prediction, the kind of forecast that moves behavioral science away from cost accounting dullness. But with one exception,[14] Burgoon's experiments have never provided clear-cut evidence that violating another person's expectations in *either* direction will produce that desired effect.

Some state legislatures have adopted a "Lemon Law"—a statute requiring auto dealers to replace a buyer's new car when it has a major defect that continues to persist despite the shop's best attempts to fix it. Do repeated failures to validate the wisdom of standing too near or too far imply that Burgoon ought to trade in her expectancy violations model for a new nonverbal theory? Definitely not.

Taken as a whole, Burgoon's expectancy violation model continues to meet the criteria of a good scientific theory (see Chapter 3). Her theory advances a reasonable explanation for the effects of proxemic violations. The explanation she offers is relatively simple and getting simpler all the time. The theory has testable hypotheses that the theorist is willing to adjust when her tests don't support the prediction. Finally, the model offers practical advice on how to better achieve important communication goals. Could we ask for anything more? Definitely yes.

For one thing, Burgoon could sharpen her definition of *arousal* and develop a systematic program to measure whether or not it really increases with proxemic violation.[15] She could also work to tighten her basic conclusion. When she states that "rewarding communicators *frequently accrue* the most favorable communication outcomes by violating rather than conforming to expectancies," the qualifying word *frequently* reveals the less-than-certain state of her theory.[16] Scholars searching for a nonverbal communication covering law could wish for a more definitive statement. On the basis of Burgoon's excellent record of ongoing research and theory adjustment, I anticipate that she'll soon offer a revised violations model which will meet these expectations.

QUESTIONS TO SHARPEN YOUR FOCUS

1. What *proxemic* advice would you give to communicators who believe they are seen as *unrewarding*?

2. The results of *empirical research* have caused Burgoon to revise her theory. Which change has most dramatically altered the original expectancy violations model?

3. The sign on the door of a restaurant reads: "No shoes, no shirt, no service." What are other posted notices that communicate nonverbal expectations?

4. Is it possible to adopt Birdwhistell's stance of *cultural relativism* yet still accept the basic predictions of the current expectancy violations model?

A SECOND LOOK

Recommended resource: Judee K. Burgoon, "A Communication Model of Personal Space Violations: Explication and an Initial Test," *Human Communication Research*, Vol. 4, 1978, pp. 129–142.

Original statement: Judee K. Burgoon and Stephen B. Jones, "Toward a Theory of Personal Space Expectations and Their Violations," *Human Communication Research*, Vol. 2, 1976, pp. 131–146.

Theory revision: Judee K. Burgoon, "Nonverbal Violations of Expectations," in *Nonverbal Interaction*, John Wiemann and Randall Harrison (eds.), Sage, Beverly Hills, Calif., 1983, pp. 77–111.

Expanding the theory to multiple nonverbal cues: Judee K. Burgoon and Jerold Hale, "Nonverbal Expectancy Violations: Model Elaboration and Application to Immediacy Behaviors," *Communication Monographs*, Vol. 55, 1988, pp. 58–79.

Interpretation of expectancy violation: Judee Burgoon, Deborah Newton, Joseph Walther, and E. James Baesler, "Nonverbal Expectancy Violations and Conversational Involvement," *Journal of Nonverbal Behavior*, Vol. 13, No. 2, 1989, pp. 97–119.

Nonverbal arousal: Judee K. Burgoon, Douglas Kelley, Deborah Newton, and Maureen Keeley-Dyreson, "The Nature of Arousal and Nonverbal Indices," *Human Communication Research*, Vol. 16, 1989, pp. 217–255.

Expanding the theory to eye contact: Judee K. Burgoon, Deborah Coker, and Ray Coker, "Communicative Effects of Gaze Behavior: A Test of Two Contrasting Explanations," *Human Communication Research*, Vol. 12, 1986, pp. 495–524.

Expanding the theory to intercultural contexts: Judee Burgoon, "Applying a Comparative Approach to Expectancy Violations Theory," in *Comparatively Speaking: Communication and Culture Across Space and Time*, Jay Blumler, Jack McLeod, and Karl Rosengren (eds.), Sage, Newbury Park, Calif., 1992, pp. 53–69.

CHAPTER 8

Semiotics
of Roland Barthes

What do the following six things have in common?

1. Perspiration on the faces of actors in the film *Julius Caesar*
2. Red wine and a steak cooked rare
3. The brain of Albert Einstein donated to science
4. Diamond-studded G-strings worn by "artistic" dancers in striptease shows
5. A magazine photograph of a young African soldier saluting the French flag
6. The exaggerated grimace of a pro wrestler when an opponent tightens his hammerlock

According to the French writer Roland Barthes, each of these items is a nonverbal *sign* waiting to be read. Interpreting signs is the task of semiologists, and at his death in 1980, Barthes (rhymes with "smart") held the Chair of Literary Semiology at the College of France. In his book *Mythologies*, he sought to decipher the cultural meaning of a variety of nonverbal signs, including the six mentioned here. He concluded that each of these signs perpetuates the dominant values of society. Take the sweat on the brow of the Romans in *Julius Caesar*, for example:

> Sweat is a sign. Of what? Of moral feeling. Everyone is sweating because everyone is debating something within himself; we are here supposed to be in the locus of a horribly tormented virtue, that is the very locus of tragedy, and it is sweat which has the function of conveying this. . . . To sweat is to think—which evidently rests on the postulate, appropriate to a nation of businessmen, that thought is a violent, cataclysmic operation, of which sweat is only the most benign symptom.[1]

I selected this brief passage to introduce Barthes because it illustrates both the focus and style of his writing. Although semiology (or semiotics as it is better known in America) is concerned with *anything that can stand for some-*

thing else, Barthes concentrates on interpreting *visual* signs. His ultimate goal is to explain how seemingly straightforward signs pick up ideological or connotative meaning and work to maintain the cultural status quo. He realized that few moviegoers would consciously link perspiration with a put-down of reflective thought, but the subtlety of the message was all the more reason for a semiotic critique.

Barthes' interpretation of Roman sweat also provides a sample of his pithy use of language. Unlike most intellectuals, he frequently wrote for the popular press and occasionally appeared on television to comment on the foibles of the French middle class. His academic colleagues found his statements witty, disturbing, flashy, overstated, or profound in turn—but never dull. He obviously made them think. With the exception of Aristotle, the four volume *International Encyclopedia of Communication* contains more references to Barthes than any other theorist I present in this book.[2]

Since semiotics is discussed more in Europe than in America, you probably don't hear the term bandied about at the student union or in late-night bull sessions. So before moving to Barthes' analysis of signs, I'll introduce the field of semiotics in more detail.

SURVEYING THE FIELD OF SEMIOTICS: WHERE TO DRAW THE LINE

The term *semiology* was coined by Swiss linguist Ferdinand de Saussure in the early 1900s. He used it to refer to a potential science that might investigate the nature of signs, study their impact on society, and state the laws that govern them. He was quite tentative about the exact boundaries of this new scientific field and wasn't even sure whether scholars would want to explore it. "Since it does not yet exist," he said, "one cannot say for certain that it will exist."[3] But he thought semiology had a right to exist and wanted to carve out a place for its future study—just in case. His discipline was linguistics, but he regarded the study of verbal signs as just one branch of the yet-to-be-developed overarching field of semiology. Saussure himself never pursued an interest in nonverbal signs.

During Barthes' lifetime, semiology acquired the basic forms of respected scholarship—a professional society, The International Association for Semiotic Studies; and an academic journal, *Semiotica*. In addition to an interest in verbal codes, semiotics welcomed the study of meaning through smell, taste, touch, tone of voice, gesture, proxemics, music, visual images, and systems of objects. Perhaps because almost all human activity fits under that broad semiotic umbrella, scholars had difficulty agreeing on the proper focus of semiotic research. Participants at the 1974 International Semiotics Conference in Milan were split fifty-fifty between those who were positive they knew what semiotics was and those who were certain they didn't. Umberto Eco of Italy summarized the chaotic proceedings with an ironic reference to Saussure's initial aspirations for the creation of semiology, "We have spoken about semiotics, therefore semiotics exists."[4]

The History of Semiology

By permission of Johnny Hart and Creators Syndicate.

In his book *A Theory of Semiotics*, Eco gives an unexpected twist to the word *semiotics* that I find helpful in understanding the field's domain. He defines semiotics as the "theory of the lie." Follow his thought process in the passage below as he moves step-by-step to reach that conclusion:

> Semiotics is concerned with everything that can be taken as a sign. A sign is everything which can be taken as significantly substituting for something else. This something else does not necessarily have to exist or to actually be somewhere at the moment in which a sign stands for it. Thus semiotics is in principle the discipline studying everything which can be used in order to lie. If something cannot be used to tell a lie, conversely it cannot be used to tell the truth; it cannot in fact be used "to tell" at all.[5]

Normally, we regard lying as a verbal pursuit. When faced with a contradiction between *what* is said and *how* it's said, however, we tend to believe the nonverbal signs. "Seeing is believing," we say. "Talk is cheap." Movies like *The Sting* and *House of Games* remind us that professional con artists, or "grifters," are successful in their deceptions because they are adept at lying nonverbally. Therefore, Eco's definition of a sign as "anything that can be used to lie" embraces both verbal and nonverbal signs.

Mystery stories can also expand our understanding of semiotics. When fictional detectives like Sherlock Holmes or Nero Wolfe search for clues to the identity of a culprit, they don't expect to find something as obvious as fingerprints on a smoking gun. It's the small "telltale signs" that trip up the guilty party. Consider, for instance, this conversation between Holmes and his foil, Watson. Watson confesses that he "sees nothing." "On the contrary, Watson," Holmes counters, "You can see everything. You fail, however to reason from what you see. You are too timid in drawing your inferences."[6]

As you will see in the rest of the chapter, Barthes was not timid about drawing inferences from everyday signs. He referred to the semiologist's workplace as "the kitchen of meaning," and entered it every day as an enthusiastic semiotic chef.

> Semiology is not a Cause for me; it is not a science, a discipline, a school, a movement with which I identify my own person. . . . Then what is Semiology for me? It is an adventure.[7]

WRESTLING WITH SIGNS

Barthes initially described his semiotic theory as an explanation of "myth." He later substituted the term *connotation* to label the ideological baggage that signs can carry wherever they go, and most students of Barthes' work regard *connotation* as a better word choice to convey his true concern.

Barthes' theory of connotative meaning won't make sense to us, however, unless we first understand the way he views the structure of signs. His thinking was strongly influenced by the ideas he discovered in Saussure's *Course in General Linguistics.* I'll use portions of Barthes' essay on pro wrestling à la Hulk Hogan to illustrate two core semiotic principles that Barthes restated over and over in his writing.

1. A Sign Is the Combination of a Signifier and a Signified

The distinction between the signifier and the signified can be seen in Barthes' graphic description of the body of a wrestler who was selected by the promotor because he typified the repulsive slob.

> As soon as the adversaries are in the ring, the public is overwhelmed with the obviousness of the roles. As in the theatre, each physical type expresses to excess the part which has been assigned to the contestant. Thauvin, a fifty-year-old with an obese and sagging body . . . displays in his flesh the characters of baseness. . . . I know from the start that all of Thauvin's actions, his treacheries, cruelties and acts of cowardice, will not fail to measure up to the first image of ignobility he gave me. . . . The physique of the wrestlers therefore constitutes a basic sign, which like a seed contains the whole fight.[8]

According to Barthes, the image of the wrestler's physique is the *signifier.* The concept of ignobility or injustice is the *signified.* The combination of the two—the villainous body—is the *sign.*

This way of defining a sign differs from our customary usage of the word. We would probably say that the wrestler's body *is a sign of* his baseness—or whatever else came to mind. But Barthes considers the wrestler's body to be just *part* of the overall sign; it's the signifier. The other part is the concept of hideous baseness. The signifier isn't a sign of the signified. Rather, they work together in an inseparable bond to form a unified sign.

Barthes' description of a sign as the correlation between the signifier and the signified came directly from Saussure. The Swiss linguist visualized a sign as a piece of paper with writing on both sides—the signifier on one side, the signified on the other. If you cut off part of one side, an equal amount of the other side automatically goes with it.

Is there any logical connection between the image of the signifier and the content of the signified? Saussure insisted that the relationship was arbitrary—one of correlation rather than of cause and effect. Barthes wasn't so sure. He was willing to grant the claim of Saussure (and I. A. Richards) that words have no inherent meaning. For example, there is nothing about *referee* as a verbal sign that makes it stand for the third party in the ring who is inept at making Thauvin follow the rules. But nonverbal signifiers seem to have a natural affinity with their signifieds. Barthes noted that Thauvin's body was so repugnant that it provoked nausea. He classified the relationship between signifiers and signifieds as "quasi-arbitrary." After all, Thauvin really did strike the crowd as vileness personified.

2. A Sign Does Not Stand on Its Own: It Is Part of a System

Barthes entitled his essay "The World of Wrestling," for like all other semiotic systems, wrestling creates its own separate world of interrelated signs.

> Each moment in wrestling is therefore like an algebra which instantaneously unveils the relationship between a cause and its represented effect. Wrestling fans certainly experience a kind of intellectual pleasure in *seeing* the moral mechanism function so perfectly. . . . Wrestlers, who are very experienced, know perfectly how to direct the spontaneous episodes of the fight so as to make them conform to the image which the public has of the great legendary themes of its mythology. A wrestler can irritate or disgust, he never disappoints, for he always accomplishes completely, by a progressive solidification of signs, what the public expects of him.[9]

Barthes notes that the grapplers' roles are tightly drawn. There is little room for innovation; the men in the ring work within a closed system of signs. By responding to the unwavering expectation of the crowd, the wrestlers are as much spectators as the fans who cheer or jeer on cue.

Wrestling is just one of many semiotic systems. Barthes also explored the cultural meaning of designer clothes, French cooking, automobiles, Japanese gift giving, household furniture, urban layout, and public displays of sexuality. He attempted to define and classify the features common to all semiotic systems. This kind of structural analysis is called *taxonomy*, and Barthes' book *Elements of Semiology* is a "veritable frenzy of classifications."[10] Barthes later admitted that his taxonomy "risked being tedious," but the project strengthened his conviction that semiotic systems function the same way despite their apparent diversity.

Barthes believed that the significant semiotic systems of a culture affirm the status quo. The mythology that surrounds a society's crucial signs displays the world as it is today—however chaotic and unjust—as *natural*, *inevitable*, and *eternal*. The function of myth is to bless the mess. We now turn to Barthes' theory of connotation, or myth, which suggests how a seemingly neutral or inanimate sign can accomplish so much.

THE YELLOW RIBBON TRANSFORMATION: FROM FORGIVENESS OF STIGMA TO PRIDE IN VICTORY

According to Barthes, not all semiological systems are mythic. Not every sign carries ideological baggage. How is it that one sign can remain emotionally neutral while other signs acquire powerful inflections or connotations that suck people into a specific worldview? Barthes contends that a mythic or connotative system is a *second-order semiological system*—built off a preexisting sign system. The sign of the first system becomes the signifier of the second. A concrete example will help us understand Barthes' explanation.

In a 1989 article appearing in the *American Journal of Semiotics*, Donald and Virginia Fry of Emerson College examined the widespread American practice of displaying yellow ribbons during the Mideast hostage crisis.[11] They traced the transformation of this straightforward yellow symbol into an ideological sign. Americans' lavish display of yellow ribbons during Operation Desert Storm a decade later adds a new twist to the Frys' analysis. I'll update their yellow ribbon example to illustrate Barthes' semiotic theory.

"Tie a Yellow Ribbon Round the Ole Oak Tree" was the best-selling pop song of 1972 in the United States.[12] Sung by Tony Orlando and Dawn, the lyrics express the thoughts of a convict in prison who is writing to the woman he loves. After three years in jail, the man is about to be released and will travel home by bus. Fearing her possible rejection, he devises a plan that will give her a way to signal her intentions without the potential embarrassment of a face-to-face confrontation.

Since he'll be able to see the huge oak planted in front of her house when the bus passes through town, he asks her to use the tree as a message board. If she still loves him, wants him back, and can overlook the past, she should tie a yellow ribbon around the trunk of the tree. He will know that all is forgiven and join her in rebuilding a life together. But if this bright sign of reconciliation isn't there, he'll stay on the bus, accept the blame for a failed relationship, and try to get on with his life without her.

The yellow ribbon is obviously a sign of acceptance, but one not casually offered. There's a taint on the relationship, hurts to be healed. Donald and Virginia Fry label the original meaning of the yellow ribbon in the song as "forgiveness of a stigma."

Yellow ribbons in 1991 continued to carry a "we want you back" message when U.S. armed forces fought in Operation Desert Storm. Whether tied to trees, worn in hair, or pinned to lapels, yellow ribbons still proclaimed, "Welcome home." But there was no longer any sense of shameful acts to be forgiven or disgrace to be overcome. Vietnam was ancient history and America was the leader of the "new world order." Hail the conquering heroes.

The mood surrounding the yellow ribbon had become one of triumph, pride, and even arrogance. After all, hadn't we intercepted Scud missiles in the air, guided "smart bombs" into air-conditioning shafts, and "kicked Saddam Hussein's butt across the desert"? People were swept up in a tide of "yellow fever." More than 90 percent of U.S. citizens approved of America's actions in Iraq. The simple yellow ribbon of personal reconciliation now served as a blatant sign of nationalism. What had originally signified forgiveness of a stigma now symbolized pride in victory.

THE MAKING OF MYTH: STRIPPING THE SIGN OF HISTORY

According to Barthes' theory, the shift from "forgiveness of stigma" to "pride in victory" followed a typical semiotic pattern. Figure 8.1 shows how it's done.

Barthes claimed that every ideological sign is the result of two interconnected sign systems. The first system is strictly descriptive—the signifier image and the signified concept combining to produce a denotative sign. The three elements of the sign system based on the "Tie a Yellow Ribbon . . ." lyrics are marked with Arabic numerals at the top left portion of the diagram. The three segments of the connotative system are marked with Roman numerals. Note that the sign of the first system does double duty as the signifier of the Gulf war connotative system. According to Barthes, this lateral shift, or connotative sidestep, is the key to transforming a neutral sign into an ideological tool. Follow his thinking step-by-step through the diagram.

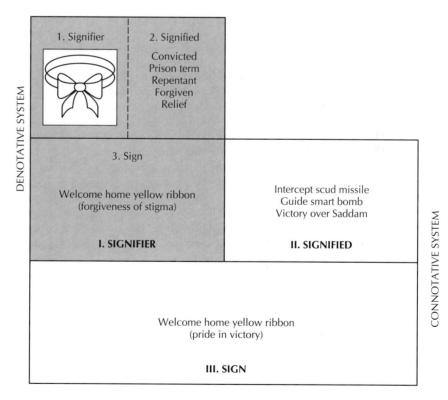

FIGURE 8.1

Connotation as a Second-Order Semiotic System (Adapted from Barthes, "Myth Today.")

The signifier (1) of the denotative sign system is the image of a yellow ribbon that forms in the mind of the person who hears the 1972 song. The content of the signified (2) includes the stigma which comes from the conviction of a crime and a term in jail, the prisoner's willingness to take responsibility for the three-year separation, and the explosive release of tension when the Greyhound passengers cheer at the sight of the oak tree awash in yellow ribbons. The corresponding denotative sign (3) is "forgiveness of a stigma." For those who heard the song on the radio, the yellow ribbon sign spoke for itself. It was a sign rich in regret and relief.

Current usage takes over the sign of the denotative system and makes it the signifier (I) of a secondary (connotative) system. The "welcome home" yellow ribbon is paired with the mythic content of a signified (II) that shouts to the world, "Our technology can beat up your technology." But as the symbol of the yellow ribbon is expropriated to support the myth of American nationalism, the sign loses its historical grounding.

As a mere signifier of the connotative system, the yellow ribbon is no longer rooted in the details of the song. It ceases to stand for three years of hard time in prison, repentance or wrongdoing, or forgiveness that gains meaning because there is so much to be forgiven. Now in the service of the mythic semiotic system, the yellow ribbon becomes empty, timeless, a form without substance. According to Barthes, that doesn't mean that the meaning of the original denotative sign is lost:

> The essential point in all this is that the form does not suppress the meaning, it only impoverishes it, it puts it at a distance, it holds it at one's disposal. One believes that the meaning is going to die, but it is a death with reprieve; the meaning loses its value, but keeps its life, from which . . . the myth will draw its nourishment.[13]

In the connotative system, the generalized image of a yellow ribbon is now paired with the signified content of victory in the Persian Gulf war as seen on CNN. But since the signifier can't recall a historical or cultural past, the mythic sign (III) of which it is a part carries the "crust of falsity."[14] For example, there's no sense of American culpability in supplying arms to Saddam Hussein until the time he invaded Kuwait. And since mythic communication is unable to imagine anything alien, novel, or other, the sign sweeps away second thoughts about civilian deaths in Baghdad. The transformed yellow ribbon is now a lofty sign which allows no room for nagging doubts that love of oil may have been our country's prime motivation for championing the United Nation's "humanitarian" intervention.

UNMASKING THE MYTH OF A HOMOGENEOUS SOCIETY

Barthes was convinced that only those with semiotic savvy can spot the hollowness of connotative signs. For most Americans, the yellow ribbon will continue to elicit an unreflective "we're number one" feeling of national pride. Of course, it goes without saying that people will love their country. But that's precisely the problem with mythic signs. They *go without saying*. They don't explain, they don't defend, and they certainly don't raise questions. So it's up to the semiologist to deconstruct the mythic system.

Throughout his life, Roland Barthes deciphered and labeled the ideologies foisted upon the naive consumer of images. Although the starting-point signifiers vary—Einstein's brain, steak and wine, a stripper's G-string, an African saluting the French tricolor—Barthes concluded that society's connotative spin always ends up the same. Mythic signs reinforce the dominant values of their culture.

How do ideological signs enlist support for the status quo? According to Barthes, they do it by transforming history into nature—pretending that current conditions are the natural order of things. As with the yellow ribbon, everything that is personal, conditional, cultural, and temporal disappears. We are left with a sign that makes the world seem inevitable and eternal. Barthes' analysis calls to mind the final words of the "Gloria Patria," a choral response that many Christians sing in worship:

> As it was in the beginning,
> Is now and ever shall be,
> World without end. Amen. Amen.

For believers, singing these words about anything or anyone but God would be heresy. Without granting the exception, Barthes would concur. All his semiotic efforts were directed at unmasking what he considered the heresy of those who controlled the images of society—the naturalizing of history.

CRITIQUE: WILL THE REAL SEMIOLOGIST PLEASE STAND UP?

Although Barthes is undeniably a pivotal figure in the development of semiotics, his approach to signs is just one of many. Some scholars regard American philosopher Charles Peirce rather than Saussure as the founder of semiotics. Yet neither man nor most of their intellectual descendants shared Barthes' agenda of deconstructing myth. This doesn't mean that Barthes' theory was wrong in its aim or explanation, but the diversity does suggest that there is no single semiotic theory. Novelist Walker Percy (*The Moviegoer, The Second Coming, Thanatos*) sums up the perennial problem faced by semiotics:

> Semiotics runs the risk of being about everything and hence about nothing. At best a loose and inchoate discipline, semiotics is presently in such disarray that all sorts of people call themselves semioticists and come at the subject from six different directions.[15]

During his lifetime, Barthes headed in at least six different directions in his own thinking about signs. Oxford University Fellow Terry Eagleton writes that Barthes was horrified by any type of orthodoxy.[16] When his theory of connotation became the established wisdom in intellectual circles, he quickly shifted his semiotic ground. As Eugen Simion reports, Barthes "does not mind plotting in secret against the doctrine of his own making."[17] Whatever the reason, Barthes later disavowed two principles that undergird his theory of myth and thus offered his own critique.

Principle 1: Every Sign Has Meaning

Barthes abandoned this belief after spending a year in Japan, a country he called "The Empire of Signs." He observed a number of rites and practices which convinced him that some signs have no signified:[18]

> There is no hidden meaning in Kabuki theatre. "The face dismisses any signified."
>
> The ceremonial bow salutes no one. "The form is empty."
>
> The signified flees from wrapped packages. "What the Japanese carry . . . are actually empty signs."
>
> Haiku poetry wages a war against meaning.
>
> > How admirable he is
> > Who does not think "Life is ephemeral"
> > When he sees a flash of lightning!

To the westerner, lack of significance is nonsense. In the Empire of Signs, signs can be void of all meaning.

Principle 2: Denotation Precedes Connotation

In Barthes' original semiotic model, signs started out "connotatively inno-cent." Only after denotation was established could a connotative inflection be added. But Barthes later inverts the relationship of denotation and connota-tion:

> Denotation is not the first meaning, but pretends to be so; under this illusion, it is ultimately no more than the *last* of the connotations (the one which seems to both establish and to close the reading).[19]

How can we have any confidence in Barthes' semiotic theory when the theorist himself has abandoned his creation? Surprisingly, many semiologists believe Barthes was right the first time and therefore discount his revision. Is there a chance that Barthes would have returned to his original point of view? Probably not; but given Barthes' fondness for doing the unexpected, maybe so.

We'll never know for sure. Barthes was struck and killed by a laundry truck just outside the College of France in 1980. You'll have to decide on your own whether or not Barthes' initial semiotic construction meets the criteria of a good theory. One hint, however. Despite Saussure's hope for a *science* that explores the nature of signs, semiotics is definitely a *humanistic* endeavor and should be judged on that basis.

QUESTIONS TO SHARPEN YOUR FOCUS

1. Eco defines a *sign* as "anything that can be used to lie." Can you think of any human activity that doesn't fit within the study of *semiotics*?

2. What is the *signifier* and *signified* of something you are wearing right now?

3. Why did Barthes think it was crucial to *unmask* or *deconstruct* the original *denotation* of a sign?

4. "It's not over 'til the fat lady sings." What are the denotative *signifier*, *signified*, and *sign* to which this statement refers? What *connotative shift* has altered the meaning of the original sign?

A SECOND LOOK

Recommended resource: Roland Barthes, *Mythologies*, Annette Lavers (trans.), Hill and Wang, New York, 1972, especially "The World of Wrestling" and "Myth Today," pp. 15–25, 109–159.

Classification of semiotic system: Roland Barthes, *Elements of Semiology*, Annette Lavers and Colin Smith (trans.), Hill and Wang, New York, 1968.

Essays on semiotics: Roland Barthes, *The Semiotic Challenge*, Richard Howard (trans.), Hill and Wang, New York, 1988.

Semiology of Saussure: Ferdinand de Saussure, *A Course in General Linguistics*, McGraw-Hill, New York, 1966.

Introduction to semiotics: Arthur Asa Berger, *Signs in Contemporary Culture*, Sheffield Publishing, Salem, Wisc., 1989.

Further investigation of semiotics: Kaja Silverman, *The Subject of Semiotics*, Oxford University Press, New York, 1983.

Japanese signs: Roland Barthes, *Empire of Signs*, Richard Howard (trans.), Hill and Wang, New York, 1982.

Semiotic switches later in life: Roland Barthes, "Inaugural Lecture, College de France," in *A Barthes Reader*, Susan Sontag (ed.), Hill and Wang, New York, 1982, pp. 457–478.

PART THREE

Intrapersonal Communication

SELF-CONCEPT

Think back to the day your high school year-book arrived. If you're like most people, you quickly leafed through to find a picture of yourself. You breathed a sigh of relief when you found that the photograph wasn't faded, blurred, or cropped off across the top of your head. After you saw that the image was clear, you began to worry about how you looked in the midst of all your classmates' pictures.

There are two issues here—identity and self-esteem. *Identity* is the image we see when we look at ourselves, the denotation of self-concept. *Self-esteem* is how we feel about that image, the connotation of self-concept.

None of us has just one mind's-eye photograph that faithfully records our "true self." It's more accurate to think of identity as an album of mental snapshots that depict us in flux—smiling, frowning, mugging at the camera, and so forth. George Herbert Mead's theory of symbolic interactionism says that these pictures are given to us by the signifi-cant others in our lives as they respond to our presence. As poet Ralph Waldo Emerson wrote, each close companion

> Is to his friend a looking-glass
> Reflects his figure that doth pass.[1]

Chapter 9 explores Mead's theory of how our "looking-glass self" develops, and the effect it has on our subsequent behavior. Symbolic interactionism claims that the perceived reaction of significant others shapes our personal self-portrait. The theory has little to say about self-esteem.

Having a clear view of who we are is not enough. We also want to like what we see. Since researchers can't enter the darkroom of the mind, there's no direct way to measure inner regard. Others may be able to spot our overall attitude toward self through our facial expression or body posture, but any attempt to uncover complex feelings of esteem must

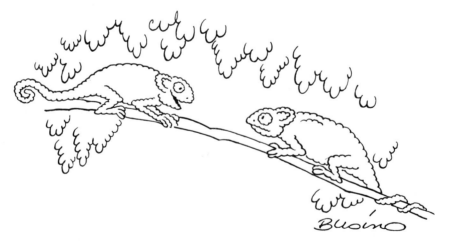

"Of course you're going through an identity crisis—you're a chameleon."

© 1974 SR/World. Reprinted by permission of Orlando Busino.

110

rely on verbal self-reports. These can be the stories we tell about ourselves or our multiple responses to an "I am . . ." sentence-completion test. Using either method, a content analysis reveals that self-esteem is made up of four inner feelings.

1. A Sense of Competence. Almost a hundred years ago, pioneer psychologist William James suggested a self-esteem formula that balances two opposing factors:[2]

$$\text{Self-esteem} = \frac{\text{Competence}}{\text{Expectation}}$$

We can raise our self-regard either by getting better at what we're doing or by lowering our expectations.

2. A Sense of Self-Determination. Do we feel that we control our own outcomes, or does it seem that our lives are held hostage by fate and powerful others? People who feel in charge of their lives tend to have greater self-esteem than those who believe they have no say in their own destiny.

3. A Sense of Togetherness. We like ourselves better when we sense a basic consistency among our beliefs, emotions, and actions. Conversely, self-alienation is the noxious feeling that arises when our outward behavior doesn't match our inner convictions or when our emotions seem to be those of a stranger. We can bolster a sense of congruence by telling stories about ourselves that pull together fragments from our past. A consistent narrative convinces others and ourself that our life is really of one piece.

4. A Sense of Moral Goodness. Even in an anything-goes world which scoffs at moral absolutes, we want the feeling that our lives are ethically okay, approved, validated. CMM theorists Barnett Pearce and Vernon Cronen note that

> the creation of moral orders seems to be one of the few universal features of human soci-

eties. All peoples indicate what can be done, what must be done, what is prohibited, and what is beyond their responsibility. Any description of human social arrangements that does not recognize these distinctions and their places in social structure and action is incomplete.[3]

Chapter 38 presents a variety of ethical standards that help people determine the difference between right or wrong, good or bad, and virtue or vice in their communication choices.

If you possess all four of these inner convictions, you probably don't sit gazing at your own photo. Introspection is a killer; the more time we spend as the object of our own attention, the less satisfied we will be. Probably the single best way to build self-esteem is to lose ourselves in a cause that compels us to look outward at others rather than inward at ourselves.

Identity and self-esteem are important factors in the way we communicate. A clear identity reduces uncertainty. Our talk will be more spontaneous, confident, and direct when we have a clear image of who we are. On the other hand, think of the eighth-grade boy who is just entering puberty. He never knows what sound will emerge when he opens his mouth. Sometimes his voice is a rich baritone; other times it cracks into a high squeak. The uncertain youngster usually ends up mumbling or not saying anything at all.

Self-esteem strongly affects verbal participation. People who like themselves tend to participate freely in groups; people who are down on themselves hold back. Esteem is also linked with persuasion. Those with high self-regard initiate more attempts to persuade others than do those with a low opinion of self. Chronic self-doubters are more easily swayed by influence attempts than are people who possess great self-confidence. Self-esteem colors what we hear and what we say.

CHAPTER 9

Symbolic Interactionism
of George Herbert Mead

Symbolic interactionism is the somewhat chaotic yet fascinating collection of observations, maxims, and propositions that sprang from the mind of sociologist George Herbert Mead. Mead never systematized his ideas or wrote down his thoughts. His students at the University of Chicago pulled together class notes and conversations with their mentor and published *Mind, Self, and Society* after his death in 1934. It was only then that his chief disciple, Herbert Blumer, coined the term *symbolic interactionism.*

UNSCIENTIFIC SPECULATION OR AN ARTISTIC MODEL OF LIFE

Symbolic interactionism isn't so much a theory (as outlined in Chapter 1) as it is a perspective or an orientation. Its fluid boundaries, imprecise definitions, and undisciplined approach don't lend themselves to an easy summary. There are no *Cliffs Notes* for this one. Taken as a whole, Mead's ideas are rather like a Rorschach inkblot test—what you see depends on your background and desires.

Vagueness is an integral quality of the interactionist approach. Its adherents see it as an artistic model of life, and neither life nor art proceeds in straight lines. Transactions between people are awesomely complicated and can only be understood fully when they aren't dissected and examined under a microscope. Mead and his followers view traditional scientific analysis of human behavior as "reductionistic"—forcing individuals to appear more similar and less complex than they really are. Of course, any attempt to reduce Mead's ideas to a few understandable principles is vulnerable to the same charge.

But symbolic interactionism is too important to bypass just because it's somewhat enigmatic and defies easy analysis. Some of the theories presented in later chapters draw heavily on Mead's insights. Even if this weren't so, the approach is worth discussing because it contains Mead's in-depth inquiry into the nature and origin of the self. His ideas won't make sense, however, unless you understand what Mead thinks are the key distinctions between human beings and animals.

UNIQUE QUALITIES OF THE HUMAN ANIMAL: REFLECTION, INTENTION, AND USE OF SYMBOLS

When our female basset hound was less than one year old, I took her to dog obedience school. Bowser flunked. At the first class she emitted an odor that was irresistible to half the canine students. Our hound was in heat. The male dogs paid attention to Bowser rather than to their owners, and the angry instructor told me to take her home.

Explaining the problem to my 6-year-old daughter was tough. Later I overheard Sharon scolding an appropriately sad-looking basset: "Bowser, you're a bad girl. You shouldn't be so attractive to those boy dogs. Next time don't be such a flirt." I couldn't help smiling because Sharon was assuming human attributes in a dumb beast. Mead would have found it ridiculous as well. The distinction between human beings and animals is the starting point of symbolic interactionism.

Contrast Bowser's experience with this imaginary scene at a typical college. Art, who considers himself the campus stud, has a Friday night date with Yvonne. While they are sitting together in her car, he catches a whiff of her perfume. Being a man of the world, he immediately recognizes the provocative scent as "My Sin." He's pretty sure she's sending him a message and prepares for an amorous night. But he hesitates to make a move because he's not certain of her intention. Maybe she just likes the smell of the perfume she's chosen.

Despite the similarity of sexual desire triggered by scent, Mead would highlight three crucial differences in male response to Bowser and Yvonne. First, the dogs' reactions were immediate and automatic. Mead calls this a "conversation of gestures." Once the other dogs picked up Bowser's signal, they advanced without delay or choice. Art, however, paused and considered his options. If Art had lunged for Yvonne with no sign of reflection, one can imagine her telling her roommate, "That guy is an animal."

A second difference has to do with intention. Sharon's stern lecture was funny because she attributed purpose to Bowser's erotic odor. In reality, our dog was merely programmed by her biological clock. But Art figured there was a reason behind Yvonne's choice of fragrance. Should he interpret her perfume as an invitation, or did it merely signify a preference for the scent?

The biggest gap between people and puppies is the use of symbols. Unlike animals, Art and Yvonne are both capable of assigning words to represent the act of mating. *My sin, intercourse, making love,* or hundreds of other terms may be used to refer to sex. It is this peculiar human ability to interact through the use of symbols that gives symbolic interactionism its name.

SYMBOLIC NAMING CREATES THE SELF

As human beings, we have the ability to name things. We can designate a concrete object (rock), identify an action (throw), or refer to an abstract idea (vandalism). Occasionally a word sounds like the thing it describes (*smack, thud, crash*), but usually the names we use have no logical connection with the object at hand. Symbols are arbitrary signs. There's nothing inherently small, soft, or cuddly in the word *kitten*. It's only through talk with others—symbolic interaction—that we come to ascribe that meaning and develop "a universe of discourse."

Mead believed that symbolic naming is the basis for society. The biblical book of Genesis states that Adam's first job was to name the animals—the dawn of civilization. Although "Me Tarzan, you Jane" is a primitive utterance, it's still light years ahead of the utterance of Cheetah the chimp, who can only chatter.

Throughout history, language has been the repository for names of important objects. The more crucial something is to our well-being, the more names we use to describe its nuances. Eskimos use over thirty separate words to communicate shades of difference when talking about snow.[1]

Interactionists claim that the "extent of knowing is the extent of naming." Although language is like a prison that confines us, we have the potential to push back the walls and bars as we master more words. You know from your own experience of taking the SAT or ACT College Board exams that half of the questions center on vocabulary. The construction of the test obviously reflects agreement with the interactionist claim that intelligence is the ability to symbolically label everything we encounter. Mead would agree with the title of the *Reader's Digest* feature, "It Pays to Enrich Your Word Power."

Why this concern with naming in a section on self-concept? The answer is that to Mead and other interactionists there is one kind of naming that's of prime importance—the symbolic labels we give to ourselves.

To use a name for oneself is to acquire a self. Recall that the Sapir-Whorf hypothesis maintains that we won't see things for which we don't have words. We need terms to label our inner experience. Without language there would be no self-concept. In normal times, a name gives a semblance of consistency and stability to our otherwise uncertain existence. Conversely, literature is filled with characters who undergo a name change to mark a radical transformation in personality. The New Testament figure Saul of Tarsus becomes Paul after a religious conversion experience. The good Dr. Jekyll becomes the evil Mr. Hyde. But these are proper names. Interactionists care most about the descriptive terms people use to define themselves.

Bernhard Goetz's controversial shooting of four young men on a New York subway illustrates how names create the self. Four scruffy-looking youths (two holding screwdrivers) asked Goetz for five dollars. Goetz could have labeled the episode "a joke," "panhandling," or "redistribution of wealth." But he defined the incident as "a robbery," naming himself "vigilante" rather than "victim." Most self-references don't result in a prison term (Goetz) or paralysis for life (one young man), but the names we use to define ourselves usually have great personal significance.

TAKING THE ROLE OF THE OTHER

As you might imagine, Mead doesn't consider naming the self a straightforward pursuit. The complex process starts with our cognitive ability to play with symbols. Whenever we face a new interpersonal situation, our typical human response is to hesitate so that we can mentally play out different scenarios.

Think of Art as he faces a possible perfume come-on. Unless this is a familiar situation to him, he'll pause to imagine a half-dozen different possibilities. "If I say this, then she'll probably do that. But if I go with Plan B, I think she'll laugh at me. Of course I could wait for her to say something first, and then respond with. . . ." Mead calls this inner dialogue "minding."

Minding is the pause that's reflective. It's the two-second delay while we mentally rehearse our next move, test alternatives, anticipate reactions. Mead says we don't need any encouragement to look before we leap. We naturally talk to ourselves in order to sort out the meaning of the situation. Art will act differently if he concludes that Yvonne's perfume is a carefully crafted invitation rather than a sweet-smelling cologne casually splashed on without erotic intent.

If he is to make an accurate judgment, Art needs to place himself mentally outside his body so that he can taste, see, hear, smell, and feel what it's like to be Yvonne. Mead refers to this cognitive drama as "taking the role of the other." "It is through taking this role of the other that he is able to come back on himself and so direct his own process of communication."[2]

Art may have a tough time imagining Yvonne's attitude and response. People who are fixated on their own desires and those who wield power often lack the sensitivity to invest time and effort in understanding another person. But symbolic interactionists claim that role taking is the essence of being human.

LOOKING-GLASS SELVES FORM A GENERALIZED OTHER

In Harper Lee's novel *To Kill a Mockingbird*, Scout stands on Boo Radley's porch and recalls her father's words, "you never really know a man until you stand in his shoes and walk around in them."[3] That's a clear statement of what symbolic interactionism means by role taking. The young, impulsive girl tastes what it's like to be a shy, emotionally fragile man. Note that she doesn't become him. That would be *Invasion of the Body Snatchers*. She does, however, look out at the world through his eyes. More than anything else, what she sees is herself.

We're now close to Mead's idea of self-concept. He doesn't believe that we get a glimpse of who we are through introspection. Rather, we paint our self-portrait by "taking the role of others," imagining how we look to them. Interactionists call that mental image "the looking-glass self."

Not all mirrors reflect the same image. Art may pick up vibrations that Yvonne thinks he's gross, whereas others might have projected kinder impressions. Art will form an aggregate picture from the perceived judgments of the people who are important to him. Don't expect these significant others to be a cross section of those who know him. We tend to choose friends and lovers who will help us sustain a favorable image. Mead labels this weighted composite view "the generalized other." It represents the attitude of the community around us. The generalized other also constitutes the major portion of what he calls "the self."

THE SELF AS "I"; THE SELF AS "ME"

Symbolic interactionists are convinced that the self is a function of language. Without talk there would be no self-concept. Since my symbolic interaction (talk) is always in flux, it follows that there is no little statue of Em Griffin that's the real me. Having such a doll-sized replica at the core of my being would suggest that the self is a fixed-in-stone, tangible object. According to Mead, this isn't so. The self is an ongoing process combining the "I" and the "me."

The "I" phase is the self's spontaneous driving force. The "I" is novel, unpredictable, and unorganized. For those of you who are intrigued with brain hemisphere research, Mead's "I" is akin to right-brain impulsiveness and creativity.

The "I" is the source of motivation, the springboard of activity, the subject or origin of action. Art's desire to pursue Yvonne is part of this "I." We know little about the "I" because it's forever elusive. Trying to examine the "I" phase of self is like viewing a snowflake through a lighted microscope. The very act causes it to vanish.

The "me" can be viewed as an object—the generalized other. Remember that in grammar school you learned to use the personal pronoun *me* in a sentence as the object of a verb. Because of the role-taking capacity of the human race, we can stand outside our bodies and view ourselves as objects. This reflexive experience is like having the Goodyear blimp hover overhead, transmitting back video shots of our actions. Mead described the process this way: "If the 'I' speaks, the 'me' hears. If the 'I' strikes, the 'me' feels the blow."[4]

There is no "me" at birth. The "me" develops only through continual symbolic interaction—first with family, next with playmates, then in institutions such as schools. As a sociologist, Mead saw this process as socialization. The "me" is the organized community within the individual. That's the reason his followers entitled his book, *Mind, Self, and Society.*

Think of the "me" as the product in a Baskin-Robbins 31 Flavors ice cream store. Just as there are many flavors, so there is more than one "me." Some flavors on the board never change. Vanilla, chocolate, mint chocolate chip, butter pecan, and pralines and cream account for 50 percent of sales. If for some reason a manager decided to remove these standbys, the store would soon close. In the same way, our stable and well-accepted "me's" offer consistency and permanence in our life. Through the eyes of others I view myself as a husband, teacher, father, and believer in God. Divorce, getting fired from my job, the loss of a child, or the loss of faith would undoubtedly create in me a crisis of identity. Symbolic interactionists view the "me" as the reason we obey laws, comply with the wishes of others, and generally enact the role of solid citizen.

But something inside us (the "I") wants novelty. We have an appetite to eat and sell exotic ice cream flavors—baseball bubble gum, candy-date, licorice twist. For example, I love flying an ultralight airplane that cruises at thirty-five miles per hour—with the wind in my hair and the bugs in my teeth. I also am the king of junk food junkies. Will others accept these weird "me's"? Ultimately our acceptance is determined by whether we can successfully float these public selves. As for Art, if Yvonne and all the other women on campus reject his advances and laugh in his face, he won't be able to sustain his self-image as a stud. Community reaction dictates keeping traditional ice cream flavors in stock.

RESEARCH BY PARTICIPANT OBSERVATION

Mead believed that symbolic interaction research can be accomplished only through an individual's own interpretation of his or her life. He valued personal letters, diaries, and autobiographical accounts. He had little sympathy for clinically controlled behavioral experiments. The results might be quantifiable, but the lifeless numbers ignore the meaning that the experience had for the person. With the exception of the work of Manford Kuhn at the University of Iowa, early interactionists shared Mead's antistatistical bias. Kuhn sought to measure self-concept through the use of a twenty-item sentence-completion test. The four building blocks of self-esteem cited in the brief introduction to self-concept were culled from data generated by his technique. But interpretive analysis continues to be the pivotal research of symbolic interactionism.

Participant observation is the approach of the ethnographer who systematically sets out to share in the life of the people under study. (See Chapter 24 for an extended discussion of ethnography.) Participant observation allows people to create the categories for the social scientist instead of having the social scientist try to fit life experiences into predetermined categories. The researcher adopts the stance of an interested, yet ignorant, visitor who needs instruction and will let the observations generate the conclusions. There's always the danger that the investigator will lose his or her objectivity and get sucked into another world. More than one anthropologist has been caught up in voodoo while examining the cult in Haiti. Mead thought it worth the risk. He saw involvement as the only way to discover how people interpret their symbols. Wranglers are fond of saying that the only way to understand horses is to smell like a horse, eat from a trough, and sleep in a stall. That's participant observation! Undoubtedly, Mr. Ed's stable lad was a symbolic interactionist.

SELF-FULFILLING PROPHECY

The implication of symbolic interactionism is that each of us has a significant impact on how others view themselves. A person's identity is shaped not by his or her own actions but by our reactions. That kind of power is often referred to as "self-fulfilling prophecy," the tendency for our expectations to

Reprinted from The Saturday Evening Post © 1973.

evoke responses that confirm what we originally anticipated. The process is nicely summed up by Eliza Doolittle, a girl from the gutter in George Bernard Shaw's play *Pygmalion*: "the difference between a lady and a flower girl is not how she behaves, but how she's treated."[5]

A sobering short story called "Cipher in the Snow" tells the true account of a boy who is treated as a nonentity by his parents, teachers, and other children. Their negative responses gradually reduce him into what they perceive him to be—nothing. He eventually collapses and dies in a snow-bank for no apparent reason. The interactionist would describe his death as symbolic manslaughter.

CRITIQUE: THOUGHTS TOO FAR REMOVED FROM EXPERIENCE

Most readers of *Mind, Self, and Society* are struck by the inconsistent way Mead used terms like *self, role, minding, I, me,* and *generalized other.* Perhaps Mead was precise when he stated his ideas, but their exact meaning was lost in the years before his students compiled the manuscript. Whatever the explanation, this lack of clarity makes any objective test of the theory impossible.

But even if its predictions had sharp edges, the theory would be less than satisfying because it deals only with the rational side of humanity. People are seen as competent manipulators of symbols, capable of pure reason. The self is disembodied from the hunk of flesh that carries it around. Philosophers refer to this separation of mind and body as "idealism," and it runs counter to a philosophy like that of Outward Bound, which assumes that identity is altered under physical and emotional stress. Even those of us who never had the peak experience of a wilderness trek can understand that headache and heartache are ever-present factors in self-evaluation.

The idealism inherent in the theory is undoubtedly the reason symbolic interactionism all but ignores the most fascinating aspect of the self: self-esteem. Mead's discussion of the looking-glass self focuses only on self-image—the identity side of self-concept. He had little to say about emotion, values, or put-downs from those who hold power over us—the stuff of which self-evaluation is made. A few followers have tried to address these issues, but most seem comfortable to rehash their leader's teachings. This silence on self-esteem is a major drawback.

Despite these shortcomings, symbolic interactionism is a remarkable endeavor. It has greater breadth than any other theory discussed in this book. I could have easily presented it in the section on messages, interpersonal communication, or cultural context. As you read about Pearce and Cronen's coordinated management of meaning, Delia's constructivism, Burke's dramatism, Fisher's narrative paradigm, Tannen's genderlect, and Kramarae's muted group theory, realize that each of these theorists owes an intellectual debt to ideas that originated with Mead. That impressive list of significant others could give a boost to any theorist's looking-glass self.

QUESTIONS TO SHARPEN YOUR FOCUS

1. What do *symbolic interactionists* believe are the crucial differences between *human beings* and *animals*? What would you add or take off the list?

2. As Mead used the terms, are your *looking-glass self* and your *me* the same thing? Why or why not?

3. Think of a time in your life when your *self-concept* changed dramatically. Do you believe that society-induced *self-fulfilling prophecy* played a major role in the shift?

4. Is symbolic interactionism a theory of *identity*, *self-esteem*, or both?

A SECOND LOOK

Recommended resource: Herbert Blumer, "Symbolic Interaction: An Approach to Human Communication," in *Approaches to Human Communication*, Richard W. Budd and Brent Ruben (eds.), Spartan Books, New York, 1972, pp. 401–419.

A fuller treatment: Herbert Blumer, *Symbolic Interactionism: Perspective and Method*, Prentice-Hall, Englewood Cliffs, N.J., 1969.

Original source: George Herbert Mead, *Mind, Self, and Society*, University of Chicago, Chicago, 1934.

Later developments: Manford H. Kuhn, "Major Trends in Symbolic Interaction Theory in the Past Twenty-Five Years," *The Sociological Quarterly*, Vol. 5, 1964, pp. 61–84.

Communication issues: Bruce E. Bronbeck, "Symbolic Interactionism and Communication Studies: Prolegomena to Future Research," in *Communication and Social Structures*, D. R. Maines and C. J. Couch (eds.), Charles C. Thomas, Springfield, Ill., 1988, pp. 323–340.

Systematizing Mead's ideas: John D. Baldwin, *George Herbert Mead*, Sage, Newbury Park, Calif., 1986.

Collected articles: Jerome Mannis and Bernard Meltzer (eds.), *Symbolic Interaction*, Allyn and Bacon, Boston, 1978.

Participant observation: Erving Goffman, *The Presentation of Self in Everyday Life*, Doubleday, Garden City, N.Y., 1959.

Empirical research: Manford Kuhn and Thomas McPartland, "An Empirical Investigation of Self-Attitudes," *American Sociological Review*, Vol. 19, 1954, pp. 68–76.

Consideration of power: Peter Hull, "Structuring Symbolic Interaction: Communication and Power," *Communication Yearbook 4*, Dan Nimmo (ed.), Transaction Books, New Brunswick, N.J., 1980, pp. 49–60.

Self-fulfilling prophecy: Robert K. Merton, *Social Theory and Social Structure*, Free Press, New York, 1957.

Application: Jean Mizer, "Cipher in the Snow," *Today's Education*, Vol. 53, November 1964, pp. 8–10.

MOTIVATION

Most communication theories describe behavior. They try to answer the "what" questions of interaction: What did she say? What is his response? What actions are they planning to take? Theories of motivation are an attempt to answer the "why" questions. They seek to go behind the behavior and discover the internal cause or reason for the action.

Motivation is usually defined as our stable disposition to satisfy specific needs—

food, sleep, sex, affection, accomplishment, power, novelty, beauty, and so forth. When these needs are unfulfilled, they goad us to action. It's as if we each had a miniature person with a stick inside our bellies. He or she pokes the point of the stick against our stomach wall just when we're trying to rest. Where the stick jabs and how. hard it's pushed determines the nature and extent of our behavior. When the ache becomes too bothersome, we rouse ourselves and do

"In my view, management overrates the motivational appeal of mackerel."

Drawing by Stevenson; © 1991 The New Yorker Magazine, Inc.

whatever we must do to get rid of the irritant. Once we have taken care of the pain, we can lie down and relax until we feel the next motivational prod.

Many theories of motivation approximate this model. The stick they describe is a single factor that relentlessly goads everyone throughout life. For example, three Austrian psychiatrists each assumed there is a universal drive that activates human behavior, but they disagreed as to what it is. Sigmund Freud saw that stick as pleasure, especially sex. Alfred Adler regarded the drive for power as the motive force behind all actions. And Viktor Frankl postulated a need for meaning in life that leaves us uncomfortable until we have an ultimate purpose for living.

The problem with metaphors like the person-with-the-stick image is that they can lead to false conclusions. Is there really just one stick that prods everyone in the same direction? It would seem that a sophisticated theory of human motivation would account for multiple inclinations.

Harvard psychologist David McClelland postulates three social needs—the need for achievement, the need for affiliation, and the need for power. He believes that everyone experiences them in varying amounts, and that the recurrent concern to satisfy these distinct needs "energizes, orients, and selects behavior."[1]

Measuring the relative strength of the three needs can be a tricky process. People may not be aware of their desire for achievement, affiliation, or power, so the validity of self-reports is questionable. But the judgment of outside observers is no more reliable. Since a motive can't be seen, we can only infer its presence by the apparent effect it has on another's behavior.

McClelland tries to surmount these difficulties by analyzing the imagery that emerges in a story-writing exercise. He shows people ambiguous photographs of men and women in natural settings and asks them to write stories about the characters. Who are these people in the picture? What do they want? What are they thinking? What will they do?

McClelland assumes that communication reflects our unconscious motivation. He is convinced that the stories which emerge can be systematically analyzed in a way that reveals the writer's underlying pattern of needs. He categorizes the imagery of each narrative according to the extent it reflects a concern for the social goals of achievement, affiliation, or power.

People who are high in need for achievement tend to write stories about doing things better—outperforming someone else, reaching a personal goal, creating something unique, or working hard at a task for a long time. People who are high in need for affiliation usually write stories in which at least one character wants to establish, maintain, or restore a warm, personal relationship. Their desires could run the gamut from friendly, social activity to deep, long-lasting intimacy. People who are high in need for power typically write stories that contain accounts of strong actions, powerful emotional responses, expressed concern for reputation, and unsolicited advice—all indicative of a desire to have an impact on others.

McClelland's theory of motivation is highly respected in the field of psychology, yet has had little impact among communication scholars. The exact opposite holds true for Abraham Maslow's theory of motivation presented in Chapter 10. Although many psychology texts on motivation completely ignore Maslow's hierarchy of needs, his view of people striving toward self-actualization has inspired the authors of a number of applied communication texts.

There are quite a few similarities between the works of Maslow and McClelland. Both men were trained as psychologists. Their theories avoid simplistic analyses, suggesting rather that people are motivated by more than one need. Each man has offered a comprehensive theory describing needs that are distinctively human. And neither theory gives a special status to communication. Instead, verbal and nonverbal communication is regarded as behavior subject to all the motivational forces which affect other activities.

Despite such similarities, the two theories are quite diverse. McClelland sees individual motive patterns as relatively stable. Maslow, on the other hand, allowed for and expects change. McClelland believes the three social needs for achievement, affiliation, and power can each exert a strong force on a person at the same time. Maslow was certain that at a given stage in a person's life, he or she feels only a single pull. While Mc-

Clelland doesn't speak to the issue of human nature as either good or bad, Maslow was vocal in his belief that humans possess an innate goodness which can only be subverted by many years of being denied the basic needs of life.

Maslow rejected the traditional view of motivation that treats needs as irritants to be temporarily soothed until they flare up again. He became suspicious of this mosquito-bite model because it didn't describe the people he thought were most productive in life. He saw them as drawn rather than driven. As you read about Maslow's hierarchy of needs, decide whether his theory of motivation describes the inner forces that affect the person you know best—you.

CHAPTER 10

Hierarchy of Needs
of Abraham Maslow

Think of someone who fits the following description: loving, fair, realistic, relaxed, self-sufficient, spontaneous, creative, nice. Make sure he or she also has an honest directness, a playful spirit, a history of successful risk taking, and a way of moving through life that seems effortless.

This is the kind of extraordinary person Brandeis University psychologist Abraham Maslow considered when he devised a theory of motivation fifty years ago. They are a rare breed—the Olympic medal winners of the human race. To Maslow, it made sense to examine the finest specimens of the species. So in order to discover exemplary qualities in the human race, he studied the lives of Abraham Lincoln, Albert Einstein, Jane Addams, Eleanor Roosevelt, Frederick Douglass, Martin Buber, Albert Schweitzer, and a few dozen others representing his definition of the brightest and the best.

THE THIRD FORCE: A REACTION TO PESSIMISTIC DETERMINISM

Maslow realized that his method was a radical departure from the two standard psychological approaches to the study of human nature. The Freudian psychoanalytic school emphasized people's destructive tendencies. Consistent with the survival-of-the-fittest views of Charles Darwin , Freud saw no moral difference between people and animals. We may walk upright, but there's no reason to believe we'll act that way. Maslow thought that Freud's pessimism was a logical result of looking at the dark side of the human psyche. "The study of crippled, stunted, immature, and unhealthy specimens can yield only a cripple psychology and a cripple philosophy."[1]

The behaviorism of B. F. Skinner offers little more hope. Since students of motivation spend most of their time studying the behavior of white rats, it's no wonder they construct need models based solely on hunger, thirst, sex, and the avoidance of pain. If we must do animal research, Maslow asked, why not study the playfulness of monkeys or the affectionate loyalty of dogs? He was also critical of behaviorists' tendency to ignore unique characteristics. When they finally get around to looking at people, they lop off individual differences and reduce warm bodies to cold statistical averages.

Maslow's hierarchy of needs offers an alternative to what he saw as the depressing determinism of both Freud and Skinner. To call attention to the differences between his optimistic view and their denial of human freedom and dignity, he labeled his approach the "Third Force." Maslow was convinced that when scientists finally examined the noble examples of human development, they would discover that people are basically trustworthy, self-protecting, and self-governing. Our innate tendency is toward growth; we are even capable of love. Maslow's theory is bullish on the human race.

DEFICIENCY NEEDS MUST BE SATISFIED FOR GROWTH TO OCCUR

Maslow was not stupid. He could read the newspaper as well as anybody else and was saddened by the daily reports of inhuman deceit and violence. But that was exactly his point. Lying, cheating, stealing, and murder are not what he thought human nature was meant to be. These are aberrant behaviors that occur when legitimate human needs are thwarted. To borrow a line spoken by a gang member to Officer Krupke in the 1962 Academy Award winning movie *West Side Story*, "I'm depraved on account of I'm deprived."[2]

According to Maslow's theory, there are four types of needs that must be satisfied before a person can act unselfishly. As Figure 10.1 shows, the needs are arranged in a hierarchical order. The upward climb is made by satisfying one set of needs at a time. The most basic drives are physiological. After that comes the need for safety, then the desire for love, and then the quest for

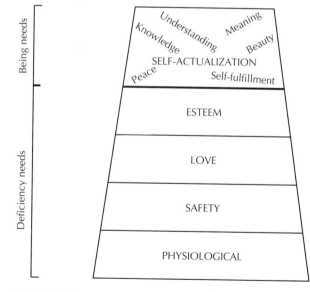

FIGURE 10.1
Maslow's Hierarchy of Needs (Adapted from Goble, *The Third Force.*)

esteem. Note the softening of terminology used to describe the move up the ladder. We're *driven* to satisfy the lower needs, but we're *drawn* to meet the higher ones.

Maslow referred to the four lower needs as "deficiency needs" because their lack creates a tension within us. He saw nothing wrong with the human desire to scratch where we itch. As long as we can work to satisfy the cravings, we're moving toward growth. It's when a repressive society or a warped individual curtails our freedom to satisfy our needs that we become ill. Satisfying needs is healthy. Blocking gratification makes us sick.

The urge to fulfill needs is potent but not overpowering. Maslow thought that the Freudian label *instinct* overstated the case. Maslow used the term *instinctoid* to designate a less insistent motivational force. People *can* resist the pull of physiological, safety, love, and esteem needs, but it's not easy.

The instinctoid label also means that these needs are universal urges and not created by culture, as the behaviorist would claim. Although everyone has the same set of the needs, our ways of fulfilling those needs can be different. You could meet your need to belong (love and be loved) by going to a party, whereas your roommate might go for a quiet walk with a friend. Despite these different means of gratification, our common desire for love makes us brothers or sisters under the skin.

LOWER NEEDS TAKE PRIORITY UNTIL MET

There is nothing unique about Maslow's focus on physical, safety, love, and esteem needs. Other theorists include these four in their lists of basic needs. The genius of the hierarchy is its concept of prepotency. A *prepotent need* is the one that has the greatest power or influence over our actions. Maslow claimed that everyone has a prepotent need, but the need will differ among individuals. You might be motivated by a craving for love, while I may be motivated by a desire for esteem. Which need is prepotent for a given individual? According to Maslow, a person's prepotent need is the *lowest unmet need* in the pyramid.

Not surprisingly physical drives take priority in Maslow's system. Almost all motivational theorists regard the needs for food and other physical necessities as powerful and primary urges. Fortunately for many people, these basic wants are usually well satisfied. What happens when there is plenty of bread and the belly is full day after day? Maslow described the shift in motivation that occurs when survival needs are met:

> At once other (and higher) needs emerge, and these, rather than physiological hungers, dominate the organism. And when these in turn are satisfied, again new (and still higher) needs emerge, and so on. As one desire is satisfied, another pops up to take its place.[3]

What follows is a brief description of the deficiency needs in the order Maslow predicted they occur.

Physiological Needs

Physiological needs are basic: The body craves food, liquid, sleep, oxygen, sex, freedom of movement, and a moderate temperature. When any of these are in short supply, we feel the distressing tension of hunger, thirst, fatigue, shortness of breath, sexual frustration, confinement, or the discomfort of being too hot or cold. These irritants compel us to seek the missing commodity so that our body can return to homeostasis—a system in balance or at rest.

As long as the body feels substantially deprived, it marshals all its energies in the service of satisfying these demands. Responding like a heat-seeking missile, a dog or cat invariably finds the one patch of sunlight that provides a warm place to doze. On the physiological level, Maslow sees people as no different. But once these physical needs are met regularly, they no longer exert pressure. A need fulfilled no longer motivates.

Weight Watchers advises that the time to go to the grocery store is after a complete meal. When we've had enough to eat, food becomes relatively unimportant. As hunger and the other physiological needs are met, the need for security kicks in.

Safety Needs

The safety needs operate mainly on a psychological level. Naturally we try to avoid a poke in the eye with a sharp stick. But once we've managed a certain level of physical comfort, we'll seek to establish stability and consistency in a chaotic world. When he talked about security, Maslow pictured the child who strives for predictability and certainty. For instance, most kids enjoy a set bedtime routine and grow visibly distressed if a parent tries to short-circuit the ritual. Their safety needs require a consistent and secure world that offers few surprises.

Unfortunately, life doesn't always cooperate. Some of you who come from a broken or dysfunctional home know the cringing fear of waiting for the next fight or the other shoe to fall. Many adults go through life stuck on this level and act as if catastrophe will happen any moment. Political appeals for law and order are aimed at people whose insecurities have never been quieted. Maslow also placed religious inclination on the safety rung because he saw that tendency as an attempt to bring about an ordered universe with no nasty shocks.

Love and Belongingness Needs

The love or belongingness needs come into play after the physiological and security drives are satisfied. Gratification is a matter of degree rather than an either-or accomplishment. But once a need has been significantly satisfied over a long period of time, it becomes functionally absent. The action switches to the next highest level, in this case, love.

"I think we've satisfied all our basic needs."
Drawing by Koren; © 1991 The New Yorker Magazine, Inc.

Maslow's concept of belonging combines the twin urges to give and receive love. Giving love is different from the passion of rock music lyrics that announce, "I want you, I need you, I'm going to have you." That's raw sex. And giving love is more than the maternal instinct implanted by nature. For Maslow, giving love is seeking to fill a void by understanding and accepting selected others. Receiving love is a way of staving off the pangs of loneliness and rejection. The man who attains this level will "feel keenly, as never before, the absence of friends, or a sweetheart, or a wife, or children."[4]

Even though it's higher in the hierarchy than physical or safety needs, the desire for love and belonging is similar in that it motivates only when a person feels a deficit. According to Maslow, love loses its pull when you've had enough. Thirty years ago he suggested that the desire for love and belonging was the lowest level of unmet need for most Americans. If the continuing popular appeal of *Cheers* reruns on television is a reliable indicator, his assessment still holds true today.

Maslow notes that the need for love is more fragile than the needs that go before. For example, this need is nonexistent in the psychopath, who feels no desire for warmth or affection. And some people get their esteem and belongingness wires crossed. They want respect before they want love. But for most of us, the prepotent order is as Maslow depicted it:

Physiological → Safety → Love → Esteem

Esteem Needs

The esteem needs are of two types. There's self-esteem, which is the result of competence or mastery of tasks. Harvard psychologist David McClelland calls this "need for achievement." There's also the attention and recognition that come from others. Wanting this admiration is part of what McClelland labels "need for power." McClelland assumes that individual differences in needs are tied to personality, and they change slowly if at all. Maslow, on the other hand, believes that repeated shifts in motivation are possible when a person is in a supportive environment.

Consider the real-life case of Tony, who seemed to have everything going against him, yet he has risen to the esteem level in the hierarchy of needs. Tony was raised in the inner city of Chicago, the seventh child in a Hispanic family of twelve that lacked legal status in the United States. With his father working a minimum-wage job, Tony never had enough to eat. The lack of health care and sufficient heat in the winter guaranteed that Tony's childhood would center on his physical wants.

When Tony was 12 years old, extended welfare benefits plus financial aid from a local church combined to raise his family slightly above the poverty line. As food, warmth, and medical attention silenced his body's chronic aches, Tony began to worry about the twin threats of the immigration service and street gangs. He had risen to the safety level in Maslow's hierarchy.

The Amnesty Act of 1986 took away the fear of deportation, and a high school coach recruited him for an after-hours wrestling program that removed him from the constant hassle with gang members. With safety no longer a major concern, Tony started to feel the pull of his previously dormant needs to love and to belong.

As Maslow would have predicted, the last few years of Tony's life have been characterized by an increased interest in his brothers and sisters, friendship with his wrestling buddies, and a mutual fascination with a girl named Helen. Although his needs for love are only partially fulfilled, Tony now talks about making something of his life and has applied for financial aid to enter college. Maslow would cite these initial efforts as evidence that Tony has worked his way up to the esteem level of the hierarchy.

Contrast Tony's experience with a man who has been brought up in a comfortable, secure, loving environment. He has never known physical want, experienced danger, or felt separation from the people he loves. Unlike Tony, he will probably take for granted the blessings he already has. Because of the constant gratification he's received, this person might put up with all sorts of hardship, danger, and loneliness in order to gain a sense of worth. He might even die for a cause. Maslow notes that it's easier to make sacrifices when you're never faced chronic deprivation. There are few martyrs from the ranks of those who have to struggle for existence.

SELF-ACTUALIZATION: THE ULTIMATE GOAL

Maslow described the need for self-actualization as "the desire to become more and more what one is, to become everything that one is capable of becoming."[5] People feel this gentle but persistent tug to maximize their potential only after they have satisfied their basic deficiency cravings. Obviously, the comic strip character Charlie Brown, who bemoans the curse of great potential, has yet to reach that point.

Self-actualization can take many forms, depending on the individual. These variations may include the quest for knowledge, understanding, peace, self-fulfillment, meaning in life, or beauty. For instance, the aesthetic person operating on this level may feel physically ill when driving past an ugly array of fast-food restaurants with garish neon signs. But the need for beauty is neither higher nor lower than the other needs at the top of the pyramid. Self-actualization needs aren't hierarchically ordered.

You'll recall that Maslow set out to study fully functioning people who had grown past the discontent and restlessness that characterize the lower-order needs of the hierarchy. He found very few. People who fit his criteria turned out to be mature in years as well as in the process of living. Each was dedicated to a task or calling which would benefit others. Since they weren't people who need people, they were free to pursue a cause or vocation.

Most of us have trouble imagining ourselves on this transcendent plane, so Maslow developed a device that would give the uninitiated a glimpse of the self-actualized life. He asked people to describe the single most joyous, happy, or blissful moment of their life. Perhaps you'd recount a religious experience, a moment of sexual ecstasy, or a time when a piece of music took you to the heights. This peak experience would provide a taste of the fulfillment available to those who get beyond the deficiency needs.

Maslow's vision of self-actualization as the highest human attainment became a rallying point for Carl Rogers, Rollo May, Erich Fromm, and other humanistic psychologists. If not the founder of the human potential movement, Maslow certainly is a father figure to those who are part of the if-it-feels-good-do-it tradition. It's hard to imagine hordes of people lined up to hug Leo Buscaglia had not Maslow paved the way.

RESEARCH SUPPORTS THE MOTIVES BUT NOT THE ORDER

No one can seriously question the impact of Maslow's theory. Millions of people have been affected by his ideas. But truth isn't determined by a head count. How has the hierarchy stood up under scientific scrutiny? The results are mixed. Hundreds of empirical studies have supported the motivational force of physical, safety, love, and esteem needs. But the same studies have failed to discover a hierarchical or prepotent arrangement.

In the late 1960s a Dutch industrial psychologist, Gerald Huizinga, attempted to validate the theory in the workplace. Because of its scope and different cultural setting, Huizinga's study is one of the more ambitious attempts to verify the principles of the hierarchy. He surveyed over 600 managers drawn from five industries in the Netherlands. His sample included people from production, personnel, research and development, finance, and top management. They ranged in age from 20 to 65, and their educational backgrounds extended from the Dutch equivalent of grade school to university graduates.

Huizinga's book-length write-up demonstrates that he is a true believer in Maslow's theory. Yet no matter how many ways he analyzed the data, there was simply no evidence that workers had a single dominant need, much less that the need diminished in strength when gratified.

Despite the lack of systematic empirical support, it's hard to dismiss the idea that one overriding need governs our behavior until the desire is satisfied. When the body hurts, concerns for security, love, and esteem do seem to be pushed into the background. A true test of prepotency can only be made in a longitudinal study which lasts over a decade or more. The long time span would give the researcher a chance to spot whether or not changes in motivation follow the upward pattern that Maslow predicted.

VALIDATION OF THE HIERARCHY IN RELIGIOUS CONGREGATIONS

Not all truth comes out of a laboratory or from a survey questionnaire. Sensitive observers of the human scene can often spot a relationship before the behavioral scientist devises a way to test for it. Keith Miller is a Protestant pastor, lecturer, and writer who believes that Maslow's prepotency principle is validated in the makeup of religious congregations.

Impoverished people respond to a vision of heaven as a large banquet table that satisfies their physical needs. Believers on the safety level of the hierarchy are predisposed to favor pastors who preach about eternal security from the terrors of Hell. Those who are fortunate enough to have risen above the safety level tend to look down on adherents of "that old-time religion." They want assurance that God is love. But that warm message strikes many worshipers on the esteem level as self-indulgent. Faith to them means a sense of worth that comes from doing something of lasting value in God's world. And finally, individuals who feel tugs toward self-actualization respond most to calls for meditation and study.

Miller feels that all five approaches are legitimate, but each will seem ridiculous when viewed from above or sterile when viewed from below. He obviously finds Maslow's hierarchy a valuable analytical tool. Not all observers are so positive.

CRITIQUE: MASLOW AS THE FATHER OF THE "ME GENERATION"

In a scathing critique entitled "Stepping Off Maslow's Escalator," social critic Daniel Yankelovich accuses Maslow of providing intellectual justification for the selfish individualism of the last two decades. Before agreeing with the charge, remember that Maslow's original cluster of self-actualized individuals consisted of people who no longer felt the tug of deficiency needs and were freed up to help others. Somehow this selfless component has been ignored by Maslow's disciples, and self-fulfillment has come to mean "look out for number one." Yankelovich notes that it's not fair to blame Maslow for the excesses of his followers, yet in the end he does so.

Perhaps Maslow was overly optimistic about human goodness. His idea of an innate, positive direction is hard to accept after watching a film on the Holocaust or reading reports of torture from Amnesty International. Certainly we have the *capacity* for good. But history doesn't support the claim that being trustworthy, loyal, helpful, friendly, courteous, kind, and so forth, is the dominant human tendency.

Maslow's theory of motivation does have a healthy emphasis on freedom of choice. He believes that the ability to respond is what makes us fully human. With this in mind, one might wish that he had placed more emphasis on responsible, unselfish commitment to others. For the past few thousand years, communication professionals have recommended that speakers concentrate on the needs of their audience rather than focusing on their own desires. In spite of the turned-in focus of the last decade, the advice still seems sound.

QUESTIONS TO SHARPEN YOUR FOCUS

1. Maslow's *humanistic* approach was a reaction against Freudian and behavioristic psychology. How does the *"Third Force"* differ from these other two approaches?

2. Given that *safety* needs are lower in the *hierarchy* than needs for *love* and *esteem*, how is it possible that people might willingly die for their country?

3. What has been the single most joyous, happy, or blissful moment of your life? Does that *peak experience* square with Maslow's description of *self-actualization* as an unselfish state?

4. Is there any place for delayed gratification within Maslow's theory of motivation?

A SECOND LOOK

Recommended resource: Abraham H. Maslow, *Motivation and Personality*, 2d ed., Harper & Row, New York, 1970.

Original statement: Abraham H. Maslow, "A Theory of Human Motivation," *Psychological Review,* Vol. 50, 1943, pp. 370–396.

Recommended secondary source: Frank Goble, *The Third Force,* Grossman, New York, 1970.

Field research: Gerald Huizinga, *Maslow's Hierarchy in the Work Situation,* Wolters-Noordhoff, Groninggen, Netherlands, 1970.

Religious application: Keith Miller, *The Becomers,* Word, Waco, Tex., 1973, pp. 89–109.

Critique: Daniel Yankelovich, "Stepping Off Maslow's Escalator," in *New Rules: Searching for Self-Fulfillment in a World Turned Upside Down,* Random House, New York, 1981, pp. 234–243.

Critique: Andrew Neher, "Maslow's Theory of Motivation: A Critique," *Journal of Humanistic Psychology,* Vol. 31, No. 3, 1991, pp. 89–112.

PERCEPTION

A story about three umpires captures some of the key issues of perception. One umpire states flatly, "Some's balls, some's strikes—I calls them as they is." The second umpire was less sure reality was easy to see. "Some's balls, some's strikes—I calls them as I sees them." The third understands that, for all practical purposes, reality is in the eye of the beholder. "Some's balls, some's strikes—but they ain't nothin' till I calls them!"

No serious student of perception would join the first umpire in believing we can accurately perceive the true features of another human being. Early studies in the field adopted the stance of the second umpire and sought to isolate the systematic errors we make when viewing others. The effort resulted in a short list of common perceptual biases:[1]

1. We tend to assume that others are like us. We imagine that their emotional reactions to events are the same as ours. More often than not, we're wrong.

2. We see what we expect to see. Even impartial umpires aren't immune to the influence of past experience. Ted Williams was the last .400 hitter in baseball. A catcher once complained when Williams took a belt-high pitch down the heart of the plate and the umpire called it a ball. The umpire responded coldly, "Mr. Williams will let you know when the ball is in the strike zone."

3. First impressions are hard to shake. Researchers label this fact the "law of primacy." It may be because we adjust later views to fit our first picture, or perhaps we get tired of taking in new data. Nonetheless, our final portrait of another usually bears a striking resemblance to the initial image.

4. We notice characteristics we don't like more readily than those we do. Pleasant feelings come across in a muted blur, but the distressing emotions of fear, anger, disgust, and boredom stand out in bold relief. It's easy to ignore ten positives in a letter of recommendation and focus on the one item of criticism.

Most modern perceptual theorists align themselves with the third umpire. He recognizes that reality is not so much a matter of what's going on *out there* as it is of what's going on *in here*—in his mind. When the fans yell, "The ump needs glasses," the issue is not one of optics.

We organize our social perceptions into comprehensive patterns. In that sense, we all subscribe to our own implicit theory of personality. We assume that certain traits go together. When we hear that another person is warm, we're likely to conclude that he or she is also honest and sensitive. Stereotypes are the result of implicit personality theories which are no longer responsive to new data. "Don't confuse me with the facts," says the stubborn theorist within us, "My mind is made up."

The umpire who calls balls and strikes has a standard of judgment published in a rule book, and that makes the job easier. When we categorize people, however, we must make up the rules as we go along. As you will read in Chapter 12, constructivists like Jesse Delia claim that people exhibit varying degrees of cognitive complexity as they form their impressions of others. According to Delia, people who are cognitively complex in their interpersonal perceptions of others have a greater capacity to create effective per-

"We think Dawson and Debronski are still talking, but it could be a Greek vase."
Reproduced by permission of Punch.

son-centered messages than those who think in simplistic black-and-white terms. In addition to the existence of a rule book with published criteria, there are two other reasons why the umpire's job is easier:

1. Players may complain about a call, but the umpire behind the plate doesn't have to contend with the ball's squawking that it was misperceived. That's not the situation between people. British psychotherapist R. D. Laing maintained that "human beings are constantly thinking about others and about what others are thinking about them, and

what others think they are thinking about the others, and so on."[2] He called this speculation the "spiral of reciprocal perspectives," and he said we usually guess wrong. Worse yet, we fail to realize our misunderstanding, so the "fantasy coefficient" between us rises while the whirling spiral gathers into a hurricane force that destroys relationships. Laing was convinced that our inability to experience another person's experience dooms us to a lifetime of misperception.

2.   Except in the case of beanballs thrown at a batter's head, the umpire doesn't need to worry about what the pitcher meant to do. Yet you and I are constantly faced with judging the intentions of others. Chapter 11 presents Fritz Heider's theory of attribution. The theory deals with the assignment of praise or blame based on the assumed intentions of the actor.

Heider, Delia, and Laing would contend that the process of interpersonal perception takes more than a keen eye and a pure heart. Even a slow-motion instant replay doesn't begin to sort out all that's happening. Perception involves more than just the five senses of sight, sound, touch, taste, and smell. At its root, perception is interpretation.

CHAPTER 11

Attribution Theory
of Fritz Heider

My wife, Jean, served on a jury in a federal case involving conspiracy, racketeering, drug dealing, armed robbery, and extortion. The seven defendants were accused of being the lieutenants in the "Little Mafia" gang which terrorized a Chicago neighborhood. The gang leader had escaped from police custody and was on the FBI's most-wanted list.

The key government witness was an ex-gang member named Larry. Larry was called "the Canary" by the defendants because he turned informer. For two months Jean listened to the testimony and tried to figure out whether Larry's story was credible. Was his behavior on the witness stand that of a pathological liar, a rejected pal seeking revenge, a petty crook who would say anything to save his own skin, or an honest witness dedicated to the truth? Fritz Heider, the Austrian-born father of attribution theory, said that we all face the same task Jean confronted—trying to figure out personality from behavior.

Heider, who became a psychologist and taught at the University of Kansas, said that attribution is the process of drawing inferences. We see a person act and immediately reach conclusions that go beyond mere sensory information. Suppose Larry yawns while on the stand. Is he bored, afraid, tired, or indifferent? Jean will search for an explanation that makes sense to her. Heider would have seen her as a naive psychologist bringing common sense to bear on an interpersonal judgment. If he were crafting the theory today, he might well describe Jean and all of us as Judge Wapner stand-ins, rendering decisions in a people's court of everyday life.

We're constantly told we shouldn't judge others. Attribution theory says we can't help it. Like my wife, who had to listen to Larry's testimony for a week, we're inundated with sensory data, some of it contradictory. Faced with this information overload, we make personality judgments in order to explain otherwise confusing behavior. For example, although Jean had earlier thought Larry was a credible witness, she wondered why Larry yawned when describing how a gang member struck a victim on the head with a baseball bat. She made a snap judgment that he was callously indifferent to human suffering.

In addition to our need for clarity, there's another reason for making causal inferences from behavior. We want to know what to expect in the future. Prediction is a survival skill. During the third week of the trial, Jean came face-to-face with one of the defendants outside a train station. Mildly anxious, she quickly turned aside. Accurate attributions can help us know which people might do us harm.

ATTRIBUTION: A THREE-STEP PROCESS

Attribution is a three-step process through which we perceive others as causal agents. Suppose you are stopped at a red light, and the driver in the car ahead flips an empty soda can into the gutter. Before the light turns green, you mutter the three thoughts that cross your mind:

I saw that! (Perception of the action)

You meant to do that! (Judgment of intention)

You're a slob! (Attribution of disposition)

The process of attribution is diagramed in Figure 11.1. I visited the courtroom the day ex-gang member Larry described the baseball bat attack, so I'll use my reactions to illustrate Heider's chain of causal inference. Jean experienced her own attributional sequence as she heard the testimony that day. Since her private world differs from mine, however, I can write with certainty only about one person's experience—my own.

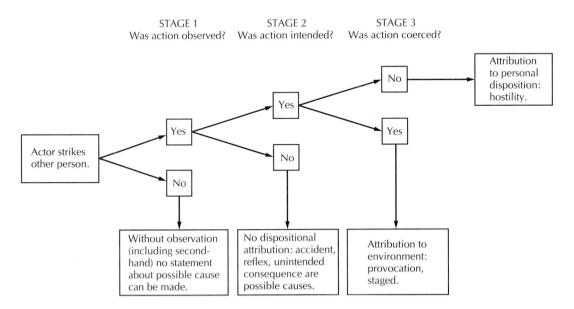

FIGURE 11.1
The Process of Attribution (From Shaver, *An Introduction to Attribution Processes.*)

Step 1: Perception of the Action

The courtroom was on the twenty-first floor of the Federal Building. A well-dressed, handsome man carrying a bag of donuts dashed toward the elevator just as the doors were closing. I slapped my hand against the breaker bar to hold the car, receiving enthusiastic words of thanks and the offer of a donut. We traded a few friendly comments until we got off at the same floor. It turned out we were both headed for the south courtroom. A few minutes later I learned that his name was Brian, and I also heard testimony of how he used a Louisville Slugger to beat up a cocaine addict who hadn't paid for his drug.

Was Brian observed? Yes, Larry was an eyewitness and gave an account of the act. My perception was secondhand through Larry's description, but Jean had told me the night before that she thought Larry was a credible witness. My vicarious observation of the scene triggered the start of the attribution chain. If I hadn't heard the story, the process would never have started.

I'm sure that my perception of the action was subject to all the biases listed in the introduction to this section. It was initially difficult to picture such a brutal act performed by Brian because that contradicted my initial image of a generous, joking Brian. This first impression, which was formed on the elevator, was one of warmth, a trait that casts a halo over all other qualities.

I like to think of myself as a good judge of character, so my continuing desire to see Brian in a favorable light could well have compromised the integrity of my courtroom listening. That's why jurors are excused "for cause" when personal motivation prevents their being impartial. Despite these biases, the new information crashed into my world and I moved to the second stage of causal attribution.

Step 2: Judgment of Intention

Since Larry's words convinced me that Brian was present when the man was struck with a bat, the next question was, To what extent had Brian wanted it done? That may sound like a strange way to ask the question, but Heider didn't consider intention as an either-or matter. He identified five sliding scale positions of personal causation. We can see these gradations reflected in the American legal code. Suppose for a moment that the victim had died. Our judgment of intention could place the killing blow into five different categories before the law.[1]

1. Association.   Despite the testimony, maybe Brian didn't direct the attack, swing the bat, or even know the man who did. He was merely in the vicinity at the time. Chance proximity is no reason to assign causality. We hope we are past the stage of killing the messenger who brings bad news. To impute guilt by association would be irrational. Not guilty.

2. Causality.   Perhaps the event took place at a sandlot baseball game. Brian took a mighty swing at a pitch that fooled him, and the bat slipped out of his hands, striking the unlucky fellow standing forty feet away in foul territory. It's true that Brian's hand was the ultimate cause of death, but he had no motive or desire to do harm, and that is what a coroner's jury would rule. Accidental death.

3. Justifiability.   Suppose the event took place in Brian's apartment. Returning from work, Brian surprised an intruder who came at him with a knife. Brian grabbed the bat, which was propped in the corner, and swung it to protect himself. Some might wonder about excessive force, but most people would see it as self-defense. Justifiable homicide.

4. Foreseeability.   Picture Brian trying to hit fly balls to a group of friends in a crowded park. It's a dangerous game from the start. Angry at his inability to get the ball in the air, he impulsively flings the bat aside, blindsiding a man playing with his children nearby. That would be reckless homicide. Brian might honestly claim that he never meant to hurt anybody, but the law would regard him as responsible for the outcome of his careless act. Manslaughter.

5. Intentionality.   None of the scenarios above captures the purposeful nature of the attack Larry described. I saw Brian as the sole cause of the attack and was convinced he meant to destroy. The police would label it "premeditated homicide." We'd call it murder.

Common Biases in Judging Intention

Because I'm illustrating attribution theory in a courtroom setting, I've cast judgment of intention in legal terms. But Heider emphasized that the issue transcends accountability before the law. We're really dealing with moral culpability—perceived responsibility in the court of public opinion. When we judge another's motives, we move past Sergeant Joe Friday's dispassionate "Just the facts, ma'am," and enter the realm of values, "shoulds," and "oughts." It's easy for bias to shade our judgment. Three volumes of attribution research edited by Harvey, Ickes, and Kidd verify the human tendencies described in Heider's original work.[2]

1.   We tend to hold others more responsible for negative results than for positive outcomes. If the first-year student who sits next to us in class flunks a test, he's stupid. If he aces it, we're more likely to think he's lucky.

2.   We tend to hold others more responsible for not trying than for incompetence. It's worse to be lazy than to lack ability.

3.   We tend to hold others more responsible when they aim to improve their position rather than avoid loss. For example, we judge more

"I hit Big Angie eight times with the fire ax and then threw him into the East River because of peer pressure."

Artist unknown.

harshly a hungry person who steals food than we do a well-fed person who won't willingly share it.

4. We tend to hold others more responsible for their outcomes when we fear the same thing may happen to us. A veteran skydiver haughtily claimed that anyone who "bounced" got what he or she deserved. The skydiver used defensive attribution as reassurance that death by sudden impact always happens to someone else.

5. We tend to hold others more responsible than we hold ourselves. Apparently, we use a double standard as we decide who should be held accountable for mistakes and errors. When things turn out badly for others, we assume it's their fault; but for our own failures, we tend to blame circumstances or other people. We see others as causal agents, but we give ourselves an excuse.

All our biased judgments involve a decision between personal and environmental control. This tension is a crucial ingredient in the third step of attribution. Having taken notice of Brian's aggressive action and believing that it was an unprovoked and wanton attack with malicious intent, I'm now in a position to make a dispositional attribution.

Step 3: Attribution of Disposition

Heider defined attribution as an effort to "predict and control the world by assigning transient behavior to relatively unchanging dispositions."[3] You can see that process in my train of thought as I heard the testimony about the assault:

> That was a brutal attack. Brian's a brute! I can't imagine bashing someone over the head when they haven't done anything to hurt me. I wonder if he's insane. No, there was nothing crazy about how he acted on the elevator. And there wasn't any pressure from the gang leader to do the job. Brian offered to work the guy over for $500, yet he didn't even need the money. No doubt about it; he's a brute and he'll probably be violent again.

Note how quickly I jumped from behavior to disposition. I assumed that people who *do* things like that *are* like that. Heider said that's typical. As naive psychologists, we constantly assess how much an action is due to personality as opposed to environmental pressure. When judging others, our tendency is to discount external factors and put our thumb on the character side of the scale.

ATTRIBUTIONS DEPEND ON PERCEIVED FREEDOM OF CHOICE

The key issue is choice. If we see others as compelled to act as a result of circumstances beyond their control, we won't assign their behavior to enduring traits of character. I tried to consider the possibility that Brian was driven by madness, coerced by his boss, or forced to the act by financial need. These mitigating circumstances would short-circuit the attributional chain. But I couldn't find any outside explanation which would account for the severity of the action.

Heider stated that we judge an actor's freedom as proportional to the difficulty of performing the act. It's not easy to crack someone's skull. It takes tremendous desire and exertion to lay waste the human head. Being face-to-face with the victim makes it even harder. (Dante condemned the designer of the catapult to an inner circle of Hell. By giving a warrior a means to achieve death without having a visual link to the victim, the inventor made killing easier.[4]) Since Brian performed this difficult task with apparent ease, I considered him as having true choice, his act free of constraint. I therefore attributed to Brian a cluster of personality traits and attitudes consistent with volitional violence. My conclusion: Brian is a hardened criminal.

Don't be surprised that I ended up explaining Brian's behavior by the type of person he is rather than by the circumstances surrounding the attack. None of us is immune from the bias that Stanford psychologist Lee Ross calls the "fundamental attribution error."[5] It is the tendency for observers to underestimate situational influences and overestimate dispositional influences upon behavior. Whether it's a police officer's callous reaction that the rape victim was "asking for it," the football coach's analysis that a player missed a tackle because he didn't try hard enough, or parents' assumption that the crumpled fender on the family car is due to their son's carelessness, we assume that people are responsible for the things that happen to them.

This extended account of judgment may give you the impression that attribution is a prolonged, conscious deliberation which takes place only in formal settings of guilt or innocence. Not so. Causal inferences are usually subconscious snap judgments made whenever we see others in action. Our judgments deal with praise as well as blame. Heider's theory has generated thousands of studies that blanket the map of interpersonal relations. One of the fascinating extensions of the theory is the work of Cornell University psychologist Daryl Bem, who is interested in the way we look at our own actions.

SELF-PERCEPTION: A SPECIAL CASE OF ATTRIBUTION

Bem is concerned with the dispositional labels we assign to ourselves. He claims we don't have favored status when it comes to figuring out our own prevailing moods. Our weak internal signals may give clues to our attitudes or emotions, but behavior is the acid test that confirms or rejects our intuition. So we watch ourselves act and then draw conclusions about our inner disposition just like outside observers do.

Conventional wisdom suggests that behavior follows attitude: "I play tennis because I like it." Bem's radical behaviorism says it works the other way around: "I like tennis because I play it." Later in the book we'll see that cognitive dissonance theory also predicts that actions precede attitude, but Bem explains the sequence on the basis of self-perception. We see ourselves put a dollar in a beggar's cup and decide that we are compassionate.

Emotions work the same way. You might think it's safe to assume that a fellow knows when he is sexually aroused. Not necessarily, according to Bem. He cites a study by Stuart Valins, a research psychologist at the State University of New York (SUNY) at Stony Brook. College men were wired with fake electrodes that supposedly picked up their heartbeat and amplified it through a speaker for them to hear. The experimenter occasionally varied the bogus biofeedback as the males looked at pictures of nude women. The men reported being most "turned on" by the photos that were associated with a change in heartbeat.

Some cynic has suggested that love is a feeling you feel you're feeling when you feel you're feeling a feeling. The statement is consistent with Bem's description of self-attribution. We aren't sure what we feel, so we look to behavioral clues to fill in the gaps. "It must be love cuz my heart skipped a beat."

CRITIQUE: RENDERING A VERDICT

Heider suggested that people systematically evaluate causes of behavior in a commonsense search to understand why things happen. If Heider was right, however, some of the jurors Jean was with failed to get the message. After ten days of bickering, nine were convinced of the defendants' guilt; three saw them as innocent. One jury member chose to ignore all the evidence, relying instead on a gut feeling that the men were innocent. In reaction to this member's stubborn refusal to discuss wiretap recordings, another juror lay on the floor for days and wouldn't discuss anything.

The jury's bizarre behavior illustrates a serious weakness in Heider's case. Like Mead's symbolic interactionism (see Chapter 9), attribution theory stresses human rationality and ignores the role of emotion. Heider described the process as one of making "causal inferences," but are we the detached observers of the human scene that the phrase suggests? It may be more accurate to describe the attribution process as "jumping to conclusions." And Heider's naive psychologists might be more correctly labeled "self-serving perverters of the truth."

Just as Jean and the other jurors had to decide whether to believe the testimony of Larry the Canary, so you and I must render a verdict on the validity and usefulness of attribution theory. A vote to reject means we still need to find a way to explain our quick judgments of personality based on behavior. But if we find Heider's attribution principles to be true beyond a reasonable doubt, sheer human decency requires us to resist some of the built-in biases that tilt our perceptions.

The chief culprit is our consistent tendency to assume that other people are the sole cause of their actions, that they are free to move in any direction they want. In the absence of overwhelming evidence to the contrary, we'd be much closer to the truth if we viewed others as enclosed in a maze of environmental constraints. Most people on welfare aren't poor because they're too lazy to work. Pilot error is only part of the story in airplane accidents. There are times when others really can't help being late. In short, other people's lives are just as complicated as ours.

In spite of its questionable ability to deal with the passionate side of relationships, attribution theory provides a helpful analysis of the way we parcel out praise or blame. It has stimulated thousands of research studies that investigate the way people interpret the behavior they see. The last two articles suggested in A Second Look attempt to explain the apparent irrational behavior of jurors. Heider's ideas may not be perfect, but as the theory itself suggests, few objects of our judgment are as good or as bad as we want to give them credit for being.

QUESTIONS TO SHARPEN YOUR FOCUS

1. What happens when we *observe* an action but decide that the other person had no *intention* to do it?

2. Tracy's coffee ends up all over Lacy's new shirt. Before you jump to the conclusion that Lacy is a slob, can you construct a scenario for the five categories of causation—*association, causality, justifiability, foreseeability, intentionality?*

3. What steps could you take to make certain that you don't commit the *fundamental attribution error?*

4. According to attribution theory, what is it that we *attribute* to other people?

A SECOND LOOK

Recommended resource: Kelly G. Shaver, *An Introduction to Attribution Processes,* Lawrence Erlbaum Associates, Hillsdale, N.J., 1983.

Original conception: Fritz Heider, "Social Perception and Phenomenal Causality," *Psychological Review,* Vol. 51, 1944, pp. 358–374.

Fuller development: Fritz Heider, *The Psychology of Interpersonal Relations,* John Wiley & Sons, New York, 1958.

Fundamental attribution error: L. D. Ross, "The Intuitive Psychologist and His Shortcomings: Distortions in the Attribution Process," in *Advances in Experimental Social Psychology,* Vol. 10, Leonard Berkowitz (ed.), Academic Press, New York, 1977, pp. 173–220.

Relational attributions: John H. Harvey, Terri L. Orbuch, and Ann L. Weber (eds.), *Attributions, Accounts, and Close Relationships,* Springer-Verlag, New York, 1992.

Alternative approach to person perception: Mary K. Babcock, "The Dramaturgic Perspective: Implication for the Study of Person Perception," *European Journal of Social Psychology,* Vol. 19, 1989, pp. 297–309.

Self-perception principle: Daryl Bem, "Self-Perception Theory," in *Advances in Experimental Social Psychology,* Vol. 6, Leonard Berkowitz (ed.), Academic Press, New York, 1972, pp. 2–62.

Heartbeat study: S. Valins, "Cognitive Effects of False Heart-Rate Feedback," *Journal of Personality and Social Psychology,* Vol. 4, 1966, pp. 400–408.

Research updates: J. H. Harvey, W. Ickes, and R. F. Kidd (eds.), *New Directions in Attribution Research,* Vols. 1–3, Lawrence Erlbaum Associates, Hillsdale, N.J., 1976, 1978, 1981.

Further extensions: J. H. Harvey and Gifford Weary (eds.), *Attribution: Basic Issues and Applications,* Academic Press, San Diego, 1985.

Jury psychology: Gerald Miller, "Social Cognition, the Unwanted Juror?" in *Social Cognition and Communication,* Michael Roloff and Charles Berger (eds.), Sage, Beverly Hills, Calif., 1982, pp. 227–254.

Jury simulation research: Wayne Weiten and Shari S. Diamond, "A Critical Review of the Jury Simulation Paradigm: The Case of Defendant Characteristics," *Law and Human Behavior,* Vol. 3, 1979, pp. 71–93.

CHAPTER 12

Constructivism
of Jesse Delia

Some theories rely on a measuring device. The theory of gravity depends on a scale to gauge the crucial factor of force. Constructivism is like that. The critical instrument is psychologist Walter Crockett's Role Category Questionnaire (RCQ) printed below.[1] Take ten minutes to respond to the items. Consider the time spent part of the cost of learning the theory and an investment to gain new insight about yourself.

ROLE CATEGORY QUESTIONNAIRE

Think of people about your same age whom you know well. Select one person that you like, and also pick someone you dislike. Once you have two specific people in mind, spend a moment to mentally compare and contrast them in terms of personality, habits, beliefs, and the way they treat others. Don't limit yourself to similarities and differences between the two; let your mind play over the full range of characteristics that make them who they are.

Now take a piece of paper and for about five minutes describe the person you enjoy so that a stranger would understand what he or she is like. Skip physical characteristics, but list all of the attributes, mannerisms, and reactions to others that identify who he or she is. Please do that now.

When you've finished the description, do the same thing for the person you don't like. Again, write down any and all personal characteristics of actions that you associate with that person. Please spend about five minutes for this description.

COGNITIVE COMPLEXITY OF INTERPERSONAL IMPRESSIONS

The Role Category Questionnaire is designed to sample the interpersonal constructs that we carry around in our head in order to make sense out of the world. Constructs are the templates or stencils we fit over reality to bring order out of chaos. Like sets of opposing terms (hot-cold, good-bad, fast-slow), constructs are contrasting features we use to classify perceptions. The police artist has an identification kit with which an eyewitness can construct the face of a suspect. By systematically altering the shape of the chin, size of the nose, distance between the eyes, line of the hair, and so forth, the crime observer can build a likeness of the person in question. But the RCQ doesn't bother with physical features. It centers on the categories of personality and action that we use to define the character of another person.

The arena of politics offers a familiar example of the way we use constructs to describe another individual. All of us have our own bipolar dimensions of judgment that we apply to politicians. Some typical scales are liberal-conservative, honest-crooked, competent-inept. The politically astute observer may draw on dozens of these interpretive orientations to describe shades of difference. There are conservatives, and there are *Southern* conservatives. Then there are Southern *fiscal* conservatives. Some of them are *military interventionists,* and so forth. On the other hand, those who are politically apathetic may use only one value-laden construct as they watch the six o'clock news—hero or bum.

Researchers who use the RCQ are trying to determine the respondent's degree of cognitive complexity. They are called "constructivists" because they are more concerned with the structure of the writer's constructs than with the actual judgments being made. A person could have a dazzling network of constructs in one area of life but operate on the Neanderthal level in other fields. Constructivists aren't interested in the subtle nuances of sound we hear on a compact disc system, distinctions we see in the new tax law, or the variety of techniques we have to hit a topspin lob. Their domain is the complexity of our interpersonal impressions.

Someone has said that there are two kinds of people in the world—those who think there are two kinds of people in the world, and those who don't. The constructivist believes that the first kind of person is cognitively immature, because he or she is able to see others only in terms of black or white. But the second kind of person has grown into a sophisticated observer of the human scene, capable of picturing people using a vast range of colors, shades, and hues. When it comes to thinking about people, the Role Category Questionnaire was designed to separate the adults from the kids.

THE THREE FACES OF COGNITIVE COMPLEXITY: DIFFERENTIATION, ABSTRACTION, AND ORGANIZATION

Because of limitations of space, you read a compressed version of the official RCQ instructions. You will also get a shorthand account of the scoring procedure. If you're going to put much weight on the results, consult the article on the RCQ by Brant Burleson and Michael Waltman (see A Second Look). Burleson is one of the main researchers in a constructivist network headed by Jesse Delia, chairman of the speech communication department at the University of Illinois.

Figure 12.1 displays a sample response to the RCQ in tabular form. The descriptions can be scored for three different facets of cognitive complexity: differentiation, abstraction, and organization.

Differentiation is defined as the number of separate personality constructs used to describe the target person. The terms *friendly, nice,* and *everybody likes him* may seem similar, but the fact that the respondent used different words is evidence of three distinct constructs.

Abstraction is the degree to which the respondent sees visible behavior in terms of internal traits, motives, and dispositions. To say that Roger has a *funny way of talking* may be true, but the judgment shows little sign of an intricate psychological process at work. Claiming that he's *insensitive* requires a mental leap that goes beyond surface observation.

Organization has to do with the recognition and reconciliation of conflicting impressions. The respondent's *but* in Item 26 shows an awareness of a seeming inconsistency between Roger's insecurity and arrogance. The attempt to harmonize the apparent contradiction indicates a high capacity for complex thought.

Gordon (liked peer)	Roger (disliked peer)
1. Very funny	20. Hurried
2. Concerned for the poor	21. Never has time
3. Watches his budget	22. Successful writer
4. Athletic	23. Insensitive
5. Sharp	24. Confuses other people
6. Competent	25. Everybody knows him
7. Friendly	26. Insecure but acts...
8. Totally sincere	27. ... arrogant to cover it up
9. Nice	xx Has pimples
10. Enthusiastic	28. Funny way of talking
xx Short haircut	29. Smart
11. Likes to swear	30. Irritating laugh
12. Loyal	xx Tennis elbow
xx Friendly	
13. Called in time of trouble	
14. Good handball player	
15. Everybody likes him	
16. Good buddy	
17. Religious	
18. Solid student	
19. Good ole boy	
xx Irish	

FIGURE 12.1
Sample Role Category Questionnaire

SCORING THE ROLE CATEGORY QUESTIONNAIRE FOR COMPLEXITY

Scoring for differentiation is easy, but analyzing the test for abstraction and organization is both tricky and cumbersome. Because the three measures correlate moderately well, most researchers are content to count the number of constructs and assume they've tapped the entire dimension of cognitive complexity. We'll score it the same way.

Add up the number of different descriptions you used to describe both people. As a rule of thumb, consider that each new term represents an additional construct. Seeing Gordon as both *sharp* and *competent* earns two points. That's also true with Roger's *hurried* and *never has time*. But there are exceptions to the one-term-equals-one-construct rule.

Adjectives and adverbs that merely modify the extent of a characteristic don't score extra points. Thus *very funny* and *totally sincere* each receive just one point. Since idioms such as *good ole boy* have a single referent, they get a single point as well. Physical descriptions and demographic labels say nothing about character, so we skip over them. That eliminates *short haircut, Irish, has pimples,* and *tennis elbow*. It's possible that the writer may associate these with personality traits, but without any hint in that direction we can't count them. And, of course, the repetition of *friendly* doesn't increase the total. Apart from these rules, close calls should get the benefit of the doubt and score an extra point.

The person who took this test used thirty constructs—more than most. Curiously, Delia and his colleagues seldom publish means and standard deviations on the RCQ. They state that they're more interested in the relative position of the score as opposed to the absolute number. That doesn't give the uninitiated much of a clue to what a score might mean, but the few reports of scores from adult populations show averages between twenty and twenty-five.

Is the test a good measure of cognitive complexity? Delia makes a good case for its validity. He points out that any individual differences in adult thought process should emerge as relatively stable over time. This standard has been met through good test-retest reliability. His claim that cognitive complexity develops with a child's chronological age should be reflected in progressively higher scores as youngsters grow older. This also happens.

Finally, he notes that a pure test of personality should not be confounded by other character traits or extraneous factors. Research has established that scores on the RCQ are independent of IQ, empathy, writing skill, and extroversion. Some critics have charged that it's merely a measure of loquacity or wordiness, but constructivists maintain that high scores on this free-response test take more than the gift of gab.

Now that you have an idea of what's involved in cognitive complexity, we'll consider the main hypothesis of constructivism. To help us grasp the theory's predictions, we'll look at its practical implications, even though the team assembled by Delia ignores applied research because it detracts from theoretical issues.

PERSON-CENTERED MESSAGES

Constructivists claim that people who are cognitively complex in their perceptions of others have a communication advantage over those with less developed mental structures. Intricate thought patterns give them the capacity to create "person-centered messages." As Delia uses the phrase, it refers to "messages which reflect an awareness of and adaptations to subjective, affective and relational aspects of the communication contexts."[2]

If you've taken a public speaking course, your instructor undoubtedly stressed the importance of audience analysis. Once you know the backgrounds and attitudes of your listeners, you can make adjustments in your speech that will increase the chances of reaching your goal. There are many terms to describe this ability. Communication practitioners call it "listener adaptation" or "rhetorical sensitivity." Business executives refer to being "market-driven," and educators speak of being "process-oriented." Whatever we call it, the creation of person-centered messages is a sophisticated communication skill. Constructivists say that cognitively complex people can do it especially well.

Note that they don't claim the person always *does* it, only that he or she has a capacity that others don't. Possessing a deluxe set of interpersonal constructs affords the opportunity to focus on the unique features of the target person. It's like a golfer carrying a bag that contains a full set of irons and woods. Just as the golfer may select the wrong club, the cognitively complex communicator doesn't automatically encode better messages. Fatigue, pressure to conform, or dozens of other situational factors can mute the advantage. Constructivists state repeatedly that cognitive complexity is a "necessary but not sufficient cause of person-centered messages." In statistical terms, this means that there is a "significant but moderate correlation" between a score on the RCQ and the creation of person-centered messages.

ALTERING MESSAGE CONTENT TO MATCH COMMUNICATION PURPOSE

Let's apply this insight to the almost impossible task of being a resident adviser in a college dormitory. Consider the job description of Kristin, a typical R.A. For a modest cut in the cost of room and board, she's expected to be all things to all women. But Kristin didn't apply to be an R.A. for reasons of money. As a caring, people-oriented individual, she wants to treat each student on her corridor as a unique individual and provide a personalized bridge between the student and the school. To accomplish this goal, she needs to master the following diverse types of communication.

Comforting. Suppose a freshman is homesick or has broken up with her boyfriend. Kristin needs to help her manage the distress without minimizing, ignoring, or challenging the hurt the girl is feeling. If Kristin is good at her job, she'll display the counselor's skill of legitimatizing the emotion while placing it in perspective.

Regulating. Sometimes Kristin feels like a campus cop. The school rules clearly prohibit men from staying in the rooms overnight. As an R.A., Kristin has a duty to enforce the rules, but she wants to do it by pointing out the interpersonal consequences for everyone involved rather than creating a scene by threatening punishment or calling in the dean of students.

Persuading. The women on her floor voted unanimously to have a picnic. It's not supposed to be a couples affair, but some of them are now hanging back because they wouldn't be coming with a date. Sophisticated influence requires that any attempt to persuade those without dates to come must be strategically cast in terms of *their* needs and desires rather than Kristin's.

Relationship Building. Kristin enjoys building others' self-esteem. If she's particularly sharp, she will affirm their desirable qualities without conveying a binding expectation that they should always remain as they are. It takes skill to give others positive feedback in a way that preserves their autonomy. It's even a greater challenge to be an evenhanded third-party advocate when conflict rages between roommates.

Explaining. A new phone system has been installed, and it's Kristin's job to explain how it works. She isn't trying to convince anybody of anything. Her aim is to create understanding by presenting the information in a way that builds on what the students already know instead of stubbornly insisting "that's just the way it is."

According to constructivism, a cognitively complex Kristin will tend to craft person-centered messages that are appropriate to her specific communication purpose. A less capable R.A. won't.

RESEARCH LINKING COMPLEXITY WITH FLEXIBILITY

Delia and his colleagues have gathered abundant support to back up their claim that a person who has the capacity to make complex interpersonal judgments also has an ability to construct person-centered messages. Ruth Ann Clark and Delia's study of second- to ninth-grade schoolchildren is a prototype of constructivist research.

Clark and Delia focused on the children's ability to adapt persuasive appeals to different target listeners. After taking the RCQ orally, the kids role-played three different persuasive tasks. One was to convince a woman they didn't know to keep a lost puppy.

Naturally, the quality of messages differed. Some children showed no realization that the woman's perspective on the matter might be different from their own. Other kids recognized the difference but failed to adapt their message to this reality. A more sophisticated group took notice of the difference and made an attempt to refute the counterarguments they knew their

appeal would raise. The best messages also stressed the advantages that would come to her if she would comply with the request.

Constructivists claim that strategic adaptation is a developmentally nurtured skill. Consistent with their theory, Clark and Delia found that the quality of messages improved as the age of the children increased. But differences in construct differentiation not due to chronological age also had a significant impact. Cognitively complex students were two years ahead of their same-aged classmates in ability to encode person-centered messages. This result is typical of constructivist findings. The connection between construct differentiation and sophisticated message strategies is well established. But the question of *why* they should be linked remains unanswered.

PURSUING THE CAUSAL MECHANISM

Clark and Delia originally assumed that high cognitive complexity enabled the communicator to do a better job of social perspective taking. You'll recall that Mead and other symbolic interactionists (see Chapter 9) claim that taking the role of the other is a mental gymnastic we perform prior to viewing our looking-glass self. But constructivists have talked about taking the role of the other as an intervening variable in the process of creating messages that achieve our goal. Figure 12.2 shows how perspective taking could be a middle step between complexity and audience adaptation.

The Clark and Delia data can easily be interpreted in light of the children's mental potential to trade places with the woman they were talking to about keeping the lost puppy. Youngsters started with the original core message they wanted the lady to accept. ("Keep the puppy.") Older kids who possessed cognitive complexity beyond their years showed an ability to imagine what the woman was thinking. ("My husband will think I'm a sucker for every stray in town.") Armed with this knowledge, they adapted to the perspective of their target. ("Having a dog for a companion will take away

FIGURE 12.2
Possible Mediating Effect of Social Perspective Taking

some of the loneliness you feel at night when your husband is out of town. He'll feel better that you've got a furry friend.")

While all this sounds plausible, Delia and his colleagues have grown increasingly uncomfortable with perspective taking as the *sole* explanation of cognitive complexity's impact. Mental role-playing is such a slippery concept that it's hard to know what's going on when a person does it. Even when perspective taking is tightly defined, it still shows only a 25 percent overlap with cognitive complexity.

Delia's new thrust is to explain the effect of cognitive complexity in terms of pursuing *multiple* goals. Most communication situations have a certain ambiguity. Consider Kristin's intentions as she walks in on Barb and Ken at 3:30 A.M. If she has multiple and interconnected ways of interpreting her experience with others, she'll realize that whatever she says has to work on four or five different levels. As an R.A. she's required to regulate Barb's behavior, but she wants to do it without causing Barb loss of face. She wants to forestall conflict between Barb and her absent roommate and at the same time persuade Ken to leave without a fuss. Finally, she hopes that all of this can serve to draw her closer to Barb instead of driving a wedge between them. A rather ambitious agenda.

Perhaps mentally complex people like Kristin understand the complicated nature of reality, whereas someone who defines the situation more simplistically might barge in on Ken and Barb and yell, "Both of you get the hell out of here." Constructivists are now testing to see if people who score high on the RCQ define interpersonal situations in a way different from that of those who possess fewer interpersonal constructs.

CRITIQUE: CATEGORIES OF WEAKNESS—TEST VALIDITY, PRACTICAL APPLICATION, AND READABILITY

Most critics fault constructivists for their total reliance on the RCQ as the measure of cognitive complexity. Whatever the test measures, it doesn't seem to match up with what others mean by the term *cognitive complexity*. Doubt about the questionnaire's validity puts the constructivist in the precarious position of saying in effect, "Everyone's wrong except me."

But what if the constructivist is right? What difference does it make if cognitive complexity as measured by the RCQ makes us better communicators? That finding seems of little importance until the theory addresses the question of how people can improve that part of the mind.

In the first documented dialogues centering on communication theory, Plato raised the question of whether rhetoric was a knack or an art.[3] The question still seems appropriate. If cognitive complexity is a knack or fixed trait that can't be developed, the knowledge of its effect has limited value. We may even do a disservice to people by labeling them "simplistic thinkers." But if mental complexity is an art that can be mastered through conscious method, constructivist researchers need to spell out how black-and-white thinkers can start seeing shades of gray. So far this type of applied research has been low on the constructivist agenda.

An additional problem is one of form rather than substance. Constructivist literature is hard to read. Perhaps the long sentences, polysyllabic words, and heavy style make sense in a convoluted way. If you were fashioning a theory that values abstract constructions, you'd probably be hesitant to write in simple subject-verb-object sentences.

But constructivist prose doesn't mask the common search of those who share the same system of ideas. Delia has made a strong call for a "reflective analysis of the implicit assumptions and ordering principles underlying research questions and methods."[4] He's launched a research program that models that commitment, and others have enlisted in the cause. As one of the few well-known theories about communication to spring from within the discipline, constructivism is especially worthy of your consideration.

QUESTIONS TO SHARPEN YOUR FOCUS

1. How many points for *differentiation* would the phrase "humorous and totally funny" score on the *Role Category Questionnaire?*

2. Look at the "Calvin and Hobbes" cartoon on page 152. How would constructivists explain Calvin's success in getting a horsey ride from his father?

3. At times, people with *high cognitive complexity* are less successful at reaching their *communication goal* than are people with low cognitive complexity. Is this failure a challenge to the validity of constructivism?

4. Sometimes during an argument a kid will chide another with the words "Aw, grow up!" According to constructivists, the phrase offers good advice in a way that's poor. Why?

A SECOND LOOK

Recommended resource: Brant R. Burleson, "Cognitive Complexity," in *Personality and Interpersonal Communications*, J. C. McCroskey and J. A. Daly (eds.), Sage, Beverly Hills, Calif., 1987, pp. 305–349.

Comprehensive statement: Jesse Delia, Barbara J. O'Keefe, and Daniel J. O'Keefe, "The Constructivist Approach to Communication," in *Human Communication Theory*, Frank E. X. Dance (ed.), Harper & Row, New York, 1982, pp. 147–191.

Role category questionnaire: Brant R. Burleson and Michael S. Waltman, "Cognitive Complexity: Using the Role Category Questionnaire Measure," in *A Handbook for the Study of Human Communication,* Charles Tardy (ed.), Ablex, Norwood, N.J., 1988, pp. 1–35.

Research review: Daniel J. O'Keefe and H. E. Sypher, "Cognitive Complexity Measures and the Relationship of Cognitive Complexity to Communication: A Critical Review," *Human Communication Research,* Vol. 8, 1981, pp. 72–92.

Role-taking study: Ruth Ann Clark and Jesse Delia, "Cognitive Complexity, Social Perspective-Taking, and Functional Persuasive Skills in Second- to Ninth-Grade Students," *Human Communication Research,* Vol. 3, 1977, pp. 128–134.

Person-centered research: Brant R. Burleson, "The Constructivist Approach to Person-Centered Communication: Analysis of a Research Exemplar," in *Rethinking Communication,* Vol. 2, Brenda Dervin, Lawrence Grossberg, Barbara J. O'Keefe, and Ellen Wartella (eds.), Sage, Newbury Park, Calif., 1989, pp. 29–46.

Multipurpose messages: Barbara J. O'Keefe and Jesse Delia, "Impression Formation and Message Production," in *Social Cognition and Communication,* M. E. Roloff and C. R. Berger (eds.), Sage, Beverly Hills, Calif., 1982, pp. 33–72.

Interface between constructivism and attribution theory: Steven R. Wilson, Michael G. Cruz, and Kil Ho Kang, "Is It Always a Matter of Perspective? Construct Differentiation and Variability in Attributions About Compliance Gaining," *Communication Monographs,* Vol. 59, 1992, pp. 350–367.

PART FOUR

Interpersonal Communication

RELATIONSHIP DEVELOPMENT

Consider your relationship with the person you are closer to than anyone else in the world. Is it one of "strong, frequent and diverse interdependence that lasts over a considerable period of time?"[1] That's how UCLA psychologist Harold Kelley and eight co-authors define *close relationship*. Note that their definition could apply in situations where the parties don't even like each other. Most other theorists reserve the term *closeness* for relationships that also include a positive bond.

The intimacy found in families, friendships, and romantic pairs has much in common. Whatever the context, a close relationship offers enjoyment, trust, sharing of confidences, respect, mutual assistance, and spontaneity. Romance offers passion and exclusiveness as well.

Some people seem to have a "recurrent preference or readiness for experience of close, warm, and communicative exchange with others."[2] This is how Loyola (Chicago) motivational researcher Don McAdams defines the need for intimacy. Unlike those who pursue friendship or love as a means to an end (business contacts, a game of tennis, sexual fulfillment), people high in need for intimacy regard relationships as terminal—ends in themselves.

Consistent with the popular image of the "inexpressive male," gender research shows that the majority of "people who need people" are women. But the difference in masculine and feminine approaches to relationships appears to have more to do with culture than chromosomes (see Chapter 34). Men tend to define closeness in terms of proximity, shared experience, cooperation, and touch with a sexual partner. Women associate intimacy with trust, shared conversation, and emotional support. It's the difference between "doing" and "being."

University of Chicago economist Gary Becker won the 1992 Nobel Prize in economics on the basis of his introduction of supply and demand market models to predict the behavior of everyday living—including love and marriage. News commentators expressed skepticism that matters of the heart could be reduced to cold numbers, but the economic metaphor has dominated social science discussion of interpersonal attraction for the last three decades. The basic assumption of most relational theorists is that people interact with others in a way so as to maximize their personal benefits and minimize their personal costs.

Numerous parallels exist between the stock market and the personality market:

Law of supply and demand. A rare, desirable characteristic commands higher value on the exchange.

Courting of a buyer. Most parties in the market prepare a prospectus that highlights their assets and downplays their liabilities.

Laissez faire rules. "Let the buyer beware." "All's fair in love and war." "It's a jungle out there."

Expert advice. Daily newspapers around the country carry syndicated advice columns by Sylvia Porter and Ann Landers. Whether the topic is money or love, both columnists advise cautious risk taking.

Investors and traders. Investors commit for the long haul; traders try to make an overnight killing.

BERRY'S WORLD reprinted by permission of NEA, Inc.

Although the economic model of personal relationships may strike you as cynical and degrading, consider how humanist author Erich Fromm sums up contemporary love in his renowned book *The Art of Loving*: "Two persons thus fall in love when they feel they have found the best object available on the market, considering the limitations of their own exchange value."[3]

We will look at a specific theory of social exchange under the topic of relationship maintenance (see Chapter 16), but a profit-loss analysis of early encounters shows that interpersonal attraction is a good indicator of future relational development. We seem to be attracted to people we view as potentially rewarding. Physical attractiveness is a reliable draw, especially during early encounters. Unless another's striking appearance makes us feel ugly, we automatically assume that good-looking equals "good." The same principle holds true with competence. We like the reflected glory that comes from being with a winner.

Decades of scientific research support Dale Carnegie's conclusion in *How to Win Friends and Influence People*: "Give honest, sincere appreciation. Be . . . lavish in your praise."[4] Circumstances also play a role. We often grow fond of people we see repeatedly, especially in cooperative situations or at times of stress. Yet all these factors have proved to be less important than similarity of attitudes and values. We like those who are like us.

Although attraction provides the motivation for a close relationship with another person, wanting and getting are separate issues.

Irwin Altman and Dalmas Taylor distinguish between desire and deed in their theory of social penetration processes, presented in Chapter 13. They discuss attraction within a traditional reward-cost framework, yet they suggest that intimacy can be realized only when both parties show vulnerability through self-disclosure.

Not all theorists believe that an economic model appropriately describes relational development. Charles Berger would agree with Altman and Taylor that self-disclosure, reciprocity, liking, and similarity are key issues in the growth of friendship or romance. But Berger claims that reduction of uncertainty—not potential outcome value—is the overriding concern that links these issues during the early stages of a relationship. Chapter 14 presents Berger's uncertainty reduction theory—scholarship that is particularly noteworthy because it is the first scientifically oriented theory to be proposed by a speech communication scholar.

The two theories in this section regard communication as the means by which people can develop close relationships. Yet neither theory suggests that all relationships proceed on a straight-line trajectory toward that goal. In fact, most relationships never get close. Even when both parties are drawn together by a strong mutual attraction, they face many forces at work inside and outside the relationship which make intimacy elusive.

Yet surprisingly, people do become friends or lovers for life. The durability of the bond seems due to their willingness to invest resources in the relationship. Longevity has less to do with what each party gets out of a relationship than with what each one puts into it.

CHAPTER 13

Social Penetration Theory
of Irwin Altman & Dalmas Taylor

A friend in need is a friend indeed.
Neither a borrower or a lender be.

A rolling stone gathers no moss.
Still waters run deep.

To know him is to love him.
Familiarity breeds contempt.

Proverbs are the wisdom of the ages boiled down into short, easy-to-remember phrases. There are probably more maxims in use about interpersonal relationships than about any other topic. But are these truisms dependable? As we can see in the pairings above, the advice they give often seems contradictory.

Consider the plight of Pete, a new freshman student at a residential college, as he enters the dorm to meet his roommate for the first time. Pete has just waved good-bye to his folks and already feels a sharp pang of loneliness as he thinks of his girl back home. He worries about how she'll feel about him when he goes home at Thanksgiving. Will she illustrate the reliability of the old adage that "absence makes the heart grow fonder," or will "out of sight, out of mind" be a better way to describe the next few months?

Pete finds his room and immediately spots the familiar shape of a lacrosse stick. He's initially encouraged by what appears to be a common interest, but he's also fascinated by a campaign button that urges him to vote for a candidate for Congress who is on the opposite end of the political spectrum from Pete. Will "birds of a feather flock together" hold true in their relationship, or will "opposites attract" better describe their interaction?

Just then Jon, his roommate, comes in. For a few minutes they trade the stock phrases that give them a chance to size up each other. Something in Pete makes him want to tell Jon how much he misses his girlfriend, but a deeper sense of what is an appropriate topic of conversation on first meeting someone prevents him from sharing his feelings quite this soon. On a sub-conscious level, perhaps even a conscious one, Pete is torn between acting on the old adage "misery loves company," or on the more macho one, "big boys don't cry."

Pete obviously needs something more than commonsense sayings to help him understand relational dynamics. A few years before Pete was born, Irwin Altman and Dalmas Taylor proposed a theory called "social penetration process" that explains how relational closeness develops. Altman is a social psychologist at the University of Utah, and Taylor is now dean of liberal arts at Wayne State University in Detroit. They would predict that Pete and Jon will end up as best friends only if they proceed in a "gradual and orderly fashion from superficial to intimate levels of exchange as a function of both immediate and forecast outcomes."[1] In order to capture the process, we first have to understand the complexity of people.

PERSONALITY STRUCTURE: A MULTILAYERED ONION

Altman and Taylor compare people to onions. This isn't their attempt at commentary on the human capacity to offend. It is their description of the multilayered nature of personality. Peel the outer skin from an onion, and you'll find another beneath it. Remove that layer and you'll expose a third, and so on. Pete's outer layer is his public self that's accessible to anyone who cares to look. The outer layer includes a myriad of details that certainly help describe who he is but are held in common with others at the school. On the surface, people see a tall, 18-year-old male, a business major from Michigan who lifts weights and gets lots of phone calls from home.

If Jon can look beneath the surface, he'll discover the semiprivate attitudes that Pete reveals only to some people. Pete is sympathetic to liberal causes, deeply religious, and is prejudiced against fat people.

Pete's inner core is made up of his values, self-concept, unresolved conflicts, and deeply felt emotions. This is his unique private domain which is invisible to the world but has a significant impact on the areas of his life that are closer to the surface. Perhaps not even his girlfriend or parents know his most closely guarded secrets about himself.

CLOSENESS THROUGH SELF-DISCLOSURE

Pete becomes accessible to others as he relaxes the tightened boundaries and makes himself vulnerable. This can be a scary process, but Altman and Taylor believe it's only by allowing Jon to penetrate well below the surface that Pete can draw truly close to his roommate.

There are many ways to show vulnerability. Pete could give up the territoriality that marks his desk and dresser drawers as his private preserve, share his clothes, or read a letter from his girl out loud. Nonverbal paths to openness include mock roughhousing, eye contact, and smiling. But the main route to deep social penetration is through self-disclosure.

Figure 13.1 helps you imagine a wedge being pushed point first into an onion. The depth of penetration represents the degree of personal disclosure. To get to the center, the wedge must first slice through the outer layers. Altman and Taylor claim that on the surface level this kind of biographical information exchange takes place easily, perhaps at first meeting. But they picture the layers of onion skin as tougher and more tightly wrapped as the wedge nears the center.

Recall that Pete was hesitant to share his longing for his girlfriend with Jon. If he admits these feelings, he's opening himself up for some heavy-handed kidding or emotional blackmail. In addition, once the wedge has penetrated deeply, it will have cut a passage through which it can return again and again with little resistance. Future privacy will be difficult. Realizing both of these factors, Pete may be extra cautious about exposing his true feelings. Perhaps he'll fence off this part of his life for the whole school term. According to social penetration theory, a permanent guard will limit the closeness these two young men can achieve.

THE DEPTH AND BREADTH OF SELF-DISCLOSURE

The depth of penetration is the degree of intimacy. Figure 13.1 diagrams the closeness Jon has gained if he and Pete become good friends during the year. In their framework of social penetration theory, Altman and Taylor have outlined the following observations about the process that will have brought Pete and Jon to this point:

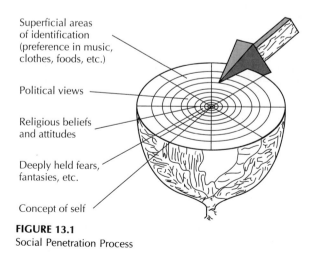

Superficial areas of identification (preference in music, clothes, foods, etc.)

Political views

Religious beliefs and attitudes

Deeply held fears, fantasies, etc.

Concept of self

FIGURE 13.1
Social Penetration Process

1. Peripheral items are exchanged more frequently and sooner than private information. While the point of the wedge has barely reached the intimate area, the trailing edges have cut a wide swath through the outer rings. The relationship is still at a relatively impersonal level ("big boys don't cry"). While at the communication department of the University of Wisconsin at Milwaukee, researcher Arthur VanLear (who is now at the University of Connecticut) analyzed the content of conversation in developing relationships. His study showed that 14 percent of talk revealed nothing about the speaker, 65 percent dwelled on public items, 19 percent shared semiprivate details, and only 2 percent disclosed intimate confidences. Further penetration will bring Pete to the point where he can share deeper feelings ("misery loves company").

2. Self-disclosure is reciprocal, especially in the early stages of relational development. The theory predicts that new acquaintances like Pete and Jon will reach roughly equal levels of openness, but it doesn't explain why. Pete's vulnerability could make him seem more trustworthy, or perhaps his initial openness makes transparency seem more attractive. It's also possible that the young men feel a need for emotional equity, so that a disclosure by Pete leaves Jon feeling uneasy until he's balanced the account with his own payment—a give-and-take exchange in which each party is sharing deeper levels of feeling with each other. Whatever the reason, social penetration theory asserts a law of reciprocity.

3. Penetration is rapid at the start but slows down quickly as the tightly wrapped inner layers are reached. Instant intimacy is a myth. Not only is there internal resistance to quick forays into the soul, there are societal norms against telling too much too fast. Most relationships stall before a stable intimate exchange is established. For this reason, these relationships fade or die easily following separation or a slight strain. A comfortable sharing of positive and negative reactions is rare. When it is achieved, relationships become more important to both parties, more meaningful, and more enduring.

4. Depenetration is a gradual process of layer-by-layer withdrawal. A warm friendship between Pete and Jon will deteriorate if they begin to close off areas of their lives that had earlier been opened. Relational retreat is a sort of taking back of what has earlier been exchanged in the building of a relationship. Altman and Taylor compare the process to a movie shown in reverse. Surface talk still goes on long after deep disclosure is silenced. Relationships are likely to terminate not in an explosive flash of anger but in a gradual cooling off of enjoyment and care.

While depth is crucial to the process of social penetration, breadth is equally important. Note that the diagram in Figure 13.1 shows an onion with sections, much like an orange. The produce manager at a market might quibble with the segmentation, but it accurately represents how Pete's life is cut into different areas—family, sports, dating, studies, health, and so forth. It's quite possible for Pete to be candid about every intimate detail of his

*"Bob, as a token of my appreciation for this wonderful lunch I would like
to disclose to you my income tax returns for the last four years."*

Drawing by Ziegler; © 1984 The New Yorker Magazine, Inc.

romance, yet remain secretive about his father's alcoholism or his own minor
dyslexia. Because only one area is accessed, the relationship depicted in the
onion drawing is typical of a summer romance—depth without breadth. Of
course, breadth without depth describes the typical "Hi, how are you?"
casual relationship. A model of true intimacy would show wedges inserted
deeply into every area.

REGULATING CLOSENESS ON THE BASIS OF REWARDS AND COSTS

Right after their first encounter, Pete will sort out the pluses and minuses of
being with Jon. According to Altman and Taylor, he'll calculate a bottom-line
reward-cost ratio. This index of relational satisfaction refers to "the balance of
positive and negative experience in a social relationship." For their reward-
cost analysis, Altman and Taylor draw heavily on the ideas of Thibaut and
Kelley, which are presented in Chapter 16.

Early in a relationship, physical appearance, mutual agreement, and
similar backgrounds are seen as benefits ("birds of a feather flock together").
Disagreement and deviance from what's expected are negatives. But as the
relationship changes, so does the nature of interaction that friends find
rewarding. Deeper friendships that thrive on common attitudes and spoken

appreciation can tolerate and even enjoy surface diversity ("opposites attract").

If there's a large surplus of positives over negatives, Pete will think it worthwhile to open his life a bit to Jon. If the negatives outweigh the positives, he'll be more likely to avoid future interaction. Since they've been assigned as roommates, Pete doesn't have the option to withdraw physically from Jon. But a negative assessment may cause him to hold back emotionally for the rest of the year.

Evaluating rewards is a tricky business. Even if we convert intangible benefits into quantifiable figures, their psychological impact may vary. Altman and Taylor have the following three observations about relational rewards and costs:

1. Given two interactions with the same profit-loss ratios, the one with the higher numbers is a greater stimulant to vulnerability. If Pete is aware of a dozen advantages and three disadvantages to rooming with Jon, that 12:3 ratio offers more incentive to closeness than if there were only four benefits and one drawback, a 4:1 ratio.

2. The amount of a reward is not the same thing as the satisfaction it gives. A thousand dollars is a windfall of delight for a struggling student but a pittance to a millionaire. We judge the value of a reward by comparing it to a baseline of past experience. If Pete first senses a coolness from Jon but later feels warmth and approval, it will heighten his desire for closeness more than if he'd received uninterrupted warmth from the start.

3. The result from each interaction is stored in the individual's memory. Experiences that take place early in a relationship can have a huge impact because they constitute such a large proportion of the total relational history. One unpleasant experience out of ten is merely troublesome; one out of two can end a relationship before it really begins.

So we can see, in summary, that the rate of social penetration between Pete and Jon will depend on the surplus of rewards over costs. Each fellow will consider the past, forecast the future, and adjust the rate of approach accordingly. When income merely offsets expense, the relationship will plateau. When costs exceed rewards, it will decline.

CRITIQUE: PULLING BACK FROM SOCIAL PENETRATION

Social penetration is an established and familiar explanation of how closeness develops, yet over 300 subsequent studies suggest that the path to intimacy described on the previous pages is not completely accurate. Just as Altman and Taylor describe friends as continually reappraising their relationship in light of new experiences, it makes sense for us to reevaluate the theory's predictions that fail to be supported by real-life data.

Contrary to the initial prediction that reciprocity of self-disclosure would be highest in the exploratory stage of relationships, VanLear found mutual sharing most frequently in the semiprivate middle range of penetration. The discrepancy may be due to the unexpected speed of self-revelation. The evidence shows friendships form by a quick thrust of the disclosure blade rather than a measured insertion. University of Mississippi psychologist John Berg discovered that college roommates often decide within a few weeks whether or not they will stay together the following year.

The original theory made no mention of the gender difference in vulnerability, but Altman and Taylor's latest summary of research concludes that males are less open than females. If Pete and Jon were Pam and Joan, the breadth, depth, and pace of disclosure would likely be greater.

The initial statement of Altman and Taylor's theory described the breakup of relationships as a reverse penetration process in which both parties methodically seal off inner layers of their lives and slowly drift apart. In order to test this hypothesis, Chicago psychologists Betsy Tolstedt, at Hines Hospital, and Joseph Stokes, at the University of Illinois, analyzed the conversation of long-term romantic partners at the time when their relationships were falling apart. They discovered that feelings of pain and anger caused the process of breaking up to be more chaotic than the theory would predict. Consistent with reports from marriage counselors, their findings indicate that the depth of self-disclosure often increases dramatically in the final stages of deterioration.

Altman has had second thoughts about his basic assumption that openness is the predominant quality of relationship development. He speculates that the desire for privacy may counteract what he first thought was a unidirectional quest for intimacy. He now proposes a "dialectic model," which assumes that "human social relationships are characterized by openness or contact and closedness or separateness between participants."[2] He believes that the tension between openness and closedness results in cycles of disclosure and withdrawal. There is no guarantee that Pete's waves of accessibility will be in sync with the ebb and flow of Jon's openness. Two recent studies by VanLear confirm that there is periodic cycling between openness and closedness in both friendships and romantic relationships. Chapter 17 shows how other communication scholars have continued to develop a dialectical perspective. Long-term closeness is a chancy prediction.

Although Altman and Taylor have found it necessary to modify the original theory, their image of wedges penetrating deeply into a multilayered onion has proved to be a helpful model of intimacy development. If Pete and Jon are typical roommates, they will likely limit the other to partial penetration. But as long as mutual vulnerability produces more pleasure than pain, they will continue to draw closer.

University of North Dakota psychologist Paul Wright believes that Pete and Jon could reach a point of such closeness that their relationship would no longer be driven by a self-centered concern for personal gain. When friendships have what Wright calls "an intrinsic, end-in-themselves quality," people regard good things happening to their friends as rewards in themselves. Jon would get just as excited about Pete's successful employment interview as he would if he got the job himself. This kind of selfless love is rare. When it does occur, it develops only through an extended process of social penetration.

QUESTIONS TO SHARPEN YOUR FOCUS

1.   The onion model in Figure 13.1 is sectioned into eight parts, representing the *breadth* of a person's life. How would you label these eight regions of interest in your life?

2.   *Depth* of self-disclosure involves great potential *cost*. When will people take that risk?

3.   Social penetration theory is usually thought of as a theory of *self-disclosure*. What are some other ways of showing *vulnerability* in a relationship?

4.   The romantic truism "to know her is to love her" seems to contradict the relational adage "familiarity breeds contempt." Given the principles of social penetration theory, can you think of a way both statements might be true?

A SECOND LOOK

Recommended resource: Irwin Altman and Dalmas Taylor, *Social Penetration: The Development of Interpersonal Relationships*, Holt, New York, 1973.

State of the art: Dalmas Taylor and Irwin Altman, "Communication in Interpersonal Relationships: Social Penetration Processes," in *Interpersonal Processes: New Directions in Communication Research*, Michael Roloff and Gerald Miller (eds.), Sage, Newbury Park, Calif., 1987, pp. 257–277.

Dialectic revision: Irwin Altman, Anne Vinsel, and Barbara Brown, "Dialectic Conceptions in Social Psychology: An Application to Social Penetration and Privacy Regulation," in *Advances in Experimental Social Psychology*, Vol. 14, Leonard Berkowitz (ed.), Academic Press, New York, 1981, pp. 107–160.

Reward-cost analysis: Dalmas Taylor and Irwin Altman, "Self-Disclosure as a Function of Reward-Cost Outcomes," *Sociometry*, Vol. 38, 1975, pp. 18–31.

Self-disclosure reciprocity: C. Arthur VanLear, "The Formation of Social Relationships: A Longitudinal Study of Social Penetration," *Human Communication Research*, Vol. 13, 1987, pp. 299–322.

Cycles of self-disclosure: C. Arthur VanLear, "Testing a Cyclical Model of Communicative Openness in Relationship Development: Two Longitudinal Studies," *Communication Monographs*, Vol. 58, 1991, pp. 337–361.

Depenetration: Betsy Tolstedt and Joseph Stokes, "Self-Disclosure, Intimacy, and Depenetration Process," *Journal of Personality and Social Psychology*, Vol. 46, 1984, pp. 84–90.

Study of roommates: John Berg, "Development of Friendship between Roommates," *Journal of Personality and Social Psychology*, Vol. 46, 1984, pp. 346–356.

Intrinsic rewards of friendship: Paul H. Wright, "Self-Referent Motivation and the Intrinsic Quality of Friendship," *Journal of Social and Personal Relationships*, Vol. 1, 1984, pp. 115–130.

CHAPTER 14

Uncertainty Reduction Theory

of Charles Berger

No matter how close two people eventually become, they always start out as strangers. Let's say you've just taken a job as a driver for a delivery service over the Christmas holidays. After talking with the other drivers, you conclude that your income and peace of mind will depend on working out a good relationship with Heather, the radio dispatcher. All you know for sure about Heather is her attachment to Hannah, a 100-pound Labrador retriever who never lets Heather out of her sight. The veteran drivers joke that it's hard to tell the difference between the voices of Heather and Hannah over the radio. With some qualms you make arrangements to meet Heather (and Hannah) over coffee and donuts before your first day of work. You really have no idea what to expect.

Charles Berger believes that it's natural to have doubts about our ability to predict the outcome of initial encounters. Berger, a professor of communication, who is now at the University of California, Davis, notes that "the beginnings of personal relationships are fraught with uncertainties."[1] Unlike social penetration and social exchange theories, which try to forecast the future of a relationship on the basis of projected rewards and costs (Chapters 13 and 16), Berger's uncertainty reduction theory focuses on how human communication is used to gain knowledge and create understanding.

> Central to the present theory is the assumption that when strangers meet, their primary concern is one of uncertainty reduction or increasing predictability about the behavior of both themselves and others in the interaction.[2]

Berger agrees with Heider's notion (Chapter 11) that our main purpose in talking to people is to "make sense" out of our interpersonal world. That's why you're having breakfast with a stranger and her dog. If you brought your own hound to the meeting, chances are the two dogs would circle and sniff each other, trying to get some idea of what their counterpart was like.

Humans are no different; we're just a bit more subtle as we use symbols instead of smells to reach our conclusions.

UNCERTAINTY REDUCTION: TO PREDICT AND EXPLAIN

Berger's focus on predictability is straight from Shannon and Weaver's information theory (Chapter 4). "As the ability of persons to predict which alternative or alternatives are likely to occur next decreases, uncertainty increases."[3] But he also owes a debt to Heider's view of people as intuitive psychologists. We need to predict *and* explain. If Heather's going to bark at you on the radio, you want to understand why.

Berger notes that there are at least two kinds of uncertainty that you face as you set out for your first meeting with Heather. Because you aren't sure how you should act, one kind of uncertainty deals with *behavioral* questions. Should you shake hands? Who pays for the donuts? Do you pet the dog? Often there are accepted procedural protocols to ease the stress that behavioral uncertainty can cause. Good manners go beyond common sense.

A second kind of uncertainty focuses on *cognitive* questions aimed at discovering who the other person is as a unique individual. What does Heather like about her job? What makes her glad? Sad? Mad? Does she have other friends, or does she lavish all her attention on Hannah? When you first meet a person, your mind may conjure up a wild mix of his or her potential traits and characteristics. Reducing cognitive uncertainty means acquiring information that allows you to discard many of these possibilities. That's the kind of uncertainty reduction Berger's theory addresses.

AN AXIOMATIC THEORY: CERTAINTY ABOUT UNCERTAINTY

Berger proposes a series of axioms to explain the connection between his central concept of uncertainty and seven key variables of relationship development: verbal output, nonverbal warmth, information seeking, self-disclosure, reciprocity, similarity, and liking.[4] Axioms are traditionally regarded as self-evident truths which require no additional proof. (All people are created equal. The shortest distance between two points is a straight line. What goes up must come down.) Here are Berger's seven truths about initial uncertainty.

> *Axiom 1:* Given the high level of uncertainty present at the onset of the entry phase, as the amount of verbal communication between strangers increases, the level of uncertainty for each interactant in the relationship will decrease. As uncertainty is further reduced, the amount of verbal communication will increase.

When you first sit down with Heather, the conversation will be halting and somewhat stilted. As words begin to flow, you'll discover things about each other which make you feel more confident in each other's presence. When your comfort level rises, the pace of the conversation will pick up.

Axiom 2: As nonverbal affiliative expressiveness increases, uncertainty levels will decrease in an initial interaction situation. In addition, decreases in uncertainty level will cause increases in nonverbal affiliative expressiveness.

When initial stiffness gives way to head nods and tentative smiles, you'll have a better idea of who Heather is. This assurance leads to further signs of warmth—prolonged eye contact, forward body lean, pleasant tone of voice.

Axiom 3: High levels of uncertainty cause increases in information-seeking behavior. As uncertainty levels decline, information-seeking behavior decreases.

What is it about Heather that prompted the other drivers to warn you not to start off on the wrong foot? You simply have no idea. Like a bug with its antennae twitching, you carefully monitor what she says and how she acts in

"I always know what Harry's going to say, and he always knows what I'm going to say, so, by and large, we just don't bother."

Drawing by Gahan Wilson; © 1986 The New Yorker Magazine, Inc.

order to gather clues about her personality. But you become less vigilant after she explains her pet peeve with drivers who complain about their assignments on the radio. Whether or not you think her irritation is justified, you begin to relax because you have a better idea of what to expect.

> *Axiom 4:* High levels of uncertainty in a relationship cause decreases in the intimacy level of communication content. Low levels of uncertainty produce high levels of intimacy.

Like Altman and Taylor (Chapter 13), Berger equates intimacy of communication with depth of self-disclosure. Demographic data revealing that Heather was raised in Toledo and that you are a communication major are relatively nonintimate. These typify the opening gambits of new acquaintances who are still feeling each other out. Heather's admission that she feels more loyalty from Hannah than from any person is a gutsy admission that raises the intimacy level of the conversation to a new plane. People express attitudes, values, and feelings when they have a good idea what the listener's response will be.

> *Axiom 5:* High levels of uncertainty produce high rates of reciprocity. Low levels of uncertainty produce low levels of reciprocity.

Self-disclosure research confirms the notion that people tend to mete out the personal details of their lives at a rate that closely matches their partner's willingness to share intimate information.[5] Reciprocal vulnerability is especially important in the early stages of a relationship. The issue seems to be one of power. When knowledge of each other is minimal, we're careful not to let the other one-up us by being the exclusive holder of potentially embarrassing information. But when we already know the ups and downs of a person's story, an even flow of information seems less crucial. Berger would not anticipate long monologues at your first get-together with Heather; future meetings might be a different story.

> *Axiom 6:* Similarities between persons reduce uncertainty, while dissimilarities produce increases in uncertainty.

The more points of contact you establish with Heather, the more you'll feel you understand her inside and out. If you are a dog lover, the two of you will click. If, however, you are partial to purring kittens, Heather's devotion to this servile beast will cause you to wonder if you'll ever be able to figure out what makes her tick.

> *Axiom 7:* Increases in uncertainty level produce decreases in liking; decreases in uncertainty produce increases in liking.

This axiom suggests that the more you find out about Heather, the more you'll appreciate who she is. It directly contradicts the cynical opinion that "familiarity breeds contempt," affirming instead that "to know her is to love her."

THEOREMS: THE LOGICAL FORCE OF UNCERTAINTY AXIOMS

Once we grant the validity of the seven axioms, it's tempting to pair two of them together to produce additional insight into relational dynamics. The combined axioms yield an inevitable conclusion when inserted in the well-known pattern of deductive logic:

$$\text{If } A = B$$
$$\text{and } B = C$$
$$\text{then } A = C$$

Berger does this for all possible combinations, thereby generating twenty-one theorems. For example:

> If similarity reduces uncertainty (axiom 6)
> and reduced uncertainty increases liking (axiom 7)
> then similarity and liking are positively related (theorem 21)

In this case, the result isn't exactly earthshaking. The connection between similarity and liking is a long-established finding in research on interpersonal attraction.[6] But viewed as a whole, these twenty-one logical extensions sketch out a rather comprehensive theory of interpersonal development—all based on the importance of reducing uncertainty in human interaction.

Instead of listing all twenty-one theorems, I've plotted the relationships they predict in Figure 14.1. The chart reads like a mileage table you might find in a road atlas. Select one axiom along the top and another down the side. The intersection between the two shows the number of Berger's theorem and the type of correlation it asserts. A plus sign ($+$) shows that the two interpersonal variables rise or fall together. A minus sign ($-$) indicates that as one increases, the other decreases. Will the warmth of Heather's nonverbal communication increase as the intimacy of her self-disclosure deepens? Theorem 7 says it will. Suppose you grow fond of Heather as a friend. Will you seek to find out more about her? Theorem 17 says you won't. (More on this later.)

ADDED THOUGHTS ON THE QUEST TO KNOW

Although Berger first proposed the entire axiom and theorem system of uncertainty reduction theory in a 1975 paper with Northwestern University colleague Richard Calabrese, he continued to add new insights on the process over the next decade. Three additions significantly expanded the theory.

1. Motivation to Search for Information

Axiom 3 clearly states that the inability to predict and explain people's actions when you first meet is the reason you want to find out more about them. Interpersonal ignorance is not bliss. It's frustrating! But Berger later contended that our drive to reduce uncertainty about new acquaintances gets an extra boost from any of three prior conditions:[7]

	Ax 1 Verbal Communication	Ax 2 Nonverbal Warmth	Ax 4 Self-Disclosure	Ax 3 Information Seeking	Ax 5 Reciprocity	Ax 7 Liking	Ax 6 Similarity
Ax 1 Verbal Communication		1 +	2 +	3 −	4 −	5 +	6 +
Ax 2 Nonverbal Warmth	1 +		7 +	8 −	9 −	10 +	11 +
Ax 4 Self-Disclosure	2 +	7 +		12 −	13 −	14 +	15 +
Ax 3 Information Seeking	3 −	8 −	12 −		16 +	17 −	18 −
Ax 5 Reciprocity	4 −	9 −	13 −	16 +		19 −	20 −
Ax 7 Liking	5 +	10 +	14 +	17 −	19 −		21 +
Ax 6 Similarity	6 +	11 +	15 +	18 −	20 −	21 +	

FIGURE 14.1

Theorems of Uncertainty Reduction Theory (Adapted from Berger and Calabrese, "Some Explorations in Initial Interaction and Beyond.")

a. *Anticipation of future interaction*   We know we're going to see them again.

b. *Incentive value*   They have something we want.

c. *Deviance*   They act in a weird way.

Heather hooks you on all three counts. You know you're going to be dealing with her for the next few weeks, she can make you or break you financially according to the routes she assigns, and she has this strange attachment to Hannah. According to Berger, when you add these three factors to your natural curiosity, you'll *really* want to solve the puzzle of who she is.

2.   Strategies for Removing Doubt

Berger has initiated an extensive program of research to accurately catalogue how people "find out things about others in order to reduce their uncertainty about them." He reports three different approaches,[8] and the person groping for answers will probably use all three.

a. *Passive strategy*   We unobtrusively observe others as they live their lives. This fly-on-the-wall tactic works best when the subject of our investigation is spotted reacting to other people in an informal or "backstage" setting. That way he or she will remain unaware of our interest and scrutiny and won't be put on guard. (This strategy sounds like normal "scoping" behavior on any college campus.)

b. *Active strategy*   We ask a third party for information. We realize that the mutual acquaintance will probably give a highly slanted account, but most of us have confidence in our ability to filter out the bias and discern the true underlying character. We can also alter the environment (move chairs, arrange for background music, plan a disruption within the group) to see how the other person reacts. As with the passive approach, we still have no face-to-face communication with the other person.

c. *Interactive strategy*   We can ask other people to talk about themselves. This is the quickest route to reduce uncertainty, but a questioner can only go so far. Continual probing in social settings begins to take on the feel of a cross-examination or "the third degree." Our own self-disclosure offers an alternative way to elicit information from others without seeming to pry. By being transparent we create a safe atmosphere for others to respond in kind—something they may feel obligated to do. Berger reminds us that any interactive response we receive may be selective or deceptive.

3.   A New Axiom

Many communication researchers have moved uncertainty reduction theory beyond the confines of two strangers meeting for the first time. Berger applauds this extension. "The broadening of the theory's scope suggests the potential usefulness of reconceptualizing and extending the original formulation."[9] The first work he cites is a longitudinal study of romantic relationships among unmarried couples who had been together for about a year. Malcolm Parks (Michigan State University) and Mara Adelman (University of Washington) discovered that men and women who communicate more often with their partners' family and friends have less uncertainty about the person they love than those whose relationships exist in relative isolation.[10] Networking couples also tend to stay together. On the basis of these findings, Berger offers an additional axiom to augment the original seven.

> **Axiom 8:** Shared communication networks reduce uncertainty, while lack of shared networks increases uncertainty.

Berger's incorporation of this axiom into his formal design generates seven new theorems about interpersonal development. If theorems 22 through 28 were plotted in Figure 14.1, you could see that "shared communication networks" correlates positively (+) with every variable except information seeking and reciprocity. For example, theorem 28 states that "shared communication networks and liking are positively related."

Intercultural theorists have seized on uncertainty reduction theory for its possible insights into the communication differences that are glaringly evident when east meets west or north meets south. When you think about it, culture is the ultimate shared communication network. When we leave the comfort of the familiar and become strangers in a strange land, our uncertainty level soars. William Gudykunst at California State, Fullerton, has adopted and adapted Berger's theory to communication between Americans and people of Japan or Korea. Gudykunst claims that reducing uncertainty and the anxiety that often accompanies it is the key to bridging the culture gap.[11] But he's also convinced that uncertainty has a different feel in Southeast Asia than it does in the United States and northern Europe. I'll wait to describe Gudykunst's extension of uncertainty reduction theory until I introduce his anxiety/uncertainty management theory in the section on intercultural communication (see Chapter 34). For now it is enough to realize that Berger's ideas have triggered extensive research by other communication scholars.

CRITIQUE: NAGGING DOUBTS ABOUT UNCERTAINTY

In a state-of-the-art update on uncertainty reduction theory, Charles Berger admits that his original statement contained "some propositions of dubious validity."[12] Critics quickly point to theorem 17, which predicts that the more you like people, the less you'll seek information about them. It's hard to imagine a less defensible position.

> Frankly, it is not clear why information-seeking would decrease as liking increased other than being required by deductive inference from the axiomatic structure of uncertainty reduction theory. In fact, it seems more reasonable to suggest that persons will seek information about and from those they like rather than those they dislike.[13]

That's the blunt assessment shared by Kathy Kellermann of the University of California, Santa Barbara, who originally participated in Berger's research program. We might be willing to dismiss this apparent error as only one glitch out of twenty-one theorems, but the tight logical structure which is the genius of the theory doesn't provide that option. Theorem 17 is dictated by axioms 3 and 7. If the theorem is wrong, the axioms are suspect. Kellermann targets the motivational assumption of axiom 3 as the problem.

Axiom 3 assumes that lack of information invariably triggers a search for knowledge. But Kellermann and Rodney Reynolds of the University of Hawaii studied motivation to reduce uncertainty in more than a thousand students at ten universities, and they found that "wanting knowledge rather than lacking knowledge is what promotes information-seeking in initial encounters with others."[14] Their conclusion is illustrated by the story of a teacher who asked a boy, "What's the difference between *ignorance* and *apathy*?" The student replied, "I don't know, and I don't care." (He was right!) Kellermann and Reynolds also failed to find that anticipated future interaction, incentive value, or deviance gave any motivational kick to information seeking as Berger claimed they would. So it seems that Berger's suggestion of a universal drive to reduce uncertainty during initial interaction is questionable at best, yet it still remains part of the theory.

The strongest attack on the theory comes from Michael Sunnafrank at the University of Minnesota in Duluth. He challenges Berger's claim that uncertainty reduction is the key to understanding early encounters. Consistent with Altman and Taylor's social penetration model presented in the previous chapter, Sunnafrank insists that the early course of a relationship is guided by its "predicted outcome value."[15] He's convinced that maximizing rewards is more important than figuring out personality. If this is true, you'll be more concerned with establishing a smooth working relationship with Heather at your first meeting than you will be in figuring out what makes her tick.

Who is right, Berger or Sunnafrank? Which is more important to people when they first meet each other—uncertainty reduction or predicted outcome value? Initial head-to-head tests favor projected rewards as the paramount issue. For example, Theodore Grove and Doris Werkman had their Portland State students talk with both an able-bodied stranger and a physically handicapped stranger. When conversing with someone in a wheelchair, students' apprehension (projected outcome value) won out over curiosity (desire to reduce uncertainty).[16]

Berger doesn't think a real contest between uncertainty reduction and predicted outcome value is possible. He says that any predictions you make about the payoffs of working with Heather are only as good as the quality of your current knowledge. To the extent you are uncertain of how an action will affect the relationship, predicted outcome value has no meaning.

Even though the validity of Berger's original uncertainty reduction theory is in doubt, his analysis of initial interaction is a major contribution to communication scholarship. He recently observed that "the field of communication has been suffering and continues to suffer from an intellectual trade deficit with respect to related disciplines; the field imports much more than it exports."[17] Uncertainty reduction theory was an early attempt by a scholar trained within the discipline to reverse that trend. His success at stimulating critical thinking among his peers can be seen by the fact that every author cited in this chapter is a member of a communication faculty.

Although some of Berger's axioms may not perfectly reflect reality, his focus on the issue of reducing uncertainty is at the heart of communication inquiry. Appealing for further dialogue and modification rather than a wholesale rejection of the theory, Berger asks:

> What could be more basic to the study of communication than the propositions that (1) adaptation is essential for survival, (2) adaptation is only possible through the reduction of uncertainty, and (3) uncertainty can be both reduced and produced by communicative activity?[18]

It's a sound rhetorical question.

QUESTIONS TO SHARPEN YOUR FOCUS

1. An *axiom* is a self-evident truth. Which one of Berger's axioms seems least self-evident to you?

2. Check out *theorem 13* in Figure 14.1. Does the predicted relationship between *self-disclosure* and *reciprocity* match the forecast of social penetration theory?

3. Under what conditions does Berger think our *curiosity* about another person is almost irresistible?

4. The relationship between *information seeking* and *liking* in *theorem 17* is only one out of twenty-one original predictions. Why do critics take doubts about its validity so seriously?

A SECOND LOOK

Recommended resource: Charles R. Berger, "Communicating Under Uncertainty," in *Interpersonal Processes: New Directions in Communication Research*, Michael Roloff and Gerald Miller (eds.), Sage, Newbury Park, Calif., 1987, pp. 39–62.

Original statement: Charles Berger and Richard Calabrese, "Some Explorations in Initial Interaction and Beyond: Toward a Developmental Theory of Interpersonal Communication," *Human Communication Research*, Vol. 1, 1975, pp. 99–112.

Strategies for uncertainty reduction: Charles R. Berger, "Beyond Initial Interaction: Uncertainty, Understanding, and the Development of Interpersonal Relationships," in *Language and Social Psychology*, H. Giles and R. St. Clair (eds.), Blackwell, Oxford, 1979, pp. 122–144.

Further development: Charles R. Berger and J. J. Bradac, *Language and Social Knowledge: Uncertainty in Interpersonal Relations*, Arnold, London, 1982.

Current state of the art: Charles R. Berger and William B. Gudykunst, "Uncertainty and Communication," in *Progress in Communication Sciences*, Vol. 10, Brenda Dervin and Melvin Voigt (eds.), Ablex, Norwood, N.J., 1991, pp. 21–66.

Motivation to reduce uncertainty: Kathy Kellerman and Rodney Reynolds, "When Ignorance Is Bliss: The Role of Motivation to Reduce Uncertainty in Uncertainty Reduction Theory," *Human Communication Research*, Vol. 17, 1990, pp. 5–75.

Measuring uncertainty: Glen W. Clatterbuck, "Attributional Confidence and Uncertainty in Initial Interaction," *Human Communication Research*, Vol. 5, 1979, pp. 147–157.

Comparison with other uncertainty theories: Charles R. Berger, "Uncertainty and Information Exchange in Developing Relationships," in *A Handbook of Personal Relationships*, Steve Duck (ed.), John Wiley and Sons, New York, 1988, pp. 239–255.

Intercultural extension: William B. Gudykunst, "Culture and the Development of Interpersonal Relationships," *Communication Yearbook 12*, James Anderson (ed.), Sage, Newbury Park, Calif., 1989, pp. 315–354.

Critique: Michael Sunnafrank, "Predicted Outcome Value During Initial Interactions: A Reformulation of Uncertainty Reduction Theory," *Human Communication Research*, Vol. 13, 1986, pp. 3–33.

RELATIONSHIP MAINTENANCE

The term *maintenance* may call to mind an auto repair shop where workers with oil-stained coveralls and grease under their fingernails struggle to fix a worn-out engine. The work is hard, the conditions are messy, and the repair is best performed by mechanics who have some idea of what they're doing.

This image of rugged work is appropriate when thinking about the ongoing effort required to maintain a close relationship. In many ways, forming a close bond is much easier than sustaining it. The beginning stages of intimacy are often filled with excitement at discovering another human being who sees the world as we do, with the added touch of wonder that the person we like likes us as well. As the relationship becomes more established, however, conflict, jealousy, distrust, and boredom can be the friction that threatens to pull the engine apart. The owner's manual of a new "Intimacy" should warn that periodic maintenance is necessary for driving longevity.

"Fourteen people love me, 22 people like me, 6 people tolerate me, and I have only 3 enemies. Not bad for a little kid, huh?"

Cartoon by Scott. Appeared in Saturday *Review*, April 17, 1976.

In as much as the image of auto upkeep and repair communicates the importance of "servicing" a relationship, the metaphor of mechanical labor is appropriate. But personal relationships aren't inanimate objects with interchangeable parts that can be adjusted with a wrench. Since the widespread growth of medical HMOs (Health Maintenance Organizations), many people now associate the term *maintenance* with holistic care for a living organism.

Humanistic communication writer John Stewart refers to a pair's personal relationship as a "spiritual child" which is born as the result of their coming together.[1] His analogy stresses that a relationship requires continual care and nurture for sustained growth. When people ignore the spiritual children they've created, the results are sick and puny relationships. Although Stewart thinks it's impossible to totally kill a relationship as long as one of the parents is still alive, child abuse or abandonment results in a stunted or maimed relationship.

Figure RM.1 lists fifty maintenance strategies grouped into twelve overarching categories. In addition to offering a provocative checklist for analyzing your own efforts at relational maintenance, the classification offers a helpful way to introduce the three theories which focus on this topic.

Chapter 15 presents Paul Watzlawick's interactional view of dysfunctional relationships. He compares the typical family as an interconnected system. Like it or not, what happens to one individual in the system has an impact on every other member. He believes that an excess or absence of overt talk about communication is a symptom of a family in trouble. This problem would show up in the metacommunication categories (C and D) in the list of strategies. His emphasis on the potentially positive effects of using a therapist or counselor to help reframe family communication patterns suggests the benefits of seeking outside help (K).

I've already previewed John Thibaut and Harold Kelley's social exchange theory under the topic of relationship formation. As you will see in Chapter 16, they view interpersonal behavior as the logical result of rewards and costs in the external environment (A). From a social exchange perspective, antisocial and prosocial maintenance strategies (E and F) are attempts to exercise relational control through the use of selective rewards and punishments.

Although the strategies listed in Figure RM.1 were compiled by communication researcher Leslie Baxter, she is uneasy with the implication that the goal of maintenance and repair is to restore a relationship to its original condition. She is convinced that romantic couples are caught in conflicting strategic desires for integration and separation (I and J), stability and change (G and H), expression and privacy (B). For Baxter, relationship maintenance isn't as much about achieving stability as it is about coping with the stress inherent in every intimate bond. Chapter 17 presents her dialectical perspective.

STRATEGY TYPES AND EXAMPLES OF RELATIONAL MAINTENANCE

A. Changing external environment
   1. Barren and hostile ("I get us to focus on a mutual enemy or an adverse external condition.")
   2. Fertile and benign ("I have candlelight dinner with my spouse.")

B. Communication strategies
   3. Talk ("I spend more time talking with my spouse.")
   4. Symbolic contact ("I call my spouse during the day just to say 'Hi'. ")
   5. Openness and honesty ("I am open and honest with my spouse.")
   6. Talk about the day ("I talk about my day with my spouse.")
   7. Share feelings ("I share my feelings with my spouse.")

C. Metacommunication
   8. Talk about the problems ("I talk about the problems in our relationship with my spouse.")
   9. Interim progress reports ("I have regular, periodic, talks about our relationship with my spouse.")
   10. Cooling off before talking ("I wait until I've cooled off before I discuss our problem with my spouse.")
   11. Tell spouse his or her faults ("I tell my spouse his or her faults and the damage they do to our relationship.")

D. Avoid metacommunication
   12. ("I keep quiet and let our problem pass.")

E. Antisocial strategies
   13. Argument ("I argue or fight with my spouse.")
   14. Ultimatums ("I give my spouse an ultimatum or I threaten to end the relationship.")
   15. Insolence ("I am rude, insulting, impolite, and disrespectful to my spouse.")
   16. Sullenness ("I sulk, pout, give my spouse the silent treatment.")
   17. Hyper-criticalness ("I nag and criticize my spouse.")
   18. Being obstinate ("I am stubborn, I refuse to give in to or compromise with my spouse.")
   19. Verbally imply relationship has no future ("I tell my spouse that the marriage has no future.")
   20. Break contact ("I walk out of the house without telling my spouse when I will return.")
   21. Act cold ("I give my spouse the cold shoulder.")
   22. Refuse self-disclosure ("I don't provide my spouse with my customary degree of disclosure about myself.")
   23. Refuse favors ("I refuse to supply my spouse with my usual favors or I refuse to accept favors I plainly need from my spouse.")
   24. Threaten exclusiveness/common space/common future ("I have an affair, pretend to have an affair, or flirt with a third party.")

FIGURE RM.1
Fifty Strategies for Relational Maintenance in Marriage (From Baxter and Dindia, ''Marital Partners' Perceptions of Marital Maintenance Strategies.'')

F. Prosocial strategies

25. Be nice ("I am courteous and polite to my spouse, I show my spouse respect.")
26. Be cheerful ("I am cheerful, good-natured and pleasant to my spouse.")
27. Refrain from criticism ("I refrain from criticizing my spouse.")
28. Give in ("I give in to my spouse or compromise with my spouse.")
29. Verbally imply relationship has future ("I bring up topics such as buying a home or having children that indicate the relationship will be there in the future.")
30. Being warm ("I am friendly, kind, sympathetic, understanding, and supportive of my spouse.")
31. Listening better ("I try to be a better listener to my spouse.")
32. Doing favors ("I do a favor for my spouse.")
33. Insuring exclusiveness/common space/common future ("I assure my spouse of my fidelity.")

G. Ceremonies

34. Origin celebrations ("I remember my spouse's birthday, our wedding anniversary, Valentine's Day.")
35. Reminiscence ("I reminisce with my spouse about past pleasurable experiences we shared together.")
36. Discuss the end of the relationship ("I discuss with my spouse what it would be like if the relationship ended through divorce or death.")
37. Piacular ceremonies ("I kiss and make up with my spouse.")
38. Communion celebrations ("I have us eat out at a favorite expensive restaurant.")
39. Verbal expressions of affection ("I tell my spouse I love him or her.")
40. Nonverbal expressions of affection ("I hug and kiss my spouse.")
41. Compliments ("I compliment my spouse.")
42. Gift-giving ("I give my spouse a gift.")

H. Anti-rituals/spontaneity

43. ("I surprise my spouse.")

I. Togetherness

44. Time together ("I spend more time with my spouse.")
45. Shared activity ("I do more things with my spouse.")
46. Spend time with network ("I spend time with my spouse together with our children, family, or friends.")

J. Seeking/allowing autonomy

47. ("I allow my spouse time to be alone or to do things with other people, and I take time to be alone or to do things with other people.")

K. Seeking external assistance

48. Seeking outside help ("I seek help outside our marriage; for example, I have us attend a marriage encounter or go to a marriage counselor.")
49. Joint use of prayer/religion ("I pray with my spouse or attend church with my spouse.")
50. Individual use of prayer/religion ("I pray by myself for guidance about our marriage.")

CHAPTER 15

The Interactional View
of Paul Watzlawick

The Franklin family is in trouble. A perceptive observer could spot their difficulties despite their successful façade. Sonia Franklin is an accomplished pianist who teaches advanced theory and technique to students in her own home. Her husband Stan will soon become a partner in a Big Eight accounting firm. Their daughter Laurie is an honor student, an officer in her high school class, and the number two player on the tennis team. But Laurie's younger brother, Mike, has dropped all pretense of interest in studies, sports, or social life. His only passion is drinking beer and smoking pot.

Each of the Franklins reacts to Mike's substance abuse in different, but less than helpful, ways. Stan denies that his son has a problem. Boys will be boys, and he's sure Mike will grow out of this phase. The only time he and Mike actually talked about the problem, Stan said, "I want you to quit drinking—not for me and your mother—but for your own sake."

Laurie has always felt responsible for her kid brother and is scared because Mike is getting "wasted" every few days. She makes him promise that he'll quit using and continues to introduce him to her straight friends in the hope that he'll get in with a good crowd.

Sonia worries that alcohol and drugs will ruin her son's future. One morning when he woke up with a hangover, she wrote a note to the school saying Mike had the flu. She also called a lawyer to help Mike when he was stopped for drunk driving. Although she promised never to tell his father about these incidents, she chides Stan for his lack of concern. The more she nags, the more he withdraws.

Mike feels caught in a vicious circle. Smoking pot helps him relax, but then his family gets more upset, which makes him want to smoke more, which . . . During a tense dinner table discussion he lashed out: "You want to know why I use? Go look in a mirror." Although the rest of the family sees Mike as "the problem," psychologist Paul Watzlawick would describe the whole family system as disturbed. He formed his theory of social interaction by looking at dysfunctional patterns within families in order to gain insight about healthy communication.

THE FAMILY AS A SYSTEM

Picture a family as a mobile suspended from the ceiling. Each figure is connected to the rest of the structure by a strong thread tied at exactly the right place to keep the system in balance. Tug on any string, and the force sends shock throughout the whole network. Sever a thread, and the entire design tilts in disequilibrium.

The threads in the mobile analogy represent communication rules that hold the family together. Watzlawick believes that in order to understand the movement of any single figure in the family system, one has to examine the communication patterns among all its members. He regards the communication that the family members have among themselves about their relationships as especially important.

Watzlawick (pronounced VAHT-sla-vick) is a long-term research associate at the Mental Health Institute, Palo Alto, California, and an adjunct faculty member at the Stanford University Medical Center. He is one of about twenty scholars and therapists who were inspired by and worked with anthropologist Gregory Bateson. The common denominator that continues to draw the Palo Alto Group together is a commitment to study interpersonal interaction as part of an entire system. They reject the idea that individual motives and personality traits determine the nature of communication within a family. In fact, the Palo Alto researchers care little about *why* a person acts in a certain way, but they have a great interest in *how* that behavior affects everyone in the group.

A systems approach to family relationships defies simplistic explanations of why people act as they do. For example, some pop psychology books on body language claim that a listener standing in a hands-on-hips position is skeptical about what the speaker is saying. Watzlawick is certainly interested in the reaction others have to this posture, but he doesn't think that a particular way of standing should be viewed as part of a cause-and-effect chain of events:

$$a \rightarrow b \rightarrow c \rightarrow d$$

Relationships are not simple, nor are they "things" as suggested by the statement, "We have a good relationship." Relationships are complex functions in the same sense that mathematical functions link multiple variables:

$$x = b^2 + \frac{2c}{a} - 5d$$

Just as x will be affected by the value of a, b, c, or d, so the hands-on-hips stance could be due to a variety of attitudes, emotions, or physical conditions. Maybe the stance does show skepticism. But it also might reflect boredom, a feeling of awkwardness, aching shoulder muscles, or self-consciousness about middle-aged "hip-handles."

Watzlawick uses the math metaphor throughout his book *Pragmatics of Human Communication.* You'll recall from the introduction to the Verbal Messages section that the term *pragmatics* refers to the relationship between signs and behavior, not to the practicality of words. Along with co-authors Janet Beavin and Don Jackson, Watzlawick presents five axioms that describe the "tentative calculus of human communication." These make up the "grammar of conversation," or, to use another analogy that runs through the book, "the rules of the game."

There is nothing particularly playful about the game the Franklins are playing. Psychologist Alan Watts says that "life is a game where rule No. 1 is: This is no game, this is serious."[1] Watzlawick defines game as "sequences of behavior governed by rules." Even though Sonia and Stan are involved in an unhealthy "game without end" of nag-withdrawal-nag-withdrawal, they continue to play because it serves a function for both of them. (Sonia feels superior; Stan avoids hassles with his son.) Neither party may recognize what's going on, but their rules are a something-for-something bargain. Mike's drinking and his family's distress may fit into the same category. (Getting drunk not only relieves tension temporarily, it's a great excuse for sidestepping the pressure to excel, which is the name of the game for the Franklins.)

The network of communication rules which governs the Franklins' interaction makes it extremely difficult for any of them to change their behavior. Watzlawick, Beavin, and Jackson use the label *family homeostasis* to describe what many family counselors agree is the tacit collusion of family members to maintain the status quo. Interactional theorists believe that we'll fail to recognize this destructive resistance to change unless we understand five basic axioms, or rules, of communication.

Axiom 1: One Cannot Not Communicate

You've undoubtedly been caught in situations where you feel obliged to talk but would rather avoid the commitment to respond that's inherent in all communication. For example, you come home from a date, and your mother meets you inside the door and says, "Tell me all about it." Or perhaps you need to study, but your roommate wants to chat.

In an attempt to avoid communication, you could bluntly state that your test the following morning makes studying more important than socializing. But voicing your desire for privacy can stretch the rules of good behavior and often results in an awkward silence that speaks loudly about the relationship.

You could flood your mother with a torrent of meaningless words about the evening, merely say it was "fine" as you duck into your room, or plead tiredness, a headache, or a sore throat. Watzlawick calls this the "symptom strategy" and says it suggests, "*I* wouldn't mind talking to you, but something stronger than *I*, for which I cannot be blamed, prevents me." But whatever you do, it would be naive not to realize that your mother will analyze your behavior for clues about the evening's activities. His face an immobile mask, Mike Franklin may mutely encounter his parents. But he communicates in spite of himself by his facial expression and the fact of his silence.

Axiom 2: Human Beings Communicate Both Digitally and Analogically

The car I drive has a combination of analogical and digital instruments. The rise and fall of the needle on the gas gauge is analogous to the level of the gasoline in the tank. The reading is approximate, but one quick look is enough to picture the overall fuel situation. The odometer gives a digital readout. It's quite exact, yet I still have to translate the meaning of the 12,452 miles recorded last year. There is nothing about these five digits that suggests the actual quantity they represent. The shape of the numbers, for instance, in no way indicates several thousand of anything. The numbers are merely an agreed-upon code that General Motors and I both understand. After deciphering the digital symbols, I still have to figure out what the numbers signify in terms of wear and tear on tires or trade-in value. Analogical communication represents things by likeness; digital communication refers to things by name.

Watzlawick sees language as digital communication. With few exceptions, words have no similarity to the things or ideas they describe. He regards most nonverbal communication as analogical. Tone of voice, facial expression, and touch reliably mirror gradations of feeling. That's why Mike can't hide his emotions from his parents or sister. His overall negative mood leaks out nonverbally.

According to Watzlawick, problems arise when we digitally label the nonverbal acts which analogically represent inner feelings. Suppose Mike gives his mother flowers on her birthday. Should Sonia define the gift as a sign of affection, a bribe for future help when he's in trouble, restitution for past hurt, or . . . ? If Mike stammers, sweats, and looks at the ground when he tells his sister that he's kept his promise of abstinence, is his nonverbal behavior a sign of falsehood or fear? It's hard to translate accurately between verbal and nonverbal channels.

Axiom 3: Communication = Content + Relationship

The heading is a shorthand version of the formal axiom: "Every communication has a content and relationship aspect such that the latter classifies the former and is therefore metacommunication."[2] Watzlawick chose to rename the two aspects of communication that Gregory Bateson had originally called "report" and "command." Report or content is *what* is said. Command or relationship is *how* it's said. Figure 15.1 outlines the distinction that is crucial to the interactional model.

Content	Relationship
Report	Command
What is said	How it's said
Digital	Analogical
Verbal channel	Nonverbal channel
Cognitive	Affective
Computer data	Computer program
Words	Punctuation
Communication	Metacommunication

FIGURE 15.1
Interactional View of Two Aspects of Communication

Neither the equation above nor the contrasting terms in Figure 15.1 quite capture the way relationship surrounds content and provides a context or atmosphere for interpretation. It's the difference between data fed into a computer and the program that directs how the data should be processed. In written communication, punctuation gives direction as to how the words should be understood. Shifting a question mark to an exclamation mark alters the meaning of the message. Right? Right! In spoken communication, however, it is the tone of voice, emphasis on certain words, facial cues, and so forth, that direct how the message was meant to be interpreted.

Watzlawick refers to the relational aspect of interaction as "metacommunication." It is communication about communication. Metacommunication says, "This is how I see myself, this is how I see you, this is how I see you seeing me . . ." According to Watzlawick, metacommunication usually fades into the background when relationships are healthy. When a family is in trouble, however, metacommunication dominates the discussion. Mike Franklin's dinner-table outburst is an example of pathological metacommunication that shakes the entire family system. The Palo Alto Group is convinced it would be a mistake for the Franklins to ignore Mike's attack in the hope that the tension will go away. Sick family relationships only get better when family members are willing to talk with each other about their patterns of communication.

Axiom 4: The Nature of a Relationship Depends on How Both Parties Punctuate the Communication Sequence

Consider the relational tangle described in one of the "Knots" composed by R. D. Laing to describe sick family systems:[3]

He can't be happy
> when there's so much suffering in the world

She can't be happy
> if he is unhappy
> She wants to be happy

He does not feel entitled to be happy

She wants him to be happy
> and he wants her to be happy

He feels guilty if he is happy
> and guilty if she is not happy

She wants both to be happy

He wants her to be happy

So they are both unhappy

The poem describes a discouraging cycle:

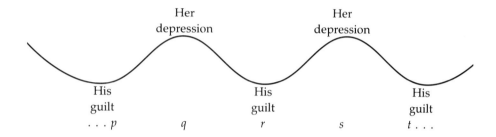

Outside observers see a reciprocal pattern of guilt and depression that has no beginning or end. But the woman enmeshed in the "knot" punctuates the sequence by starting at point *p*, *r*, or *t*. She thus regards the man as selfish, the cause of her unhappiness. Equally ensnared in the system, the man punctuates the sequence by designating her depression at point *q* or *s* as the initial event. Therefore, he sees his guilt as the result of her being a happiness junkie. Asking either of them, "Who started it?" would merely feed into their fruitless struggle for control.

Watzlawick notes that "what is typical about the sequence and makes it a problem of punctuation is that the individual concerned conceives of himself only as reacting to, but not as provoking, these attitudes.[4] This is true for both adult Franklins. Stan sees himself as withdrawing from Sonia only because of her constant nagging. Sonia feels certain that she wouldn't harp on the issue if Stan would face the problem of Mike's drinking.

Axiom 5: All Communication Is Either Symmetrical or Complementary

The final axiom continues to focus on analogical communication. While definitions of *relationship* include the issues of belongingness, affection, trust, and intimacy, the interactional view pays particular attention to questions of control, status, and power. Remember that Bateson's original label for analogical communication was *command*. According to Watzlawick, symmetrical interchanges are based on equal power; complementary communication is based on differences in power. He makes no attempt to label one as good and the other as bad. Healthy relationships have both kinds of communication.

In terms of ability, the women in the Franklin family have a symmetrical relationship; neither one tries to control the other. Sonia has expertise on the piano; Laurie excels on the tennis court. Each of them performs without the other's claiming dominance. Fortunately, their skills are in separate areas. Too much similarity can set the stage for an everything-you-can-do-I-can-do-better competition.

Sonia's relationship with Mike is complementary. Her type of mothering is strong on control. She hides the extent of Mike's drinking from his father, lies to school officials, and hires a lawyer on the sly to bail her son out of trouble with the police. By continuing to treat Mike as a child, she maintains their dominant-submissive relationship. Although complementary relationships aren't always destructive, the status difference between Mike and the rest of the Franklins is stressing the family system.

The interactional view holds that there is no way to label a relationship on the basis of a single verbal statement. Judgments that an interaction is either symmetrical or complementary require a sequence of at least two messages—a statement from one person, and a response from the other. While at Michigan State University, communication researchers Edna Rogers-Millar and Richard Farace devised a coding scheme to categorize ongoing marital interaction on the crucial issue of who controls the relationship.

One-up communication (↑) is movement to gain control of the exchange. A bid for dominance includes messages that instruct, order, interrupt, change topics, disconfirm, or fail to support what the other person said. One-down communication (↓) is movement to yield control of the exchange. The bid for submission is evidenced by agreement with what the other person said. Despite Watzlawick's contention that all discourse is either symmetrical or complementary, Rogers-Millar and Farace code one-across communication (→) as well. They define it as movement toward neutralizing control.

Figure 15.2 presents the matrix of possible relational transactions. The pairs which are circled show a symmetrical interaction. The pairs in triangles indicate complementary relations. The pairs in squares reveal transitory communication. Rogers-Millar's later research showed that bids for dominance (↑) do not necessarily result in successful control of the interaction (↑ ↓).[5]

TRAPPED IN A SYSTEM WITH NO PLACE TO GO

Family systems are highly resistant to change. This inertia is especially apparent in the home of someone who has an addiction. Each family member occupies a role that serves the status quo. In the Franklin family, Mike, of course, is the one with "the problem." With the best of intentions, Sonia is the "enabler" who cushions Mike from feeling the pain caused by his chemi-

Response to Message

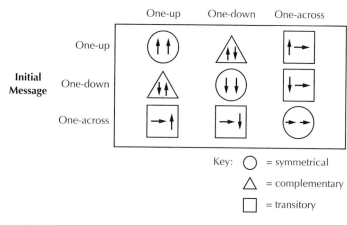

Key: ◯   = symmetrical

△   = complementary

▢   = transitory

FIGURE 15.2
Matrix of Transactional Types (Adapted from Rogers-Millar and Farace, "Analysis of Relational Communication in Dyads: New Measurement Procedures.")

cal abuse. Stan is the "deny-er," while Laurie is the family "hero" who compensates for her brother's failure. Family therapists note that when one person in a distressed family gets better, another member often gets worse. If Mike stopped drinking and using pot, Laurie might quit the tennis team, ignore her studies, or start smoking marijuana herself. Dysfunctional families confirm the adage "the more things change, the more they stay the same."

Watzlawick sees family members as often caught in a "double bind," which Bateson originally described. Parental messages such as "you ought to love me" or "be spontaneous" place children in an untenable position. The children are bound to violate some aspect of the injunction no matter how they respond. (Love can only be freely given; spontaneity on demand is impossible.) The paradox of the double bind is that the high-status party in a complementary relationship insists that the low-status person act as if the relationship were symmetrical—which it isn't. Stan's *demand* that his son stay sober for his *own sake* places Mike in a no-win situation. He can't obey his dad and be autonomous at the same time.

CHANGING THE GAME BY CHANGING THE RULES

How can the Franklin family break out of their never-ending game and experience real change in the way they relate to each other? According to Watzlawick, effective change for the whole family will come about only when members are helped to step outside the system and see the self-defeating nature of the rules under which they're playing. He calls this process of changing the punctuation "reframing."

*"I don't want you to go for a walk because I want you to go for a walk.
I want you to go for a walk because you want to go for a walk."*

Drawing by Maslin; © 1988 The New Yorker Magazine, Inc.

To reframe . . . means to change the conceptual and/or emotional setting or viewpoint in relation to which a situation is experienced and to place it in another frame which fits the "facts" of the same concrete situation equally well or even better, and thereby changes its entire meaning.[6]

Watzlawick compares reframing to the process of waking up from a bad dream. He points out that during a nightmare you may run, hide, fight, scream, jump off a cliff, or try dozens of other things to make things better, but nothing really changes. Relief comes only when you step outside the system by waking up. Without the intervention of a timely alarm clock or a caring roommate, relief can be a long time coming.

Reframing is the sudden "ah-hah" of looking at things in a new light. Watzlawick cites the classic case of Tom Sawyer, who faced the drudgery of whitewashing a fence on a summer afternoon. He transformed the onerous task into an opportunity for pleasure and profit by "allowing" his friends to pay him for a chance to take a turn with the bucket and brush.

For the Franklins, reframing means they must radically change their perspective. First and foremost, they need to recognize that Mike's addiction is a disease over which he has no control. His drinking is not a sign of moral weakness or a voluntary rebuff of his family's values. He drinks because he's an alcoholic. Second, the Franklins need to abandon the fruitless search for someone to blame. Despite Mike's look-in-the-mirror accusation, the members of his family aren't responsible for his addiction. Alcoholics Anonymous (AA) assures them that they didn't cause it, they can't cure it, and they can't control it. It's a disease.

The reference to control suggests a third reframing task for the Franklins. They must admit that their so-called solutions are as much a problem as their son's drinking. Mike will never seek treatment for his illness as long as his family continues to shield him from the consequences of his behavior. Reframing will help Sonia see that writing excuses and hiring lawyers may be less caring than letting her son get kicked out of school or allowing his driver's license to be suspended.

Adopting a tough-love perspective can usually be accomplished only with outside help. For Watzlawick, this means a therapist. Self-help groups called Families Anonymous (FA) offer an alternative way to reframe the family network. Just as AA gives support to the recovering alcoholic, FA offers support for those who face chemical dependency within their own families. At each meeting, participants read aloud a brief selection entitled "Helping," in which they pledge to avoid manipulation, control, overprotectiveness, and any attempts to make the addicted family member fit a standard or image. The reading closes with radical words for worried parents: "I can change myself. Others I can only love."[7] That's changing the game by changing the rules.

CRITIQUE: THE PLUS AND MINUS OF RELATIONAL CALCULUS

The interactional view of the Palo Alto Group has encouraged communication scholars to go beyond narrow cause-and-effect assumptions. You can see the influence of a systems approach in Pearce and Cronen's coordinated management of meaning (see Chapter 6), Fisher's interact system model of decision emergence (see Chapter 21), and Weick's model of organizing process (see Chapter 23). But because they focus on form rather than content, systems theories are hard to prove. Watzlawick's axiom that one cannot not communicate is a case in point. *Communication Studies*, the journal of the Central States Communication Association, carried a series of articles attacking and defending this popular principle, but it's hard to imagine what kind of evidence an author could summon that would settle the controversy once and for all.

The interactional view also reveals some conceptual fuzziness. Watzlawick's axioms define metacommunication as the analogical, nonverbal features of messages—a raised eyebrow from Laurie, a haughty tone from Sonia, Mike's slouch in a chair. But when Watzlawick discusses how to bring about change in a disturbed family system, he refers to *talk* about relationships as metacommunication. His advice on explicit talk about relationships is also confusing. He often recommends a frank discussion of family communication rules yet states elsewhere that this focus can be destructive. He offers no guidelines as to when it helps and when it hurts.

Despite this confusion, the Palo Alto Group has made a lasting impact on the field of communication by focusing on the distinction between the content and relationship aspects of messages. The publication of *Pragmatics of Human Communication* marked the beginning of widespread study of the ways communication reflects and shapes relational development.

QUESTIONS TO SHARPEN YOUR FOCUS

1. What is the difference between *digital* and *analogical* communication? Which type of communication takes away the option of not communicating?

2. For decades the United States and the former Soviet Union were engaged in a nuclear arms race. How does Watzlawick's axiom about the *punctuation of communication sequences* explain the belligerence of both nations?

3. Can you make up something your instructor might say that would place you in a *double bind*? Under what conditions would this be merely laughable rather than frustrating?

4. Read one of the letters printed in the "Ann Landers" or "Dear Abby" column of your daily newspaper. How could you *reframe* the situation the writer describes?

A SECOND LOOK

Recommended resource: Paul Watzlawick, Janet Beavin, and Don Jackson, *Pragmatics of Human Communication*, W. W. Norton, New York, 1967.

Seminal ideas of the Palo Alto Group: Gregory Bateson, "Information and Codification," in *Communication*, Jurgen Ruesch and Gregory Bateson (eds.), W. W. Norton, New York, 1951, pp. 168–211.

System theory: B. Aubrey Fisher, "The Pragmatic Perspective of Human Communication: A View from System Theory," in *Human Communication Theory*, Frank E. X. Dance (ed.), Harper & Row, New York, 1982, pp. 192–219.

Control, metacommunication, and context: Arthur Bochner and Dorothy Krueger, "Interpersonal Communication Theory and Research: An Overview of Inscrutable Epistemologies and Muddled Concepts," in *Communication Yearbook 3*, Dan Nimmo (ed.), Transaction Books, New Brunswick, N.J., 1979, pp. 197–211.

Relational control: L. Edna Rogers and Richard Farace, "Analysis of Relational Communication in Dyads: New Measurement Procedures," *Human Communication Research*, Vol. 1, 1975, pp. 222–239.

Changing a system: Paul Watzlawick, John H. Weakland, and Richard Fisch, *Change*, W. W. Norton, New York, 1974.

Pathological punctuation: R. D. Laing, *Knots*, Pantheon Books, New York, 1970.

Family systems of alcoholics: Sharon Wegscheider, *Another Chance: Hope and Health for the Alcoholic Family*, Science and Behavior Books, Palo Alto, Calif., 1981.

Case studies of family pathology: Jules Henry, *Pathways to Madness*, Random House, New York, 1971.

Whether one cannot not communicate: Theodore Clevenger, Jr., "Can One Not Communicate? A Conflict of Models," *Communication Studies,* Vol. 42, 1991, pp. 340–353.

Critique: Carol Wilder, "The Palo Alto Group: Difficulties and Directions of the Interactional View for Human Communication Research," *Human Communication Research*, Vol. 5, 1979, pp. 171–186.

CHAPTER 16

Social Exchange Theory
of John Thibaut & Harold Kelley

In 1959 Perry Smith and Dick Hickock invaded a Kansas farmhouse in a senseless robbery that netted under $50. After tying up the four family members in separate rooms, they blasted them with a shotgun to eliminate all witnesses. Two months later the men were captured and placed in separate interrogation rooms. The police had enough evidence to convict them for parole violation and passing bad checks, but the evidence for murder was thin. The prosecutor needed a confession.

Truman Capote's book *In Cold Blood* describes the dilemma faced by Smith and Hickock. Shortly after the crime, they had agreed to stick together so that they could back up their planned alibi if arrested. Yet held in isolation, each doubted the other's will or ability to hold out. Smith saw Hickock as a convincing liar, but thought his "guts were unreliable." Similarly, Hickock feared dying on the gallows because he thought Smith would lose his nerve.

Often in jointly committed homicides, the suspect who turns state's evidence gains immunity while the other one, who feigns innocence, gets the death penalty. This differential treatment provides a strong temptation to cop out. But admitting guilt doesn't always achieve leniency. If both suspects confess, the government has more evidence than it needs to convict for murder, and both killers get a life sentence. Yet if both stonewall, the prosecutor can get a conviction only on a lesser charge. This is the classic prisoner's dilemma: Confess the crime or maintain innocence?

THE OUTCOME MATRIX AS A MIRROR OF LIFE

Figure 16.1 diagrams the interdependence of Smith and Hickock. This 2 x 2 matrix is the central analytical device of John Thibaut and Harold Kelley's social exchange theory. Thibaut was professor of psychology at the University of North Carolina until his death in 1986; Kelley continues to use the outcome matrix at UCLA to examine how people decide what to do in their relationships. I urge you to work through the potential outcome values shown in each matrix presented in the chapter. The placement of the numbers at the

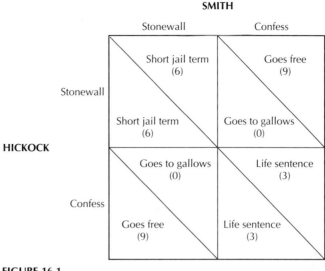

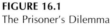

FIGURE 16.1
The Prisoner's Dilemma

intersection of two behaviors reflects Thibaut and Kelley's conviction that our relational outcomes are always linked with the actions of others.

The column headings show the two choices open to Smith; the row labels describe Hickock's same options. The four cells inside the box reveal the consequences of the various behavioral combinations. Smith's outcomes are in the upper right corner of each cell. Hickock's are in the lower left portion. For example, if Smith confesses while his partner stands mute, he goes free and Hickock dies.

The numbers in parentheses are attempts to quantify the values of different outcomes. Thibaut and Kelley let a single number represent the rewards minus the costs of a given course of action. For example, Smith might mentally sum up the benefits of a life sentence as a $+14$. He'd have the relief of escaping execution, a chance for human contact, plenty of time to watch TV, and perhaps a shot at parole later on. Of course the downside of a life term in jail would cancel out most of those benefits. Smith's costs, which he might mentally rate as a -11, would include permanent loss of freedom, guards' continually telling him what to do, boredom, and fear of violence from other prisoners. Since the outcome of an interaction equals rewards $(+14)$ minus costs (-11), Smith would regard the consequence of a mutual confession as a bleak $+3$.

The idea of totaling potential benefits and losses to determine behavior isn't new. Since philosopher John Stuart Mill stated his philosophy of utilitarianism,[1] there's been a compelling logic to the minimax principle of human behavior. The minimax principle claims that people seek to maximize their benefits and minimize their costs. So the higher the number in an outcome matrix, the more attractive the behavior that might make it happen.

It would be nice if every interaction offered both parties a chance to get their optimum outcome at the same time. Unfortunately, the world's not set up that way. As with the prisoner's dilemma, there's the potential for one person's gain to come at the other's expense. Thibaut and Kelley describe the prisoner's dilemma matrix as "bilaterally discordant" and believe it offers a good way to study conflict between people.

Social exchange theory assumes that we can accurately anticipate the payoffs of a variety of interactions. Our minds are like computers, and a computer analysis is only as good as the data that are fed in. Garbage in; garbage out. To the authors of the theory, the data we get are remarkably reliable. Not only can Hickock see that twin confessions will result in a life sentence for him, he can also understand that they'll produce the same effect for Smith.

The 2 x 2 matrix plots either-or decisions, but most human encounters require a much larger map to represent the multiple options of both parties. Despite this complexity, Thibaut and Kelley believe that members of a dyad, as well as outside observers, can realistically grasp the potential outcomes shown across the grid. In addition, the participants have the sense to choose what's best.

The best choice is not always the one associated with the highest number on the board. Take a look at Smith's and Hickock's options. There's no doubt that freedom is the most desirable outcome, yet if each man confesses in the hope of avoiding prison, they will both end up behind bars for the rest of their lives. As is the case when playing a game of checkers, it's not enough to know you want to advance your marker to the far side of the board to gain a king; you also must credit your opponent's desire to do the same. Success requires that you take into account what the other player is likely to do.

The need for a strategy of anticipation leads some to refer to this exchange approach as "game theory." However, Thibaut and Kelley want to avoid the head-butting, win-lose, adversarial tone that goes with seeing the other as an opponent in a game. The internal cost of conflict cuts into the worth of an outcome; its resolution is value added. For this reason, they prefer the term *interdependence theory.* Whatever label we use, successful players learn to synchronize their moves with the actions of others.

COMPARING THE RESULTS: IS EVERYBODY HAPPY?

It may have occurred to you that a life sentence could mean something quite different to Smith than to Hickock. Social exchange theory presents two standards of comparison by which to evaluate a given outcome, whether in prison or under more normal circumstances. The first benchmark deals with relative satisfaction—how happy or sad an interpersonal outcome makes a participant feel. Thibaut and Kelley call it the *comparison level.*

A person's comparison level (CL) is the threshold above which an outcome seems attractive. If your CL for clerical employment is an hourly wage

"So the prince and the princess lowered their expectations and lived reasonably contentedly forever after."

of $8, you would be satisfied working for $9 an hour but feel exploited if you received only $7 for your labor.

Satisfaction depends on expectation, which is shaped by prior experience, especially gripping events of the recent past. A run of bad outcomes can make previously distasteful results more palatable. A string of successes whets the appetite for a gourmet feast.

If Smith's memory is filled with killers who either go free or merely get token jail terms, his CL will be at +7 or so, and a life sentence rated at +3 will seem a cruel joke. In spite of his murderous brutality, even a moderate term in jail will strike him as unfair. Hickock, on the other hand, may see execution as the likely result of committing homicide. As a former convict, he knew men who went to the gallows. With a CL of only $+2$, a life sentence at $+3$ might look quite attractive.

COMPARING THE RESULTS: IS EVERYONE GOING TO STICK AROUND?

Thibaut and Kelley suggest that there is a second standard by which we evaluate the outcomes we receive. They call it the *comparison level of alternatives* (CL_{alt}), and the level is pegged by the best payoffs available outside the current relationship. CL_{alt} is the worst outcome a person will accept and still stay in a relationship. As more attractive outside possibilities become available, or as existent outcomes slide below an established CL_{alt}, instability increases. This may sound like a stock market analysis rather than a description of interpersonal relationships. Not surprisingly, some advocates of a social exchange approach refer to it as a "theory of economic behavior."

CL_{alt} doesn't speak to the issue of attraction or satisfaction. A woman could be happy in her job, yet leave for a new position which offers even higher pay, better working conditions, or a more interesting assignment.

Relative Value of Outcome, CL, CL_{alt}	State of the Relationship
Outcome > CL > CL_{alt}	Satisfying Stable Dependent
Outcome > CL_{alt} > CL	Satisfying Stable Nondependent
CL_{alt} > CL > Outcome	Not satisfying Break relationship Happy elsewhere
CL_{alt} > Outcome > CL	Satisfying Unstable Happier elsewhere
CL > CL_{alt} > Outcome	Not satisfying Break relationship Continue unhappy
CL > Outcome > CL_{alt}	Highly unsatisfying Can't break away Dependent and unhappy

FIGURE 16.2
Six Relational Typologies (Adapted from Roloff, *Interpersonal Communication: The Social Exchange Approach.*)

Conversely, she might remain in a loveless marriage because the high cost of exit lowers the attractiveness of the best outside alternative. Social workers describe the plight of a battered wife as "high cost, low rewards." Yet she often remains with her abusive husband because the option of being alone in the world appears worse. (Outcome > CL_{alt}.) She'll end the relationship only when she perceives an outside alternative which promises a better life (CL_{alt} > Outcome).

Nonvoluntary relationships have an extremely low CL_{alt}. Smith and Hickock each tried to escape from custody and failed. Their only alternative to the unwanted dilemma was suicide, an outcome on a par with execution. Thibaut and Kelley arbitrarily set CL_{alt} at zero in a payoff matrix, so that's why every outcome but hanging is shown as positive in the prisoner's dilemma. Even without the three absolute values of Outcome, CL, and CL_{alt}, the rank order reveals a lot about the state of relational health. Figure 16.2 outlines the six possibilities.

The last row at the bottom of the figure describes the plight of Hickock and Smith during the long months in prison before their trial. The shorthand notation on the left indicates a situation in which their comparison level desires and expectations are greater than the actual outcomes they receive, yet jail is better than the only alternatives available—suicide or execution. Most people in prison find themselves in a hapless and hopeless position.

DEPENDENCE FOSTERS CONTROL

In addition to distinctions in attractiveness and stability, Figure 16.2 separates relationship types on the basis of power. Consider the tie that exists between you and your mother. Her power over you is directly proportional to the amount of dependence you have on her for the benefits of life. If she is your only source for college tuition, wise counsel, emotional support, and fudge brownies, her ability to govern your life is great. If you can easily get the benefits she offers someplace else, you avoid interdependence. When outcomes exceed CL_{alt} by a large margin, dependence is great. Thibaut and Kelley make no claim that this is either good or bad. They merely point out the link between dependence and control. Their discussion of power involves three different forms of control.

1. Reflexive Control. The ability to reward yourself is reflexive control. It's pulling your own strings, taking responsibility for your own outcomes, being your own best friend. This is what Jane has in the first matrix of Figure 16.3. By choosing to do whatever behavior "X" represents, she can give good things to herself regardless of Dick's response. Self-provided rewards are portable. They continue to provide independence when carried into new relationships. These appear nonexistent for Smith and Hickock, since the best outcome each man can achieve on his own is a life sentence.

2. Fate Control. The ability to affect another's outcomes regardless of

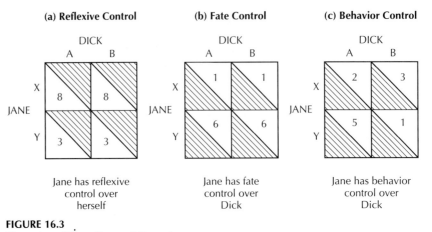

FIGURE 16.3
Illustration of Three Forms of Control

what he or she does is fate control. In the second matrix of Figure 16.3, Jane has fate control over Dick. She can exercise this power with tender, loving care or jerk him around unmercifully. Either way, he can't do a thing about it as long as they're together. His only recourse is the one available in most low-power situations—break off the relationship. Massive environmental fate control has removed even that option for Smith and Hickock. They've got to deal with each other, and each one by confessing can condemn the other to a lifetime in prison—or worse. That's mutual fate control.

3. Behavior Control.   The ability people have to change another's behavior through variations of their own is behavior control. It doesn't necessarily generate high outcomes; it's simply the power to move the other person around the matrix. By shifting her choice from behavior X to behavior Y in the third matrix of Figure 16.3, Jane gives Dick a strong inducement to act toward her in option A rather than option B. Hickock was the first to admit guilt in the Kansas murder case. Foreknowledge of his partner's confession would have given Smith a great impetus to abandon his claim of innocence.

People within interdependent relationships juggle the three forms of control, usually in some blend of mutuality. Mutual reflexive control is the power of individuals to make what they want come true in their own lives. Mutual fate control is the power they have to make what they want come true in others' lives. Mutual behavior control is the power they have to resolve the conflict that's generated by the clash of the first two kinds.

TRANSFORMING CONFLICT INTO COOPERATION

Thibaut and Kelley present a number of matrices which stimulate real-life conflicts. As with the prisoner's dilemma, the games come with intriguing titles: Chicken, Battle-of-the-Sexes, Threat, Zero-Sum. Social exchange theory

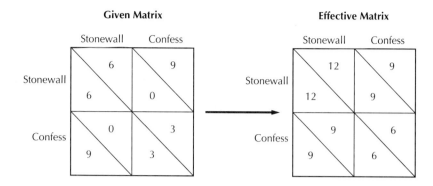

FIGURE 16.4
Prisoner's Dilemma Transformation: Maximizing Joint Outcomes

assumes that once the outcome values of a situation are known, prediction of a player's moves is automatic. However, life is rarely that simple. Playing for points, jelly beans, or money, people who are thrust into these conflict scenarios continually act contrary to what outsiders see as their own interest. Usually the variant choices reflect a prosocial, nonselfish bias. Players act less selfishly than the theory predicts.

Rather than abandon the basic principle of maximizing rewards and minimizing costs, Thibaut and Kelley speculate that people caught up in conflict reconceptualize the situation to relieve tension. Anxious participants mentally alter the numbers so that they are in effect responding to a matrix different from the one they were given. The transformation process Thibaut and Kelley describe is similar to the reframing that Watzlawick considers the only hope for dysfunctional family systems (see Chapter 15).

Figure 16.4 shows a prisoner's dilemma transformation that regards good things happening to the other man as of equal value to benefits for self. Systems theorists would say that the individuals have redefined the system so that it now includes the other person. The subjective shift to joint outcomes clearly makes stonewalling the desirable choice. The men no longer face a dilemma. Although there's no evidence that either Smith or Hickock added their partner's rewards into their own benefit mix, some close friends and lovers obviously do.

The revised theory sketches other transformations that people use to resolve interpersonal conflict and reduce the inner agony of making hard decisions. An altruistic strategy flip-flops the payoffs within a given cell. If Hickock claims sole responsibility for the crimes, Smith can go free. A concern for justice prefers equal prison terms of whatever length over differential treatment. A competitive mind-set places a premium on getting a personal outcome as good or better than the other killer. ("I'd rather we both hang than you get off easier than me.") Truman Capote reports that this was Hickock's thinking at the time he confessed, and both men did hang.

The field of interpersonal influence has a long tradition of studying group norms. Norms are the stated and implicit rules of a group that identify the range of acceptable behavior. Often couched in moral terms, these principles provide a basis for action when the situation is confusing. Social exchange theory describes norms as socially rewarded transformations aimed at curbing the use of raw power. The language of prison reveals that there is indeed an enforced honor among thieves. Labels of "cheat," "fink," or "snitch" add to the cost of squealing on a buddy, so the classic prisoner's dilemma looks different from within the walls.

Another set of moral transformations comes into play when people deal with each other over time. For example, parents promote a turn-taking norm as a way to reduce conflict among their children. Children who adopt this stance do so in the hope that it will work to their advantage in the long run. For Smith and Hickock, this was not an option; they had only one chance to resolve their prisoner's dilemma.

CRITIQUE: WEIGHING THE OUTCOMES OF SOCIAL EXCHANGE THEORY

Thibaut and Kelley's social exchange theory is an ambitious attempt to quantify and calculate the friction of interdependence. Altman and Taylor's wholesale use of the reward-cost analysis for social penetration theory (see Chapter 13) shows the value of the exchange approach. Yet some students regard mathematical models of human interaction as foreign territory. They balk when asked to cross the borders of the outcome matrix and work through the numbers of comparison levels, transformations, and fate control. They could avoid culture shock by first immersing themselves in the theory's rich description of power.

But even those who appreciate Thibaut and Kelley's technical analysis must ask hard questions about the theory's basic assumptions: Can a complex blend of advantages and disadvantages be reliably reduced to a single number? Do individuals respond so selfishly that they always opt to do what they calculate is in their own best interest? Are the suggested transformations testable refinements of a solid theory, or are they just shotgun attempts to salvage faulty hypotheses?

Although negative answers would cast doubt on the theory's validity, the research findings stimulated by the social exchange approach offer helpful insights on conflict resolution. In prisoner's dilemma situations, for example, the chance to communicate increases cooperation dramatically. A single play presents greater temptation to zap a partner than does continual interdependence. Once trust is broken, it's hard to restore joint collaboration.

Research confirms that there are different reasons for noncooperation. People with a competitive mind-set regard the prisoner's dilemma as a chance to take advantage of a weaker opponent. Folks with a high need for affiliation fear that others will exploit them, so they adopt a defensive strategy. The end result is the same—an unwinable war. The ironic conclusion is that pursuit of selfish interest provides fewer personal benefits than does a concern for the general welfare. That insight alone makes social exchange theory attractive. For all but the most severe critic, the outcome exceeds the comparison level.

QUESTIONS TO SHARPEN YOUR FOCUS

1. Many people refer to social exchange theory as *game theory*. In what ways does a game metaphor seem to fit the ideas of Thibaut and Kelley?

2. Suppose you are caught using Velcro on the back of your campus parking permit so it can be transferred to other cars. You could get a warning, a $20 fine, or have your permit revoked. In the end, on what will your *happiness* depend?

3. The theory talks about *reflexive control, fate control,* and *behavior control.* If you could have power in only one of these areas, which kind would you want?

4. "There is no greater love than this: to lay down one's life for one's friends."[2] Given the *minimax principle* of human behavior, how is such a sacrifice possible?

A SECOND LOOK

Recommended resource: Harold H. Kelley and John W. Thibaut, *Interpersonal Relationships*, John Wiley & Sons, New York, 1978.

Original statement: John W. Thibaut and Harold H. Kelley, *The Social Psychology of Groups*, John Wiley & Sons, New York, 1959.

Theory revision: Harold H. Kelley, *Personal Relationships: Their Structures and Processes*, Lawrence Erlbaum Associates, Hillside, N.J., 1979.

Prisoner's dilemma: Anatole Rapoport and Albert Chammah, *Prisoner's Dilemma*, University of Michigan, Ann Arbor, 1965.

Real-life conflict: Truman Capote, *In Cold Blood*, Random House, New York, 1965.

Integration with other exchange theories: Richard M. Emerson, "Social Exchange Theory," *American Sociological Review*, Vol. 35, 1976, pp. 335–362.

Conflict from an exchange perspective: Michael E. Roloff, *Interpersonal Communication: The Social Exchange Approach*, Sage, Beverly Hills, Calif., 1981, pp. 87–114.

Transformations: Victor M. H. Borden and George Levinger, "Interpersonal Transformations in Intimate Relationships," in *Advances in Personal Relationships*, Vol. 2, Warren Jones and Daniel Perlman (eds.), Jessica Kingsley, London, 1991, pp. 35–56.

simple, but it means so much more when I do this." Sarah then closes together the thumb and forefinger of each hand to form interlocking links of a chain and continues:

> Now it means to be joined in a relationship—separate, but one. That's what I want. But you think for me—think for Sarah—as though there were no "I." "She will be with me, quit her job, learn how to play poker, leave Orin's party, learn how to speak." That's all *you*, not me. Until you let me be an "I" the way you are, you can never come inside my silence and know me. And I won't let myself know you. Until that time, we can't be like this—joined.

2. Predictability/Novelty (Internal Dialectic of Stability/Change)

Berger's uncertainty reduction theory makes a strong case for the idea that people want predictability in their relationships (see Chapter 14). Baxter doesn't question this human search for certainty, but she's convinced that Berger makes a mistake by ignoring our opposing desire for novelty. We want at least a little mystery, a bit of spontaneity, a touch of surprise from our partner. Without the spice of variety to season our time together, the relationship becomes bland, boring, and ultimately, emotionally dead.

The dialectic of predictability/novelty weaves through Sarah and James' relationship. As she admits at the end of the film, Sarah constantly uses her anger to push James away. When this doesn't work, she withdraws from the conversation. The emotional distance is safe and predictable. We see this recurring hit-and-run tactic when James, in street clothes, crouches down at the edge of a swimming pool and begins to declare his love to Sarah, who is in the water. She quickly kicks away from the side of the pool. But the patterned interaction takes a novel twist when James loses his balance as he imploringly says, "Sarah, I think I'm falling in lo—, into the pool with you." His unexpected entry into the water breaks through her defenses and she swims to him for their first kiss.

Not all surprises are welcome. As the love relationship between James and Sarah deepens, he promises he will never ask her to speak. Yet in a moment of passion, he begs her just once to say his name. Despite his protest that the plea "just came out," this sudden request shatters a comfortable routine. In this case Sarah desires predictability, whereas James wants novelty. Throughout much of the film their desire are the other way around, but the dialectic is continually present.

3. Openness/Closedness (Internal Dialectic of Expression/Privacy)

Halfway through *Children of a Lesser God*, James asks Sarah, "What do you hear? I mean, is it just silence?" Sarah's response indicates the depth of her isolation, "No one has ever gotten in there to find out." James then asks if she will ever let him in, but his question is met only with stillness—Sarah's silence. From this scene we might conclude that Sarah is simply an extremely private person; yet earlier in the film she had openly revealed the humiliating details of adolescent sexual encounters. The two scenes seem contradictory.

You might recall that Irwin Altman, one of the founders of social penetration theory, ultimately came to the conclusion that self-disclosure and privacy operated in a cyclical or wavelike fashion over time.[6] Baxter picks up on Altman's recognition that relationships aren't on a straight-line path to intimacy. She sees the pressures for openness and closedness waxing and waning like phases of the moon. Her dialectical perspective suggests that a person's need to "tell all" is countered by a natural desire for secrecy. If Sarah's communication seems somewhat schizophrenic, it's because the dialectical forces for transparency and discretion are hard to balance.

4. Revelation/Concealment (External Dialectic of Expression/Privacy)

Just as the contradiction between autonomy and connection is the central tension a couple confronts within their relationship, the decision about what to tell others is the fundamental dilemma partners face with their social networks. Baxter notes that each of the possible advantages of "going public" is offset by corresponding potential dangers.

1. Approval from significant others could legitimize the relationship, but there's no guarantee their support will be forthcoming.
2. Partners get an added pleasure from confiding their joy with friends and family, but those hearing the news may be indiscreet and gossip with others.
3. The act of sharing with another may strengthen ties with that confidant, but he or she could feel jealous of the new relationship.
4. Public disclosure is a relational rite of passage signaling a partner that the tie that binds them together is strong. But this kind of reassurance comes at the cost of privacy—a nonrecurring resource that gives a couple some breathing room to work out problems.

Aware that strategic management of their "public relations" is a crucial matter, most couples mete out information bit by bit to carefully selected friends. But occasionally news of their bond "leaks out" through nonverbal behavior. This happened with James and Sarah. Mr. Franklin, the school's director, sees James running barefoot from Sarah's apartment. Franklin conveys his knowledge of the romance when he later returns James' shoe—retrieved from the bottom of the swimming pool. The only verbal acknowledgment that either man gives of this new state of affairs is Franklin's indirect warning, "Be careful, Jimbo."

At a later date James declares to Franklin, "It's Sarah and me! I love her." He also broadcasts the relationship by bringing Sarah to a faculty party at the director's house. But his early attempts to hide his love for Sarah reflect the conceal-reveal tension that Baxter calls the "dialectical linchpin" of a couple's link with the outside world.

5. Conventionality/Uniqueness (External Dialectic of Stability/Change)

The school where James teaches discourages innovation. During the employment interview the headmaster warns James that no one there is trying to change the world. The message is clear—go along to get along.

Baxter notes that society has a stake in seeing its relational patterns reproduced. Excessive uniqueness makes others feel uncomfortable. But pressure to conform is only one force a couple feels. Since a carbon-copy relationship doesn't provide the sense of uniqueness necessary for intimacy, a close pair also experiences a pressure to be different. Here again, the couple is caught in a dilemma.

James ignores the headmaster's advice to conform. His love affair with Sarah is anything but conventional. He is "normal"; she cannot hear and does not speak. He's a trained professional; she scrubs floors. The couple argue often and their confrontations are punctuated with obscene gestures. They don't "fit in." Yet even in the midst of their maverick relationship, James assumes that he and Sarah will enact traditional roles. They will marry and have children; she will quit her job; he will take care of her. The contradictory forces of conventionality and uniqueness are always at work.

6. Inclusion/Seclusion (External Dialectic of Integration/Separation)

According to Baxter, a couple needs an abundance of privacy until the two parties have worked out a unique code of meanings and the relationship has jelled. In American culture, deliberate exclusion of outsiders is an act that crystallizes the pair as a social unit. But even for the most devoted partners, tolerance for isolation wears thin after a while. Other people can be a source of stimulation to overcome the ho-hum predictability which settles in on a secluded pair. Third parties can also provide the social support that legitimatizes the relationship of friends or lovers.

In *Children of a Lesser God,* Sarah and James spend almost all their free time alone with each other. Attempts to integrate their dyadic subculture with larger social networks turn out to be dismal flops. Sarah is patronized by the faculty at the headmaster's poker party. She also feels alienated from James' students who are learning to talk. James feels equally left out in the frantic silence of signing at a reception where all the guests are deaf. He peevishly blows across the top of a Coke bottle just to hear a sound. James and Sarah's fictional relationship is still fresh when the film ends, but the couple's inability to work out a balance between inclusion and seclusion with outsiders doesn't bode well for the future of their relationship.

STRATEGIES FOR COPING WITH DIALECTICAL TENSIONS

Confronted with the ongoing contradictions cited above, how is it that some close relationships manage to survive and, in a few instances, thrive? Baxter suggests six fundamental strategies that people use in order to cope with the opposing pressures that come with the relational territory. As you will see, some of the strategies are used more often than others and not all prove equally satisfying.

1. Selection is the strategy of continually responding to one pole of a dialectic while ignoring the other. For example, throughout much of the film, Sarah opts for autonomy over connection, closedness instead of open expression, and novelty in lieu of predictability. Sarah isn't necessarily pleased with the choices she's made, and in this she is similar to many who try to avoid contradiction by giving in to one pull over the other. In an in-depth study of more than 100 people in romantic relationships, Baxter discovered that parties who used selection strategies were often dissatisfied with how they handled the tension between autonomy and connection with their partner.[7]

2. Cyclic alternation between contrasting poles is the process of separating the dialectical forces over time by responding to one pull now, the other pull later. According to Baxter, this first-one-then-the-other strategy is the predominant response of partners to the autonomy-connection paradox. The wavelike pattern certainly describes James' efforts to connect with Sarah. His moves to draw close emotionally and physically are interspersed with fierce arguments or solitary retreats into music that only he can hear. These times of autonomy end with an apology, and then a new cycle of connection-seeking behavior begins.

3. Segmentation is a separation tactic by which partners compartmentalize different aspects of their relationship. Some issues and activities resonate with one dialectical tug, while other concerns and actions resonate with the opposing pull. Sarah, for example, is transparent with James about her history with boys and her feelings of anger, but her reason for avoiding speech is a topic that is taboo in their relationship.[8] Baxter found that segmentation is the predominant strategy individuals use to handle the openness/closedness and novelty/predictability contradictions. Couples who segment their lives by injecting novelty into a predictable (committed) relationship report greater satisfaction than those who deal with the dialectic of change through selection or cyclic alteration.

4. Moderation is a compromise approach that seeks to neutralize or buffer the full force of each dialectical pole. For example, James tries to deal with the openness/closedness dilemma through small talk with Sarah the first few times they meet. She won't play the moderation game, so he abandons the attempt. The couples Baxter surveyed report very few instances of strategic moderation, but that may be because downplaying conflict comes so naturally that they weren't even aware they did it.

5. Disqualification is Baxter's term for indirect or equivocal communication which seeks to defuse or ignore the full force of contradiction. Recall that Janet Bavelas recommended strategic ambiguity when people were in a no-win situation (see Chapter 4). While walking with Sarah, James deflects a serious question from her with a humorous comment. She stops and signs,

"You can't communicate with someone when your mind is busy amusing yourself." He sheepishly admits, "You're right, I'm sorry." James obviously felt bad that he dodged the issue, but Baxter thinks that intentional vagueness can be a wonderfully adaptive strategy when a person is caught in the double bind of conflicting expectations. Not many of her respondents recalled instances of disqualification, but like James, those who did seemed less than satisfied over how they had dealt with the internal dilemma of expression.

6. Reframing is an effort to redefine the contradiction in a way that the two opposing forces are no longer regarded as opposites. Consistent with Watzlawick's theory of reframing (see Chapter 15) and Thibaut and Kelley's parallel notion of "transformation" (see Chapter 16), Baxter's findings indicate that pairs who use this strategy are more satisfied with their relationship. Unfortunately, they are also rare. Since only a few people in her study mentioned reframing, Baxter offers some examples of how creative redefinition might take place. A "traditional" married couple might redefine their relationship as unique because they've stayed together for thirty-two years. Or a man might reframe a boring visit with his wife's relatives as an occasion for autonomy. ("Being with her people is a sacrifice I choose to make.")

The final scene in *Children of a Lesser God* shows Sarah reunited with James, yet wanting to reframe their relationship. She asks, "Do you think we could find a place where we can meet—not in silence, and not in sound?" From Leslie Baxter's dialectical perspective, the answer is in doubt. Even if the couple were to find such a place, other contradictions would intrude. That's why relationships are continually in flux. Hollywood might offer the impression that James and Sarah "lived happily ever after," but a true-to-life tag line for their story might read, "and the struggle continues." That realistic assessment might sound discouraging. Yet when we appreciate the fact that healthy relationships need both autonomy and connection, novelty and predictability, closeness and openness, a guarantee of ongoing dialectical work seems more like a promise than a threat.

CRITIQUE: PROBLEMS IN DETERMINING DILEMMAS

Baxter describes the strategy of reframing contradictions as a sophisticated and complex effort, one not fully appreciated by parties early in their relational development. The same comments apply to her dialectical perspective. Most scholars who have studied personal relationships for a number of years are no longer comfortable singling out self-disclosure, reduction of uncertainty, or predicted outcome value as the key variable of interpersonal dynamics. A dialectical model of close relationships provides an appealing alternative to the simplistic input-output logic of other theories.

Perhaps relational investigators have been slow to recognize dialectical pressures because most research techniques lack the capacity to spot contradictions. Consider, for example, the typical unidimensional attitude scale that asks a person to provide a single response:

What do you want from your partner?

Intimacy   : ____ : ____ : ____ : ____ : ____ : ____ : ____ :   Independence

Most researchers would interpret a midscale response as the mark of a person who is undecided or has no opinion. Yet he or she may feel anything but wishy-washy on the issue. As virtually every relational theorist taking a dialectical perspective would point out, the respondent might crave intimacy *and* independence, yet have no way to register these dual desires on a forced-choice scale. Unless the question provides the option of simultaneously marking an X at each end of the scale, the ongoing dialectical tension will remain hidden from view.

Does Baxter's theory correctly identify the specific contradictions that are inherent in close relationships? Are the arenas of integration/separation, stability/change, and expression/privacy the main sites of stress where the push-pull of dynamic tensions are played out? The question is worrisome because other dialectical theorists generate different lists of opposing forces. For example, William Rawlins, a Purdue University researcher who examines communication among best friends, fails to spot a novelty-predictability contradiction. He does, however, find a judgment-acceptance paradox. Perhaps this difference is due solely to the fact that Rawlins studies friendships while Baxter concentrates on romantic relationships, but in this early stage of dialectical research, there are contradictions among theorists as to what the relational contradictions actually are.

From Baxter's perspective, knowing the exact content of the relational struggle is less important than recognizing the fact that the struggle goes on. She gets discouraged when professionals imply that healthy relationships are the result of nothing but self-disclosure, assertiveness, uncertainty reduction, empathic listening, or any other single communication variable. That kind of tunnel vision fails to credit the tremendous achievement of couples who survive and thrive in the ongoing dialectical tensions of human existence.

QUESTIONS TO SHARPEN YOUR FOCUS

1. How many different synonyms and terms can you list that capture what Baxter means by the word *dialectic?*

2. Which dialectic does Baxter see as the primary strain within the relationship? Which one does she see as fundamental to a couple's relationship with others?

3. Which of the thirteen theories already discussed would Baxter consider *simplistic* or *antidialectical?*

4. Do you regard Baxter's dialectical perspective as a *scientific* or a *humanistic* theory? Why?

A SECOND LOOK

Recommended resource: Leslie A. Baxter, "A Dialectical Perspective on Communication Strategies in Relationship Development," in *A Handbook of Personal Relationships*, Steve Duck (ed.), John Wiley & Sons, New York, 1988, pp. 257–273.

Relationship maintenance: Leslie A. Baxter, "A Dialogic Approach to Relationship Maintenance," in *Communication and Relational Maintenance*, D. J. Canary and L. Stafford (eds.), Academic Press, San Diego, Calif., 1993.

Relationships in flux: Richard Conville, *Relational Transitions*, Praeger, New York, 1991.

Relational implications of Bakhtin's worldview: Leslie A. Baxter, "Thinking Dialogically about Communication in Personal Relationships," in *Structure in Human Communication*, Richard L. Conville (ed.), Greenwood Publishing Group, Westport, Conn., 1994.

Study of people in romantic relationships: Leslie A. Baxter, "Dialectical Contradictions in Relationship Development," *Journal of Social and Personal Relationships*, Vol. 7, 1990, pp. 69–88.

Autonomy vs. connection: Barbara Montgomery, "Communication as the Interface between Couples and Culture," in *Communication Yearbook 15*, Stanley Deetz (ed.), Sage, Newbury Park, Calif., 1992, pp. 475–507.

Dialectical tensions with external parties: Leslie A. Baxter, "The Social Side of Personal Relationships: A Dialectical Perspective," in *Social Context and Relationship*, Vol. 3, Steve Duck (ed.), Sage, Newbury Park, Calif., 1993.

Friendship dialectics: William Rawlins, *Friendship Matters: Communication, Dialectics, and the Life Course*, Aldine de Gruyter, New York, 1992.

INFLUENCE

We live in a world of intentional interpersonal influence. It's hard to walk through the day without having two or three people try to persuade you to spend time, energy, or money on something they value. Communication theorists ignore attempts that rely on brute force. There is, however, an active group of researchers who are concerned solely with changes in outward behavior. They study the verbal strategies people use to elicit compliance to their wishes.[1]

Studies of compliance-gaining strategies usually ask people to imagine being in an uncomfortable interpersonal situation—the guy next door is hosting a wild midnight party, your roommate's guest has already stayed a week, you need to borrow a car from someone you barely know. The researcher then asks you what tactics you would use to get the other person to do what you want. Typically, you would be asked to rank a predetermined list of compliance-gaining strategies—promises, threats, explanations, hints, compliments, warnings, accusations, direct requests, and so forth.

Advocates of compliance-gaining inquiry stress the importance of finding out what verbal strategies people actually use, rather than focusing on what they might do or could say to achieve their goal. Although the studies provide rich descriptive data, to this point they haven't been theory-based. There has been little explanation of why people select the tactics they do, prediction of what they would do next time, evaluations of how well the tactics work, or concern with application to other situations.

In contrast with the effort to catalogue compliance-gaining strategies, most persuasion theorists focus on voluntary shifts in attitude that come in response to verbal messages. Attitudes are internal responses made up of what people think, feel, and intend to do. Since attitudes can be known only through self-report, researchers often end up asking lots of questions:

"What do you honestly believe?" (*Cognitive*)

"Is your heart really in it?" (*Affective*)

"What do you plan to do?" (*Behavioral*)

For many years attitude theorists defined the combined answers as a person's "predisposition to respond." But the marginal relationship between stated opinion and subsequent behavior has proved a continual embarrassment for those who claim that attitudes predict actions.

Richard Petty and John Cacioppo group theories of attitude change into seven major approaches:[2]

1. Conditioning and Modeling. Approaches that assume people seek to "maximize their benefits and minimize their costs." Persuasion is successful when people vicariously observe or directly experience rewards for "right" opinions and behavior. Social exchange theory (see Chapter 16) and social learning theory (see Chapter 31) operate within this framework.

2. Message-Learning. Approaches that place a premium on the content of persuasion. Lasting influence depends on attention, comprehension, and retention of messages.

3. Perceptual-judgmental. Approaches that are less concerned with what a message states than how it is interpreted by the person who hears it. The same message can strike two people as radically different. Chap-

Drawing by Booth; © 1977 The New Yorker Magazine, Inc.

ter 18 presents Sherif, Sherif, and Nebergall's social judgment theory. It examines the effect of different amounts of discrepancy between the position advocated and the stand of the recipient.

4. Motivational. Approaches that focus on needs as forces for change. We've already considered Maslow's hierarchy as an umbrella theory of human motivation, but persuasion scholars concentrate on the need for consistency as a stimulus to attitude change. Chapter 19 outlines Leon Festinger's theory of cognitive dissonance, which predicts the specialized circumstances under which attitudes shift to line up with behavior.

5. Attributional. Approaches that stress the power of self-fulfilling prophecy. Rather than raise resistance by pointing out a lack or failing in the other person, the advocate affirms the existence of the desired attitude as if it were already firmly in place.

6. Combinatory. Approaches that consider the way new ideas are weighted and averaged into previously held beliefs. These theories employ precise mathematical models to describe the way information is processed.

7. Self-Persuasion. Approaches that regard self-generated arguments as more potent agents of change than any external message. The process can be triggered by role-playing, by active involvement in a cause, or merely by wrestling with ideas that are linked to the attitude.

Despite the fact that some of these approaches offer conflicting explanations for changes in attitude, no one set of theories has emerged as the best way to view the persuasion process. Petty and Cacioppo's elaboration-likelihood model attempts to pull together the wisdom found in each school of thought. They see two distinct routes to attitude change. The central route involves active consideration of message content; the peripheral route uses the credibility of the message source and other persuasion cues to determine response. Petty and Cacioppo's model explores the likelihood that people will use the central route. Chapter 20 presents their theory.

CHAPTER 18

Social Judgment Theory
of Muzafer Sherif

My son Jim is an airline pilot. As he walks through the airport he hears all sorts of comments about air safety. I've listed below eleven statements that reflect the range of attitudes he has heard expressed. Read through these opinions, and taste the diversity of viewpoint they represent.

1. Air traffic controllers are overworked.
2. All life is risk. Flying is like anything else.
3. Complex jet planes are disasters waiting to happen.
4. The crowded skies are a myth.
5. Flying is safer than taking a train.
6. Many pilots are flying while they are under the influence of alcohol.
7. The most dangerous part of flying is the drive to the airport.
8. Most mistakes are fatal at 30,000 feet.
9. There are old pilots. There are bold pilots. There are no old, bold pilots.
10. American pilots are the best-trained in the world.
11. United States government regulations ensure well-maintained airplanes.

Take a few minutes to mark your reactions to these statements. If you follow each instruction given below before jumping ahead to the next one, you'll have a chance to experience what social judgment theory predicts.

1. To begin, read through the items again and underline the single statement that most closely represents your point of view.
2. Now look back and see whether any other items seem reasonable. Circle the numbers in front of these acceptable statements.
3. Reread the opinions and determine the one that strikes you as most objectionable. Run a line through the whole sentence.
4. Finally, cross out the numbers in front of any other statements that

are objectionable to you. By crossing out these unreasonable ideas, it's possible that all eleven statements will end up marked one way or another. It's also possible that you'll leave some items unmarked.

ATTITUDES AS LATITUDES: ACCEPTANCE, REJECTION, AND NONCOMMITMENT

I've just taken you through on paper what social judgment theory says happens in the head. We hear a message and immediately judge where it should be placed on the attitude scale in our mind. According to Carolyn Sherif, Muzafer Sherif, and Roger Nebergall, this subconscious sorting out of ideas occurs at the instant of perception. We weigh every new idea by comparing it with our present point of view. They call their analysis of attitudes "the social judgment-involvement approach," but most scholars refer to it simply as "social judgment theory." Although Carolyn Sherif is the first author of the book describing the process, it is commonly acknowledged that her husband took the lead in the theory's development and testing.

A psychologist who was associated with the University of Oklahoma, Muzafer Sherif had already published two landmark studies demonstrating how individuals are influenced by reference groups, groups that members use to define their identity. His "robber's cave" study explored intergroup conflict; his "autokinetic effect" research stimulated scores of later studies analyzing conformity pressure. Both studies found that people's perceptions are altered dramatically by group membership. Social judgment theory extended his concern with perception to the field of persuasion.

Sherif believed that each of the four steps listed above is necessary to determine your attitude toward airline safety. He wrote that an "individual's stand is not represented adequately as a point along a continuum. Different persons espousing the same position may differ considerably in their tolerance around this point."[1]

He saw an attitude as an amalgam of three zones. The first zone is called the "latitude of acceptance." It's made up of the item you underlined and any others you circled as acceptable. A second zone is the "latitude of rejection." It consists of the opinions you crossed out as objectionable. The leftover statements, if any, define the "latitude of noncommitment." These were the items that you found neither objectionable nor acceptable. They're akin to marking "undecided" or "no opinion" on a traditional survey.

Suppose Jim encounters a man named Ned who is grumbling in the airport about the dangers of flight. Jim wants to persuade Ned that flying is safer than sleeping in his own bed. Social judgment theory recommends that he try to figure out the breadth and location of Ned's three latitudes before presenting his case. Figure 18.1 shows where Ned places those eleven statements along the mental yardstick he uses to gauge safety. Armed with knowledge about the location and breadth of the three latitudes, my son

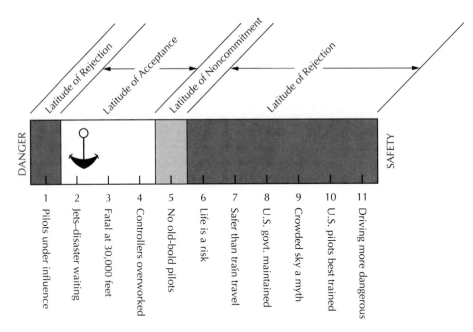

FIGURE 18.1
Sample Cognitive Map Concerning Air Safety

would realize that Ned's high ego-involvement in the topic of air safety will cause him to twist any words of reassurance.

THE CERTAINTY OF THOSE WHO CARE

The theory predicts that the higher Ned's ego-involvement, the harder it will be to persuade him to change his position. Ego-involvement refers to how crucial the issue is in his life. Is it important? Is it central to his well-being? Does he think about it, dream about it, stew over it? Some folks walking through Concourse A are mere visitors. Perhaps they're simply eating at the airport restaurant, meeting Aunt June's plane, or picking up a suitcase for a friend. They are for safety and against crashes, but it's not their major concern. They have low ego-involvement.

For others the issue is central. As frequent flyers, they swap horror stories with fellow travelers of near misses, read accounts of accidents in the newspaper, and break into a cold sweat when they recall a rough landing on a foggy night. People who fit this profile are highly ego-involved. Some even join an airline passenger association that lobbies Congress for stricter regulations concerning air safety. Sherif formally defined high ego-involvement as "membership in a group with a known stand."

Ned's mental profile shows high ego-involvement. The first indication is that his latitude of noncommitment is almost nonexistent. Sherif regarded a wide latitude of noncommitment as a reliable sign of low ego-involvement, but Ned has only one statement in that category. He may not be sure about old, bold pilots, but he has definite opinions on everything else. He sees safety as a black-and-white issue. Persons with low ego-involvement see more grays.

Note Ned's extended latitude of rejection. There's a solid band on the safety side that spans over six gradations of opinion. A wide latitude of rejection is a sign of high ego-involvement. Ned cares. He has intense feelings about the potential dangers of flying.

The statement he agreed with most (jets are disasters waiting to happen) is marked with an anchor. Sherif said that's what our favored position does; it anchors all our other beliefs. If air safety were only a casual concern for Ned, it would be fitting to represent his stand with a small anchor that could easily be dragged to a new position. But since his fear of flying is great, a hefty anchor is more appropriate.

Although people can feel passionately about middle-of-the-road positions, the theory states that massive attitude anchors are usually found toward the ends of the scale. Extreme positions and high ego-involvement go together. That's why religion, sex, and politics are taboo topics in the wardroom of a U.S. Navy ship at sea. When passions run deep, radical opinions are common and there's little room for diversity.

CONTRAST: DISTANCING THE MESSAGE

The term *social judgment-involvement* describes the linkage that Sherif saw between perception and ego-involvement. Highly committed people have large latitudes of rejection. Any message which falls within that range will be perceived by them as more discrepant from their anchor than it really is. Sherif called this process "contrast." The message is mentally pushed away to a position that is farther out, and the hearer doesn't have to deal with it as a viable option worthy of consideration.

All of this is bad news for Jim. Suppose he walks up to Ned and calmly explains that the crowded skies are a myth. On his last five flights he's never seen another plane, much less had to dodge one. If Ned hears it correctly, that message is a 9 on his mental scale.

Social judgment theory says he probably won't hear it right. Unless a speaker is crystal clear, the contrast effect telescopes all unacceptable positions and pushes them farther away. Jim's supposedly reassuring words of ample separation between aircraft will register at a 10 or 11 rather than a 9. The theory then warns that any time a message falls within our latitude of rejection, we'll react negatively. The more extreme it seems, the more we'll shift in the opposite direction. Despite Jim's well-intentioned effort, his words will strike nervous Ned as self-serving propaganda and the fearful flyer will end up at a 2, even more skeptical.

"I'm happy to say that my final judgment of a case is almost always consistent with my prejudgment of the case."

Drawing by Dana Fraden; © 1973 The New Yorker Magazine, Inc.

ASSIMILATION: EMBRACING THE MESSAGE

Jim might have used perceptual distortion to his advantage. Sherif described a process of "assimilation," which is the exact opposite of contrast. It's the rubber band effect that draws an idea toward the hearer's anchor so that it seems to be almost his or her opinion. Assimilation takes place when a message falls within the latitude of acceptance.

Suppose Jim tells Ned that air traffic controllers are overworked. Although that message is at 4 on Ned's cognitive map, he will hear it as more similar to his anchoring attitude than it really is, perhaps a 3. Sherif predicted that Ned would then shift his stance in the direction of Jim's message, maybe ending up at 2.25. Persuasion has occurred.

Sherif reduced interpersonal influence to the issue of the distance between the message and the hearer's position:

Stripped to its bare essential, the problem of attitude change is the problem of the degree of discrepancy from communication and the felt necessity of coping with the discrepancy.[2]

The greater the discrepancy, the more hearers will adjust their attitudes *as long as the message is within their latitude of acceptance*. But people feel no compulsion to respond to messages in their latitude of rejection. They may even be turned off by the persuasive attempt and end up more opposed to the idea than they were originally.

PRACTICAL ADVICE FOR THE PERSUADER

Sherif would have advised Jim to avoid messages that claim flying is safer than driving or train travel. Ned simply won't believe them, and they may push him even deeper into his antiaviation stance. For maximum influence, Jim should select a message that's right on the edge of Ned's latitude of acceptance. Admit that radar operators are overworked, but stress the care pilots take to compensate for possible controller mistakes. Or use the statement about the old, bold pilot, showing him how the airline systematically screens out daredevils. According to social judgment theory, this strategy will result in a small amount of positive persuasion.

Jim wants more. But Sherif would have cautioned that it's all Jim can get in a one-shot attempt. If he were talking to an open-minded person with a broad latitude of acceptance, a bigger shift would be possible. But when he's dealing with a highly ego-involved traveler, he has to work within a narrow range. True conversion from one end of the scale to the other is a rare phenomenon. The only way to get large-scale change is through a series of small, successive movements. Persuasion is a gradual process.

It's also a social process. The lack of interpersonal bond between Jim and Ned limits the amount of influence that's possible. If Ned heard strong reassurances of airline safety from his friends and family, it might occasion a major shift. Sherif noted that "most dramatic cases of attitude change, the most widespread and enduring, are those involving changes in reference groups with differing values."[3]

EVIDENCE THAT ARGUES FOR ACCEPTANCE

Research on the predictions of social judgment theory requires a highly ego-involving issue. One fascinating study employed a topic vitally important to college students—sleep.[4] Before the study most of the undergraduates accepted the conventional wisdom that the human body functions best with eight hours of sleep a night. They read an article written by an expert in the field that claimed young adults actually need much less. The message was the same for all with one crucial difference. Some students were told they needed eight hours, some seven, some six, and so on, right down the line. The final group actually read that humans need no sleep at all! They then had a chance to give their opinion.

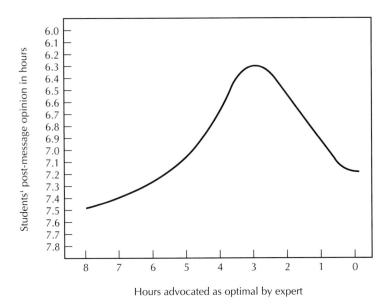

FIGURE 18.2

Sleep Study Results (Adapted from Bochner and Insko, "Communicator Discrepancy, Source Credibility and Opinion Change.)"

Sherif's theory suggests that the fewer hours recommended, the more students will be swayed until they begin to regard the message as patently ridiculous. The results shown in Figure 18.2 confirm this prediction. Persuasion increased as the hours advocated were reduced to three, a message which caused students to revise their estimate of optimum sleep down to 6.3 hours. Anything less than three hours fell outside their latitude of acceptance and ceased to be as effective.

Three things have become clear as the theory has been tested:

1. A highly credible speaker can stretch the hearer's latitude of acceptance. When the "expert" in the sleep study was a Nobel Prize-winning physiologist rather than a YMCA director, persuasion increased.

2. Ambiguity can often serve better than clarity. When Jimmy Carter ran for the presidency he said, "I want a government as good as the people who support it." Nobody knew exactly what he meant, so the statement fell within their latitude of acceptance. George Bush's somewhat vague reference to a "kinder, gentler nation" seemed to have the same beneficial effect.

3. There are some people who are dogmatic on every issue. "Don't confuse me with the facts," they say. "My mind is made up." These cantankerous souls have a chronically wide latitude of rejection.

My favorite applied social judgment story comes from a university development director I know who was making a call on a rich alumnus. He anticipated that the prospective donor would give as much as $10,000. He made his pitch and asked what the wealthy businessman could do. The man protested that it had been a lean year and that times were tough—he couldn't possibly contribute more than $20,000. The fund-raiser figured that he had seriously underestimated the giver's latitude of acceptance and that $20,000 was on the low end of that range. Without missing a beat he replied, "Trevor, do you really think that's enough?" The alumnus wrote a check for $25,000.

CRITIQUE: HOW WIDE IS YOUR LATITUDE OF ACCEPTANCE?

How do you feel about the fund-raising ploy described above? It obviously worked, but the application of social judgment theory raises some ethical questions. Is it legitimate for politicians to be intentionally vague so they can appeal to everyone? Or consider my son's worthy desire to allay the fears of the flying public. The theory claims Jim will be more effective by presenting a soft-sell message at midscale rather than stating his sincere conviction that flying is safer than driving. Is this honest?

There are two nonmoral problems you need to ponder as well. The first has to do with validity. Social judgment theory predicts an attitudinal backlash when the message falls deep within the latitude of rejection. Most research, including the sleep study, fails to find it. The radical claim that we need never sleep continued to have a positive, although diminished, impact. The second problem has to do with practical application. How can we know where the three latitudes fall for another person? That's what audience analysis and market research is all about, but it's hard to imagine Jim handing Ned a questionnaire in the departure lounge.

Despite these drawbacks, social judgment theory is an elegant conception of the persuasion process. There's an intuitive appeal to the idea of crafting a message that's positioned right at the edge of the listener's latitude of acceptance in order to be as effectively discrepant as possible. That's my recommendation to Jim as he confronts a variety of air travelers. I wonder in which of his three latitudes my fatherly advice will fall.

QUESTIONS TO SHARPEN YOUR FOCUS

1. How does the concept of *attitudes as latitudes* help you understand your attitude toward the various requirements of this course?

2. Suppose you find out that the fellow sitting next to you is *highly ego-involved* in the issue of gun control. Based on social judgment theory, what are three predictions about him that you might reasonably make?

3. What practical advice does social judgment theory offer to you if you want to ask your boss for a raise?

4. Do you have any *ethical qualms* about applying the wisdom of social judgment theory? Why or why not?

A SECOND LOOK

Recommended resource: C. Kiesler, B. Collins, and N. Miller, *Attitude Change*, John Wiley & Sons, New York, 1969, Chapter 6, pp. 238–301.

Original conception: Carolyn Sherif, Muzafer Sherif, and Roger Nebergall, *Attitude and Attitude Change: The Social Judgment-Involvement Approach*, W. B. Saunders, Philadelphia, 1965.

Theory update: D. Granberg, "Social Judgment Theory," in *Communication Yearbook 6*, M. Burgoon (ed.), Sage, Beverly Hills, Calif.,1982, pp. 304–329.

Ego-involvement: W. W. Wilmot, "Ego-Involvement: A Confusing Variable in Speech Communication Research," *Quarterly Journal of Speech*, Vol. 57, 1971, pp. 429–436.

Attitudes as latitudes: Kenneth Sereno and Edward Bodaken, "Ego-Involvement and Attitude Change: Toward a Reconceptualization of Persuasive Effect," *Speech Monographs*, Vol. 39, 1972, pp. 151–158.

Sleep study: S. Bochner and C. Insko, "Communicator Discrepancy, Source Credibility and Opinion Change," *Journal of Personality and Social Psychology*, Vol. 4, 1966, pp. 614–621.

Robber's cave study: Muzafer Sherif, "Experiments in Group Conflict," *Scientific American*, Vol. 195, 1956, pp. 54–58.

Autokinetic effect study: Muzafer Sherif and Carolyn Sherif, *Social Psychology*, Harper, New York, 1969.

Contemporary treatment: Daniel J. O'Keefe, "Social Judgment Theory," in *Persuasion: Theory and Research*, Sage, Newbury Park, Calif., 1990, pp. 29–44.

CHAPTER 19

Cognitive Dissonance Theory

of Leon Festinger

Aesop tells a story about a fox that tried in vain to reach a cluster of grapes which dangled from a vine above his head. The fox leapt high to grasp the grapes, but the delicious-looking fruit remained just out of reach of his snapping jaws. After a few attempts the fox gave up and said to himself, "These grapes are sour, and if I had some I would not eat them."[1]

DISSONANCE: DISCORD BETWEEN BEHAVIOR AND BELIEF

Aesop's fable, the source of the phrase "sour grapes," also paints a picture of what former Stanford University social psychologist Leon Festinger meant by "cognitive dissonance." It is the distressing mental state caused by an "inconsistency between how a person acts and what he knows."

The fox's retreat from the grape arbor clashed with his knowledge that the grapes were tasty. By changing his attitude toward the grapes, he provided an acceptable explanation for his behavior.

Festinger regarded cognitive dissonance as similar to hunger. It is an aversive drive which could be represented as a separate layer on Maslow's hierarchy: "Dissonance acts in the same way as a state of drive or need or tension."[2] It motivates us to change either our behavior or belief in an effort to avoid an unpleasant feeling. The more important the issue and the greater the discrepancy between behavior and belief, the higher the magnitude of dissonance that we'll feel. In extreme cases cognitive dissonance is like our cringing response to fingernails being scraped on a blackboard—we'll do anything to get away from the awful sound.

229

THREE HYPOTHESES: WAYS TO REDUCE DISSONANCE
BETWEEN ATTITUDES AND ACTIONS

The focus of cognitive dissonance theory is attitude change. Festinger's original statement of the theory suggested three mental mechanisms people use to ensure that their attitudes are consonant with their actions. These hypotheses have proved to be of great interest to persuasion practitioners. I'll illustrate the three hypotheses in the context of a nonprofit organization's attempt to raise money for economic development in the third world.

About 10 percent of the people in the world are starving. A number of private voluntary organizations send food to impoverished countries like Somalia, Bosnia, and Haiti in order to provide immediate hunger relief. A smaller group of agencies tries to develop self-help skills in people that will enable them to escape from the poverty that causes starvation. The difference between relief and development is captured in the well-known saying, "Give a man a fish and he'll eat for a day; teach a man to fish and he'll eat for life."

Opportunity International is a nonprofit development organization that overcomes poverty by creating jobs. Opportunity lends money to men and women who have shown a motivation and talent to run a small business. The borrowed capital permits owners to expand their successful enterprise, thus generating new jobs for people who were unemployed. With a payback rate of 90 percent, Opportunity is then able to recycle the funds to create more jobs. Consistent with a philosophy of enabling a person to fish, the agency helps the entrepreneur acquire nets so that many people can feed their families. The organization has a fifteen-year track record of turning every $500 contributed into a job that lasts year after year.

Thousands of families are now self-supporting because of the ability of Opportunity's board and staff to persuade private donors to contribute money for loans and technical assistance. The success and failure of their fund-raising effort illustrate the hypotheses of cognitive dissonance theory.

Hypothesis 1: Selective Exposure Prevents Dissonance

Festinger claimed that people avoid information that is likely to increase dissonance. We tend to choose reading material and television programs that are consistent with our existing beliefs. Association with like-minded people buffers us from ideas that might cause discomfort. By taking care to "stick with our own kind," we can maintain the relative comfort of the status quo.

Selective exposure explains the response to mass-produced fund-raising letters, most of which are thrown into the trash unopened. A picture of a starving child on the envelope only serves to warn a nondonor that the message inside will induce guilt, so the words don't get read. Premium offers, teaser questions to arouse curiosity, and envelopes with no return address or organizational logo are standard ways to get around selective exposure. Many organizations purchase mailing lists of people who have responded to other hunger appeals. But Opportunity learned early in its history that ninety cents out of every new dollar raised by mail solicitation goes to pay for the cost of fund-raising. The mass marketer's ways of overcoming resistance to dissonance seemed both ineffective and unethical.

German psychologist Dieter Frey surveyed all the pertinent research on selective exposure and concluded that the avoidance mechanism doesn't kick in if we don't regard the dissonant information as a threat.[3] For example, a person may be induced to look at unwanted information about world hunger if it is attractively embedded in popular music ("We Are the World") or in literature (*The Grapes of Wrath*). Warm personal relationships are an even better guarantee that another will consider dissonant information. Opportunity raises a million dollars each year. Two-thirds of that amount comes from a dozen board members and their personal contacts.

Hypothesis 2: Postdecision Dissonance Creates a Need for Reassurance

According to Festinger, close-call decisions generate huge amounts of internal tension. The more important the issue, the longer a person agonizes over two equally attractive options; and the greater the difficulty involved in reversing the decision, the more dissonance a person will feel after deciding what to do. Sometimes referred to as the "morning-after sensation," the second thoughts that plague us after a tough choice motivate us to seek reassuring information and social support for our decision.

The classic example of postdecision dissonance is the turmoil experienced after a person signs a contract to buy a new car. The cost is high, there are many attractive models from which to choose, and the down payment commits the customer to go through with the purchase. It's not unusual to find a customer in the library poring over the pages of the *Consumer Reports* auto issue *after* placing an order. The buyer is seeking information that will quiet nagging doubts.

Most contributors feel conflicting demands for the money they give. A husband's or wife's uneasiness, an appeal from another worthy cause, or the ever-present possibility of financial crisis can cause a donor to waver in his or her commitment after signing a pledge card. Opportunity makes a conscious attempt to have its president or a board member spend time with the person after he or she has indicated an intent to give. The presence of someone who is also making a large donation reduces much of the postdecision dissonance.

Hypothesis 3: Minimal Justification for Action Induces a Shift in Attitude

Persuasion researchers have long distinguished between public compliance and private acceptance. But before cognitive dissonance theory, it seemed natural to think of inner attitude and outward behavior as the beginning and end of a cause-and-effect sequence. If you wanted to persuade people to contribute money for hunger relief, you first had to persuade them to care about the plight of famine victims in Somalia.

Attitude → Behavior

Festinger's minimal justification hypothesis reverses the sequence. He suggested that the best way to stimulate compassion in others is to get them to do something tangible to help solve the problem. (For "where your treasure is, there your heart also."[4])

Behavior → Attitude

But Festinger attached one important condition. Instead of giving potential donors a flood of reasons to contribute, cut back the incentive to the point where it is the least amount that will secure the donation.

> Thus if one wanted to obtain private change in addition to mere public compliance, the best way to do this would be to offer just enough reward or punishment to elicit overt compliance.[5]

A practical example may clarify the logic of Festinger's advice.

As a volunteer fund-raiser for Opportunity, I've taken two separate trips with potential donors to view the work in the Dominican Republic. We toured the places of business, heard each owner's story, and talked to the workers who had jobs because of a loan. These on-site project visits are Opportunity's most effective fund-raising strategy.

Participants pay their own way. A group can opt for a luxury tour or a bare-bones experience. The first group I led decided to go first-class—four-star hotel, fine restaurants, and a lavish cultural show at night. Travelers on the second trip chose the economy route—a hotel without air-conditioning, street-vendor food, and souvenirs from a local market. Both groups gave generously at the end of the trip; their immediate public response was the same. However, the first-class travelers are no longer involved with the organization, whereas those who ate yucca roots continue to contribute.

Festinger would have interpreted the difference in terms of incentives. People on the first trip had abundant reason to go to Latin America. It was a wonderful minivacation on the exotic Caribbean with a "do gooder" activity thrown in. No dissonance was aroused. But the second group had insufficient justification for the cost and discomfort they incurred. They had to generate their own reasons for taking the trek, and the work of Opportunity was the obvious candidate. ("Why am I willing to pay big bucks to travel to a hot and dusty place? Because this work of helping the poor is so valuable.")

TRACKING DOWN THE CAUSE AND EFFECT OF DISSONANCE

The noncommonsensical nature of the minimal justification hypothesis generated a great deal of hostility in social science circles. Theorists who interpreted all behavior as the result of incentives seemed affronted at the notion that rewards might hurt a cause rather than help it. The controversy stimulated a mass of studies from advocates and detractors of the surprising prediction. It all began with the famous $1/$20 experiment.

Would I Lie to You?

Festinger and James Carlsmith recruited Stanford University men to participate in a psychological study of unknown purpose. As each man arrived at the lab, he was assigned the boring and repetitive task of sorting a batch of spools into lots of twelve and turning square pegs a quarter turn to the right. The procedure was designed to be both monotonous and tiring. At the end of an hour the experimenter approached the subject and made a request. A student assistant had supposedly failed to show up, and the researcher needed someone to fill in by telling a potential female subject in the waiting room how much fun the experiment was. Dissonance researchers call this "counter-attitudinal advocacy." We'd call it lying.

Some of the men were promised $1 to express enthusiasm about the task; others were offered $20. It is comforting to know that six of the men refused to take part in the deception, but most students tried to recruit the young woman. The typical conversation was similar for both payment conditions:

> SHE: "I heard it was boring."
> HE: "Oh no, it's really quite interesting."

What did differ were privately expressed attitudes after the study was over. Students who lied for $20 confessed that they thought the task of sorting spools was dull. Those who lied for $1 maintained that it was much more enjoyable. (Festinger and Carlsmith practiced their own form of deception in the study—subjects never received the money which was promised.)

By now you should have a pretty good idea of how dissonance theorists analyze the results. They note that $20 was a huge sum of money (worth more than $50 in today's economy). If a student felt qualms about telling a "white lie," the cash was a ready justification. Thus he felt little or no tension between his action and attitude. But the men who lied for a dollar had lots of cognitive work to do. The logical inconsistency of saying a boring task was interesting had to be explained away through an internal dialogue:

> I'm a Stanford man. Am I the kind of guy who would lie for a dollar? No way.
> Actually what I told the girl was true. The experiment was a lot of fun.

Festinger says that $1 was just barely enough to induce compliance to the experimenter's request, so students had to create another justification. They changed their attitudes toward the task to bring it into line with their behavior.

You can probably think of alternative ways to account for Festinger and Carlsmith's findings. The study has been replicated and modified many times in an effort to close off loopholes that would admit other explanations. The results have made it necessary to qualify Festinger's minimal justification hypothesis. Today most persuasion researchers accept a revised version of cognitive dissonance theory.

Saving Face: The Rationalizing Animal

University of California social psychologist Elliot Aronson was attracted to cognitive dissonance theory because of Leon Festinger's startling minimal justification prediction. He quickly determined that the theory in its original form had some "conceptual fuzziness." It failed to state the conditions under which a person would definitely experience dissonance. Early disciples of Festinger would settle disputes by saying, "If you want to be sure, ask Leon."

Aronson concluded that the issue isn't *logical* inconsistency, but *psychological* inconsistency. We aren't rational animals; we are rationalizing animals who want to appear reasonable to ourselves. He interprets the $1/$20 experiment as a study of self-esteem maintenance. "If dissonance exists, it is because the individual's behavior is inconsistent with his self-concept."[6] The Stanford men were in a bind because they regarded themselves as decent, truthful human beings. If they had seen themselves as liars, cheats, or jerks, they would have felt no tension.

DILBERT reprinted by permission of UFS, Inc.

According to Aronson, the amount of dissonance a person can experience is directly proportional to the effort he or she has invested in the behavior. Since Marine boot camp is tougher than basic training in the regular Army, Aronson would expect a recruit to feel greater tension if he violated the norms of the Marine Corps. The harder it is to get into a group, the more an initiate values membership. Rarely does a football player brag that his coach schedules light workouts.

The principle of effort is reflected in the 80/20 rule of fund-raising. No matter what the cause, 80 percent of the resources come from 20 percent of the donors. These people aren't passive check writers. They also invest time and energy. Volunteers often increase their own contribution shortly after asking someone else for money. The principle of effort explains why Opportunity travelers who put up with rugged conditions are the ones who have maintained long-term involvement.

Even the reactions of Aesop's fox make sense in light of the animal's low investment of energy. Aronson points out that the fox wouldn't think the grapes were sour if he had spent the whole afternoon jumping to get them. Attitudes follow behavior because of the effort we've committed.

Personal Responsibility for Bad Outcomes

As a predictor of dissonance, Aronson's fear of looking foolish proved better than Festinger's logical inconsistency. But it remained for University of Texas researcher Robert Wicklund and his colleague from the University of Kansas, Jack Brehm, to establish the definitive conditions under which counterattitudinal advocacy leads to change in conviction. They showed that "personal responsibility for undesirable consequences" is the ultimate cause of dissonance.

Wicklund and Brehm say that choice and foreseeability are the necessary ingredients for a sense of personal responsibility. It's possible to conceive of a situation in which volunteer fund-raisers might feel responsible for a bad situation and thus experience dissonance.

Since the breakup of the Soviet Union, the Agency for International Development (U.S. AID) and private voluntary organizations have encouraged Opportunity to open partner agencies in Bulgaria and other former eastern bloc countries. Suppose a married couple who are Opportunity board members have doubts about supporting expansion into a non-third-world country that has no recent history of entrepreneurial motivation or expertise. Then imagine Opportunity's president asking the couple to host a coffee in their home to solicit money from friends for a new Bulgarian agency. The president doesn't apply pressure; he merely lets the volunteers know he'd appreciate the effort. The board members worry that funds raised might not help the poor, but they ultimately comply with the president's request.

This would be a classic case of minimal justification for a public behavior that runs counter to private belief. If it turns out that the money doesn't create jobs for the poor, the board members would feel personally responsible for their friends' contributions being wasted. No one forced the couple to ask for money, and they had some reason to anticipate that using the funds in Bulgaria was money down the drain. Choice and foreseeability make them susceptible to dissonance when things turn out bad. Since they can't undo their public commitment to the Bulgarian work, the dissonance they feel will cause them to change their attitude. Wicklund and Brehm would predict that the couple will gloss over the Bulgarian failure and become ardent boosters of the eastern European program.

CRITIQUE: DISSONANCE OVER DISSONANCE

Despite extensive revisions, cognitive dissonance theory still has weaknesses. In Chapter 3, I illustrated the problem of testability with my boyhood pal's ''never-miss shot'' on his driveway basketball court. In the same way, cognitive dissonance is the never-miss prediction of communication theory. When it works, the results are spectacular. When it doesn't, the true believer merely accepts the negative result as tacit evidence that the person in question didn't feel enough dissonance. In other words, the theory can't be proved wrong.

Chapter 3 also recommends simplicity. Many critics think that by appealing to dissonance as an explanation of opinion change, Festinger and his colleagues have been unduly complicated. Although not arguing with the predictions of dissonance theory, Daryl Bem claims that self-perception is a much simpler interpretation of the research data.

You'll recall from the chapter on attribution theory (Chapter 11) that Bem believes we judge our internal dispositions the same way others do—by observing our behavior. Bem ran his own $1/$20 study. People heard a recording of a Stanford man's enthusiastic account of the boring task. Some were told he received $1 for lying to the female subject; others were told he received $20. From this simple description of behavior, people were able to predict correctly that $20 liars would continue to believe the task boring, and that $1 liars would think it interesting. If others need only observe our actions in order to know how we feel, why should we need more? Bem is convinced we determine our attitude by watching ourselves act. Appeals to cognitive dissonance only cloud the scene.

Yet dissonance theory in its present form has made a significant contribution to the field of attitude change. Its implications for the persuader are clear. High-pressure tactics may get immediate compliance, but they won't get long-term commitment. The hard sell is out; the soft sell is in.

The persuader who desires lasting attitude change should give enough incentive to induce others to act, but not so much that they regard it as an offer they can't refuse. The wise advocate makes certain that people who respond have a good understanding of the future implications of their decision. Then if things turn sour, the new convert won't.

QUESTIONS TO SHARPEN YOUR FOCUS

1. Cognitive dissonance is a distressing mental state. When did you last experience this *aversive drive?* Why might you have trouble answering that question?

2. The results of Festinger's famous *$1/$20 experiment* can be explained in a number of different ways. What explanation satisfies you?

3. Suppose you want your friends to change their sexist attitudes. What advice does the *minimal justification hypothesis* offer?

4. Where would Festinger have placed the *need for consonance* on Maslow's hierarchy of needs (see Chapter 10)?

A SECOND LOOK

Recommended resource: Elliot Aronson, "The Rationalizing Animal," *Psychology Today,* May 1973, pp. 46–51.

Original statement: Leon Festinger, *A Theory of Cognitive Dissonance,* Stanford University, Stanford, Calif., 1957.

Secondary resource: Daniel J. O'Keefe, "Cognitive Dissonance," in *Persuasion: Theory and Research,* Sage, Newbury Park, Calif., 1990, pp. 61–78.

Selective exposure: Dolf Zillmann and Jennings Bryant (eds.), *Selective Exposure to Communication,* Lawrence Erlbaum Associates, Hillsdale, N.J., 1985.

$1/$20 experiment: Leon Festinger and James Carlsmith, "Cognitive Consequences of Forced Compliance," *Journal of Abnormal and Social Psychology,* Vol. 58, 1959, pp. 203–210.

Saving face: Elliot Aronson, "The Theory of Cognitive Dissonance: A Current Perspective," in *Advances in Experimental Social Psychology,* Vol. 4, Leonard Berkowitz (ed.), Academic Press, New York, 1969, pp. 2–34.

Personal responsibility: Robert Wicklund and Jack Brehm, *Perspectives on Cognitive Dissonance,* Lawrence Erlbaum Associates, Hillsdale, N.J., 1976.

Theory development: Anthony Greenwald and David Ronis, "Twenty Years of Cognitive Dissonance: Case Study of the Evolution of a Theory," *Psychological Review,* Vol. 85, 1978, pp. 53–57.

State of the art: Joel Cooper and Russell Fazio, "A New Look at Dissonance Theory," in *Advances in Experimental Social Psychology,* Vol. 17, Leonard Berkowitz (ed.), Academic Press, Orlando, Fla., 1984, pp. 229–266

Self-perception: Daryl Bem, "Self-Perception: An Alternative Interpretation of Cognitive Dissonance Phenomena," *Psychological Review,* Vol. 74, 1967, pp. 183–200.

Fund-raising: Thomas Broce, *Fund Raising,* 2d ed., University of Oklahoma, Norman, 1986.

CHAPTER 20

Elaboration Likelihood Model
of Richard Petty & John Cacioppo

Like a number of women whose children are out of the home, Rita Francisco has gone back to college. Her program isn't an aimless sampling of classes to fill empty hours. She has enrolled in every course that will help her become a more persuasive advocate. Rita is a woman with a mission.

Rita's teenage daughter was killed when the car she was riding in smashed into a stone wall. The girl's eighteen-year-old boyfriend lost control on a curve while going eighty miles per hour. Rita's son walks with a permanent limp as a result of injuries received when a high school girl plowed through the parking lot of a 7-Eleven on a Friday night. When police obtained a DUI (driving under the influence) conviction, it only fueled Rita's resolve to get young drivers off the road. She works to convince anyone who will listen that the minimum age for a driver's license should be raised to twenty-one.

This is a tough sell on any college campus. While her classmates can appreciate the tragic reasons underlying her fervor, few subscribe to her drastic solution. Rita realizes that students could easily dismiss her campaign as the ranting of a hysterical woman and is determined to develop the most effective persuasive strategy possible. She wonders if she would have more success by presenting well-reasoned arguments for raising the driving age or lining up highly credible people to endorse her proposal.

THE CENTRAL ROUTE VS. THE PERIPHERAL ROUTE: ALTERNATIVE PATHS TO PERSUASION

Ohio State psychologist Richard Petty thinks Rita is asking the right question. He conducted his Ph.D. dissertation study using the driver's license topic while testing the relative effectiveness of high-source credibility and strong-message arguments. He found that the results varied depending on which of two mental routes to attitude change a listener happened to use. Petty labeled the two processes the "central route" and the "peripheral route." He sees the distinction as helpful in reconciling much of the conflicting data of persuasion research. Along with Ohio State colleague John Cacioppo, he launched an intensive program of study to discover the best way for the persuader to activate each route.

The central route involves message elaboration. Elaboration is "the extent to which a person carefully thinks about issue-relevant arguments contained in a persuasive communication."[1] People using the central route scrutinize the ideas, try to figure out if they have true merit, and mull over their implications. It's an attempt to process the new information rationally.

The peripheral route offers a shorthand way to accept or reject a message "without any active thinking about the attributes of the issue or the object of consideration."[2] Instead of doing extensive cognitive work, recipients rely on a variety of cues which allow them to make quick decisions. Robert Cialdini of Arizona State University lists six cues which trigger a "click, whirr" programmed response.[3] These cues allow us to fly the peripheral route on automatic pilot:

1. Reciprocation—"You owe me."
2. Consistency—"We've always done it that way."
3. Social proof—"Everybody's doing it."
4. Liking—"Love me, love my ideas."
5. Authority—"Just because I say so."
6. Scarcity—"Quick, before they're all gone."

Petty and Cacioppo discuss the two routes to attitude change as if they are mutually exclusive. They repeatedly refer to the trade-off between message elaboration and persuasive cues. Although the authors acknowledge that the choice is not an all-or-nothing process, their model treats the two basic routes as distinct paths. Figure 20.1 shows a simplified version of the elaboration likelihood model (ELM) as it applies to Rita's situation. We'll work down the model one level at a time in order to understand Petty and Cacioppo's predictions about the likelihood of Rita's message being considered and tested (mentally elaborated) by students at her college.

MOTIVATION FOR ELABORATION: IS IT WORTH THE EFFORT?

Petty and Cacioppo assume that people are motivated to hold correct attitudes. The authors admit that we aren't always logical, but they think we make a good effort not to kid ourselves in our search for truth. We want to maintain reasonable positions.

Yet a person can only scrutinize a limited number of ideas. We hear so many persuasive messages that we would experience a tremendous information overload if we tried to interact with every variant thought we heard. The only way to solve this problem is by being "lazy" toward most issues in life. Petty and Cacioppo claim we have a large-mesh mental filter which allows

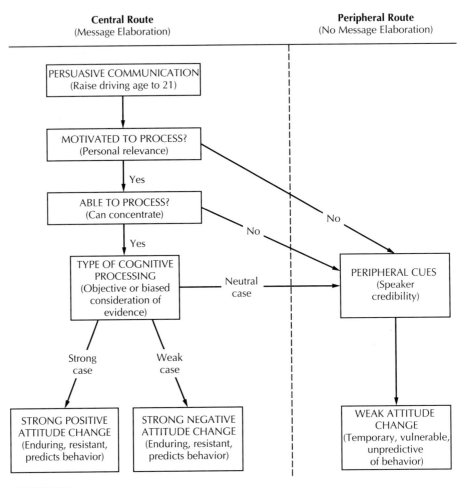

Central Route
(Message Elaboration)

Peripheral Route
(No Message Elaboration)

FIGURE 20.1
The Elaboration Likelihood Model (Adapted from Petty and Cacioppo, ''The Elaboration Likelihood Model of Persuasion.'')

items we regard as insignificant to flow through without being processed. But statements about things that are personally relevant are trapped and tested. In the terms of social judgment theory, we're motivated to elaborate only ideas with which we are highly ego-involved.

There are few things in life more important to the young American than the right to drive. A license is the closest thing our society has to an adolescent rite of passage. For some it is a passport to freedom. It seems unlikely, therefore, that students would regard Rita's recommendation as trivial. Yet raising the age requirement would have less personal relevance to a twenty-two-year-old senior than it would to the incoming student fresh out of high school. ELM's authors would regard the younger student as more highly motivated to grapple with Rita's proposal.

Petty and Cacioppo maintain that as long as people have a personal stake in accepting or rejecting an idea, they will be much more influenced by what a message says than by the characteristics of the person who said it. But when a topic is no longer relevant, it gets sidetracked to the periphery of our mind where credibility cues take on a greater importance. Without the motivation of personal relevance, there will be no elaboration.

ABILITY FOR ELABORATION: CAN THEY DO IT?

Once people have shown an inclination to think about the content of a message (motivation), the next issue is whether or not they are *able* to do so. Since Rita's immediate audience consists of men and women who have duly impressed a college admissions officer, you would think the question of ability would be moot. But issue-relevant thinking (elaboration) takes more than intelligence. It also requires an opportunity to concentrate.

Distraction disrupts elaboration. Rita's classmates will be hard-pressed to think about her point of view if it's expressed amid the din of the student union snack bar where you can't hear yourself think. Or perhaps she presents her solution for highway safety when the students are trying to concentrate on something else—an upcoming exam, a letter from home, or an instant mental replay of the winning shot in an intramural basketball game.

Rita may face the same challenge as television advertisers who have only the fleeting attention of viewers. Like them, Rita can use repetition to ensure that her main point comes across, but too much commotion will short-circuit a reasoned consideration of the message, no matter how much repetition is used. In that case, students will use the peripheral route and judge the message by cues which indicate whether Rita is a competent and trustworthy person.

TYPE OF ELABORATION: OBJECTIVE VS. BIASED THINKING

As you can see from the downward flow in the central path of their model (Figure 20.1), Petty and Cacioppo believe that motivation and ability strongly increased the likelihood that a message will be elaborated in the minds of listeners. Yet as social judgment theory suggests, they may not process the information in a fair and objective manner. Rita could have the undivided attention of students who care deeply about the right to drive but discover that they've already built up an organized structure of knowledge concerning the issue.

When Rita claims that teenage drivers are more dangerous than older motorists because they have twice as many accidents, a student may counter with the fact that teenagers drive twice as many miles and are therefore just as safe as adults. Whether or not the statistics are true or the argument is valid isn't the issue. (As we saw in the last chapter, typical ways of resolving cognitive dissonance aren't especially rational.) The point is that those who

Reprinted from the Saturday Evening Post © 1989.

already know a lot about driving safety will probably be biased in the way they process Rita's message.

Petty and Cacioppo refer to biased elaboration as top-down thinking in which a predetermined conclusion colors the supporting data underneath. They contrast this with objective elaboration, or bottom-up thinking, which lets facts speak for themselves. Biased elaboration merely bolsters previous ideas. Perhaps you've seen a picture of Rodin's famous statue, *The Thinker*, a man sitting with his head propped in one hand. If the thinker already has a set of beliefs to contemplate, Petty and Cacioppo's research shows that additional thought will merely fix them in stone. Rita shouldn't assume that audience elaboration will always help her cause; it depends on whether it's biased elaboration or objective elaboration.

ELABORATED ARGUMENTS: STRONG, WEAK, AND NEUTRAL

If Rita manages to win an unbiased hearing from students at her school, Petty and Cacioppo say her cause will rise or fall on the perceived strength of her arguments. The two theorists have no absolute standard for what distinguishes a cogent argument from one that's specious. They simply define a strong message as one which generates favorable thoughts when it's heard and scrutinized.

Petty and Cacioppo predict that thoughtful consideration of strong arguments will produce major shifts in attitude change in the direction desired by the persuader. Suppose Rita states the following:

> National Safety Council statistics show that drivers in the sixteen to twenty age group account for 15 percent of the miles driven in the United States, yet they are responsible for 40 percent of the deaths that occur on the highway.

This evidence could give cause for thought. Her fellow students may not be comfortable with the facts, but some of them might find the statistics quite compelling. According to the ELM, the enhanced thinking of those who respond favorably will cause their change in position to persist over time, resist counterpersuasion, and predict future behavior—the "triple crown" of interpersonal influence.

However, persuasive attempts that are processed through the central route can have dramatically negative effects as well. Despite her strong convictions, Rita may be able to make only a weak case for changing the current law.

> Raising the legal driving age would allow the secretary of state's office to reduce its backlog of work. This would give government officials time to check driving records so they could keep dangerous motorists off the road.

This weak argument is guaranteed to offend the sensibilities of anyone who thinks about it. Rather than compelling listeners to enlist in Rita's cause, it will only give them a reason to oppose her point of view more vigorously. The elaborated idea will cause a boomerang effect that will last over time, defy other efforts to change it, and break out into behavior. These are the same significant effects that the elaborated strong argument produces, but in the other direction.

Rita's ideas could produce an ambivalent reaction. Listeners who give careful consideration to her ideas may end up feeling neither pro nor con toward the evidence. Their neutral or mixed response obviously means that they won't change their attitudes as a result of processing through the central route. But just like those who were unmotivated or unable to elaborate ideas from the start, these listeners switch over to the peripheral route where they come under the influence of nonmessage cues.

PERIPHERAL CUES: AN ALTERNATIVE ROUTE OF INFLUENCE

Although the majority of this chapter has dealt with the central route to attitude change, most messages are processed on the peripheral path.

Signposts along the way direct the hearer to favor or oppose the persuader's point of view without ever engaging in an inner dialogue over the merits of the proposal. Petty and Cacioppo call the resultant shifts "attitude changes without issue-relevant thinking."

As explained earlier, the hearer who has chosen the peripheral route relies on a variety of cues as an aid in reaching a quick decision. The most obvious cues are tangible rewards linked to agreement with the advocate's position. Food, sex, and money are traditional inducements to change. I once overheard the conclusion of a social exchange between a college senior and a young woman who was trying to persuade him to donate blood in order to fulfill a class assignment. "Okay it's agreed," she said. "You give blood for me today, and I'll have you over to my place for dinner tomorrow night." Although this type of transaction has been going on for centuries, Petty and Cacioppo would still describe it as peripheral. Public compliance to the request for blood—yes. Private acceptance of its importance—not likely.

For many students of influence, speaker or source credibility is the most interesting cue on the peripheral route. Four decades of research confirm that people who both are likable and have expertise on the issue in question can have a persuasive impact regardless of what arguments they present. Who Rita is speaks so loudly that some students won't hear what she says. Which students? According to Petty and Cacioppo, the unmotivated, the unable, or the undecided students who switched to the peripheral path.

Listeners who believe that Rita's twin tragedies have given her wisdom beyond their own will shift to a position slightly more sympathetic to her point of view. The same holds true for those who see her as pleasant and warm. But there are students who will regard her grammatical mistakes as a sign of ignorance, or they'll be turned off by a maternal manner that reminds them of a lecture from Mom. These peripheral route critics will become a bit more skeptical of Rita's position. Note that attitude change on this outside track can be either positive or negative, but either way it doesn't have the robust persistence, invulnerability, or link to behavior that we see in change that comes from message elaboration.

SCRUTINIZING THE EVIDENCE

Over the past decade Petty and Cacioppo have conducted more than fifty experiments to test the basic assumptions of the model. The typical study varies personal relevance, argument strength, and source credibility. The results consistently verify that motivation is a key determinant as to which of the distinctive routes to attitude change will be used:

1. The central route is used on issues of high personal relevance; people are persuaded mostly by strong evidence.
2. The peripheral route is used on issues of low personal relevance; people are persuaded mostly by source credibility cues.

In addition to ego-involvement with the subject matter, these studies confirm three other factors that make elaboration more likely:

1. Motivation for focused thought is higher when people feel solely responsible to evaluate the message.

2. Motivation also increases when the hearer has a high personal need for cognitive clarity and an awareness that many independent sources are advocating the same thing.

3. Listener ability to evaluate the message thoughtfully goes up when the arguments are relatively simple to understand and are repeated a few times.

CHOOSING A ROUTE: PRACTICAL ADVICE FOR THE PERSUADER

Petty and Cacioppo's advice for Rita (and the rest of us) is clear. She needs to determine the likelihood that her listeners will give their undivided attention to evaluating her proposal. If it appears that they have the motivation and ability to elaborate the message, she had best come armed with facts and figures to support her case. A pleasant smile, emotional appeals, or a reputation as a safety expert won't make any difference.

Since it's only by thoughtful consideration that her listeners could experience a lasting change in attitude, Rita probably hopes they can go the central route. But it's difficult to build a compelling persuasive case. If she fails to do her homework and presents weak arguments, the people who are ready to think will shift their attitude to a more antagonistic position.

If Rita determines that her hearers are unable or unwilling to think through the details of her plan, she'll be more successful choosing a delivery strategy that emphasizes the package rather than the contents. This could include a heartrending account of her daughter's death, a smooth presentation, and an ongoing effort to build friendships with the students. Perhaps bringing homemade cookies to class or offering rides to the mall would aid in making her an attractive source.

Some of the most effective peripheral cues are endorsements from highly popular or respected public figures. Rita is sure that students appreciate Bill Cosby and David Letterman. And she suspects that the words of test pilot Chuck Yeager and race-car driver Mario Andretti might carry some weight on the topic of motor safety. By somehow associating her message with these credible people she can achieve a slight change in student attitudes. Yet it probably wouldn't last long, stand up to attack, or affect their behavior. Petty and Cacioppo say that a small and fragile change is all that can be expected through the peripheral route.

It's not likely that Rita will get many people to elaborate her message in a way that ends up favorably for her cause. Most persuaders avoid the central route because the audience won't go with them or they find it is too difficult to generate compelling arguments. But Rita really doesn't have a choice.

Having a driver's license is so important to most of these students that they'll be ready to dissect every part of her plan. They won't be won over by a friendly smile. Rita will have to develop thoughtful and well-reasoned arguments if she is to change their minds. Given the depth of her conviction, it's worth a try.

CRITIQUE: ELABORATING THE MODEL'S WEAKNESS

Despite the impressive research support for Petty and Cacioppo's ELM, the theory has been criticized for setting up a false "forced choice" model of information processing. Michigan State University communication professor James Stiff insists that it's possible for a person to ponder evidence and be influenced by characteristics of the communicator *at the same time*. He suggests that the routes are more elastic than Petty and Cacioppo presume. Stiff presents a parallel processing model which describes optimal influence as a combination of intensive elaboration and moderate attention to source credibility.[4] The ELM authors respond by saying that their model doesn't rule out the possibility of people's using both routes simultaneously, but they reiterate that there is no evidence to suggest that it happens.

Petty and Cacioppo's research program has focused more on listeners' motivation and ability to elaborate messages than it has on the strength of the arguments they hear. Perhaps this omission is due to the difficulty of testing how good a case the speaker actually made. Petty and Cacioppo define a good message as "one containing arguments such that when subjects are instructed to think about the message, the thoughts they generate are fundamentally favorable."[5] In other words, the arguments are regarded as strong if the people are persuaded, but weak if folks are turned off. Like cognitive dissonance theory, ELM seems to have its own "never-miss shot." Until such time as the ELM theorists can identify what makes a case weak or strong apart from its ultimate effect on the listener, it doesn't make much sense to include argument strength as a key variable within the model.

Yet even if Cacioppo and Petty's conceptual map is too simplistic or their view of argument strength is too slippery, their elaboration likelihood model is impressive because it pulls together and makes sense out of diverse research results that have puzzled communication theorists for years. For example, why do most people pay less attention to the communication than they do to the communicator? And if speaker credibility is so important, why does its effect dissipate so quickly? ELM's explanation is that few listeners are motivated and able to do the mental work that is required for a major shift in attitude. The two-path hypothesis also helps clarify why good evidence and reasoning can sometimes have a life-changing impact but usually make no difference at all.

Attitude-change research often yields results that seem confusing or contradictory. Petty and Cacioppo's ELM takes many disjointed findings and pulls them together into a unified whole. This integrative function of the elaboration likelihood model makes it a valuable theory of influence.

QUESTIONS TO SHARPEN YOUR FOCUS

1. Can you think of five words or phrases that capture the idea of *message elaboration?*

2. What *peripheral cues* do you usually monitor when someone is trying to influence you?

3. Petty and Cacioppo want to persuade you that their elaboration likelihood model is a mirror of reality. Do you process their arguments for its accuracy through your *central route* or your *peripheral route? Why not the other way?*

4. Students of persuasion often wonder whether *high credibility* or *strong arguments* sway people more? How would ELM theorists respond to that question?

A SECOND LOOK

Recommended resource: Richard E. Petty and John T. Cacioppo, *Communication and Persuasion: Central and Peripheral Routes to Attitude Change,* Springer-Verlag, New York, 1986.

ELM integration of persuasion approaches: Richard E. Petty and John T. Cacioppo, *Attitudes and Persuasion: Classic and Contemporary Approaches,* W. M. C. Brown, Dubuque, Iowa, 1981.

Effect of involvement: Richard E. Petty and John T. Cacioppo, "Involvement and Persuasion: Tradition versus Integration," *Psychological Bulletin,* Vol. 107, 1990, pp. 367–374.

Secondary resource: Daniel J. O'Keefe, "Elaboration Likelihood Model," in *Persuasion: Theory and Research,* Sage, Newbury Park, Calif., 1990, pp. 95–129

Postulates and research: Richard E. Petty and John T. Cacioppo, "The Elaboration Likelihood Model of Persuasion," in *Advances in Experimental Social Psychology,* Vol. 19, Leonard Berkowitz (ed.), Academic Press, Orlando, Fla., 1986, pp. 124–205.

Message arguments versus source credibility: Richard E. Petty, John T. Cacioppo, and R. Goldman, "Personal Involvement as a Determinant of Argument-Based Persuasion," *Journal of Personality and Social Psychology,* Vol. 41, 1981, pp. 847–855.

Driver's license study: Richard Petty, "A Cognitive Response Analysis of the Temporal Persistence of Attitude Changes Induced by Persuasive Communications." Unpublished doctoral dissertation, Ohio State University, Columbus, 1977.

Effects of evidence: John Reinard, "The Empirical Study of the Persuasive Effects of Evidence: The Status After Fifty Years of Research," *Human Communication Research,* Vol. 15, 1988, pp. 3–59.

Effects of credibility: H. W. Simons, N. M. Berkowitz, and R. J. Moyer, "Similarity, Credibility and Attitude Change: A Review and a Theory," *Psychological Bulletin,* Vol. 73, 1970, pp. 1–16

Mindless cues: Robert B. Cialdini, *Influence: Science and Practice,* 2d ed., Scott Foresman, Glenview, Ill., 1988.

Critiques of ELM: "Forum: Specifying the ELM," *Communication Theory,* Vol. 3, 1993. (Mark Hamilton, John Hunter, and Franklyn Boster, "The Elaboration Likelihood Model as a Theory of Attitude Formation: A Mathematical Analysis," pp. 50–65. Paul Mongeau and James Stiff, "Specifying Causal Relationships in the Elaboration Likelihood Model," pp. 65–72. Mike Allen and Rodney Reynolds, "The Elaboration Likelihood Model and the Sleeper Effect: An Assessment of Attitude Change Over Time," pp. 73–82.)

PART FIVE

Group and Public Communication

DECISION MAKING

ORGANIZATIONAL COMMUNICATION

PUBLIC RHETORIC

DECISION MAKING

A cynic once said that a camel is a horse put together by a committee. Though many share this pessimistic view, the results of research in schools, business, and government show that problem-solving groups often come up with solutions that are superior to anything thought of by individual members. Referred to as "synergy," the recurrent finding that the whole is more than the sum of its parts has stimulated efforts to explain the typical process of group decision making.

Forty years ago, Robert Bales of Harvard University developed a method of discussion analysis which distinguishes twelve types of verbal behavior. A typical committee meeting requires the classification of ten to fifteen comments a minute. Figure DM.1 shows Bales' revised list of categories and some of the interrelationships he built into his system of observation.

The middle area of Bales' system (sections B and C) is for statements that focus on accomplishing the group task. The outer areas (sections A and D) are for comments that reflect relationships within the group. By coding everything a person says, an observer using Bales' categories is able to develop a profile of preferred interaction style for each group member. The results confirm that some people concentrate on getting the job done, while others are much more concerned with social-emotional issues. Task-oriented individuals are the pistons that drive the group machine. Relationship-oriented mem-

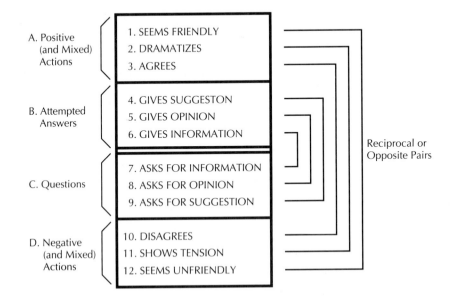

FIGURE DM.1
Categories for Interaction Process Analysis (From Bales, *Personality and Interpersonal Behavior.*)

bers are the lubricant that prevents excessive friction from destroying the group. Good groups require both kinds of people.

Bales anticipated that groups would follow a simple developmental pattern:

Questions → Attempted answers → Positive and negative reactions

While this idealized sequence proved too simplistic, he did find that groups trying to reach a consensus on a major problem would often move through three general phases: orientation, evaluation, and control. Chapter 21 presents B. Aubrey Fisher's four-phase theory of decision emergence, which provides a similar, yet more comprehensive, explanation of group progress.

You can see in Figure DM.1 that Bales' twelve categories are divided into a half-dozen reciprocally matched pairs. *Asks for information* is balanced by *gives information. Seems friendly* is juxtaposed with *seems unfriendly.* The only pair which doesn't present an obvious mirror image is *dramatizes—shows tension.* Bales originally called category 2 *relieves tension,* but because the jokes and stories placed

"There are no great men, my boy . . . only great committees."
Drawing by Chas. Addams; © 1975 The New Yorker Magazine, Inc.

here often serve to get a group moving when it's stuck, he decided that the term *dramatizes* is a more accurate label.

Bales found that good groups maintain a rough balance between each of the six pairs. For example, a group can move smoothly through the orientation stage when people hear answers (category 6) to their questions about the nature of their task (category 7). But the group gets stuck if members seek facts that no one has, or if everyone volunteers information that nobody wants.

Bales found that a 2 : 1 ratio of positive to negative comments was optimum for social-emotional category pairs (1 and 12, 2 and 11, 3 and 10). Although a high proportion of cutting remarks could tear a group apart, he discovered that a healthy dose of voiced skepticism was necessary to reach a quality decision. Examining classic blunders in U.S. foreign policy, Irving Janis agrees that an inordinate desire for group unity can cause groups to make bad decisions. His theory of groupthink is the subject of Chapter 22.

Fisher, Janis, and Bales are optimistic that decision-making groups can reach synergy. If it's true that a camel is a horse put together by a committee, we should remember that the ungainly looking beast turns out to be an ideal solution for a group of desert nomads.

CHAPTER 21

Interact System Model of Decision Emergence
of B. Aubrey Fisher

Throughout the twentieth century, group members involved in decision-making tasks have been urged to follow educator-philosopher John Dewey's pattern of reflective thinking. The six-step logical process parallels a doctor's approach to treating a patient:

1. Recognize symptoms of illness.
2. Diagnose the cause of the ailment.
3. Establish criteria for wellness.
4. Consider possible remedies.
5. Test to determine which solutions will work.
6. Implement or prescribe the best solution.

Despite its widespread use in discussion-leadership training, the late B. Aubrey Fisher, a communication professor at the University of Utah, judged Dewey's system to be "of little value as a *guide for groups* involved in making decisions." Fisher noted that although reflective thinking can help individuals figure out good solutions, not all decisions faced by a group are problems to be solved, and rationality isn't always the ultimate test of an effective outcome. Decisions are worthless unless they're implemented, so member commitment to the solution is sometimes more important than reaching the logical or right decision.

Consider the appointment of Juan Ladamora to a joint faculty-student search committee which has the task of recommending a candidate to be the new dean of students. The former dean resigned under fire when minority groups on campus produced convincing evidence of systematic discrimination in college housing and employment. Juan is a Filipino undergraduate chosen by the president to represent Asian students on campus. He is joined by an African-American graduate student, the presidents of a sorority and the local chapter of NOW, an avowed homosexual, and three faculty members from different departments. The president of the college has instructed the committee to submit a single name that all eight can enthusiastically support and sell to their constituent groups. As Juan walks across campus to attend the first meeting, he wonders what twists and turns the course of the discussion will take. That's precisely the question that Fisher's interact system model of decision emergence is designed to answer.

THE DECISION-MAKING GROUP AS AN OPEN SYSTEM

Fisher viewed groups as systems in the same way that telephone companies, football teams, and Detroit auto assembly lines are systems. They are "a set of units bound by a definable context within which the component units interact with each other."[1] Although there are differences, AT&T is quite similar to General Telephone, the Chicago Bears are like the San Francisco Forty-Niners, and putting together a Taurus has much in common with assembling a Saturn. Fisher thought it reasonable to expect that Juan's search committee will reach a decision in roughly the same way as a problem-solving group at IBM or a jury deliberating the fate of a defendant does. His interact system model tries to capture the similarities.

Some systems theorists would regard the eight individuals on the search committee as the basic units of analysis, and therefore concentrate their efforts on understanding the relationships among group members. They would see the committee as a closed system, its decision a predictable result of the nature of the people appointed.

Not so with Fisher. He would have viewed Juan's committee as an open system which can interact with outsiders, generate new information, and adapt to change. He thought Bales' social-emotional categories were extra baggage that distract the observer from the crucial elements of a task group system that is open to input from the outside. He focused on what was said regardless of who said it or of the feelings that surrounded the comment. Fisher didn't believe that the initial mix of personalities dictates the final outcome. He was convinced that the verbal interaction does.

A GROUNDED THEORY OF GROUP DEVELOPMENT

Given his systems orientation, Fisher began his study of decision making with the belief that all groups go through similar phases or stages before reaching consensus. Just as people experience birth, childhood, maturity, and death, he assumed that groups share a common life cycle. But he was careful not to anticipate the number or nature of these phases.

Most scientifically oriented theorists begin with a core idea. Berger is convinced that people who have just met are concerned with reducing uncertainty. Festinger was certain that inconsistency causes dissonance. Petty and Cacioppo believe there are two routes to persuasion. These researchers then formulate hypotheses, axioms, postulates, or corollaries which spell out the specific implications of their central tenet. Finally, they test their predictions by applying them to real-life situations to see if they fit. This deductive approach is reflected in the organization of chapters you've already read. The report of research usually comes after the statement of theory.

Fisher feared that a preliminary conclusion would bias the way the results are interpreted. He wanted to base his theory on what actually happens rather than on what people expect or think ought to happen. He was committed to having data generate the theory rather than the other way around. He called this "grounded theory"; the label refers to the idea that principles are constructed on a solid base of direct observation and evidence rather than on mere inference or speculation.

CODING TASK INTERACTION

Fisher's research required a means of separating the statements of group members based on their reaction to a specific decision proposal. Suppose Juan's group is considering limiting its search to off-campus candidates. Any statement Juan makes on that topic could be classified according to Fisher's system of observation. But comments not anchored to the decision proposal would be ignored by the person using Fisher's system. When he summarized the procedure he used in his own research, Fisher reported that "any interaction considered to be serving purely a procedural or socializing function, i.e. nontask function, was coded into an 'et cetera' category and excluded from the data."[2] That means that statements which Bales would rate as "seems friendly/unfriendly," "dramatizes," or "shows tension" were not recorded.

Figure 21.1 shows the ultimate categories that Fisher used to classify verbal responses to a decision proposal. The original system had a slot for "summarizes," but it was used so seldom that he dropped it from the analysis. The "disagreement" category is a later addition put in for balance. Statements in parentheses illustrate things Juan might say which would be assigned to that particular category.

FOUR PHASES OF DECISION EMERGENCE

Fisher applied his coding system to ten nonclassroom groups facing major decisions. The groups ranged in size from four to twelve members, in duration from twenty-five minutes to thirty hours, and in age of participants from teens to sixties. Some groups were all male, some were all female, and some were mixed. He sought this variety to ensure that any recurrent pattern wasn't due to similarity of group composition. Like Juan's committee, all ten groups had tasks that required consensus, and all achieved that goal.

The data collected were analyzed on two levels. Fisher totaled the frequency of eight types of verbal "acts" that took place at various times

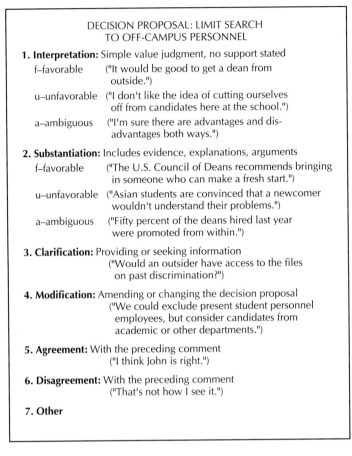

DECISION PROPOSAL: LIMIT SEARCH
TO OFF-CAMPUS PERSONNEL

1. Interpretation: Simple value judgment, no support stated

f–favorable   ("It would be good to get a dean from outside.")

u–unfavorable   ("I don't like the idea of cutting ourselves off from candidates here at the school.")

a–ambiguous   ("I'm sure there are advantages and disadvantages both ways.")

2. Substantiation: Includes evidence, explanations, arguments

f–favorable   ("The U.S. Council of Deans recommends bringing in someone who can make a fresh start.")

u–unfavorable   ("Asian students are convinced that a newcomer wouldn't understand their problems.")

a–ambiguous   ("Fifty percent of the deans hired last year were promoted from within.")

3. Clarification: Providing or seeking information
("Would an outsider have access to the files on past discrimination?")

4. Modification: Amending or changing the decision proposal
("We could exclude present student personnel employees, but consider candidates from academic or other departments.")

5. Agreement: With the preceding comment
("I think John is right.")

6. Disagreement: With the preceding comment
("That's not how I see it.")

7. Other

FIGURE 21.1
Fisher's Categories of Verbal Interaction Applied to Hypothetical Task Group
(From Fisher, "Decision Emergence: Phases in Group Decision Making.")

throughout the life of the groups. These isolated acts can be symbolized as a series of separate statements:

Figure 21.2 shows what percentage of the time each type of statement was used.

Fisher also examined statements in combination with what went before or came after. The paired progression below shows how these "interacts" were formed:

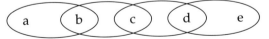

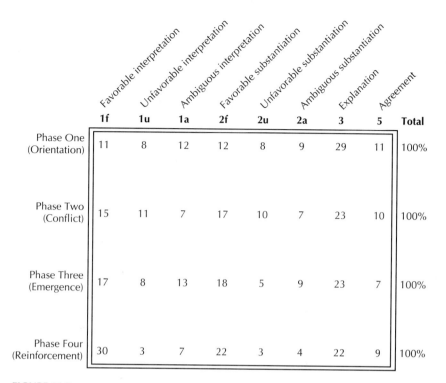

	Favorable interpretation	Unfavorable interpretation	Ambiguous interpretation	Favorable substantiation	Unfavorable substantiation	Ambiguous substantiation	Explanation	Agreement	
	1f	**1u**	**1a**	**2f**	**2u**	**2a**	**3**	**5**	**Total**
Phase One (Orientation)	11	8	12	12	8	9	29	11	100%
Phase Two (Conflict)	15	11	7	17	10	7	23	10	100%
Phase Three (Emergence)	17	8	13	18	5	9	23	7	100%
Phase Four (Reinforcement)	30	3	7	22	3	4	22	9	100%

FIGURE 21.2

Percentage of Interaction Response Coded for Each Category (From data in Fisher, "Decision Emergence: Phases in Group Decision Making.")

The next four sections of the chapter describe significant interact trends. Both the act and interact analyses suggest that consensus is reached in a four-phase sequence of decision emergence:

$$Orientation \rightarrow Conflict \rightarrow Emergence \rightarrow Reinforcement$$

Phase 1: Orientation

The first phase is characterized by a great amount of clarification and agreement. Clarification seems to serve two functions. First, it reduces the uncertainty members feel as they begin their task. Every new group has a "shakedown" period in which members become acclimated and try to figure out the choices that are open to them. Second, a request for clarification is also a way to express disagreement without disturbing the peace ("I'm not sure I understand what you're saying").

The high amount of agreement discovered by Fisher appears to be a way to keep the conversational ball rolling in the middle of start-up tension. Although group members concur with a broad range of statements, agreement especially follows statements that are ambiguous (1a/5, 2a/5). Members can't tell at that point which way the group will go, and agreeing with ambiguous interpretations and substantiations is a way to keep options open.

There are other indications of tentativeness in the orientation phase. Unfavorable responses are lower than in the second phase. Also, favorable interpretations are rarely reinforced with another favorable interpretation (1f/1f). Fisher concluded that many of the ambiguous comments reflect a safe way to express tentative agreement with the decision proposal. His assumption is supported by the nonassertive way ideas are presented during Phase 1 ("I may be wrong, but perhaps. . . . ").

Phase 2: Conflict

The transition from phase 1 to phase 2 can be spotted by the decline of ambiguity and the increase in strong reactions—both favorable and unfavorable. The tentativeness of the orientation stage is replaced by certainty and vehemence ("You have to. . . . "). As attempts to persuade increase, people form coalitions with other like-minded members. It's not unusual to have a back-to-back string of favorable interpretations (1f/1f) spoken by participants who discover they react the same way.

In all probability, Juan will get caught up in the controversy and identify with one side or the other. Perhaps Juan, the black graduate student, and one of the professors are adamant that the whole student personnel department is tainted by racism. Of course, it's possible that he or someone else will withdraw from the conflict. But as polarization increases, not to take a stand is uncharacteristic. Unfavorable substantiation (2u) is higher in phase 2 than at any other time, another indication that conflict is now the norm.

Individual roles solidify in the latter half of the conflict phase. Leadership emerges from the ranks of the majority and those in the minority begin to recognize that they are fighting a losing battle. The move to phase 3 is more prolonged and less distinct than the other phase transitions.

Phase 3: Emergence

Groups can take only so much conflict. As the discussion slides into a new pattern, it becomes obvious to all which way the group is heading. Yet the group won't reach consensus if one side loses and the winners gloat. The take-no-prisoners combativeness of the second phase softens so that those who are outnumbered are given an opportunity for strategic withdrawal. Ambiguity becomes the path of retreat. "If conflict was a clash of favorable and unfavorable opinions, emergence is . . . a semi-clash of favorable and ambiguous opinion."[3]

Ambiguous statements (1a,2a) are heard just as often in the emergence phase as in the orientation stage. But Fisher described their function quite differently. Ambiguity served as tentative agreement in phase 1, but here it reflects muted disapproval. Unfavorable statements (1u,2u) are fewer, and ambiguity becomes a way station on the dissenter's journey to embracing the group decision ("I just wondered . . . ").

Fisher originally hoped to be able to pinpoint the exact time that a decision was reached but concluded that this was an unrealistic goal. He could only say with certainty that the third phase lasts longer than the others, the group attains unanimity toward the end of that stage, and the term *emergence* captures the gradual nature of the process. Juan may never know for sure when the committee reached a consensus on seeking an outside candidate.

Phase 4: Reinforcement

Although the final phase is brief compared with the stages that came before, it is vital for creating group solidarity. Members have an increasing awareness that the decision has already been made, and even those originally opposed have a deepening commitment to the final outcome. The reinforcement stage is like the idealized Old West where "seldom is heard a discouraging word." This is evidenced by the virtual disappearance of unfavorable reactions. Dissent may be constructive during the conflict and emergence phases because disagreement can stimulate innovative ideas. But controversy in phase 4 would be a hindrance to a spirit of unity.

According to Fisher, this absence of disruptive talk reflects real agreement rather than mere avoidance of conflict. In this final phase, favorable interpretation and substantiation (1f,2f) accounted for over 50 percent of everything that was said. Analysis of the interacts shows that almost all the positive reinforcement is given to statements favoring the decision proposal (1f/5, 2f/5).

"Wait a minute, you guys—I've decided to make it unanimous after all."
Drawing by Vietor; © 1978 The New Yorker Magazine, Inc.

Fisher characterized the reinforcement stage as a time of uninhibited joviality. Members engage in loud laughter, verbal backslapping, and mutual congratulations on a job well done. No matter which candidate the search committee ultimately settles on, Juan will walk away from the final meeting with a warm glow, convinced that the person they've nominated will seek racial justice on campus.

VARIATIONS ON A THEME

Fisher was the first to admit that not all groups go through the four-phase developmental sequence. His interact model is designed to apply to groups that need to reach a consensus on issues of major importance to members. Don't expect to see the sequence in operation over mundane matters or when the majority rules through a quick vote.

Fisher also noted that variations are common. Effective members shift from phase to phase, altering their verbal behavior as appropriate. But sometimes a group will get stuck in a phase because one member is unable to adjust to changing conditions. This could be due to interpersonal insensitivity, but usually it's because he or she has a hidden agenda that drives every comment. Either way, the group gets bogged down and is unable to progress to the succeeding phase.

Other group researchers agree with the overall thrust of Fisher's model, if not with its details. Bales found a three-step group progression. And like Fisher, he called the first period a time of orientation. The categories that predominate in his evaluation period match the interactions in Fisher's conflict phase. Bales didn't spot a distinct time of emergence, but his final period of control has some similarity with Fisher's reinforcement phase.

Perhaps the greatest outside confirmation of Fisher's four phases comes from a survey of group process literature undertaken by B. W. Tuckman, who is now dean of education at Florida State University. Before the interact system model was published, Tuckman synthesized previous research and concluded that groups go through a developmental cycle of *forming, storming, norming,* and *performing.* Not only do the labels rhyme, they also seem to match the four phases that Fisher discovered.

PRACTICAL IMPLICATIONS OF DECISION PHASES

Unlike Bales' categories, which have been used by a variety of consultants to analyze specific groups and their members, Fisher's verbal categories have served mainly as a tool to establish his four-phase hypothesis. The theory itself, however, is highly useful. If Fisher has correctly identified the stages of decision emergence, the perceptive leader can spot the phase a group is in and avoid saying things that might sabotage the natural process. In fact, any member who regards consensus as a goal would do well to heed advice based on Fisher's research:

Phase 1—Realizing that ambiguity serves the function of tentative agreement, don't press for specifics during this orientation period. Since requests for clarification often mask disagreement, don't assume you already have unanimity and push for closure.

Phase 2—Arguments are natural and necessary in the conflict stage. Insist that members fight fairly, but don't try to smooth over controversy that the group needs to hear.

Phase 3—At this point, dissenters use vague comments as a means to give in somewhat gracefully. Don't short-circuit their acquiescence by demanding total commitment.

Phase 4—Let people enjoy their new found unity. An overflow of positive reinforcement increases the likelihood that members will stick by the decision after the meeting.

CRITIQUE: AN EMERGING CONSENSUS ON THE INTERACT MODEL

Although there is widespread agreement in the field of group dynamics that decision-making groups go through a somewhat predictable process, the interact system model has its critics. One of them was B. Aubrey Fisher himself. Later in his life he regarded his decision to ignore nonverbal interaction as a mistake. He became even more convinced that relational issues shouldn't be excluded:

> The original purpose of the investigation which discovered these four phases was to observe verbal task behavior free from the confounding variables of the socioemotional dimension. That purpose, of course, was doomed to failure. The two dimensions are interdependent.[4]

The omission of relational issues is particularly shortsighted when there are large discrepancies in the power wielded by certain members of the group. Consider Juan's involvement on the joint faculty-student search committee. We can expect his comments to be a bit circumspect if one of the faculty members is also his professor in a required psychology course. There's also the issue of cultural differences. Juan might be more opposed to a proposal than anyone else sitting at the table, but his Filipino upbringing would make direct criticism unlikely. Fisher's classification method doesn't record these subtle interpersonal dynamics. As University of Minnesota communication researcher Dean Hewes notes in his critique of interaction category systems, "That complexity, if it does exist, does not disappear from the phenomenon under investigation simply by requiring that coders ignore it."[5]

Despite the problems with Fisher's categories, most observers applaud his efforts to capture the process of group development through analysis of verbal interacts. The mere categorization of single statements wouldn't have revealed the different functions of ambiguity in phase 1 and phase 3. It's not only helpful to know what Juan said during the search committee's deliberations, it's important to understand where it came in the flow. As all systems theorists note, sequence is crucial.

QUESTIONS TO SHARPEN YOUR FOCUS

1. Could a well-prepared group leader plan out the first few *interacts* of a *decision-making process*?

2. Fisher believed that *ambiguous* statements in the group serve a different function in the *emergence phase* than they do in the *orientation phase*. How do they differ? How could he tell?

3. What changes would you expect if Fisher has advocated a *closed systems* theory rather than an *open systems* theory?

4. Fisher's interact systems model has been criticized for ignoring the effect of *emotion* on communication. Which of the other theories already presented are open to that charge?

A SECOND LOOK

Recommended resource: B. Aubrey Fisher and Donald Ellis, "Anatomy of Communication in Decision-Making Groups: Improving Effectiveness," in *Small Group Decision Making*, 3d ed., McGraw-Hill, New York, 1990, pp. 170–200.

Brief summary: B. Aubrey Fisher, "Decision Emergence: The Social Process of Decision Making," in *Small Group Communication: A Reader*, 4th ed., R. S. Cathcart and L. A. Samovar (eds.), Wm. C. Brown, Dubuque, Iowa, 1984, pp. 149–156.

Theoretical assumptions: B. Aubrey Fisher and Leonard C. Hawes, "An Interact System Model: Generating a Grounded Theory of Small Groups," *Quarterly Journal of Speech*, Vol. 57, 1971, pp. 444–453.

Quantitative analysis: B. Aubrey Fisher, "Decision Emergence: Phases in Group Decision Making," *Speech Monographs*, Vol. 37, 1970, pp. 53–66.

Quantitative analysis: B. Aubrey Fisher, "The Process of Decision Modification in Small Discussion Groups," *Journal of Communication*, Vol. 20, 1970, pp. 51–64.

Research update: Kenneth Cissna, "Phases in Group Development: The Negative Evidence,"*Small Group Behavior*, Vol. 15, 1984, pp. 3–32.

Critique: Dean Hewes, "The Sequential Analysis of Social Interaction,"*Quarterly Journal of Speech*, Vol. 65, 1979, pp. 56–73.

Systems approach: B. Aubrey Fisher, "The Pragmatic Perspective of Human Communication," in *Human Communication Theory*, Frank E. X. Dance (ed.), Harper & Row, New York, 1982, pp. 192–219.

Early review of literature: B. W. Tuckman, "Developmental Sequence in Small Groups," *Psychological Bulletin*, Vol. 63, 1965, pp. 384–399.

Reflective thinking: John Dewey, *How We Think*, Heath, New York, 1910.

CHAPTER 22

Groupthink
of Irving Janis

Two days after his inauguration in 1961, President John F. Kennedy received a briefing from the CIA on a secret plan for a small-scale invasion of Cuba. First suggested by Richard Nixon when he was vice president under Eisenhower, the plan called for the secret arming, training, and transportation of an elite fighting force of Cuban exiles who would spearhead a popular uprising against the Castro government.

Political historians agree that the close group of Kennedy advisers represented some of the brightest and best minds to serve the country. The secretary of defense was Robert McNamara, who had worked his way up to the presidency of Ford Motor Company. Dean Rusk, secretary of state, was former head of the Rockefeller Foundation. McGeorge Bundy, national security adviser, had been the dean of arts and sciences at Harvard University, and he was joined by the school's outstanding historian, Arthur Schlesinger. Combined with the political savvy of President Kennedy and his brother Robert, who was attorney general, these men brought a vast collective intellect to bear on any governmental decision.

Yet after two months of deliberation, the group unanimously approved the disastrous Bay of Pigs invasion. Three days after the initial landing, all the 1,400 invading troops were either dead or in prison camps, the United States' moral and political leadership in the world was seriously undermined, and Castro's position was solidified. He has now outlasted seven American presidents.

THE BAY OF PIGS DECISION: A PERFECT FAILURE

Once the decision was made, everything went wrong. The president originally approved the plan on the basis that America's link with the rebels could be kept hidden. Yet a week before the invasion, American newspapers reported CIA efforts to recruit volunteer fighters in Miami and described the "secret" training camps in Guatemala. The top-level group assumed that a surprise attack by propeller-driven bombers could destroy the Cuban air force while its planes were on the ground. Yet, because Castro's forces were on

263

alert, Cuban planes became airborne. The superior jets knocked out half of the unmarked United States planes, sank or drove away the four supply ships, and bombed the invading troops as soon as they hit the beach.

The Kennedy advisers were counting on the high morale of the invasion brigade to triumph over weak and undisciplined Cuban troops. In reality, the exiles were discontented and split into factions even before they were surrounded by 20,000 well-trained Cuban soldiers. Ignoring evidence that most Cubans supported Castro and his government, the group had great hopes that the invasion would touch off sabotage and uprisings among a populace that was anti-Castro. Because of this wishful thinking, the president and his advisers planned no viable escape route for the troops in case the invasion failed. Two years later they ransomed the prisoners with food and medical supplies worth $53 million. The whole effort was a grand fiasco.

Irving Janis, a Yale social psychologist, is fascinated with the question of how a blue-ribbon group could make such a terrible decision. He is convinced that their grievous error wasn't an isolated instance limited to Democratic administrations or presidential cabinets experiencing a shaky start. He believes he can spot the same group dynamic at work in other tragic White House decisions—Roosevelt's complacency before Pearl Harbor, Truman's invasion of North Korea, Johnson's escalation of the Vietnam war, and Nixon's Watergate break-in and Reagan's Iran-Contra scandal coverups. Janis doesn't regard the presidential advisors as stupid, lazy, or evil. Rather, he sees them as victims of "groupthink."

GROUPTHINK: A CONCURRENCE-SEEKING TENDENCY

Janis defines *groupthink* as "a mode of thinking that people engage in when they are deeply involved in a cohesive in-group, when the members' strivings for unanimity override their motivation to realistically appraise alternative courses of action."[1] According to his definition, groupthink occurs only when cohesiveness is high. It requires that members share a strong "we-feeling" of solidarity and desire to maintain relationships within the group at all costs.

Janis pictures this kind of group as having a "warm clubby atmosphere." The description is similar to what a perceptive black man had in mind when a friend asked him what clubs he would like to join when integration became a reality. His answer: "Only one. I'd like to be part of the 'good ole boys club.' That's where the 'insider' deals are made."[2]

Most students of group process regard members' mutual attraction to each other as an asset. Marvin Shaw, University of Florida psychologist and the author of a leading text in the field, states this conviction in the form of a general hypothesis which has received widespread research support: "High-cohesive groups are more effective than low-cohesive groups in achieving their respective goals."[3] But Janis believes that the "superglue" of solidarity which bonds people together often causes their mental processes to get stuck:

"Now, let's hear it for good old Al, whose idea this Group Think was in the first place."
Drawing by Whitney Darrow, Jr.; © 1972 The New Yorker Magazine, Inc.

> The more amiability and esprit de corps among members of a policy-making in-group, the greater is the danger that independent critical thinking will be replaced by groupthink, which is likely to result in irrational and dehumanizing actions directed against out-groups.[4]

Janis is convinced that the consensus-seeking tendency of close-knit groups can cause them to make inferior decisions.

SYMPTOMS OF GROUPTHINK

What are the signs that group loyalty is causing members to adopt a groupthink mentality? Janis lists eight symptoms of groupthink which show that concurrence seeking is leading a group astray. He illustrates them with reference to the Bay of Pigs decision.

1. Illusion of Invulnerability.   Members of the Kennedy inner circle felt they could do no wrong. Schlesinger describes the "new frontiersmen" as having tremendous confidence in the Kennedy magic. "Euphoria reigned; we thought for a moment that the world was plastic and the future unlimited."[5]

2. Belief in Inherent Morality of the Group.   Under the sway of group-think, members automatically assume the rightness of their cause. Like King Arthur's knights of the round table, the president's men never questioned whether they were on the side of truth, justice, and goodness. The first symptom shows that the group overestimates its power. This one indicates that it overestimates its morality.

3. Collective Rationalization.   The Kennedy team members continually reassured one another that the international community would believe there was no United States involvement, that the Cuban air force could be wiped out with a single strike, and that the invasion would trigger an anti-Castro revolt. They didn't question these beliefs despite considerable evidence that they were wrong. "Hear no evil, see no evil, speak no evil."[6]

4. Out-Group Stereotypes.   Kennedy and his advisers pictured the Cuban air force as obsolete, the army as weak, and Castro as stupid. None of these simplistic perceptions were accurate. But rationalizations and stereotypes serve to keep a group close-minded toward counteropinions.

5. Self-Censorship.   Schlesinger had grave doubts about the invasion, but he was a weak voice in the Cabinet room. "I can only explain my failure to do more than raise a few timid questions by reporting that one's impulse to blow the whistle on this nonsense was simply undone by the circumstances of discussion."[7] He didn't want to be an isolated, dissenting voice, disrupting the harmony of the Kennedy team. Self-censorship and the final three symptoms show the pressure toward uniformity so central to groupthink.

6. Illusion of Unanimity.   Although each member of the group might have held private opinions which differed from the party line, the group perpetuated the fiction that all were in agreement. Schlesinger describes the meetings as taking place in a "curious atmosphere of assumed consensus." No one wanted to be first to pour sand into the gears of a well-oiled machine. Everyone took silence for consent.

7. Direct Pressure on Dissenters.   Consciously or not, the president structured the discussion in a way that suppressed negative reactions. When a member voiced a mildly discrepant view, Kennedy would call for an immediate straw poll on the entire plan without discussion of the merits of the specific argument. Furthermore, the will to go forward with the invasion became associated with virility. Anyone who stated a reservation might have his manhood called into question.

8. Self-Appointed Mindguards.   "Mindguards" protect a leader from assault by troublesome ideas. Bobby Kennedy assumed that role when he privately confronted a doubtful Schlesinger. "You may be right or you may be wrong, but the President has made his mind up. Don't push it any further. Now is the time for everyone to help him all they can."[8]

GROUPTHINK IN EVERYDAY LIFE

Most of us will never have the opportunity to counsel with presidents and kings on affairs of state, but Janis maintains that groupthink can occur whenever members consider loyalty to the group more important than the action it decides to take. I attend a church that places a high value on close, warm relationships among its members. This is particularly true for the governing board of elders, a group of twenty-four men and women who have known each other for many years, spend time together praying, and occasionally go on a weekend retreat for joint planning and renewal. Led by a pastor who models a deep faith in God, the group represents the company of the committed within the church.

A few years ago the board adopted a midyear budget increase that assumed a jump in annual giving of $300 per family. The amiable tone of discussion and final concurrence among the board members didn't prepare them for the angry protest from the congregation. In hindsight, group members ruefully recall that they were swept up in groupthink.

The pastor provided a collective rationalization for the group by citing an authority on church growth who claimed congregations don't resent special appeals for fund-raising. Any questions about the church's ability to raise the money were quickly laid to rest with easy reassurances that our members always respond to a challenge. How could we fail when the money was for such a good cause? The enthusiasm within the stewardship subcommittee established a norm for the entire board. An emotional appeal from a popular member stilled further dissent. One man later admitted, "I had inner qualms, but I thought I was the only one. I felt like a vote to go slow was a vote against God."

You can probably think of your own example of groupthink from campus life. At my school there was a cohesive group of athletes who evidenced all eight symptoms described by Janis. Known as "The Boys," they wanted to end their college career with a prank that would commemorate their closeness. A week before graduation they kidnapped the campus security officer. Quite a few shared doubts about the scheme with their girlfriends before the act, yet not one raised an objection when the group discussed the plan. None of the boys wanted to shatter the feeling of solidarity or appear to be afraid. For some, it was indeed the end of their college career.

IT DOESN'T ALWAYS HAPPEN

Although Janis sees groups that are highly attractive to members as especially prone to making bad policy decisions, he doesn't believe that all cohesive

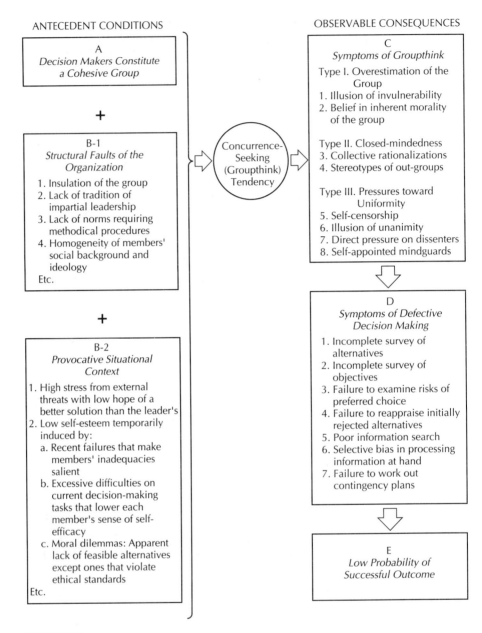

FIGURE 22.1
Theoretical Analysis of Groupthink (From Janis, *Groupthink*, 2d edition)

groups end up succumbing to groupthink. Cohesiveness is a necessary but not sufficient condition for excessive concurrence seeking. Figure 22.1 shows his formal model of groupthink.

Box A shows that cohesiveness is a major cause of groupthink. But the likelihood of concurrence-seeking behavior increases when there are structural faults within the organization (box B-1) and the policy decision has to be made during a time of high stress and low self-esteem (box B-2). The secret of short-circuiting the groupthink process lies in altering the factors in the B boxes that act as catalysts in cohesive groups. The items easiest to change are the first three in box B-1 concerning insulation of the group, impartial leadership, and procedural methods.

As a counterpoint to the Bay of Pigs fiasco, Janis analyzes the Cuban missile crisis, which the Kennedy team faced eighteen months later. A CIA spy photo provided conclusive evidence that Russian technicians were setting up nuclear missiles on Cuban soil less than a hundred miles from the United States shoreline. The cohesive core of the Kennedy policy team was the same as it again tried to determine how to react toward Cuba. The resultant naval blockade brought the world closer to nuclear war than it has ever been, but Janis sees no signs of sloppy thinking as the group devised its strategy to force the Soviets to back down.

I suppose the ultimate proof that the group adopted a good plan to avoid nuclear disaster is that we're alive to read about their deliberations. But in box D of Figure 22.1, Janis provides a checklist of defective decision-making symptoms that would confirm a bad decision had been made even if the planners succeeded and avoided an atomic holocaust. None of these characteristic symptoms were evident in the missile-crisis discussion.

By changing the structural faults of the policy process (see box B-1 of Janis' model), President Kennedy guaranteed that every proposal would get a vigorous appraisal. Following the Bay of Pigs catastrophe, he established procedural norms which encouraged dissent and guaranteed outside evaluation. The specific measures he took illustrate Janis' prescriptions for avoiding groupthink.

REMEDIES FOR GROUPTHINK

Since many groups have no set procedures to ensure close scrutiny of favored solutions, Janis recommends assigning the role of critical evaluator to every member. Instead of representing their own constituency or narrow area of expertise, each participant would take on responsibility for the entire plan. Kennedy told Cabinet members during the Cuban missile crisis that they were all to act as "skeptical generalists." He also guaranteed hard-look assessments by appointing two devil's advocates. His brother Bobby irritated the group with his continual probing on the morality of a preemptive air strike, but in the end the group chose a route that achieved their goals while maintaining the value of human life—no one was killed. Of course, a leader's request for critical comments is a hollow exercise if he or she shows irritation or cuts off debate when the group starts to savage a cherished idea.

Leaders climb to the top by being "take-charge" people. But the very force of personality which placed them in authority can have a chilling effect on group candor. If the opinion of a well-liked leader becomes known, it can quickly become the group norm. Some leaders are able to switch into a nondirective role, but most hemorrhage internally when they try not to reveal their preference too soon. Janis' prescription for open inquiry is to have the leader periodically leave the group so that members will feel free to express their personal views. President Kennedy intentionally stayed away from some meetings in order that those who might be intimidated by his presence would speak. Robert Kennedy noted that there was more true give-and-take when the president wasn't in the room.

Because a close-knit group at the top of an organization is insulated from outside opinions, Janis suggests breaking up into subgroups that work simultaneously on the same issue. Each subgroup can draw on the expertise of trusted subordinates who are encouraged to give their advice freely. The subgroups then come back together and compare notes. This method increases the chance of a security leak, and some critics claim that consensus is reached only through sheer exhaustion, but it served Kennedy well during the Cuban missile crisis. There's always the danger that any of these techniques will create more conflict than the group can handle, but Janis thinks it's worth the risk.

CRITIQUE: AVOIDING UNCRITICAL ACCEPTANCE OF GROUPTHINK

Janis calls for greater critical assessment of proposals lest they be adopted for reasons other than merit. Since his description of groupthink in government has received great popular approval, it seems only fair to cite a number of problems with his theory that give cause for pause.

1. The theory continues to be vague. The original definition of groupthink as a mode of thinking among people who are actively involved in a cohesive group is confusing. Although his later designation of groupthink as a "consensus-seeking tendency" tightens the concept, it's still uncertain what criteria he uses to measure cohesiveness or the way it interacts with the other factors in the model presented in Figure 22.1. Would Janis regard the Kennedy team's discussion of Cuban missiles as a great example of avoiding groupthink if the Russians had responded to the naval blockade by declaring war?

2. Even when Janis is specific, the rationale behind his theory isn't always convincing. Jeanne Longley and Dean Pruitt, who write from the perspective of business (Cummins Engine Co.) and education (State University of New York at Buffalo), claim that there's no theoretical basis for tying together the eight symptoms of groupthink. The symptoms seem to come from a grab bag of after-the-fact case studies. A belief in the inherent morality of the in-group and a stereotyping of out-groups have no logical relationship with concurrence-seeking activity.

3. Janis makes little attempt to link his ideas with other traditions in group dynamics. This is uncharacteristic for an experimental social psychologist who has a long list of scientific publications. He could view groupthink as premature consensus in a faulty process that skips over the conflict stage crucial to Fisher's four-phase sequence:

Orientation → Conflict → Emergence → Reinforcement

Janis ignores the pioneer work of Bales on the need for balance in positive and negative reactions in group discussion. He makes little use of the extensive research on conformity, deviance, or group polarization. Surprisingly, Janis is as insular in his analysis as the committees he accuses of being under the sway of groupthink.

4. Janis places a negative value on cohesiveness, whereas most other researchers find it a positive asset. Longley and Pruitt speculate that this may be because Janis focuses on wrenching policy dilemmas, while mainstream research deals with everyday, mundane problems. Up to this point Janis hasn't differentiated group tasks according to their difficulty or the gravity of their consequences. Perhaps the distinction would provide a way for Janis to integrate his historical analysis into a broader body of knowledge about the effect of cohesiveness on a variety of group decisions.

In spite of these multiple difficulties, Janis' concept of groupthink continues to capture the imagination of those who have seen close-knit groups make terrible decisions. The 1986 space shuttle *Challenger* disaster could have been avoided had the NASA launch team openly discussed the misgivings of the Morton Thiokol engineer who worked with the O-rings that ultimately failed. But after being ridiculed by his superiors and co-workers as a sky-is-falling alarmist, the engineer would only voice a mild protest before retreating into the safety of silence. He simply said that launching the shuttle in freezing temperatures would be "an act away from goodness." As subsequent events made clear, so is groupthink.

QUESTIONS TO SHARPEN YOUR FOCUS

1. Janis defines *groupthink* as a *consensus-seeking tendency*. What alternative terms would you use to describe the same group phenomenon?

2. Suppose your instructor leads a classroom discussion about whether communication theory should be a required course for majors. Which of the eight *symptoms of groupthink* do you think would emerge? Why?

3. Janis claims that groupthink is triggered by a combination of (1) *group cohesiveness*, (2) *structural faults* within the organization, and (3) *stressful circumstances*. Which of these three precipitating factors is easiest to change?

4. What other theories covered in the book are consistent with Janis' groupthink hypothesis?

A SECOND LOOK

Recommended resource: Irving Janis, *Groupthink,* 2d ed., Houghton Mifflin, Boston, 1982.

Original statement: Irving Janis, *Victims of Groupthink,* Houghton Mifflin, Boston, 1972.

Decision-making context: Irving Janis and Leon Mann, *Decision Making,* Free Press, New York, 1977.

Popular summary: Irving Janis, "Groupthink," *Psychology Today,* November 1981, pp. 43–46 and 74–75.

Kennedy presidency: Arthur Schlesinger, *A Thousand Days,* Houghton Mifflin, Boston, 1965.

Historical perspective: Gregory Herek, Irving Janis, and Paul Huth, "Decision Making During International Crises," *Journal of Conflict Resolution,* Vol. 31, 1987, pp. 203–226.

Integration with group dynamics literature: Gregory Moorhead, "Groupthink: Hypothesis in Need of Testing," *Group and Organization Studies,* Vol. 7, 1982, pp. 429–444.

Groupthink in the laboratory: Carrie Leana, "A Partial Test of Janis' Groupthink Model: Effects of Group Cohesiveness and Leader Behavior on Defective Decision Making," *Journal of Management,* Vol. 11, 1985, pp. 5–17.

Critique: Jeanne Longley and Dean G. Pruitt, "Groupthink: A Critique of Janis's Theory," in *Review of Personality and Social Psychology,* Vol. 1, Ladd Wheeler (ed.), Sage, Beverly Hills, Calif., 1980, pp. 74–93.

ORGANIZATIONAL COMMUNICATION

Organizational theorists offer a variety of helpful ways to view what's going on when people come together for complex activity. Most organizational analysis considers communication to be the central task of management. The five approaches below use different metaphors to picture the place of communication in corporate life.

1. The Mechanistic Approach. This classical approach visualizes organizations as machines designed to accomplish specific goals. According to this metaphor, workers are interchangeable parts that function smoothly as long as their range of motion is clearly defined and their actions are lubricated with an adequate hourly wage. Whether working under a supervisor on the General Motors assembly line, a manager at the golden arches of McDonalds, or a militaristic coach in the NFL, employees receive downward communication about how to do their job. Human engineering places a premium on control, efficiency, and rationality. However, the cool impersonality of management may grind down any sense of personal responsibility or human creativity among the work force.

2. The Human Relations Approach. In direct contrast to the mechanistic model, the human relations approach sees individuals as the essential ingredients of any organization. Workers are people, and people are not necessarily the unmotivated, passionless robots the classical school assumes them to be. Strongly influenced by Abraham Maslow's image of people ascending a hierarchy of needs at their own rate, the human relations approach suggests that leaders concentrate on fulfilling the needs of individual members (see Chapter 10). Two-way communication with workers is an executive's most important job. Humanistic managers assume that given the opportunity to get involved in a challenging task, people respond with enthusiasm and creativity. "Satisfied workers will be productive workers."

3. The General Systems Approach. The word *system* is used to describe many of the important realities of our life—weather system, telephone system, accounting system, digestive system, defense system. *System* refers to the overall process that transforms raw material or inputs from the environment (warm air, messages, numbers, food, soldiers) into finished products or outputs (thunderstorms, communication, balance sheets, energy, armies). In each case the whole is greater than the sum of its parts. Chapter 23 presents Karl Weick's model of organizations as information systems—coordinated activities in need of constant realignment in order to survive in a changing environment.

4. The Political Approach. The mechanistic, human relations, and general systems approaches fail to address the internal conflicts that surface in every organization. Strikes, lockouts, discrimination, sexual harassment, "old boy" networks, and corporate wheeler-dealers are the surface symptoms of an internal struggle for power that never stops. Yet office politics aren't necessarily dysfunctional. Proxy fights, labor negotiations, workplace coalitions, company rules, and grapevine gossip can be analyzed as natural ways to redistribute power throughout the organization.

273

*"And so you just threw everything together? . . . Mathews,
a posse is something you have to organize."*

5. The Cultural Approach. Symbolic interactionists (see Chapter 9) assume that human beings act toward things on the basis of meanings that the things have for them. A cultural approach looks for the shared meanings which are unique to a given group of people. Anthropologist Clifford Geertz discovers the interpretive framework of a culture by studying its heroes, values, stories, jokes, rituals, taboos, myths, and legends. Chapter 24 applies his method to the task of analyzing a corporate culture. For Geertz and other symbolic anthropologists, culture is not something an organization has, it is something an organization is.

CHAPTER 23

Information Systems Approach to Organizations

of Karl Weick

My father worked at a large metropolitan newspaper. I was 6 years old when he first took me to experience the final hour before the morning edition was "put to bed." The place was alive with activity—shouted orders, quick telephone calls, copy boys running last-minute changes to the composing room. The whole scene was like watching a huge animal struggling for survival.

Many systems theorists regard the image of a living organism as an appropriate metaphor to apply to all organizations. One model fits all. Even though mosquitoes, sparrows, trout, and polar bears represent vastly different species in the animal kingdom, they all have systems to provide for nourishment, respiration, reproduction, and elimination of bodily waste.

Karl Weick is uncomfortable comparing organizations to live *bodies*, but he definitely regards organizing as a lively *process*. Weick is the Rensis Likert Professor of Organizational Behavior and Psychology at the University of Michigan. Whether he's examining a publishing company, IBM, the city council, or a local jazz band, Weick focuses on the common process of organizing (verb) rather than the static structure of the organization (noun). He sees his approach as capturing a slice of life; traditional analysis is like performing an autopsy.

Weick equates organizing with information processing. Information is the common raw material that all organizations process. But the communication an organization receives is often equivocal. That means a given message has more than one possible interpretation. Weick's model of organizing describes how people make sense out of these confusing verbal inputs. Since we share some familiarity with the species of organizational animal known as "college,'' I'll use academic life at a university to illustrate the features of his model. As you will discover, Weick draws heavily on ideas already discussed in earlier chapters.

THE PURPOSE OF ORGANIZING: REDUCING EQUIVOCALITY

Shannon and Weaver's information theory (see Chapter 4) defined communication as the reduction of uncertainty, a lessening of what you don't know now about what is going to happen next. Weick regards the process of organizing the same way:

> The activities of organizing are directed toward the establishment of a workable level of certainty. An organization attempts to transform equivocal information into a degree of unequivocality with which it can work and to which it is accustomed.[1]

You probably experience the highest degree of uncertainty in a course at the start of the term. The first session is often a stylized version of the game Twenty Questions: Will there be a final exam? Are all the readings in the text? Is a theory different from a model? Does communication require conscious intent?

"Let me get this straight now. Is what you want to build a jean factory or a gene factory?"
From the Wall Street Journal—Permission Cartoon Features Syndicate.

You may have concerns different from those of your classmates, but everyone seeks to remove ambiguity from the environment. By midterm much of your uncertainty will be gone. The lessening of ambiguity won't be due to buildings, offices, or equipment. Organizing is the human interaction of discussions, interviews, lectures, readings, experiences, and making sense of experiences. Yet the process may appear to be quite disorganized.

Fifty years before Alan Bloom's back-to-the-basics book *The Closing of the American Mind*, University of Chicago Chancellor Robert Hutchins bemoaned the chaos that confronts the young adult who steps onto the university campus. There are courses running from art to zoology, but Hutchins claimed that neither the students nor the professors can integrate truths presented within a department, much less between separate disciplines. Weick agrees that "university organizations have *goals* that are inconsistent, ill defined, and loosely coupled; *technology* that no one understands; and *participants* who vary in how much time and effort they invest in the organization."[2] But he doesn't share Hutchins' pessimism.

Weick believes that the degree of complexity and diversity within the organization needs to match the level of ambiguity of the data it processes. He calls this "requisite variety." Since university students and faculty are dealing with vast amounts of confusing information, Weick is convinced they will fail to accomplish their varied tasks of "sense making" unless they organize in a complicated array of interpersonal networks. He advises deans and department heads not to panic in the face of disorder. Instead, he encourages members who are working in an equivocal information environment to "complicate themselves." Most organizations function quite well even though no one knows for sure what's going on.

THE UNIVERSITY AS A LOOSELY COUPLED SYSTEM

Business consultants often describe organizations according to the mechanistic approach—employees are cogs in a corporate machine which is geared to produce widgets. Weick adopts the general systems approach, but he thinks the principles of mechanical engineering have little to offer the student of organizational life. Rather than using a mechanical model, he prefers a biological one, the same type used in the Bible to describe relationships in the early Christian church:

> For the body does not consist of one member but of many. . . . If the ear should say, "Because I am not an eye, I do not belong to the body," that would not make it any less part of the body. If the whole body were an eye, where would be the hearing? . . . God arranged the organs in the body, each one of them, as he chose. . . . There are many parts, yet one body. The eye cannot say to the hand, "I have no need of you."[3]

The passage illustrates the interconnectedness that Weick regards as the primary feature of organizing life. Sometimes the bonds are tight. For example, McDonalds' quality-control directives ensure that the french fries you get near campus will taste like the ones served under the golden arches in your home neighborhood. In other cases the linkage is quite loose. A drought in Idaho may adversely affect the taste of potatoes served in McDonalds *and* the student union cafeteria. But almost all events are coupled to each other in some way.

In order that you might experience loose coupling firsthand, Weick urges you to tour buildings on your campus and note whether there are more statues and busts of college donors than there are of famous people. He claims that this seemingly isolated feature of university life could well be linked with a closed-stack policy in the library, the percentage of the campus budget that goes for beautification, the average distance from faculty offices to washrooms, and whether or not faculty names are listed alphabetically or by academic rank.

Weick describes the basic unit of interconnectedness as the *double interact.* Fisher's theory of system interacts (see Chapter 21) examined what group members said and the response of others. But a double interact consists of three elements—act, response, and adjustment. You write a research proposal, the professor says it's too wordy, you cut it down to a single page.

Student ⟸⟹ Professor

Double interact loops are the tightly coupled building blocks of every organization. These communication cycles are the reason Weick focuses more on relationships within an organization than he does on an individual's talent or performance. He believes that many outside consultants gloss over the importance of the double interact because they depart the scene before the effects of their recommended action bounce back to have an impact on the actor.

The university is a prime example of double interacts in a loosely coupled system. Loose coupling refers to the fact that feedback loops in the classics department have little in common with the double interacts occurring in the school of business, and neither set is tightly linked with the cycles of information within the building and grounds side of the organization. Although Hutchins deplored the absence of common goals and commitment, Weick sees it as a strength. Loose coupling allows the university to absorb shocks, scandals, and stupidity without destroying the system. An incompetent professor, surly registrar, or dull student won't be cause to shut the doors.

THE UNIVERSITY AS A SYSTEM OPEN TO THE ENVIRONMENT

In 1844 Charles Darwin's *The Origin of the Species* presented his theory of evolution.[4] His survival-of-the-fittest position is quite simple. Organisms live in a harsh environment. Some are not well suited to survive and thus quickly die. Others have whatever it takes to live; they reproduce. Natural selection results in a form of life better suited to its surroundings:

Variation → Selection → Retention

Weick applies Darwin's theory to organizations. He thinks we should consider the social-cultural environment as a jungle where survival is the name of the game, an ultimate goal even more important than accomplishing the stated aims of the organization. The March of Dimes is a case in point. That charitable organization was founded for the specific purpose of funding research to discover a way to prevent polio. In 1954 Dr. Jonas Salk discovered a vaccine for the virus, and in 1960 Dr. Albert Sabin developed an effective oral strain that virtually ended the crippling childhood disease. One might think that the charity would celebrate victory and gratefully disband. But the March of Dimes fund-raising system proved to have greater resistance to death than polio. The organization adapted to a changing environment by switching its focus to birth defects, and thirty years later is still soliciting money.

Weick contends that some people organize in a way better adapted to survive than do others. The fierce competition among schools for new students and the steady disappearance of small private colleges support his view. Weick notes one major difference between biological evolution and group survival, however. A given animal is what it is; variation comes through mutation. But the nature of an organization can change when its members alter their behavior. University of Colorado economist Kenneth Boulding labels adaptation through change "survival of the fitting."

My childhood visit to my father's office left a lasting impression of organizational fluidity. He pointed out the official organizational chart which hung on the wall. The bold vertical lines of authority flowing down the pyramid gave the impression of a controlled and orderly flow of communication. But then he pulled his unofficial pencil version from the top drawer of his desk. It was smudged with erasures and cluttered by dotted lines crisscrossing the page. "That's who is really talking to each other this week," he said. Weick would have liked my father's approach. He tells managers to continually "rechart the organizational chart."

THE THREE-STAGE PROCESS OF SOCIAL-CULTURAL EVOLUTION

According to Weick, social-cultural evolution is a three-stage process that begins with enactment:

Enactment → Selection → Retention

Enactment: Don't Just Sit There; Do Something

The term *ivory tower* is often used to suggest that universities are separate and aloof from the world that surrounds them. Weick regards any notion of fixed barriers between an organization and its environment as erroneous. Consider the relationship between a university basketball team and its various publics. In addition to double interacts with the players, the coach has to respond to professors' calling for strict academic standards, alumni's clamoring for victory, reporters' wanting interviews, television's dictates for odd starting times, the administration's demands for ethical recruitment, and the whims of parents and high school coaches who are convinced that their boy is the next Michael Jordan.

The example not only shows the absence of firm boundaries that mark where an organization stops and the environment begins, it is also consistent with Weick's belief that organizations create their own environment. Achieving a slot in the NCAA playoffs will create alumni pride, a climate certain to result in increased giving. In the terms of open-systems theory, the environment is as much an output as it is an input. Through the process of enactment, people organizing together invent their environment rather than merely discover it.

Action is the root idea of en*act*ment. Weick is convinced that the failure to act is the cause of most organizational ineffectiveness. He advises the manager to wade into the swarm of equivocal events and "unrandomize" them. The only way a leader can fail the test of organizing is by doing nothing.

I recently had the opportunity to watch Weick's advice played out in discussions between the young president of a small church-affiliated college and male students who petitioned the administration for condom dispensers in the dorm. Although the proposal for coin-operated machines in the men's washrooms was specific, the meaning behind the request was equivocal. Did the ad hoc group have a sincere concern about the danger of AIDS and unwanted pregnancy on campus, or were they using the issue as a way to attack the moral fiber of the school? Was the request an admirable case of student activism or merely a challenge to all authority?

As soon as he heard about the issue, the president, William Hill, set up a series of meetings and informal discussions to clarify the situation. Although talking about the issue may not strike you as bold action, remember that Weick regards processing information as the essence of organizing. President Hill's act of initiating honest dialogue created a positive climate among students and gave him a basis for selecting a specific interpretation of their behavior.

Selection: Respond Now; Plan Later

Weick defines *selection* as "retrospective sense making." It is an organizer's answer to the recurring question of meaning: "Knowing what I know now, should I change the way I label and connect the flow of experience?" But we can only interpret actions that we've already taken. That's why Weick thinks chaotic action is better than orderly inaction. Common ends and shared means are the result of effective organizing, not a prerequisite. Planning comes after enactment.

President Hill received information which he could interpret in different ways (equivocality). He immediately invited the six students making the request to come to his office to talk (enactment). After the meeting was over, he looked back on the dialogue and tried to imagine a reasonable history that led up to the conference (selection). Weick says that Hill had two organizational tools to help make his selection—rules and cycles.

Assembly *rules* are stock responses that have served well in the past and have become standard operating procedure. Whether codified in oral tradition or stated in the company manual, these rules represent the corporate wisdom about how to process information. Undoubtedly, Hill's school has a pool of guidelines relevant to the student request for condom dispensers:

All requests should be put in writing.

Never appear to give in to student pressure.

In sexual matters, just say no.

Controversial issues should be sent to the trustees.

Yet each of these rules seems less than satisfying in this many-faceted situation. Weick would claim their inadequacy is due to the ambiguity inherent in the request. Rules are fine when equivocality is low, but they fail to remove uncertainty from a situation when many conflicting interpretations are possible.

The second tool for selection is the act-response-adjustment *cycle* of the double interact. These verbal loops can take the form of interviews, meetings, open briefings, conferences, phone calls, discussions, exchange of memos, working lunches, or chats over the watercooler. Like a full turn of the crank on an old-fashioned clothes wringer, each communication cycle squeezes equivocality out of the situation. Weick claims the more equivocal the information an organization has to process, the more communication cycles it requires to reduce ambiguity to an acceptable level. He postulates an inverse relationship between rules and cycles. As cycles increase to handle complex data, reliance on rules goes down.

A series of communication cycles between Hill and Bob Lott (spokesman for the petitioning group) went a long way to reduce uncertainty that each had about the other's intent:

HILL: It's great to see that students care about social issues on campus.

LOTT: Thanks for being willing to talk with us right away. The former president would have ignored the issue, and we'd never get a straight answer.

HILL: This one is a tough issue. When it comes to AIDS, there's no such thing as safe sex with more than one partner. Condoms aren't 100 percent effective.

LOTT: We don't want to encourage loose behavior, but sometimes in a moment of passion during dorm visitation a guy and a girl may have sex without taking proper precautions. Chaplain Thurgood at Pinehurst College said, "I'd do anything in my power to prevent one abortion or one case of AIDS." That's how we feel.

HILL: I feel the same way. But I fear that your suggestion would encourage dangerous sex rather than make it safe. Would you guys be willing to cut out closed-door visitation to reduce the risk?

LOTT: (Long pause) We'll have to think that one over.

You may or may not agree with either man's stance, but through this sequence of double interacts both parties eliminated potential misinterpretations of the other's actions. Hill rejected the notion that students were trying to embarrass the school, but he also concluded that they weren't willing to sacrifice their visitation rights to achieve public health goals. Hill ultimately decided against installing condom dispensers. Although Hill's decision was not popular with the students, because of his openness to discuss the issue in a reasoned manner, they did not perceive him as a weak leader or an authoritarian prude. The positive cast that each put on the other's behavior is consistent with Weick's preference for affirmation over criticism. In Hill's and Lott's case, the foundation for positive interpretations had been laid through the president's participation in pickup games of basketball in the gym.

Although much of Weick's overall model remains to be tested, two innovative studies confirm that organizational members employ rules to process unambiguous data, but use communication cycles to process highly equivocal information. Organizational communication professors Linda Putnam of Texas A and M University and Ritch Sorenson of Iowa State University designed a sixteen-hour simulation for two imaginary fireworks companies, periodically feeding in messages of varying ambiguity. Members applied more rules when the meaning was clear, fewer rules when the meaning was obscure. Northern Illinois University communication professor Gary Kreps ran a field test on the year-long proceedings of a university faculty senate. He gauged the equivocality of twenty-four separate motions and then tracked the debate within the body. As Weick predicted, equivocal proposals generated more double interacts among members than motions which appeared straightforward. Taken together, these studies show that there is an inverse relationship between rules and cycles that varies according to input ambiguity.

Retention: Treat Memory as a Pest

Retention in organizations is like biological reproduction in nature. It's the way systems remember. President Hill's college isn't as loosely coupled as a state university, so his manner of responding to the condom proposal may become a dominant action in corporate policy. But even small schools aren't so tightly knit that a leader's actions and interpretations automatically become the norm for all college staff. Most employees will never hear how the president responded, much less recall it at a later date.

Weick thinks that's fortunate: Too much retention creates a network of rules that reduces a person's flexibility to respond to complex information.

Weick recognizes that some degree of collective memory provides stability for people who are working together. What is a corporate image if not a record of interpersonal relationships, casual maps of how things work within the organization, and stories of successful penetrations of the outside environment? That's why universities publicize faculty and student achievements, preserve accounts of experiences on campus, and catalogue the honors received by famous alumni. But the weight of tradition can stifle the flexibility needed to ensure survival in an uncertain future. Weick seeks an ongoing tension between stability and innovation. He fears that managers give too much credence to past experience and suggests they should "treat memory as a pest." The 1990s decline of corporate giants like IBM, Sears, and General Motors suggests that he is right.

Weick urges leaders to continually discredit much of what they think they know—to doubt, argue, contradict, disbelieve, counter, challenge, question, vacillate, and even act hypocritically. Company manuals are collections of recipes which suggest that each course will turn out right if you follow the rules. Weick prefers the crazed-chef approach, which encourages the cook to make up the recipe as he or she goes along. Organizations fail because they lose flexibility by relying too much on the past.

CRITIQUE: THE PLUSES AND MINUSES OF METAPHOR

Karl Weick manages to do what few systems theorists have done in the past—make a general theory interesting. He accomplishes this through a variety of provocative metaphors, vivid examples, and startling statements. He writes that "all interesting theories share the quality that they constitute an attack on the assumptions taken for granted by an audience."[5] He guarantees attention by continually challenging the conventional wisdom of managers who seek to simplify procedures and minimize conflict.

His sociocultural application of Darwin's evolution theory shares the advantages and drawbacks of all metaphors. On the positive side, the biological model explains the hard-to-understand concept of systems in terms of something we know intimately—our body. It also highlights features of organizations that we might otherwise miss—the ultimate goals of survival, the body's ability to innovate, and especially, its constant exchange with the environment.

Yet the living-information-systems model has its danger. It would be easy to become so caught up in the figure of speech that the metaphor becomes an ideology. Some who regard organizations as actual living organisms have taken the way the body *is* as evidence of how an organization *ought* to be. For example, many apologists for the free enterprise system offer social Darwinism as justification for cutthroat capitalism. Or we might argue that since the healthy body has a functional unity, any conflict within an organization is a sign of illness. Weick, however, doesn't treat the metaphor as proof, and he shouldn't be held responsible for the mistakes of people who do. What he has done is to offer a provocative theory which has stimulated a great deal of discussion. If his theory strikes you as somewhat equivocal, consider the ambiguity an occasion for double interacts with your instructor to reduce the uncertainty.

QUESTIONS TO SHARPEN YOUR FOCUS

1. Weick takes a *systems approach* to organizing. Can you name three other theories from earlier chapters that are systems theories? Do they all describe *open systems*?

2. Compare and contrast Weick's view of *social-cultural evolution* with Darwin's view of *biological survival of the fittest*. How are they similar? How are they different?

3. Is your family organization *tightly* or *loosely coupled*? How does it deal with *equivocal information* from the outside environment? Does this method of processing information help or hinder its survival?

4. Does Weick's advocacy of *retrospective sense making* apply to your learning in this course? When would *rules* serve well? What opportunities do you have for *double interacts*?

A SECOND LOOK

Recommended resource: Karl E. Weick, *The Social Psychology of Organizing*, 2d ed., Addison-Wesley, Reading, Mass., 1979.

Theory update: Karl E. Weick, "Organizing Improvisation: 20 Years of Organizing," *Communication Studies*, Vol. 40, 1989, pp. 241–248.

Living system metaphor: Gareth Morgan, "Nature Intervenes: Organizations as Organisms," in *Images of Organization*, Sage, Beverly Hills, Calif., 1986, pp. 39–76.

Loosely coupled systems: J. Douglas Orton and Karl E. Weick, "Loosely Coupled Systems: A Reconceptualization." *Academy of Management Review*, Vol. 15, 1990, pp. 202–223.

Academic organization: Karl Weick, "Educational Organizations as Loosely Coupled Systems," *Administrative Science Quarterly*, Vol. 21, 1976, pp. 1–21.

Retrospective sense making: Anne Donnellon, Barbara Gray, and Michael Burgoon, "Communication, Meaning, and Organized Action," *Administrative Science Quarterly*, Vol. 31, 1986, pp. 43–55.

Rules and equivocal messages: Linda Putnam and Ritch Sorenson, "Equivocal Messages in Organizations," *Human Communication Research*, Vol. 8, 1982, pp. 114–132.

Cycles and ambiguous proposals: Gary Kreps, "A Field Experimental Test and Reevaluation of Weick's Model of Organizing," in *Communication Yearbook 4*, Dan Nimmo (ed.), Transaction Books, New Brunswick, N.J., 1980, pp. 389–398.

Critique of Weick's model: B. Aubrey Fisher, "The Enactment of Communication," Annual meeting of the Speech Communication Association, 1980.

CHAPTER 24

Cultural Approach to Organizations
of Clifford Geertz

Princeton anthropologist Clifford Geertz writes that "man is an animal suspended in webs of significance that he himself has spun.[1] He pictures culture as those webs. In order to travel across the strands toward the center of the web, an outsider must discover the common interpretations that hold the society together. Culture is shared meaning, shared understanding, shared sense making.

Geertz has conducted field research in the islands of Indonesia and on the Moroccan highlands, rural settings remote from industrial activity. His best-known monograph is an in-depth symbolic analysis of the Balinese cockfight. Geertz has never written a treatise on the bottom line, never tried to decipher the significance of the office Christmas party, and never met a payroll, a disqualifying sin in the eyes of many business professionals. Yet despite his silence on the topic of big business, Geertz's interpretive approach has proved useful in making sense of organizational activity. Many analysts have come to view employees of IBM, CBS, and AT&T as members of distinct tribes rather than corporate clones cut from the same gray flannel cloth.

CULTURE AS A METAPHOR OF ORGANIZATIONAL LIFE

The use of culture as a root metaphor was undoubtedly stimulated by western fascination with the economic success of Japanese corporations. When American business leaders traveled to the Far East to study methods of production, they discovered that the superior quantity and quality of Japan's industrial output had little to do with technology, but was due to the workers' shared cultural value of group loyalty. Organizing looks radically different depending on how people in the host culture structure meaning. Communal face-saving in Japan is foreign to the class antagonism of Great Britain, or the we're-number-one competitive mind-set of the United States.

*"Before we head into the annual meeting, gentlemen, I thought a quick
little review of just who we are might be in order."*
© 1974, Henry R. Martin.

Today the term *corporate culture* means different things to different people. Some observers use the phrase to describe the surrounding environment which constrains a company's freedom of action. (U.S. workers would scoff at singing a corporate anthem at the start of their working day.) Others use the term to refer to a quality or property of the organization. (Acme Gizmo is a friendly place to work.) They speak of *culture* as synonymous with *image*, *character*, or *climate*. But writers Mike Pacanowsky at the University of Colorado Communication Department and Nick O'Donnell-Trujillo at Southern Methodist University Communication Department are committed to Geertz's symbolic approach, which considers culture as more than a single variable in organizational research:

> Organizational culture is not just another piece of the puzzle; it is the puzzle. From our point of view, culture is not something an organization has; a culture is something an organization *is*.[2]

WHAT CULTURE IS; WHAT CULTURE IS NOT

Geertz admits that the concept of culture as "systems of shared meaning" is somewhat vague and difficult to grasp. Unlike popular usage that equates culture with concerts and art museums, he refuses to use the word to signify "less primitive." No modern anthropologist would fall into the trap of classifying people as high-or-low-culture.

Culture is not whole or undivided. Geertz points out that even close-knit societies have subcultures and countercultures within their boundaries. Employees in sales and accounting eye each other warily—the first group calling the accountants "number crunchers" and "bean counters," the second group in turn labeling members of the sales force "fast talkers" and "glad-handers." Despite their differences, both groups may regard blue-collar bowling as a strange ritual compared with their normal weekend round of golf.

Organizational theorists Harrison Trice of Cornell University and Janice Beyer of the University of Texas state that culture has two basic components:

(1) its substance, or the network of meanings contained in its ideologies, norms, and values; and (2) its forms, or the practices whereby these meanings are expressed, affirmed and communicated to members.[3]

Trice and Beyer present a typology of cultural forms which include rites, ceremonies, rituals, myths, legends, stories, folklore, and artifacts. Geertz calls these expressions of culture "an ensemble of texts . . . which the anthropologist strains to read over the shoulder of those to whom they properly belong."[4]

The elusive nature of culture prompts Geertz to label its study a "soft science." It is not an experimental science in search of law, but an interpretive one in search of meaning. The corporate observer is one part scientist, one part drama critic.

The fact that all symbols require interpretation is nicely captured in a story about Pablo Picasso recorded by York University (Toronto) writer Gareth Morgan.[5] "It isn't how she really looks." When asked by the painter how she really looked, the man produced a photograph from his wallet. Picasso's comment: "Small, isn't she?"

THICK DESCRIPTION: WHAT ETHNOGRAPHERS DO

Geertz refers to himself as an ethnographer. Just as geographers chart the physical territory, ethnographers map out social discourse. They observe, they record, they analyze. There's no shortcut for the months of participant observation required to collect an exhaustive account of interaction. Without that raw material, there would be nothing to interpret. Geertz spent years in Indonesia and Morocco. MIT organizational researcher John Van Maanen studied the socialization of recruits for a big-city police force by joining the rookie class at the training academy. Like Geertz, he was completely open about his research goals, and he participated fully in the three-month class. He then spent four months riding in a squad car with a novice and a veteran—eight to ten hours a day, six days a week. Clearly, ethnographers commit to the long haul.

The daily accounts of intensive observation invariably fill the pages of many ethnographers' notebooks. The visual image of these journals stacked on top of each other would be sufficient justification for Geertz to refer to ethnography as "thick description." However, the term describes the intertwined layers of common meaning that underlie what a particular people say and do. Analysis of corporate culture requires interpretation as well as observation. Geertz calls this the "said" of interaction. It's not enough to preserve copies of office memos or to make transcripts of meetings. The "said" of thick description is the ethnographer's best guess at the thought, gist, or meaning that lies behind what the participants are saying.

Thick description starts with a state of bewilderment. "What the devil's going on?" Geertz asks himself as he wades into a new culture. The only way to reduce the puzzlement is to observe as if one were a stranger in a foreign land. That may be difficult for a manager who is already enmeshed in a specific corporate culture. He or she may overlook many of the signs that point to common interpretation. Worse yet, the manager may assume that office humor or the company grapevine has the same significance for people in this culture as for those in a previous place of employment. Geertz says it will always be different.

Behaviorists would probably consider employee trips to the office watercooler of little interest. If they did regard water breaks worth studying, they would tend to note the number of trips and length of stay for each worker. Ethnographers would be more interested in the significance the seemingly mundane activity had for the employees. Instead of a neat statistical summary, they'd have pages of dialogue at the watercooler. Geertz fears that a frequency count would only bleach human behavior of the very properties that interest him. But he would be particularly sensitive to the stories that were told and the rites that evolved. Although they don't limit themselves to these forms, ethnographers find that stories and rites provide a particularly helpful access to the unique shared meanings within an organization.

THE SYMBOLIC INTERPRETATION OF STORY

Stories that are repeated over and over provide a convenient window through which to view corporate webs of significance. Trice and Beyer define story as "a narrative based on true events—often a combination of truth and fiction."[6] Pacanowsky and O'Donnell-Trujillo ask, "Has a good story been told that takes you to the heart of the matter?"[7] They focus on the scriptlike qualities of narratives which line out an employee's part in the company play. Although workers have room to improvise, the anecdotes provide clues as to what it means to perform a task in this particular theater. Stories capture memorable performances and pass on the passion the actor felt at the time.

Pacanowsky and O'Donnell-Trujillo suggest three types of narrative which dramatize organizational life. *Corporate stories* carry the ideology of management and reinforce company policy. Every McDonalds franchisee hears about the late Ray Kroc, who, when he was chairman of the board, picked up trash from the parking lot when he'd visit a store.[8] *Personal stories* are those which company personnel tell about themselves, often defining how they would like to be seen within the organization. *Collegial stories* are positive or negative anecdotes told about others in the organization. Since these aren't usually sanctioned by management, these accounts pass on how the organization "really works."

Throughout most of my life, I've had access to some of the cultural lore of Dixie Communications, a medium-sized corporation which operates a television station and newspaper in a southern city. Like so many other regional companies, Dixie has been taken over by an out-of-state corporation that has no local ties. The brief narratives below are shorthand versions of stories heard again and again throughout the company.

> Although the original publisher has been dead for twenty-five years, employees fondly recall how he would spend Christmas Eve with the workers in the press room. Their account is invariably linked with reminders that he initiated health benefits and profit sharing long before it became a union demand. (Corporate)

> The publisher ran another newspaper in the north and so was away much of the time. No announcement was ever made about when he would return. When the janitor polished the brass banister in the main lobby and hummed "Happy Days Are Here Again," everyone knew "the big brass" would arrive shortly. (Corporate)

> The current comptroller is the highest-ranking "local boy" in the corporation. He often tells the story about the first annual audit he performed long before computers were installed. Puzzled when he ran across a bill for fifty pounds of pigeon feed, he discovered that the company used homing pigeons to send in news copy and circulation orders from a town across the bay. The story usually concludes with an editorial comment about pigeons being more reliable than the new machines. His self-presentation reminds listeners that he has always been cost-conscious, yet it also aligns him with the human side of the "warm people versus cold machines" issue. (Personal)

> The theme of absentee ownership runs throughout many of the stories told around the plant. On-site inspections by the CEO of the parent company are limited to overnight stays. The man comes straight from the airport carrying his suitcase. Rumor has it that he brings it to carry the cash profits back up north. The term *carpetbagger* is often part of the story. (Collegial)

> Shortly after the takeover, a department head encouraged the new publisher to meet with his people for a few minutes at the end of the day. The new boss declined the invitation on the grounds of efficiency: "To be

quite candid, I don't want to know about a woman's sick child or a man's vacation plans. That kind of information makes it harder to fire a person." Spoken in a cold, superior tone, the words *quite candid* are always part of the story. (Collegial)

CULTURAL UNIQUENESS VS. COMMON THEMES

Geertz cautions against any analysis which says, "This story means . . ." Cultural myths contain a mosaic of significance and defy a simplistic one-on-one translation of symbols. Yet taken as a whole, the five stories above reveal an uneasiness with the new management. This interpretation is consistent with repeated metaphorical references to the old Dixie as "family" and the new Dixie as "a faceless computer."

These warm-cold images emerge in other organizations as well. Is it possible that corporate cultures are more similar than Geertz would be willing to admit? An essay written by Stanford management professor Joanne Martin and three co-authors claims that although each corporate culture thinks its stories are unique, every workplace narrative is really a symbolic answer to one of only seven questions:

1. What do I do when my boss breaks the rules?
2. Is the big boss human?
3. Can the little person rise to the top?
4. Will I be fired?
5. Will the organization help if I have to move?
6. How will the boss react to mistakes?
7. How will the organization react to obstacles?

The Dixie stories seem to speak to the themes of questions 2 and 4, but Geertz would caution against assuming that all stories fit this mold. The thicker the description of an organization becomes, the more we'll become aware of the exceptional nature of members' sense of shared meaning. Despite their similar functions, training, and technology, the *New York Times*, the *Cleveland Plains Dealer*, the *Denver Post*, and Dixie Communications have distinct corporate systems of beliefs and values. A change of job is a switch in culture.

RITES: THE MORE THINGS CHANGE, THE MORE THEY STAY THE SAME

Geertz wrote about the Balinese rite of cockfighting because the contest represented more than a game. "It is only apparently cocks that are fighting there. Actually it is men." The cockfight is a dramatization of status. "Its function is interpretive: It is a Balinese reading of Balinese experience, a story they tell themselves about themselves."[9]

According to Trice and Beyer, a *rite* consists of

relatively elaborate, dramatic planned sets of activities that consolidate various forms of cultural expressions into one event, which is carried out through social interaction, usually for the benefit of an audience.[10]

They list six types of rites which have latent social consequences that go beyond their obvious public purpose:

1. Rites of passage (basic training in the military)
2. Rites of degradation (firing top executives)
3. Rites of enhancement (award ceremonies)
4. Rites of renewal (training seminars)
5. Rites of conflict resolution (collective bargaining)
6. Rites of integration (office Christmas party)

Over a generation ago, workers in the classified advertising department at Dixie created an integrative rite which survives to the present. The department is staffed by over fifty telephone sales representatives who work out of a large common room. At Dixie, these representatives not only take the phoned-in "two lines/two days/two dollars" personal ads, they also initiate callbacks to find out if customers were successful and might want to sell other items. Compared with similar operations at other papers, classified advertising at Dixie is a major profit center which has low employee turnover. The department continues to have the "family atmosphere" of premerger Dixie.

Most of the phone representatives are women under the age of 40. They regard Max, the male manager who has held the position for over thirty years, as a "father confessor"—a warm, nonjudgmental person with a genuine concern for their lives. Whenever a woman has a baby, Max visits her in the hospital and offers help to those at home preparing for her return. Women announce their pregnant status by taping a dime within a large picture frame on the outer wall of Max's office, inscribing their name and anticipated day of delivery.

This rite of integration serves multiple functions for the women:

At a time of potential anxiety, it is an occasion for public affirmation from the larger community.

The rite is a point of contact between work and those outside of Dixie. Employees often take pride in describing the ritual to customers and friends.

Although the dime-on-the-wall practice originated with the workers, the authorized chronicle of decades of expected births proclaims a sense of permanence. It says in effect: "The company doesn't consider motherhood a liability; your job will be here when you get back."

From the management's standpoint, the rite ensures that there will be no surprises. Max has plenty of time to schedule the employee's maternity leave, arrange for another salesperson to cover her accounts, and anticipate stresses that she might be encountering. Trice and Beyer note that rites of passage guarantee a continuity of the social order: "The rites help assure that new occupants can be treated like the old, and thus will cause little disturbance or uncertainty in ongoing social relations."[11]

It is tempting to read economic significance into the fact that employees use dimes to symbolize this major change in their lives. But the women involved refer to the small size of the token rather than its monetary value. Geertz would caution that this is *their* story, and we should listen to *their* interpretation.

THE MANAGER AS CHANGE AGENT

The current popularity of the cultural metaphor is undoubtedly due to business leaders' desire to shape interpretation within their organization. Symbols are the tools of management. Executives don't operate forklifts or produce widgets; they create vision, state goals, process information, send memos, and engage in other symbolic behavior. If they believe that culture is the key to commitment, productivity, and sales, the possibility of changing culture becomes a seductive idea. Planting organizational stories and establishing rites would seem an ideal way to create a corporate myth.

But can culture be created? Geertz regards shared interpretations as naturally emerging from all members rather than consciously engineered by managers. Leaders may articulate a new vision in a fresh vocabulary, but it is the people who smile, sigh, snicker, or scoff. For example, Martin Luther King's "I Have a Dream" speech, discussed in the next chapter, was powerful because he touched a chord that was already vibrating within millions of listeners.

Shared meanings are hard to dispel. Symbol watchers within a company quickly discount the words of management if they don't square with performance. The erratic executive of a large company wrote a text on leadership and had the nerve to ask a middle manager if she had purchased the book. "I don't need to read the book," was her gutsy reply, "I've seen the play."

Yet even if culture *could* be changed, there still remains the question of whether it *should* be. Symbolic anthropologists have traditionally adopted a nonintrusive style appropriate to examining fine crystal—look, admire, but don't touch. Managers who regard themselves as agents of cultural change create bull-in-a-china-shop fears for consultants who have ethical concerns about how their corporate analyses might be used. University of Massachusetts management professor Linda Smircich notes that ethnographers would draw back in horror at the idea of using their data to extend a tribal priest's control over the population, yet most communication consultants are hired by top management to do just that.

CRITIQUE: IS THE CULTURAL APPROACH USEFUL?

By now you understand that Geertz would regard the quest to alter culture as both inappropriate and virtually impossible. This purist position exposes him to criticism from pragmatists who want not only to understand organizational communication but also to influence it. While granting that culture is a helpful metaphor, pragmatists point out that most employees join a company long after they've been socialized into the values of the larger society. They also claim that unique corporate cultures are rare. Most organizations have a series of bureaucratic rules and procedures that seem to replace the shared interpretations which are Geertz's "superglue" of culture. Pragmatists also despair of having the time or funding to carry out the thick description Geertz's view of culture dictates.

None of these objections attack the basic validity of an interpretive approach that takes corporate communication seriously. Contrary to the traditional approach of consultants who are funded by the organizations they study, the purpose of thick description is not to help managers increase production or get things running smoothly. The aim of symbolic analysis is to create a better understanding of what it takes to function effectively within a given culture. In most organizations, members are free to decide whether or not they want to belong. A sensitive cultural analysis could help them make an intelligent choice. Perhaps managers fail to appreciate the value of thick description because they have yet to make an effort to sort out the webs of significance within their organization. The answer, like culture, is a matter of interpretation.

QUESTIONS TO SHARPEN YOUR FOCUS

1. Based on the concept of organizational culture as *systems of shared meaning,* how would you describe the culture at your school to a prospective student?

2. An *ethnographer's* thick description of your college culture would be more than a pile of notes describing activities on campus. What else is involved in *thick description?*

3. Can you identify specific *rites of passage, degradation, enhancement, renewal, conflict resolution,* and *integration* at your school?

4. What *favorite story* do you tell to others about your current or most recent place of employment? Would you classify it as a *corporate, personal,* or *collegial* narrative? Why?

A SECOND LOOK

Recommended resource: Clifford Geertz, *The Interpretation of Cultures,* Basic Books, New York, 1973. (See especially "Thick Description: Toward an Interpretive Theory of Culture," pp. 3–30; and "Deep Play: Notes on the Balinese Cockfight," pp. 412–453.)

Cultural metaphor: Gareth Morgan, "Creating Social Reality: Organizations as Cultures," in *Images of Organization,* Sage, Newbury Park, Calif., 1986, pp. 111–140.

Current scholarship: Peter J. Frost, Larry F. Moore, Meryl Reis Louis, Craig C.

Lundberg, and Joanne Martin (eds.), *Reframing Organizational Culture,* Sage, Newbury Park, Calif., 1991.

Thick description: John Van Maanen, "Observations on the Making of Policemen," *Human Organization,* Vol. 32, 1973, pp. 407–418.

Stories as performance: Michael Pacanowsky and Nick O'Donnell-Trujillo, "Organizational Communication as Cultural Performance," *Communication Monographs 50,* 1983, pp. 127–147.

Functions of story: Mary Helen Brown, "Defining Stories in Organizations: Characteristics and Functions," *Communication Yearbook 13,* James A. Anderson (ed.), Sage, Newbury Park, Calif., 1990, pp. 162–190.

Rites: Harrison Trice and Janice Beyer, "Studying Organizational Cultures Through Rites and Ceremonials," *Academy of Management Review,* Vol. 9, 1984, pp. 653–669.

Alternative views of corporate culture: Linda Smircich, "Concepts of Culture and Organizational Analysis," *Administrative Science Quarterly,* Vol. 28, 1983, pp. 339–358.

Corporate stories: Joanne Martin, Martha Feldman, Mary Jo Hatch, and Sim Sitkin, "The Uniqueness Paradox in Organizational Stories," *Administrative Science Quarterly,* Vol. 28, 1983, pp. 438–453.

A reader: Peter Frost, Larry Moore, Meryl Louis, Craig Lundberg, and Joanne Martin (eds.), *Organizational Culture,* Sage, Beverly Hills, Calif., 1985.

Managing organizational culture: Sonja A. Sackmann, "Managing Organizational Culture: Dreams and Possibilities," *Communication Yearbook 13,* James A. Anderson (ed.), Sage, Newbury Park, Calif., 1990, pp. 114–148.

Nonmanagerial orientation: Michael Pacanowsky and Nick O'Donnell-Trujillo, "Communication and Organizational Cultures," *Western Journal of Speech Communication,* Vol. 46, 1982, pp. 115–130.

Japanese organization: John Junkerman, "Life on the Fast Lane at Datsun," in *Creative Organization Theory,* Gareth Morgan (ed.), Sage, Newbury Park, Calif., 1989, pp. 174–180.

PUBLIC RHETORIC

Despite what you read in the newspapers, *rhetoric* is not necessarily a dirty word. For citizens in ancient Greece, knowing how to speak was part of their democratic responsibility. Rhetorical ability was a survival skill in the rough-and-tumble politics of the Roman Forum. Following the decay of Rome, the church explored the use of rhetoric to preserve and spread the faith. As the Renaissance took hold, the study of rhetoric moved to the university, where it became a core subject of the trivium—logic, grammar, and rhetoric. In each setting, teachers and practitioners championed the art of rhetoric as a means of ensuring that speakers of truth would not be at a disadvantage when trying to win the hearts and minds of an audience.

Rhetoric is "an action humans perform when they use symbols for the purpose of communicating with one another."[1] Although this definition is broad, it centers attention on the intentional act of using words to have an effect. I use the term *public rhetoric* in this section to refer to a speaking context in which the speaker has an opportunity to monitor and adjust to the response of his or her immediate audience. Rhetoricians have always had a special interest in judicial argument, legislative debate, political rallies, religious sermons, and messages given at special celebrations.

The Greeks and Romans divided the study of rhetoric into five parts, or disciplines:

1. *Invention*—discovery of convincing arguments
2. *Arrangement*—organizing material for best impact
3. *Style*—selection of appropriate language
4. *Delivery*—coordinating voice and gestures
5. *Memory*—mastery and rehearsal of content

With the possible exception of memory, these "five canons of rhetoric" require that a speaker first analyze and then adapt to a specific group of listeners. We can, of course, react to the idea of audience adaptation in two different ways. If we view speakers who adjust their message to fit a specific audience in a positive light, we'll praise their rhetorical sensitivity and flexibility. If we view them negatively, we'll condemn them for their cynical pandering and lack of commitment to the truth. Rhetorical thought across history swings back and forth between these two conflicting poles. The words of most rhetoricians reflect the tension they feel between "telling it like it is" and telling it in a way that the audience will listen.

The Greek philosopher Plato regarded rhetoric as mostly flattery. Far from seeing it as an art, he described rhetoric as a "knack"—similar to cooking or the clever use of cosmetics. Both are attempts to make things seem better than they really are.[2] Yet despite his scorn, Plato imagined an ideal rhetoric based on a speaker's understanding of listeners with different natures and dispositions.

> He must then discover the kind of speech that matches each type of nature. When that is accomplished, he must arrange and adorn each speech in such a way as to present complicated and unstable souls with complex speeches, speeches exactly attuned to every changing mood of the complicated soul—while the simple soul must be presented with a simple speech.[3]

Plato never developed his conception of an ideal rhetoric, but his student Aristotle did. More than 2,000 years ago, Aristotle's *Rhetoric* systematically explored the topics of speaker, message, and audience. Chapter 25 presents his theory of rhetoric, the majority of which has stood the test of time. His ideas form a large proportion of the advice presented in contemporary public speaking texts. Aristotle defined rhetoric as the art of discovering all available means of persuasion, but this conception doesn't solve the problem of how to get audiences to listen to hard truths.

Religious rhetors live within the same paradox. In many ways the apostle Paul seemed to personify the lover of diverse souls that Plato had earlier described. In his first letter of the Corinthians, Paul reminds the people of Corinth that he made a conscious decision to let his message speak for itself ("My speech and my proclamation were not with plausible words of wisdom"[4]). Yet further on in the letter he outlines a conscious rhetorical strategy ("I have become all things to all people, that I might by all means save some"[5]). Four centuries later, Augustine continued to justify the conscious use of rhetoric by the church. Why, he asked, should defenders of truth be long-winded, confusing,

and boring, when the speech of liars was brief, clear, and persuasive?

The tension between the logic of a message and the appeal it has for an audience wasn't easily resolved when the university became the seat of rhetoric. British orator Francis Bacon sought to integrate the two concerns when he wrote that "the duty of rhetoric is to apply Reason to Imagination for the better moving of the will."[6] French scholar Peter Ramus offered a more radical solution to the problem. He split the five canons of rhetoric into two parts. Invention, arrangement, and memory became the province of logic. That left only style and delivery for rhetoricians to explore, and for centuries rhetoric was more concerned with form than substance.

American teachers of rhetoric rediscovered Aristotle in the early 1900s. As outlined in Chapter 2, neo-Aristotelianism became *the* standard for rhetorical research and practice. But not all scholars are content to analyze speeches using Aristotle's categories of logical, emotional, and ethical proof. Three twentieth-century rhetoricians have offered conscious alternatives to Aristotle's way of thinking.

I. A. Richards' "new rhetoric" is the first option. I've already discussed his study of

FRANK & ERNEST reprinted by permission of NEA, Inc.

misunderstanding and its remedies in Chapter 5. Kenneth Burke offers a second "new rhetoric." He claims that speaker identification with an audience is a better way to understand the human drama than Aristotle's "old rhetoric" of persuasion. Walter Fisher argues that the "rational world paradigm" of Aristotle is too limited. He regards all communication as story and offers his "narrative paradigm" as a new way to understand both private and public rhetoric. I present Burke's

dramatism in Chapter 26 and Fisher's narrative paradigm in Chapter 27.

Despite the claims of newness by Richards, Burke, and Fisher, each theorist has to deal with the old question that Aristotle faced: "How do you move an audience without changing your message or losing your integrity?" As you read, see which theorist comes up with an answer that's most satisfying to you.

CHAPTER 25

The Art of Rhetoric
of Aristotle

Aristotle was a student of Plato in the golden age of Greek civilization, four centuries before the birth of Christ. He became a respected instructor at Plato's Academy but disagreed with his mentor over the place of public speaking in Athenian life.

Athens was filled with self-appointed professors who used public speaking for fame and profit. Called Sophists, these "hired guns" gave speeches, wrote speeches, and taught others to give speeches. Some of them did so without apparent concern for the truth of their message. Plato scoffed at the Sophists' oratorical devices, dismissing their crowd-pleasing techniques as similar to the knack of cookery or the flattering use of cosmetics—both of which he perceived as being aimed at making something appear better than it really is. His suspicion is mirrored today in the negative way people use the term *mere rhetoric* to label the speech of "tricky" lawyers, "mealy mouthed" politicians, "spellbinding" preachers, and "fast-talking" salespeople.

Aristotle, like Plato, deplored the demagoguery of speakers' using their skill to move an audience while showing a casual indifference to the truth. Yet unlike Plato, he saw the tools of rhetoric as a neutral means by which the orator could either accomplish noble ends or further fraud: "Rightly employed, they work the greatest blessings; wrongly employed, they work the utmost harm." Aristotle believed that truth has a moral superiority which makes it more acceptable than falsehood. But unscrupulous opponents of the truth may fool a dull audience unless an ethical speaker uses "all possible means of persuasion" to counter the error. Speakers who neglect the art of rhetoric have only themselves to blame when their hearers choose falsehood. Success requires wisdom *and* eloquence.

Both the *Politics* and *Ethics* of Aristotle are polished and well-organized books compared with the rough prose and arrangement of his text on rhetoric. The *Rhetoric* apparently consists of Aristotle's reworked lecture notes for his course at the Academy. Despite the uneven nature of the writing, the *Rhetoric* is a searching study of audience psychology. Sophistic training for public address required rote memorization of famous speeches; the training handbooks contained little more than various techniques to stir up emotional response from the masses. Speaking was performance. But Aristotle raised rhetoric to a science by systematically exploring the effects of the speaker, the speech, and the audience. He regarded the speaker's use of this knowledge as an art. Quite likely, the text your communication department uses for its public speaking classes is basically a contemporary recasting of the audience analysis provided by Aristotle 2,300 years ago.

RHETORIC: MAKING PERSUASION PROBABLE

Aristotle saw the function of rhetoric as the discovery in each case of "all available means of persuasion." He never spelled out what he meant by persuasion, but his concern with noncoercive methods makes it clear that he ruled out force of law, torture, and war. His threefold classification of speech situations according to the nature of the audience shows that he had affairs of state in mind.

The first in Aristotle's classification is courtroom (forensic) speaking, which addresses judges who are trying to decide the facts of a person's guilt or innocence. Supreme Court nominee Clarence Thomas' testimony before the Senate Judiciary Committee is a case of judicial rhetoric centering on accusation and defense. The second, political (deliberative) speaking, is aimed at legislators or voters who decide future policy. The 1992 presidential debates gave George Bush, Bill Clinton, and Ross Perot a chance to sway undecided voters. The third, ceremonial (epideictic) speaking, heaps praise or blame upon another for the benefit of spectators. Lincoln gave his Gettysburg Address in order to honor "the brave men, living and dead, who struggled here."

Because his students were familiar with the question-and-answer style of Socratic dialogue, Aristotle classified rhetoric as a counterpart or offshoot of dialectic. Dialectic is one-on-one discussion; rhetoric is continuous discourse to a group. Dialectic is a search for truth; rhetoric tries to demonstrate truth that's already been found. Dialectic answers general philosophical questions; rhetoric addresses specific, practical ones. Dialectic deals with certainty; rhetoric deals with probability. Aristotle saw this last distinction as particularly important: Rhetoric is the art of discovering ways to make truth seem more probable to an audience that isn't completely convinced.

RHETORICAL PROOF: LOGOS, ETHOS, PATHOS

According to Aristotle, the available means of persuasion are based on three kinds of proof: logical (*logos*), ethical (*ethos*), and emotional (*pathos*). Logical proof comes from the line of argument in the speech, ethical proof is the way the speaker's character is revealed through the message, and emotional proof is the feeling the words draw out of the hearers. Some form of *logos*, *ethos*, and *pathos* is present in every public presentation, but perhaps no other modern-day speech has brought all three proofs together as effectively as Martin

Luther King, Jr.'s "I Have a Dream" speech delivered to civil rights marchers in Washington, D.C., in 1963. We'll look at this speech throughout the rest of the chapter to illustrate Aristotle's rhetorical theory.

Case Study: "I Have a Dream"

At the end of August 1963, a quarter of a million people assembled at the Lincoln Memorial in a united march on Washington. The rally capped a long, hot summer of sit-ins protesting racial discrimination in the south. (The film *Mississippi Burning* portrayed one of the tragic racial conflicts of that year.) Two months before the march, President John F. Kennedy submitted a civil rights bill to Congress which would begin to rectify the racial injustices, but its passage was seriously in doubt. The organizers of the march hoped that it would put pressure on Congress to outlaw segregation in the south, but they also wanted the demonstration to raise the national consciousness about economic exploitation of blacks around the country.

Martin Luther King shared the platform with a dozen other civil rights leaders, each limited to a five-minute presentation. King's successful Montgomery, Alabama, bus boycott, freedom rides, and solitary confinement in a Birmingham jail set him apart in the eyes of demonstrators and TV viewers. The last of the group to speak, King had a dual purpose. In the face of a Black Muslim call for violence, he urged blacks to continue their nonviolent struggle without hatred. He also implored white people to get involved in the quest for freedom and equality, to be part of a dream fulfilled rather than contribute to an unjust nightmare.

A few years after King's assassination, I experienced the impact his speech had had upon the African-American community. Teaching public address in a volunteer street academy, I read the speech out loud to illustrate matters of style. The students needed no written text. As I came to the last third of the speech, they recited the eloquent "I have a dream" portion word for word with great passion. When we finished, all of us had moist eyes.

David Garrow, author of the Pulitzer Prize-winning biography of King, called the speech the "rhetorical achievement of a lifetime, the clarion call that conveyed the moral power of the movement's cause to the millions who watched the live national network coverage."[1] King shifted the burden of proof onto those who opposed racial equality. Aristotle's three rhetorical proofs can help us understand how he made the status quo of segregation an ugly option for the moral listener.

Logical Proof: Lines of Argument That Make Sense

Aristole focused on two forms of logical proof—the *enthymeme* and the *example*. He regarded the enthymeme as "the most effective among the various forms of persuasion." An enthymeme is merely an incomplete version of a formal syllogism. Logicians might create the following syllogism out of one of King's lines of reasoning:

Major premise: All men are created equal.

Minor premise: I am a man.

Conclusion: I am equal to other men.

Typical enthymemes, however, leave out a premise which is already accepted by the audience: "All men are created equal, . . . I am equal to other men." In terms of style, the enthymeme is more artistic than a stilted syllogistic argument. But as University of Wisconsin rhetorician Lloyd Bitzer notes, Aristotle had a greater reason for advising the speaker to suppress the statement of a premise which the listeners already believe.

> Because they are jointly produced by the audience, enthymemes intuitively unite speaker and audience and provide the strongest possible proof. . . . The audience itself helps construct the proof by which it is persuaded. [2]

Most rhetorical analysis looks for enthymemes embedded in one or two lines of text. In the case of "I Have a Dream," the whole speech is one giant enthymeme. If the logic of the speech were to be expressed as a syllogism, the reasoning would be as follows:

Major premise: God will reward nonviolence.

Minor premise: We are pursuing our dream nonviolently.

Conclusion: God will grant us our dream.

King used the first two-thirds of the speech to establish the validity of the minor premise. White listeners are reminded that blacks have been "battered by the storms of persecution and staggered by winds of police brutality." They have "come fresh from narrow jail cells," and are "veterans of creative suffering." Blacks are urged to meet "physical force with soul force," not to allow "creative protest to degenerate into physical violence," and never to "satisfy our thirst for freedom by drinking from the cup of bitterness and hatred." The movement is to continue nonviolent.

King used the last third of the speech to establish his conclusion; he painted the dream in vivid color. It included King's hope that his four children would not be "judged by the color of their skin, but by the content of their character." He pictured an Alabama where "little black boys and black girls will be able to join hands with little white boys and white girls as sisters and brothers." And in a swirling climax, he shared a vision of all God's children singing, "Free at last, free at last. Thank God Almighty we are free at last." But he never articulated the major premise.

This line of argument makes no sense unless King and his audience were already committed to the truth of the major premise—that God would reward their commitment to nonviolence. Aristotle stresses that audience analysis is crucial to the effective use of the enthymeme. The centrality of the church in American black history, the religious roots of civil rights protest, and the crowd's frequent response of "My Lord" suggest that King knew his audience well. He never stated what to them was obvious, and this strengthened rather than weakened his logical appeal.

The enthymeme uses deductive logic—moving from global principle to specific truth. Arguing by example uses inductive reasoning—drawing a final conclusion from specific cases. Since King mentioned few examples of discrimination, it might appear that he failed to use all possible means of logical persuasion. But pictures of snarling police dogs, electric cattle prods used on peaceful demonstrators, and signs over drinking fountains stating "Whites only" appeared nightly on TV news. As with the missing major premise of the enthymeme, King's audience supplied their own vivid images. He helped his listeners interpret this evidence by the rich use of metaphor.

Aristotle wrote, "Easy learning is naturally pleasant to all. . . . It is metaphor above all else that gives clearness, charm, and distinction."[3] Metaphors are a type of example, and King was a master of metaphor:

> The Negro lives in a *lonely island* of poverty in the midst of a *vast ocean* of material prosperity.

> To rise from the *dark and desolate valleys of segregation* to the *sunlit path of racial justice.* (italics added)

King's use of metaphor was not restricted to images drawn from nature. Perhaps his most convincing metaphor was an extended analogy picturing the march on Washington as people of color coming to the federal bank to cash a check written by the Founding Fathers. America had defaulted on the promissory note and had sent back the check marked "insufficient funds." But the marchers refused to believe that the bank of justice was bankrupt, that the vaults of opportunity were empty. These persuasive images gathered listeners' knowledge of racial discrimination into a powerful flood of reason:

> Let justice roll down like waters
> and righteousness like a mighty stream.[4]

Ethical Proof: Perceived Source Credibility

According to Aristotle, it's not enough for a speech to contain plausible argument. The speaker must *seem* credible as well. Many audience impressions are formed before the speaker ever begins. As poet Ralph Waldo Emerson cautioned over a century ago, "Use what language you will, you can never say anything but what you are."[5] Some who watched Martin Luther King on television undoubtedly tuned him out because he was black. But Aristotle was more interested in audience perceptions that are shaped by what the speaker does or doesn't say. In the *Rhetoric* he identified three qualities which build high source credibility—intelligence, character, and goodwill.

1. Perceived Intelligence.   The quality of intelligence has more to do with shared values than it does with training at Plato's Academy. Audiences judge intelligence by the overlap between their beliefs and the speaker's ideas. (My idea of an agreeable speaker is one who agrees with me.) King

"I see our next speaker needs no introduction. . . ."
© 1975; Reprinted courtesy of Bunny Hoest.

quoted the Bible, the United States Constitution, the patriotic hymn "My Country 'tis of Thee," Shakespeare's *King Lear,* and the Negro spiritual "We Shall Overcome." With the exception of bomb-throwing terrorists and racial bigots, it's hard to imagine anyone with whom he didn't establish a strong value identification.

2. Character.   Character has to do with the speaker's image as a good and honest person. Even though he and other blacks were victims of "unspeakable horrors of police brutality," King warned against a "distrust of all white people" and against "drinking from the cup of bitterness and hatred." It would be difficult to maintain an image of the speaker as an evil racist while he was being charitable toward his enemies and optimistic about the future.

3. Goodwill.   Goodwill is a positive judgment of the speaker's intention toward the audience. Aristotle thought it possible for an orator to possess extraordinary intelligence and sterling character, yet still not have the listeners' best interest at heart. King was obviously not trying to reach "the vicious racists" of Alabama, but no one was given a reason to think that King bore them ill will. His dream included "black men and white men, Jews and Gentiles, Protestants and Catholics."

Although Aristotle's comments on *ethos* were stated in a few brief sentences, no other portion of his *Rhetoric* has received such close scientific scrutiny. The results of sophisticated testing of audience attitudes show that his three-factor theory of source credibility stands up remarkably well. Listeners definitely think in terms of authoritativeness (intelligence) and trustworthiness (character). Sometimes goodwill seems to fold into questions of character, and at other times into a dimension of speaker dynamism or energy surfaces. But whether the third category of credibility is goodwill or dynamism, Martin Luther King exuded all three.

Emotional Proof: Striking a Responsive Chord

Aristotle believed that the effective speaker must know how to stir up various emotions in the audience. He catalogued a series of opposite feelings, then explained the conditions under which each mood is experienced, and finally described how the speaker can get an audience to feel that way. If his advice sounds familiar, it may be a sign that human nature hasn't changed much in 2,300 years.

Anger (vs. Mildness).   Aristotle's discussion of anger was an early version of Freud's frustration-aggression hypothesis. People feel angry when they are thwarted in their attempt to fulfill a need. Remind them of interpersonal slights, and they'll become irate. Show them that the offender is sorry, deserves praise, or has great power, and the audience will calm down.

Love or Friendship (vs. Hatred).   Consistent with present-day research on attraction, Aristotle considered similarity as the key to mutual warmth. The speaker should point out common goals, experience, attitudes, and desires. In the absence of these positive forces, a common enemy can be used to create solidarity.

Fear (vs. Confidence).   Fear comes from a mental image of potential disaster. The speaker should paint a vivid word picture of the tragedy, showing that its occurrence is probable. Confidence can be built up by describing the danger as remote.

Shame (vs. Shamelessness).   We feel embarrassed or guilty when loss is due to our own weakness or vice. The emotion is especially acute when a speaker recites our failings in the presence of family, friends, or those we admire.

Indignation (vs. Pity).   We all have a built-in sense of fairness. As the producers of *60 Minutes* have discovered, it's easy to arouse a sense of injustice by describing an arbitrary use of power upon those who are helpless.

Admiration (vs. Contempt).   People admire moral virtue, power, wealth, and beauty. By demonstrating that an individual has acquired life's goods through hard work rather than mere luck, admiration will increase.

THE FIVE CANONS OF RHETORIC

Although the organization of Aristotle's *Rhetoric* is somewhat puzzling, scholars and practitioners synthesize his words into four distinct standards for measuring the quality of a speaker: the construction of an argument (invention), ordering of material (arrangement), selection of language (style), and techniques of delivery. Later writers add memory to the list of skills the accomplished speaker must master. As mentioned in the introduction to this section on public rhetoric, the five canons of rhetoric have set the agenda of public address instruction for over 2,000 years. Aristotle's advice strikes most students of public speaking as refreshingly up to date.

Invention. Aristotle claimed that people have places in their minds for stock arguments that they find convincing. Cornell University literature professor Lane Cooper explained: "In these special regions the orator hunts for arguments as a hunter pursues game."[6] Although individuals differ, Aristotle believed that most listeners respond to a speaker who contrasts the possible with the impossible, greater good with lesser good, important matters with trivial concerns, and what occurred in the past with what can happen in the future. King's "I Have a Dream" speech followed this latter line of argument. He moved from what was to what could be.

Arrangement. According to Aristotle, you should avoid complicated schemes of organization. "A speech has two parts. . . . You state your case and you prove it."[7] The introduction should capture attention, establish your credibility, and make clear the purpose of the speech. The conclusion should remind your listeners what you've said and leave them feeling good about you and your ideas. Like speech teachers today, Aristotle decried the practice of starting with jokes that have nothing to do with the topic, insistence on three-point outlines, and waiting until the end of the speech to reveal the main point.

Style. A good style is clear. "Language which does not convey a clear meaning fails to perform the function of language." Speakers can increase clarity by using vivid examples, creating fresh metaphors, and talking in everyday words. An effective oral style appeals to the ear rather than the eye. King's "I Have a Dream" looks chopped up when written, but its staccato style was perfect for a massive live audience.

Memory. Aristotle's students needed no reminder that good speakers are able to draw upon a collection of ideas and phrases stored in the mind. But Roman teachers of rhetoric found it necessary to stress the importance of memory. In our present age of word processing and TelePrompTers, memory seems to be a lost art. Yet the stirring conclusion of King's speech departed from his prepared text and effectively pulled together lines he had used before.

Delivery. Audiences reject delivery that seems planned or staged. Naturalness is persuasive; artifice, just the reverse. Any form of presentation which calls attention to itself takes away from the speaker's proofs.

CRITIQUE: STANDING THE TEST OF TIME

For many teachers of public speaking, criticizing Aristotle's *Rhetoric* is like doubting Einstein's theory of relativity or belittling Shakespeare's *King Lear*.

Yet the Greek philosopher often seems less clear than he urged his students to be. Scholars are puzzled by a failure to define the exact meaning of *enthymeme,* a confusing system of classifying metaphor according to type, and the blurred distinctions between deliberative (political) and epideictic (ceremonial) speaking. At the beginning of the *Rhetoric,* Aristotle promised a systematic study of *logos, ethos,* and *pathos,* but he failed to follow that three-part plan. Instead, it appears that he grouped the material in a speech-audience-speaker order.

Some present-day critics are bothered by the *Rhetoric's* view of the audience as passive. Speakers in Aristotle's world seem to be able to accomplish any goal as long as they do their speech preparation with careful thought and an accurate audience analysis. Other critics wish Aristotle had considered a fourth component of rhetoric, the situation. Any analysis of King's address apart from the context of the march on Washington would certainly be incomplete.

In the eyes of some readers, Aristotle waffled on the ethical issue of persuasive speaking. Book One of the *Rhetoric* took the position that it's wrong to play on the emotions of an audience ("One might just as well make a carpenter's rule crooked before using it as a measure").[8] Book Three said that impression management is the central task of the speaker. Yet ethicists today continue to struggle with the same dilemma, so perhaps this is just another example of the timeless wisdom of the *Rhetoric.* Referring to Aristotle's manuscript in a rare moment of sincere appreciation, the French cynic, Voltaire, declared what many speech teachers would echo today: "I do not believe there is a single refinement of the art that escapes him."[9]

QUESTIONS TO SHARPEN YOUR FOCUS

1. For most people today, the term *rhetoric* has bad associations. What synonym or phrase captures what Aristotle meant, yet doesn't carry a negative connotation?

2. What *enthymemes* have advocates on each side of the abortion issue employed in their public *deliberative rhetoric*?

3. Aristotle divided *ethos* into issues of *intelligence, character,* and *goodwill.* Which quality is most important to you when you hear a classroom lecture?

4. Most scholars who define themselves as *rhetoricians* identify with the humanities rather than the sciences. Can you support the claim that Aristotle took a *scientific approach to rhetoric*?

A SECOND LOOK

Recommended resource: *Aristotle on Rhetoric,* translated and with an introduction and notes by George A. Kennedy, Oxford University, New York, 1991.

Standard reference: *The Rhetoric of Aristotle,* translated and with an introduction by Lane Cooper, D. Appleton, New York, 1932.

Rhetoric as art: George A. Kennedy, "Philosophical Rhetoric," in *Classical Rhetoric*, University of North Carolina, Chapel Hill, 1980, pp. 41–85.

Rhetoric as science: James L. Golden, Goodwin F. Berquist, and William E. Coleman, *The Rhetoric of Western Thought*, Kendall/Hunt, Dubuque, Iowa, 1976, pp. 25–39.

Enthymeme: Lloyd F. Bitzer, "Aristotle's Enthymeme Revisited," *Quarterly Journal of Speech*, Vol. 45, 1959, pp. 399–409.

Metaphor: Samuel Levin, "Aristotle's Theory of Metaphor," *Philosophy and Rhetoric*, Vol. 15, 1982, pp. 24–46.

Dimensions of source credibility: J. C. McCroskey, "Scales for the Measurement of Ethos," *Speech Monographs*, Vol. 33, 1968, pp. 67–72.

Speaker charisma: H. W. Simons, N. M. Berkowitz, and R. J. Moyer, "Similarity, Credibility and Attitude Change: A Review and a Theory," *Psychological Bulletin*, Vol. 73, 1970, pp. 1–16.

Audience resistance: Raymond A. Bauer, "The Obstinate Audience," *American Psychologist*, Vol. 19, 1964, pp. 319–329.

Analysis of King's speech: Alexandra Alvarez, "Martin Luther King's 'I Have a Dream,'" *Journal of Black Studies*, Vol. 18, 1988, pp. 337–357.

King's oral rhetoric: Carolyn Calloway-Thomas and John Louis Lucaites (eds.), *Martin Luther King, Jr., and the Sermonic Power of Public Discourse*, University of Alabama, Tuscaloosa, 1993.

King's written rhetoric: Martin Luther King, Jr., "Letter from a Birmingham Jail," in *Why We Can't Wait*, Harper & Row, New York, 1963, pp. 77–100.

March on Washington: David J. Garrow, *Bearing the Cross*, William Morrow, New York, 1986, pp. 231–286.

CHAPTER 26

Dramatism

of *Kenneth Burke*

American audiences want straightforward advice from their film critics. Gene Siskel and Roger Ebert created the successful television show *Sneak Previews* by describing a movie's plot, showing a brief clip, commenting on the quality of acting, and recommending whether people should see the film or skip it. The thumbs-up–thumbs-down nature of their judgment leaves little room for trying to discern the writer's purpose or the director's motivation. In this sense, Siskel and Ebert are *reviewers* of cinema rather than *critics*.

Kenneth Burke, on the other hand, is a critic. Along with the symbolic theorists we've already discussed (Pearce and Cronen, Barthes, Mead, Geertz), Burke believes that language is a strategic human response to a specific situation. "Verbal symbols are meaningful acts from which motives can be derived." He considers clusters of words as dances of attitudes. According to Burke, the critic's job is to figure out why a writer or speaker selected the words that were choreographed into the message. The task is ultimately one of assessing motives.

Now in his nineties, Burke picks his way through the human "motivational jungle" using the tools of philosophy, literature, psychology, economics, linguistics, sociology, and communication. He spent his young adult years in Greenwich Village, a New York bohemian community which included e. e. cummings and Edna St. Vincent Millay. Like many intellectuals during the depression of the 1930s, Burke flirted with communism but was disillusioned by Stalin's intolerance and brutality. Although he never earned a college degree, he taught for fifteen years at Bennington College in Vermont and filled visiting lectureships at Harvard, Princeton, Northwestern, and the University of Chicago.

Burke's writing shows an intellectual breadth and depth that leads admirers to refer to him as a Renaissance man. He calls himself a "gypsy scholar" and responds to questions about his field of interest by asking, "What am I but a word man?" *Dramatism* is Burke's favorite word to describe what he sees going on when people open their mouths to communicate.

For Burke, life is not *like* a drama; life *is* drama. The late Harry Chapin (who happened to be Burke's grandson) captured some of the tragedy and comedy of everyday life by putting words to music in "story songs." My personal favorite is "Cat's in the Cradle," the timeless tale of a father too busy to spend time with his son. Any male who hears the song realizes that he has a part in the drama rather than being a passive listener.

The latest somebody-done-somebody-wrong song on the radio makes it clear that a critic's skills could be helpful in understanding human motivation. But it wasn't until 1952 that University of Illinois rhetorician Marie Hochmuth Nichols alerted the field of speech to the promises of Burke's dramatistic methodology.[1] Since that time, thousands of communication scholars have used his perspectives of identification, dramatistic pentad, and guilt-redemption cycle as ways to analyze public address.

IDENTIFICATION: WITHOUT IT, THERE IS NO PERSUASION

Although a great admirer of Aristotle's *Rhetoric*, Burke is less concerned with enthymeme and example than he is with a speaker's overall ability to identify with an audience.

> The key term for the "old rhetoric" was *persuasion* and its stress upon deliberative design. The key term for the "new rhetoric" is *identification* and this may include partially unconscious factors in its appeal.[2]

Identification is the common ground that exists between speaker and audience. Burke uses the word *substance* as an umbrella term to describe a person's physical characteristics, talents, occupation, background, personality, beliefs, and values. The more overlap there is between the substance of the speaker and the substance of the listener, the greater the identification. Behavioral scientists use the term *homophily* to describe perceived similarity between speaker and listener, but Burke prefers religious language to scientific jargon. Borrowing from Martin Luther's description of what takes place at the communion table, Burke says identification is "consubstantiation." The theological reference calls to mind the oft-quoted Old Testament passage where Ruth pledges solidarity with her mother-in-law, Naomi: "For where you go I will go, and where you lodge I will lodge; your people shall be my people, and your God my God."[3] That's identification.

Audiences sense a joining of interests through style as much as through content. Burke says the effective communicator can show consubstantiality by giving signs in language and delivery that his or her properties are the same as theirs. The style of a typical tent evangelist probably turns off a cosmopolitan New Yorker more than the content of the message. The mood and manner of revival-style preaching signal a deep division between the evangelist and the urbane listeners. To the extent that the speaker could alter the linguistic strategy to match the hearers' sophisticated style, they'd think the speaker was "talking sense."

Burke says that identification works both ways. Audience adaptation not only gives the evangelist a chance to sway the audience, it also serves to help

"As unbelievable as it may seem to you today, this court was once a puppy, too."
Drawing by Barsotti; © 1988 The New Yorker Magazine, Inc.

the preacher fit into the cultural mainstream. But identification in either direction will never be complete. If nothing else, our tennis elbow or clogged sinuses constantly remind us that we are separate from the rest of the human race. But without some kind of division in the first place, there would be no need for identification. And without identification, there is no persuasion.

THE DRAMATISTIC PENTAD

Burke regards persuasion as the communicator's attempt to get the audience to accept his or her view of reality as true. The "dramatistic pentad" is a tool to analyze how the speaker tries to do it. The five-pronged method is a shorthand way to "talk about their talk about." Burke's pentad directs the critic's attention to five crucial elements of the human drama—act, scene, agent, agency, and purpose.

> In a well-rounded statement about motives, you must have some word that names the act (names what took place in thought or deed), and another that names the scene (the background of the act, the situation in which it occurred); also you must indicate what person or kind of person (agent) performed the act, what means or instruments he used (agency), and the purpose.[4]

Although Burke is an advocate of creativity, he believes the critic's choice of labels should be constrained by the language that the speaker actually selects. Burke recommends a content analysis that identifies key terms on the basis of frequency and intensity of use. The speaker's "God term" is the word to which all other positive words are subservient. When critics discover the God term, they should avoid dictionary definitions as a way of determining its exact meaning. A speaker's God term is best understood by the other words that cluster around it, known by the company it keeps. In like fashion, a "Devil term" sums up all that a speaker regards as bad, wrong, or evil. Consistent with the Sapir-Whorf hypothesis described in the section on verbal messages, Burke's analysis sees words as "terministic screens" which dictate interpretations of life's drama.

Burke illustrates the importance of taking language seriously by having the reader imagine a parallel pentad with substitute terms:

act	scene	agent	agency	purpose
response	situation	subject	stimulus	target

He says that the dramatistic pentad on the top assumes a world of intentional action, whereas the scientific terms on the bottom describe motion without purpose.

The dramatic pentad is deceptively similar to the standard journalistic practice of answering who, what, where, when, why, and how in the opening paragraph of a story. Because Burke regards himself as an interpreter rather than a reporter, he's not content merely to label the five categories. By evaluating the ratio of importance between individual pairs (scene versus agent, agent versus act), the critic determines which element provides the best clue to the speaker's motivation.

The pentad offers a way to determine why the speaker selected a given rhetorical strategy to identify with the audience. When a message stresses one element over the other four, it reveals a speaker's philosophy or worldview.

Act.   A critic's label for the act pictures what was done. A speech which features dramatic verbs demonstrates a commitment to realism.

Scene.   The description of the scene gives a context for where and when the act was performed. Public speaking which emphasizes setting and circumstance downplays free will and reflects an attitude of situational determinism ("I had no choice").

Agent.   The agent is the person or people who performed the act. Some messages are filled with references to self, mind, spirit, and personal responsibility. This focus on character and the agent as instigator is consistent with philosophical idealism.

Agency.   Agency is the means the agent used to do the deed. A long description of methods or technique reflects a ''get-the-job-done'' approach which springs from the speaker's mind-set of pragmatism.

Purpose.   The speaker's purpose is the stated or implied goal of the address. An extended discussion of purpose within the message shows a strong desire on the part of the speaker for unity or ultimate meaning in life, common concerns of mysticism.

Burke is somewhat confusing in his use of the terms *purpose* and *motivation*. Is his concern for purpose (as one of the five terms of the pentad) separate from his quest for underlying motivation, which the entire dramatistic metaphor is designed to uncover? Perhaps it's the distinction between an immediate localized goal, and the ultimate direction of all human activity. According to this view, the pentad can be seen as offering a static photograph of a single scene in the human drama. The guilt-redemption cycle, the third perspective, would be the plot of the whole play.

GUILT-REDEMPTION CYCLE: THE ROOT OF ALL RHETORIC

The immediate purpose of a speech may vary according to the scene or agent, but Burke is convinced that the ultimate motivation of all public speaking is to purge ourselves of an ever-present, all-inclusive sense of guilt. Guilt is his catch-all term to cover every form of tension, anxiety, embarrassment, shame, disgust, and other noxious feelings that he believes are intrinsic to the human condition. His ''Definition of Man'' is a discouraging counterpoint to the optimism we've seen in Abraham Maslow and Carl Rogers. (Like most writers of an earlier generation, Burke used the word *man* to designate human beings of both genders. Given his record of using words to startle and create wonder, as he nears the age of 100, one wonders if he might suddenly recast his definition in exclusively feminine symbols. But in order to remain faithful to what he wrote, I won't alter his gender-loaded references.)

> Man is
> the symbol-using inventor of the negative
> separated from his natural condition by instruments
> of his own making
> goaded by the spirit of hierarchy
> and rotten with perfection.[5]

Burke starts out by acknowledging our animal nature, but like Mead (see Chapter 9), he emphasizes this uniquely human ability to create, use, and abuse language. The rest of his definition makes it clear that the capacity to manipulate symbols is not an unmixed blessing. The remaining lines suggest three linguistic causes for the sense of inner ''pollution.''

By writing ''inventor of the negative,'' Burke claims that it's only through manmade language that the possibility of choice comes into being. There is no "Don't" or "Thou shalt not" in nature. Symbolic interaction is a precondition of "no-ing."

The phrase "separated from his natural condition by instruments of his own making" bounces off the traditional description of a human as a "tool-using animal." Here again, Burke suggests that our technological inventions get us into trouble. Murphy's Law states that anything that can go wrong will.[6] When it comes to interpersonal relations, Burke thinks Murphy was an optimist.

Burke writes extensively about hierarchies, bureaucracies, and other ordered systems which rank how well people observe society's negative rules. He's convinced that no matter how high you climb on the performance ladder, you'll always feel a strong sense of embarrassment for not having done better. The guilt-inducing high priests of the hierarchy are the professional symbol users of society—teachers, lawyers, journalists, artists, and advertising copy writers.

The final phrase, "rotten with perfection," is an example of what Burke calls "perspective by incongruity." The device calls attention to a truth by linking two incongruous words. Burke uses the technique to point out that the harder we strive to be perfect, the more rotten we feel. The realization of a "perfect 10" (Ten Commandments, Bo Derek, an Olympic dive) only intensifies our sense of imperfection. Perfection makes us more aware of our "original sin" and heightens our desire to find someone on whom we can dump our load of guilt. Burke believes that getting rid of guilt is the basic plot of the human drama. At its root, rhetoric is the public search for a perfect scapegoat.

Redemption Through Victimage

Those who have rejected or never had a religious commitment may be impatient with Burke's continual use of theological terms. Surprisingly, he makes no claim to be a man of faith, nor does he ask his readers to believe in God. Regardless of whether or not you accept the Christian doctrine of human sin and divine redemption, Burke claims that the "purely social terminology of human relations can not do better than to hover about that accurate and succinct theological formula."[7] He regards theology as a field that has fine-tuned its use of language and urges the social critic to look for secular equivalents of the major religious themes of guilt and purification. This quest has brought him to view rhetoric as a continual pattern of redemption through victimage.

Burke says that the speaker has two choices. The first option is to purge guilt through self-blame. Described theologically as "mortification," this route requires confession of sin and a request for forgiveness. Even obvious candidates (Richard Nixon, Ted Kennedy, Ollie North, Gary Hart) find it excruciatingly difficult to admit publicly that they are the cause of their own grief. Since it's much easier for people to blame their problems on someone else—the second option—Burke suggests we look for signs of victimage in every rhetorical act. He's sure we'll find it.

Victimage is the process of designating an external enemy as the source of all our ills. The list of candidates is limited only by our imagination—eastern liberals, Muslim fundamentalists, the Colombian drug cartel, the military-industrial complex, blacks, Communists, Jews, chauvinistic males, homosexuals, the police, rich capitalists, and so forth. Since Operation Desert Storm, Americans would probably nominate Iraq's president Saddam Hussein, whose massively callous acts make him seem the personification of evil. Perfect guilt requires a perfect victim. God terms are only as powerful as the Devil terms they oppose.

Burke is not an advocate of redemption through victimization, but he says he can't ignore the historical pattern of people uniting against a common enemy ("congregation through segregation"). We've already discussed his claim that identification is the central strategy of the new rhetoric. The easiest way for an orator to identify with an audience is to lash out at whatever or whomever the people fear (My friend is one who hates what I hate).

A RHETORICAL CRITIQUE OF HITLER'S BATTLE

Almost all of Burke's applied criticism is more appropriate for a course in literature than a study in speech communication. He did, however, create one piece of rhetorical criticism which distinctly analyzes public speaking using dramatistic principles. Before America entered World War II, Burke interpreted the rhetorical strategy of Adolf Hitler by comparing his public performance with his ideas written in *Mein Kampf*, a book Burke calls "the well of Nazi magic." Instead of examining one particular speech, the study looks at Hitler's rhetoric as a "body of identification."

Although he doesn't use his dramatistic pentad as an organizational scheme, Burke employs each of its five concepts to "discover what kind of 'medicine' this medicine-man has concocted":[8]

Act: Propagandistic speeches

Scene: Post-World War I turmoil

Agent: Hitler, the prophetic leader

Agency: Mass rallies

Purpose: Unification of Germany

Burke observes that "the yearning for unity is so great that people are always willing to meet you halfway if you will give it to them by fiat,. . . regardless of the facts."[9] Hitler employed many methods to promote unification, but his most powerful device was casting the "International Jew" as the devil incarnate—a scapegoat to blame for all the nation's ills, guaranteeing "purification by dissociation":

Hence if one can hand over his infirmities to a vessel, or "cause," outside the self, one can battle an external enemy instead of battling an enemy within. And the greater one's internal inadequacies, the greater amount of evils one can load upon the back of "the enemy."[10]

Burke concludes that Hitler's appeal relied on "a bastardization of fundamentally religious patterns of thought" which offered a noneconomic interpretation of economic ills. "This *materialization* of a religious pattern is, I think, one terrifically effective weapon of propaganda." But just because something works doesn't mean it's right. Dramatism doesn't require that Burke remain ethically neutral toward Hitler or his methods. "It may well be that people, in their human frailty, require an enemy as well as a goal. Very well: Hitlerism itself has provided us with such an enemy."[11]

CRITIQUE: EVALUATING THE CRITIC'S ANALYSIS

Kenneth Burke is perhaps the foremost rhetorician of the twentieth century. Burke writes about rhetoric; other rhetoricians write about Burke. Universities offer entire courses on Burkean analysis. On two separate occasions the Speech Communication Association of America featured the man and his ideas at its national convention. The Kenneth Burke Society holds conferences and competitions which give his followers the opportunity to discuss and delight over his wide-ranging ideas. He obviously has something to say.

The problem for the beginning student is that he says it in such a roundabout way. Burke is closely tied to symbolic interactionism (see Chapter 9), and complexity seems to be characteristic of much of the writing within that tradition. Even advocates like Nichols feel compelled to explain why Burke is frequently confusing and sometimes obscure: "In part the difficulty arises from the numerous vocabularies he employs. His words in isolation are usually simple enough, but he often uses them in new contexts."[12] Clarity is compromised further by Burke's tendency to flood his text with literary allusions. Unless a student is prepared to grapple with Coleridge's "The Rime of the Ancient Mariner," Augustine's *Confessions*, and Freud's *The Psychopathology of Everyday Life*—all on the same page—Burke's mental leaps and breadth of scholarship will prove more frustrating than informative.

Yet Burke enthusiasts insist that the process of discovery is half the fun. Like a choice enthymeme, Burke's writing invites active reader participation as he surrounds an idea. And no matter what aspect of rhetoric that idea addresses, the reader will never again be able to dismiss words as "mere rhetoric." Burke has done us all a favor by celebrating the life-giving quality of talk.

Without question, the dramatistic pentad is the feature of Burke's writing that has gained the most approval. The integrated procedure offers five artistic "cookie cutters" for the critic to use in slicing human interaction into digestible, bite-sized morsels. Many have found it helpful in pinpointing a speaker's motivation and the way the speech functions to serve that need or desire.

Burke's concept of rhetoric as identification is a major advance in a field of knowledge which many scholars had thought complete. Rather than opposing Aristotle's definition, he has given it a contemporary luster by showing that common ground is the foundation of emotional appeal. Communication scientists can't test Burke's claim that unconscious identification produces behavior and attitude change, but they can confirm that perceived similarity facilitates persuasion.

Of all Burke's motivational principles, his strategies of redemption are the most controversial. Perhaps that's because his "secular religion" takes God too seriously for those who don't believe, yet not seriously enough for those who do. Both camps have trouble with Burke's unsubstantiated assumption that guilt is the primary human emotion which underlies all public address. There's no doubt that Hitler's speeches exploited a guilt-scapegoat linkage, but whether the same religious drama is played out in every Rotary Club speech is another matter.

I appreciate Burke's commitment to an ethical stance that refuses to let desirable ends justify unfair means. He urges speakers not to make a victim out of someone else in order to become unified with the audience. True believers in the dramatistic gospel maintain that it's unwise to talk about communication without some understanding of Burke. The inclusion of this chapter is my response to their claim.

QUESTIONS TO SHARPEN YOUR FOCUS

1. Burke says that without *identification*, there is no persuasion. A number of the theories already covered deal with ideas or principles akin to identification. Can you name five?

2. Burke encourages the *rhetorical critic* to discover communicators' *motives* by analyzing the *God terms* and *Devil terms* they use. What are his God terms and Devil terms?

3. Apply the *dramatistic pentad* to the nonverbal rhetoric of a TGIF party on campus. Which of the five elements of the pentad would you stress to capture the meaning of that human drama?

4. Burke claims that all rhetoric ultimately serves to *expiate guilt through victimage*. If he's right, is it the speaker, the listener, or the victim's guilt that is being purged?

A SECOND LOOK

Recommended resource: Sonja Foss, Karen Foss, and Robert Trapp, *Contemporary Perspectives on Rhetoric*, Waveland, Prospect Heights, Ill., 1985, pp. 153–188.

Dramatism: Kenneth Burke, "Dramatism," in *The International Encyclopedia of the Social Sciences*, Vol. 7, David L. Sills (ed.), Macmillan, New York, 1968, pp. 445–451.

Identification: Kenneth Burke, A *Rhetoric of Motives*, Prentice-Hall, Englewood Cliffs, N.J., 1950, pp. 20–46.

Pentad: Kenneth Burke, *A Grammar of Motives*, Prentice-Hall, Englewood Cliffs, N.J., 1945, pp. xvii–xxv.

Guilt-redemption: Kenneth Burke, "On Human Behavior Considered 'Dramatistically,'" in *Permanence and Change*, Bobbs-Merrill, Indianapolis, 1965, pp. 274–294.

Human nature: Kenneth Burke, "Definition of Man," in *Language as Symbolic Action*, University of California, Berkeley, 1966, pp. 3–24.

Devil terms: Elizabeth Walker Mechling and Jay Mechling, "Sweet Talk: The Moral Rhetoric Against Sugar," *Central States Speech Journal*, Vol. 34, 1983, pp. 19–32.

Burkean critique of Hitler: Kenneth Burke, "The Rhetoric of Hitler's 'Battle,'" in *The Philosophy of Literary Form*, Louisiana State University, Baton Rouge, 1941, pp. 191–220.

Application to speech communication: Marie Hochmuth Nichols, "Kenneth Burke and the New Rhetoric," *Quarterly Journal of Speech*, Vol. 38, 1952, pp. 133–144.

Limits of dramatism: James W. Chesebro, "Extensions of the Burkean System," *Quarterly Journal of Speech*, Vol. 78, 1992, pp. 356–368.

Feminist critique: Celest Michelle Condit, "Post-Burke: Transcending the Substance of Dramatism," *Quarterly Journal of Speech*, Vol. 78, 1992, pp. 349–355.

He swore that this time he was through with her for keeps, but of course he wasn't. When he finally found her, she was lying passed out in a highly specialized establishment located above an adult bookstore, and he had to pay the management plenty to let her out of her contract. She'd lost her front teeth and picked up some scars you had to see to believe, but Hosea had her back again and that seemed to be all that mattered.

He changed his sandwich board to read "God is love" on one side and "There's no end to it" on the other, and when he stood on the street corner . . . nobody can say how many converts he made, but one thing that's for sure is that, including Gomer's, there was seldom a dry eye in the house.[5]

NARRATION AND PARADIGM: DEFINING THE TERMS

Fisher defines *narration* as "symbolic actions—words and/or deeds—that have sequence and meaning for those who live, create, or interpret them."[6] Hosea's life and Buechner's account of it clearly qualify as narrative. But Fisher's definition is broad and is especially notable for what it doesn't exclude. On the basis of his further elaboration,[7] I offer this expanded paraphrase of the definition above:

> Narration is communication rooted in time and space. It covers every aspect of our lives and the lives of others in regard to character, motive, and action. The term also refers to every verbal or nonverbal bid for a person to believe or act in a certain way. Even when a message seems abstract—is devoid of imagery—it is narration because it is embedded in the speaker's ongoing story that has a beginning, middle, and end, and it invites listeners to interpret its meaning and assess its value for their own lives.

Under Fisher's expanded definition, the didactic God-is-love phrase on Hosea's sandwich board is the premise for the *Greatest Story Ever Told*. Those who dwell in the story cannot help loving as Hosea did. When the term *narrative* is applied this way, we may have trouble imagining any serious communication which doesn't qualify as narration. That's precisely Fisher's point. He believes that all messages are best viewed as story, not necessarily in their form, but because they cause us to spin out their implications for the way we live *our* story.

Fisher uses the term *paradigm* to refer to a "conceptual framework." You'll remember from Heider's attribution theory and Delia's constructivism that person perception is not so much a matter of the physics of sight and sound as it is one of interpretation (see Chapters 11 and 12). Meaning isn't inherent in events; it's attached at the workbench of the mind. A paradigm is a universal model which calls for people to view events through a common interpretive lens.

In *The Structure of Scientific Revolutions*, Thomas Kuhn argues that an accepted paradigm is the mark of a mature science. Responding to this challenge, communication scientists in the 1970s sought to discover a universal model that would explain communication behavior.[8] Fisher's narrative paradigm is a humanistic counterpart to their efforts. Fisher offers a way to understand all communication and to direct rhetorical inquiry. He doesn't regard the narrative paradigm as a specific rhetoric. Rather, he sees it as "the foundation on which a complete rhetoric needs to be built. This structure would provide a comprehensive explanation of the creation, composition, adaptation, presentation, and reception of symbolic messages."[9]

PARADIGM SHIFT: FROM RATIONAL-WORLD PARADIGM TO NARRATIVE PARADIGM

Fisher begins his book *Human Communication as Narration* with a reference to the opening line of the Gospel of John: "In the beginning was the word (*logos*)." He notes that the Greek word *logos* originally included story, reason, rationale, conception, discourse, thought—all forms of human communication. Imagination and thought were not yet distinct. The story of Hosea and Gomer was *logos*.

According to Fisher, the writings of Plato and Aristotle reflect the early evolution from a generic to a specific use of *logos*—from story to statement. *Logos* had already begun to refer only to philosophical discourse, a lofty enterprise that relegated imagination, poetry, and other aesthetic concerns to a second-class status. Rhetoric fell somewhere between *logos* and poetic. It was the bastardized offspring of the somewhat seamy union between "pure logic" on the one hand and emotional stories that would stir up passions on the other. The Greek citizen concerned with truth alone should steer clear of rhetoric and consult an expert on wisdom—the philosopher.

Fisher notes that 2,000 years later the scientific revolution dethroned the philosopher-king. For the last few centuries the only knowledge that seems to be worth knowing in academia is that which can be spotted in the physical world. The person who wants to understand the way things are needs to check with a doctor, a scientist, an engineer, or other technical expert. Despite the elevation of technology and the demotion of philosophy, both modes of decision making are similar in their elitist tendencies "to place that which is not *formally* logical or which is not characterized by *expertise* within a somehow subhuman framework of behavior."[10] Fisher sees philosophical and technical discussion as the scholars' standard approach to knowledge. He calls this mind-set the *rational-world paradigm*.

Fisher lists five assumptions of the prevailing rational-world paradigm. See if they match what you've been taught all along in school.

1. People are essentially rational.
2. We make decisions on the basis of arguments.
3. The type of speaking situation (legal, scientific, legislative) determines the course of our argument.

4. Rationality is determined by how much we know and how well we argue.

5. The world is a set of logical puzzles that we can solve through rational analysis.

Viewed through the rational-world paradigm, the story of Hosea is ridiculous. Hosea's marriage to Gomer is irrational. The only logical conclusion is that the man had an unhealthy sexual obsession with a destructive woman. Buechner's words present no plausible argument why Hosea's willingness to let Gomer walk all over him is a superior strategy to separation or divorce. Other than the Old Testament passage, the author offers no evidence that Hosea and Gomer are historical characters, that any kind of god exists, or that this supreme being actually commanded Hosea to marry a whore. The claim that Hosea and Gomer's dysfunctional marriage illustrates the divine-human relationship has no basis in fact. The story is absurd.

Fisher is convinced that the assumptions of the rational-world paradigm are too limited. He calls for a new conceptual framework (a paradigm shift) in order to better understand human communication. His narrative paradigm is built on five assumptions similar in form to the rational-world paradigm, but quite different in content.

1. People are essentially storytellers.

2. We make decisions on the basis of good reasons.

3. History, biography, culture, and character determine what we consider good reasons.

4. Narrative rationality is determined by the coherence and fidelity of our stories.

5. The world is a set of stories from which we choose, and thus constantly re-create, our lives.

Viewing human beings as storytellers who sometimes argue is a major conceptual shift. For example, in a logical system, values are emotional nonsense. From the narrative perspective, however, values are the "stuff" of stories. Working from a strictly logical standpoint, aesthetic proof is irrelevant, yet within a narrative framework, style and beauty play a pivotal role in determining whether or not we get into a story. Perhaps the biggest shift in thinking has to do with who is qualified to assess the quality of communication. Whereas the rational-world model holds that only experts are capable of presenting or discerning sound arguments, the narrative paradigm maintains that, armed with a bit of common sense, almost any of us can spot a good story. Fisher would say that each of us will make his or her judgment about Buechner's account of Hosea (or any story) based upon *narrative rationality*.

NARRATIVE RATIONALITY: COHERENCE AND FIDELITY

According to Fisher, not all stories are equally good. Even though there's no guarantee that people won't adopt a bad story, he thinks that everybody

THE DYING ART OF STORYTELLING

Drawing by M. Stevens; © 1989 The New Yorker Magazine, Inc.

applies the same standards of narrative rationality to whatever stories he or she hears. The idea of narrative rationality is closer to Kenneth Burke's concept of *identification* than it is to the *logos* of Aristotle. Can we identify with the story of a marriage between a prophet and a prostitute? Fisher believes that our answer depends on whether or not Buechner's account meets the twin tests of *narrative coherence* and *narrative fidelity*.

Narrative Coherence: Does the Story Hang Together?

Narrative coherence has to do with how probable the story appears to the hearer. Does the narrative "hang together"? Do the people and events it portrays seem to be of one piece? Are they part of an organic whole? Do the characters act consistently?

Buechner's version of Hosea and Gomer's relationship translates this ancient tale of unrequited love into a contemporary setting. To the extent that his modern-day references to roll calls in school, adult bookstores, and heavy lipstick consistently portray the present, the story has structural integrity. Fisher regards the internal consistency of a narrative as similar to lines of argument in a rational-world paradigm. In that sense, his narrative paradigm doesn't discount or replace logic. Instead, Fisher lists logic as one, but only one, of the factors that affect narrative coherence.

Stories hang together when we're convinced that the narrator hasn't left out important details, fudged the facts, or ignored other plausible interpretations. We often judge the coherence of a narrative by comparing it with other stories we've heard that deal with the same theme. How does Buechner's account of a man's love for a prostitute stack up against films like *Pretty Woman*, *Never on Sunday*, or *The World of Suzie Wong*? To the extent that Gomer's selfish behavior seems more realistic to us than the heart-of-gold motivation of pretty woman Julia Roberts, we'll credit Buechner's biblical update with coherence.

For Fisher, the ultimate test of narrative coherence is whether or not we can count on the characters to act in a reliable manner. We are suspicious of accounts where characters behave ''uncharacteristically''; we tend to trust stories of people who show continuity of thought, motive, and action. Whether you regard Buechner's Hosea as a wonderfully forgiving husband or a nauseatingly spineless wimp, the constancy of his love for Gomer in spite of her unfaithfulness is a thread that gives the fabric of the story a tight weave.

Narrative Fidelity: Does the Story Ring True?

Narrative fidelity is the quality of a story that causes the words to strike a responsive chord in the life of the listener. A story has fidelity when it rings true with the hearers' experience, squares with the stories they might tell about themselves.

Have we, like Gomer, ever been caught up in the party scene, cheated on a faithful lover, been forgiven when we didn't deserve it, or shed tears over the hurt we've caused ourselves and others? To the extent that the details of the story portray the world we live in, the narrative has fidelity.

Fisher's book *Human Communication as Narration* has the subtitle *Toward a Philosophy of Reason, Value, and Action.* He believes a story has fidelity when it provides a logic of good reasons to guide our future actions. When we buy into a story, we buy into the type of character we should be. Thus, values are what set the narrative paradigm's logic of good reasons apart from the rational-world paradigm's mere logic of reasons.

Fisher regards some stories as more truthful and humane than others and is convinced that people have a natural tendency to prefer these accounts. What are the specific values that guide hearers as they gauge a story's truth or fidelity? Fisher imagines the response of an ideal audience, one composed of people like the self-actualized individuals that Maslow so admired (see Chapter 10).

> It appears that there is a permanent public, an actual community existing over time, that believes in the values of truth, the good, beauty, health, wisdom, courage, temperance, justice, harmony, order, communion, friendship, and oneness with the Cosmos—as variously as those values may be defined or practiced in ''real'' life.[11]

Fisher believes that these virtues shape our logic of good reasons, our commonsense response to the story. If we are convinced that this audience of good people would squirm in discomfort at the stupid codependence of the prophet, the narrative will lack fidelity. But inasmuch as we think that these ideal auditors would applaud Hosea's love and forgiveness of Gomer, Buechner's words will have the ring of truth.

APPLYING THE PARADIGM

Unlike Kenneth Burke's dramatistic pentad presented in the previous chapter, Walter Fisher's narrative paradigm is not introduced as a tool for rhetorical criticism. Yet he still believes that a narrative perspective can help us understand what goes on in human communication. In *Human Communication as Narration*, Fisher uses the principles of narrative coherence and narrative fidelity to analyze various types of communication. He explains why a sometimes inarticulate President Ronald Reagan was aptly known as "The Great Communicator." He examines the false values of Willy Loman that lead to his downfall in *Death of a Salesman*. And he explores the consequences of adopting the rival philosophies embedded in the stories of two Greek thinkers—Socrates and Callicles. According to Fisher, the very fact that the narrative paradigm can be applied to this wide range of communication genres is strong evidence of its validity.

If Fisher is right, the narrative paradigm should provide insight into whatever the key communication issue of the day happens to be. I'm writing this chapter one week after Bill Clinton was elected President of the United States. The narrative paradigm would hold that American voters selected Bill Clinton's story over George Bush's story.

Consider first the issue of coherence. During the campaign, both candidates struggled with presenting coherent stories. President Bush attacked Governor Clinton's integrity for waffling about his efforts to avoid the draft during the Vietnam war. Clinton charged that the former vice president's statements about the Iran-Contra scandal were inconsistent. Bush's words about the illegal sales of guns to Iran (and when he knew it) struck many voters as contradictory. The President faced an even greater problem of inconsistency on the crucial issue of the failed economy. He told the country that he would launch a vigorous program to bring the nation out of its long-term recession, but people wondered why, if he really had a plan, hadn't he put it into effect during his first term in office?

As for narrative fidelity, the values expressed by Bill Clinton resonated with the American public more than those espoused by George Bush and the Republican party in 1992. President Bush championed "family values," but working mothers and single parents felt excluded from the family. Bush seemed equally removed from the people on bread-and-butter economic issues. When asked in the second debate how he was personally affected by economic hard times, Bush visibly struggled with the question. To the audience, it was obvious that he just didn't "get it."

Clinton, on the other hand, identified with citizens who were hurt by economic uncertainty and high unemployment. Challenged in a town meeting to show that he knew the cost of a gallon of milk, a loaf of bread, and a pair of blue jeans, Clinton's answers showed that he understood the plight of the consumer. On election day, voters indicated that Bill Clinton's common-man-of-the-people-from-a-place-called-Hope story had greater fidelity than George Bush's things-will-get-better-if-you-trust-my-leadership story. As Walter Fisher suggests, we can gain new insight into political communication when we view an election campaign as conflicting stories vying for listener acceptance.

CRITIQUE: DOES FISHER'S STORY HAVE COHERENCE AND FIDELITY?

Fisher's narrative paradigm offers a fresh alternative to the neo-Aristotelian analysis which has dominated rhetorical thinking in the field of speech communication. His approach is radically democratic. When communication is viewed as narrative, people don't need specialized training to figure out whether a story holds together or has the ring of truth. Anyone with a little common sense is a competent rhetorical critic.

Of course, Fisher's theory is itself a story, and as you might expect, not everyone accepts his narrative tale. Critics dispute whether all communication really is story and whether Fisher's logic of good reasons is true to life. Ironically, the first concern is a matter of coherence and the second raises the issue of fidelity.

Fisher's claim that all communication is story begs two questions:

1. Are there any forms of communication where coherence is not an appropriate standard? University of Kansas rhetorical critic Robert Rowland suggests that some types of science fiction don't even try to make narrative sense. If he's right, the discovery of a communication genre unconcerned with consistency is a serious blow to Fisher's universal claim.

2. Even if we sign on to Fisher's sweeping statement that all human communication is narration, does this truth offer any meaningful insight? Fisher's definition of narration may be so broad that saying discourse is story may not be saying much. The problem is similar to popular psychology's wholesale diagnosis of families as dysfunctional. If the "dysfunctional" label is attached to every family system, the term loses descriptive power. Perhaps by labeling all communication as narration, Fisher has purchased coherence at the cost of clarity.

Other critics charge that Fisher's logic of good reasons is the soft spot of his narrative paradigm. According to Fisher, a story's good reasons are good because they appeal to the values of the people who are likely to hear the tale. But one shortcoming of the narrative paradigm is its failure to specify how to recognize the values of a story and the values of an audience to see if they coincide.

William Kirkwood at East Tennessee State University claims there is a bigger problem with the logic of good reasons. Kirkwood says that a standard of narrative fidelity implies that good stories cannot and perhaps should not go beyond what people already believe and value. He charges that the logic of good reasons encourages writers and speakers to adjust their ideas to people rather than people to their ideas, and thus denies the "rhetoric of possibility."[12]

Fisher thinks this is ridiculous. He explicitly states that people have the capacity "to formulate and adopt new stories that better account for their lives or the mystery of life itself."[13] Certainly, the forgiveness that Hosea extends to Gomer goes beyond anything most of us have ever experienced on a human level, yet the story still strikes a responsive chord in many who hear it. Perhaps a good story can extend our aspirations to a level that we couldn't have imagined before we first heard the tale.

Is all communication story, and do we judge every message we hear on the basis of whether it holds together and rings true with our values? If you take Fisher's ideas seriously, you won't need me or a trained rhetorician to give you the final word. Like everyone else, you can spot the difference between a good and a bad story.

QUESTIONS TO SHARPEN YOUR FOCUS

1. Using Fisher's definition of *narration*, can you think of any types of communication that don't fit within the *narrative paradigm*?

2. Fisher claims that the *rational-world paradigm* dominates western education. Can you list courses you've had at college that adopt the assumptions of this conceptual framework?

3. What is the difference between *narrative coherence* and *narrative fidelity*?

4. You apply a *logic of good reasons* to the stories you hear. What are the *values* you hold that cause you to accept or reject Buechner's story of Hosea?

A SECOND LOOK

Recommended resource: Walter R. Fisher, *Human Communication as Narration: Toward a Philosophy of Reason, Value, and Action,* University of South Carolina, Columbia, 1987.

Original statement: Walter R. Fisher, "Toward a Logic of Good Reasons," *Quarterly Journal of Speech,* Vol. 64, 1978, pp. 376–384.

Subsequent development: Walter R. Fisher, "Narration as a Human Communication Paradigm: The Case of Public Moral Argument," *Communication Monographs,* Vol. 51, 1984, pp. 1–22.

Storytelling and narrativity in communication research: Journal of Communication, Vol. 35, No. 4, 1985, entire issue.

Paradigms: Thomas Kuhn, *The Structure of Scientific Revolutions*, University of Chicago, Chicago, 1962.

Modern stories from the past: Frederick Buechner, *Peculiar Treasures*, Harper & Row, New York, 1979.

Story of an election: "Special Election Issue," *Newsweek,* November/December 1992.

Critique: Robert C. Rowland, "On Limiting the Narrative Paradigm: Three Case Studies," *Communication Monographs*, Vol. 56, 1989, pp. 39–54.

Critique: Barbara Warnick, "The Narrative Paradigm: Another Story," *Quarterly Journal of Speech*, Vol. 73, 1987, pp. 172–182.

PART SIX

Mass Communication

MEDIA AND CULTURE

Early mass communication theorists assumed that print and electronic media have an enormous power to mold opinion, arouse feelings, and sway behavior. They viewed the mass audience as defenseless and relatively passive—a herd of sheep that is easy prey for manipulative advertising or clever propaganda. The "powerful effects" model likened media messages to bullets fired from a machine gun into a crowd. A similar metaphor pictured print, film, and radio as hypodermic needles that inject something directly into the patient. The ability of Goebbel's Nazi propaganda to mobilize anti-Semitic feeling in the 1930s gave credence to the cause-and-effect notion of media influence.

Even while the United States movie industry cranked out patriotic films in the 1940s to bolster the national war effort, American social scientists began to question the tradition of powerful effects. Voting-behavior studies showed that audiences were much more active, resistant, and obstinate than had been first imagined. Media sociologists Elihu Katz of Hebrew University and Paul Lazarsfeld of Columbia University characterized society as "a honeycomb of small groups bound by a rich web of personal ties and dependencies"[1] that help shield the individual from media influence. This "limited effects" model recommends looking at differences between people in order to explain the relatively small and scattered impact of mass media.

One line of research consistent with a limited-effects view examines reader, listener, and viewer motivation for attending to a particular type of message. For example, the "uses and gratifications" approach suggests that viewers are selective in the kinds of TV programs they watch.[2] People wanting *information* may tune in *The MacNeil/Lehrer NewsHour* on public television; individuals seeking to clarify their *personal identity* may watch *Donahue*; viewers searching for clues about *social interaction* may turn on *All My Children*; and people looking for *entertainment* may select *Wheel of Fortune*. Of course, some shows might satisfy all four desires, but most programs will affect only those who are predisposed to respond. Advocates of the limited-effects position believe that media constitute only one set of factors that influence people.

The European study of mass communication has focused on broad cultural issues rather than on specific media effects. Because the mass media standardize the symbolic environment, continental scholars have developed a list of questions that they believe every researcher should address.[3]

1. What is the mediating role of culture? Does culture constrain the media, or do the media alter culture?

2. Do the media reflect the diversity of a culture, or do they only portray the ideology of the dominant group within society?

3. What should be the crucial focus of mass communication study—the content of the message or the technology of the media?

4. What research methods are appropriate for analyzing the impact of the media—the quantitative statistical measures of social scientists or the qualitative textual analyses of literature, ethnography, and philosophy?

CATHY © 1983 Cathy Guisewite. Dist. by Universal Press Syndicate.
Reprinted with permission. All rights reserved.

5. What is the role of the media specialist—neutral administrator of research funded by government and business or critic of societal injustice?

The three theories in this section speak to these cultural issues. Marshall McLuhan's theory of technological determinism (see Chapter 28) regards our present cultural upheaval as a direct result of the information explosion fostered by television and the computer. His belief that "the medium is the message" contrasts with George Gerbner's view that the violent *content* of television programming cultivates a climate of fear (see Chapter 29). Stuart Hall is impatient with Gerbner's attempt to support cultivation theory with survey data, but he agrees with Gerbner's claim that the media play a key role in maintaining the status quo. Casting his critical theory (see Chapter 30) within a Marxist framework, Hall sees himself as an advocate of people who are systematically relegated to the margin of society.

Although McLuhan, Gerbner, and Hall reject the simplistic "hypodermic needle" model of mass media influence, their theories do represent a return to the concept of powerful effects. Despite their differences on a number of the crucial issues, each man believes that the media have a powerful effect because they articulate, interpret, and help create a society's culture. The media mediate culture.

28

Technological Determinism
of Marshall McLuhan

In the late 1960s, the top-ranked television show across the United States was Rowan and Martin's *Laugh-In*—a fast-paced, off-beat comedy that launched the careers of Lily Tomlin and Goldie Hawn. The weekly format included words of wisdom from the program's poet-philosopher, Henry Gibson. He got a good laugh with a one-liner: "Marshall McLuhan, what are you doin'?"

Marshall McLuhan was the director of the Center for Culture and Technology at the University of Toronto. The writers of *Laugh-In* popped in McLuhan's name because he was already popular. The mild-mannered Canadian appeared on the cover of *Time*, had a walk-on role in Woody Allen's *Annie Hall*, and was the subject of an extensive *Playboy* interview.

Coming to his study of media and culture through a background in English literature, McLuhan pictured himself as a blind man tapping his cane in all directions to discover the nature of his media environment. He referred to his ideas as "probes," the tentative gropings of one who takes "the numb stance of the technological idiot." But there was nothing tentative about McLuhan's prophetic message. When asked what he was doing, the "Oracle of the Electronic Age" said he was telling all who would listen that we live at a unique time in history. The new electronic media have radically altered the way people think, feel, and act. We're in the midst of a revolution, yet most of us have yet to understand that the world will never be the same.

COMMUNICATION INVENTIONS: THE BALANCE POINTS OF HISTORY

McLuhan divided all human history into four periods, or epochs—a tribal age, a literate age, a print age, and an electronic age. He claimed the transitions between periods were neither gradual nor evolutionary. In each case the world was wrenched from one era into the next because of new developments in communication technology. The schematic in Figure 28.1 represents the

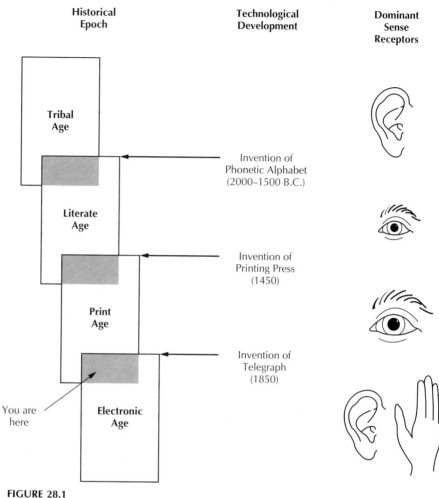

FIGURE 28.1
Marshall McLuhan's Media Map of History

Canadian professor's view of history. As you can see, he thought that those of us born in the twentieth century are living on the cusp of history.

According to McLuhan, the crucial inventions that changed life on this planet were the phonetic alphabet, the printing press, and the telegraph. He was certain that their developers had little idea at the time that their technological innovations would revolutionize society, but if we'd only bother to open our eyes, we'd see that the phonetic alphabet catapulted the human race into an age of literacy and that Gutenberg's press launched the industrial revolution.

For the past 3500 years of the Western world, the effects of media—whether it's speech, writing, printing, photography, radio or television—have been systematically overlooked by social observers. Even in today's revolutionary electronic age, scholars evidence few signs of modifying this traditional stance of ostrichlike disregard.[1]

What almost everyone fails to see, said McLuhan, is that people alive today are caught up in a third radical breakthrough. Whatever answer Samuel Morse received when he first tapped out "What hath God wrought?" on his telegraph, the reply clearly didn't anticipate the social upheaval the electronic media would create.

WE SHAPE OUR TOOLS AND THEY IN TURN SHAPE US

At its core, McLuhan's theory is technological determinism. He held that inventions in technology invariably cause cultural change. Whereas Karl Marx's economic determinism argued that changes in modes of *production* determine the course of history, McLuhan concluded that it is specifically changes in modes of *communication* that shape human existence.

Belief in the pivotal role of communication innovation wasn't original with McLuhan. Noting the effect of the railroad in the wilderness, fellow Canadian Harold Innis had already suggested that sudden extensions of communication are reflected in cultural disturbances. But McLuhan was unique in claiming that channels of communication are the primary cause of cultural change. Family life, the workplace, schools, health care, friendship, religious worship, recreation, politics—nothing remains untouched by communication technology. Whereas Emerson regarded an institution as "the lengthened shadow of a man," McLuhan was sure that cultural institutions are lengthened shadows of human inventions—specifically the alphabet, the printing press, and the electronic media. As with all his ideas, he had a catchy way of putting it: "We shape our tools and they in turn shape us."

McLuhan regarded communication inventions as pivotal because he considered every new form of media innovation to be an extension of some human faculty. The book is an extension of the eye. The wheel is an extension of the foot. Clothing is an extension of the skin. Electronic circuitry (especially the computer) is an extension of the central nervous system. You can see by these examples that McLuhan avoids a narrow definition of media. Media are anything that amplify or intensify a bodily organ, sense, or function. Media not only extend our reach and increase our efficiency, they also act as a filter to organize and interpret our social existence.

THE MEDIUM IS THE MESSAGE

McLuhan was convinced that the way we live is largely a function of the way we process information. The phonetic alphabet, the printing press, and the telegraph were turning points in human history because they changed the way people thought about themselves and their world. Tom Wolfe, an analyst of popular culture, summarizes McLuhan's thesis:

> The new technologies . . . radically alter the entire way people use their five
> senses, the way they react to things, and therefore, their entire lives and the
> entire society. It doesn't matter what the content of a medium like TV
> is . . . twenty hours a day of sadistic cowboys caving in people's teeth
> or . . . Pablo Casals droning away on his cello.[2]

McLuhan said it more succinctly: "The medium is the message."

Students of McLuhan continue to debate what the Canadian theorist meant by this apparently simple equation. Sometimes he seemed to indicate that the words we choose are irrelevant ("The content or message of any particular medium has about as much importance as the stenciling on the casing of an atomic bomb"). On other occasions he made the significance of the symbols a matter of degree ("I'm not suggesting that content plays *no* role—merely that it plays a distinctly subordinate role"). Either way, he obviously believed that a medium changes people more than the sum of all the messages of that medium. He warns that the content of a medium "is like the juicy piece of meat carried by the burglar to distract the watchdog of the mind." The same words spoken face-to-face, printed on paper, or presented on television provide three different messages.

The word *message* lends itself to a pun which further illustrates McLuhan's conviction that the media work us over. "The medium is the *massage*," he claimed. The image he offers is of a burly masseur pommeling his client's body rather than giving him a soothing back rub. Television roughs up its viewers. He also described the turbulent 1960s with another variation on the theme: "The medium is the *mass-age*." Although McLuhan obviously had fun with his play on words, he was serious about the core idea. Be it oral, written, or electronic, the primary channel of communication changes the way we perceive the world. The dominant medium of any age dominates people.

PARSING THE PAST: A MEDIA ANALYSIS OF HISTORY

McLuhan supported his thesis of technological determinism by interpreting the sweep of human history from a media perspective.

1. The Tribal Age: An Acoustic Place in History

According to McLuhan, the tribal village was an acoustic place where the senses of hearing, touch, taste, and smell were developed far beyond the ability to visualize. The right hemisphere of the brain dominated the left hemisphere. The ear was king; hearing was believing. Members of this oral culture were unable to adopt the role of the detached observer—they acted and emotionally reacted at the same time. Conformity to the group was the rule rather than the exception.

McLuhan claimed that "primitive" people led richer and more complex lives than their literate descendants because the ear, unlike the eye, is unable to select the stimuli it takes in.

> By their dependence on the spoken word for information, people were drawn together into a tribal mesh: and since the spoken word is more emotionally laden than the written—conveying by intonation such rich emotions as anger, joy, sorrow, fear—tribal man was more spontaneous and passionately volatile.[3]

Then someone invented letters.

2. The Age of Literacy: A Visual Point of View

McLuhan wrote that the phonetic alphabet fell into the acoustic world like a bombshell, installing sight at the head of the hierarchy of senses. People who could read exchanged an ear for an eye. Of course, the reader is free to disagree, illustrating McLuhan's belief that a private, left-brain "point of view" becomes possible in a visual society. Both writer and reader are separate from the text. Literacy jarred people out of collective tribal involvement into "civilized" private detachment. Print made it possible to leave the tribe without being cut off from a flow of information.

McLuhan also claimed that the phonetic alphabet established the line as the organizing principle in life. In writing, letter follows letter in a connected, orderly line. Logic is modeled on that step-by-step linear progression. According to McLuhan, when literate people say, "I don't follow you," they mean, "I don't think you are logical." He alleged that the invention of the alphabet fostered the sudden emergence of mathematics, science, and philosophy in ancient Greece. He cited the political upheaval in colonial Africa as evidence that literacy triggers an ear-to-eye switch which isolates the reader.

3. The Print Age: Prototype of the Industrial Revolution

If the phonetic alphabet made visual dependence possible, the printing press made it widespread. In *The Gutenberg Galaxy*, McLuhan wrote that repeatability is the most important characteristic of movable type, and a run of 100,000 copies of his book suggests that he's right. Because the print revolution demonstrated mass production of identical products, McLuhan called it the forerunner of the industrial revolution.

He saw other unintended side effects of Gutenberg's invention. The rise of nationalism followed the homogenization of fluid regional tongues into a fixed national language. Printing deified not only the Gutenberg Bible, but all written words. The press turns words into The Word, and McLuhan labeled literate people "natural suckers" for propaganda. But he regarded the fragmentation of society as the most significant outcome of the new innovation:

> Printing, a ditto device, confirmed and extended the new visual stress. It created the portable book, which men could read in privacy and in isolation from others.[4]

Many libraries have the words "The truth will set you free" carved in stone above the main entrance.[5] McLuhan said that the books inside free readers to be alienated from others in their literate culture. Like easel painting, the printed book glorifies individualism.

4. The Electronic Age: The Rise of the Global Village

According to McLuhan, the power of the printed word is over: "The age of print . . . had its obituary tapped out by the telegraph." Of course Samuel Morse's invention was only the first of the electronic communication devices that would make the corner Radio Shack seem like a magic shop to previous generations.

Telegraph   Telephone   Radio
Film projector   Phonograph
Television   Photocopier   Answering machine
Computer   VCR   Compact disc
Holograph   Cellular phone   FAX

"You see, Dad, Professor McLuhan says the environment that man creates becomes his medium for defining his role in it. The invention of type created linear, or sequential, thought, separating thought from action. Now, with TV and folk singing, thought and action are closer and social involvement is greater. We again live in a village. Get it?"

Drawing by Alan Dunn; © 1966 The New Yorker Magazine, Inc.

Before his death in 1980, McLuhan predicted that even the staggering cultural impact of this communication hardware would be insignificant compared with the upheaval caused by the computer software to come.

McLuhan insisted that the electronic media are retribalizing the human race. Instant communication has returned us to a prealphabetic, oral tradition where sound and touch are more important than sight. We've gone "back to the future."

> The day of the individualist, of privacy, of fragmented or "applied" knowledge, of "points of view" and specialist goals is being replaced by the over-all awareness of a mosaic world in which space and time are overcome by television, jets and computers—a simultaneous, "all-at-once" world in which everything resonates with everything else as in a total electrical field.[6]

McLuhan pictured all of us as members of a single global village. The electronic media bring us in touch with everyone, everywhere, instantaneously. Closed human systems no longer exist. The rumble of empty stomachs in Somalia or artillery in Sarajevo vibrates in the living rooms of Seattle. As the first postliterate generation, privacy for us is a luxury or a curse of the past. The planet is like a general store where nosy people keep track of everyone else's business—a twelve-way party line or an Ann Landers column "writ large." Citizens of the world are back in acoustic space.

Linear logic is useless in the electronic society that McLuhan described. Acoustic people no longer inquire, "Do you see my point?" Instead we ask, "How does that grab you?" What we feel is more important than what we think.

TELEVISION IS A COOL MEDIUM

The purpose of McLuhan's media-cultural analysis was to explain the social unrest of the 1960s and focus attention on the unprecedented changes that were still ahead as society moved fully into the electronic era. Because television had just become the dominant communication medium, most of McLuhan's efforts centered on describing the fundamental nature and revolutionary power of TV.

McLuhan classified media as either *hot* or *cool*. Hot media are high-definition channels of communication and are usually beamed at a single sense receptor. Print is a hot, visual medium. So are photographs and motion pictures. They package lots of data in a way that requires little work on the part of the viewer. McLuhan would have labeled the text of this book "hot" but judged the cartoons as "cool." Cool media's low-definition display draws a person in, requiring high participation to fill in the blanks.

McLuhan said a lecture is hot; discussions are cool. The hard sell is hot; the soft sell is cool. Plato's syllogisms were hot; Aristotle's enthymemes were cool. Despite radio's claim to be "the theater of the mind," he called it hot because the broadcast wave carries detailed information over a single channel. Yet he considered the telephone cool because its personal nature demands a response.

Note the parallel between McLuhan's categories of hot and cool and the distinctions between left-brain and right-brain functions. Hot media tend to be highly visual, logical, and private. They are organized to communicate packets of discrete information. Cool media tend to be aural, intuitive, and emotionally involving. Unlike the hot camera which focuses on the figure in the foreground, cool (right-brain) media clarify the surrounding context and let perceivers insert themselves into the story. People naturally think of television as a visual medium, but McLuhan disputed that notion. He classified TV as an aural and tactile medium—very, very cool.

Television is cool because it requires involvement and participation to fill in its vague and blurry image. The low-definition video display presents a series of widely spaced dots which viewers must connect on their internal mental screens. Unlike radio or print, television doesn't bypass either sight or sound. You can probably study while listening to the radio, but television doesn't work well as background.

LIVING ON THE EDGE OF AN ERA: SOME EXAMPLES

McLuhan supported his interpretation of history by offering numerous examples of media-induced change. I'll cite some of the evidence he offered in the areas of politics, education, and sex and drugs. I'll also include events that took place after he died, but which lend added credence to his ideas. I'm confident that McLuhan would have drawn on these subsequent events to support his theory of technological determinism.

Politics

Political leaders in the electronic age can survive without vision, but they can't make it without charisma. Larry King, Ted Koppel, and David Letterman are late-night heroes because they know how to talk to the nation on TV in the personal style the town crier used in a preprint era. McLuhan said that "the political candidate who understands TV—whatever his party, goals or beliefs—can gain power unknown in history."[7] Political journalists scoffed when Bill Clinton played his saxophone on MTV and hosted an economic summit in the style of a television talk-show host. But the soon-to-be president showed that the generation gap was really a communication gap. He understood that baby boomers are children of the boom box rather than the soap box.

In 1969, McLuhan observed that "the Western world is being revolutionized by the electric media as rapidly as the East is being Westernized."[8] The iron curtain could keep western people, products, and paper out of eastern Europe, but it couldn't stop the electronic media from carrying the message of freedom from other parts of the global village. Few recognized the extent of the electronic revolution, however. Thus the sudden collapse of the Communist-bloc governments of eastern Europe in 1989 shocked political pundits. Based on his belief that social reality is determined by communication technology, McLuhan probably would have been surprised that it took so long.

Education

McLuhan charged that people living in the midst of innovation often cling to what *was*, as opposed to what *is*. He considered the educational establishment a prime example. By the time Johnny starts school, he has already watched over 10,000 hours of television. According to McLuhan, the child craves in-depth involvement, not linear detachment. "But suddenly, he is snatched from the cool, inclusive womb of television and exposed—within a vast bureaucratic structure of courses and credits—to the hot medium of print."[9] Johnny's friend Jenny discovers that unlike *Sesame Street*, her Tuesday class isn't sponsored by the number 4. Words plod along a blackboard one by one rather than prance in patterns on a user-friendly screen. McLuhan claimed that today's child knows that going to school is an interruption to his or her education. Because the teacher still considers video an audiovisual *aid* rather than the primary tool of learning, the information level for Jenny and Johnny takes a dip when they walk into the classroom.

The acoustic media are a threat to an educational establishment that has a vested interest in books. The establishment runs the schools as "intellectual penal institutions" with visual, print-minded teachers as mindguards. The result is a triumphant and bitter cry of "School's out forever" in Alice Cooper's countercultural song.[10] The irony, from McLuhan's perspective, is that it is school—not hard rock—which stands against culture. If teachers would "plunge into the vortex of electronic technology," they could turn an outdated "ivory tower" into a modern-day "control tower."

Sex and Drugs

One of McLuhan's more controversial claims was that TV is a tactile medium as well as an acoustic one. He contended that "TV tattoos its message directly on our skins," and linked that "fact" to increased interpersonal touch, nudity, and public sexuality of recent decades. Because television is a medium of touch, when we "turn on" the set, we do the same thing to ourselves. McLuhan's first book, *The Mechanical Bride*, anticipated current fascination with the sensual possibilities of virtual reality.[11] He thought that the sexual revolution which began in the 1960s was the inevitable consequence of youth's trying to cope with the tension created by living in the historical seam between two conflicting media cultures.

He felt the same way about drugs. McLuhan regarded the use of marijuana, cocaine, and LSD as an attempt to achieve empathy with an electric environment that offers the potential of an all-at-once, total involvement of the senses. As a devout Catholic, McLuhan was less than enthusiastic about the use of hallucinogenic drugs, but he tried to avoid moral judgments. When asked about the legalization of mind-expanding drugs, McLuhan responded:

> My personal point of view is irrelevant, since all such legal restrictions are futile and will inevitably wither away. You could as easily ban drugs in a retribalized society as outlaw clocks in a mechanical culture.[12]

CRITIQUE: HOW COULD HE BE RIGHT? BUT WHAT IF HE IS?

Pop artist Andy Warhol said that sometime in life every person enjoys fifteen minutes of fame. Marshall McLuhan had fifteen years. Academics tend to be suspicious of their colleagues who make money and become famous, so perhaps the man's enormous popularity gave added impetus to critics' scorn for his methods and message. The pages of *McLuhan: Hot & Cool* and *McLuhan: Pro & Con* are filled with denunciation:

> "[McLuhan] prefers to rape our attention rather than seduce our understanding."[13]

> "He has looted all culture from cave painting to *Mad* magazine for fragments to shore up his system against ruin."[14]

> "The style . . . is a viscous fog through which loom stumbling metaphors."[15]

By labeling his ideas "probes" rather than "theory," McLuhan may have hoped to deflect criticism. But if this was his stratagem, it obviously didn't work. Fairleigh Dickinson communication professor Paul Levinson referred to McLuhan's "charming contempt for logic," but not everyone was charmed. George Gordon, chairman of the department of communication at Fordham University, labels his work "McLuhanacy" and dismisses it as totally worthless. Gordon stated, "Not one bit of *sustained* and *replicated* scientific evidence, inductive or deductive, has to date justified any one of McLuhan's most famous slogans, metaphors, or dicta."[16] Indeed, it's hard to know how one could prove that the phonetic alphabet created Greek philosophy, the printing press fostered nationalism, or that television is a tactile medium.

Since deterministic theories maintain that everything in life is connected to a single factor—economics (Marx), sex (Freud), media (McLuhan)—there's no way to stand objectively outside the theory to support or discredit its claims. For those who regard testability as a mark of good theory, McLuhan's leaps of faith are a major hindrance to taking his ideas seriously. McLuhan, however, dismissed his detractors by describing them as left-brain critics who are incapable of understanding right-brain concepts. From within his system, who's to say that he is wrong?

Tom Wolfe reverses the question: "What if he's *right*? Suppose he is what he sounds like—the most important thinker since Newton, Darwin, Freud,

Einstein and Pavlov?"[17] This kind of praise for McLuhan's ideas is more typical of media practitioners than academic theorists. Tony Schwartz, the acknowledged leader in the field of political advertising, credits McLuhan for his insight that attitudes are not ideas you put into a person with words. They are emotional responses that can be drawn out of people through association with familiar sounds. Electronic media don't instruct—they strike a responsive chord.

Malcolm Muggeridge echoes McLuhan's media-as-message dictum in his analysis of religious broadcasting. Drawing on his former experience as BBC television host and editor of the British humor magazine *Punch,* Muggeridge proclaims the folly of believing that the message of God's love can be presented on TV without being polluted. He notes, "Nothing TV deals with becomes more grand, beautiful, mysterious, or complicated."[18] He likens the efforts of TV evangelists to the misguided labor of a piano player in a brothel, pounding out the hymn "Abide with Me" in order to edify customers and inmates alike. The medium *is* the message.

Although it would be difficult to find anyone today who accepted all, or even most, of McLuhan's ideas, his historical analysis has heightened awareness of the possible cultural effects of new media technologies. Other scholars have been more tempered in their statement and rigorous in their documentation. But none has raised media consciousness to the level achieved by McLuhan with his catchy statements or dramatic metaphors. Economist Kenneth Boulding, who heads the Institute of Behavioral Sciences at the University of Colorado, captured both the pro and con reactions to McLuhan by using a metaphor of his own: "It is perhaps typical of very creative minds that they hit very large nails not quite on the head."[19]

QUESTIONS TO SHARPEN YOUR FOCUS

1. Why does McLuhan particularly target the inventions of the *phonetic alphabet,* the *printing press,* and the *telegraph* as crucial for an understanding of culture?

2. McLuhan considers a motion picture film viewed in a theater a *hot medium.* Using his own rational for television as a *cool medium,* can you defend the thesis that film should be classified "cool" as well?

3. What news have you seen recently on TV that illustrates McLuhan's belief that we now live in a *global village*?

4. Can you conceive of any way that McLuhan's theory of *technological determinism* could be proved false?

A SECOND LOOK

Recommended resource: Playboy interview: Marshall McLuhan, *Playboy,* March 1969, pp. 53, 53–54, 56, 59–62, 64–66, 68, 70.

Impact of print media: Marshall McLuhan, *The Gutenberg Galaxy,* University of Toronto, Toronto, 1962.

Impact of electronic media: Marshall McLuhan, *Understanding Media,* McGraw-Hill, New York, 1964.

Hemispherical dominance: Marshall McLuhan and Eric McLuhan, "Culture and Communication: The Two Hemispheres," in *Laws of Media,* University of Toronto, Toronto, 1988, pp. 67–91.

McLuhan once over lightly: Marshall McLuhan and Quentin Fiore, *The Medium Is the Massage,* Random House, New York, 1967.

Early vs. late McLuhan: Bruce E. Gronbeck, "McLuhan as Rhetorical Theorist," *Journal of Communication,* Vol. 31, 1981, pp. 117–128.

Intellectual roots: Harold Innis, *The Bias of Communication,* University of Toronto, Toronto, 1964.

Methodology: Paul Levinson, "McLuhan and Rationality," *Journal of Communication,* Vol. 31, 1981, pp. 179–188.

Critique: Gerald Stearn (ed.), *McLuhan: Hot & Cool,* Dial Press, New York, 1967.

Critique: Raymond Rosenthal (ed.), *McLuhan: Pro & Con,* Funk & Wagnalls, New York, 1968.

Critique: G. N. Gordon, "An End to McLuhanacy," *Educational Technology,* January 1982, pp. 39–45.

Resonance in practice: Tony Schwartz, *The Responsive Chord,* Anchor, Garden City, N.Y., 1973.

Religious broadcasting: Malcolm Muggeridge, *Christ and the Media,* Eerdmans, Grand Rapids, Mich., 1977.

CHAPTER 29

Cultivation Theory
of George Gerbner

What are the odds that you'll be involved in some kind of violent act within the next seven days? 1 out of 10? 1 out of 100? 1 out of 1,000? 1 out of 10,000?

According to George Gerbner, the answer you give may have more to do with how much TV you watch than with the actual risk you face in the week to come. Gerbner, former dean of the Annenberg School of Communication at the University of Pennsylvania, claims that heavy television users develop an exaggerated belief in "a mean and scary world." The violence they see on the screen cultivates a social paranoia that resists notions of trustworthy people or safe environments.

Like Marshall McLuhan, Gerbner regards television as the dominant force in shaping modern society. But unlike McLuhan, who viewed the medium as the message, Gerbner is convinced that TV's power comes from the symbolic content of the real-life drama shown hour after hour, week after week. At its root, television is "story," and a society's stories give "a coherent picture of what exists, what is important, what is related to what, and what is right."

Until recently, the only acceptable storytellers outside the home were those passing down religious tradition. Today, the TV set is a key member of the household, with virtually unlimited access to every person in the family. Television dominates the environment of symbols, telling most of the stories, most of the time. Gerbner claims that people now watch television as they might attend church, "except that most people watch television more religiously."

What do they see in their daily devotions? According to Gerbner—violence. During the turmoil of the late 1960s, the National Commission on the Causes and Prevention of Violence suggested that violence is as American as cherry pie.[1] Instead of being a deviant route to power, physical force and its threat are traditional ways people gain a larger slice of the American dream. Gerbner says that violence "is the simplest and cheapest dramatic means to demonstrate who wins in the game of life and the rules by which the game is played." Those who are immersed in the world of TV drama learn these "facts of life" better than occasional viewers.

Gerbner's voice is only one of many that proclaims a link between communication media and violence. Critics have publicly warned against the chaotic effects of comic books, rock music, and video games as well as television. But the man who for many years was the editor of the *Journal of Communication* thinks that TV is a special case. For almost two decades he spearheaded an extensive research program that monitored the level of violence on television, classified people according to how much TV they watch, and compiled viewer perceptions of potential risk and other sociocultural attitudes. His cultivation explanation of the findings is one of the most talked-about and argued-over theories of mass communication.

AN INDEX OF VIOLENCE

Alarmed parents, teachers, and critics of television assume that the portrayal of violence has been escalating. But is the level of dramatic aggression really on the rise? Gerbner and his colleagues sought to develop an objective measure which would allow TV's friends and foes to discuss the trend on the basis of fact rather than feeling. They defined dramatic violence as "the overt expression of physical force (with or without a weapon, against self or others) compelling action against one's will on pain of being hurt and/or killed or threatened to be so victimized as part of the plot."[2]

The definition rules out verbal abuse, idle threats, and pie-in-the-face slapstick. But it includes the physical abuse presented in a cartoon format. When the coyote pursuing the roadrunner is flattened by a steamroller, or Batman dispatches the Joker's henchmen with a BAM! SOCK! POW!, Gerbner labels the scene violent. He also counts auto crashes and natural disasters. From an artistic point of view, these events are no accident. The screenwriter inserted the trauma for dramatic effect. Characters die or are maimed just as effectively as if they'd taken a bullet in the chest.

For over a decade, Annenberg researchers randomly selected a week during the fall season and videotaped every prime-time (8 to 11 P.M.) network show. They also recorded programming for children on Saturday and Sunday (8 A.M. to 2 P.M.). After counting up the incidents that fit their definition, they gauged the overall level of violence with a formula that included the ratio of programs that scripted violence, the rate of violence in the programs that did, and the percentage of characters involved in physical harm and killing. They found that the annual index is remarkably stable.

EQUAL VIOLENCE, UNEQUAL RISK

Gerbner reports that regardless of whether the dramas are *Matlock, In the Heat of the Night, Homicide: Life on the Street,* or dozens of forgettable shows canceled after a thirteen-week run, the cumulative portrayal of violence varies little from year to year. Two-thirds of prime-time programs contain actual bodily harm or threatened violence. *The Cosby Show, Murphy Brown,* and *Cheers* are not typical. Dramas that include violence average five traumatic incidents per viewing hour. Almost all the weekend children's shows major in mayhem. They average twenty cases an hour. By the time the typical TV viewer graduates from high school, he or she has observed 13,000 violent deaths.

On any given week, two-thirds of the major characters are caught up in some kind of violence. Heroes are just as involved as villains, yet there is great inequality as to age, race, and gender of those on the receiving end of physical force. Old people and children are harmed at a much greater rate than young or middle-aged adults. In the pecking order of "victimage," blacks and Hispanics are killed or beaten more than their Caucasian counterparts. Gerbner notes that it's risky to be "other than clearly white." It's also dangerous to be female. The opening lady-in-distress scene is a favorite dramatic device to galvanize the hero into action. And finally, blue-collar workers "get it in the neck" more often than white-collar executives.

If insurance companies kept actuarial tables on the life expectancy of television characters, they'd discover that the chance of a poor, elderly black woman's avoiding harm for the entire hour is almost nil. The symbolic vulnerability of minority-group members is even more striking given their gross underrepresentation in TV drama. Gerbner's analysis of the world of television records that 50 percent of the people are white, middle-class males, and women are outnumbered by men 3 to 1. Although one-third of our society is made up of children and teenagers, they appear as only 10 percent of the characters on prime-time shows. Two-thirds of the United States labor force have blue-collar or service jobs, yet that group constitutes a mere 10 percent of the players on television. Blacks and Hispanics are only occasional figures, but the elderly are by far the most excluded minority. Less than 3 percent of the dramatic roles are filled by actors over the age of 65.

In sum, the Annenberg logs reveal that people on the margin of American society are put into a symbolic double jeopardy. Their existence is understated, but at the same time their vulnerability to violence is overplayed. When written into the script, they are often made visible in order to be a victim. Not surprisingly, these are the very people who exhibit the most fear of violence when the TV set goes off.

ESTABLISHING A VIEWER PROFILE

Equipped with the sure knowledge of TV drama's violent content, Gerbner and his associates gathered surveys of viewer behavior and attitudes. Although some later researchers have tried to create saturation exposure in an experimental setting, Gerbner says the nature of his cultivation hypothesis makes testing in the laboratory impossible. He believes that the effects of heavy TV viewing can be seen only after years of slow buildup. The pervasive presence of television also rules out a control group. Gerbner regards everyone as a consumer. His questions merely aim at distinguishing between "light" and "heavy" users.

"You do lovely needlepoint, grandma, but. . ."
Reproduced by permission of Punch.

Most of Gerbner's work establishes a self-report of two hours a day as the upper limit of light viewing. He labels heavy viewers as those who admit an intake of four hours or more. There are more heavy viewers, but each group makes up about one-fourth of the general population. Gerbner also refers to the heavy viewer as "the television type," a more benign term than the current "couch potato" with its twin allusions to steady diets of television and potato chips.

Gerbner claims that television types don't turn on the set in order to watch *Roseanne* or *Northern Exposure*. They simply want to watch television per se. Light viewers are more selective, turning the set off when a favorite program is over. Gerbner's reason for distinguishing the audience is to test whether those with heavy viewing habits regard the world as more dangerous than those with occasional or light viewing habits. Cultivation theory predicts they do.

PLOWING THE MIND: DEEP FURROWS VS. ONCE OVER LIGHTLY

Believing that violence is the backbone of TV drama and knowing that people differ in how much TV they see, Gerbner sought to discover the "cultivation differential." That's his term for "the difference in the percent giving the 'television answer' within comparable groups of light and heavy viewers." His annual survey targeted four attitudes.

    1. *Chances of involvement with violence.* The question at the start of the chapter addresses this issue. Those with light viewing habits predict that their weekly odds of being a victim are 1 out of 100; those with heavy viewing habits fear the risk to be 1 out of 10. Actual crime statistics indicate that 1 out of 10,000 is more realistic. Of course, the prediction of those with heavy viewing habits may be due to their greater willingness to justify physical aggression. Children who are habitual TV watchers agree that it's "almost always all right [to hit someone] if you are mad at them for a good reason."

2. *Fear of walking alone at night.* Not surprisingly, more women than men are afraid of dark streets. But for both sexes, the fear of victimization correlates with time spent in front of the tube. People with heavy viewing habits tend to overestimate criminal activity, believing it to be ten times worse than it really is. In actuality, muggers on the street pose less bodily threat than injury from cars.

3. *Perceived activity of police.* People with heavy viewing habits believe that 5 percent of society is involved in law enforcement. Their video world is peopled with police, judges, and government agents. People with light viewing habits estimate a more realistic 1 percent. Gerbner's television type assumes that police officers draw their guns almost every day, which is not true.

4. *General mistrust of people.* Those with heavy viewing habits are suspicious of other people's motives. They subscribe to statements that warn people to expect the worst:

   "Most people are just looking out for themselves."
   "In dealing with others, you can't be too careful."
   "Do unto others before they do unto you."

   Gerbner calls this cynical mind-set the "mean world syndrome."

The Annenberg evidence suggests that the minds of heavy TV viewers become fertile ground for sowing thoughts of danger. If cultivation of the nonstop viewer does indeed occur, what's the mechanism that plows a furrow in their brow? Gerbner presents two explanations of how cultivation takes place—mainstreaming and resonance.

MAINSTREAMING

Mainstreaming is Gerbner's word to describe the process of "blurring, blending and bending" that those with heavy viewing habits undergo. He thinks that through constant exposure to the same images and labels, television types develop a commonality of outlook. Radio stations segment the audience to the point where programming for left-handed truck drivers who bowl on Friday nights is a distinct possibility. But TV producers seek to "attract the largest possible audience by celebrating the moderation of the mainstream." Television homogenizes its audience so that those with heavy viewing habits share the same orientations, perspectives, and meanings with each other. We shouldn't ask how close this collective interpretation is to the mainstream of culture. According to Gerbner, television *is* the mainstream.

He illustrates the mainstream effect by showing how television types blur economic and political distinctions. TV glorifies the middle class, and those with heavy viewing habits assume that label no matter what their income. But those with light viewing habits who have blue-collar jobs accurately describe themselves as working-class people.

In like fashion, those with heavy viewing habits position themselves as political moderates. Most characters in TV dramas frown on political extremism—right or left. This middle-of-the-road ethic is apparently picked up by the constant viewer. It's only from the ranks of sporadic TV users that Gerbner finds people who label themselves "liberal" or "conservative."

Social scientists have come to expect political differences between rich and poor, blacks and whites, Catholics and Protestants, city dwellers and farmers. Those distinctions still emerge when sporadic television viewers respond to the survey. But Gerbner reports that traditional differences disappear among those with heavy viewing habits. It's as if the light from the TV set washes out any sharp features that would set them apart.

Even though those with heavy viewing habits call themselves moderates, the Annenberg team notes that their position on social issues is decidedly conservative. Constant watchers consistently voice opinions in favor of low taxes, more police protection, and stronger national defense. They are against big government, free speech, homosexuals in the military, the Equal Rights Amendment, abortion, interracial marriage, open-housing legislation, and busing to achieve integration.

Saturation viewing seems to bend television types toward the political right, although they do support greater funding of social security, health services, and education. Gerbner labels the mix of attitudes and desires the "new populism" and sees its rise as evidence that those with heavy viewing habits are sucked into the mainstream. The almost complete overlap between the "new populism" and the policies of Ronald Reagan could explain the former president's reputation as being the "great communicator" when he went directly to the people on television. His message was like an old friend they'd grown up with on prime-time TV.

RESONANCE

Gerbner also explains the constant viewer's greater apprehension by the process of *resonance*. Many viewers have had at least one firsthand experience with physical violence—armed robbery, rape, bar fight, mugging, auto crash, military combat, or a lover's quarrel that became vicious. The actual trauma was bad enough. But he thinks that a repeated symbolic portrayal on the TV screen can cause the viewer to replay the real-life experience over and over in his or her mind: "The congruence of the television world and real-life circumstances may 'resonate' and lead to markedly amplified cultivation patterns."

Constant viewers who have experienced physical violence get a double dose.

For three years I was a volunteer advocate in a low-income housing project. Although I felt relatively safe walking through the project, police and social workers told stories of shootings and stabbings. Even peace-loving residents were no strangers to violence. I can't recall ever entering an apartment where the TV was silent. Gerbner would expect that the daily diet of symbolic savagery would reinforce people's experience of doorstep violence, making life even more frightening. The hesitation of most tenants to venture outside their apartments would seem to confirm his resonance assumption.

The mainstreaming and resonance hypotheses are after-the-fact explanations for Gerbner's main finding that for those who heavily watch television, the world is a scary place. He says that most media effects research focuses on the few people who imitate the violence they see on TV.

> But it is just as important to look at the large majority of people who become more fearful, insecure, and dependent on authority; and who may grow up demanding protection and even welcoming repression in the name of security.[3]

CRITIQUE: TV'S CULTIVATION OF FEAR—A WEAK RELATIONSHIP

For most observers, Gerbner's claim that the dramatic content of television creates a fearful climate makes sense. How could the habitual viewer watch so much violence without its having a lasting effect? Yet cultivation theory has drawn fierce criticism from its detractors. Since the late 1970s communication journals have been filled with the sometimes bitter charges and counter-charges of critics and supporters.

The controversy begins with the relatively weak relationship that Gerbner and his colleagues have been able to establish between heavy viewing and fear of violence. Although more often than not the two go together, the overlap isn't great enough to be able to predict the presence of heavy fear from the knowledge of heavy viewing. The linkage is loose.

Some opponents claim that the correlation is so slight that it should be discounted and the theory abandoned. A few suggest that the small positive relationship exists only because the Annenberg group mishandled the data. For example, University of Chicago sociologist Paul Hirsch charges that Gerbner conveniently glossed over the fact that nonviewers were actually among the most fearful people in his sample. Conversely, cultivation advocates believe that the results would be more impressive if Gerbner had controlled for factors other than time spent in front of the TV.

University of Wisconsin researchers Robert Hawkins (journalism and mass communication) and Suzanne Pingree (women's studies) note that not all prime-time programming is drama. They found a cultivation effect with crime adventures, game shows, and cartoons, but not with comedy, news, documentaries, sports, or variety shows.

Researchers who take a "uses and gratifications" approach believe that viewer motivation makes a difference. Gerbner assumes that those with heavy viewing habits watch TV "more by the clock than the program," but he never made an effort to separate those people who are ritualistic in their behavior from those who watch with a purpose. Cable television gives even those with heavy viewing habits a chance to be selective.

Although cultivation theory claims to predict who will experience fear of victimization, Gerbner measures only the perceived probability that violence will occur. Purdue mass communication researchers Glenn Sparks and Robert Ogles remind us that our feeling of fear depends on (1) how awful the event would be if it happened, (2) how well we think we'd cope if it did, and (3) the odds we think it will. Since the Annenberg group ignores the first two factors, they really only gauge the *likelihood* of victimization. By lumping together all types of programs, neglecting viewer motivation, and failing to accurately measure fear, Gerbner makes it almost impossible to establish a strong relationship between viewing TV drama and feeling fear.

Even if Gerbner established that television types are always anxious, we couldn't be certain that it is TV which cultivates that fear. Correlation doesn't prove causality. Perhaps people who are already scared watch television to escape their fears rather than the other way around. Indiana University media research Dolf Zillmann thinks that the cognitive dissonance principle of selective exposure (see Chapter 19) explains Gerbner's data better than the idea of cultivation. He notes that television drama "almost always features the triumph of justice." He's not suggesting that fearful people *like* symbolic violence, but its portrayal seems to be necessary for the good guys to win and the bad guys to lose.

There's also the possibility that both Gerbner and Zillmann are wrong. Perhaps neither fear nor heavy viewing is the cause of the other, but each is caused by a common third factor that Gerbner didn't even measure. That prospect led University of Toronto researchers Anthony Doob and Glenn Macdonald to canvas four of their city's neighborhoods that had varying rates of crime. The researchers assumed that "people who watch a lot of television may have a greater fear of being victims of violent crime because, in fact, they live in more violent neighborhoods." (You're not paranoid if they really are out to get you.) When the effect of neighborhood was removed, the effect of television was reduced to almost nothing. Only in the most risky district did a viewer's fear increase in proportion to the number of programs watched. Gerbner maintains that this one exception illustrates his resonance principle in action, but the study severely undermines the cultivation hypothesis.

Students of mass communication are left with a popular, yet questionable, theory of media influence. The intuitive logic of a connection between television and fear is strong. The research supporting it is mixed. And any notion of direct cause and effect is weak. Gerbner's claim that "ritualistic exposure to television's repetitive force" cultivates "pervasive fear and mistrust" is somewhat like fine TV drama. It's worth watching as long as we realize it may contain an element of fiction.

QUESTIONS TO SHARPEN YOUR FOCUS

1. How would you change Gerbner's *definition of dramatic violence* so that his index of TV violence would measure what you think is important?

2. What type of people are underrepresented in television drama? What type of people are overrepresented? Who are the victims of symbolic violence on the screen?

3. How do your *political* and *social values* differ from the *mainstream* attitudes of Gerbner's *television type*?

4. If heavy viewing of televised violence doesn't *cause* viewer fear of a mean and scary world, how do you explain Gerbner's findings that they go together?

A SECOND LOOK

Recommended resource: George Gerbner, Larry Gross, Michael Morgan, and Nancy Signorielli, "Living with Television: The Dynamics of the Cultivation Process," in *Perspectives on Media Effects,* Jennings Bryant and Dolf Zillmann (eds.), Lawrence Erlbaum Associates, Hillsdale, N.J., 1986, pp. 17–40.

Violence index: George Gerbner, Larry Gross, Marilyn Jackson-Beeck, Suzanne Jeffries-Fox, and Nancy Signorielli, "Cultural Indicators: Violence Profile No. 9," *Journal of Communication,* Vol. 28, No. 3, 1978, pp. 176–207.

Mainstreaming and resonance: George Gerbner, Larry Gross, Michael Morgan, and Nancy Signorielli, "The 'Mainstreaming' of America: Violence Profile No. 11," *Journal of Communication,* Vol. 30, No. 3, 1980, pp. 10–29.

Research update: Robert Ogles, "Cultivation Analysis: Theory, Methodology and Current Research on Television-Influenced Constructions of Social Reality," *Mass Communication Research,* Vol. 14, 1987, pp. 43–53.

New directions: Nancy Signorielli and Michael Morgan (eds.), *Cultivation Analysis: New Directions in Media Effects Research,* Sage, Newbury Park, Calif., 1989.

Type of programming: Robert Hawkins and Suzanne Pingree, "Uniform Messages and Habitual Viewing: Unnecessary Assumptions in Social Reality Effects," *Human Communication Research,* Vol. 7, 1981, pp. 291–301.

Neighborhood factor: Anthony Doob and Glenn Macdonald, "Television Viewing and Fear of Victimization: Is the Relationship Causal?" *Journal of Personality and Social Psychology,* Vol. 37, 1979, pp. 170–179.

Behavioral critique: Paul Hirsch, "The 'Scary World' of the Nonviewer and Other Anomalies," *Communication Research,* Vol. 7, 1980, pp. 403–456.

Humanistic critique: Horace Newcomb, "Assessing the Violence Profile Studies of Gerbner and Gross," *Communication Research,* Vol. 5, 1978, pp. 264–282.

Fear vs. likelihood of violence: Glenn G. Sparks and Robert M. Ogles, "The Difference Between Fear of Victimization and the Probability of Being Victimized: Implications for Cultivation," *Journal of Broadcasting & Electronic Media*, Vol. 34, No. 3, 1990, pp. 351–358.

Direction of cause: Dolf Zillmann and Jacob Wakshlag, "Fear of Victimization and the Appeal of Crime Drama," in *Selective Exposure to Communication*, Dolf Zillmann and Jennings Bryant (eds.), Lawrence Erlbaum Associates, Hillsdale, N.J., 1985, pp. 141–156.

CHAPTER 30

Critical Theory
of Stuart Hall

Critical theorists view the mass media as a means by which the haves of society gain the willing support of the have-nots to maintain the status quo. Although these critics differ in many particulars, they typically share a reformist agenda which includes three aims:

1. To raise the public awareness that entertainment and news media promote the interest of the dominant groups of society. Critical theorists stop short of charging an establishment conspiracy to oppress the poor and the powerless, but they do say that media content tends to cover up unjust social relations.

2. To analyze the symbolic means by which capitalism is made attractive to workers who suffer economic exploitation. Critical theorists take an interpretive approach to communication studies.

3. To expose the so-called neutral stance of American communication study as myth. Critical theorists refer to statistical research which shows low media impact as "administrative" because it serves the dominant cultural ideology. They consider inquiry funded by big business and government as no more impartial than would be a report on the satisfying life of chickens drawn up by Colonel Sanders.

Stuart Hall is a British professor of sociology at Open University, Milton Keynes, England. He is only one of a large group of European scholars who are critical of traditional media scholarship because it ignores power relationships. I have chosen to present his particular brand of critical theory because of the increasing influence his ideas are having in American academic circles. A specific case of media-aided domination may help you understand his cultural analysis.

Maria Ortiz works as a cashier at a Wal-Mart discount store in Aurora, Illinois—a city on the edge of the Chicago metropolitan area made famous by *Wayne's World*. Maria is a single parent with two preschool-age children. Even though she works full-time and has medical benefits, her $6.00-per-hour wage puts her well below the poverty line. After work she picks up her children at a day-care center, fixes dinner, and goes through an extended bedtime ritual. Then she collapses in front of the TV set for a cops-and-robbers show, the evening news, and a bit of Jay Leno or *Nightline.*

Maria's stressful life grows more uncertain when workers at the local Caterpillar tractor plant go on strike. An already depressed local economy turns worse and as sales at the store plummet, her boss warns of possible layoffs. At this point, Maria begins to watch television less for entertainment and more for current information on the talks between labor and management at the Caterpillar plant. Hector, who lives in the apartment next door, is walking the picket line and she knows he's making three times the money she is. She can't understand why he and his fellow workers don't agree to terms with the company and go back to work. Perhaps if Ross Perot were in charge of Caterpillar, the strike would be settled and things would get better for everyone.

Stuart Hall explores the connection between what Maria sees on her television screen and her faith in the American way. He has less concern about the technological nature of the TV medium Maria watches or the dramatic violence she sees than he does over the nature of the violence being done to her in the workplace. There is no question in Hall's mind that megacorporations like Wal-Mart are taking unfair advantage of Maria and millions of other workers, but he doesn't see any reason to assume that the economic exploitation would be less under Ross Perot. He thinks it's tragic that Maria accepts the capitalistic system as basically fair and that she feels that everything would be okay if the right man were in charge. He's convinced that Maria's naiveté is due in part to the way the media report power disputes. He blames American mass communication scholarship for ignoring the relationship of media and the maintenance of an unjust social order.

THE MEDIA ARE IDEOLOGICAL

Hall believes the media function to maintain the dominance of those already in positions of power. The media serve the Sam Waltons, Donald Trumps, and Ross Perots of the world; they exploit the Maria Ortizes. Hall says that the communication field continues to be "stubbornly sociologically innocent." He is "deeply suspicious of and hostile to empirical work that has no ideas because that simply means that it does not know the ideas it has."[1] Noncritical researchers represent their work as pure science with no presuppositions, but every media theory by its very nature has ideological content. For example, the whole field of market research is based on the value that capitalism is good.

As for mainstream mass communication research in the United States, he believes that it serves the myth of democratic pluralism—the pretense that society is held together by common norms including equal opportunity, respect for diversity, one person-one vote, individual rights, rule of law. The usual finding that the media have little effect celebrates the political claim that democracy works. Such research claims that the American dream has been empirically verified, and science beckons developing countries to become "fully paid up members of the consensus club."

Hall claims that typical research on individual voting behavior, brand loyalty, or response to dramatic violence fails to uncover the struggle for power that the media mask. He thinks it's a mistake to treat communication as a separate academic discipline (a view which may not endear him to your instructor). Academic isolation tends to separate messages from the culture they inhabit:

> All the repetition and incantation of the sanitized term *information*, with its cleansing cybernetic properties, cannot wash away or obliterate the fundamentally dirty, semiotic, semantic, discursive character of the media in their cultural dimensions.[2]

Therefore, Hall refers to his work as "cultural studies" rather than "media studies," and in the decade of the seventies he directed the Center for Contemporary Cultural Studies (CCCS) at the University of Birmingham.

Under Hall, the staff of CCCS sought to articulate their perception of the cultural struggle between the haves and the have-nots. Hall uses the term *articulate* in the dual sense of "speaking out" on oppression and "linking" that subjugation with the communication media because they provide the terrain where meaning is shaped. He says he doesn't seek to be a "ventriloquist" for the masses, but does desire to "win some space" where their voices can be heard. The effort to jar people loose from their entrenched power positions often requires harsh words, but a "cozy chat among consenting scholars" won't dissolve the ideology that glues together communication theory.

The language Hall uses reflects his commitment to a broad Marxist interpretation of history. Since the stated aim of critical theory is to unmask power, he says critical theory is valid if it "deconstructs" the current structure of media research and intervenes in the lives of people like Maria Ortiz. As far as he's concerned, the truth of critical theory is established by its ability to raise consciousness of the media's role in preserving the status quo.

MARXISM WITHOUT GUARANTEES

Classical Marxism reduces all of life to matters of money. Economics is the base. Everything else—social life, politics, religion, culture—is superstructure determined by underlying economic realities. However, Marx wouldn't regard Maria's Catholic faith, Hispanic background, Democrat voter registration, or television viewing habits as unimportant. He wrote that superstructure is a necessary part of "reproducing the conditions of production." But he saw class distinctions based on money at the root of the entire social system. Within a capitalistic economy, the communication media merely reflect the exploitation of labor.

Hall rejects Marx's economic determinism. It's true that most English aristocracy vote Conservative while the working classes join the ranks of Labour, but he doesn't believe there's a necessary one-on-one relationship between wealth and political thought. He wants to erase the stereotypical image of the "great, immovable class battalions heaving their ascribed ideological luggage about the field of struggle, with their ideological number-plates on their backs."[3] He replaces this image with the concept of *overdetermination*. The term suggests that every action has multiple causes. Although Hall doesn't draw the connection, what he labels "overdetermination" is the same principle that systems theorists call "equifinality." Both perspectives avoid simplistic cause-and-effect description.

Although economic class is a major factor in how a person reacts, so are race and gender. Each of these factors, and others as well, could account for a particular ideology. As a Jamaican black who immigrated to England as a young adult, Hall found that his color was often as important as his economic class in the way people reacted to him. Working-class racism is difficult to analyze using the orthodox Marxist tools of base and superstructure. So Hall regards the golden rule of Marxism—"the one who has the gold, rules"—as an oversimplification. The leading ideology of a society doesn't precisely mirror the thoughts of the ruling class. It's only by rejecting the money-equals-power equation that Hall is able to explain a working-class cashier's desire to have Ross Perot take over a discount chain which Hall believes should belong to her and the other workers.

He continues to maintain that the inherent contradictions in capitalism will result in an ongoing struggle between those who do the work and those who reap the profits. But his "Marxism without guarantees" avoids an economic determinism which would claim, for example, that advertisers dictate the editorial content of the news. He knows that his theory is not pure Marxism, but he says that he'd rather be "right but not rigorous" than "rigorous but wrong."

HEGEMONY: SUBTLE SWAY OF THE HAVES OVER THE HAVE-NOTS

Hall and other critical theorists repeatedly refer to the concept of *hegemony* when they describe the cultural role of the media. The term is not familiar to most Americans, perhaps because it disturbingly labels United States foreign policy in the twentieth century. *Hegemony* can be defined as "preponderant influence or authority, especially one nation over another."

Third-world nations are convinced that the word describes western exports of news and entertainment. They cite the almost global monopoly of AP and Reuters news services, the foreign-language editions of *Time,* and the broadcast signal of CNN—all of which virtually ignore life in developing countries and give a northern hemisphere inflection to world events. People in Bolivia smoke packs of Marlboros, watch Indiana Jones, and listen to Michael Jackson, but most citizens of Boston know nothing of that poorer country. Many third-world leaders call for a "new information order" which offsets western ideology and represents the interests of the less affluent nations. Hall is sympathetic to their plight but uses hegemony to describe the way media impose the leading-class ideology on the rest of society within capitalistic nations. As with other concepts, he clarifies his understanding of hegemony by stating what it is not.

Hegemony is not force. The leading coalition of interests in a society doesn't gain leadership over the working classes through coercion of the army, police, or courts. Instead, the "culture industries" of art and communication produce a definition of reality that is favorable to the ruling class. For example, in 1986 the Motion Picture Academy awarded eleven Oscars to *Out of Africa*, a film which glorified a privileged, white European woman's efforts to help impoverished Kenyan natives. It bypassed *The Color Purple,* an artistic masterpiece which gave testimony to the indomitable spirit of women in the black underclass. Spike Lee's *Malcolm X* fared no better, but at least African-Americans could go to the movie theater and see a person of their race lifted up. With the exception of *Stand and Deliver*—the story of Jaime Escalante's success as a math teacher—Hollywood has offered no real-life role model for Mexican-American children to emulate. Cultural leadership is the most effective form of power, winning Maria Ortiz's active consent despite the fact that her granting of it means continual subordination.

Hegemony is not total. Ruling-class values form only part of the dominant cluster, and ideological victory is only temporary mastery in a particular theater of conflict. Hall says the question is not whether the robber baron ethics of people like Perot, Walton, and Trump will wipe out a concern for economic justice. It won't. The issue is relative balance of power at any point in history.

Hegemony is not a plot. Journalists in democratic countries are not controlled by the state; broadcasters aren't ideological agents of their political masters. Just as native speakers may not understand the syntax or grammar of their language, so most reporters and commentators don't realize their bias toward the status quo. Their very insistence on journalistic independence lends credibility to their words. Viewers trust Peter Jennings, Tom Brokaw, and Dan Rather more than the officials whose statements the anchormen report. Nevertheless, Hall is convinced that these journalists give an *unconscious* turn to the news of the day.

Hegemony isn't merely reflected in the media; it's reinforced there. Some observers maintain that broadcast and print journalism simply report what is going on in the world. Hall denies that "news selects itself" and denounces the "window on the world" model of media function. The real role of the media is "production of consent" rather than "reflection of consensus." His critical theory holds that TV messages never deliver a single meaning. "They are rather, the site of a plurality of meanings, in which one is preferred and offered to the viewers, over the others, as the most appropriate."[4]

ENCODING THE DOMINANT IDEOLOGY

We have already seen that, for Hall, ideology and class outlook may not always be the same. Ideologies are mental frameworks:

> the languages, the concepts, categories, imagery of thought, and the systems of representation—which different classes and social groups deploy in order to make sense of, define, figure out and render intelligible the way society works.[5]

We might naturally assume that ideologies are clusters of ideas, but Hall regards them as structures, not content. Ideologies are subcultures, ways to code reality, classification schemes, rules of the semantic game. What Hall would regard as Maria Ortiz's ideology, she would call common sense.

Hall believes that Maria's ideology will be partly shaped by what she sees on her TV screen. Since television is the dominant "means of signification" in our society, he considers it the terrain over which the struggle to define events must be waged. This battle for meaning can't be resolved by consulting a dictionary. People with different ideologies usually have little argument over the denotation of a word. For example, both sides in the Caterpillar tractor dispute agree that a strike refers to employees' refusing to work. But the feelings surrounding the term—the connotations—aren't fixed.

How will the public regard the strike at Caterpillar? Will they see it as a threat to the public interest, a breakdown of cooperation? Or will they hail it as a triumph of solidarity, a creative response to greedy injustice? If the last two interpretations would sound strange on the eleven o'clock news, Hall says it's because the media give an ideological spin to each story—a kind of body English which favors those in power.

According to Hall, the typical broadcast interview simply takes for granted that rising wage demands are the sole cause for inflation; shareholder pressure for higher dividends is never mentioned. Or consider the annual crisis in funding public assistance. It's almost always linked to "welfare cheating" rather than to high fees charged by doctors, hospitals, and pharmacies. Yet according to the Chicago-based Institute for Economic Policy, 57 percent of every welfare dollar ends up in the hands of medical providers. Hall sees no bias in the media in their denotation of the day's events. But connotations are fragments of ideology through which collective meaning is achieved. This is the emotional ground over which Maria's interpretation must be contested. As you may recall, it was also the chief concern of Roland Barthes' semiotic analysis (see Chapter 8).

With all the channels of mass communication in the unwitting service of the ruling elite, Hall has trouble believing ("pessimism of the intellect") that the powerless can change the system. Yet he is determined ("optimism of the will") to do everything he can to expose and alter the media's structuring of reality.

"Your royal command has been obeyed, Highness. Every town crier in the land is crying: 'Old King Cole is a merry ole soul.' Before nightfall we'll have them all believing it."

Copyright © 1970 Reprinted by permission of Saturday Review and Edward Frascino.

He cites one small victory by activists in the organized struggle to establish that black is beautiful. By insisting on the term *black* rather than *Negro* or *colored*, people of African heritage give dignity in the 1970s to what was once a racial slur. Jesse Jackson's call for an African-American identity is a continuing effort to control the use of symbols. This is not a matter of mere semantics as some would charge. Although there is nothing inherently positive or negative in any of these racial designations, the connotative difference is important because the effects are real. A similar campaign has transformed the term *Jamaican*. When Hall went to England it had an immigrant feel. Today it conjures up romance, rum and Coke, and reggae music. The ideological fight is a struggle to capture language. Hall sees those on the margin of society doing semantic battle on a media playing field that's never quite level.

THE OBSTINATE AUDIENCE

Just because the media present a preferred interpretation of human events is no reason to assume that the audience will correctly "take in" the offered ideology. I once heard Robert Frost read his famous poem "Stopping by Woods on a Snowy Evening." After completing the last stanza—

> These woods are lovely, dark and deep,
> But I have promises to keep,
> And miles to go before I sleep,
> And miles to go before I sleep.[6]

—the New England poet said in a crusty voice, "Some people think I'm talking about death here, but I'm not." Yet poems, like media depictions, have a life of their own. Despite his words, I have continued to interpret the verse as referring to obligations to be met before we die.

Hall holds out the possibility that Maria Ortiz may be equally obstinate by resisting the dominant ideology and translating the message in a way more congenial to her class attitude. He outlines three decoding options:

1. Operating inside the dominant code. The media produce the message; the masses consume it. The audience "reading" coincides with the "preferred reading." (Maria believes she can receive a fair wage even though stockholders get capital gains.)

2. Applying a negotiable code. The audience assimilates the leading ideology in broad outline but opposes its application in specific cases. (Maria accepts the free enterprise system but advocates radical measures to correct abuses of hourly wage employees.)

3. Substituting an oppositional code. The audience sees through the establishment bias in the media presentation and mounts an organized effort to demythologize the news. (The Retail Trade Worker's Union publishes a memo documenting Wal-Mart's plans to open new outlets only where labor can be hired on a part-time basis at minimum wage.)

Hall has a genuine respect for the ability of people to resist assimilation. The idea of America as a melting pot has never been accurate. The image only survives as a political ploy. (Sociologists, in fact, prefer the "salad-bowl" metaphor.) He doesn't regard the masses as cultural dupes who are easily manipulated by those who control the media, but he is unable to predict when and where the resistance will spring up.

Even though Hall is less than specific about how scholars should research questions of media and culture, he's categorical in his denunciation of the scientific community's potential to find the answers. Critical theory rejects the "body counts" of a survey research which is "consistently translating matters that have to do with signification, meaning, language, and symbolization into crude behavioral indicators." Yet in recent years Hall has stated that extensive empirical work is required to establish the validity of critical claims. He is somewhat vague about what shape that research would take, but others who share his ideology offer detailed evidence of media hegemony.

In their book *Mapping Hegemony*, Robert Goldman and Arvind Rajagopal catalogue CBS news accounts of a labor dispute between coal miners and the mine owners. Their detailed analysis offers convincing proof that media coverage framed the conflict as a miners-versus-the-public-interest contest. The mine owners got a pass.

CRITIQUE: CRITICIZING CRITICAL THEORY

In his early work, Marshall McLuhan was highly critical of television. Hall accuses McLuhan of being co-opted by the media establishment in later years. He characterizes McLuhan's final position as one of "lying back and letting the media roll over him; he celebrated the very things he had most bitterly attacked." No one has ever accused Stuart Hall of selling out to the dominant ideology of western society. Many, however, question the wisdom of performing scholarship under an ideological banner.

Do value commitments inevitably compromise the integrity of research? Former Surgeon General C. Everett Koop lamented that pro-choice researchers always conclude that abortion does no psychological harm to the mother, whereas pro-life psychologists invariably discover that abortion leaves long-term emotional scars. Not surprisingly, the findings of the economically conservative American Enterprise Institute in Washington, D.C., differ greatly from the conclusions reached at the Center for Contemporary Cultural Studies under the direction of Hall. Ever since Copernicus thought the unthinkable thought that the earth is not the center of the universe, truth has prospered by investigating what *is*, separately from what we think it *ought* to be. Hall seems to blur that distinction.

Is Hall's analysis of culture superior to the work of other critical theorists? Without a standard of truth, there seems to be no reliable way to evaluate the quality of media criticism. One person's research conclusions are as good as another's. Hall has served the field of mass communication well by identifying hidden ideologies but as yet offers no basis for preferring one over another. Liberation theology in Latin America reaches many of the same Marxist conclusions arrived at by Hall, but that movement cites Jesus' concern for the poor as its ultimate validation. Hall offers no court of appeal. Embracing his cultural analysis is an act of faith or personal preference.

Hall's most positive contribution to mass communication study is his constant reminder that it's futile to talk about meaning without considering power at the same time. Cliff Christians, director of the Institute for Communication Research at the University of Illinois and a leading writer in the field of media ethics, agrees with Hall that the existence of an idealistic communication situation where no power circulates is a myth. Christians is lavish in his praise of Hall's article, which I've listed as the recommended resource: "His essay, like the Taj Mahal, is an artistic masterpiece inviting a pilgrimage."[7]

Many adherents to critical theory believe that Hall's cultural analysis would not do justice to the full complexity of Maria Ortiz's life. Some spot a heavy masculine cast to his thinking that would seem to ignore her gender. Others despair at Hall's high level of philosophical abstraction. They fear that he would be unable to make a convincing local analysis of the way Maria interprets her life while watching a rerun of *Dallas* on TV.

John Fiske at the University of Wisconsin shares Hall's critical approach to mass communication, but he claims that Hall has underestimated the ability of a person like Maria to resist social control. She's quite capable of enjoying the saga of J.R. without getting sucked into the ideology of Texas takeovers. Fiske also thinks Hall's cultural analysis suffers by not dealing with questions of what gives Maria pleasure and how she has fun.

Despite these numerous criticisms, Stuart Hall has attracted tremendous interest and a large following. Samuel Becker, chairman of the communication studies department at the University of Iowa, describes himself as a besieged empiricist and notes the irony of Hall's attack. Hall knocks the dominant ideology of communication studies, yet he "may himself be the most dominant or influential figure in communication studies today."[8]

QUESTIONS TO SHARPEN YOUR FOCUS

1. *Hegemony* is not a household word in the United States. How would you explain what the term means to your roommate? Can you think of a metaphor or analogy that would help clarify this critical concept?

2. What is the nature of Hall's complaint about *American media scholarship*?

3. Hall articulates the position that the *media encode the dominant ideology of our culture*. If you do not now agree with his thesis, what *evidence* could he muster that would convince you that he's right?

4. Check back to Roland Barthes' theory of *semiotics* (see Chapter 8). How are Barthes' and Hall's perspectives similar?

A SECOND LOOK

Recommended resource: Stuart Hall, "Ideology and Communication Theory," in *Rethinking Communication Theory*, Vol. 1, Brenda Dervin, Lawrence Grossberg, Barbara O'Keefe, and Ellen Wartella (eds.), Sage, Newbury Park, Calif., 1989, pp. 40–52. (See also multiple reactions following.)

Marxist interpretations: Samuel Becker, "Marxist Approaches to Media Studies: The British Experience," *Critical Studies in Mass Communication*, Vol. 1, 1984, pp. 66–80.

Open Marxism: Stuart Hall, "The Problem of Ideology—Marxism Without Guarantees," *Journal of Communication Inquiry*, Vol. 10., No. 2, 1986, pp. 28–44. (The whole issue is devoted to Stuart Hall.)

Ideology of the media: Stuart Hall, "The Rediscovery of 'Ideology': Return of the Repressed in Media Studies," in *Culture, Society and the Media*, Michael Gurevitch, Tony Bennett, James Curran, and Janet Woollacott (eds.), Methuen, London, 1982, pp. 56–90.

Media bias: Stuart Hall, I. Connell, and L. Curti, "The 'Unity' of Current Affairs Television," in *Working Papers in Cultural Studies No. 9*, Center for Contemporary Cultural Studies, University of Birmingham, Birmingham, England, 1976, pp. 51–93.

Critical analysis of the political right: Stuart Hall, *The Hard Road to Renewal: Thatcherism and the Crisis on the Left*, Verso, London, 1988.

Journalistic bias toward status quo: Stuart Hall, "A World at One with Itself" and "The Determination of News Photographs," in *The Manufacture of News*, Stanley Cohen and Jock Young (eds.), Sage, Beverly Hills, Calif., 1981, pp. 147–156 and 226–243.

Center for Contemporary Cultural Studies: Stuart Hall, Dorothy Hobson, Andrew Lowe, and Paul Willis (eds.), *Culture, Media, Language*, Hutchinson, London, 1980.

Media hegemony: Robert Goldman and Arvind Rajagopal, *Mapping Hegemony: Television News Coverage of Industrial Conflict*, Ablex, Norwood, N.J., 1991.

The active audience: John Fiske, *Television Culture*, Methuen, London, 1987.

Articulation of black: Stuart Hall, "Signification, Representation, Ideology: Althusser and the Post-Structuralist Debates," *Critical Studies in Mass Communication*, Vol. 2, 1985, pp. 91–114.

Critical theory in American communication study: Hanno Hardt, "The Return of the 'Critical' and the Challenge of Radical Dissent: Critical Theory, Cultural Studies, and American Mass Communication Research," in *Communication Yearbook 12*, James A. Anderson (ed.), Sage, Newbury Park, Calif., 1989, pp. 558–600.

Overview of critical theories: "Ferment in the Field," *Journal of Communication*, Vol. 33, No. 3, 1983.

MEDIA EFFECTS

In 1940, before the era of television, a team of researchers from Columbia University headed by Paul Lazarsfeld descended on Erie County, Ohio, an area that had reflected national voting patterns in every twentieth-century presidential election. By surveying people once a month from June to November, the interviewers sought to determine how the press and radio affected the people's choice for the upcoming presidential election.[1]

Contrary to the then accepted "hypodermic needle" model of direct media influence, the researchers found little evidence that voters were swayed by what they read or heard. Political conversions were rare. The media seemed merely to reinforce the decisions of those who had already made up their minds.

Lazarsfeld attributed the lack of media effect to "selective exposure." Republicans avoided articles and programs that were favorable to President Franklin Roosevelt; Democrats bypassed news stories and features sympathetic to Republican Wendell Willkie. In the 1950s, Leon Festinger's theory of cognitive dissonance (see Chapter 19) provided a convincing explanation of why people pay attention only to ideas they already believe. The principle of selective exposure didn't always test out in the laboratory, where people's attention was virtually guaranteed, but in a free marketplace of ideas it accounted for the limited short-term effects of mass communication.

The Erie County results forced media analysts to recognize that friends and family affect the impact of media messages. They concluded that print and electronic media influence masses of people only through an indirect "two-step flow of communication." The first stage is the direct transmission of information to a small group of people who stay well informed. In the second stage, these opinion leaders pass on and interpret the messages to others in face-to-face discussion.

The two-step flow theory surfaced at a time of rapid scientific advancement in the fields of medicine and agriculture. The model accurately described the diffusion of innovation among American doctors and farmers in the 1950s, but the present era of saturation television has made alterations necessary. The first step of the revised two-stage theory of media influence is the transmission of information to a mass audience. The second step is validation of the message by people who the viewer respects.[2]

In 1953 Fredric Wertham's *Seduction of the Innocent* documented the glorification of violence in comic books.[3] Since then, mass communication researchers have sought to establish a relationship between media usage and aggression. Ad hoc studies have produced conflicting results, but two theory-based programs of research have established causal links between television and violent behavior.

You might recall from Glenn Sparks' analysis of the Cindy Crawford ad for Pepsi-Cola that the excitation transfer theory of Dolf Zillmann recognizes that TV has the power to stir up strong feelings.[4] Although we use labels like "fear," "anger," "sex," "humor," and "love" to describe these emotional states, the physiological response is the same no matter what kind of TV program elicited the response. It's easy to get our emotional wires crossed when the show is over. On the basis of his work at Indiana University, Zillmann says that the heightened state of arousal takes a while to dissipate, and the leftover excitation can amplify any mood we

CALVIN AND HOBBES © 1987 WATTERSON. Dist. by Universal Press Syndicate.
Reprinted with permission. All rights reserved.

happen to be feeling. If a man is mad at his wife, the emotional stimulation he gets from televised aggression can escalate into domestic violence. But Zillmann says that the arousal which comes from an erotic bedroom scene or a hilarious comedy often has the same effect.

Excitation transfer can account for violent acts performed immediately after TV viewing. But Albert Bandura's social learning theory takes it a step further and predicts that the use of force modeled on television today may erupt in antisocial behavior years later. Although Bandura's theory can explain imitation in many contexts, Chapter 31 applies it specifically to the vicarious learning of aggression through television.

Communication scholars have shown surprisingly little interest in studying the dynamics of television advertising. However, practitioner Tony Schwartz theorizes that commercials are effective when they strike a responsive chord within the viewer.[5] He says that media persuasion is not so much a matter of trying to put an idea into consumers'

heads as it is seeking to draw an emotional response out of them. The best commercials use sight and sound to resonate with an audience's past experience.

The last two theories in this section were instrumental in reestablishing a powerful-effects view of mass communication. Chapter 32 outlines McCombs and Shaw's conception of the agenda-setting function of the media. They say journalists don't try to tell people what to think, but the selection of news in the broadcast and print media automatically dictates what the public will think about. Chapter 33 presents Noelle-Neumann's spiral of silence. Her theory describes the chilling effect of public opinion on the expression of unpopular views. She believes the process is accelerated when every media outlet echoes the same idea over and over.

Although each of the theories in this section has a different explanation for the media's influence, all three take the approach that electronic and print communication mold rather than mirror public opinion.

CHAPTER 31

Social Learning Theory
of Albert Bandura

If you've taken an introductory course in economics, you're already familiar with the policy planner's dilemma of deciding whether to allocate limited resources for guns or for butter. The problem is usually posed to illustrate the impersonal market forces of supply and demand, profit and loss. Yet planners are people, and most individuals come to the war-or-peace decision points of life having already developed preferred responses. Northwestern psychologist Donald Campbell calls these tendencies "acquired behavioral dispositions," and he suggests six ways that we learn to choose one option over another.

1. *Trial-and-error experience* is a hands-on exploration that might lead to tasting the butter and squeezing the trigger, or perhaps the other way around.

2. *Perception of the object* is a firsthand chance to look, admire, but don't touch a pistol and a pound of butter at close range.

3. *Observation of another's response to the object* is hearing a contented sigh when someone points the gun or spreads the butter on toast. It is also seeing critical frowns on faces of people who bypass the items in a store.

4. *Modeling* is watching someone fire the gun or melt the butter to put it on popcorn.

5. *Exhortation* is the National Rifle Association's plea to protect the right to bear arms or Willard Scott's commercial message urging us to use real butter.

6. *Instruction about the object* is a verbal description of the gun's effective range or of the number of calories in a pat of butter.

Campbell claims that direct trial-and-error experience creates a deep and long-lasting acquired behavioral disposition, while perception has somewhat less effect, observation of response even less, and modeling less still. Exhortation is one of the most used but least effective means to influence attitudes or actions.

Stanford psychologist Albert Bandura agrees that conversation is not an effective way of altering human behavior, but he thinks that classical learning theory's preoccupation with trial-and-error learning is shortsighted. "Coping with the demands of everyday life would be exceedingly trying if one could arrive at solutions to problems only by actually performing possible options and suffering the consequences."[1] His social learning theory concentrates on the power of example.

THE SPREAD OF TV VIOLENCE THROUGH MODELING

Bandura's major premise is that we can learn by observing others. He considers vicarious experience to be the typical way that human beings change. He uses the term *modeling* to describe Campbell's two midrange processes of response acquisition (observation of another's response and modeling), and he claims that modeling can have as much impact as direct experience.

Social learning theory is a general theory of human behavior, but Bandura and people concerned with mass communication have used it specifically to explain media effects. Bandura warned that "children and adults acquire attitudes, emotional responses, and new styles of conduct through filmed and televised modeling."[2] George Gerbner (see Chapter 29) was concerned that television violence would create a false climate of fear. Albert Bandura cautioned that TV might create a violent reality that was worth fearing.

Bandura's warning struck a responsive chord in parents and educators who feared that escalating violence on TV would transform children into bullies. Although he doesn't think this will happen without the tacit approval of those who supervise the children, Bandura regards anxiety over televised violence as legitimate. That stance caused network officials to blackball him from taking part in the 1972 *Surgeon General's Report on Violence.*[3] It is doubtful whether TV sets will ever bear an inscription similar to that on packs of cigarettes: "Warning: The Surgeon General has determined that TV violence may turn your child into an insensitive brute." But if Bandura had been picked as a member of the research team, the report would have been more definitive in pointing out the causal link between television violence and aggressive behavior.

Consider the case of Tyler Richie, a shy 10-year-old boy who has been raised on a Saturday-morning diet of superheroes. After school he's absorbed for an hour in helping Nintendo's Mario Brothers fight their way out of danger. He then catches the last half of a *Rockford Files* rerun on a local station and sees that even mild mannered James Garner regards violence as the best option when his Pappie is in trouble. After dinner, Ty laughs at the fake fighting of roller derby and wrestling on sports cable. He then slips a cassette of *Dirty Harry* into the VCR and settles back for some hard-core violence. "Go ahead and make my day," he drawls as Clint Eastwood appears on the screen.

The combined four hours that Ty spends in front of the screen represent a typical day for boys in his class at school. Bandura considers "gentle" Ty a likely candidate to someday clobber his sister, shoot a prowler, or use criminal force to get his own way. Social learning theory postulates three necessary stages in the causal link between television violence and actual physical harm to another: attention, retention, and motivation.

Attention: "I Never Thought of That Before"

Because advertising rates are tied directly to a program's share of the market, television professionals are experts at gaining and holding attention. Practitioners are committed to the drawing power of dramatized personal injury and physical destruction. According to Bandura, televised violence will grab Ty's attention because it is simple, distinctive, prevalent, useful, and depicted positively.

1. *Simple.* There's nothing very subtle about punching someone in the face. Drawn-out negotiations and attempts at reconciliation are complicated, but even a child can understand a quick right to the jaw. In order to avoid confusion, the good guys wear white hats.

2. *Distinctive.* The characters on the screen take risks that don't fit the ordered pattern of Ty's life. That's why Action Jackson pays his own way on commercial stations, while Mr. Rogers' ten-minute sweater change requires a subsidy on public television. Prosocial behavior like sharing, sympathy, control of anger, and delayed gratification appears dull when compared with violent action sequences.

3. *Prevalent.* Bandura cites Gerbner's index of violence (see Chapter 29) to show that television portrays "the big hurt." Over 80 percent of prime-time programs contain violent acts. That figure rises to over 90 percent for weekend cartoon shows. With Nintendo sweeping America and more than half of the nation's families owning a VCR, violence on demand is easy to arrange.

4. *Useful.* Social critics decry the gratuitous violence on television, but Bandura denies that aggression is unrelated to the story line. The scenes of physical force are especially compelling because they suggest that violence is a preferred solution to human problems. Violence is presented as a strategy for life.

5. *Positive.* On every type of program, television draws in viewers by placing attractive people in front of the camera. There are very few overweight bodies or pimply faces on TV. When the winsome star roughs up a few hoods to help the lovely young woman, aggression is given a positive cast.

Using violence in the race for ratings not only draws an attentive audience, it transmits responses that we, as viewers, might never have considered before. The media expand our repertoire of behavioral options far beyond what we would discover by trial and error and in ways more varied than we would observe in people we know. The unthinkable no longer is.

Retention: "I Figured Out What I Was Doing Wrong"

Bandura says it's fortunate that people learn from vicarious observation, since mistakes could prove costly or fatal. Without putting himself at risk, Ty is able to discover that a knife fighter holds a switchblade at an inclined angle of forty-five degrees and that he jabs up rather than lunging down. Ty can pick up this bit of "street smarts" from an admired Harry or a despised Scorpio, and learning takes place whether the fictional model is rewarded or punished for his action. We hope that Ty will never have an occasion to put his knowledge into practice. It's certainly unlikely that he'll walk out of the house and immediately mimic the action he has learned; instantaneous reproduction is uncommon. In contrast to classical learning theory, Bandura says we can learn novel behavior without any practice or direct reinforcement for its consequences. The action will lie dormant, available for future use, as long as we remember it.

Memory is a cognitive function, so Bandura's theory moves beyond mere behaviorism. Like most other communication theorists, he believes that the ability to use symbols sets humans apart from the limited stimulus-response world of animals. "Humans don't just respond to stimuli, they interpret them."[4]

Bandura says that we store events in two ways—through visual images and through verbal codes. Ty may have a vivid picture in his mind of Clint Eastwood leveling an unswerving Colt .45 Magnum revolver. If so, repeated instant mental replays (with Ty in the role of enforcer) will ensure that he remembers how to point a gun in the future. The more he exercises the image, the stronger the memory will be in the future.

Bandura is convinced, however, that major gains in vicarious learning

CALVIN AND HOBBES © 1989 WATTERSON. Dist. by Universal Press Syndicate.

come when the observer develops a conscious awareness of the technique involved. These insights are stored verbally. Ty will take a giant step toward becoming a dead shot when he can sort out the visual image of Clint Eastwood into generalized principles:

"Hold the weapon with both hands."

"Don't jerk the trigger; squeeze it."

"Aim six inches low to compensate for the recoil."

Bandura says that learning through modeling is more a matter of abstracting rules than mimicry. It's not simply "monkey see, monkey do."

The entire acquisition process described by Bandura is a spectator sport. That's why television teaches violence so well. Ty doesn't have to actually do the aggressive behavior; fantasy rehearsal in his mind will keep the act a live option for the future. If he ever does point a gun in anger, the act of force, after years of mental role-playing, will set his acquired behavioral disposition into granite. "The highest level of observational learning is achieved by first organizing and rehearsing the modeled behavior symbolically, and then enacting it overtly."[5]

Motivation: "Why Not Do It? It Worked Out Fine for Them"

We observe many forms of behavior in others that we never perform ourselves. Without sufficient motivation, Ty may never imitate the violence he sees on TV. Bandura uses the term *motivation* to refer to the rewards and punishments Ty imagines will accompany his use of physical force. Would he go to jail for blowing away an enemy, remain anonymous if he dropped a brick from a highway overpass, or gain status for punching out a jerk who was hassling a friend? Note that these questions concern potential outcomes rather than sanctions already experienced. Bandura cautions that "the widely accepted dictum that behavior is governed by its consequences fares better for anticipated than for actual consequences."[6]

Most reinforcement theorists recognize that Ty's expectations for future rewards or punishment come in part from external sources such as parents, friends, and teachers. Bandura says that the effects of TV violence will be greatly diminished if a youngster's parents punish or disapprove of aggression. He contends that unconditional love and approval merely encourage self-actualized tyrants.

Yet Ty also shares a responsibility for his own actions. The latest version of social learning theory places increasing emphasis on self-regulation. Bandura is uncomfortable with any form of determinism. He doesn't believe that people are "buffeted by environmental stimuli," nor does he accept the notion that they are "driven by inner forces." He sees external and internal rewards working together in a "reciprocal determination" to influence behavior. But social learning theory focuses on *vicarious* reward as a third factor which causes acquired responses to break out into action.

Television models do more than teach novel styles of conduct. When people on television are punished for being violent, that punishment reinforces society's sanctions against acting above or outside the law. But when other characters in the story accept or applaud the use of force, that approval weakens inhibitions the viewer may have about hurting people. Producers, writers, and directors are quick to argue that action sequences end up by showing that crime doesn't pay. Armed robbers, rapists, murderers, and terrorists are brought to justice by the final fade-out. But Bandura isn't worried about the bad guys glorifying violence. It's the aggression of the good guys that troubles him. Crime may not pay on television, but physical force does.

Consider the potential encouragement of violence offered by the 1989 motion picture *Batman*. In the first week of its release in the United States, over 10 million patrons watched the Joker's creative sadism amid squeals of delight in the theaters. While the average young male in the audience might have difficulty identifying with the bizarre Jack Nicholson, Michael Keaton looked like Everyman in his low-key portrayal of the wealthy young avenger. The producer, Jon Peters, wanted a story line that would provide "a great opportunity to have this guy kick some ass,"[7] which Batman does. In the end, Bruce Wayne gets the satisfaction of avenging his parents' murder, praise from the grateful mayor of the city, and the adoration of the adorable Kim Basinger. These vicarious rewards would seem to justify almost any vigilante action. The filmmakers would claim that *Batman* is mere fantasy; Bandura would probably call it an effective classroom for life.

"YOU BIG BULLY, QUIT PICKING ON THAT CLOWN"

Bandura and his students ran a series of experiments to study social learning of aggression through television. He used a three-foot-high inflated plastic Bobo doll as the potential victim. The clown figure had a heavy sand base that made it pop back up after being knocked down. Nursery school boys and girls saw a film in which an adult male or female model assaulted the clown. The kids themselves then had a chance to "play" with the Bobo doll without adult supervision.

Figure 31.1 shows two of the attacks the female model performed, with typical matching behavior of a girl who saw the film. Since children in the control group didn't normally say and do these things, the experiment demonstrated that the youngsters had acquired the new, aggressive behavior by watching the film.

Some children saw a version in which the adult model was rewarded with candy, soda pop, and praise for being a "strong champion." Others heard the model scolded: "Hey there, you big bully, you quit picking on that clown." As the adult retreated, he or she tripped and fell, and then received a humiliating spanking with a rolled up magazine.

Consistent with social learning theory, Bandura found that children ex-

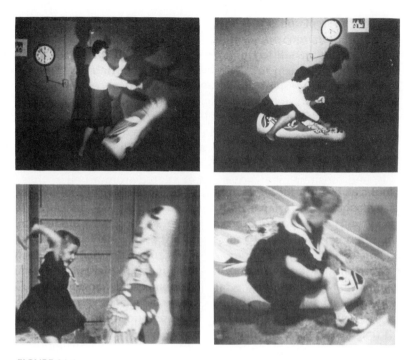

FIGURE 31.1
Child's Imitation of Adult Aggressive Behavior as Observed on Film (From Bandura,
Ross, and Ross, "Imitations of Aggressive Film-Mediated Models.")

hibited more aggression when the adult models were rewarded for their attack on the Bobo doll than when they were punished. Yet given enough inducement by the experimenter, most children were able to copy the hostile actions. Bandura concludes that reinforcement doesn't affect the learning of novel responses, but it does "determine whether or not observationally acquired competencies will be put into use." He discovered that the same antisocial learning took place when the aggressor was a cartoon character (Herman the Cat), rather than a human model. In other studies he discovered that removal of restraint is greatest for boys when the model is male and greatest for girls when the model is female. Consistent with traditional gender-based roles, boys were more violent than girls.

AROUSED OR DRAINED: TWO ALTERNATIVES TO IMITATION

Although Bandura discusses television violence in terms of modeling, there are alternative interpretations of the effect that dramatized aggression has on an audience. Dolf Zillmann and other instigation theorists agree with Bandura that viewers are aroused when they see simulated violence on the screen.[8] But arousal researchers note that people also get excited watching suspense, comedy, or sexy bedroom scenes. If a viewer turns on the set feeling somewhat angry, the emotions these programs stir up can fuel a full-blown hatred that may spill over into physical aggression. According to instigation theorists, it's the *arousal* in the violent programs that stimulates aggression, not the imitation processes Bandura emphasizes. Instigation is an idea which sounds plausible, but an appeal to arousal fails to explain how viewers learn new techniques. Nor can it account for a violent action breaking out years after it was modeled on television.

Favored by media apologists, catharsis theory, on the other hand, suggests that the depiction of physical force actually reduces aggression.[9] The theory maintains that many viewers are filled with pent-up anger, hostility, and tension. Like excess steam vented from a boiler, these destructive impulses are safely drained off through exposure to fantasy violence. (The catharsis theory sees Rambo and psychiatric counselors as serving the same function.) The notion that violent drama can be healthy traces back to Aristotle's belief that Greek tragedy served to purge feelings of grief and fear. The problem with the catharsis claim is that there is no evidence to support it. Most efforts to demonstrate that a heavy dose of televised violence reduces aggression end up showing the opposite. People may *feel* better, but they *get* worse.

CRITIQUE: A POSITIVE, BUT WEAK, CAUSAL RELATIONSHIP

Bandura states that "theories must demonstrate predictive power." Social learning theory's claim that fantasy violence teaches and encourages real aggression tests out splendidly in the laboratory, where other factors can be held constant, but only passably in the field. One ten-year study tracked 460 third-grade boys until they were 19 years old.[10] The young men in the study who had watched a great amount of televised violence as children were more aggressive than those who had been occasional viewers. However, those who were more aggressive as kids showed no tendency to watch more televised violence when they grew up. The twin findings support Bandura's claim that fantasy aggression leads to the real thing. But childhood viewing habits accounted for only 10 percent of the difference in later aggression.

Although this 10 percent figure may sound rather small, even a small effect from media violence can add up to a significant social problem when a program has an audience of 30 million people. If only 1 out of every 10,000 viewers imitates an act of violence, the fictional drama had produced at least 3,000 new victims.

Social learning theory shares the problem of almost all reinforcement theories—it doesn't predict what the learner will regard as positive. Ty may be turned off by the machismo of John Wayne ("A man's got to do what a man's got to do"), yet relish the lean intensity of Clint Eastwood. Forecasting taste is risky business. Bandura's theory is also vulnerable to the charges of Stuart Hall, which were presented in the previous chapter. Bandura's research epitomizes everything in the American media-effects tradition that

Hall disdains. Yet social learning theory is relevant to many of the crucial cultural issues Hall and other social theorists discuss.

Modeling clarifies why highly publicized suicides and drug overdoses (Marilyn Monroe, Ernest Hemingway, Janis Joplin, John Belushi) are followed by sharp upswings of self-inflicted death.[11] It also helps us understand why political assassinations (Robert Kennedy, Martin Luther King, Jr., Malcolm X) occur in clusters. Vicarious observation explains the spread of Gandhi's innovative tactics of militant nonviolence to racial and antiwar protest.

The theory predicts that publicizing airline hijackings and terrorist kidnappings will result in increased political violence. It implies that news coverage of urban riots will promote further disorder when it shows video clips of joyous looters rather than the human misery of a destroyed neighborhood.

Social learning theory also has useful observations about the antisocial results of pornography. Vicarious reinforcement explains how men can maintain a "rape myth" in the face of overwhelming evidence that women are angered and sickened by the mere idea of sexual assault. The pornographic portrayal of abducted females stirred to sexual ecstasy by their captors encourages men to hang on to a dehumanizing rationalization that women secretly want to be taken by force. Although sexually explicit films are used beneficially by dysfunction clinics to lower inhibitions and teach foreplay technique, Bandura warns that continuous exposure to erotic fantasy may hinder sexual satisfaction. The simulated wild passion portrayed in every encounter sets up an unreasonably high expectation that normal lovemaking can't match.

Bandura doesn't advocate tight artistic censorship or governmental controls on news reporting, but his concern with these issues shows social learning theory's usefulness in matters of death, power, and passion. Bandura doesn't claim that television is the only way people acquire behavioral dispositions. But he has established that the media are an important ingredient in the formative mix. Ty is learning today; perhaps he will be acting out tomorrow.

QUESTIONS TO SHARPEN YOUR FOCUS

1. Effective modeling requires *attention, retention,* and *motivation.* How does *cognition* play a part in each of these steps?

2. How do you respond to the claim that television doesn't promote *viewer violence* because villains are *punished* rather than *rewarded* for their cruel behavior?

3. If you were designing a further *Bobo doll study* with children, what else would you want to explore about *modeling* or *imitation*?

4. Is it possible that both Bandura's *social learning theory* and Zillmann's *excitation transfer theory* could be right at the same time?

A SECOND LOOK

Recommended resource: Alexes Tan, "Social Learning of Aggression of Television," in *Perspectives on Media Effects,* Jennings Bryant and Dolf Zillmann (eds.), Lawrence Erlbaum Associates, Hillsdale, N.J., 1986, pp. 41–55.

Initial statement: Albert Bandura and Richard Walters, *Social Learning and Personality Development,* Holt, Rinehart and Winston, New York, 1963.

General theory: Albert Bandura, *Social Learning Theory,* Prentice-Hall, Englewood Cliffs, N.J., 1977.

Later cognitive emphasis: Albert Bandura, *Social Foundations of Thought and Action: A Social Cognitive Theory,* Prentice-Hall, Englewood Cliffs, N.J., 1986.

Acquired behavioral dispositions: Donald Campbell, "Social Attitudes and Other Acquired Behavioral Dispositions," in *Psychology: A Study of a Science,* Vol. 6, S. Koch (ed.), McGraw-Hill, New York, 1963, pp. 94–172.

Classic learning theory: B. F. Skinner, *Beyond Freedom and Dignity,* Knopf, New York, 1971.

Bobo doll study: Albert Bandura, Dorothea Ross, and Sheila Ross, "Imitations of Aggressive Film-Mediated Models," *Journal of Abnormal and Social Psychology,* Vol. 66, 1963, pp. 3–11.

Longitudinal study: M. Lefkowitz, L. Eron, L. Walker, and L. Huesmann, *Growing Up to Be Violent: A Longitudinal Study of the Development of Aggression,* Pergamon, New York, 1977.

Pornography: James Check and Neil Malamuth, "Pornography and Sexual Aggression: A Social Learning Theory Analysis," in *Communication Yearbook 9,* Margaret McLaughlin (ed.), Sage, Beverly Hills, Calif., 1986, pp. 181–213.

CHAPTER 32

Agenda-Setting Function
of Maxwell McCombs & Donald Shaw

For some unexplained reason, in June 1972, five unknown men broke into the Democratic National Committee headquarters looking for undetermined information. It was the sort of local crime story that rated two paragraphs on page 17 of *The Washington Post*. Yet editor Ben Bradlee and reporters Bob Woodward and Carl Bernstein gave the story continual high visibility even though the public initially seemed to regard the incident as trivial.

President Nixon dismissed the break-in as a "third-rate burglary," but over the following year Americans showed an increasing public awareness of Watergate's significance. Half of the country became familiar with the word *Watergate* over the summer. By April of 1973 that figure had risen to 90 percent. When television began gavel-to-gavel coverage of the Senate hearings on the matter a year after the break-in, virtually every adult in the United States knew what Watergate was about. Six months later President Nixon protested, "I am not a crook," and a half-year after that he was forced from office because the majority of citizens and their representatives had decided that he was.

THE AGENDA: NOT WHAT TO THINK, BUT WHAT TO THINK ABOUT

Journalism professors Maxwell McCombs and Donald Shaw regard Watergate as a perfect example of the agenda-setting function of the mass media. They were not surprised that the Watergate issue caught fire after months on the front page of *The Washington Post*. McCombs and Shaw believe that the "mass media have the ability to transfer the salience of items on their news agenda to the public agenda." They aren't suggesting that broadcast and print personnel make a deliberate attempt to influence listener, viewer, or reader opinion on the issues. Reporters in the free world have a deserved reputation for independence and fairness. But McCombs and Shaw say that we look to news professionals for cues on where to focus our attention. "*We judge as important what the media judge as important.*"[1]

Although McCombs and Shaw first referred to the agenda-setting function of the media in 1972, the idea that people desire a media assist to determine political reality had already been voiced by a number of current events analysts. In an attempt to explain how the United States had been drawn into World War I, Pulitzer Prize-winning author Walter Lippmann claimed that the media act as a mediator between "the world outside and the pictures in our heads."[2] McCombs and Shaw often quote University of Wisconsin political scientist Bernard Cohen's observation concerning the specific function the media serve: "The press may not be successful much of the time in telling people what to think, but it is stunningly successful in telling its readers what to think about."[3]

Starting with the Kennedy-Nixon contest in 1960, political analyst Theodore White wrote the definitive account of four presidential elections. Independently of McCombs and Shaw, and in opposition to the then current wisdom that mass communication had limited effects upon its audience, White came to the conclusion that the media shaped the election campaigns:

> The power of the press in America is a primordial one. It sets the agenda of public discussion; and this sweeping political power is unrestrained by any law. It determines what people will talk and think about—an authority that in other nations is reserved for tyrants, priests, parties and mandarins.[4]

A THEORY WHOSE TIME HAD COME

McCombs and Shaw's agenda-setting theory found an appreciative audience among mass communication researchers. The prevailing selective exposure hypothesis (see Chapter 19) claimed that people would attend only to news and views that didn't threaten their established beliefs. The media were seen as merely stroking preexistent attitudes. After two decades of downplaying the influence of newspapers, magazines, radio, and television, the field was disenchanted with this limited-effects approach. Agenda-setting theory boasted two attractive features: It reaffirmed the power of the press while still maintaining that individuals were free to choose.

The notion of an agenda-setting function was consistent with a "uses and gratifications" approach that analyzes the different motives people have for watching television.[5] The division of attitude into affective evaluation and cognitive salience was already paralleled by Sherif's social judgment theory (see Chapter 18). In social judgment terms, McCombs and Shaw don't claim that the media alter recipients' latitudes of acceptance or change their anchored opinions. The authors do predict, however, that press and television cause audience ego-involvement in the issue to rise and fall in response to media emphasis.

Agenda-setting theory represents a back-to-the-basics approach to mass communication research. Like the initial Erie County voting studies,[6] the focus is on election campaigns. The theory predicts a cause-and-effect relationship between media content and voter perception. Although later work explores the conditions under which the media priorities are most influential, the theory rises or falls on its ability to show a match between the media's

"Dad, if a tree falls in the forest, and the media aren't there to cover it, has the tree really fallen?"

agenda and the public's subsequent rank-order of concerns. McCombs and Shaw support their main hypothesis with results from surveys they took while working together at the University of North Carolina in Chapel Hill. (McCombs is now at the University of Texas.) Their analysis of the 1968 race for president between Richard Nixon and Hubert Humphrey set the pattern for later agenda-setting research. The study provides an opportunity to examine in detail the type of quantitative survey research that Stuart Hall and other critical theorists so strongly oppose.

MEDIA AGENDA AND PUBLIC AGENDA: A CLOSE MATCH

McCombs and Shaw's first task was to measure the media agenda. They determined that Chapel Hill residents relied on a mix of nine print and broadcast sources for political news—two Raleigh papers, two Durham papers, the out-of-state edition of *The New York Times, Time, Newsweek,* and the CBS and NBC evening news.

They established *position* and *length* of story as the two main criteria of prominence. For newspapers, the front-page headline story, a three-column story on an inside page, and the lead editorial were all counted as evidence of significant focus upon an issue. For newsmagazines, the requirement was an opening story in the news section or any political issue to which the editors devoted a full column. Prominence in the television news format was defined by placement as one of the first three news items or any discussion which lasted over forty-five seconds.

Because the agenda-setting hypothesis refers to substantive issues, the researchers discarded news items about campaign strategy, position in the polls, and the personality of the candidates. The remaining stories were then sorted into fifteen subject categories, which were later collapsed into five major issues. A composite index of media prominence revealed the following order of importance: foreign policy, law and order, fiscal policy, public welfare, and civil rights.

In order to measure the public's priorities, McCombs and Shaw asked Chapel Hill voters to outline what they considered the key issues of the campaign, regardless of what the candidates might be saying. People who were already committed to a candidate were dropped from the pool of respondents. The researchers assigned the specific answers to the same broad categories used for media analysis. They then compared the aggregate data from undecided voters with the composite description of media content. The rank of the five issues on both lists was nearly identical.

WHAT CAUSES WHAT?

McCombs and Shaw believe that the hypothesized agenda-setting function of the media is responsible for the almost perfect correlation they found between the media and public ordering of priorities.

$$\text{Media agenda} \rightarrow \text{Voters' agenda}$$

But as the critique of cultivation theory suggested, correlation is not causation. It's possible that newspaper and television coverage simply reflects public concerns that already exist.

$$\text{Voters' agenda} \rightarrow \text{Media agenda}$$

The results of the Chapel Hill study could be interpreted as support for the notion that the media are just as market-driven in their news coverage as they are in programming entertainment. The findings are impressive but equivocal. A true test of the agenda-setting hypothesis must be able to show that a matching public agenda lags behind the media schedule of priorities.

Figure 32.1 diagrams just such a delayed relationship that agenda-setting predicts. Although McCombs and Shaw's 1968 study wasn't designed to spot a time lapse, later research on the theory measures the salience of issues two or three times during the campaign. The results so far are promising, but not conclusive. About one-half of the published studies do show that media prominence appears a while before public concern. The delay is often about four months. But the failure to find a consistent time lag between the two raises the possibility that media and public agendas might both be caused by a

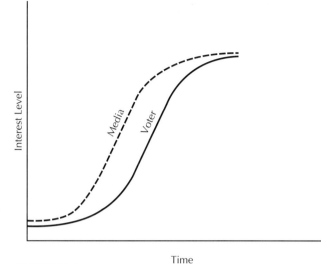
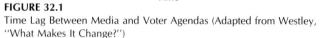

FIGURE 32.1
Time Lag Between Media and Voter Agendas (Adapted from Westley, "What Makes It Change?")

third variable—reality. Perhaps they are similar because they both mirror what is actually happening in the world.

Pennsylvania State University communication researcher Ray Funkhouser performed an exhaustive retrospective search for newsmagazine stories during the year 1960 to 1970. He charted the rise and fall of media attention on issues and compared these trends with annual Gallup poll responses to a question about "the most important problem facing America." As with less ambitious agenda-setting studies, Funkhouser's study found a strong relationship between media and public priorities. But he was doubtful that the Gallup poll responses really measured people's personal, emotional concerns:

> The correspondence between news articles and public opinion may be nothing more than the public's regurgitating back to the pollster what is currently in the news, with little or no relation to what the respondent himself feels is important.[7]

Although Funkhouser's results failed to establish a definite chain of influence from media to the general public, they do make it clear that the twin agendas aren't mere reflections of reality. The number of American troops in Vietnam increased until 1968, but news coverage peaked two years before. The same was true of urban violence and campus unrest. Press interest cooled down while cities and colleges were still heating up. It appears that Walter Lippmann was right—the actual environment and the pictures in our mind are two different worlds.

FINE-TUNING THE THEORY

The lack of clear-cut support for an overall agenda-setting hypothesis has stimulated McCombs and Shaw to identify conditions under which media influence appears strongest. Even in their original study, they filtered out voters who were already committed to a candidate. As the theory became more sophisticated, they postulated a "need for orientation" as a crucial factor in people's willingness to let the news media shape their thinking. Referred to by some as an "index of curiosity," it combines relevance and uncertainty. Because I am a dog and cat owner, any story about cruelty to animals always catches my attention (high relevance). I have ambivalent feelings about scientific progress coming from experimentation on live animals (high uncertainty). According to McCombs and Shaw, this combination would make me attuned to media emphasis on a candidate's position on vivisection. If the editors of *Time* or at ABC think it's important, I would think it's important.

Given sufficient motivation to read the article, there is some evidence that a newspaper story has greater agenda-setting power than a parallel piece on the evening news. Perhaps that's because television gives limited coverage to a large number of stories; TV news is seldom more than a headline service. Unless the vivisection story is given in-depth treatment on *60 Minutes, Nightline,* or *The McNeil/Lehrer NewsHour,* television doesn't take time to go beyond the bare facts to explain what they mean. Showing a picture of a dead dog stirs emotions, but it doesn't raise questions of laboratory ethics, medical training, or scientific inquiry. By framing a story within a larger context, the print media can point out its significance for the reader.

Even as McCombs and Shaw refine their theory, other analysts are asking why one issue is featured in the media and another ignored. How does the news become the news?

WHO SETS THE AGENDA FOR THE AGENDA SETTERS?

Recall that Funkhouser found that topic selection in newsmagazines was out of sync with actual national and world events. In fact, 75 percent of the stories that come across a news desk are never printed or broadcast. Obviously, news doesn't select itself. Who sets the agenda for the agenda setters?

One view regards a handful of news editors as the guardians, or "gatekeepers," of political dialogue. Nothing gets put on the political agenda without the concurrence of eight men—the operation chiefs of Associated Press, *The New York Times, The Washington Post, Time, Newsweek,* ABC, NBC, and CBS. Although there is no evidence to support right-wing conservative charges that the editors are part of a liberal, eastern-establishment conspiracy, these key decision makers are undeniably part of a media elite that doesn't represent a cross section of U.S. citizens. The media elite consists of middle-aged, Caucasian males who attend the same conferences, banquets, and parties. As Watergate demonstrated, when one of them "puffs" a story, the rest of the nation's media climb aboard. Once *Time* headlined the 1988 presidential contest between George Bush and Michael Dukakis as "The Nice Man vs. The Ice Man," the candidates' personality became the election issue.

An alternative view regards the candidates themselves as the ultimate source of issue salience. In 1988, George Bush successfully focused media attention on Willie Horton, a convict who raped and murdered a woman while he was on a furlough from a prison in Massachusetts. Bush's media handlers (sometimes referred to as "spin doctors") turned the tragedy into a commentary on the Democratic governor's liberalism, and not a day went by without some effort to smear Dukakis with Horton's crime. By winning the election, Bush inherited the power to raise any issue to national prominence with a few remarks. But as Nixon discovered with Watergate, he was unable to suppress an issue which might prove uncomfortable. President Bush tried to dismiss the economic recession as a "mild technical adjustment." The press and the people decided it was major.

Current thinking on news selection targets the increasing role of "interest aggregations." The term was coined by Columbia University sociologist Robert Merton to refer to clusters of people who demand center stage for their one overriding concern, whatever it might be—antiabortion, antiwar, anticommunism, antipollution, anti-free trade, antiflag desecration. As the examples indicate, these groups usually rally around a specific action which they oppose. They stage demonstrations, marches, and other media events so that television and press will be forced to cover their issue. The net effect is that various power centers are vying for the right to be heard. The media seem to pay attention to those who grab it.

ARE THE ISSUES THE REAL CAMPAIGN ISSUE?

In the Chapel Hill research report, McCombs and Shaw note that "a considerable amount of campaign news was *not* devoted to discussion of the major political issues, but rather to an *analysis of the campaign itself.*" News of campaign events, position in the polls, and candidate strategy accounted for 47 percent of the media's political focus. Since the most salient issue (foreign policy) received only 10 percent of the coverage, it's safe to conclude that the real issue in the campaign was the campaign. Most agenda-setting research since the prototype study finds that the media assign the highest news value to questions of campaign strategy. The ultimate issues are, Who is going to win? and How is the candidate going to do it?

While a doctoral candidate at the University of Pennsylvania, John Carey studied the political agenda during an off-year congressional election. He compared the media analysis of the campaign to the color commentary on a televised pro football game:

> The general game plan was laid out; strengths and weaknesses of supporting elements like the party organization were analyzed; field conditions like inflation and unemployment were considered; the present score (i.e. the polls) was

matched against scores earlier in the game to see where the momentum was going; psychological elements like poor crowd reaction were suspected of taking a toll on one side; and key plays . . . were brought back again and again in a form of instant replay.[8]

Viewers seem to relish the rich smorgasbord of analysis that dominates political coverage. Their appetite for "inside dope" suggests that agenda-setting theory may be dealing with only the leftovers.

CRITIQUE: AN UNCERTAIN AGENDA

Although McCombs and Shaw assume that the agenda-setting function of media is an established fact, the research base of almost two decades supports a conclusion of "probable" rather than "proven." Procedural problems cloud many of the studies that support a causal link. Measures of media coverage are well standardized, but methods for determining the public's agenda vary widely across the research program.

There continue to be nagging questions about the direction of the effect. It seems reasonable to assume that the media's agenda informs the voters' agenda, rather than the other way around. But the possibility that media priorities merely reflect public opinion hasn't been eliminated. It's still premature to conclude that the agenda-setting function of the media is a "done deal."

Although McCombs and Shaw's basic prediction is straightforward, the theory which has evolved is best applied only in narrowly defined situations. Consider the following limitations:

1. The original theory spoke only to the matter of issue salience during political campaigns. Later extensions expand its scope to candidate image and to some nonpolitical topics, but the effects hypothesis basically applies to the concerns of voters.

2. The agenda-setting hypothesis describes the media's effect only on those who have a desire for political guidance. People with a low "need for orientation," those already committed to candidates, and consumers who use the media purely for entertainment aren't expected to be swayed by media priorities.

3. The media have less effect on local issues or matters with which the reader or viewer has hands-on experience. The agenda-setting prediction seems to work out best on issues of foreign affairs, urban violence (when the audience doesn't live in the ghetto), and other areas where the media's secondhand reality is our only source of information. The pocketbook issues of unemployment, inflation, and taxes are less susceptible to media dictates. All these qualifications seem to chip away at the significance of McCombs and Shaw's hypothesis.

Despite the problems listed above, the agenda-setting function of the mass media has earned a firm place in media-effects literature. McCombs and Shaw have established a plausible case that some people look to print and broadcast news during election campaigns for clues to guide them on deciding which issues are important. Agenda-setting theory also provides a needed reminder that news stories are just that—stories. The message always requires interpretation. For these reasons, McCombs and Shaw have accomplished the function they ascribe to the media. Agenda-setting theory is now part of the mass communication agenda.

QUESTIONS TO SHARPEN YOUR FOCUS

1. If the media aren't telling you what to think, why is their ability to tell you *what to think about* so important?

2. What *type of person under what type of circumstances* is most susceptible to the media's *agenda-setting function?*

3. Who do you think sets the agenda for the *agenda makers?* News editors? The President? The people? Political action committees? Reporters? Friends of reporters? Stockholders? Advertisers?

4. Is there a recent issue that *news reporters and commentators* are now talking about all the time that you and the people you know don't care about? Do you think you'll still be apathetic four months from now?

A SECOND LOOK

Recommended resource: David L. Protess and Maxwell McCombs (eds.), *Agenda Setting: Readings on Media, Public Opinion, and Policymaking,* Lawrence Erlbaum Associates, Hillsdale, N.J., 1991.

Brief summary: Maxwell McCombs and Sheldon Gilbert, "News Influence on Our World of Pictures," in *Perspectives on Media Effects,* Jennings Bryant and Dolf Zillmann (eds.), Lawrence Erlbaum Associates, Hillsdale, N.J., 1986, pp. 1–15.

Theory and research summary: Werner J. Severin and James W. Tankard, Jr., *Communication Theories and Origins, and Uses in the Mass Media,* Longman, New York, 1992, pp. 207–229.

Prototype election study: Maxwell McCombs and Donald Shaw, "The Agenda-Setting Function of the Mass Media," *Public Opinion Quarterly,* Vol. 36, 1972, pp. 176–187.

Time lag study: G. Ray Funkhouser, "The Issues of the 60's: An Exploratory Study in the Dynamics of Public Opinion," *Public Opinion Quarterly,* Vol. 37, 1973, pp. 62–75.

Review of research: Donald Shaw and Maxwell McCombs, *The Emergence of American Political Issues: The Agenda-Setting Function of the Press,* West, St. Paul, Minn., 1977.

Current state of theory and research: "Symposium: Agenda Setting Revisited," *Journal of Communication,* Vol. 43, No. 2, 1993, pp. 58–127.

Research update: Everett M. Rogers and James W. Dearing, "Agenda-Setting Research: Where Has It Been, Where Is It Going?" *Communication Yearbook 11,* James A. Anderson (ed.), Sage, Newbury Park, Calif., 1988, pp. 555–594.

Watergate: David Weaver, Maxwell McCombs, and Charles Spellman, "Watergate and the Media: A Case of Agenda-Setting," *American Politics Quarterly,* Vol. 3, 1975, pp. 458–472.

Presidential campaign: Theodore White, *The Making of the President 1972,* Bantam, New York, 1973.

How news becomes news: Maxwell McCombs and Donald Shaw, "Structuring the 'Unseen Environment,'" *Journal of Communication,* Vol. 26, No. 2, 1976, pp. 18–22.

Campaigns as agendas: John Carey, "How Media Shape Campaigns," *Journal of Communication,* Vol. 26, No. 2, 1976, pp. 50–57.

Capturing media attention: Bruce Westley, "What Makes It Change?" *Journal of Communication,* Vol. 26, No. 2, 1976, pp. 43–47.

Critique: Gene Burd, "A Critique of Two Decades of Agenda-Setting Research," in David L. Protess and Maxwell McCombs (eds.), *Agenda Setting: Readings on Media, Public Opinion, and Policymaking,* Lawrence Erlbaum Associates, Hillsdale, N.J., 1991, pp. 291–294.

CHAPTER 33

Spiral of Silence
of Elisabeth Noelle-Neumann

The 1980 presidential election seemed too close to call. Polls reported that President Jimmy Carter and challenger Ronald Reagan were in a virtual dead heat over the last two months of the campaign. But according to Elisabeth Noelle-Neumann, professor emeritus of communications research at the Institut für Publizistik in Germany, most pollsters asked the wrong question. Instead of asking, "Who do you plan to vote for?" they should have asked, "Who do you think will win the election?"

They would have discovered that even while voter preference was holding equal, the expectation that Reagan would win was growing from week to week. Noelle-Neumann notes that the apparent discrepancy makes it look like the second question was posed on a different planet, but she claims that people's assessment of the political climate, and especially their forecast of future trends, are early, reliable indicators of what will happen in an election. In Carter's case they were. The night before the vote, Democratic pollster Pat Caddell came to the President and sadly announced that the contest was over. Millions of voters were taking part in a last-minute swing for Reagan. The actual vote the next day buried Carter in a Republican landslide.

Noelle-Neumann's spiral of silence is a theory that explains the growth and spread of public opinion. As founder and director of the Allensbach Institute (the German counterpart to America's Gallup poll organization), she has come to recognize the power of public opinion. Along with philosopher John Locke, she regards public opinion as a *tangible force* that keeps people in line. Locke outlined three forms of law—divine, civil, and opinion. He claimed that the law of opinion is the only law by which people really abide.[1] Whether in politics, ethics, or matters of fashion, Noelle-Neumann defines public opinion as "opinions on controversial issues that one *can* express in public without isolating oneself."[2]

The term *spiral of silence* refers to the increasing pressure people feel to conceal their views when they think they are in the minority. Noelle-Neumann believes that television accelerates the spiral, but to grasp the role of the mass media in the process we first must understand people's extraordinary sensitivity to the ever-changing standard of what society will tolerate.

AN UNCANNY GIFT: PERCEIVING THE CLIMATE OF OPINION

Noelle-Neumann is constantly amazed at the human ability to discern the climate of public opinion accurately. Science has fixed on five bodily receptors through which people sense their environment: eye (sight), ear (sound), tongue (taste), nose (smell), skin (touch). Only half facetiously, the veteran pollster postulates a "quasi-statistical organ"—a sixth sense which provides trustworthy information about what society in general is thinking and feeling. It's as if people come equipped with antennae that quiver to every shift in the social breeze. How else, she says, can we account for the fact that "when a swing in the climate occurs for or against a party, a person, or a particular idea, it seems to be sensed everywhere at almost exactly the same time, by [everybody]."[3] Without benefit of random samples, interview schedules, or frequency distributions, average people can tell which way the wind is blowing before the scientific polls sample the climate of public opinion.

Noelle-Neumann recommends two questions to sample the barometric readings inside people's heads:

1. "Regardless of your personal opinion, do you think most people. . . ?" [present climate]
2. "Will more or less people think this way a year from now?" [future forecast]

People rarely respond, "How should I know?" or "I'm no prophet." She believes that assessing the public mood, present or future, is the most natural thing in the world for people to do. Thirty years of survey experience has convinced her that people usually get it right. Even when they misread the present, they invariably can spot future trends. For example, near the end of every year her Allensbach Institute asks a representative sample of German men and women, "Do you look forward to the coming year with hopes or with fears?" The level of optimism expressed shows no relationship to economic growth in the year the question is asked, but it gives an uncanny forecast of the actual rise or fall in the growth rate of the nation's GNP for *the following year*.

The human ability to spot momentum in public tastes and opinions is not used frivolously. Noelle-Neumann says it requires an unbelievable expenditure of energy to figure out which ideas are on the increase and which are on the decline. The tremendous concentration required to monitor social trends makes sense only when compared with a greater strain—the danger of isolating oneself with an opinion that has gone out of style. "The effort spent in observing the environment is apparently a smaller price to pay than the risk of losing the goodwill of one's fellow human beings—of becoming rejected, despised, alone."[4]

THE FEAR OF ISOLATION

According to Noelle-Neumann, the fear of isolation is the centrifugal force that accelerates the spiral of silence. She draws heavily on the famous conformity research of Swarthmore psychologist Solomon Asch to support her claim. Asch demonstrated that people will ignore the plain evidence of their senses and yield to perceived group pressure.[5]

Look at the lines above. Which line—A, B, or C—is the same length as line X? The answer seems obvious, and left on his or her own, everyone picks line A. But put an individual in a group of experimental confederates who unanimously state that line B is the right answer, and the unsuspecting subject will feel great anxiety. Thoughts of isolation are very real to the person who considers standing firm: "Will these folks frown, argue, or curse my stubbornness? Worse yet, will they snicker or laugh at me? If I say what I really think, will they turn away in contempt or kick me out of the group?" Asch found that most people placed in this stressful situation would conform at least some, if not all, of the time.

Is fear of isolation a trait peculiar to Americans? Noelle-Neumann rejects that possibility on the basis of Yale psychologist Stanley Milgram's follow-up study conducted in Europe. Milgram selected France and Norway as nations with strikingly diverse cultures—the first one highly individualistic, the other with a strong sense of cohesiveness. As he anticipated, Norwegians conformed more than the French. But like their American counterparts, the majority of people in both groups were unable to stand firm in the face of group pressure.

Noelle-Neumann also considers the possibility that people conform more out of a desire to identify with a winner than to avoid isolation. For example, after an important election is over, a greater percentage of people report voting for the victor than the ballot totals would indicate. But she doesn't consider false reports as attempts to belatedly climb on the bandwagon and bask in reflected glory. Rather, she interprets the petty lies as a defensive strategy to avoid the social stigma that comes from being a deviant on value-laden issues. Even though a go-along-to-get-along approach might brand a person as a conformist or a hanger-on, Allensbach respondents indicate that rejection is even worse.

Banishment from the group, long-term solitary confinement, and sanctioned public ridicule are regarded as cruel punishments in most parts of the world. Noelle-Neumann says that only the criminal or moral hero doesn't care what society thinks. The rest of us want the peace and contentment that comes from belonging. Nobel Prize-winner Mother Teresa affirms Noelle-Neumann's analysis: "The worst sickness is not leprosy or tuberculosis, but the feeling of being respected by no one, of being unloved, deserted by everyone."[6]

A TIME TO SPEAK AND A TIME TO KEEP SILENT

Since people can tell when they are out of sync with public opinion and they fear being isolated for holding views that aren't in favor, we could expect those who see themselves in the minority to keep silent. This is precisely what Elisabeth Noelle-Neumann predicts:

> Individuals who . . . notice that their own personal opinion is spreading and is taken over by others, will voice this opinion self-confidently in public. On the other hand, individuals who notice that their own opinions are losing ground, will be inclined to adopt a more reserved attitude.[7]

She is not suggesting that the latter group will easily abandon an unpopular conviction and change their minds. People aren't weather vanes. But men and women who realize they are fighting a headwind may duck their heads and keep their own counsel. Their silence will probably pass unnoticed or be taken as tacit agreement, so they won't be hassled. People in the United States who spoke out against Operation Desert Storm had to be either very brave or very foolish.

"One final question: Do you now own or have you ever owned a fur coat?"

Drawing by M. Stevens; © 1989 The New Yorker Magazine, Inc.

In the first 1988 presidential debate, George Bush invoked the "L word." He called Michael Dukakis a liberal—"a card-carrying member of the ACLU," an organization which defended atheists, criminals, and child pornographers. Millions of liberals around the country winced at this verbal body blow to their position. Conservatism had been on the rise for over a decade; liberalism had been in retreat. Liberals could have protested that the American Civil Liberties Union also defended patriot Ollie North, or that Bush's positions on social security, Medicare, and relations with China were originally advocated by liberals. But consistent with Noelle-Neumann's prediction, they found it safer to suffer in silence.

The Allensbach Institute has discovered an effective way to find out whether people are willing to speak out in favor of their viewpoint. Suppose, for example, that the topic is abortion. They would ask:

> Assume that you have five hours of train travel ahead of you, and somebody [next to you] begins to talk about abortion. Would you like to talk with this person or would you rather not talk?[8]

The train test reveals a series of factors which determine the likelihood that people will voice their opinions. The first factor is by far the most important.

1. Those who favor the majority position are more willing to express their views than those who belong to the minority faction. "Feeling in harmony with the spirit of the age loosens the tongue."

2. If perception of the present opinion climate doesn't match a person's forecast for the future, willingness to speak out depends more on the future trend.

3. People are more willing to speak to those who share their thoughts than to those who disagree. When you fear isolation, friends are safer than foes.

4. Low self-esteem will cause a person to remain mute. The Allensbach team identifies these individuals by their agreement with a survey statement about relationships: "I know very few people."

5. Males, young adults, and people of the middle and upper classes find it easier to speak out.

6. Existing law encourages people to express their opinion when they feel outnumbered. The Supreme Court's *Roe v. Wade* decision emboldened "closet pro-choice" women who had been fearing public reprisal.

7. Various camps differ in their readiness to stand up for their convictions. Vice President Spiro Agnew's label of "silent majority" touched a responsive chord in the early 1970s among conservatives who were prone to silence.

THE ACCELERATING SPIRAL OF SILENCE

You now have the building blocks that Noelle-Neumann uses to construct her model of public opinion:

Human ability to gauge trends of public sentiment.

Individuals' justifiable fear of isolation.

People's hesitancy to express minority views.

She integrates these factors in the following description of the plight of those who sense minority status. Her summary of the theory reveals that they are indeed caught in a spiral of silence.

> People . . . live in perpetual fear of isolating themselves and carefully observe their environment to see which opinions increase and which ones decrease. If they find that their views predominate or increase, then they express themselves freely in public; if they find that their views are losing supporters, then they become fearful, conceal their convictions in public and fall silent. Because the one group express themselves with self-confidence whereas the others remain silent, the former appear to be strong in public, the latter weaker than their numbers suggest. This encourages others to express themselves or to fall silent, and a spiral process comes into play.[9]

Figure 33.1 pictures the journey of minority factions down the spiral of silence. The ball represents people who sense a slight discrepancy between their position and the prevailing public opinion, much like President Jimmy Carter's supporters in the early fall of 1980. Up to this point they felt comfortable expressing their views in public, perhaps even displaying campaign buttons or bumper stickers. But then the nagging fear of isolation—insistent as the pull of gravity—convinces them to be more circumspect in what they say. Bumper stickers disappear, and they avoid arguments with Reaganites. Carter hasn't lost any voting strength; only the outward fervor has tapered off. However, the Republican clamor for Reagan is undiminished, so Carter backers get the impression of a dip in support for their man.

Carter's people have now come full circle. Their political antennae register a relative shift in public sentiment even before it shows up in the polls. Reagan's apparent strength becomes a self-fulfilling prophecy because it causes Democrats to see a widening gap between themselves and the majority opinion. To an even greater degree, they draw back from public scrutiny, and thus begin another lap on the accelerating downward spiral toward silence. The greater the perceived discrepancy between the prevailing public opinion and their own viewpoint, the more they feel the force of society's demand that they give in. Finally, the pressure to conform becomes so great that some who are most fearful of isolation switch sides. The result is a surprising (but predictable) landslide for Ronald Reagan.

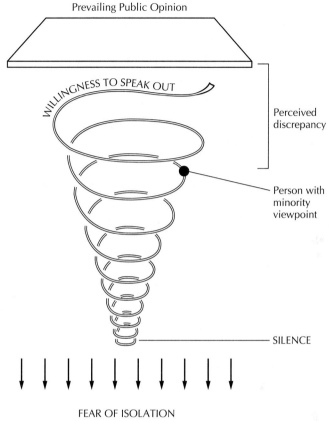

Prevailing Public Opinion

WILLINGNESS TO SPEAK OUT

Perceived discrepancy

Person with minority viewpoint

SILENCE

FEAR OF ISOLATION

FIGURE 33.1
The Downward Spiral Toward Silence

THE POWERFUL ROLE OF THE MASS MEDIA

Noelle-Neumann believes that the media accelerate the muting of the minority in the spiral of silence. Although every human being comes equipped with a quasi-statistical organ with which to analyze the climate of public opinion, that early warning system requires data to process. Direct observation gives us only a small proportion of the information we use; the print and electronic media provide most of our knowledge about the world around us. Marshall McLuhan said that individual media are extensions of specific physical senses. Noelle-Neumann regards *all* media forms as agents of that hypothetical sixth sense, but she isn't convinced that they always serve well.

For decades after the 1940 Erie County voter study, American media sociologists insisted that selective exposure on the part of the reader or viewer neutralized any persuasive effect that the print and broadcast media might have. Like other European scholars, Noelle-Neumann rejects the view that the media only reinforce preexisting beliefs. She admits that selective exposure may limit attitude change through the written word. Given the existing variety of newspapers, magazines, and current events literature, it's quite possible for a reader to avoid contrary opinions. But she thinks television is a different matter. She says, "The effects of mass media increase in proportion to the degree in which selective perception is made difficult."[10] A fictional account of a crooked poker game in a small rural town illustrates her claim.

A farm worker regularly received his wages at the end of the day on Friday. Each week he then walked to the local tavern and lost all his money gambling in a back-room poker game of five-card draw. After a few months a friend took him aside and advised, "Don't play with those guys any more—they're cheating you blind." "Oh I know the game is rigged," the farmhand replied, "but it's the only game in town."

Television is often the only game in town, yet Noelle-Neumann says that media researchers usually fail to recognize that fact. They try to test for media effects in the laboratory, but they can't re-create the "ubiquity, consonance, and cumulation" that give TV its power. She is referring to television's all-surrounding presence, its single point of view, and the constant repetition of its message. These factors override selective exposure and bias a whole nation's judgment of the prevailing opinion. How powerful does Noelle-Neumann think the broadcast media are?

> I have never found a spiral of silence that goes against the tenor of the media, for the willingness to speak out depends in part upon sensing that there is support and legitimation from the media.[11]

Thus Noelle-Neumann agrees with Stuart Hall's assessment (and pessimism) concerning the media's intrusive role in democratic decision making. She ascribes a function to the media that goes one step beyond agenda setting. The media in general and television in particular not only tell us what to think about, they provide the sanctioned view of what everyone else is thinking.

Given the media's role in crystallizing public opinion, media access becomes crucial for those who desire to shape the public mood. It's no longer enough for potential opinion leaders to have well-thought-out positions and the courage of their convictions. They must be ready, willing, and *able* to command media attention. This gives anybody with an assault rifle, friends in high places, or inherited wealth an advantage over the average citizen in programming that quasi-statistical organ that readers and viewers possess.

As an example of a false consensus promoted by the media, Noelle-Neumann cites the negative attitude of her country's journalists toward the overall German character. In the 1950s and 1960s, commentators consistently bad-mouthed German materialism, rudeness, and love for authority. These and other negative stereotypes permeated the media. Data from the Allensbach Institute show that the continual pounding took its toll. The Institute's annual survey included an item about the German character: "Generally speaking, what do you consider to be the best qualities of the German?" In 1952 only 4 percent of the people answered, "Don't know of any." That figure rose to 14 percent in 1962. By 1972, 20 percent of the people were unable to voice a single positive trait. Noelle-Neumann concludes that the mass media can make a majority look like a minority. Television transmits public opinion; television also creates it.

DUAL EVIDENCE: SURVEY RESEARCH AND CLASSIC AUTHORS

The German character survey is only one of many research studies that Noelle-Neumann presents to support a spiral of silence explanation of how fads in fashion, ideas, and politics can take hold. Most of the studies involve reports of German attitudes toward issues and politicians unfamiliar to North Americans, but researchers in the United States have collected similar supporting data. For example, University of Wisconsin researchers Carroll Glynn and Jack McLeod discovered evidence that bolsters a spiral of silence interpretation of Ronald Reagan's surprising landslide victory referred to at the start of the chapter.[12]

Noelle-Neumann suggests that portions of the spiral of silence have been recognized by philosophers and social historians throughout the last few centuries. She draws upon the insights of Locke, Hume, Rousseau, Goethe, and James Madison in the *Federalist Papers* to illustrate the force and consolidation of public opinion. She believes that Alexis de Tocqueville's analysis of the decline of religion before the French Revolution was the first to describe the entire spiraling process:

> People still clinging to the old faith were afraid of being the only ones who did so, and as they were more frightened of isolation than of committing an error, they joined the masses even though they did not agree with them. In this way, the opinion of only part of the population seemed to be the opinion of all and everybody, and exactly for this reason seemed irresistible to those who were responsible for this deceptive appearance.[13]

CRITIQUE: QUESTIONS AT THE CORE OF THE SPIRAL

University of Chicago sociologist Mihaly Csikszentmihalyi regards Elisabeth Noelle-Neumann's spiral of silence as "the most original, comprehensive, and useful" theory of public opinion yet proposed.[14] Yet he and other scholars raise serious questions about specific parts of the theory that they consider overly simplistic. For example, progressive silence may be the typical response of those who see themselves outnumbered, but how often are people really convinced that they hold a minority view? Critics of Noelle-Neumann's theory suggest that she is overly optimistic about the human faculty to assess the public mood. Instead of labeling social perception as an "uncanny gift," they think the words *pluralistic ignorance* are more appropriate.[15] The term describes people's mistaken assumption that everyone thinks like they do. Those who share the dominant opinion tend toward arrogance; those in the minority are guilty of wishful thinking. But both groups think that more people share their opinions than really do.

Noelle-Neumann agrees that people lose their quasi-statistical talent if they "crawl into a hole" to avoid disturbing ideas, but she sees this kind of behavior as the exception rather than the rule. It's unclear at this point who is right. Pluralistic ignorance would explain why Agnew's "silent majority" phrase touched a sympathetic nerve in the American public, but its existence would undermine a basic assumption of spiral of silence theory.

Critics also point out that there are people who will never be silenced by threats of isolation. Even though their cause appears hopeless, they continue to voice their opinions—whether through conviction or obstinacy. Noelle-Neumann acknowledges that a vocal minority remains at the top of the spiral in defiance of threats of isolation. She refers to these outspoken believers as *"hard-core* nonconformists." Although she suggests no way to identify these stubborn folks ahead of time, her 1991 update of spiral of silence theory tries to clarify the nature and the role of these hard-core advocates.

Csikszentmihalyi asks, "Are these individuals idiots without a sense of shame, or are they persons with superior self-confidence who are relatively independent of social approval?"[16] Noelle-Neumann's answer is that the resolute hard core is not composed of secure people with especially deep-seated beliefs. Rather they are "a minority who have been overpowered and relegated to a completely defensive position in public."[17] They are willing to speak out because they have nothing to lose. By clinging to the past, they've already been isolated. Despite this less than flattering assessment, Noelle-Neumann regards these stubborn and vocal deviants as the only hope for future swings in public sentiment.

> The chance to change or mold public opinion is reserved to those who are not afraid of being isolated. By saying and doing the unpopular, by shocking, they . . . can carry their ideas to supremacy.[18]

French social-psychologist Serge Moscovici agrees with Noelle-Neumann's assessment, but he doesn't believe she does justice to the pervasive impact of committed deviants on public opinion. Moscovici has spent his professional life explaining how opinions and attitudes of the majority are susceptible to change by the influence of a minority that stands firm. He considers Noelle-Neumann's discussion of a hard-core minority an afterthought or "finagle factor" to cover the times when the main features of her theory fail to account for shifts in the public mood.

But for Noelle-Neumann, hard-core advocates are exceptions. Most of us slide easily down the spiral of silence. As nonconformist Henry David Thoreau wrote about his own civil disobedience: "It is always easy to break the law, but even the bedouins in the desert find it impossible to resist public opinion."[19]

QUESTIONS TO SHARPEN YOUR FOCUS

1. How does Noelle-Neumann's definition of *public opinion* reflect the basic assumptions of her *spiral of silence?*

2. Is our hypothetical *quasi-statistical sixth sense* better at picking up current public opinion or predicting future public opinion? What is the rationale for your answer?

3. According to Noelle-Neumann's *train test*, under what circumstances would you expect it likely that a person would remain silent about a controversial issue?

4. Have you ever been part of a vocal *hard-core minority?* How did you withstand the *force of public opinion?*

A SECOND LOOK

Recommended resource: Elisabeth Noelle-Neumann, "The Theory of Public Opinion: The Concept of the Spiral of Silence," in *Communication Yearbook 14,* James A. Anderson (ed.), Sage, Newbury Park, Calif., 1991, pp. 256–287.

Full statement: Elisabeth Noelle-Neumann, *The Spiral of Silence,* University of Chicago, Chicago, 1984.

Early statement: Elisabeth Noelle-Neumann, "The Spiral of Silence: A Theory of Public Opinion," *Journal of Communication,* Vol. 24, No. 2, 1974, pp. 43–51.

Public opinion polling: Elisabeth Noelle-Neumann, "Turbulences in the Climate of Opinion: Methodological Applications of the Spiral of Silence Theory," *Public Opinion Quarterly,* Vol. 41, 1977, pp. 143–158.

American fear of isolation: Solomon E. Asch, "Effects of Group Pressure Upon the Modification and Distortion of Judgments," in *Group Dynamics: Research and Theory,* Dorwin Cartwright and Alvin Zander (eds.), Row, Peterson, Evanston, Ill., 1953, pp. 151–162.

European fear of isolation: Stanley Milgram, "Nationality and Conformity," *Scientific American,* Vol. 205, 1961, pp. 455–461.

Role of mass media: Elisabeth Noelle-Neumann, "Mass Media and Social Change in Developed Societies," in *Mass Media and Social Change,* Elihu Katz and Tamas Szecsko (eds.), Sage, London, 1981, pp. 137–166.

Hard-core minorities: Serge Moscovici, "Silent Majorities and Loud Minorities," in *Communication Yearbook 14,* James A. Anderson (ed.), Sage, Newbury Park, Calif., 1991, pp. 298–308.

Classical testimony: Elisabeth Noelle-Neumann, "Public Opinion and the Classical Tradition: A Reevaluation," *Public Opinion Quarterly,* Vol. 43, 1979, pp. 143–156.

Carter-Reagan election study: Carroll Glynn and Jack McLeod, "Public Opinion du Jour: An Examination of the Spiral of Silence," *Public Opinion Quarterly,* Vol. 48, 1984, pp. 731–740.

Analysis and application: D. Garth Taylor, "Pluralistic Ignorance and the Spiral of Silence: A Formal Analysis," *Public Opinion Quarterly*, Vol. 46, 1982, pp. 311–335.

Powerful effects-minimal effects: Elisabeth Noelle-Neumann, "The Effect of Media on Media Effects Research," *Journal of Communication*, Vol. 33, No. 3, 1983, pp. 157–165.

Critique: Carroll J. Glynn and Jack M. McLeod, "Implications of the Spiral of Silence Theory for Communications and Public Opinion Research," in *Political Communication Yearbook 1984*, Keith R. Sanders, Lynda Lee Kaid, and Dan Nimmo (eds.), Southern Illinois University, Carbondale, 1985, pp. 43–65.

PART SEVEN

Cultural Context

INTERCULTURAL
COMMUNICATION

When we think of *culture*, most of us picture a place—the South American culture of Brazil, the Mid-East culture of Saudi Arabia, or the Far East culture of Japan. But Gerry Philipsen, a professor of communication at the University of Washington who specializes in intercultural communication, says that culture is not basically geographical. Nor is it essentially political or a matter of race. Philipsen describes *culture* as "a socially constructed and historically transmitted pattern of symbols, meanings, premises, and rules."[1] At root, culture is a code.

Ethnographers study the speech and nonverbal communication of people in order to crack the code. We've already looked at Mead's reliance on *participant observation* (see Chapter 9) and Geertz's use of *thick description* (see Chapter 24) to unravel the complex web of meanings that people share within a society or culture. In like manner, Philipsen spent three years in a multiethnic, blue-collar Chicago neighborhood studying what it means to speak like a man in "Teamsterville."[2]

The home of the late mayor Richard J. Daley and a place where the "Grabowski fans" of Mike Ditka's football world feel at home, Teamsterville is a place where men regard talk as a sissy way to deal with women and children. Talk is also seen as an ineffective tool to get what you want from someone in authority. Philipsen found that speaking in Teamsterville is reserved for street-corner camaraderie.

> Speech is seen as an instrument of sociability with one's fellows, as a medium for asserting communal ties and loyalty to a group, and serves—by its use or disuse, or by the particular manner of its use—to signal that one knows one's place in the world.[3]

As Philipsen heard when he first walked into a bar, "We don't want no yahoos around here."[4]

Philipsen spent a year analyzing the communication patterns of the "Nacirema" (read *American* backward). Typified by concern for "real communication" as opposed to "mere talk," Nacirema speech values *close, supportive,* and *open* communication.

Donal Carbaugh, professor of communication at the University of Massachusetts, analyzed the Nacirema ritual of talk about talk as enacted five times a week on the popular TV talk show *Donahue*.[5] He discovered the cardinal rule of conversation on *Donahue* is that "the presentation of 'self' is the preferred communication activity," and that "statements of personal opinions count as proper 'self' presentations." Everyone has a moral right to present "self" through his or her opinions, and to have those opinions respected. Any ethical statements that appeal to universal standards of conduct are regarded as attempts to infringe on the rights of others. As for the place of communication in the Nacirema culture—whatever the problem is, communication is the answer.

For years, the *Donahue* show was taped in a Chicago television studio within five miles of Teamsterville, yet the two cultures these communities reflect seem to be worlds apart. Just how different are the two cultures? Is there a way to measure the relative discrepancy between any two patterns of communication or systems of meanings? From a study of multinational corporations in more than fifty countries, Dutch researcher Geert Hofstede concluded that there are four crucial dimensions on which to compare cultures.[6]

1. *Power* distance—the extent to which the less powerful members of society accept that power is distributed unequally (Americans—low; Japanese—moderate).

2. *Masculinity*—clearly defined sex roles with male values of success, money, and things as dominant in society (Americans—high; Japanese—extremely high).

3. *Uncertainty avoidance*—the extent to which people feel threatened by ambiguity and create beliefs and institutions to try to avoid it (Americans—low; Japanese—extremely high).

4. *Individualism*—people look out for themselves and their immediate family as opposed to identifying with groups responsible to take care of them in exchange for group loyalty (Americans—extremely high; Japanese—low).

Most researchers agree that Hofstede's distinction between individualism and collectivism is the crucial dimension of cultural variability. The *we*-centered focus of Teamsterville sets it apart from individualistic American society in general, and the extreme *I*-centered preoccupation of its Nacirema subculture in particular. Cultural anthropologist Edward Hall was the first to label the communication style of collectivistic cultures *"high-context,"* and the style of individualistic cultures *"low-context."* The designation divides peoples on the basis of how they interpret messages.

A high-context communication or message is one in which most of the information is ei-

Cat and fish enduring cultural exchange.
Permission: John S. P. Walker.

ther in the physical context or internalized in the person, while very little is in the coded, explicit part of the message. A low-context communication is just the opposite, i.e., the mass of information is vested in the explicit code.[7]

Hall says that people in every culture communicate both ways. The difference is one of focus. Collectivistic Japanese have a message-context orientation; individualistic Americans rely more on message content.

The term *cross-cultural communication* is usually reserved for theory and research that compares specific interpersonal variables such as conversational distance, self-disclosure, or styles of conflict resolution across two or more different cultures. Chapter 35 presents Stella Ting-Toomey's face-negotiation theory of conflict management. Her theory is typical of a cross-cultural approach to communication.

William Gudykunst used a similar comparative approach when he first explored how the predictions of Berger's uncertainty reduction theory might need to be modified to accommodate cultural differences (see Chapter 14). He was intrigued with the possibility that high-context speakers might be more in doubt about a stranger's decorum or ability to act appropriately than they are with attitude similarity, self-disclosure, or other typical low-context concerns. But along with Barnett Pearce and Vernon Cronen (see Chapter 6), Gudykunst has grown increasingly interested in issues of intercultural communication. What happens when a stranger tries to communicate effectively within a different culture? Chapter 34 presents Gudykunst's model of anxiety/uncertainty management that tries to answer that question.

CHAPTER 34

Anxiety/Uncertainty Management Theory
of William Gudykunst

During my first sabbatical leave from Wheaton College I spent a month in the Philippine Islands. When a Filipino couple heard that I was coming to their country, they asked me to spend a week with them on an "academic adventure." Ping and Lena were former graduate students of mine who occasionally taught at Mickelson College, a small church-related school in the remote province of the Davao del Sur. Lena had used a text of mine for a course at the school, and she invited me to be the commencement speaker at their graduation.

The students and staff at Mickelson are Belaan Indians. After their native tongue they speak a dialect of Cebuano. English is their third language and is taught in the school. To get to their campus from Manila, I had to fly first on a jet, then on a propeller plane. The trip continued by jeep and concluded with a six-hour pump boat ride over open water. Ping and Lena explained that the 100 students and 10 faculty faced multiple threats of disease, violent weather, Communist-Muslim insurgency, and piracy—in that order. Located on the top of a small mountain, the school had no electricity or running water. A banner in their chapel proclaimed, "Lo, I am with you alway even unto the end of the world."[1] I felt I was there.

ENTER THE STRANGER

Bill Gudykunst's anxiety/uncertainty management theory focuses on cross-cultural encounters between cultural in-groups and strangers. Gudykunst is professor of communication at California State University, Fullerton, and he developed his interest in intercultural communication when he served as an intercultural relations specialist for the U.S. Navy in Japan. His job was to help naval personnel and their families adjust to living in a foreign culture.

Gudykunst assumes that at least one person in an intercultural encounter is a *stranger*.[2] Through a series of initial crises, strangers experience both

403

uncertainty and anxiety. They aren't sure how to behave, and they don't feel secure. Gudykunst says that anxiety and uncertainty are separate issues and that communication between strangers and in-group members is affected by interpersonal as well as intercultural factors. But because strangers are hyper-aware of cultural differences, other distinctions blur together, and they usually overestimate the effect of ethnolinguistic identity on the behavior of people in an alien society.

As a stranger in a strange land, I experienced all the thoughts and feelings that Gudykunst describes. But lest we get hung up on our own doubts and insecurities, Gudykunst reminds us that my hosts at Mickelson were subject to the same intercultural forces that affected me. It was a novel situation for them as well. I was only the second Caucasian visitor they'd had at their school in a decade.

Gudykunst has revised his anxiety/uncertainty management theory several times. The early versions cast his ideas into axioms written from the standpoint of the stranger. His latest statement flips the perspective and describes intercultural encounters with strangers as experienced by members of the in-group. In an effort to avoid the ethnocentric trap of thinking that my view of the world is the way it *really* is, I'll illustrate Gudykunst's theory by applying it to the situation of my Philippine Belaan hosts. They wanted to bridge the culture gap through effective communication just as much as I did.

EFFECTIVE COMMUNICATION: A RESULT OF MINDFUL ALTERNATIVES

Gudykunst uses the term *effective communication* to refer to the process of minimizing misunderstandings. He notes that other authors use a variety of terms to convey the same idea—*accuracy, understanding, isomorphic attributions,* or *basic communications fidelity.*[3] According to Gudykunst, effective communication between Pol Quia, the president of Mickelson, and me would not necessarily require that we draw close, share similar attitudes, or even speak with clarity—as welcome as these outcomes might be. Gudykunst would consider our communication effective if Pol and I could accurately predict and explain each other's behavior to the extent that these actions tied into our discussion. In other words, no big surprises.

Figure 34.1 diagrams Gudykunst's basic theory of anxiety/uncertainty management. The theory is designed to explain effective interpersonal and intergroup communication in general, and intercultural communication in particular.

The box at the far right of Figure 34.1 represents that goal. Gudykunst asserts that cutting down on misunderstanding is hard work, especially when the stranger comes from a wildly different culture. I'll work back through the flowchart to show how he thinks a meeting of minds might occur. As Gudykunst's term *mindfulness* suggests, he doesn't think it happens by accident.

Like brushing our teeth or turning out the lights before we go to sleep,

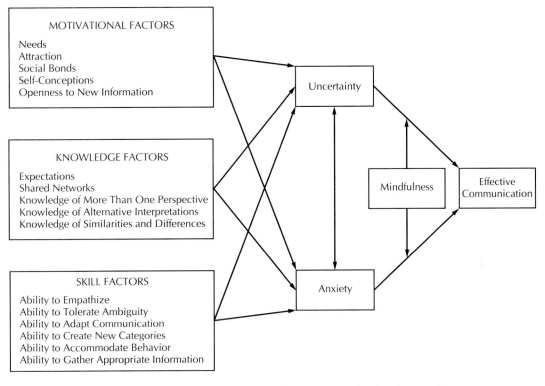

FIGURE 34.1
A Schematic Representation of the Basic Theory (Omitting Cultural Variability) (From Gudykunst, "Toward a Theory of Effective Interpersonal and Intergroup Communication: An Anxiety/Uncertainty Management (AUM) Perspective.")

much of our everyday conversation seems to be part of a set routine. The way we answer the phone, place an order at McDonalds, or kid around with our friends becomes so habitual that we can do it without thinking. Someone watching us play out our lives could easily spot a number of *scripts* we follow when we communicate with others.

Scripted behavior may serve us well when the roles are familiar and all the players know their lines, but Gudykunst cautions that mindless conversation in a cross-cultural situation can escalate the tension and confusion that's already there. In order to reduce anxiety and uncertainty rather than create more, Pol Quia needs to pay attention to what he says and how I respond. I need to monitor my words and Pol's reaction as well.

William Howell, one of Gudykunst's mentors at the University of Minnesota, suggests at least four levels of communication competence.[4]

1. *Unconscious incompetence.* We misinterpret others' behavior and aren't even aware we're doing it. Ignorance is bliss.

2. *Conscious incompetence.* We know that we're misinterpreting others' behavior but don't do anything about it.

3. *Conscious competence.* We think about our communication and continually work at changing what we do in order to become more effective.

4. *Unconscious competence.* We've developed our communication skills to the point that we no longer have to think about how we speak or listen.

Gudykunst defines *mindfulness* as stage 3 in Howell's model. Someone operating at stage 4 may look and feel like a "natural," but situations with strangers are often so fluid that unconscious competence can quickly turn into oblivious incompetence. The intercultural communicator who tries to fly on automatic pilot may quickly crash and burn. Cognitive choice, on the other hand, moderates the destructive force of doubt or fear.

ANXIETY AND UNCERTAINTY: TWIN OFFSPRING OF CULTURAL VARIABILITY

As the title of his theory suggests, Gudykunst believes that anxiety and uncertainty are the basic causes of communication failure in intercultural situations. These two causes of misinterpretation are closely related, yet Gudykunst sees them as different in a few crucial ways. Uncertainty is cognitive; anxiety is affective. Uncertainty can be retrospective; anxiety anticipates what is yet to come.

Gudykunst takes his ideas of uncertainty straight from Charles Berger's uncertainty reduction theory (see Chapter 14). Uncertainty includes the doubts we have about our ability to predict the outcome of our encounters with strangers. For example, would my gift of an *Encyclopaedia Britannica* to the Mickelson library be regarded as an educational treasure or an insensitive judgment of their academic resources? In that sense, uncertainty looks to the future. Yet it refers to the past as well.

As we mentally review an intercultural encounter, uncertainty describes our inability to explain why any of us acted as we did. For example, why did students carry cases of Coke up the mountain when I arrived at Mickelson? Was this effort in recognition of my status as honored visitor, an accommodation to my queasy North American stomach, or a tacit statement that there would be nothing stronger to drink during my stay? I wasn't sure.

Uncertainty is a thought; anxiety is a feeling. Gudykunst defines anxiety as "the feeling of being uneasy, tense, worried, or apprehensive about what might happen."[5] Just as players in Thibaut and Kelley's prisoner's dilemma game might feel anxious about an anticipated unpleasant social exchange (see Chapter 16), so both strangers and in-group members eye the future warily when their differences make mutual satisfaction seem unlikely. The district superintendent expressed this form of fear the night before graduation.

I had just delivered a forty-minute address to students and their families at the senior-class baccalaureate ceremony. Because most of the Belaan par-

Shrew People: quick, carnivorous, usually nocturnal beings; smaller but more vicious than the better-known Mole People; eat five times their own body weight every day; cannibals.

ents spoke no English, I stopped every few sentences for the superintendent to translate my words into their tongue. Therefore, the forty minutes consisted of twenty minutes of message plus twenty minutes of interpretation. After I was through, the obviously worried man took me aside and explained the local rhetorical facts of life. What I had said was fine, he told me, but it was way too brief. Unless I spoke at the graduation ceremony the next day for at least an hour—without an "interrupter"—the local citizens would regard the ceremony as of little consequence and the students would lose face. Now *I* was worried.

The experience points up the extent to which anxiety and uncertainty are linked to the degree of difference between the culture of the in-group and the culture from which the stranger comes. Gudykunst's model in Figure 34.1 doesn't portray the place of cultural variability, yet his words make it clear that the wider the cultural gap, the higher the levels of anxiety and uncertainty that everyone will experience.

Anxiety and uncertainty aren't always bad. Gudykunst recognizes that a minimal level of anxiety and uncertainty will keep us from getting bored—motivate us to communicate better. But once they climb above a threshold of useful stimulation, anxiety and uncertainty are the causes of failed communication. As Gudykunst writes of the uncertainty that accompanies intercultural contact, he pictures the push-pull dialectic of novelty/prediction that Leslie Baxter described for all relationships (see Chapter 17). In like manner, stranger-group anxiety is akin to the tension created by the connection/autonomy contradiction. Both are natural and even helpful in intercultural contacts, but when cultural differences are great, they can quickly escalate to levels that destroy effective communication.

Gudykunst draws on Hofstede's dimensions of culture as a helpful way to gauge cultural variation.[6] According to Hofstede's research, the Philippines and the United States are almost identical in their strong emphasis on masculinity and high tolerance for ambiguity. But the two cultures diverge sharply on the dimension of power position and collectivism versus individualism. I was a low-context egalitarian individualist invading the world of high-context hierarchical collectivists. No wonder they had some doubts and fears to overcome when I arrived.

CROSS-CULTURAL COMMUNICATION COMPETENCE

The far left column of Figure 34.1 pulls together many factors that cause uncertainty and anxiety to rise or fall in a specific cross-cultural encounter. Don't let Gudykunst's label of "Superficial Causes" fool you into thinking that they are unimportant. Some of these motivational, knowledge, and skill variables explain why Mickelson faculty and students were able to communicate effectively with me during that first encounter and why I've gone back to Davao del Sur three times in the last ten years. Gudykunst calls these factors "superficial" only because they ultimately lead back to his central themes of anxiety and uncertainty.

In the latest version of his theory, Gudykunst organizes these multiple factors along traditional lines of *communication competence*. By way of illustration, consider the speakers who are highly competent in public speaking classes at your school. Students who get A's usually evidence three qualities—motivation, knowledge, and skill. It takes all three to be truly effective.

Some speakers have something to say (knowledge) and want to say it (motivation), but they leave the audience squirming because they don't have the skill to eliminate the *and ah's* and *you know's* from their delivery. The motivation and skill of a second group of speakers demonstrate that they have the gift of gab, but listeners quickly tune out their smooth-sounding talk if they don't know their audience. And a third group of speakers have the requisite knowledge and skill to be effective, but their motivation to stand up and speak in front of others is definitely lacking. Either they just don't care or they're scared out of their mind.

Gudykunst lays out thirty-eight separate axioms that specify the causal links from individual factors of motivation, knowledge, and skill to his key variables of anxiety and uncertainty. I'll present ten of the axioms that I've found especially helpful in understanding my initial encounter with the native Filipino students and faculty at Mickelson College. As you will see, these axioms draw heavily on ideas advanced by other communication theorists. In that sense, anxiety/uncertainty management theory is a great review of much that you've already read in earlier chapters.

Motivation Factors

Axiom 1: An increase in our need for a sense of group inclusion will produce an increase in our anxiety.

Although I was raised in the individualistic culture of the United States, my personal prepotent need on Maslow's hierarchy is the desire for love or belongingness (see Chapter 10). My Filipino hosts are part of a collectivist society that emphasizes social identity. As axiom 1 suggests, our mutual strong needs for affiliation increased our initial edginess when we first met.

Axiom 13: An increase in our attraction to strangers will produce an increase in our ability to decrease our anxiety and in our ability to reduce predictive and explanatory uncertainty.

At the end of my visit, Pol told me that our relationship was solidified with laughter. It started when I was afraid of crossing a ravine on a felled coconut tree, so I crawled across on all fours like an animal. The Belaans began to giggle at the ridiculous sight, and I couldn't help laughing with them. After that, whenever the conversation got dull, someone would grunt like a pig and we'd all break out laughing. As social penetration theory predicts, attraction led to vulnerability and self-disclosure (see Chapter 13).

Knowledge Factors

Axiom 18: An increase in our cognitive complexity will produce an increase in our ability to reduce our predictive and explanatory uncertainty.

Delia's constructivism assumes that cognitively complex people are best equipped to take the perspective of others (see Chapter 12). As I talked with Bing Quia, the wife of Mickelson's president, she showed that she didn't think of people in either-or categories. Perhaps her interpersonal flexibility was due to her wider knowledge of the Filipino society—she was the only adult at the school who wasn't Belaan by birth. Whatever the reason for her ability to differentiate personality constructs, Bing seemed to be able to sense my thoughts and feelings and express them to others in the group.

> *Axiom 20:* An increase in our awareness of strangers' violations of our positive expectations and/or their confirming our negative expectations will produce an increase in our anxiety and a decrease in our ability to reduce our predictive and explanatory uncertainty.

Burgoon extended her expectation violation model to include verbal violations in intercultural contexts (see Chapter 7). Early in our conversations I asked the faculty of the school to tell me about problems they encountered as teachers. My bluntness was an invitation for public embarrassment. The question violated their expectation that I would take care not to say anything that would cause them to lose face. The talk became tense. This was the low point of my five-day visit.

> *Axiom 26:* An increase in our knowledge of strangers' language (or dialect) will produce a decrease in our anxiety and an increase in our ability to reduce our predictive and explanatory uncertainty.

Richards proposed his "new rhetoric" to study misunderstanding and its remedies (see Chapter 5). One of those remedies was his 850-word lexicon of Basic English. Although I didn't speak Cebuano or the local Belaan dialect, the faculty and students of Mickelson had a command of my native language that exceeded Richards' minimum vocabulary. As a result, they were able to dispel a number of their doubts and fears about my response to being on their campus. Of course, I benefited just as much.

> *Axiom 28:* An increase in the similarity we perceive between ourselves and strangers will produce a decrease in our anxiety and an increase in our ability to reduce our predictive uncertainty.

Burke uses the term *identification* to refer to the similarities that make communion possible (see Chapter 26). Despite our cultural differences, the folks at Mickelson and I shared a common religious faith and a common concern with education. As if these similarities didn't provide enough common ground, I was shipwrecked with the district superintendent in a violent thunderstorm. As Maslow suggested, our responses during this "peak experience" gave us both a new understanding of who each of us were and what we could expect from each other (see Chapter 10).

> *Axiom 30:* An increase in our shared networks will produce a decrease in our anxiety and an increase in our ability to reduce our predictive and explanatory uncertainty.

This axiom is a direct extension of the one Berger added to his original uncertainty reduction theory (see Chapter 14). My former graduate students, Ping and Lena, were the only people the Mickelson staff and I knew in common, but they acted as enthusiastic go-betweens as they sponsored me and endorsed my hosts.

Skill Factors

> *Axiom 31:* An increase in our ability to create new categories will produce an increase in our ability to manage our anxiety and an increase in our ability to reduce our predictive and explanatory uncertainty.

For my Filipino hosts, who constantly struggled to survive in a harsh environment, my presence posed an additional complication. With some hesitation, one of the Belaan men asked me what they should do with my body if I were to die while I was there. After some thought, I suggested cremation—a novel suggestion in this remote province. He replied that they were open to the idea as long as they could send the ashes back to my family in America. Weick notes that double interacts are preferable to rules for dealing with equivocal information in a hostile environment (see Chapter 23). By initiating a communication cycle of speech act, response, and adjustment, my hosts increased their options and felt better in the process.

> *Axiom 32:* An increase in our ability to tolerate ambiguity will produce an increase in our ability to manage our anxiety.

Given the slow pace of life in a rural setting without telephone, television, or daily mail, students at Mickelson found it difficult to understand my concern to return to Manila on a specific day. After a few questions, however, they seemed to accept this stranger's preoccupation with schedule as a puzzle not worth worrying about. Even though I was the visitor to their culture, I sensed that they were slowly compiling a Geertz-type "thick description" of my cultural values without having to make immediate sense of what they observed (see Chapter 24).

> *Axiom 33:* An increase in our ability to empathize will produce an increase in our ability to reduce our predictive and explanatory uncertainty.

Rogers' existential theory postulates that empathic understanding is a necessary condition of relational health (see Chapter 3). It's even less of a stretch to imagine how the skill of empathic listening could reduce uncertainty about a stranger's motives and actions. On several occasions I discussed aspects of my personal life with Porferio, the district superintendent. His steady gaze and comfortable silences gave me the feeling that he was tasting what it was like to be me. If so, he was also reducing his uncertainty about his American visitor.

These ten examples provide a sample of the multiple factors that Gudykunst claims affect the anxiety and uncertainty that people experience when a stranger comes into their midst. The continual tie-in with other communication theory and research demonstrates Gudykunst's belief that intercultural communication is an extension rather than an exception to principles of interpersonal communication. It's all a matter of degree. The stranger the stranger, the more everyone involved has to work mindfully at overcoming anxiety and uncertainty.

CRITIQUE: OVERWHELMED BY CULTURAL VARIABLES

You may remember that Michael Sunnafrank is a severe critic of uncertainty reduction theory—the theory that was the original catalyst for anxiety/uncertainty management theory (see Chapter 14). Yet even Sunnafrank acknowledges the impact and scope of Gudykunst's work: "Unarguably the most prolific communication research program in the 1980s is being conducted by Gudykunst and his associates."[7] Although Gudykunst is best known for his insights into intercultural encounters, his theorizing also incorporates intrapersonal, interpersonal, and intergroup levels of analysis. This flood of scholarship continues unabated in the 1990s as Gudykunst continually revises and extends the application of his theory.

There is a danger, however, that the student of communication could easily be overwhelmed and confused by the sheer quantity and detail of Gudykunst's theoretical predictions. Berger's original uncertainty reduction theory contained seven axioms that generated twenty-one theorems when they were paired in all possible combinations. In contrast, Gudykunst's theory sets forth a total of forty-nine axioms! He holds out the possibility of pairing the axioms of anxiety/uncertainty management theory in the same way. Hypothetically, the 49 axioms could spawn 1,176 theorems. Although Gudykunst notes that it would be inappropriate to link every possible pair, he doesn't offer clear guidance on which axioms shouldn't be combined. Even if he had only a few hundred theorems, they would still violate the scientific criterion of relative simplicity.

When presenting an earlier version of his theory that contained only thirteen axioms, Gudykunst outlined the effort he had taken to make the theory as uncomplicated as possible. He also forecast that "further simplification should occur in future versions of the theory."[8] Obviously, this hasn't happened. Applying his own expressed standard, the current anxiety/uncertainty management theory is a step in the wrong direction.

Gudykunst maintains that the large number of axioms is not excessive. In fairness to his point of view, all the axioms focus on the causes or effects of anxiety and/or uncertainty. Most of them appear to be elaborations or refinements of axiom 39, which summarizes the main thrust of the theory.

> *Axiom 39:* When we are mindful of the process of communication, a decrease in our anxiety about interacting with others *and* an increase in the accuracy of predictive and explanatory certainty regarding others' behavior will produce an increase in the effectiveness of our communication.

Yet even this core axiom is conditional as it seeks to incorporate the dialectical tension referred to earlier. Gudykunst adds that "anxiety and uncertainty below our minimum threshold will not produce increases in our effectiveness; anxiety and uncertainty above our maximum threshold will produce decreases in effectiveness." Perhaps all the qualifications are necessary to capture the complexity of life, but this is a very intricate theory.

Stella Ting-Toomey, Gudykunst's colleague at California State, Fullerton, questions whether the whole uncertainty reduction approach doesn't reflect a western bias. She notes that the implicit goal of uncertainty reduction is to control one's environment—a theme that is "highly valued by Western, individualistic cultures but not necessarily by Eastern collectivistic cultures."[9] If she is right, my Filipino hosts were less concerned about dealing with their uncertainty about me than I was in managing my uncertainty about them. Perhaps, as Ting-Toomey suggests, these people of the east link communication effectiveness with issues of *relational intuition, relational fate,* and *relational letting go.*

The issue Ting-Toomey raises is more far-reaching than the relative importance of reducing uncertainty. What's at stake is the question of whether or not a panhuman theory of intercultural communication is possible.[10] You'll have a chance to consider the issue of comparative theory and east-west differences when you read about Ting-Toomey's face-negotiation theory in the next chapter.

QUESTIONS TO SHARPEN YOUR FOCUS

1. In what situations might *mindfulness* hinder rather than help *effective communication?*

2. When might *anxiety and uncertainty reduction* not facilitate effective communication?

3. Which of the ten *superficial causes* of anxiety and uncertainty that I discussed would apply to communication between teenagers and the elderly?

4. Think of the most culturally diverse cross-cultural communication situation you've ever encountered. Which of Hofstede's four *dimensions of cultural variability* were highly discrepant?

A SECOND LOOK

Recommended resource: William B. Gudykunst, "Toward a Theory of Effective Interpersonal and Intergroup Communication: An Anxiety/Uncertainty Management (AUM) Perspective," in *Intercultural Communication Competence,* R. L. Wiseman and J. Koester (eds.), Sage, Newbury Park, Calif., 1993, pp. 33–71.

Initial formal statement: William B. Gudykunst, "Uncertainty and Anxiety," in *Theories in Intercultural Communication,* Young Yun Kim and William B. Gudykunst (eds.), Sage, Newbury Park, Calif., 1988, pp. 123–156.

Preliminary statement: William B. Gudykunst, "A Model of Uncertainty Reduction in Intercultural Encounters," *Journal of Language and Social Psychology*, Vol. 4, 1985, pp. 79–97.

Uncertainty reduction roots: Charles R. Berger and Richard Calabrese, "Some Explorations in Initial Interactions and Beyond," *Human Communication Research*, Vol. 1, 1975, pp. 99–112.

Integration of identity and uncertainty perspectives: William B. Gudykunst and Mitchell R. Hammer, "The Influence of Social Identity and Intimacy of Interethnic Relationships on Uncertainty Reduction Processes," *Human Communication Research*, Vol. 14, 1988, pp. 569–601.

Application: William B. Gudykunst, "Diplomacy: A Special Case for Intergroup Communication," in *Communicating for Peace*, Felipe Korzenny and Stella Ting-Toomey (eds.), Sage, Newbury Park, Calif., 1990, pp. 19–39.

Turning theory into practical advice for communicating with strangers: William B. Gudykunst, *Bridging Differences: Effective Intergroup Communication*, Sage, Newbury Park, Calif., 1991.

Mindfulness: Ellen J. Langer, *Mindfulness*, Addison-Wesley, Reading, Mass., 1989.

Critique: Stella Ting-Toomey, "Culture and Interpersonal Relationship Development: Some Conceptual Issues," in *Communication Yearbook 15*, James A. Anderson (ed.), Sage, Newbury Park, Calif., 1989, pp. 371–382.

CHAPTER 35

Face-Negotiation Theory
of Stella Ting-Toomey

For the past year I've served as a volunteer mediator at a metropolitan center for conflict resolution. My role as a mediator is to help people in conflict reach a voluntary agreement that satisfies both sides. I'm not a judge or a jury, and I work hard not to make moral judgments about who's right and who's wrong. A mediator acts as a neutral third party whose sole job is to facilitate the process of negotiation. That doesn't mean it's easy.

Most disputants come to the center in a last-ditch effort to avoid the cost and intimidation of a day in court. The service is free, and we do everything possible to take the threat out of the proceedings. But after failing or refusing to work out their differences on their own, people walk in the door feeling various degrees of anger, hurt, fear, confusion, and shame. On the one hand, they hope that the negotiation will help resolve their dispute. On the other hand, they doubt that talk around a table will soften hard feelings and change stubborn responses that seem to be set in stone.

The professional staff of the center instruct volunteers in a model of negotiation that maximizes the chance of people's reaching a mutually acceptable agreement. From the first day of training, the staff insist that "the mediator controls the process, not the outcome." Figure 35.1 lists a number of techniques that mediators use to ensure progress without suggesting the shape of the solution. Used artfully, the techniques work well. Despite the initial hostility of conflicting parties, 70 percent of the negotiations end in freely signed and mutually kept agreements.

The model of negotiation doesn't work equally well for everyone, however. Although the center serves a multiethnic urban area, old-timers note that the number of people of Asian origin seeking conflict mediation is disproportionately small. On rare occasions when Japanese, Vietnamese, Chinese, or Koreans do come to the office, the discussion seems to go round and round without getting anywhere. Even when participants reach agreement, they seem more relieved than pleased.

Stella Ting-Toomey's face-negotiation theory explains these cultural differences in response to conflict. A communication department colleague of Gudykunst at California State University, Fullerton, Ting-Toomey assumes

415

Assurance of impartiality: "Neither of you have met me before, right? I haven't got a stake in what you decide."

Guarantee of confidentiality: "What you say today is strictly between us. I'll rip up my notes before you leave the room."

Nonjudgmental listening: "I don't know anything about what brought you here. Beth, we'll start with you. Please tell me what happened."

Disputant equality: "Nate, thanks for not interrupting while Beth was telling her story. Now it's your turn. What do you want to tell me?"

Avoid "why" questions: Harmful—"Why did you do that?" Helpful—"What would you like to see happen?"

Validate feelings while defusing their force: "I can understand that you felt mad when you found the bike was broken."

Frequent summarization: "I'd like to tell you what I've heard you say. If I don't get it right, fill me in. Beth, I hear three concerns. . . ."

Blame self, not them: "Nate, I'm sorry. That slipped by me. Say it again so that I can get it right."

Private conferences: "I wanted to meet privately with you to see if there's anything you want to tell me in confidence that you didn't feel you could say with Beth in the room." (Always meet individually with both parties.)

Reframe issues of "right" and "wrong" into interests: "Beth, I'm not sure I understand. Tell me, how will Nate's going to jail give you what you need?"

Avoid advice: Harmful—"Here's a suggestion that might solve your problem." Helpful—"How do you think this issue might be settled?"

Brainstorming: "Let's see how many different solutions you can think of that might solve the problem. Just throw out any ideas you have and we'll sort through them later to see which ones might help."

Role play: "Nate, do you have any thoughts about what would make Beth comfortable?"

Mutual stroking: "I appreciate your hard work on this problem. I feel optimistic that both of you can come to an agreement."

Don't get stuck: "Let's move on to the issue of insurance. We can come back to this later on."

Reality testing: "How realistic is it to think that the bike can be put back in mint condition?"

Consider the alternative: "What are you going to do if you don't reach an agreement today?"

Reminder of voluntary participation: "This is your deal. No option is unreasonable as long as it serves what both of you need. But don't sign anything you aren't happy with. Either of you can walk out at any time."

Move toward agreement: "You've already agreed on a number of important issues. I'm going to begin to write them down."

No assignment of guilt: Harmful—"Nate admits he broke the bicycle and apologizes for his carelessness." Helpful—"Nate agrees to pay $140. Beth agrees to drop all charges."

Highly specific written agreements: "Nathanial Stamos agrees to pay Elizabeth Greenfield an amount of one hundred forty dollars with a money order delivered to her apartment at 792 East Highland at 7:00 P.M. Friday, November 5, 1993."

FIGURE 35.1
Techniques of Third-Party Mediation

that people of every culture are always negotiating "face"—their public self-image. Our identity can always be called into question, and the anxiety and uncertainty churned up by conflict render us especially vulnerable. Face-negotiation theory postulates that the facework of people from individualistic, low-context cultures like the United States will be strikingly different from the facework of people from collectivistic, high-context cultures like Japan or Korea. According to Ting-Toomey, when the facework is different, the style of handling conflict will vary as well.

HIGH-CONTEXT CULTURE VS. LOW-CONTEXT CULTURE

I've already introduced Edward Hall's distinction between high- and low-context cultures in the introduction to this intercultural section. You'll recall that he uses these labels to refer to the relative importance of context when interpreting a message within a given culture. In a low-context society, what is said has great significance; meaning is found in words. Words are less important in a high-context society; meaning is couched in the nature of the situation and the relationship. Since Ting-Toomey bases her face-negotiation theory on the distinction that Hall makes, I'll contrast high- and low-context cultures in greater detail.

In order to help you draw a mental picture of the differences and to avoid the tongue-twisting verbiage of high-context–low-context labels, I'll follow the lead of cross-cultural researchers who cite Japan and the United States as classic examples of high-context and low-context cultures. Note that it would be equally appropriate to use China, Korea, Vietnam, or the Philippines to represent a high-context perspective. I could also insert Germany, Switzerland, or one of the Scandinavian societies as the model of a low-context approach. It is Ting-Toomey's grouping of national cultures within the high-context and low-context categories that separates her theory of conflict management from a mere listing of national characteristics, so feel free to make mental substitutions.

As members of a high-context culture, Hall says that the Japanese value collective needs and goals over individual needs and goals. They assume that in the long run, each individual decision affects everyone in the group. Therefore, a person's behavior is controlled by the norms of the group. This *we*-identity of the Japanese is totally foreign to the *I*-identity of the American who values individualistic needs and goals over group needs and goals. The American's behavior is governed by the personal rules of a freewheeling self that is concerned with individual rights rather than group responsibilities. Marching to a different drummer is the rule in the United States, not the exception.

Hall claims that the strong in-group identity of the Japanese people leads them to perceive others in us-them categories. Once they identify an outsider's background and group affiliation, they have few questions about the person's attitudes or feelings. Their main concern seems to be whether their guest will act appropriately within the Japanese society. People in the United States show a different curiosity. They are filled with questions about the interior life of visitors from other cultures. What do they think? What do they feel? What do they plan to do? Americans assume that every person is unique, and they reduce uncertainty by asking questions to the point of cross-examination.

As for communication, Americans believe in straight talk. Assertiveness is saying what you mean; honesty is meaning what you say. Both are highly prized. Perhaps the highest art form of explicit communication is the legal contract. A U.S. lawyer's dream is to prepare a verbal document that allows no room for interpretation. Hall says that Japanese communication is more subtle. Bluntness is regarded as rude; patience and indirection are the marks of a civilized person. What is said is less important than how it's said and who did the saying. Meaning is embedded in the setting and the nonverbal code. In Japan, the highest form of communication competency is empathy—the ability to sense what others are thinking and feeling without their having to spell it out for you.

With this understanding of the difference between high- and low-context cultures in mind, read through the description of mediation techniques in Figure 35.1. Taken as a whole, the list provides a reliable window to the values that guide this type of negotiation. Participants who come to the conflict center are treated as responsible individuals who can make up their own minds about what they want. The mediator encourages antagonists to deal directly with their differences and keeps the conversation focused on the possibility of a final agreement. While the mediator is careful never to pressure clients to reach an accord, the climate of immediacy suggests this is their best chance to put the whole mess behind them in an acceptable way and get on with their lives. The mediator works hard to make sure that the individual rights of both parties are respected.

Whether or not disputants reach an agreement, the mediation approach outlined in Figure 35.1 offers a safe place where no one need feel embarrassed. At least no one from an individualistic, low-context American culture! As it turns out, the very techniques designed to allow people to save face during negotiation pose an additional threat to face for those from a collectivistic, high-context culture. No wonder these people stay away or leave dissatisfied. Ting-Toomey's face-negotiation theory explains why this is so by sketching the different dimensions of face.

THE FOUR FACES OF FACE

Although popular western wisdom regards *face* as an Asian preoccupation, Ting-Toomey and other relational researchers find it to be a universal concern. That's because face is an extension of self-concept. In their well-developed theory of politeness, University of Cambridge linguists Penelope Brown and Stephen Levinson define face as ''the public self-image that every member of society wants to claim for himself/herself."[1] Many writers regard face as an almost tangible good that can rise or fall like soybean futures on the commodities exchange at the Board of Trade. Yutang calls face "a psychological image that can be granted and lost and fought for and presented as a gift."[2] The term includes the patrician concern for dignity, honor, and status. Yet it also covers the raw power of prideful "trash talk" after a slamdunk on the basketball court—"In your face!" Ting-Toomey simply refers to face as "the projected image of one's self in a relational situation."[3]

Although an overall view of face as public self-image is straightforward and consistent with Mead's concept of the "generalized other" (see Chapter 9), Ting-Toomey highlights two issues that turn face into a multifaceted object of study. Face means different things to different people depending on how they answer two questions. The questions probe matters of *face concern* and *face need*.

Face Concern: "Whose Face Are You Trying to Save?"

This question may seem ridiculous to most Americans or members of other individualistic, low-context cultures. Whose face do I want to protect? The answer is obvious: "Mine!" Yet Ting-Toomey reminds us that there are places in the world where face concerns focus on the other person. Even in the midst of conflict, people pay as much or more attention to maintaining the face of the other party as they do to preserving their own. Their answer to the face-concern question would honestly be a mutual "ours," or even an altruistic "yours."

Figure 35.2 plots face concern along the horizontal axis. Mediators at the conflict resolution center would fall to the right of center on the self-face–other-face scale. They are trained to willingly take the blame for glitches in the negotiation—to look bad so that others can look good. This is not a natural American response, however, and the mediation model doesn't depend on parties in conflict showing great concern for their adversary's public self-image. A grudging respect for civility is all that's required.

Face Need: "Do I Want Autonomy or Inclusion?"

Ting-Toomey's face-need question seems to come straight from the dialectical tension that Leslie Baxter discerned between autonomy and connection (see Chapter 17). Brown and Levinson refer to the need for autonomy as *negative face*, and the desire for inclusion as *positive face*.[4] Negative face is the claim for basic rights of space, privacy, and noninterference. Positive face is the claim for respect, approval, and appreciation. Most of us want to maintain both types of face—negative and positive. But Ting-Toomey states that individuals in low-context cultures like the United States focus on autonomy needs, while members of collectivistic, high-context cultures like Japan concentrate on meeting needs for inclusion.

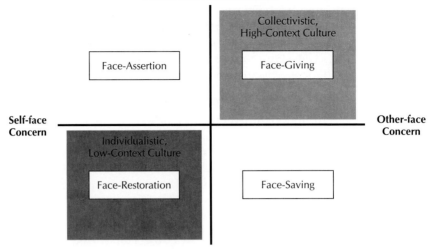

FIGURE 35.2

Two-Dimensional Grid of Facework Maintenance (Based on Ting-Toomey, "Intercultural Conflict Styles: A Face-Negotiation Theory" and "Intergroup Diplomatic Communication: A Face-Negotiation Perspective.")

Positive-face–negative-face needs are plotted on the vertical axis of Figure 35.2. Mediator behaviors of listening, encouraging, and taking the disputant's statements seriously are ways of building positive face. A side benefit of role-play is that the technique helps both parties see signs of humanity in their adversary. But overall, the model of mediation is geared to address needs for autonomy rather than inclusion. Volunteers are frequently reminded that they are mediators, not counselors.

Ting-Toomey's 2 x 2 grid of facework maintenance shown in Figure 35.2 yields four distinct ways of negotiating public self-image:

1. *Face-restoration*—give self freedom and space; protect self from other's infringement on one's autonomy.
2. *Face-saving*—signal respect of the other person's need for freedom, space, dissociation.
3. *Face-assertion*—defend and protect one's need for inclusion.
4. *Face-giving*—defend and support the other person's need for inclusion.

Ting-Toomey believes that individuals from a given society can negotiate face using any or all of these four approaches. But since these maintenance strategies spring from face concerns and face needs deeply rooted in culture, she believes that the enactment of face negotiation is culturally bound. Specifically, individualistic, low-context cultures tend to focus on face restoration. Collectivistic, high-context cultures tend to focus on face-giving. She's also convinced that these different forms of face maintenance lead to different ways of handling conflict. Reduced to bare bones, Ting-Toomey's face-negotiation theory suggests a two-step causal chain with face maintenance as the explanatory link between culture and style of conflict resolution:

Type of culture $\rightarrow$ Type of face maintenance $\rightarrow$ Type of conflict management

The embarrassment of "morning face"

FIVE STYLES OF MANAGING CONFLICT

Anyone who thinks much about interpersonal communication realizes there are different ways of handling conflict. Most students of conflict management list five distinct responses to situations where there is an incompatibility of needs, interests, or goals—avoiding, obliging, compromising, dominating, problem solving.

Suppose, for example, that you are the leader of a group of students working together on a class research project. Your instructor will assign the same grade to all of you based on the quality of the group's work, and that project evaluation will count for two-thirds of your final grade in the course. As often happens in such cases, one member of the group has just brought in a shoddy piece of work and you have only three days to go until the project is due. You don't know this group member well, but you do know that it will take three days of round-the-clock effort to fix this part of the project. What mode of conflict management will you adopt?

Avoiding: "I would avoid open discussion of my differences with the group member."

Obliging: "I would give in to the wishes of the group member."

Compromising: "I would use give-and-take so that a compromise can be made."

Dominating: "I would be firm in pursuing my side of the issue."

Problem solving: "I would exchange accurate information with the group member to solve the problem together."

Ting-Toomey maintains that avoiding, obliging, compromising, dominating, and problem solving vary according to their mix of concern for self-face and other-face. Figure 35.3 charts these five styles of conflict management according to their culture-related face concern. Obliging (smoothing), for example, is the behavior of choice for people who are concerned for the face of others, but not their own. Conversely, dominating (forcing) is the act of someone concerned with face restoration or face assertion for self, but not with face-saving or face-giving to others. As I've just done in the last two sentences, I display in parentheses alternative terms used by other scholars to describe the same strategies for managing conflict. It is my hope that the multiple labels suggest both the richness of research and the similarity of findings in the field of conflict resolution.

The two-tone shading of the conflict grid represents Ting-Toomey's prediction of cultural differences. She claims that avoiding, obliging, and compromising on the lightly shaded left are typical responses of people from collectivistic, high-context cultures. She is equally certain that members of individualistic, low-context cultures will tend to choose the dominating and problem-solving strategies of the heavily shaded right. My interethnic experience as a mediator in conflict situations squares with her predictions.

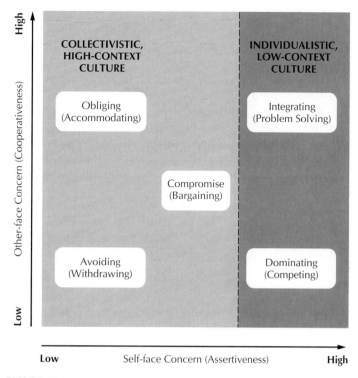

FIGURE 35.3
Five Styles of Conflict Management (Based on Ting-Toomey et al., "Culture, Face Maintenance, and Styles of Handling Interpersonal Conflict: A Study in Five Cultures.")

PUTTING FACE-NEGOTIATION THEORY TO THE TEST

Anecdotal evidence is nice, but when it comes to testing a scientific theory, rigorous controlled comparisons are necessary. The logistics of comparative research are especially challenging when trying to run a cross-cultural study. Ting-Toomey and a host of collaborators around the world tested her predictions on almost a thousand university students in Japan, China, South Korea, Taiwan, and the United States. About 200 university men and women from each country read in their own language about the potential conflict that I presented earlier between the leader and the group member who did the shoddy work. The readers were asked to put themselves in the shoes of the student leader. How would they deal with the conflict of asking a slightly known group member to redo his or her part of the project in the three days that remained? They responded to questions that probed their face concern and also provided multiple responses on a standardized survey that measures preferred styles of conflict management.

As Ting-Toomey and her colleagues anticipated, there was a strong relationship between type of culture and face concern. Students from the collectivistic, high-context Asian cultures tended to show more other-face concern; students from the individualistic, low-context culture of the United States tended to have more self-face concerns.

As face-negotiation theory predicts, the Asian students indicated they would avoid bringing up the problem altogether, try to oblige or accommodate any request the group member made, or attempt to reach some sort of compromise solution. Further confirmation for the theory came from American students' strong allegiance to dominating strategies to rectify the group project problem. They regarded doing the task done right as more important than averting an embarrassing confrontation. The one surprising finding had to do with preference for problem solving—or as others have called it, integration of viewpoints. Face-negotiation theory claims that low-context Americans would select a direct problem-solving strategy more than high-context Asians. That expectation is consistent with the indirectness of the few people from Japan, China, South Korea, and Taiwan who come to the conflict center for mediation. In this study, however, the results were just the opposite.

CRITIQUE: IS FACE REALLY NECESSARY?

The fact that Asians said they'd be more direct than Americans in their problem-solving efforts isn't a devastating blow to Ting-Toomey's theory. This is only one study, focusing on one type of conflict, measuring stated intentions rather than actual behavior. Other studies have confirmed that people who come from low-context cultures use direct problem-solving strategies in their actual relationships more than people from high-context cultures.[5] But another finding in Ting-Toomey's five-culture study gives cause to pause before we uncritically accept her proposed progression from culture type to face concern to conflict management style.

Ting-Toomey reports that there was a 38 percent overlap between culture type and face concern. That is, once you knew whether students were from Japan, South Korea, China, Taiwan, or the United States, you could explain over one-third of the variance in their attitudes toward maintaining face. In the social sciences, that's good prediction.

Ting-Toomey also reports a 58 percent overlap between culture type and style of conflict management. That is, once you knew what countries students were from, you could explain well over half of any variance in what they said they'd do to handle the conflict. Thus, Ting-Toomey found culture to be a fantastically powerful predictor of behavioral intention.

But notice that culture was a far better predictor of conflict style than it was of face concern. If the results of this study faithfully reflect cross-cultural reality, there seems to be no need to resort to the concept of "face" in order to explain culture's effect on styles of conflict management. Bringing in questions of face concern confuses rather than clarifies our understanding of cross-cultural conflict.

One of the five requirements of a good scientific theory is that it should be as simple as possible (see Chapter 3). If two theories seem to offer equally valid explanations of the world, the law of parsimony directs us to accept the less complicated one. As diagrammed earlier, Stella Ting-Toomey's face-negotiation theory uses face concerns and needs to form an explanatory link between culture and conflict management:

$$\text{Type of culture} \rightarrow \text{Type of face maintenance} \rightarrow \text{Type of conflict management}$$

If we can ignore matters of face, however, and still predict and explain style of conflict resolution from culture as well as (if not better than) when we took face into account, a simpler model is preferable:

$$\text{Type of culture} \rightarrow \text{Type of conflict management}$$

Having said all this, I must ask you to consider the possibility that my entire critique up to this point is a case of empiricism run wild. Ting-Toomey is the first to admit procedural problems which may have flawed the results of her study. For example, the paper-and-pencil conflict-resolution survey is a western construction. A good translation won't alter the western values that automatically creep into the questions. The five discrete styles of conflict management it samples may not offer eastern respondents a chance to mark what they would really do in the hypothetical situation.

Ting-Toomey's focus on matters of face is rooted in a long tradition of scholarship concerned with embarrassment, image, reputation, and status. For example, she builds on the theory and research of Brown and Levinson, who are concerned with politeness, a topic closely related to face. Working from a symbolic interactionist perspective, sociologist Erving Goffman is famous for his chronicles of backstage behavior in public places such as restaurants and mental hospitals. His ethnographic studies suggest workers drop their public mask when they walk through the door to a place that's theirs alone. Cited in the introduction to this section, cross-cultural researchers Gerry Philipsen and Donal Carbaugh would remind us that culture is a matter of shared interpretation. When a variety of people from collectivistic cultures talk about face and conflict in the same breath, we should listen to them.

Stella Ting-Toomey's analysis of four types of face is an attempt to systematize what she has heard. Her description of face concerns and face needs highlights an often ignored facet of relational maintenance in western societies and can enrich our cross-cultural sensitivity. People around the world have already answered the question, Is face really necessary? Ting-Toomey and others must now figure out how it works.

QUESTIONS TO SHARPEN YOUR FOCUS

1. Are citizens of Mexico raised in an *individualistic, low-context* culture or a *collectivistic, high-context* culture? How did you decide?

2. Can you imagine a *collectivistic, low-context* culture? Why or why not?

3. What is the difference between *face concern* and *face need?* What type of face concern and face need is involved in *face restoration?*

4. Face-negotiation theory regards *problem solving* as a typical style of conflict resolution in an individualistic society. Given that problem solving is based on *mutual face concern,* why not anticipate that the style is more typical of a collectivistic society?

A SECOND LOOK

Recommended resource: Stella Ting-Toomey, "Intercultural Conflict Styles: A Face-Negotiation Theory," in *Theories in Intercultural Communication,* Young Yun Kim and William Gudykunst (eds.), Sage, Newbury Park, Calif., 1988, pp. 213–235.

Original conception: Stella Ting-Toomey, "Toward a Theory of Conflict and Culture," in *Communication, Culture, and Organizational Processes,* William Gudykunst, L. P. Steward, and Stella Ting-Toomey (eds.), Sage, Beverly Hills, Calif., pp. 71–86.

Cross-cultural research: Stella Ting-Toomey, Ge Gao, Paula Trubisky, Zhizhong Yang, Hak Soo Kim, Sung-Ling Lin, and Tsukasa Nishida, "Culture, Face Maintenance, and Styles of Handling Interpersonal Conflict: A Study in Five Cultures," in *International Journal of Conflict Management,* Vol. 2, 1991, pp. 275–296.

Concept of face: Erving Goffman, *Presentation of Self in Everyday Life,* Doubleday, Garden City, N.Y., 1959, and *Interaction Ritual: Essays on Face-to-Face Interaction,* Doubleday, Garden City, N.Y., 1967.

High-Context–Low-Context Culture: Edward T. Hall, *Beyond Culture,* Anchor, New York, 1977, pp. 85–128.

Collectivistic-individualistic culture: Harry Tiandis, "Collectivism vs. Individualism: A Reconceptualization of a Basic Concept in Cross-Cultural Psychology," in *Cross-Cultural Studies of Personality, Attitudes and Cognition,* Macmillan, London, 1988, pp. 60–95.

Cultural variations: Geert Hofstede, *Culture's Consequences: International Differences in Work-Related Values,* Sage, Beverly Hills, Calif., 1980.

Politeness: Penelope Brown and Stephen Levinson, "Universals in Language Usage: Politeness Phenomenon," in *Questions and Politeness: Strategies in Social Interaction,* Esther N. Goody (ed.), Cambridge University, Cambridge, 1978, pp. 56–289.

Conflict mediation in the east: Ringo Ma, "The Role of Unofficial Intermediaries in Interpersonal Conflicts in the Chinese Culture," *Communication Quarterly,* Vol. 40, 1992, pp. 269–278.

Application to international negotiation: Stella Ting-Toomey and Mark Cole, "Intergroup Diplomatic Communication," in *Communicating for Peace: Diplomacy and Negotiation,* Felipe Korzenny and Stella Ting-Toomey (eds.), Sage, Newbury Park, Calif., 1990, pp. 77–95.

GENDER AND COMMUNICATION

Most of us believe that women and men interact differently. When we think about the differences (and most of us think about them a lot), we usually draw on the rich data of our lives to draw up our own minitheories of masculine-feminine communication.

For example, I recently sat from 9 A.M. to 4 P.M. in a large room at the federal courthouse with a hundred other prospective jurors. We entered as strangers, but by midmorning the women were sitting in clusters of three to seven engrossed in lively discussions. All the men sat by themselves. I thought about that stark difference as I went to my interpersonal communication class. Reviewing the class list, I realized that 70 percent of the students who took the course as an elective were female. Conversely, two-thirds of those who opted for my persuasion course were male. On the basis of this limited personal experience, I jumped to the conclusion that women talk more than men, but that their communication goal is connection rather than influence.

Stereotyping is a risky business. The distinction between women's focus on intimacy and men's concern for power has held up well under scrutiny by communication researchers. But most studies of gender differences show that women actually talk *less* than men in mixed groups.

Linguist Robin Lakoff of the University of California, Berkeley, was one of the first scholars who attempted to classify regularities of women's speech that differentiate "women-talk" from "men-talk."[1] She claimed that women's conversation is characterized by:

1. Apologies ("I'm sorry I don't know how to explain this better").
2. Indirect requests ("It's cold in here with the window open").
3. Tag questions ("That was a good movie, don't you think?").
4. Qualifiers ("I sometimes think that it's rather boring going there").
5. Polite commands ("Thanks for not smoking while we drive").
6. Precise color terms ("That's a beautiful mauve jacket").
7. Absence of coarse language ("Oh my, I left the tickets at home").
8. Speaking less, listening more.

Lakoff concluded that women's speech is marked by tentativeness and submission. She also thought that the content of women's speech was trivial.

Unfortunately, Lakoff's conclusions were based mainly on personal reflection and anecdotal evidence—much like my courthouse and classroom theorizing. After two decades of research comparing the conversational styles of men and women, we now know that patterns of gender differences are more complicated than Lakoff first suggested. Current scholarship tempers her conclusions with at least three cautions.

1. There are more similarities among men and women than there are differences.[2] If I tell you that Pat talks fast, uses big words, and holds eye contact—your chances of guessing whether Pat is male or female are just slightly better than fifty-fifty.

2.   **Among women, there is great variability of communication style. The same is true for men.** Scores on the Sex-Role Inventory, developed by Stanford University psychologist Sandra Lipsitz Bem, illustrate this within-group diversity.[3] Bem asks people to rate themselves on a series of gender-related descriptions—many related to speech. A person who marks "soft-spoken," "eager to soothe hurt feelings," and "does not use harsh language" ranks high in femininity. A person who marks "assertive," "defends own beliefs," and "willing to take a stand" ranks high in masculinity. As you might expect, males tend to fit masculine sex roles and females tend to fit feminine sex roles, but the scores from a group of people of the same sex are typically all over the map. Sometimes individuals—male or female—score high on both scales. Bem regards this combination as the best of both worlds and refers to these people with blended identities as *androgenous*. Obviously, gender-related speech isn't an either-or proposition.

3.   **Sex is a fact; gender is an idea.**[4] Within the literature of the field, the sex-related terms *male* and *female* are typically used to categorize people biologically like they do at the Olympics—by chromosomes and genitalia. On the other hand, the terms *men* and *women* or *masculine* and *feminine* are usually employed to describe an idea that's been learned and reinforced from others. When we forget that our concept of gender is a human construction, we fall into the trap of thinking that there is a real-in-nature category called "man"—a Clint Eastwood archetype who smokes Marlboros, doesn't eat quiche, won't cry, and does "what he's got to do." Sex is a given, but we negotiate or work out our concept of gender with others throughout our lives.

Both theories discussed in this section attempt to identify crucial differences between masculine and feminine styles of communication and explain why the differences persist. Chapter 36 presents Deborah Tannen's genderlect theory, which attributes misunderstanding between men and women to the fact that women's talk focuses on connection, while men communicate to achieve status and maintain independence. The "genderlect" label reflects Tannen's belief that male-female conversation is cross-cultural communication. When inevitable mistakes occur, no one is particularly to blame.

Rooted in feminist analysis, Cheris Kramarae's version of muted group theory regards talk between men and women as an unequal interchange between those who have power in the society and those who do not. As discussed in Chapter 37, Kramarae's belief is that women are less articulate than men in public because the words of our language and the norms for their use have been devised by men. As long as women's conversation is regarded as tentative and trivial, men's dominant position is secure. But just as men have a vested interest in accentuating the differences between men's and women's speech, muted group theory has a reformist agenda of contesting the masculine bias in language. Kramarae is convinced that as women become less muted, their control over their own lives will increase.

CHAPTER 36

Genderlect Styles
of Deborah Tannen

"Male-female conversation is cross-cultural communication."[1] This simple statement is the basic premise of Deborah Tannen's *You Just Don't Understand*, a book that seeks to explain why men and women often talk past each other.

Tannen is a linguistics professor at Georgetown University, and her research specialty is conversational style—not what people say but the way they say it. In her first book on conversational style she offers a microanalysis of six friends talking together during a two-and-a-half hour Thanksgiving dinner.[2]

Tannen introduces this sociolinguistic study with a quote from E. M. Forster's novel *A Passage to India:* "A pause in the wrong place, an intonation misunderstood, and a whole conversation went awry."[3] Forster's novel illustrates how people of goodwill from different cultures can grossly misunderstand each other's intentions. Tannen concludes that similar miscommunication occurs all the time between women and men. The effect may be more insidious, however, because the parties usually don't realize that they are in a cross-cultural encounter. At least when we cross a geographical border we anticipate the need to overcome a communication gap. In conversing with members of the opposite sex, Tannen notes, our failure to acknowledge different conversational styles can get us into big trouble. Most men and women don't grasp that "talking through their problems" with each other will only make things worse if their divergent way of talking is causing the trouble in the first place.

Tannen's writing is filled with imagery that underscores the mutually alien nature of male and female conversation styles. When she compared the style of boys and girls in second grade, she felt she was looking at the discourse of "two different species." For example, two girls could sit comfortably face-to-face and carry on a serious conversation about people they knew. But when boys were asked to talk about "something serious," they were restless, never looked at each other, jumped from topic to topic, and talked about games and competition. These stylistic differences showed up in older kids as well. Tannen notes that "moving from the sixth-grade boys to the girls of the same age is like moving to another planet."[4] There is no evidence that we grow out of these differences as we grow up. She describes adult men and women as speaking "different words from different worlds," and even when they use the same terms, they are "tuned to different frequencies."

Tannen's cross-cultural approach to gender differences departs from much of feminist scholarship that claims that conversations between men and women reflect men's efforts to dominate women. She assumes that male and female conversational styles are equally valid: "We try to talk to each other honestly, but it seems at times that we are speaking different languages—or at least different genderlects."5 Although the word *genderlect* is not original with Tannen, the term nicely captures her belief that masculine and feminine styles of discourse are best viewed as two distinct cultural dialects rather than as inferior or superior ways of speaking.

Tannen realizes that categorizing people and their communication according to gender is offensive to many women and men. None of us like to be told, "Oh, you're talking just like a (wo)man." Each of us regards him- or herself as a unique individual. But at the risk of reinforcing a simplistic reductionism that claims biology is destiny, Tannen insists that there *are* gender differences in the ways we speak.

> Despite these dangers, I am joining the growing dialogue on gender and language because the risk of ignoring differences is greater than the danger of naming them.6

WHEN HARRY MET SALLY: THE CLASH OF TWO CULTURES

Do men and women really live in different worlds? Tannen cites dialogue from Anne Tyler's *The Accidental Tourist,* Ingmar Bergman's *Scenes from a Marriage,* Alice Walker's *The Temple of My Familiar,* Erica Jong's *Fear of Flying,* and Jules Feiffer's *Grown Ups* to support her claim that the different way women and men talk reflects their separate cultures.

Whenever I discuss Tannen's theory in class, students are quick to bring up conversations between Billy Crystal and Meg Ryan in the 1989 Rob Reiner film *When Harry Met Sally.* I'll use the words and actions of Harry and Sally written by Nora Ephron in the film to illustrate the gender differences that Tannen proposes.

The movie begins as two University of Chicago students who have never met before share an eighteen-hour ride to New York City. Harry is dating Sally's good friend Amanda. Their different perspectives become obvious when Harry makes a verbal pass at his traveling companion just a few hours into the drive:

> SALLY: Amanda is my friend!
> HARRY: So?
> SALLY: So, you're going with her.
> HARRY: So?
> SALLY: So you're coming on to me.

HARRY: No I wasn't. . . .

SALLY: We are just going to be friends, O.K.?

HARRY: Great, friends. Best thing. [Pause] You realize of course we could never be friends.

SALLY: Why not?

HARRY: What I'm saying is . . . , and this is not a come-on in any way, shape or form . . . , is that men and women can't be friends because the sex part always gets in the way.

SALLY: That's not true. I have a number of men friends and there is no sex involved.

HARRY: No you don't. . . .

SALLY: Yes I do.

HARRY: No you don't.

SALLY: Yes I do.

HARRY: You only think you do.

SALLY: You're saying I've had sex with these men without my knowledge?

HARRY: No, what I'm saying is that they all want to have sex with you.

SALLY: They do not.

HARRY: Do too.

SALLY: They do not.

HARRY: Do too.

SALLY: How do you know?

HARRY: Because no man can be friends with a woman that he finds attractive. He always wants to have sex with her.

SALLY: So you're saying that a man can be friends with a woman he finds unattractive?

HARRY: No, you pretty much want to nail them too.

Harry next meets Sally five years later on an airplane. He surprises her when he announces that he's getting married. Sally obviously approves, but the ensuing conversation shows that they are still worlds apart in their thinking:

SALLY: Well it's wonderful. It's nice to see you embracing life in this manner.

HARRY: Yeah, plus, you know, you just get to a certain point where you get tired of the whole thing.

SALLY: What whole thing?

HARRY: The whole life of a single guy thing. You meet someone, you have the safe lunch, you decide you like each other enough to move on to dinner. You go dancing, . . . go back to her place, you have sex, and the minute you're finished you know what goes through your mind? How long do I have to lie here and hold her before I can get up and go home? Is thirty seconds enough?

SALLY: [Incredulous tone] That's what you're thinking? Is that true?

HARRY: Sure. All men think that. How long do you like to be held afterward? All night, right? See that's the problem. Somewhere between thirty seconds and all night is your problem.

SALLY: I don't have a problem.

HARRY: Yeah you do.

The casual viewer of these scenes will hear little more than two individuals quarreling about sex. Yet neither conversation is about the desirability of sex per se, but about what sex means to the parties involved. Tannen's theory of genderlect suggests that Harry and Sally's words and the way they are said reflect the separate worlds of men and women. Harry would probably regard Sally as a resident of Mr. Rogers' Neighborhood, while Sally might see Harry as coming from the Planet of the Apes. But each person obviously finds the other's view alien and threatening. Sally, as a woman, wants intimacy. Harry, as a man, wants independence.

FEMININE FOCUS ON CONNECTION VS. MASCULINE FOCUS ON STATUS

Tannen says that more than anything else, women seek human connection. Harry's initial come-on irritated Sally because he was urging her to ignore her friendship with Amanda. She was further saddened at Harry's conviction that women and men can't be friends. But she was especially shocked at Harry's later revelation that, for him, the act of sex marked the end of intimacy rather than its beginning. Both times Harry insisted that he was speaking for all men. If what Harry said was true, Sally did indeed have a problem. Harry's words implied that true solidarity with a man would be difficult to achieve, if not impossible.

According to Tannen, men are concerned mainly with status. They are working hard to preserve their independence as they jockey for position on a hierarchy of competitive accomplishment. In both conversations, Harry was the one who introduced the topic, started to argue, talked the most, and enjoyed the last word. In other words, he won. For Harry, sexual intercourse represented achievement rather than communion. "Nailing" a woman was a way to score in a never-ending game of who's on top. A woman's desire for intimacy threatened his freedom and sidetracked him from his quest to be "one up" in all his relationships.

Harry's opinion that *all* men think like he does may strike you as extreme. Tannen agrees. She believes that some men are open to intimacy, just as some women have a concern for power. You'll recall that Leslie Baxter's dialectical perspective assumes that everyone feels a tension between connection and autonomy in their relationships (see Chapter 17). Tannen agrees that many men and women would like to have intimacy *and* independence in every situation if they could, but she doesn't think it's possible. Thus the issue becomes one of priority.

> Girls and women feel it is crucial that they be liked by their peers, a form of involvement that focuses on symmetrical connection. Boys and men feel it is crucial that they be respected by their peers, a form of involvement that focuses on asymmetrical status.[7]

RAPPORT TALK VS. REPORT TALK

Why is Tannen so certain that women focus on connection while men focus on status? Her answer is that she listens to men and women talk. Just as an ethnographer pours over the words of native informants to discover what has meaning within their society, so Deborah Tannen scrutinizes the conversations of representative speakers from the feminine culture and the masculine culture in order to determine their core values. She offers numerous examples of the divergent styles she observes in everyday communication. These linguistic differences give her confidence that the connection-status distinction structures every verbal contact between women and men.

Consider the following types of talk, most of which are evident in the film *When Harry Met Sally*. At root, each of these speech forms shows that women value *rapport* talk, while men value *report* talk. Tannen suggests that you use what she calls the "aha factor" to test this assumption.

> If my interpretation is correct, then readers, on hearing my explication, will exclaim within their heads, "Aha!" Something they have intuitively sensed will be made explicit. . . . When the subject of analysis is human interaction—a process that we all engage in, all our lives—each reader can measure interpretation against her/his own experience.[8]

1. Public Speaking vs. Private Speaking

Folk wisdom suggests that women talk more than men. Tannen cites a version of an old joke that has a wife complaining to her husband: "For the past ten years you've never told me what you're thinking." Her husband caustically replies, "I didn't want to interrupt you." Tannen grants the validity of the wordy-woman–mute-male stereotype as it applies to a couple alone. She finds that women talk more than men in private conversations, and she endorses Alice Walker's notion that a woman falls in love with a man because she sees in him "a giant ear."[9] Sally continually tries to connect with Harry through words. She also shares the details of her life over coffee with her close friends Alice and Marie. But according to Tannen, Sally's rapport style of relating doesn't transfer well to the public arena where men vie for ascendancy and speak much more than women.

Harry's lecture style is typical of the way men seek to establish a "one-up" position. Tannen finds that men use talk as a weapon. The function of the long explanations they use is to command attention, convey information, and insist on agreement. Even Harry's rare self-disclosure to his buddy, Jess, is delivered within the competitive contexts of jogging, hitting a baseball in a batting cage, or watching a football game. When men retreat from the battle to the safety of their own home, they no longer feel compelled to talk to protect their status. They lay their weapons down and retreat into a peaceful silence.

Harry is unusual in that he's willing to talk about the nuances of his life with Sally. Most men avoid this kind of small talk. Yet in private conversation with Sally, Harry still speaks as though he were defending a case in court. He codifies rules for relationships, and when Sally raises a question, he announces an "amendment to the earlier rule." Men's monologue style of communication is appropriate for report, but not for rapport.

2. Telling a Story

Along with theorists Clifford Geertz and Walter Fisher (see Chapters 23 and 26), Tannen recognizes that the stories people tell reveal a great deal about their hopes, needs, and values. Consistent with men's focus on status and Billy Crystal's portrayal of Harry, Tannen notes that men tell more stories than women—especially jokes. Telling jokes is a masculine way to negotiate status. Men's humorous stories have a can-you-top-this? flavor that serves to hold attention and elevate the storyteller above his audience.

When men aren't trying to be funny, they tell stories in which they are heroes, often acting alone to overcome great obstacles. On the other hand, women tend to express their desire for community by telling stories about others. On rarer occasions when a woman is a character in her own narrative, she usually describes herself as doing something foolish rather than acting in a clever manner. This downplaying of self serves to put her on the same level with her hearers, thus strengthening her network of support.

3. Listening

A woman listening to a story or explanation tends to hold eye contact, to offer head nods, and to react with "yeah, uh-huh, mnnn, right" or other responses that indicate "I'm listening" or "I'm with you." For a man concerned with status, that overt style of active listening means "I agree with you," so he avoids putting himself in a submissive or "one-down" stance. Women, of course, conclude that men aren't listening, which is not necessarily true.

When a woman who is listening starts to speak before the other person is finished, she usually does so to add a word of agreement, to show support, or to finish a sentence with what she thinks the speaker will say. Tannen labels this "cooperative overlap." She says that from a woman's perspective, cooperative overlap is a sign of rapport rather than a competitive ploy to control the conversation. She also recognizes that men don't see it that way. Men regard any interruption as a power move to take control of the conversation, because in their world that's how it's done. Those who win the conversational game can take a don't-talk-while-I'm-interrupting-you stance and make it stick. Tannen concludes that these different styles of conversation management are the source of continuing irritation in cross-gender talk. "Whereas women's cooperative overlaps frequently annoy men by seeming to co-opt their topic, men frequently annoy women by usurping or switching the topic."[10]

4. Asking Questions

When Sally and Harry started out on their trip to New York, Sally produced a map and a detailed set of directions. Harry never used them. According to Tannen, men don't ask for that kind of help. Every admission of ignorance whittles away at the image of self-sufficiency that is so important for a man. "If self-respect is bought at the cost of a few extra minutes of travel time, it is well worth the price," she explains.[11]

Women ask questions to establish a connection with others. Even a five-minute stop at a gas station to check the best route to New York can create a sense of community, however brief. Tannen notes that when women state their opinions, they often tag them with a question at the end of the sentence ("That was a good movie, don't *you think*?"). Tag questions serve to soften the sting of potential disagreement that might drive people apart. But to men, they make the speaker seem wishy-washy.

Tannen's work on genderlect gives her the chance to speak on the lecture circuit and to do interviews on radio call-in shows. When she takes questions, she finds that women ask for information in a way that validates her expertise. Conversely, men questioners engage in a verbal sparing match, seeming satisfied only when they ask something that stumps or embarrasses her. Tannen admits that it's hard for her to understand why public face is so important to men. She quotes with approval the words of a wife in a short story: "I'd have been upset about making the mistake—but not about people *knowing*. That part's not a big deal to me." Her husband replied, "Oh, is it ever a big deal to me."[12]

5. Conflict

In the second half of *When Harry Met Sally*, Harry blows up at their friends Jess and Marie and then storms out of the room. After making an excuse for his behavior, Sally goes to him to try to calm him down.

> HARRY: I know, I know, I shouldn't have done it.
> SALLY: Harry, you're going to have to try and find a way of not expressing every feeling that you have every moment that you have them.
> HARRY: Oh, really?
> SALLY: Yes, there are times and places for things.
> HARRY: Well the next time you're giving a lecture series on social graces, would you let me know, 'cause I'll sign up.
> SALLY: Hey. You don't have to take your anger out on me.
> HARRY: Oh, I think I'm entitled to throw a little anger your way. Especially when I'm being told how to live my life by Miss Hospital Corners.
> SALLY: What's that supposed to mean?
> HARRY: I mean, nothing bothers you. You never get upset about anything.

This scene illustrates Tannen's description of most male-female strife. Men usually initiate the conflict. Since life is a contest, men are more comfortable with conflict and are less likely to hold themselves in check. By making an attempt to placate Harry and excuse his anger at their friends, Sally responds in what Tannen believes is an equally typical fashion. "To most women, conflict is a threat to connection—to be avoided at all costs."[13]

The dialogue illustrates another feature of conflict between men and women. As often happens, Sally's attempt to avert a similar outburst in the future sparks new conflict with Harry. Tannen says that men have an early warning system that's geared to detect signs that they are being told what to do. Harry bristles at the thought that Sally is trying to limit his autonomy, so her efforts backfire.

"NOW YOU'RE BEGINNING TO UNDERSTAND"

What if Tannen is right and all conversation between men and women is best understood as cross-cultural communication? Does this mean that genderlect can be taught like French, Swahili, or any other foreign language? Tannen offers a qualified "yes." She regards sensitivity training as an effort to teach men how to speak in a feminine voice, while assertiveness training is an effort to teach women how to speak in a masculine voice. But she's aware of our ethnocentric tendency to think that it's the other person who needs fixing, so she expresses only guarded hope that men and women will alter their linguistic styles.

Tannen has much more confidence in the benefits of multicultural understanding. She believes that understanding each other's styles, and the motives behind them, is a first move in overcoming destructive responses.

> The answer is for both men and women to try to take each other on their own terms rather than applying the standards of one group to the behavior of the other. . . . Understanding style differences for what they are takes the sting out of them.[14]

Tannen suggests that one way to measure whether or not we are gaining cross-gender insight is a drop in the frequency of the oft-heard lament, "You just don't understand."

Sally says that in so many words when Harry declares his love for her at a New Year's Eve party after months of estrangement. "It just doesn't work that way," she cries. Yet Harry shows that he *does* understand what's important to Sally and that he can cross the cultural border of gender to connect through rapport talk.

> Then how 'bout this way. I love that you get cold when it's seventy-one degrees out. I love that it takes you an hour and a half to order a sandwich. I love that you get a little crinkle above your nose when you're looking at me like I'm nuts. I love that after I spend a day with you I can still smell your perfume on my clothes. And I love that you are the last person I want to talk to before I go to sleep at night.

Dumbfounded, Sally realizes that Harry understands a lot more than she

"What do cats want?"

Drawing by P. Steiner; © 1990 The New Yorker Magazine, Inc.

thought he did, and he used her linguistic style to prove it. The viewer hopes that Sally has an equal understanding of report talk that is the native tongue of Harry and males who live in the land of the status hierarchy.

CRITIQUE: IS TANNEN SOFT ON RESEARCH AND MEN?

In a section entitled "Trouble Talk" in *You Just Don't Understand*, Tannen describes how women who verbally share problems with men are often frustrated by the masculine response-tendency to offer solutions. According to Tannen, women don't want advice; they're looking for the gift of understanding. When I first read this section I had the kind of "aha" reaction that she says validates her theory. I suddenly realized that her words described me. Any time my wife tells me about a problem she's facing, I tend to turn coldly analytical or dive in and try to fix it. I now know from Jean that she would rather hear me say, "I know just how you feel." Apparently Tannen's analyses of common misunderstandings between men and women have struck a responsive chord in a million other readers. *You Just Don't Understand* was on *The New York Times* best-seller list for almost a year.

But does a chorus of "aha's" mean that she's right? Psychic Jean Dixon can make ten predictions, and if only one comes true, that's the one people remember and laud her for, while they forget that the other nine turned out to be wrong. According to many social scientists, Tannen's "proof" may be like that. They charge that her theory of genderlect rests on a thin research base. For example, the men and women she studies are almost all white, middle- and upper middle-class Americans. Few of the women she describes work outside the home, discuss intellectual ideas, or are engaged in professional activities. She never substantiates her claim that all male-female conversation is cross-cultural, nor does she systematically address the issue of power differences between men and women. Tannen's neglect of power issues draws blistering attacks from many feminist scholars.

German linguist Senta Troemel-Ploetz accuses Tannen of having written a dishonest book that ignores issues of male dominance, control, power, sexism, discrimination, sexual harassment, and verbal insults. "If you leave out power," she says, "you do not understand talk."[15] The two genderlects are anything but equal. "Men are used to dominating women; they do it especially in conversations. . . . Women are trained to please; they have to please also in conversations."[16]

Contrary to Tannen's thesis that mutual understanding will bridge the culture gap between the sexes, Troemel-Ploetz believes that "men understand quite well what women want but they give only when it suits them. In many situations they refuse to give and *women cannot make them give*."[17] She thinks it's ridiculous to assume that men will give up power voluntarily. To prove her point, she suggests doing a follow-up study on men who read Tannen's best-seller. Noting that many women readers of *You Just Don't Understand* give the book to their husbands to read, Troemel-Ploetz states that if Tannen's theory is true, a follow-up study should show that these men are now putting down their papers at the breakfast table and talking empathically with their wives. She thinks it will never happen. You decide.

QUESTIONS TO SHARPEN YOUR FOCUS

1. Based on Tannen's *genderlect analysis,* do you agree with Harry that men and women can't be friends? Why or why not?

2. Apart from the topics of conflict, questions, listening, storytelling, and public versus private speaking, can you come up with your own examples of how *rapport talk* is different from *report talk?*

3. What are the practical implications for you if talk with members of the opposite sex is, indeed, *cross-cultural communication?*

4. Tannen's *"aha" factor* is similar to Carl Rogers' standard of basing our knowledge on personal experience (see Chapter 3). What are the dangers of relying solely on the "aha" factor?

A SECOND LOOK

Recommended resource: Deborah Tannen, *You Just Don't Understand*, Balantine, New York, 1990.

Conversational style: Deborah Tannen, *That's Not What I Meant!*, William Morrow, New York, 1986.

Linguistic microanalysis of conversation: Deborah Tannen, *Conversational Style: Analyzing Talk Among Friends*, Ablex, Norwood, N.J., 1984.

Strategies of conversational rapport: Deborah Tannen, *Talking Voices: Repetition, Dialogue, and Imagery in Conversational Discourse*, Cambridge University, Cambridge, 1989.

Gender differences in children's talk: Deborah Tannen, "Gender Differences in Topical Coherence: Creating Involvement in Best Friends' Talk," *Discourse Processes*, Vol. 13, 1990, pp. 73–90.

Defense of multiple methodologies: Deborah Tannen, "Discourse Analysis: The Excitement of Diversity," *Text*, Vol. 10, 1990, pp. 109–111.

Parallel view of gender differences: Carol Gilligan, *In a Difference Voice: Psychological Theory and Women's Development*, Harvard University, Cambridge, 1982.

Critique: Senta Troemel-Ploetz, "Review Essay: Selling the Apolitical," *Discourse and Society*, Vol. 2, 1991, pp. 489–502.

CHAPTER 37

Muted Group Theory
of Cheris Kramarae

Cheris Kramarae maintains that language is literally a *man*-made construction.

> The language of a particular culture does not serve all its speakers equally, for not all speakers contribute in an equal fashion to its formulation. Women (and members of other subordinate groups) are not as free or as able as men are to say what they wish, when and where they wish, because the words and the norms for their use have been formulated by the dominant group, men.[1]

According to Kramarae and other feminist theorists, women's words are discounted in our society; their thoughts are devalued. When women try to overcome this inequity, the masculine control of communication places them at a tremendous disadvantage. Man-made language "aids in defining, depreciating and excluding women."[2] Women are thus a muted group.

Kramarae is professor of speech communication and of sociology at the University of Illinois. She began her research career at that school in 1974 when she conducted a systematic study of the way women were portrayed in cartoons.[3] She found that women were notable mostly by their absence. A quick survey of the cartoon art I've used in this book will show that little has changed since Kramarae's study. Only seventeen of the fifty-eight cartoons contain female characters, and only ten of these women speak. All but two of the cartoonists are men.

Kramarae discovered that women in cartoons were usually depicted as emotional, apologetic, or just plain wishy-washy. Compared with the simple, forceful statements voiced by cartoon males, the words assigned to female characters were vague, flowery, and peppered with adjectives like *nice* and *pretty*. Kramarae noted at the time that women who don't appreciate this form of comic put-down are often accused by men of having no sense of humor or simply told to "lighten up." According to Kramarae, this type of male dominance is just one of the many ways that women are rendered inarticulate in our society. For the last twenty years Kramarae has been a leader in the effort to explain and alter the muted status of women and other minority groups.

MUTED GROUPS: BLACK HOLES IN SOMEONE ELSE'S UNIVERSE

The idea of women as a *muted group* was first proposed by Oxford University social anthropologist Edwin Ardener. In his monograph "Belief and the Problem of Women," Ardener noted the strange tendency of many ethnographers to claim to have "cracked the code" of a culture without ever making any direct reference to the half of society made up of women. Field researchers often justify this omission by reporting the difficulty of using women as cultural informants. Females "giggle when young, snort when old, reject the question, laugh at the topic," and generally make life difficult for scholars trained in the scientific (masculine) method of inquiry.[4] Ardener acknowledged the problem, but he also reminded his colleagues how suspicious they'd be of an anthropologist who wrote about the men of a tribe on the sole basis of talking only to the women.

Ardener initially assumed that inattention to women's experience was a problem of gender unique to social anthropology. But along with his Oxford co-worker Shirley Ardener, he began to realize that mutedness is due to the lack of power which besets any group that occupies the low end of the totem pole. People with little clout have trouble giving voice to their perceptions. Ardener says that their "muted structures are 'there' but cannot be 'realized' in the language of the dominant structure."[5] As a result, they are overlooked, muffled, and rendered invisible—"mere black holes in someone else's universe."[6]

Shirley Ardener cautions that a theory of mutedness doesn't necessarily imply that the muted group is always silent. The issue is whether people can say what they want to say when and where they want to say it, or must they "re-encode their thoughts to make them understood in the public domain?"[7] Cheris Kramarae is certain that men's dominant power position in society guarantees that the public mode of expression won't be directly available to women. Her extension of the Ardeners' initial concept offers insight as to why women are muted and what can be done to loosen men's lock on public modes of communication.

Kramarae argues that the ever-prevalent *public-private* distinction in language is a convenient way to exaggerate gender differences and pose separate sexual spheres of activity. Within this system the words of women are often considered as bound to the home and the "small world" of interpersonal communication—of somehow lesser importance than the words of men which resonate in the "large world" of significant political issues. She asks, "What if we had a word which pointed to the *connection* of public and private communication?"

Without such a word, I think of this textbook as a public mode of communication. I am a male. I realize that in the process of trying to present muted group theory with integrity, I may unconsciously put a masculine spin on Kramarae's ideas and the perceptions of women. In an effort to minimize this bias, I will quote extensively from Kramarae and other feminist scholars. Kramarae is just one of many communication professionals who seek to unmask the systematic silencing of a feminine "voice." I'll also draw freely on the words and experiences of other women to illustrate the communication double bind which Kramarae says is a feminine fact of life. This reliance on personal narrative is consistent with a feminist research agenda that takes women's experiences seriously.

THE MASCULINE POWER TO NAME EXPERIENCE

Kramarae starts with the assumption that "women perceive the world differently from men because of women's and men's different experience and activities rooted in the division of labor."[8] Kramarae rejects Freud's simplistic notion that "anatomy is destiny." She is certain, however, that power discrepancies between the sexes ensure that women will view the world in a way different from men. While women vary in many ways, in most cultures, if not all, women's talk is subject to male control and censorship. French existentialist Simone de Beauvoir underscored this common feminine experience when she declared: "'I am woman': on this truth must be based all further discussion."[9]

The problem facing women, according to Kramarae, is that further discussions about how the world works never take place on a level playing field. "Because of their political dominance, the men's system of perception is dominant, impeding the free expression of the women's alternative models of the world."[10]

Note that my phrase *level playing field* is a metaphor drawn from competitive team sports—an experience more familiar to men than women. This is precisely Kramarae's point. As possessors of the public mode of expression, men frame the discussion. If a man wants to contest the point about a tilted playing field, he can argue in the familiar idiom of sports. But a woman who takes issue with the metaphor of competition has to fight it out on the other fellow's linguistic home turf. (Oops, I did it again.)

Mead's symbolic interactionist perspective asserts that the extent of knowing is the extent of naming (see Chapter 9). If this is true, whoever has the ability to make names stick possesses an awesome power. Kramarae notes that men's control of the dominant mode of expression has produced a vast stock of derogatory, gender-specific terms to refer to women's talking—catty, bitchy, shrill, cackling, gossipy, chitchat, sharp-tongued, and so forth. There is no corresponding vocabulary to disparage men's conversation.

In case you think this lexical bias is limited to descriptions of speech, consider the variety of terms in the English language to describe sexually promiscuous individuals. By one count, there are twenty-two gender-related words to label men who are sexually loose—*playboy, stud, rake, gigolo, Don Juan, womanizer*, and so on. There are more than 200 words that label sexually loose women—*slut, whore, hooker, prostitute, trollop, mistress, harlot, Jezebel, hussy, concubine, streetwalker, strumpet, easy lay*, and the like.[11] Since most surveys of sexual activity show that more men than women have multiple sexual partners, there's no doubt that the inordinate number of terms describing women serves the interests of men.

In the introduction to the section on verbal messages, I introduced the Sapir-Whorf hypothesis which claims that language shapes our perception of reality. Kramarae suggests that women are silenced by not having a publicly recognized vocabulary through which to express their experience. She says that "words constantly ignored may eventually come to be unspoken and perhaps even unthought."[12] After a while, muted women may even come to doubt the validity of their experience and the legitimacy of their feelings.

MEN AS THE GATEKEEPERS OF COMMUNICATION

Even if the public mode of expression contained a rich vocabulary to describe feminine experience, women would still be muted if *their* modes of expression were ignored or ridiculed. Indeed, Kramarae describes a "good-old-boys" cultural establishment that virtually excludes women's art, poetry, plays, film scripts, public address, and scholarly essays from society's mass media. For this reason, Kramarae sees mainstream communication as "malestream" expression.

Long before Edwin Ardener noted women's absence in anthropological research, Virginia Woolf protested woman's nonplace in recorded history. The British novelist detected a certain irony about men's view of women. "Imaginatively she is of the highest importance; practically she is completely insignificant. She pervades poetry from cover to cover; she is all but absent from history."[13]

Feminist writer Dorothy Smith claims that women's absence in history is a result of closed-circuit masculine scholarship.

"The committee on women's rights will now come to order."

Reproduced by permission of Punch.

Men attend to and treat as significant only what men say. The circle of men whose writing and talk was significant to each other extends backwards in time as far as our records reach. What men were doing was relevant to men, was written by men about men for men. Men listened and listen to what one another said.[14]

As an example of men's control of the public record, Cheris Kramarae cites the facts surrounding her change of name. When she was married in Ohio, the law required her to take the name of her husband. So at the direction of the state, she became *Cheris Rae Kramer*. Later when it became legal for her to be her own person, she reordered the sounds and spelling to *Cheris Kramarae*. Many people questioned Kramarae as to whether her name change was either loving or wise. Yet no one asked her husband why he kept *his* name. Kramarae points out that both the law and the conventions of proper etiquette have served men well.

WOMEN'S TRUTH INTO MEN'S TALK: THE PROBLEM OF TRANSLATION

Assuming masculine dominance of public communication to be a current reality, Kramarae concludes that "in order to participate in society women must transform their own models in terms of the received male system of expression."[15] Like speaking in a second language, this translation process requires constant effort and usually leaves a woman wondering whether she's said it "just right." One woman writer says men can "tell it straight." Women have to "tell it slant."[16]

Think back again to Mead's symbolic interactionism (see Chapter 9). His theory describes *minding* as an automatic momentary pause before we speak in order to mentally consider how those who are listening might respond. These periods of hesitation grow longer when we feel linguistically impoverished. According to Kramarae, women have to pick and choose their words carefully in a public forum. "What women want to say and can say best cannot be said easily because the language template is not of their own making."[17]

I have gained a new appreciation of the difficulty women face in translating their experiences into man-made language by discussing Kramarae's ideas with three women friends. Marsha, Kathy, and Susan have consciously sought and achieved positions of leadership in professions where women are rarely seen and almost never heard.

Marsha is an attorney who heads her own law firm in Florida and is the first women president of the Hillsborough County Bar association. A recent area magazine article spotlighted five "power players of Tampa Bay." Norman Schwarzkopf was one; Marsha was another. Marsha attributes her success to a conscious shifting of gears when she addresses the law.

I've learned to talk like a man. I consciously lower my voice, speak more slowly, think bigger, and use sports analogies. I care about my appearance, but a women who is too attractive or too homely has a problem. A man can be drop-dead gorgeous or ugly as sin and get along OK. I've been told that I'm the most feared and respected attorney in the firm, but that's not the person I live with day by day. After work I go home and make reindeer pins out of dog biscuits with my daughters.

Kathy is an ordained minister who works with high school students. She is the most effective public speaker I ever heard in a class. Working in an organization that traditionally excludes women from "up-front" speaking roles, Kathy is recognized as a star communicator. Like Marsha, she feels women have little margin for error when they speak in public.

> Women have to work both sides to pull it off. I let my appearance and delivery say feminine—jewelry, lipstick, warm soft voice. But I plan my content to appeal to men as well. I can't get away with just winging it. I prepare carefully, know my script, use lots of imagery from the world of guys. Girls learn to be interested in whatever men want to talk about, but men aren't used to listening to the things that interest women. I rarely refer to cooking or movies like *Thelma and Louise*.

Susan is the academic dean of a professional school within a university. When her former college closed, Susan orchestrated the transfer of her entire program and faculty to another university. She recently received the Professional of the Year award in her field. When she first attended her national deans association, only eight out of fifty members were women.

> I was very silent. I hated being there. If you didn't communicate by the men's rules you were invisible. The star performers were male and they came on strong. But no one was listening; everyone was preparing their own response. The meeting oozed one-upmanship. At the reception it was all "Hail fellow well met." You wouldn't dare say, "Look, I'm having this rough situation I'm dealing with. Have you ever faced this problem?" It was only when some of the women got together for coffee or went shopping that I could be open about my experiences.

Although their status and abilities clearly show that Marsha, Kathy, and Susan are remarkable individuals, their experience as women in male hierarchical structures supports muted group theory. Kramarae says that "men have structured a value system and a language that reflects that value system. Women have had to work through the system organized by men."[18] For women with less skill and self-confidence than Marsha, Kathy, or Susan, that prospect can be daunting.

SPEAKING OUT IN PRIVATE: NETWORKING WITH WOMEN

Susan's relief at the chance to talk freely with other women deans illustrates a central tenet of muted group theory. Kramarae states that "females are likely to find ways to express themselves outside the dominant public modes of expression used by males in both their verbal conventions and their nonverbal behavior."[19]

Kramarae lists a variety of back-channel routes that women use to discuss their experience—diaries, journals, letters, oral histories, folklore, gossip, chants, art, graffiti, poetry, songs, nonverbal parodies, gynecological handbooks passed between women for centuries, and a "mass of 'noncanonized' writers whose richness and diversity we are only just beginning to comprehend."[20] She labels these outlets the female "sub-version" that runs beneath the surface of male orthodoxy.

Men are often oblivious to the shared meanings women communicate through these alternative channels. In fact Kramarae is convinced that "males have more difficulty than females in understanding what members of the other gender mean."[21] She doesn't ascribe men's bewilderment to biological differences between the sexes or to women's attempts to conceal their experience. Rather she suggests that when men don't have a clue about what women want, think, or feel, it's because they haven't made the effort to find out. When British author Dale Spender was editor of *Woman's Studies International Quarterly*, she offered a further interpretation of men's ignorance. She proposed that many men realize that a commitment to listen to women would necessarily involve a renunciation of their privileged position. "The crucial issue here is that if women cease to be muted, men cease to be so dominant and to some males this may seem unfair because it represents a loss of rights."[22] A man can dodge that equalizing bullet by innocently declaring, "I'll never understand women."

SPEAKING OUT IN PUBLIC: A FEMINIST DICTIONARY

Like other types of critical theory, feminist theory is not content to merely point out asymmetries in power. The ultimate goal of muted group theory is to change the man-made linguistic system that keeps women "in their place." According to Kramarae, reform includes challenging dictionaries that "ignore the words and definitions created by women and include many sexist definitions and examples."[23] Traditional dictionaries pose as authoritative guides to proper language use, yet because of their reliance on written male literacy sources, lexicographers systematically exclude words coined by women.

In 1985, Kramarae and Paula Treichler compiled a feminist dictionary that offers definitions for women's words that don't appear in *Webster's New International* and also presents alternative feminine readings of words that do. Reissued in 1992, the dictionary "places *women* at the center and rethinks language from that crucially different perspective."[24] Kramarae and Treichler don't claim that all women use words the same way, but they include women's definitions of approximately 2,500 words in order to illustrate women's linguistic creativity and to help empower women to change their muted status. Figure 37.1 provides a sample of brief entries and acknowledges their origin.

Amazons: The Universal Male Nightmare. (Phyllis Chesler)

Cuckold: The husband of an unfaithful wife. The wife of an unfaithful husband is just called *wife.* (Cheris Kramarae)

Depression: A psychiatric label that . . . hides the social fact of the housewife's loneliness, low self-esteem, and work dissatisfaction. (Ann Oakley)

Day care: Institutions which buy women off. They ease the immediate pressure without asking why that pressure is on *women.* (Shulamith Firestone)

Family man: Refers to a man who shows more concern with members of the family than is normal. There is no label *family woman,* since that would be heard as a redundancy. (Cheris Kramarae)

Feminist: "I myself have never been able to find out precisely what feminism is: I only know that people call me a feminist whenever I express sentiments that differentiate me from a doormat." (Rebecca West)

Gentleman: A contradiction in terms. (Laura X)

Gossip: A way of talking between women in their roles as women, intimate in style, personal and domestic in topic and setting; a female cultural event which springs from and perpetuates the restrictions of the female role, but also gives the comfort of validation. (Deborah Jones)

Guilt: The emotion that stops women from doing what they may need to do to take care of themselves as opposed to everyone else. (Mary Ellen Shanesey)

Herstory: The human story as told by women about women . . . (Anne Forfreedom)

Home: A comfortable concentration camp. (Betty Friedan)

Malfunction: Male-function. (Mary Daly)

Morals: Laws used to regulate many primitive impulses but with this little masculine exception: "All's fair in love and war." (Charlotte Perkins Gilman)

Ms.: A form of address being adopted by women who want to be recognized as individuals rather than being identified by their relationship with a man. (Midge Lennert and Norma Wilson)

Natural: Along with "normal" a word a feminist should use with extreme caution. (Sona Osman)

Pornography: Pornography is the theory and rape is the practice. (Andrea Dworkin)

Sexual harassment: Refers to the unwanted imposition of sexual requirements in the context of a relationship of unequal power. (Catharine Mackinnon)

FIGURE 37.1
Excerpts from Kramarae and Treichler's Feminist Dictionary (Kramarae and Treichler, *Amazons, Bluestockings, and Crones.*)

SEXUAL HARASSMENT: COINING A TERM TO LABEL EXPERIENCE

Perhaps more than any other single entry in the Kramarae and Treichler dictionary, the inclusion of *sexual harassment* illustrates a major achievement of feminist communication scholarship—encoding women's experience into the received language of society. Although stories of unwanted sexual attention on the job are legion, until recently women haven't had a common term to label what has been an ongoing fact of feminine life.

In 1992, the *Journal of Applied Communication Research* published thirty stories of speech communication students and professionals who were sexually embarrassed, humiliated, or traumatized by a person who was in a position of academic power. All but two of the thirty accounts came from women. As Kramarae notes, "sexual harassment is rampant but not random."[25] The anonymous story below is typical.

> He was fifty; I was twenty-one. He was the major professor in my area; I was a first year M.A. student. His position was secure; mine was nebulous and contingent on his support of me. He felt entitled; I felt dependent. He probably hasn't thought much about what happened; I've never forgotten.
>
> Like most beginning students, I was unsure of myself and my abilities, so I was hungry for praise and indicators of my intellectual merit. . . . Then, one November morning I found a note in my mailbox from Professor X, the senior faculty member in my area and, thus, a person very important to me. In the note Professor X asked me to come by his office late that afternoon to discuss a paper I'd written for him.
>
> The conversation closed with his telling me that we should plan on getting to know each other and working together closely. I wanted to work with him and agreed. We stood and he embraced me and pressed a kiss on me. I recall backing up in surprise. I really didn't know what was happening. He smiled and told me that being "friends" could do nothing but enhance our working relationship. I said nothing, but felt badly confused. . . . This man was a respectable faculty member and surely he knew more about norms for student-faculty relationships than I did. So I figured I must be wrong to feel his behavior was inappropriate, must be misconstruing his motives, exaggerating the significance of "being friendly." . . . So I planned to have an "open talk" with him.
>
> I was at a disadvantage in our "open talk," because I approached it as a chance to clarify feelings while he used it as an occasion to reinterpret and redefine what was happening in ways that suited his purposes. I told him I didn't feel right "being so friendly" with him. He replied that I was over-reacting and, further, that my small-town southern upbringing was showing. . . . I told him I was concerned that he wasn't being objective about my work, but was praising it because he wanted to be "friends" with me; he twisted this, explaining he was judging my work fairly, BUT that being "friends" did increase his interest in helping me professionally. No matter what I said, he had a response that defined my feelings as inappropriate.[26]

Muted group theory can explain this woman's sense of confusion and lack of power. Her story is as much about a struggle for language as it is a struggle over sexual conduct. As long as the professor can define his actions as "being friendly," the female student's feelings are discounted—even by herself. Had she been equipped with the linguistic tool of "sexual harassment," she could have validated her feelings and labeled the professor's advances as inappropriate and illegal.

According to Kramarae, when *sexual harassment* was first used in a court case in the late 1970s, it was the only legal term defined by women. Senatorial response to Anita Hill's testimony at the Clarence Thomas Supreme Court confirmation hearings showed that there is more work to be done before women can make their definition stick. For muted group theory, the struggle to contest man-made language continues.

CRITIQUE: IS A GOOD MAN HARD TO FIND (AND CHANGE)?

Feminist scholars insist that "the key communication activities of women's experiences—their rituals, vocabularies, metaphors, and stories—are an important part of the data for study."[27] In this chapter I've presented the words of thirty women who give voice to the mutedness they've experienced because they aren't men. I could have easily cited hundreds more. It strikes me that ignoring or discounting their testimony would be the ultimate confirmation of Kramarae's muted group thesis.

Unlike Deborah Tannen in her approach to gender differences presented in the previous chapter, Cheris Kramarae claims that questions of power are central to all human relationships. The three theories covered in the section on relationship maintenance support her contention (see Chapters 15, 16, and 17). Watzlawick's interactional view states that all communication is either symmetrical or complementary. Thibaut and Kelley's social exchange theory categorizes relationships on the basis of the reflexive, behavioral, and fate control that each party can exert. And Baxter's dialectical perspective regards the willingness to relinquish a portion of personal power as central to the tug-of-war between independence and connection. These theorists don't speak to Kramarae's assertion that we live in a patriarchal society, but their scholarship does validate her focus on control issues between men and women.

The question of men's motives is more problematic. Tannen criticizes feminist scholars like Kramarae for assuming that men are trying to control women. She acknowledges that differences in male and female communication styles sometimes lead to imbalances of power, but unlike Kramarae, she is willing to assume that the problems are caused primarily by men's and women's "different styles." Tannen cautions that "bad feelings and imputation of bad motives or bad character can come about when there was no intention to dominate, to wield power."[28]

Kramarae thinks that Tannen's apology for men's abuse of power is naive at best. She notes that men often ignore or ridicule women's statements about the problems of being heard in a male-dominated society. Rather than blaming "style differences," Kramarae points to the many ways that our political, educational, religious, legal, and media systems support gender, race, and class hierarchies. Your response to muted group theory may well depend on whether you are a beneficiary or a victim of these systems.

For men and women who are willing to hear what Kramarae has to say, the consciousness raising fostered by muted group theory can prod them to quit using words in a way that preserves inequities of power. The term *sexual harassment* is just one example of how women's words can be levered into the public lexicon and give voice to women's collective experience. Phrases like *date rape* and *glass ceiling* weren't even around when Kramarae and Treichler compiled their feminist dictionary in 1985, yet now these terms are available to label social and professional injustices that women face. Cheris Kramarae's insights and declarations of women as a group muted by men have helped shake up traditional patterns of communication between men and women.

QUESTIONS TO SHARPEN YOUR FOCUS

1. What words do you use with your same-sex friends that you don't use with members of the opposite sex? Does this usage support Kramarae's hypothesis of *male control of the public mode of expression*?

2. In a journal article about *dictionary bias*, Kramarae wrote the sentence, "I *vaginated* on that for a while."[29] Can you explain her word play in light of the principles of muted group theory?

3. Given a definition of *sexual harassment* as "unwanted imposition of sexual requirements in the context of a relationship of unequal power," can you think of a time you harassed, or were harassed by, someone else?

4. Do you tend to agree more with Tannen's genderlect perspective or Kramarae's muted group theory? To what extent does your *gender* influence your choice?

A SECOND LOOK

Recommended resource: Cheris Kramarae, *Women and Men Speaking*, Newbury House, Rowley, Mass., 1981, pp. v–ix, 1–63.

Original concept of mutedness: Edwin Ardener, "Belief and the Problem of Women" and "The 'Problem' Revisited," in *Perceiving Women*, Shirley Ardener (ed.), Malaby, London, 1975, pp. 1–27.

Annotated bibliography: Cheris Kramarae, Barrie Thorne, and Nancy Henley, "Sex Similarities and Differences in Language, Speech, and Nonverbal Communication: An Annotated Bibliography," in *Language, Gender and Society*, B. Thorne, C. Kramarae, and N. Henley (eds.), Newbury House, Rowley, Mass., 1983, pp. 151–342.

Feminist perspective in theory: Karen A. Foss and Sonja K. Foss, "Incorporating the Feminist Perspective in Communication Scholarship: A Research Commentary," in *Doing Research on Women's Communication: Perspectives on Theory and Method*, K. Carter and C. Spitzack (eds.), Ablex, Norwood, N.J., 1989, pp. 65–91.

Feminist critique of communication research: Sheryl Perlmutter Bowen and Nancy Wyatt (eds.), *Transforming Visions: Feminist Critiques in Communication Studies*, Hampton, Cresskill, N.J., 1992.

Women's words: Karen A. Foss and Sonja K. Foss, *Women Speak: The Eloquence of Women's Lives*, Waveland, Prospect Heights, Ill., 1991.

Dictionary of women's words: Cheris Kramarae and Paula Treichler, *Amazons, Blue-stockings, and Crones: A Feminist Dictionary*, 2d ed., Pandora, London, 1992.

Historical roots of feminist perspective: Lana Rakow and Cheris Kramarae (eds.), *The Revolution in Words: Righting Women, 1868–1871*, Routledge, New York, 1990.

Sexual harassment: Julia T. Wood (ed.), "Special Section—'Telling Our Stories': Sexual Harassment in the Communication Discipline," *Journal of Applied Communication Research*, Vol. 20, 1992, pp. 349–418.

PART EIGHT

Integration

ETHICAL THEORY

"Doing ethics" is hard. The complexity of ethical design making prompts some people to call the issue of moral choice a "can of worms." The tragic consequences of faulty judgments suggest the process might be more akin to sorting safely through a tangle of vipers. There was a scene in the film *Raiders of the Lost Ark* which showed Indiana Jones being lowered into a dark vault where a thick layer of slithering snakes covered the floor. The intrepid archaeologist discovered that the snakes momentarily retreated from the bright light of his torch, so he was able to secure a firm place to stand. Ethical theory offers solid ground for a moral stance. It is the light which can hold off the clamor of circumstance long enough to provide perspective on the situation.

The fantasy nature of the film was such that one could imagine Indiana Jones emerging from the cave with all the snakes straightened and bound together like sticks in a bundle of kindling wood. Although most people are suspicious of any ethical system which claims to pull together all moral quandaries into a single neatly wrapped package, normative ethical principles do offer the possibility of making "the crooked ways straight."

Chapter 38 surveys nine theories that offer guidance concerning ethical responsibility when conversing with others:

1. Epicurus' ethical egoism
2. Mill's utilitarianism
3. Kant's categorical imperative
4. Ross' self-evident duties
5. Rawls' justice as fairness
6. Aristotle's golden mean
7. Augustine's divine will
8. Buber's dialogic ethics
9. Gilligan's different voice

Each theory provides a distinct method of doing ethics. Although they disagree over what the ultimate maxim should be, advocates of the various theories agree that a consistent procedure for reaching moral decisions is preferable to relying on changing feelings or the whims of fleeting conscience. Passions of the moment often generate more heat than light, while the inner voice of conscience may be a reflection of cultural upbringing rather than a commitment to a well-thought-out position.

Levels of conscience can vary greatly from person to person. Some people with overdeveloped sensitivities require psychiatric care. Others with underdeveloped scruples end up in jail. What each person's conscience tells him or her can also change from day to day. As Bem's principle of self-attribution (see Chapter 11) and Festinger's minimal justification hypothesis (see Chapter 19) point out, inner beliefs are relatively fragile and can shift quickly to match or justify outward behavior. If ethical principles are to be a guide to future behavior rather than a rationalization of acts already performed, it's important for us to stake out our moral turf before we are thrust into a specific situation. That's the role of normative ethics.

The nine theories discussed in Chapter 38 concentrate on how best to discover the content of ethical behavior rather than focusing on *why* we should be good in the first place. The motivation to act ethically can be self-imposed, socially mandated, or divinely inspired. But regardless of the impetus, we need to have a way to determine the differ-

CALVIN AND HOBBES © 1989 WATTERSON. Dist. by Universal Press Syndicate.
Reprinted with permission. All rights reserved.

ence between right and wrong, good and bad, virtue and vice. Each of the principles represents a different vision of what constitutes the highest court of ethical appeal.

How can we decide which approach is best? Unlike behavioral theories which can be judged true or false on the basis of observable evidence, there are no metaphysical experiments by which to assess the validity of ethical first principles. Sissela Bok, author of the modern-day definitive work on lying, examines many of these positions by testing out their counsel in a number of "close call" communication situations.[1] Her ultimate criterion for accepting or rejecting a theory is whether or not she can live with the implications when the theory is consistently applied in all situations.

Chapter 38 presents four communication situations in which telling the truth *might* not be the moral thing to do. These dilemmas will give you a chance to evaluate the different ethical theories. Communication ethics is much broader than deciding where to draw the line on deception, so try not to be content with merely deciding how you would react in the four predicaments. If you find a single theory which helps you stand upright in all four cases, you're well on your way to adopting a standard of ethical conduct. Familiarity with classical ethical theory will give you some confidence that there are women and men of goodwill who share your conviction.

Communication Ethics

Stacy Murray is a communications major at a large state university. Last week the professor in her required senior seminar presented a variety of ethical theories for student consideration. Stacy had always regarded philosophical discussions as a waste of time, but after today's experiences she's not so sure. During the last twelve hours she has faced the following four situations in which lying seemed an attractive alternative:

1. The department chairman came in at the end of Stacy's morning TV production class to gather students' anonymously written evaluations of their instructor, who is under review. Stacy likes the young man who is the instructor and knows that he cares about students, but as a teacher of media technique he is hopelessly disorganized and inept. Should she ignore or downplay her instructor's defects so that he won't be in danger of losing his job, or should she tell the truth?

2. During a quick lunch in the student union, Stacy was approached by a student she knows slightly from her senior seminar. He told her he headed a group of students tutoring inner-city children every Tuesday night and asked her to volunteer. Stacy has always thought of this student as a bit of a jerk, and she is wary of being in the city after dark. Because she doesn't want to voice either of these feelings, Stacy is tempted merely to say that she is too busy.

3. The telephone rang while Stacy was having dinner with her roommate, Michelle, in their apartment. As Stacy reached to pick up the phone, Michelle blurted out, "If that's Sean, tell him I'm not here." Of course the next words Stacy heard were, "Hi, this is Sean. Is Michelle there?" As unfair as her roommate's plea might be, Stacy knows that a truthful answer will lead to a fight with Michelle.

4. When Stacy got back from studying at the library that evening, the graduate student in the next apartment asked her over for a beer. She accepted. Ordinarily Harold is a nice guy, but that night he was acting belligerent because he'd had too much to drink. When he

started talking about taking his car out for a drive, Stacy was able to sneak his keys off the desk and put them in her pocket. A few minutes later he asked accusingly, "Did you take my keys?"

Ethics has to do with the gray areas in our lives. When moral decisions are black and white, knowing what we should do is easy. We may not live up to our convictions all the time, but there's no question in our mind what we *ought* to do. I've described four situations in Stacy's life which many people would regard as close calls. The scenarios cover a broad range of issues involved in the question of verbal deception. The option of no response becomes increasingly difficult with each successive story. Lack of candor in Stacy's daytime dilemmas could be considered shading the truth, whereas the alternative to honesty in both evening situations is a boldfaced lie. The first two dilemmas are forced upon Stacy by the actions of others, while the last two are caused in part by her own actions. (She didn't have to answer the phone or pocket the keys.) It's also obvious that some of the situations are more serious—have the greater potential for harm—than others.

The ethical theories outlined in this chapter offer guidance to Stacy on how to communicate with integrity in each situation. All but the final theory fit into one of three distinctive approaches to moral decision making. The first two theories look at the consequences of behavior. Can a lie end up doing good or preventing harm? The next three theories focus on the rightness of an act regardless of whether or not it benefits the people involved. Is falsehood ever fair or just? Is it always our duty to be honest? The next group of three theories concentrates on the inner motives and character traits that make a person moral. Is the desire to tell the truth a virtue? The final theory raises the possibility that men and women could (and perhaps should) have separate ethical standards. As we work through the various theories, see which one makes the most sense to you. What theory gives you the greatest clarity as to whether or not Stacy is meeting her ethical responsibilities?

ETHICAL EGOISM: EPICURUS

Cynics maintain that people care only about themselves, that everybody is looking out for number one. Ethical egoists say that's the way it *ought* to be. Everyone should promote his or her own self-interest. The boundaries of an egoist's ethical system include only one person.

Writing a few years after Aristotle's death, Epicurus defined the good life as getting as much pleasure as possible: "I spit on the noble and its idle admirers when it contains no element of pleasure."[1] Although his position is often associated with the adage "eat, drink, and be merry," Epicurus actually emphasized the passive pleasures of friendship, good digestion and, above all, the absence of pain. He cautioned that "no pleasure is in itself evil, but the things which produce certain pleasures entail annoyances many times greater than the pleasures themselves."[2] The Greek philosopher put lying in that category.

Epicurus wrote that the wise person is prepared to lie if there is no risk of detection, but that we can never be certain our falsehoods won't be discovered. He would appreciate Stacy's desire to avoid embarrassment for herself in the student union and to keep the peace with Michelle by lying to Sean. But what if both of them find out later? As for the ugly scene with a drunken Harold, she'd do better never to have gotten involved.

A few other philosophers have echoed the Epicurean call for selfish concern. Thomas Hobbes described life as "nasty, brutish and short," and advocated political trade-offs that would gain a measure of security. Adam Smith, the spiritual father of capitalism, advised every person to seek his or her own profit. Nietzsche announced the death of God and stated that the noble soul has reverence for itself. Egoist writer Ayn Rand dedicated her novel *The Fountainhead* to "the *exaltation* of man's self-esteem and the *sacredness* of his happiness on earth."³

Modern society needs no encouragement to seek pleasure. Bobby McFerrin's egoistic advice, "Don't worry, be happy," won a Grammy award by capturing the spirit of our age. Of course, the advice of McFerrin, Rand, or Epicurus is suspect. If their counsel consistently reflects their beliefs, their words are spoken for their own benefit, not ours.

Despite the pervasive nature of egoism, most ethical thinkers denounce the selfishness of the principle as morally repugnant. How can one embrace a

"'Honesty is the best policy.' O.K.! Now, what's the <u>second-best</u> policy?"

Drawing by Dana Fradon; © 1978 The New Yorker Magazine, Inc.

philosophy which advocates terrorism as long as it brings joy to the terrorist? When the egoistic pleasure principle is compared to the life of someone like Mother Teresa, ethical egoism seems to be no ethic at all. The egoist would say, however, that the Nobel Peace Prize-winner is leading an ethical life because she takes pleasure in helping the poor. If charity becomes a burden, she should stop.

UTILITARIANISM: JOHN STUART MILL

British philosopher and economist John Stuart Mill shared the egoist's concern for outcomes, regarding an act as good or bad depending on its consequences. He applauded the Epicurean view that pleasure in life is the only consequence that matters. But Mill took great exception to Epicurus' preoccupation with his own pleasure:

> As between his own happiness and that of others, utilitarianism requires him to be as strictly impartial as a disinterested and benevolent spectator. In the golden rule of Jesus of Nazareth, we read the complete spirit of the ethics of utility. "To do as you would be done by," and "to love your neighbor as yourself," constitute the ideal perfection of utilitarian morality.[4]

Mill urged readers to seek the greatest happiness for the greatest number.

Utilitarian morality requires a hedonistic calculus similar to the moral transformations described by social exchange theory (see Chapter 16). Picture Stacy staring at the blank teacher-evaluation form as she tries to compute the positives and negatives of telling the truth. At least she has a few moments to think through consequences before writing her thoughts, a luxury she won't have that evening when the phone rings at dinner or when she is challenged by Harold.

She imagines that her instructor will be hurt by an honest evaluation; he may even lose his job. She worries that he might read the forms and recognize her writing. On the positive side, students for years to come would be happy to have a better instructor. Stacy has to balance one man's deep hurt against the smaller joys that many students would feel. Utilitarianism permits one person to be sacrificed for the good of the group, even if punishment is undeserved.

The example points up a number of problems with judging the utility of an act. Mill would ask us to cast a wide net when computing pleasure and pain, but it's impossible to figure out all the consequences ahead of time. Stacy may overlook the long-term effect that lack of candor may have upon the larger society. Although white lies and half-truths are a social lubricant, continual soft-pedaling on classroom evaluations can erode administrative confidence in student opinion. Then again, the sting of truth may cause her teacher to seek a vocation where his people-oriented skills will be highly rewarded.

There's no doubt that the principle of utility is difficult to apply in specific cases. Stacy would find it hard not to give an extra force to her own outcomes, unintentionally sliding back to an egoistic mentality. But there are ways to compensate for self-serving bias. Sissela Bok recommends adopting a "principle of veracity" which gives an initial negative weight to lies.[5] The administration of a utilitarian ethic may get complicated, but the ideal of caring about what happens to all people has a long-standing place in ethical discussion.

THE CATEGORICAL IMPERATIVE: IMMANUEL KANT

German philosopher Immanuel Kant took an entirely different approach to ethics than did Epicurus or Mill. They cared about consequences; he was concerned with the demands of reason and the moral law. They regarded an act as good or bad according to how things turned out. Kant heads the list of philosophers who define an act as right or wrong—regardless of the outcome. Kant's ethical stance is the model for Kohlberg's highest level of moral development. His condemnation of any type of lie is total:

> Truthfulness in statements which cannot be avoided is the formal duty of an individual to everyone, however great may be the disadvantage accruing to himself or another.[6]

Stacy may be able to dodge the truth by not turning in a class evaluation, refusing to answer the telephone, or telling her unattractive classmate only of her fear of getting mugged. However, confronted with Harold's direct question and penetrating stare, Kant would say that she has a moral obligation to tell the truth ("Yes, I took your keys"). Some would suggest that Harold forfeits the right to a straight answer by his drunken condition; Kant would hear none of it. Harold doesn't cease being human because his behavior is unpleasant. Stacy's lying to Harold would violate human dignity, both his and hers.

If Stacy were an egoist, she would focus on her fear that an honest answer might result in Harold's slapping her around. If she were a utilitarian, she would also worry that when Harold hears the truth, he will grab the keys and drive off into the night. Perhaps she should lie to keep someone from being killed. But Kant regarded violations of ethical duty as a fate worse than death, no matter whose life is at stake. In the words of a sports-minded colleague who teaches ethics, "Kant plays ethical hardball without a mitt."

Kant came to this absolutist position through the logic of his *categorical imperative*, a term which means "duty without exception." He stated the categorical imperative as a universal law: "Act only on that maxim which you can will to become a universal law."[7] In effect, he said we should ask the question, "What if everybody did that?" If we can't live with the answer, we have a solemn duty not to do the deed.

Stacy needs to ask herself the question, "What if everybody lied?" The answer of course is that if some words are false, all words may be false. Language is stripped of any consistent meaning. Promises would not be kept, trust would disintegrate, anarchy would reign. Since no rational being can live in a state like that, Kant's verdict is clear. Lying is always wrong! Case closed. Kant doesn't waffle on moral issues.

SELF-EVIDENT DUTIES: W. D. ROSS

British philosopher W. D. Ross agreed with Kant in one respect—ethics is a matter of doing our duty. In 1930 he published *The Right and the Good*, which recognized six basic duties:

1. Fidelity—to do no harm to others
2. Reparation—to make amends to those we have hurt
3. Gratitude—to repay those who have helped us
4. Justice—to treat people as well as they deserve
5. Beneficence—to help others when we can
6. Self-improvement—to better oneself

Kant's categorical imperative equates duty with right reason. We are obliged to do what reason dictates. Ross said we don't need a rational method to discover duty—right actions are self-evident to anyone who desires to be good. He regarded the six duties as commonsense morality that we know by intuition. His assumption gains credence when we compare the duties he listed with the Four-Way Test of Rotary International:

Is it the truth?

Is it fair to all concerned?

Will it build goodwill and better friendships?

Will it be beneficial to all concerned?

Kant claimed that all duty is absolute. He couldn't conceive of a situation where universal obligations would fundamentally conflict. Ross, on the other hand, regarded duties as conditional. He could imagine times of tragic moral choice when to fulfill one obligation on his list above is to violate another. In those cases people should act so as to fulfill their higher obligation. The six duties are ranked in order of importance. The ones higher up are "most stringent" and take precedence over those lower down.

Ross puts telling the truth at the top of the list. Whenever we enter into conversation with another, there's an implied promise that we won't lie. Stacy wasn't forced to sign up for the TV production class, talk to the fellow at lunch, answer the phone, or walk into Harold's apartment. Communication carries a "trailing duty" of fidelity.

Stacy is caught in the middle between Sean and Michelle. It's true that she has a duty to help Michelle when she can (number 5) and to show gratitude for past favors her roommate has done (number 3), but the more binding duty to avoid hurting Sean (number 1) takes precedence. Michelle might protest that a white lie would help rather than hurt everyone involved, but Ross would say that in our hearts, we know that's not right. There's really no way to argue with an intuitionist.

Most ethical thinkers are bothered that Ross seems to appeal to sentiment rather than reason. And cultural relativists scoff at the idea that people have a universal inborn standard of right and wrong. For example, ethical egoism seems little more than a concern for personal face restoration that springs from an individualistic, low-context culture. By the same token, utilitarianism parallels the concern for face-giving that is typical of a collectivistic, high-context culture.

In response to these criticisms, intuitionists use a "test of publicity" to make sure they aren't being guided by individual whim. One president of a Fortune 500 company described the test this way: "I try to act as if everything I do will be published on the front page of *The Wall Street Journal*. Most likely it will." Readers can generally agree on what's right and wrong.

JUSTICE AS FAIRNESS: JOHN RAWLS

John Rawls' theory of justice doesn't depend on intuition to determine what is right. The modern American philosopher assumes that, given a fair procedure for reaching a decision, rational people would agree to give each other equal amounts of liberty—as much freedom as possible. But differences in status, power, wealth, and intelligence give some privileged members of society unequal clout when the moral ground rules of society are hammered out. As both Stuart Hall and Cheris Kramarae suggested, the "oughts" of life get crafted to serve the vested interests of those who represent the dominant ideology (see Chapters 30 and 37).

In order to discover ethical rules that would promote freedom for everybody, Rawls creates the fiction of an ethical discussion held before we enter the world. Everyone would be required to agree on binding rules of behavior before they had any idea of which place in society they would occupy. It's his way of defining an ethical system that won't leave anyone out. Rules could not be tailor-made to serve selfish ends because it's hard to be self-serving when you don't know which "self" you'll be.

"I assume that all parties are situated behind a veil of ignorance," Rawls begins, and then goes on to describe people's fear that they might be poor, powerless, or oppressed. Freedom without real opportunity would be meaningless. Behind the veil of ignorance, rational people would craft rules of justice that would protect themselves in case fate were to put them at the bottom of the societal heap. The disadvantaged need justice. Those on top can take care of themselves.

Rawls' theory of justice protects people who are in a "one-down" position (see Rogers and Farace, who are discussed in Chapter 15). He would assume that Stacy has an ethical obligation to use her gifts to help raise the reading level of kids in the underclass. She is wrong to dismiss the request, and lying about her reasons merely compounds the injustice. Since the force of a lie is more easily sustained by those who have power, ethical rules developed behind the veil of ignorance would maintain equality by condemning deceit.

Perhaps Rawls is asking us to do the impossible. Despite a willingness to pretend being born among the downtrodden, our ethical sensitivities may be tainted by being brought up in a class of privilege, in a country of power. Even in our imagination, it's hard to go behind the veil. But Rawls' idea of the greatest benefit for the least advantaged seems to offer the strong points of utilitarianism without sharing the drawbacks. Rules devised behind a true veil of ignorance would be scrupulously fair.

THE GOLDEN MEAN: ARISTOTLE

The theories discussed up to this point are concerned with ethical *behavior*. Does an *act* produce good or bad? Is it right or wrong to *do* a certain deed? This focus undoubtedly springs from our western bias toward action. Many ancient Greek and eastern philosophers have spoken of ethics in terms of character rather than conduct, inner disposition instead of outer behavior. Hebrew and Christian scriptures praise "the pure in heart."

Aristotle took the Greek admiration for moderation and elevated it into a theory of virtue. When Barry Goldwater was selected as the Republican party's nominee for president in 1964, he boldly stated: "Extremism in the defense of liberty is no vice . . . moderation in the pursuit of justice is not virtue."[8] Aristotle would have disagreed. He assumed virtue always stands between two vices.

Consider the issue of risk taking. At one extreme is cowardliness—the cringing fear that comes from paying too much attention to danger. On the other extreme is foolhardiness—a rash disregard of possible tragic results if things turn bad. The virtue of courage occupies the middle ground. The same analysis holds for matters of money, sex, and power.

Extreme	Golden Mean	Extreme
Stinginess	Generosity	Wastefulness
Frigidity	Sensuality	Lustfulness
Weakness	Assertiveness	Aggressiveness

Aristotle sees wisdom in the person who avoids excess on either side. Moderation is best: virtue develops habits that seek to walk the middle way. He calls that path the "golden mean."

In regard to communication, Aristotle held that "falsehood is in itself mean and culpable, and truth noble and full of praise."[9] This doesn't suggest that a person must voice every unspoken thought. The golden mean for Stacy might look like this:

Extreme	Golden Mean	Extreme
Lie	Truthful statements	Tell all
Secrecy	Self-disclosure	Soul-baring

Stacy can (1) express reservations about her instructor's ability without being cruel, (2) admit her fears but not tear down the fellow who is doing the commendable task of tutoring, and (3) tell Sean on the phone that this is not a good time to talk to Michelle. Some would regard this moderate approach as "peace at any price" or "don't rock the boat." Aristotle calls temperate behavior a virtue.

DIVINE WILL: AUGUSTINE

Augustine said, "Love God and do what you will." Rather than encourage license, the statement reflects the fifth-century Catholic bishop's belief that people who truly love God will desire to bring all their actions into line with His will. Augustine drew a distinction between symbolic citizenship in the city of Babylon and the city of Jerusalem. Residents of the former are lovers of pleasure, the world, and themselves. Inhabitants of the latter are lovers of God who desire to submit to His law. "Let each one question himself as to what he loveth," Augustine wrote, "and he shall find of which [city] he is a citizen."[10]

Contemporary adherents to divine will morality may be less metaphorical, but they are equally convinced that ethics is a branch of theology. Along with the players in the rock opera *Godspell*, they pray the centuries-old prayer to

> See Thee more clearly,
> Love Thee more dearly,
> Follow Thee more nearly,
> Day by day.[11]

Augustine believed that those who sincerely desire to follow God will have no difficulty discovering His will for their lives. The Bible presents the law of the land for residents in the city of God. Speech was given to humans by God so that they could make their thoughts known to each other.

> To use speech, then, for the purpose of deception, and not for its appointed end, is a sin. Nor, are we to suppose that there is any lie that is not a sin because it is sometimes possible, by telling a lie to do service to another.[12]

The Ninth Commandment is clear—"You shall not bear false witness against your neighbor."

On the basis of his essay "On Lying," Augustine would urge Stacy to tell the truth in each situation, no matter how painful the human consequences. Unlike Kant, Augustine does recognize gradations in the seriousness of lies. Lies aimed to help others aren't as bad as those which aim to hurt. Deception to keep Harold off the road would be less wrong than false charges against Stacy's instructor made for the purpose of getting him fired. But all lies hurt our relationship with God. "If any lies . . . steal upon us, they should seek not to be justified but to be pardoned."[13]

There are two obvious questions to be posed to the person who takes a divine will position: (1) Are you sure you have the right god? (2) Are you certain you know what that higher authority wants? The *Bible*, the *Koran*, the *Tao-te Ching* aren't always explicit about what is pleasing in every situation. Even devout believers can disagree about what Stacy should do in each case. But there is general agreement among believers of various faiths that obligation to God parallels the guidelines summarized in the Hebrew scriptures:

> He has showed you, O man, what is good;
> and what does the Lord require of you
> but to do justice, and to love kindness,
> and to walk humbly with your God.[14]

DIALOGIC ETHICS: MARTIN BUBER

Martin Buber was a Soviet Jewish philosopher and theologian who immigrated to Palestine prior to World War II and died in 1965. His ethical approach focuses on relationships between people rather than on moral codes of conduct. Often referred to as "Kant with a heart," Buber used poetic language to convey the importance of our attitude toward another person: "Each should regard his partner as the very one he is."

Buber believed that true dialogue between persons is the essence of ethics. He constantly referred to the "between," the "interhuman," the "transaction," and the "mutuality" available through dialogue. Monologue creates an I-It relationship that treats the other as a thing. Dialogue creates an I-Thou relationship in which the other person is seen as created in the image of God. He agreed with Kant that people are ends, not means. We have an ethical responsibility to use things and value people rather than the other way around.

Buber used the image of the "narrow ridge" to picture the tension of dialogic living. On one side of the moral path is the gulf of subjectivism where there are no standards. On the other side is the plateau of absolutism where rules are etched in stone: "On the far side of the subjective, on this side of the objective, on the narrow ridge, where I and Thou meet, there is the realm of the Between."[15] "Living the narrow-ridge philosophy requires a life of personal and interpersonal concern, which is likely to generate a more complicated existence than that of the egoist or the selfless martyr."[16] Like Bakhtin's dialectical tension that is the "deep structure" of interpersonal relationships (see Chapter 17), Buber's narrow ridge is not a golden mean that rejects the extremes. Dialogic relationships recognize and embrace opposites: "Life is usually lived in the midst of the unity of contraries."

Although a dialogic ethic doesn't tell Stacy what she should do, Buber did say that people who desire to live uprightly with each other will put aside concerns for creating a favorable impression or sustaining an image. Truth comes from the spontaneous transparency of self with others, whereas warped communication puts all its energy into "seeming." If Stacy desires genuine dialogue, she will concentrate instead on "being." This means an honest disclosure of her anxiety about tutoring in the ghetto, a sensitive confession of her prior prejudice toward the student who asked her to tutor, and a willingness to listen to his hopes and fears. An I-Thou relationship with Harold involves discarding any sense of superiority she might feel because of his condition.

Buber may have called for moral heroics that simply can't be sustained in casual relationships. Consider the traffic jam which would result from an attempt to have an I-Thou relationship with a tollbooth collector. But his dialogic stance is the forerunner of Rogers' principle of congruence (see Chapter 3) and Maslow's self-actualized human being (see Chapter 10). Buber's emphasis on the person-in-relationship elevates open communication to a virtue.

A DIFFERENT VOICE: CAROL GILLIGAN

Carol Gilligan is professor of education in the Harvard Graduate School of Education. Her 1982 book, *In a Different Voice,* presents a theory of moral development which claims that, when they confront moral dilemmas, women tend to think and speak in an ethical voice different from that of men. Gilligan's view of gender differences parallels Tannen's analysis of men as wanting independence, women as desiring human connection (see Chapter 36). Gilligan is convinced that most men seek autonomy and think of moral maturity in terms of *justice.* She's equally certain that women desire to be linked with others and regard their ultimate ethical responsibility as one of *care.*

Gilligan says that men who are serious about ethics tend to echo the call of Kant, Ross, and Rawls to fulfill one's duty, be fair to others, and do the right thing. If it was Stan rather than Stacy who faced the four moral dilemmas posed at the start of the chapter, he'd likely make his ethical choices on the basis of personal rights, group obligations, or universal laws. For example, he would probably conclude that he ought to be honest on the class evaluation form regardless of the consequences for the teacher.

Gilligan contrasts women who care with men who are fair on the basis of the quantity and quality of feminine relationships. Individual rights, equality before the law, fair play, a square deal—all these ethical goals can be pursued without personal ties to others. Justice is impersonal. But sensitivity to others, loyalty, self-sacrifice, and peacemaking all reflect interpersonal involvement. Care comes from connection. Stacy can't respond to demands for the truth about the location of her roommate or the car keys of Harold without considering the responsibility she feels to prevent pain and alleviate suffering. She'll probably value Mill's concern for others' welfare and Buber's insistence on genuine I-Thou relationships more than insistence on abstract justice.

Although Gilligan's theory is more descriptive than proscriptive, the underlying assumption is that *the way things are* reflects *the way things ought to be*. Most ethical theorists are disturbed at the idea of a double standard—justice from some, care from others. Moral philosophy has never suggested different ethics for different groups. Every other theory covered in this chapter assumes a moral standard that applies to everyone. But readers of both sexes report that Gilligan's theory resonates with their personal experience. She even holds out the possibility that the voice of justice and the voice of care could eventually blend into a single human sound. If so, the result might be a caring law that resembles the Golden Rule—"Do unto others as you would have them do unto you."

DIFFERENT METHODS FOR DISCOVERING THE SAME TRUTH

By this time your eyes may glaze over at the variety of approaches available to those who are willing to consider ethical responsibility. Students typically have one of three reactions to the multiple options presented by ethical theorists. One response is to throw up their hands in dismay and vow not to worry about what is good, right, or noble. That's unfortunate. Even if we decide not to worry about ethics, we still are involved with ethics every day. Each choice we make has a moral component. Choosing not to select an ethical first principle is a decision to let our actions be ruled by whim or passion. Just as computers have a default drive that kicks in unless an alternative mode is chosen, so our moral choices seem to be driven by an egoistic search for pleasure unless we consciously opt for another ethical path.

A second response to the diversity of ethical theory is to pick and choose separate approaches to fit different interactions. Stacy might take an egoistic stance when required to fill out an evaluation form, adopt a utilitarian approach when asked to be a tutor, react with a Kantian inflexibility in response to her roommate's request to lie, and employ a dialogic attitude toward Harold. This pick-and-choose approach to ethical conduct seems like the medieval assertion that any practice was legitimate as long as one could find a single priest to condone it. A situational approach to morality defeats the purpose of having normative principles that are designed to provide guidance regardless of the circumstances.

The third possible response is to select one of these time-honored ways of making ethical decisions, and then live according to its dictates when you face hard choices in life. Perhaps you are bothered by the idea that two or more people can in good faith select different ethical standards. If so, remember that a basic assumption made by Mead, Maslow, Geertz, Walter Fisher, and others is that human beings are different from animals. Isn't it more human to live an "examined life" of choice rather than merely reacting to the demands of instinct? Also, consider how you would respond to adherents of each of these moral positions. Wouldn't you rather converse with almost any of them rather than with someone who claimed not to be guided by any moral principle?

In spite of their varied methods for determining where to draw the line on deception, the common counsel of each of these theorists is that Stacy should not lie. This is not to suggest that each theory is equally valid or that it makes no difference which principle we adopt as our highest court of appeal. But aligning ourselves with men and women of goodwill who have subscribed to a consistent ethical stance increases the probability that we will communicate with integrity.

QUESTIONS TO SHARPEN YOUR FOCUS

1. What is the main difference between *ethical egoism* and *utilitarianism*? Kant's *categorical imperative* and Ross' *self-evident duties*? Aristotle's *golden mean* and Buber's *dialogic ethics*?

2. Can you conceive of an action that would be *loving* but *unjust*? How about behavior that is *unloving* but *just*? Could a person act in both a loving and just manner, yet still not be *virtuous*?

3. Some of the ethical theories require a high level of mental work to figure out what is *good, right,* or *virtuous.* Others involve little or no *cognitive effort.* Which ones are "no-brainers"?

4. There's a natural link between some ethical positions and theories presented earlier in the book. What ethical theory ties in with Rogers' *existential theory*? Thibaut and Kelley's *social exchange theory*? Hall's *critical theory*?

A SECOND LOOK

Recommended resource: Sissela Bok, *Lying: Moral Choice in Public and Private Life,* Pantheon, New York, 1978.

Doing ethics: Clifford Christians, Kim Rotzoll, and Mark Fackler, "Ethical Foundations and Perspectives," in *Media Ethics,* 3d ed., Longman, New York, 1991, Chap. 1.

Ethical egoism: Edward Regis, "What Is Ethical Egoism?" *Ethics,* Vol. 91, 1980, pp. 50–62.

Utilitarianism: John Stuart Mill, *A System of Logic,* J. W. Parker, London, 1843, Book VI, Chapter XII.

Categorical imperative: Immanuel Kant, *Groundwork of the Metaphysic of Morals,* H. J. Paton (trans.), Harper Torchbooks, New York, 1964, pp. 69–71, 82–89.

Self-evident duties; W. D. Ross, *The Right and the Good,* Oxford University, Oxford, 1930, pp. 1–47.

Veil of ignorance: John Rawls, *A Theory of Justice,* Harvard University, Cambridge, Mass., 1971, pp. 136–142.

Golden mean: "Nicomachean Ethics," in *Introduction to Aristotle,* Richard McKeon (ed.), Random House, New York, 1947, pp. 331–347.

Divine will: Augustine, "On Lying" and "Against Lying," *Treatises on Various*

Subjects, Vols. 14 and 16, R. J. Deferrari (ed.), Catholic University, New York, 1952.

Dialogic ethics: Martin Buber, *Between Man and Man*, Routledge & Kegan Paul, London, 1947, pp. 1–39.

A Different Voice: Carol Gilligan, *In a Different Voice: Psychological Theory and Women's Development*, Harvard University, Cambridge, Mass., 1982.

Overview of communication ethics: Richard Johannesen, *Ethics in Human Communication*, 3d ed., Waveland Press, Prospect Heights, Ill., 1990.

COMMUNICATION THEORY

Friends who know that I've written a book about communication theory often ask which theory is the best. Although I have my personal favorites, I find myself unable to come up with a satisfying answer. I take comfort in Karl Weick's assurance that there are inevitable trade-offs in any theoretical statement. I am also convinced that his idea of categorizing theories according to the compromises their authors make is a helpful way to keep us from becoming too impatient if we spot a flaw in their construction. Creating theory isn't easy.

Weick introduces the dilemma that empirically oriented theorists face by citing University of Alberta psychologist Warren Thorngate's Postulate of Commensurate Complexity: "It is impossible for a theory of social behavior to be simultaneously general, simple or parsimonious and accurate."[1] The term *commensurate complexity* refers to the necessity of tacking on qualifications so that a

theory can account for special circumstances. Thorngate expands on his postulate:

> The more general a simple theory, the less accurate it will be in predicting specifics. . . . The more accurate a simple theory . . . , the less able it will be to account for something more than the most simple or contrived situation. . . . General and accurate theories cannot be [simple].[2]

The clock face in Figure CT.1 shows how Weick portrays the relationship of the three ideals. An hour hand pointing at two o'clock would indicate that a theory which holds true under most conditions will be, of necessity, very complicated. Because of its intricate description of attitudes as multiple latitudes, Sherif's social judgment theory comes to mind (see Chapter 18).

Sherif could have chosen to advance or retreat the hour hand in order to reduce his theory's complexity, but only at the expense

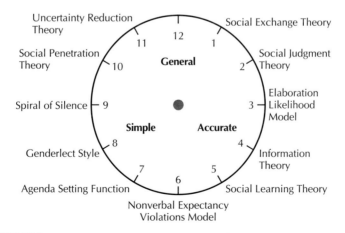

FIGURE CT.1
Classification of Selected Theories (Based on Weick's Model of Theoretical Tradeoffs.)

of generalizability or accuracy. He might have elected to limit social judgment theory's application to issues in which listeners are highly ego-involved, thus doing away with the messy problem of latitudes of noncommitment. That kind of four-o'clock treatment would be somewhat simpler and have tremendous predictive power. But Sherif was unwilling to limit the theory's usefulness to situations where attitudes were firmly anchored.

Alternatively, Sherif could have moved counterclockwise away from complexity by describing attitudes as a single point on a line, as many persuasion theorists do. A simple ten-o'clock theory could still be applied in most situations, but obviously Sherif believed its predictions would be wrong too much of the time. So, because accuracy and generalizability had high priority for Sherif, he opted for a complex theory.

In order to appreciate Weick's point about the trade-offs that confront a communication theorist, you have to be able to tell theoretical time. I'll make one circuit of the clock so that you can be clear about what the numbers represent. The placement of specific theories on the clock face reflects my evaluation of the hard priority decisions their authors have made.

I stated in Chapter 3 that a good scientific theory is useful. Since a theory placed at twelve o'clock could be applied in every situation, it would more than fulfill that requirement. But Weick suggests that there are no completely context-free approaches to social behavior. David Mortenson, a University of Wisconsin communication professor, agrees: "Communication never takes place in a vacuum; it is not a 'pure' process devoid of background or situational overtones."[3]

By giving up the fiction that their theory applies across the board, theorists at a two-o'clock position gain accuracy. A two-o'clock approach enlarges questions, adds condi-

tions, and recognizes multiple causes for the same behavior. Whereas theories which cluster near the top of the dial feature high relevancy, a clockwise shift risks being obscure in order to more accurately reflect the complexity of human behavior.

The theorist at four o'clock is pure scientist—stating, testing, and rejecting null hypotheses. Chapter 3 claimed that a good scientific theory is testable. The four-o'clock emphasis on accuracy looks for explanations that pass the test. The public often responds with, "So what?"

Description at the bottom of the dial is "context specific." When asked to predict future trends, a six-o'clock theorist responds, "It depends . . ." Quantitative research which originates here is usually run in the lab under highly contrived conditions. Qualitative research at the six-o'clock position is an interpretive collage of case study, grounded theory, participant observation, and thick description. The data are rich, but its application in other situations is limited.

Eight-o'clock theories collapse data into a single conclusion or a short list of principles which are easy to grasp. Daryl Bem offered his theory of self-perception (self-attribution) as a simpler alternative to Festinger's cognitive dissonance explanation. Like other theorists who operate from this stance, Bem is open to the charge of reductionism.

I find that students are often attracted to the ten-o'clock location on Weick's theoretical clock. It combines simplicity with relevance. Knowledge is distilled into easy-to-remember aphorisms or vivid metaphors. Intuitive hunches and inner feelings gain dignity when cast as speculative theory which is portable across situations. Of course, ten-o'clock inquiry may elevate intriguing error to a position of truth, but Weick doesn't regard the danger as necessarily fatal:

> All explanations, no matter how bizarre, are likely to be valid part of the time. It's simply

FIGURE CT.2
Anne Elk (John Cleese) Describes Her Brontosaurus Theory to Interviewer Graham Chapman on *Monty Python's Flying Circus.*

up to the originator of the idea to be smart enough or lucky enough to find those sites where the theory is accurately supported.[4]

Weick's clock-face representation of Thorngate's postulate explains why no approach in this book can avoid criticism. Each theory has at least one "soft spot" or Achilles' heel. The pursuit of two virtues is always at the expense of the third, but as Weick maintains, two out of three isn't bad. He says that theorists who try to do everything usually end up accomplishing nothing. The results are trivial, bland, and boring—easy targets for those who want to poke fun at academic pretention.

The Monty Python parody of theorizing is a case in point. The comedy troupe's brontosaurus sketch is a satire of theorists who are overly impressed with their ideas (see Figure CT.2). Appearing on a television talk show,

Anne Elk proudly presents her theory which tries to do it all:

> My theory that belongs to me . . . goes as follows and begins now. All brontosauruses are thin at one end, much thicker in the middle and then thin again at the far end. That is my theory, it is mine, and belongs to me and I own it.[5]

The theory is certainly accurate, undeniably simple, and general to the extent that it applies to every beast of that type. It is also silly. Weick recommends that theorists intentionally select their preferred position on the face of the clock, and then "relax gracefully" with the problems that go with the territory.

Although Thorndike's postulate describes the compromises inherent in scientific theories, it's not hard to imagine theorists in the humanities facing similar trade-offs. Consider two theories in the book that investigate

"For heaven's sake, Harry! Can't you just relax and enjoy art, music, religion, literature, drama and history, without trying to tie it all together?"

Reproduced by permission of Punch.

gender and communication within a society. Neither Clifford Geertz's cultural approach to gender roles in Bali nor Cheris Kramarae's version of muted group theory are able to fulfill all the requirements of a good humanistic theory discussed in Chapter 3.

Geertz's thick description of men's fight for status at a Balinese cock fight strikes a responsive chord in males around the world. The imagery he uses as he tells the story of their risky wagers has great aesthetic appeal for readers of both sexes. But the inviting prose Geertz uses and the community of agreement that he generates preclude any attempt to change Indonesian society. A reformer he is not.

Geertz's weakness is Kramarae's strength. Feminist theory is meant to challenge the unequal distribution of power perpetuated by male control of the dominant modes of expression. Although Kramarae is high on intent to reform, she doesn't expect a broad spectrum of men who hold power to agree with her analysis. As for aesthetics, abuses of power aren't pretty.

We see, therefore, that both humanistic and scientific theories involve inevitable trade-offs that always prevent a theory from being everything we might like it to be. A certain forebearance on our part is appropriate. The final chapter ahead presents a brief review of the thirty-four theories described in the book, then separates them according to their basic orientation, and finally seeks a way to pull them into a unified whole. If you should find this attempt at integration not totally satisfying, I'll hope for the same tolerance you extend to the theorists. Confusion doesn't yield easily to clarity.

CHAPTER 39

Order out of Chaos

The first goal of this final chapter is to compare and contrast the theories covered in the book according to their basic assumptions—to make order out of chaos. The classification I propose will make sense only if you are able to recall the central thesis of each theory presented in Chapters 4 through 37. The following abstracts may help you call to mind material that you read earlier in the term.

There's a danger, of course, in trying to capture the gist of a theory in only a few lines. Each chapter is already a condensation and interpretation of the author's original work. By further collapsing the content into two or three sentences (a digest of a digest), I may not do justice to the complex truth or the subtle meaning the theorist has described. I've tried to remain faithful to key phrases that the theorists employ, but the summaries aren't substitutes for the fuller descriptions and extended examples that have gone before. Remember that the capsule statements are designed merely to jog your memory in preparation for the synthesis ahead. I'll recap the theories in the same order that I have presented them.

A BRIEF REVIEW

Messages

Shannon and Weaver's information theory: In a source-channel-receiver model of signal transmission, information is defined as the opportunity to reduce uncertainty. Noise cuts the information-carrying capacity of the channel between transmitter and receiver. The way to offset noise is through increased redundancy.

Richards' meaning of meaning: Misunderstanding takes place when people assume a word has a direct connection with its referent. Words don't mean; people mean. A common past reduces misunderstanding. Definition, metaphor, feedforward, and Basic English are partial linguistic remedies for a lack of shared experience.

Reproduced by permission of Punch.

Pearce and Cronen's coordinated management of meaning: People in conversation consistently (1) achieve coherence by providing multiple frames of reference for their environment and experience, (2) coordinate their actions by negotiating rules for their activities, and (3) experience mystery as they remind themselves that there is more to life than mere factuality.

Burgoon's nonverbal expectancy violations model: Violating another person's proxemic expectations can be a superior strategy to conformity. Because distance violations are highly ambiguous, rewarding communicators can enhance their attractiveness, credibility, and persuasiveness by coming too close or staying too far away. Negatively valenced communicators should maintain a distance that others consider appropriate.

Barthes' semiotics: The significant visual sign systems of a culture affirm the status quo by suggesting that the world as it is today is natural, inevitable, and eternal. Myth makers do this by co-opting neutral denotative signs to become signifiers without historical grounding in second-order connotative semiotic systems.

Intrapersonal Communication

Mead's symbolic interactionism: Symbolic naming creates the objectified self. People develop multiple looking-glass selves by taking the role of the other.

Each of us has a significant impact on which of those multiple selves others are able to sustain.

Maslow's hierarchy of needs: People are motivated by needs which call out for satisfaction in a set order:

$$\text{Physiological} \rightarrow \text{Safety} \rightarrow \text{Belongingness} \rightarrow \text{Esteem}$$

A prepotent need fulfilled no longer motivates. The human potential for self-actualization is unleashed when the four deficiency needs are substantially met.

Heider's attribution theory: As naive psychologists, we constantly make causal inferences from the perceived behavior of others. The process involves (1) perception of action, (2) judgment of intention, and (3) attribution of disposition. We systematically err by holding people more responsible for their actions than the situation warrants.

Delia's constructivism: People who are cognitively complex in their perception of others have a greater capacity to create person-centered messages. This seems to be due to their expanded social perspective-taking ability and/or their facility to pursue multiple communication goals at the same time.

Interpersonal Communication

Altman and Taylor's social penetration theory: Interpersonal closeness proceeds in a gradual and orderly fashion from superficial to intimate levels of exchange as a function of both immediate and future outcomes. Lasting intimacy requires continual mutual vulnerability through breadth and depth of self-disclosure.

Berger's uncertainty reduction theory: When strangers meet, their primary concern is to reduce uncertainty about the other person and their relationship. As verbal output, nonverbal warmth, self-disclosure, similarity, and shared communication networks increase, uncertainty goes down—and vice versa. Information seeking and reciprocity are positively correlated with uncertainty.

Watzlawick's interactional view: Relationships within a family system are interconnected and highly resistant to change. Communication among members has both a content and relationship component. The system can be transformed only when members receive outside help to reframe the relational punctuation.

Thibaut and Kelley's social exchange theory: People act to maximize their benefits and minimize their costs. Satisfaction in a relationship depends on expectation (CL); continuation of a relationship depends on outcomes available elsewhere (CL$_{alt}$). Conflict is best resolved through mutual behavior control and prosocial transformations of perceived outcomes.

Baxter's dialectical perspective: Relationships are always in flux. Both parties experience conflicting pulls toward (1) integration and separation, (2) stability and change, and (3) expression and privacy—within their relationship and vis-à-vis their social networks. Couples cope with dialectical tension through strategies of selection, cyclic alteration, segmentation, moderation, disqualification, and reframing.

Sherif's social judgment theory: The larger the discrepancy between a speaker's position and a listener's point of view, the greater the change in attitude—as long as the message is within the hearer's latitude of acceptance. High ego-involvement usually indicates a wide latitude of rejection. Messages which fall there may have a boomerang effect.

Festinger's cognitive dissonance theory: Cognitive dissonance is an aversive drive which causes people to (1) avoid opposing viewpoints, (2) seek reassurance after a tough decision, and (3) change private beliefs to match public behavior when there is minimal justification for the action.

Petty and Cacioppo's elaboration likelihood model: Message elaboration is the central route of persuasion which produces major positive change. This occurs when the arguments are strong and people have the desire and ability to work through the ideas. By contrast, weak influence through irrelevant factors on the peripheral path is much more common.

Group and Public Communication

Fisher's interact model of decision emergence: Groups proceed through four phases in the process of reaching a consensus: (1) orientation, (2) conflict, (3) emergence, and (4) reinforcement.

Janis' groupthink: The concurrence-seeking tendency of close-knit groups can cause them to suspend critical thinking and make inferior decisions.

Weick's information systems approach to organizations: Organizing is the process of making sense out of equivocal information. Organizations survive in a hostile environment when they succeed in reducing equivocality. They evolve through a process of enactment, selection, and retention of information.

Geertz's cultural approach to organizations: Humans are animals suspended in webs of significance that they themselves have spun. An organization doesn't have a culture; it is a culture—a unique system of shared meanings. A nonintrusive ethnographic approach interprets stories, rites, and other symbolism to make sense out of corporate culture.

Aristotle's rhetoric: Rhetoric is the art of discovering all available means of persuasion. A speaker supports the probability of a message by logical, ethical, and emotional proofs. Accurate audience analysis results in effective invention, arrangement, style, delivery (and memory).

Burke's dramatism: Life is drama. The dramatistic pentad of act, scene, agent, agency, and purpose is the critic's tool to discover a speaker's motives. The ultimate motive of rhetoric is the purging of guilt. Without identification, there is no persuasion.

Fisher's narrative paradigm: People are storytelling animals; all forms of human communication are fundamentally narrative. All listeners judge a story by whether or not it hangs together and rings true with their values. Thus, narrative rationality is a matter of coherence and fidelity.

Mass Communication

McLuhan's technological determinism: Changes in communication technology—phonetic alphabet, printing press, and telegraph—radically alter the way we process sensory experience. The medium is the message. The present electronic age is a revolutionary point in human history.

Gerbner's cultivation theory: Heavy television viewers see vast quantities of dramatic violence which cultivates an exaggerated belief in a mean and scary world.

Stuart Hall's critical theory: The mass media impose the dominant ideology on the rest of society. The connotations of words and images are fragments of ideology which perform an unwitting service for the ruling elite.

Bandura's social learning theory: Children and adults acquire attitudes, emotional responses, and new styles of conduct through filmed and televised modeling. The process involves attention, acquisition, and motivation. Vicariously learned aggression can break out into antisocial behavior years later.

McCombs and Shaw's agenda-setting function: The print and broadcast media may not be successful much of the time in telling people what to think, but they are strikingly successful in telling their audience what to think about.

Noelle-Neumann's spiral of silence: People live in perpetual fear of isolating themselves and carefully monitor the environment to see which opinions increase and which ones decrease. If people sense their opinion is losing ground, they remain silent. Television's constant repetition of a single point of view accelerates the spiral of silence.

Cultural Context

Gudykunst's anxiety/uncertainty management theory: Novel situations are characterized by high levels of uncertainty and anxiety. Effective communication is made possible by our ability to mindfully manage our anxiety and reduce our uncertainty about ourselves and the people with whom we are communicating.

Ting-Toomey's face-negotiation theory: Members of collectivistic, high-context cultures have concerns for mutual face and inclusion that lead them to manage conflict with another person by avoiding, obliging, or compromising. Because of concerns for self-face and autonomy, people from individualistic, low-context cultures manage conflict by dominating or problem solving.

Tannen's genderlect styles: Male-female conversation is cross-cultural communication. Masculine and feminine styles of discourse are best viewed as two distinct cultural dialects rather than as inferior or superior ways of speaking. Men's report talk focuses on status and independence. Women's rapport talk seeks human connection.

Kramarae's muted group theory: Man-made language aids in defining, depreciating, and excluding women. Women are less articulate in public because the words and the norms for their use have been devised by men. As women cease to be muted, men cease to maintain their position of dominance in society.

ORDERING THEORIES BY THEIR SCIENTIFIC OR HUMANISTIC ROOTS

I hope that this brief review has brought to mind the richness and diversity of the theories described in these chapters. Yet it would be a mistake to consider them as thirty-four separate entities that stand alone with nothing but communication context to link them together. We need some meaningful way to bring order out of chaos.

Humboldt State communication professor Stephen Littlejohn recommends dividing communication theories into two camps according to the way their authors view knowledge.[1] Recall that the study of knowledge is called *epistemology*, and it seeks to answer the question, How do we know what we know—if we know it at all? Littlejohn describes two distinct views of the world which guide communication inquiry.

World View I regards reality as something "out there" waiting to be discovered. By taking the detached stance of a scientific observer, the World View I researcher seeks to establish cause-and-effect relationships that permit generalizations about communication. World View I theorists see communication as a linear process which can be broken down into its component parts. Laboratory and field experiments provide a method for testing hypotheses derived from general "covering laws." World View I theorists feel successful when they can predict what people are likely to do.

World View II regards reality as something that needs to be interpreted rather than discovered. Reality is constantly in flux and can only be experienced as it is lived by individuals. Everyday truth won't emerge in a controlled laboratory study, but the sensitive participant-observer can perceive patterns of human relationships in natural settings. Whereas World View I regards behavior as caused (the result of previous forces), World View II assumes human actions are freely chosen to accomplish individual purposes. World View II theorists aren't interested in research to determine universal laws that predict communication behavior. They'd rather consider the individual rules a person mentally adopts which lead to a particular communication decision. World View II theorists feel successful when they've made a perceptive interpretation of a communication event.

Littlejohn's distinction between World View I and World View II theories is a useful way to group the theories in this book. But I find the World View labels less helpful to students than the more familiar terms that appear in your college catalogue. World View I is the primary perspective of the *social sciences*. World View II is the main outlook of the *humanities and the arts*.

In the first few chapters I tried to compare and contrast the assumptions of scientific and humanistic scholarship. Now that you can look back at what each theorist proposes, you are in a better position to appreciate the different core commitments that characterize both groups. Figure 39.1 summarizes my evaluation as to whether a theory is more scientifically or humanistically oriented.

Usually it's easy to place a theory in the scientific or humanistic camp—a theoretical "no brainer" as it were. Occasionally, however, the assignment is a close-call decision. For example, Marshall McLuhan's background as a teacher of literature and the anecdotal nature of the evidence he offers might suggest a humanistic perspective. But the cause-and-effect certainty of his technological determinism tilts the balance toward science. Conversely, Leslie Baxter's dialectical perspective might seem to be rooted in science because she cites three dialectics which confront most relational pairs and uses survey research to see how couples handle the contradictions of integration/separation, stability/change, and expression/privacy. Yet she insists that personal relationships are indeterminate processes of ongoing flux and that there's no way to predict how an individual couple will work out the tensions they face. Therefore, I classify her theory as humanistic rather than scientific.

The assignments made in Figure 39.1 aren't chiseled in stone. The categorization is offered as a stimulus to integration rather than as the final word. I encourage you to work through the list of theories in order to determine whether or not you would want to switch a few of them to the opposite column. Being able to articulate a rationale for shifting a given theory is a good sign that you understand both the theory and the differences between the scientific and the humananistic endeavors. (Who knows—it also might turn out to be an essay question on your final exam.)

FOUR OPTIONS FOR SCIENTISTS AND HUMANISTS: REJECT, RESPECT, COOPERATE, MERGE

By now you probably feel more comfortable with one type of communication theory than you do with the other. I find my students almost equally divided in their preference for a humanistic or a scientific approach to the study of message meaning and behavior. What is the appropriate way to handle these differences? Is the field of speech communication best served by the two groups of scholars regarding each other as misguided adversaries, admired strangers, needed colleagues, or as partners in a mixed marriage? Without intentionally putting my thumb on the scale, I'll try to make a case for each position. Then you can decide.

1. Rejection of Inferior Scholarship

Anyone who has ever attended an academic conference knows that scholarship can be a rough-and-tumble affair. People on a search for truth commingle with teachers on a quest for tenure, and in both cases, tolerance for

	COMMUNICATION THEORY ROOTED IN THE SCIENCES	COMMUNICATION THEORY ROOTED IN THE HUMANITIES
Messages		
Information Theory	X	
Meaning of Meaning		X
Coordinated Management of Meaning		X
Nonverbal Expectancy Violations Model	X	
Semiotics		X
Intrapersonal Communication		
Symbolic Interactionism		X
Hierarchy of Needs		X
Attribution Theory		X
Constructivism		X
Interpersonal Communication		
Social Penetration Theory	X	
Uncertainty Reduction Theory	X	
Interactional View		X
Social Exchange Theory	X	
Dialectical Perspective		X
Social Judgment Theory	X	
Cognitive Dissonance Theory	X	
Elaboration Likelihood Model	X	
Group and Public Communication		
Interact System Model of Decision Emergence	X	
Groupthink		X
Information Systems Approach to Organizations		X
Cultural Approach to Organizations		X
Rhetoric	X	
Dramatism		X
Narrative Paradigm		X
Mass Communication		
Technological Determinism	X	
Cultivation Theory	X	
Critical Theory		X
Social Learning Theory	X	
Agenda Setting Function	X	
Spiral of Silence	X	
Cultural Context		
Anxiety/Uncertainty Management	X	
Face-Negotiation Theory	X	
Genderlect Style	X	
Muted Group Theory		X

FIGURE 39.1 Ordering Communication Theory Among the Sciences and Humanities

variant viewpoints is in short supply. Perhaps that's how it should be. In the debate between science and humanism, Robert Bostrom and Lewis Donahew claim that it's anti-intellectual to say that each side has something to offer. "We feel that self-deception is unhealthy, and that deception of others is even worse."[2]

Bostrom and Donahew are empiricists seeking scientific-type truth, and they launch a blistering attack against humanist theorists like Carl Rogers, Bernard Pearce and Vernon Cronen, Roland Barthes, Abraham Maslow, Paul Watzlawick, and Stuart Hall for their interpretive approach to communication study.

> Interpretivism . . . represents an intellectual nihilism in which the possibility of theory construction let alone reasoned action is impossible. . . . Theoretical anarchy and the substitution of pseudo-explanation for scientific explanation seems to us to be the inevitable results of the adoption of the interpretivist argument.[3]

Many humanists are equally critical of a scientific empiricism that claims to be value-neutral and insist on staying ideologically naive about the way big business and big government use its findings to hang onto wealth and power. Stuart Hall admits to being "deeply suspicious of and hostile to empirical work that has no ideas because that just simply means that it does not know the ideas it has."[4] Hall and other humanistic thinkers are also disparaging about social scientists' sole focus on outward behavior. He charges behavioral scientists with "consistently translating matters that have to do with signification, meaning, language, and symbolization into crude behavioral indicators, often justified in the name of a spurious scientificism."[5]

These "communication wars" between scientists and humanists are fought four times a year on the pages of the two leading journals published by the Speech Communication Association of America. The editorial policy of *Communication Monographs* is clearly pro science. Most contributors regard Harold Lasswell, Kurt Lewin, Paul Lazarsfeld, and Carl Hovland as the founding fathers of their research tradition (see Chapter 2). The *Quarterly Journal of Speech* usually prints only humanistic scholarship. Writers in *QJS* would consider Plato, Aristotle, Cicero, and Quintillion to be the founding fathers of their rhetorical tradition.

Which side is right? The answer is obviously a matter of divided opinion. But combative advocates of both groups would agree that integrity requires us to reject theory or research based on false assumptions. They insist that it would be wrong to compromise deeply held convictions to buy a homogenized peace.

2. Respect and Celebration of Differences

Princeton University philosophical pragmatist Richard Rorty comes down equally hard on scientists and humanists when either side claims an exclusive lock on truth. He agrees that there are irreconcilable differences between the two camps. Both groups are self-sealing language communities that don't—and really can't—talk to each other. The questions in one approach don't have answers in the other. In that sense, the world-view contrasts that Littlejohn described are not really separate ways of knowing, just different ways of coping. For this reason, Rorty says, the debates between the sciences and the humanities about knowledge, methodology, and human nature are "not issue(s) to be resolved, only . . . differences to be lived with."[6]

Rorty's comments remind me of Deborah Tannen's thesis that male-female conversation is cross-cultural communication (see Chapter 36). Perhaps science and humanism are best understood as distinct cultures. Although members of one culture will never completely understand the shared meaning within the other culture, they can learn to accept and appreciate the diversity.

This respect and even celebration of differences takes place to a certain extent in the field of clinical psychology. The psychoanalytic, behavioristic, and humanistic schools of therapy differ in starting point, method, and conclusion. Yet most therapists ultimately applaud any approach that helps people get better.

The field of personality assessment offers another helpful analogy. Many of you have taken the Myers-Briggs Type Indicator, a personality test that measures individual preferences on four bipolar scales.[7] The sensing-intuition scale shows how people perceive or acquire information—how they go about finding out about things. As you read through the descriptions of sensing and intuition below, consider how close they are to the epistemological positions of science and humanism.

> *Sensing:* One way to "find out" is to use your sensing function. Your eyes, ears, and other senses tell you what is actually there and actually happening, both inside and outside of yourself. Sensing is especially useful for appreciating the realities of a situation.

> *Intuition:* The other way to find out is through intuition, which shows you the meanings, relationships, and possibilities that go beyond the information from your senses. Intuition looks at the big picture and tries to grasp the essential patterns.[8]

The descriptions above suggest that there may be separate personality profiles for people who typically gravitate toward the sciences or the humanities. If there is a link between personality and world view, it makes little sense to try to talk a person out of his or her way of acquiring knowledge. Perhaps it's best to recognize that the world would be a boring place if everyone were just like us, and simply enjoy the differences.

3. Cooperation with Needed Colleagues

Even though the *reject* and *respect* options differ in emotional tone, both responses assume an insurmountable gap that separates the sciences from the humanities. Cultivation theorist George Gerbner thinks that this assessment is too bleak. Gerbner pictures a symbiotic relationship between the two world views whereby scientists and humanists help each other fulfill a promise that can't be reached by a single approach.

> Opposing science to art or humanistic scholarship presents a false dichotomy.
> . . . In communication terms, science is the human attempt to penetrate the realities of existence, and art is the effort to express them. Science thus works to make statements true while art struggles to make them compelling and believable. The two complement rather than contradict each other.[9]

Many who address the problem agree that scholars in the arts and sciences need each other, but they differ on the temporal order and the nature of the cooperative relationship. Some think that humanists think up theory, then scientists test and refine it. Others believe humanists apply theory in practical situations, but only after scientists generate and prove it. A third view suggests that humanists analyze how a message is made, while scientists analyze the effect it has on others.

It seems that everyone agrees that the strong point of science is a rigorous comparison of multiple messages, while the forte of humanism is its imaginative, in-depth analysis of a single message. Anthropologist Gregory Bateson described rigor and imagination as the two great contraries of the mind. "Either . . . by itself is lethal. Rigor alone is paralytic death, but imagination alone is insanity."[10]

Rhetorician Marie Hochmuth Nichols echoed Bateson's call for the tempering effect that the sciences and humanities can have upon each other. She claimed that "the humanities without science are blind, but science without the humanities may be vicious."[11] It wouldn't be fair to claim that science has no concern for matters of ethics. Empirical researchers are trained to be scrupulously fair in the way they collect and handle data. But the questions of value that humanists bring to communication studies can force scientists to deal with warm bodies who feel, rather than with cold impersonal statistics. Similarly, the scientists' request for hard data can act as a reality check for interpretive scholars who tend to take off on flights of fancy. If humanists can't offer evidence that allows others to reach similar conclusions, their analysis is suspect.

4. Legitimizing the Child of a Shotgun Marriage

University of Georgia speech communication professor Celeste Michelle Condit uses the analogy of a sexual liaison to describe the current relationship between social science and rhetoric in the communication discipline. Whether pure blood patriarchs of science and the humanities like it or not, she says that furtive contact between members of the two academic families has produced offspring that merge characteristics of both traditions. We should not be surprised or embarrassed if young scholars bear unmistakable resemblances to both parents.

> After all, rhetoric (the harlot of the arts) and the social science of communication (the sanctimoniously chaste youth) have been pressed up against each other for something around forty years now. Each has experienced a different torment, locked together in a tiny compartment of the university, scrapping for crumbs of academic prestige. . . . Each denies any hanky-panky, protesting respectively, that "the youth won't pay" and "she's no lady." There are signs, however, of offspring; there are increasing numbers of lines of study that borrow from the scholarly traditions of both rhetoric and social scientific communication research. Are these offspring legitimate?"[12]

Condit's tentative answer is "yes." She notes that "after years of contact with Dame Rhetoric and the crowd with which she consorts (feminist theory, hermeneutics, critical theory, & co.), some communications scientists have dropped their idealistic pose."[13] They no longer insist on covering laws, universal truth, or value neutrality. Some rhetoricians have been equally tarnished through years of contact with pragmatic scientists. They now prize rhetorical theory building above rhetorical criticism, write with technical precision rather than literary brilliance, and seem to downplay the consensus of the scholarly community as a validation of wisdom.

Instead of viewing this scientific-humanistic love child as an ugly embarrassment, Condit suggests that science and rhetoric be properly married (perhaps at an SCA convention), and that they baptize their child with the name "Understanding." She urges that Understanding receive training in research methodologies developed on both sides of the family tree—experimentation, survey research, textual analysis, and ethnography. This broad-based education in communication studies would stretch the child—and the child's teachers as well. Yet before long, the mixed-blood Understanding would outshine the pedigreed children of scientists or rhetoricians that lived in the academic neighborhood, and bring a new respectability to the family. Fact or fantasy? I encourage you to seek out your instructor's viewpoint.

A FINAL NOTE

In the Introduction I compared this book to a collection of charts—a scenic atlas of communication maps that professionals in the field consider worth viewing. I hope you've found your first look intriguing and now have a desire to explore some particular areas. I'd urge you not to be content with watching other people's travel slides; communication isn't an armchair activity. By all means consider the perspectives of Burgoon, Baxter, Burke, and all the others. But also take a look for yourself. Unlike many academic disciplines, the study of communication is one in which we're all practitioners. Remember, however, that unexamined raw experience is not education. You need to ponder, probe, speculate, and follow your hunches if you wish to take advantage of the rich data base that everyday talk provides. The two lists following this chapter could help you in your further study.

Appendix A catalogs academic journals that are particularly relevant to specific communication contexts. If you're really interested in communication theory, you need to read primary sources and understand the issues in the field. Appendix B offers my recommendation for quality movies that illustrate different aspects of the communication process. If you liked my extended references to *M*A*S*H, Children of a Lesser God,* and *When Harry Met Sally,* you may want to check out a video and cull your own examples of theoretical principles at work. Both supplements follow the organization of this book. I'd recommend sampling an equal amount of material from each list.

The field is changing rapidly. There's no reason you have to stop with a first look at communication theory or settle for a secondhand glance. You've probably been mulling over an idea not suggested in these pages. Perhaps that notion could be developed and become the focus of a new chapter in a revised edition. Choose your theoretical perspective and the communication contexts that fascinate you, and switch from casual observation to an intensive gaze. Keep looking.

QUESTIONS TO SHARPEN YOUR FOCUS

1. Which five theories summarized at the start of the chapter are your personal favorites? According to Figure 39.1, are most of them rooted in the *humanities* or the *sciences*? What does that tell you about your own *world view*?

2. How do you view the relationship between humanistic and scientific communication theory? Should scholars in opposing camps *reject, respect, cooperate,* or *merge* with each other?

3. What question do you have about communication that was not addressed by any of the theories covered in the book? Under what *communication context* would a theory that speaks to that issue best fit?

4. Based on the theories you read about this term, what's the best piece of *practical advice* you have to offer someone who wants to be a more *effective communicator*?

A SECOND LOOK

Recommended resource: "Chautauqua: Are Rhetoric and Science Incompatible?" *Communication Monographs,* Vol. 57, 1990, pp. 309–332. (Four articles.)

World-view dichotomy: Stephen Littlejohn, "An Overview of Contributions to Human Communications Theory from Other Disciplines," in *Human Communication Theory*, Frank E. X. Dance (ed.) Harper and Row, New York, 1982, pp. 243–285.

Defense of scientific approach: Robert Bostrom and Lewis Donahew, "The Case for Empiricism: Clarifying Fundamental Issues in Communication Theory," *Communication Monographs*, Vol. 59, 1992, pp. 109–129.

Defense of humanistic approach: Robyn Penman, "Good Theory and Good Practice: An Argument in Progress," *Journal of Communication Theory*, Vol. 2, 1992, pp. 234–250.

Defense of pluralism: John Waite Bowers and James J. Bradac, "Contemporary Problems in Human Communication Theory," in *Handbook of Rhetorical and Communication Theory*, Carroll Arnold and John Waite Bowers (eds.), Allyn and Bacon, Boston, 1984, pp. 871–893.

Philosophical pragmatism and the scientific-humanistic dilemma: Richard Rorty, *Philosophy and the Mirror of Nature*, Princeton University, Princeton, N.J., 1979.

Four perspectives: B. Aubrey Fisher, *Perspectives on Human Communication*, Macmillan, New York, 1978, pp. 89–242.

Research methodology: Arthur Bochner, "Perspectives on Inquiry: Representation, Conversation, and Reflection," in *Handbook of Interpersonal Communication*, Mark Knapp and Gerald Miller (eds.), Sage, Beverly Hills, Calif., 1985, pp. 27–58.

New models of communication: Brenda Dervin, Lawrence Grossberg, Barbara J. O'Keefe, and Ellen Wartella (eds.), *Rethinking Communication, Vol. 1: Paradigm Issues*, Sage, Newbury Park, Calif., 1989.

Research programs: Brenda Dervin, Lawrence Grossberg, Barbara J. O'Keefe, and Ellen Wartella (eds.), *Rethinking Communication, Vol. 2: Paradigm Exemplars*, Sage, Newbury Park, Calif., 1989.

Asian perspective: D. Lawrence Kincaid, *Communication Theory: Eastern and Western Pespectives*, Academic Press, San Diego, 1987.

Theoretical essays: Frank E. X. Dance, *Human Communication Theory*, Harper and Row, New York, 1982.

CALVIN AND HOBBES © 1987 WATTERSON. Dist. by Universal Press Syndicate.
Reprinted with permission. All rights reserved.

APPENDIX A

ACADEMIC JOURNALS THAT FOCUS ON COMMUNICATION THEORY

Overview
Communication Theory
Human Communication Research

Verbal Messages
Et cetera
Journal of Language and Social Psychology
Language

Nonverbal Messages
Human Communication Research
Journal of Nonverbal Behavior
Semiotica

Self-Concept
Journal of Abnormal and Social Psychology
Symbolic Interaction

Motivation
Journal of Personality
Motivation and Emotion

Perception
Journal of Perception and Social Psychology
Journal of Personality and Social Psychology

Relationship Development
Communication Monographs
Human Communication Research
Journal of Social and Personal Relationships

Relationship Maintenance
Human Communication Research
Journal of Social and Personal Relationships
Journal of the International Listening Association

Influence
Communication Monographs
Journal of Personal and Social Psychology
Political Communication and Persuasion

Decision Making
Group
Group and Organizational Studies
Small Group Behavior

Organizational Communication
Administrative Science Quarterly
Management Communication Quarterly

Public Rhetoric
Philosophy & Rhetoric
Quarterly Journal of Speech
Southern Communication Journal

Media and Culture
Critical Studies in Mass Communication
Journal of Communication
Media, Culture and Society

Media Effects
Communication Research
Journal of Broadcasting & Electronic Media
Journalism Quarterly
Mass Communication Research
Public Opinion Quarterly

Intercultural Communication
American Anthropologist
International Journal of Intercultural Relations

Gender and Communication
Discourse & Society
Signs: Journal of Women in Culture and Society
Women's Studies in Communication

APPENDIX B

FEATURE FILMS THAT ILLUSTRATE
COMMUNICATION THEORY

Verbal Messages
  The Conversation
  Cool Hand Luke
  Good Morning Vietnam
  Pygmalion

Nonverbal Messages
  House of Games
  The Miracle Worker
  The Sting

Self-Concept
  Breaking Away
  The Color Purple
  David and Lisa
  The Great Santini
  Mask
  My Life as a Dog

Motivation
  A Raisin in the Sun
  City Slickers
  Death of a Salesman

Perception
  Black Like Me
  The Dream Team
  Rain Man

Relationship Development
  Driving Miss Daisy
  Kiss of the Spider Woman
  Kramer vs. Kramer
  Moonstruck
  Murphy's Romance

Relationship Maintenance
  The Big Chill
  Children of a Lesser God
  The Four Seasons
  In Cold Blood
  Ordinary People
  Parenthood

Influence
  Bob Roberts
  Glengarry/Glen Ross
  Norma Rae
  Stand and Deliver
  The Verdict

Decision Making
  The Flight of the Phoenix
  Twelve Angry Men

Organizational Communication
  A Few Good Men
  The China Syndrome
  Other People's Money
  Up the Down Staircase
  Wall Street

Public Rhetoric
  Malcolm X
  Patton
  The Speeches of Martin Luther King

Media and Culture
  Being There
  Lawnmower Man
  Medium Cool
  The Year of Living Dangerously

Media Effects
  All the President's Men
  Broadcast News
  Network

Intercultural Communication
  A Passage to India
  The Chosen
  Dances with Wolves
  Do the Right Thing
  The Gods Must Be Crazy
  Witness

Gender and Communication
  Fried Green Tomatoes
  Steel Magnolias
  Thelma and Louise
  Tootsie
  When Harry Met Sally

Communication Ethics
  A Man for All Seasons
  Absence of Malice
  Chariots of Fire
  Sophie's Choice

NOTES

Chapter 1

1 Ernest Bormann, *Communication Theory*, Sheffield Publishing, Salem, Wis., 1989, p. 25.
2 Bob Garfield, "Sultry Cindy Saunters Into Pepsi's Portfolio," *Advertising Age*, January 13, 1992, p. 46. Reprinted by permission from the January 13, 1992, issue of *Advertising Age*. Contents copyright © 1992 by Crain Communications Inc.
3 George C. Homans, *The Nature of Social Science*, Harcourt, New York, 1967, p. 4.
4 Poet William Henley, "Invictus," in *The Home Book of Verse*, 9th ed., Burton E. Stevenson (ed.), Holt, Rinehart and Winston, N.Y., p. 3501.
5 C. S. Lewis, *The Abolition of Man*, Macmillan, New York, 1944, p. 309.
6 Lawrence Frey, Carl Botan, Paul Friedman, and Gary Kreps, *Investigating Communication: An Introduction to Research Methods*, Prentice-Hall, Englewood Cliffs, N.J., 1991.
7 Lana F. Rakow, "Don't Hate Me Because I'm Beautiful: Feminist Resistance to Advertising's Irresistible Meaning," *Southern Communication Journal*, Vol. 57, No. 2, 1992, p. 135.
8 *Dances with Wolves*, TIG Productions, 1990.
9 Clifford Geertz, "Thick Description: Toward an Interpretive Theory of History," *The Interpretation of Culture*, Basic Books, New York, p. 5.

Chapter 2

1 John Waite Bowers and James J. Bradac, "Contemporary Patterns in Human Communication Theory," in *Handbook of Rhetorical and Communication Theory*, Carroll Arnold and John Waite Bowers (eds.), Allyn & Bacon, Boston, 1984, p. 872.
2 Ibid.
3 Lawrence Frey, Carl Botan, Paul Friedman, and Gary Kreps, *Investigating Communication: An Introduction to Research Methods*, Prentice-Hall, Englewood Cliffs, N.J., 1991, p. 28.
4 E. Woolfson and A. Parsons, "Time," Alan Parsons Project, Arista Records, 1991.
5 J. A. Winans, "The Need for Research," *Quarterly Journal of Public Speaking*, Vol. 1, 1915, p. 22.
6 James O'Neill, "The National Association," *Quarterly Journal of Public Speaking*, Vol. 1, 1915, pp. 56–57.
7 Herbert Wichelns, "The Literary Criticism of Oratory," in *Methods of Rhetorical Criticism*, B. L. Brock and R. L. Scott (eds.), Wayne State University Press, Detroit, 1980, pp. 40–73.
8 Bernard Berelson, "The State of Communication Research," *Public Opinion Quarterly*, Vol. 23, No. 1, 1959, pp. 1–6

9 Quintilian, *Institutio Oratoria*, Vol. 4, H. E. Butler (trans.), Harvard University, Cambridge, Mass., 1958, p. 356.
10 James McCroskey, "Scales for the Measurement of Ethos," *Speech Monographs*, Vol. 33, 1968, pp. 67–72.
11 David Berlo, *The Process of Communication*, Holt, Rinehart and Winston, New York, 1960.
12 J. Donald Ragsdale, "Invention in English 'Stylistic' Rhetorics: 1600–1800," *Quarterly Journal of Speech*, Vol. 51, 1965, pp. 164–167.
13 Edwin Black, *Rhetorical Criticism: A Study in Method*, Macmillan, New York, 1965.
14 Douglas Ehninger, "Rhetoric and the Critic," *Western Journal of Speech*, Vol. 29, 1965, p. 230.
15 Parke Burgess, "The Rhetoric of Black Power: A Moral Demand," *Quarterly Journal of Speech*, Vol. 54, 1968, pp. 122–133; Robert Scott and Donald Smith, "The Rhetoric of Confrontation," *Quarterly Journal of Speech*, Vol. 55, 1969 pp. 1–8.
16 Lane Cooper, *The Rhetoric of Aristotle*, Appleton-Century-Crofts, New York, 1932, p. 6.
17 Thomas Kuhn, *The Structure of Scientific Revolutions*, 2d ed., University of Chicago Press, Chicago, 1970.
18 Carroll Arnold and Kenneth Frandsel, "Conceptions of Rhetoric and Communication," in *Handbook of Rhetorical and Communication Theory*, Carroll Arnold and John Waite Bowers (eds.), Allyn & Bacon, Boston, 1984, p. 9.

Chapter 3

1 Richard Rodgers and Oscar Hammerstein II, "The Farmer and the Cowman," from *Oklahoma!*, Rodgers & Hammerstein Library, New York, 1943, pp. 140–142.
2 Carl Rogers, "This Is Me," in *On Becoming a Person*, Houghton Mifflin, Boston, 1961, p. 16.
3 Rogers, "The Characteristics of a Helping Relationship," in *On Becoming a Person*, p. 52.
4 Rogers, "This Is Me," in *On Becoming a Person*, p. 24.
5 Karl R. Popper, *The Logic of Scientific Discovery*, Hutchinson, London, 1959, p. 59.
6 Abraham Kaplan, *The Conduct of Inquiry*, Chandler, San Francisco, 1964, p. 295.
7 Ernest G. Bormann, *Communication Theory*, Sheffield Publishing Co., Salem, Wis., 1989, p. 214.
8 Klaus Krippendorff, "The Ethics of Constructing Communication," in *Rethinking Communication, Vol. 1: Paradigm Issues*, Brenda Dervin, Lawrence Grossberg, Barbara O'Keefe, and Ellen Wartella (eds.), Sage, Newbury Park, Calif., 1989, p. 83.
9 Ibid., p. 88.
10 William H. Melody and Robert Mansell, "The Debate over Critical vs. Administrative Research: Circularity

or Challenge," *Journal of Communication*, Vol. 33, No. 3, 1983, p. 103.

11 John Stewart, "A Postmodern Look at Traditional Communication Postulates," *Western Journal of Speech Communication*," Vol. 55, 1991, p. 374.

12 David Zarefski, "Approaching Lincoln's Second Inaugural Address," in *The Practice of Rhetorical Criticism*, 2d ed., James R. Andrews (ed.), Longman, New York, 1990, p. 69.

13 Barbara Warwick, "Left in Context: What Is the Critics Role?" *Quarterly Journal of Speech*, Vol. 78, 1992, pp. 232–237.

14 Rogers, "'To Be That Self Which One Truly Is': A Therapist's View of Personal Goals," in *On Becoming a Person*, p. 171.

15 Kenneth Gergen, *Toward Transformation in Social Knowledge*, Springer-Verlag, New York, 1982, p. 109.

Verbal Messages

1 Paul Kay and Willet Kempton, "What Is the Sapir-Whorf Hypothesis?" *American Anthropologist*, Vol. 86, 1984, pp. 65–79.

2 Edward Sapir, "The Status of Linguistics as a Science," in *Selected Writings*, David Mandelbaum (ed.), University, of California, Berkeley, 1951 (1929), p. 160.

3 Noam Chomsky, *Syntactic Structures*, Mouton, The Hague, 1957; Noam Chomsky, *Aspects of the Theory of Syntax*, Massachusetts Institute of Technology, Cambridge, 1965.

4 Alfred Korzybski, *Science and Sanity*, 3d ed., International Non-Aristotelian Library, Lakeville, Conn., 1948.

5 Richard Budd, "General Semantics: An Approach to Human Communication," in *Approaches to Human Communication*, Richard Budd and Brent Ruben (eds.), Spartan Books, New York, 1972, pp. 97–119.

6 Antoine de Saint-Exupéry, *The Little Prince*, Harcourt Brace Jovanovich, San Diego, 1943, p. 67.

Chapter 4

1 Claude Shannon and Warren Weaver, *The Mathematical Theory of Communication*, Univ. of Illinois, Urbana, 1949, p. 114.

2 Ibid., pp. 3, 99.

3 Ibid., p. 100.

4 Donald Darnell, "Information Theory: An Approach to Human Communication," in *Approaches to Human Communication*, Richard Budd and Brent Ruben (eds.), Spartan Books, New York, 1972, p. 157. Used by permission.

5 Shannon and Weaver, p. 66.

6 Norbert Wiener, *The Human Use of Human Beings*, Avon, New York, 1967, p. 51.

7 Bob Goldsborough, *The Silver Spire*, Bantam Books, New York, 1992, pp. 40–41.

8 Jay Haley, "The Family of the Schizophrenic: A Model System," *Journal of Nervous and Mental Diseases*, Vol. 129, 1959, p. 359.

9 Janet Beavin Bavelas, Alex Black, Nicole Chovil, and Jennifer Mullett, *Equivocal Communication*, Sage, Newbury Park, Calif., 1990, p. 260.

Chapter 5

1 I. A. Richards, *The Philosophy of Rhetoric*, Oxford University Press, London, 1936, p. 3.

2 I. A. Richards, *Speculative Instruments*, University of Chicago Press, Chicago, 1955, p. 166.

3 Sonja Foss, Karen Foss, and Robert Trapp, *Contemporary Perspectives on Rhetoric*, 2d ed., Waveland Press, Prospect Heights, Ill., 1991, p. 28.

4 Richards, *The Philosophy of Rhetoric*, p. 3.

5 Ibid., pp. 3, 5, 7, 23.

6 Vincent Jeffries, "Virtue and Attraction: Validation of a Measure of Love," *Journal of Social and Personal Relationships*, Vol. 10, 1993, pp. 99–117.

7 Richards, *The Philosophy of Rhetoric*, p. 30.

8 I. A. Richards, *Principles of Literary Criticism*, Keagan Paul, Trench, Trubner, New York, 1924, p. 178.

9 C. K. Ogden and I. A. Richards, *The Meaning of Meaning*, Harcourt, Brace & World, New York, 1946, p. 123.

10 Aristotle, *The Poetics*, Section XXII, Leon Golden (trans.), Prentice-Hall, Englewood Cliffs, N.J., p. 41.

11 Richards, *The Philosophy of Rhetoric*, p. 93.

12 Richards, *Principles of Literary Criticism*, p. 240.

13 For an overview of general semantics, see Richard Budd, "General Semantics: An Approach to Human Communication," in *Approaches to Human Communication*," Richard Budd and Brent Ruben (eds.), Spartan Books, New York, 1972, pp. 97–119.

14 John Stewart, "A Postmodern Look at Traditional Communication Postulates," *Western Journal of Speech Communication*, Vol. 55, 1991, pp. 354–379.

Chapter 6

1 W. Barnett Pearce and Vernon E. Cronen, *Communication Action and Meaning: The Creation of Social Realities*, Praeger, New York, 1980, p. 61.

2 Suzy Kalter, *The Complete Book of M*A*S*H*, Abradale, Harry N. Abrams, Inc., New York, 1984, p. 21.

3 W. Barnett Pearce, *Communication and the Human Condition*, Southern Illinois University, Carbondale, 1989, Introduction.

4 Kalter, p. 88.

5 Ibid., p. 125.

6 Pearce, p. 77.

7 Ibid., p. 81.

8 Vernon E. Cronen, "Coordinated Management of Meaning Theory and Postenlightenment Ethics," in *Conversation on Communication Ethics*, Karen Joy Greenberg (ed.), Ablex, Norwood, N.J., 1991, p. 49.

Nonverbal Messages

1 Paul Ekman and Wallace Friesen, "The Repertoire of Nonverbal Behavior: Categories, Origins, Usage and Coding," *Semiotica*, Vol. 1, 1969, pp. 49–98.

2 Paul Ekman and Wallace Friesen, *Unmasking the Face*, Prentice-Hall, Englewood Cliffs, N.J., 1975, pp. 21–33.

3 Albert Mehrabian, *Silent Messages*, 2d ed., Wadsworth, Belmont, Calif., 1981, pp. 1–20.
4 Ray L. Birdwhistell, *Introduction to Kinesics*, University of Louisville, Louisville, Ky., 1952.

Chapter 7

1 Judee K. Burgoon, "A Communication Model of Personal Space Violations: Explication and an Initial Test," *Human Communication Research*, Vol. 4, 1978, p. 130.
2 Edward T. Hall, *The Hidden Dimension*, Doubleday, Garden City, N.Y., 1966, p. 1.
3 W. H. Auden, "Prologue: The Birth of Architecture," in *About the House*, Random House, New York, 1966, p. 14.
4 Judee K. Burgoon and Jerold Hale, "Nonverbal Expectancy Violations: Model Elaboration and Application to Immediacy Behaviors," *Communication Monographs*, Vol. 55, 1988, p. 58.
5 Burgoon, "Communication Model," p. 133.
6 Judee Burgoon, Douglas Kelley, Deborah Newton, and Maureen Keeley-Dyreson, "The Nature of Arousal and Nonverbal Indices," *Human Communication Research*, Vol. 16, 1989, p. 219.
7 Judee K. Burgoon, "Nonverbal Violations of Expectations," in *Nonverbal Interaction*, John Wiemann and Randall P. Harrison (eds.), Sage, Beverly Hills, Calif., 1983, p. 101.
8 Judee K. Burgoon, David Buller, Jerold Hale, and Mark deTurck, "Relational Messages Associated with Nonverbal Behaviors," *Human Communication Research*, Vol. 10, 1984, pp. 351–378.
9 Burgoon, "Communication Model," p. 133.
10 Ibid., p. 135.
11 Ibid., p. 130.
12 Burgoon, "Nonverbal Violations of Expectations," in *Nonverbal Interaction*, John Wiemann and Randall Harrison (eds.), Sage, Beverly Hills, Calif., 1983, p. 101.
13 Ibid., p. 86.
14 Judee Burgoon, Don Stacks, and Steven Burch, "The Role of Interpersonal Rewards and Violations of Distancing Expectations in Achieving Influence in Small Groups," *Journal of the Communication Association of the Pacific*, Vol. 11, No. 1, 1982 pp. 114–127.
15 Burgoon's conception and measurement of arousal has stimulated a vigorous public debate within the pages of *Human Communication Research*. Consult the following three articles in the order listed: (1) Judee K. Burgoon, Douglas Kelley, Deborah Newton, and Maureen Keeley-Dyreson, "The Nature of Arousal and Nonverbal Indices," *Human Communication Research*, Vol. 16, 1989, pp. 217–255; (2) Glenn Sparks and John Greene, "On the Validity of Nonverbal Indicators as Measures of Physiological Arousal," *Human Communication Research*, Vol. 18, 1992, pp. 445–471; (3) Judee Burgoon and Beth LePoire, "A Reply from the Heart," *Human Communication Research*, Vol. 18, 1992, pp. 472–482.
16 Burgoon and Hale, p. 67.

Chapter 8

1 Roland Barthes, "The Romans in Films," in *Mythologies*, Annette Lavers (trans.), Hill and Wang, New York, 1972, pp. 27–28.
2 James R. Beniger, "Who Are the Most Important Theorists of Communication?" *Communication Research*, Vol. 17, 1990, pp. 698–715.
3 Ferdinand de Saussure, *Course in General Linguistics*, Wade Baskin (trans.), McGraw-Hill, New York, 1966, p. 16.
4 Leo Pap, "Natural Signs and Nonintentive Communication," *Proceedings of the Semiotic Society of America*, Vol. 1, 1977, p. 100.
5 Umberto Eco, *A Theory of Semiotics*, Indiana University Press, Bloomington, 1976, p. 7.
6 A. Conan Doyle, "The Blue Carbuncle," in *The Adventures of Sherlock Holmes*, A & W Visual Library, New York, 1975, p. 160. (The idea of the semiologist as detective was suggested by Arthur Asa Berger in his delightful book *Signs in Contemporary Culture*, Sheffield, Salem, Wis., 1989, pp. 16–18.)
7 Roland Barthes, *The Semiotic Challenge*, Richard Howard (trans.), Hill and Wang, New York, 1988, p. 4.
8 Barthes, "The World of Wrestling," in *Mythologies*, p. 17.
9 Ibid., pp. 19, 24
10 See Barthes' use of this phrase in *The Semiotic Challenge*, p. 85. Barthes used these words to describe rhetoricians' efforts to categorize figures of speech—alliteration, hyperbole, irony, etc. The phrase is even more appropriate to characterize *Elements of Semiology*.
11 Donald Fry and Virginia Fry, "Continuing the Conversation Regarding Myth and Culture: An Alternative Reading of Barthes," *The American Journal of Semiotics*, Vol. 6, No. 2/3, 1989, pp. 183–197.
12 Irwin Levine and L. Russell Brown, "Tie a Yellow Ribbon Round the Ole Oak Tree," Levine and Brown Music, Inc., Copyright 1973.
13 Barthes, "Myth Today," in *Mythologies*, p. 118.
14 W. Thomas Duncanson, "Issues of Transcendence and Value in a Semiotic Frame," a paper presented to a joint session of the Religious Speech Communication Association and the Speech Communication Association Convention, San Francisco, Nov. 19, 1989, p. 29.
15 Walker Percy, *Lost in the Cosmos*, Farrar, Straus & Giroux, New York, 1983, p. 85.
16 Terry Eagleton, "Roland Barthes," *International Encyclopedia of Communications*, Vol. 1, Erik Barnouw (ed.), Oxford University Press, New York, 1989, p. 180.
17 "Eugen Simion on Roland Barthes: A Ghibelline Among Guelphs," *Papers on Language and Literature*, Vol. 26, 1990, p. 554.
18 Roland Barthes, *Empire of Signs*, Richard Howard (trans.), Hill and Wang, New York, 1982, pp. 47, 68, 72, 89.
19. Roland Barthes, *S/Z*, Richard Miller (trans.), Hill and Wang, New York, 1974, p. 9.

Self-Concept

1 Ralph Waldo Emerson, "Astraea," *The Works of Ralph Waldo Emerson*, Vol. III, The Nottingham Society, Philadelphia, (no date), p. 121.
2 William James, *Psychology: The Briefer Course*, Henry Holt, New York, 1892, pp. 187–188.
3 Vernon E. Cronen, "Coordinated Management of Meaning Theory and Post Enlightenment Ethics," in *Conversation on Communication Ethics*, Karen Joy Greenberg (ed.), Ablex, Norwood, N.J., p. 48.

Chapter 9

1 Kaj Birket-Smith, *The Eskimos*, Methuen, London, 1959, p. 60.
2 George Herbert Mead, *Mind, Self, and Society*, University of Chicago, Chicago, 1934, p. 254.
3 Harper Lee, *To Kill a Mockingbird*, Warner, New York, 1982, p. 282.
4 George Herbert Mead, "The Social Self," *Journal of Philosophy, Psychology and Scientific Methods*, Vol. 10, 1913, p. 375.
5 George Bernard Shaw, "Pygmalion," *Selected Plays*, Dodd, Mead, New York, 1948, p. 270.

Motivation

1 David C. McClelland, *Human Motivation*, Scott, Foresman, Glenview, Ill., 1985, pp. 223–372.

Chapter 10

1 As cited in Frank Goble, *The Third Force*, Grossman, New York, 1970, p. 14.
2 "Gee, Officer Krupke!" lyrics by Stephen Sondheim, music by Leonard Bernstein, published by G. Schirmer, New York, 1959.
3 Abraham Maslow, *Motivation and Personality*, 2d ed., Harper & Row, New York, 1970, p. 38.
4 Abraham Maslow, "A Theory of Human Motivation," *Psychological Review*, Vol. 50, 1943, p. 381.
5 Ibid., p. 382.

Perception

1 D. E. Hamachek, *Encounters with Others: Interpersonal Relationships and You*, Holt, Rinehart and Winston, New York, 1982, pp. 23–30.
2 R. D. Laing, H. Phillipson, and A. R. Lee, *Interpersonal Perception*, Springer, New York, 1966, p. 23.

Chapter 11

1 M. E. Shaw and J. L. Sulzer, "An Empirical Test of Heider's Levels in Attribution of Responsibility," *Journal of Abnormal and Social Psychology*, Vol. 69, 1964, pp. 39–46.
2 J. H. Harvey, W. Ickes, and R. F. Kidd (eds.), *New Directions in Attribution Research*, Vols. 1–3, Lawrence Erlbaum Associates, Hillsdale, N.J., 1976, 1978, 1981.
3 Fritz Heider, *The Psychology of Interpersonal Relations*, John Wiley & Sons, New York, 1958, p. 79.
4 Dionysius the Elder, 330–367 B.C. He perfected the catapult in sieges of Italian cities (Ralph Payne-Gallwey, *The Projectile-Throwing Engines of the Ancients*,

Rowman and Littlefield, Totowa, N.J., 1973, p. 5). Dante places the "tyrant of Syracuse" in the seventh circle of Hell, submerged in a stream of boiling blood (Dante Alighieri, *The Divine Comedy: Inferno*, Canto XII:107).
5 Lee Ross, "The Intuitive Psychologist and His Shortcomings: Distortions in the Attribution Process," in *Advances in Experimental Social Psychology*, Vol. 10, Leonard Berkowitz (ed.), Academic Press, New York, 1977, p. 184.

Chapter 12

1 Walter H. Crockett, "Cognitive Complexity and Impression Formation," in *Progress in Experimental Personality Research*, Vol. 2, B. A. Maher (ed.), Academic Press, New York, 1965, pp. 47–90.
2 Brant R. Burleson and Michael S. Waltman, "Cognitive Complexity: Using the Role Category Questionnaire Measure," in *A Handbook for the Study of Human Communication*, Charles Tardy (ed.), Ablex, Norwood, N.J., 1988, p. 15.
3 Plato, *Gorgias*, W. R. M. Lamb (trans.), Harvard University, Cambridge, Mass., 1967.
4 Jesse Delia, Barbara J. O'Keefe, and Daniel J. O'Keefe, "The Constructivist Approach to Communication," in *Human Communication Theory*, Frank E. X. Dance (ed.), Harper & Row, New York, 1982, p. 167.

Relationship Development

1 Harold H. Kelley, Ellen Berscheid, Andrew Christensen, John Harvey, Ted Huston, George Levinger, Evie McClintock, Letitia Anne Peplau, and Donald Peterson, *Close Relationships*, W. H. Freeman, New York, 1983, p. 38.
2 Dan P. McAdams, "Human Motives and Personal Relationships," in *Communication, Intimacy, and Close Relationships*, Valerian J. Derlega (ed.), Academic Press, Orlando, Fla., 1984, p. 45.
3 Erich Fromm, *The Art of Loving*, Harper & Row, New York, 1974, p. 3.
4 Dale Carnegie, *How to Win Friends and Influence People*, Pocket Books, New York, 1982, p. 31.

Chapter 13

1 Dalmas Taylor and Irwin Altman, "Communication in Interpersonal Relationships: Social Penetration Processes," in *Interpersonal Processes: New Directions in Communications Research*, Michael Roloff and Gerald Miller (eds.), Sage, Newbury Park, Calif., 1987, p. 259.
2 Irwin Altman, Anne Vinsel, and Barbara Brown, "Dialectic Conceptions in Social Psychology: An Application to Social Penetration and Privacy Regulation," in *Advances in Experimental Social Psychology*, Vol. 14, Leonard Berkowitz (ed.), Academic Press, New York, 1981, p. 139.

Chapter 14

1 Charles Berger, "Uncertainty and Information Exchange in Developing Relationships," in *Handbook of*

Personal Relationships, Steve Duck (ed.), Wiley, New York, 1988, p. 244.

2 Charles Berger and Richard Calabrese, "Some Explorations in Initial Interaction and Beyond: Toward a Developmental Theory of Interpersonal Communication," *Human Communication Research*, Vol. 1, 1975, p. 100.

3 Charles Berger and William Gudykunst, "Uncertainty and Communication," in *Progress in Communication Sciences*, Vol. X, Brenda Dervin and Melvin Voigt (eds.), Ablex, Norwood, N.J., 1991, p. 23.

4 Berger and Calabrese, pp. 99–112.

5 Joseph Cappella, "Mutual Influence in Expressive Behavior: Adult-Adult and Infant-Adult Dyadic Interaction," *Psychological Bulletin*, Vol. 89, 1981, pp. 101–132.

6 Ellen Berscheid and Elaine Walster, *Interpersonal Attraction*, 2d ed., Addison-Wesley, Reading, Mass., 1978, pp. 61–89.

7 Charles Berger, "Beyond Initial Interaction: Uncertainty, Understanding, and the Development of Interpersonal Relationships," in *Language and Social Psychology*, H. Giles and R. St. Clair (eds.), Basil Blackwell, Oxford, Eng., 1979, pp. 122–144.

8 Ibid.

9 Berger and Gudykunst, p. 25.

10 Malcolm Parks and Mara Adelman, "Communication Networks and the Development of Romantic Relationships: An Extension of Uncertainty Reduction Theory," *Human Communication Research*, Vol. 10, 1983, pp. 55–79.

11 William Gudykunst, "Uncertainty and Anxiety," in *Theories in Intercultural Communication*, Young Yun Kim and William Gudykunst (eds.), Sage, Newbury Park, Calif., 1988, pp. 123–156.

12 Charles Berger, "Communicating Under Uncertainty," in *Interpersonal Processes: New Directions in Communication Research*, Michael Roloff and Gerald Miller (eds.), Sage, Newbury Park, Calif., 1987, p. 40.

13 Kathy Kellermann and Rodney Reynolds, "When Ignorance Is Bliss: The Role of Motivation to Reduce Uncertainty in Uncertainty Reduction Theory," *Human Communication Research*, Vol. 17, 1990, p. 7.

14 Ibid., p. 71.

15 Michael Sunnafrank, "Predicted Outcome Value During Initial Interaction: A Reformulation of Uncertainty Reduction Theory," *Human Communication Research*, Vol. 13, 1986, pp. 3–33.

16 Theodore Grove and Doris Werkman, "Conversations with Able-Bodied and Visually Disabled Strangers: An Adversarial Test of Predicted Outcome Value and Uncertainty Reduction Theories," *Human Communication Research*, Vol. 17, 1991, pp. 507–534.

17 Charles Berger, "Communication Theories and Other Curios," *Communication Monographs*, Vol. 58, 1991, p. 102.

18 Berger, "Communicating Under Uncertainty," p. 58.

Relationship Maintenance

1 John Stewart, "Interpersonal Communication: Contact Between Persons," *Bridges Not Walls*, 5th ed., John Steward (ed.), McGraw-Hill, New York, 1990, pp. 13–30.

Chapter 15

1 Alan Watts, *The Book*, Pantheon, New York, 1966, p. 65. For other examples of Watts' use of the life-as-a-game metaphor, see Alan Watts, "The Game of Black-and-White," *The Book*, Pantheon, New York, 1966, pp. 22–46; and Alan Watts, "The Counter Game" *Psychology East & West*, Ballantine, New York, 1969, pp. 144–185.

2 Paul Watzlawick, Janet Beavin, and Don Jackson, *Pragmatics of Human Communication*, W. W. Norton, New York, 1967, p. 54.

3 R. D. Laing, *Knots*, Pantheon, New York, 1970, p. 27.

4 Watzlawick, Beavin, and Jackson, p. 99.

5 L. Edna Rogers-Millar and Frank E. Millar III, "Domineeringness and Dominance: A Transactional View," *Human Communication Research*, Vol. 5, 1979, pp. 238–245.

6 Paul Watzlawick, John H. Weaklund, and Richard Fisch, *Change*, W. W. Norton, New York, 1974, p. 95.

7 "Helping," Families Anonymous, Inc., Van Nuys, Calif., no date.

Chapter 16

1 John Stuart Mill, *Utilitarianism*, J. M. Dent & Sons, London, 1861.

2 From John 15:13, *The New American Bible*, J. P. Kennedy & Sons, New York, 1970.

Chapter 17

1 Leslie A. Baxter, "A Dialogic Approach to Relationship Maintenance," in *Communication and Relational Maintenance*, D. J. Canary and L. Stafford (eds.), Academic Press, San Diego, 1993, in press.

2 Leslie A. Baxter, "Interpersonal Communication as Dialogue: A Response to the 'Social Approaches' Forum," *Communication Theory*, Vol. 2, 1992, p. 330.

3 Leslie A. Baxter, "A Dialectical Perspective on Communication Strategies in Relationship Development," in *A Handbook of Personal Relationships*, Steve Duck (ed.), John Wiley & Sons, New York, 1988, p. 258.

4 Hugh Lofting, *The Story of Dr. Doolittle*, J. B. Lippincott, Philadelphia, 1920, pp. 81–89.

5 Baxter, "Dialectical Perspective," p. 259.

6 Irwin Altman, Anne Vinsel, and Barbara Brown, "Dialectic Conceptions in Social Psychology: An Application to Social Penetration and Privacy Regulation," in *Advances in Experimental Social Psychology*, Vol. 14, Leonard Berkowitz (ed.), Academic Press, New York, 1981, pp. 107–160.

7 All the statements in the strategy section about relational satisfaction are based on Leslie A. Baxter, "Dialectical Contradictions in Relationship Development," *Journal of Social and Personal Relationships*, Vol. 7, 1990, pp. 69–88.

8 For further information on this approach, see Leslie Baxter and William Wilmot, "Taboo Topics in Roman-

tic Relationships," *Journal of Social and Personal Relationships*, Vol. 2, 1985, pp. 253–269.

Influence

1 James Price Dillard, *Seeking Compliance: The Production of Interpersonal Influence Messages*, Gorsech Scarisbrick, Scottsdale, Ariz., 1990.
2 Richard Petty and John Cacioppo, *Attitudes and Persuasion: Classic and Contemporary Approaches*, Wm. C. Brown, Dubuque, Iowa, 1981.

Chapter 18

1 Carolyn Sherif, Muzafer Sherif, and Roger Nebergall, *Attitude and Attitude Change: The Social Judgment-Involvement Approach*, W. B. Saunders, Philadelphia, 1965, p. 222.
2 Ibid., p. 225.
3 Ibid., p. 214.
4 S. Bochner and C. Insko, "Communicator Discrepancy, Source Credibility and Opinion Change," *Journal of Personality and Social Psychology*, Vol. 4, 1966, pp. 614–621.

Chapter 19

1 Aesop, "The Fox and the Grapes," in *Aesop, Five Centuries of Illustrated Fables*, Metropolitan Museum of Art, New York, 1964, p. 12.
2 Leon Festinger, *A Theory of Cognitive Dissonance*, Stanford University, Stanford, Calif., 1957, p. 18.
3 Dieter Frey, "Recent Research on Selective Exposure to Information," in *Advances in Experimental Social Psychology*, Vol. 19, Leonard Berkowitz (ed.), Academic Press, Orlando, Fla., 1986, pp. 41–80.
4 From Jesus' "Sermon on the Mount," Matthew 6:21, *The New King James Version* of the Bible, Thomas Nelson, New York, 1982, p. 936.
5 Festinger, p. 95.
6 Elliot Aronson, "The Theory of Cognitive Dissonance: A Current Perspective," in *Advances in Experimental Social Psychology*, Vol. 4, Leonard Berkowitz (ed.), Academic Press, New York, 1969, p. 27.

Chapter 20

1 Richard E. Petty and John T. Cacioppo, *Communication and Persuasion: Central and Peripheral Routes to Attitude Change*, Springer-Verlag, New York, 1986, p. 7.
2 Richard E. Petty and John T. Cacioppo, *Attitudes and Persuasion: Classic and Contemporary Approaches*, Wm. C. Brown, Dubuque, Iowa, 1981, p. 256.
3 Robert B. Cialdini, *Influence: Science and Practice*, 2d ed., Scott, Foresman, Glenview, Ill., 1988.
4 James B. Stiff, "Cognitive Processing of Persuasive Message Cues: A Meta-Analytic Review of the Effects of Supporting Information on Attitudes," *Communication Monographs*, Vol. 53, 1986, pp. 75–89.
5 Petty and Cacioppo, *Communication and Persuasion*, p. 32.

Chapter 21

1 B. Aubrey Fisher and Leonard C. Hawes, "An Interact System Model: Generating a Grounded Theory of Small Groups," *Quarterly Journal of Speech*, Vol. 57, 1971, p. 445.
2 B. Aubrey Fisher, "Decision Emergence: Phases in Group Decision Making," *Speech Monographs*, Vol. 37, 1970, p. 55.
3 B. Aubrey Fisher, "Decision Emergence: The Social Process of Decision Making," in *Small Group Communication: A Reader*, 4th ed., R. S. Cathcart and L. A. Samovar (eds.), Wm. C. Brown, Dubuque, Iowa, 1984, p. 153.
4 B. Aubrey Fisher, *Small Group Decision Making*, 2d ed., McGraw-Hill, New York, 1980, p. 149.
5 Dean Hewes, "The Sequential Analysis of Social Interaction," *Quarterly Journal of Speech*, Vol. 65, 1979, p. 64.

Chapter 22

1 Irving L. Janis, *Victims of Groupthink*, Houghton Mifflin, Boston, 1972, p. 9.
2 Remark made to author in personal conversation.
3 Marvin E. Shaw, "Group Composition and Group Cohesiveness," in *Small Group Communication: A Reader*, 5th ed., R. S. Cathcart and L. A. Samovar (eds.), Wm. C. Brown, Dubuque, Iowa, 1988, p. 43.
4 Janis, p. 198.
5 Arthur Schlesinger, *A Thousand Days*, Houghton Mifflin, Boston, 1965, p. 214.
6 Seventeenth-century legend related to the Three Wise Monkeys carved over the door of the Sacred Stable, Nikko, Japan.
7 Schlesinger, p. 255.
8 Ibid., p. 259.

Chapter 23

1 Karl Weick, *The Social Psychology of Organizing*, Addison-Wesley, Reading, Mass., 1969, p. 40.
2 Weick, *The Social Psychology of Organizing*, 2d ed., 1979, p. 11, referring to M. D. Cohen and J. G. March, *Leadership and Ambiguity*, McGraw-Hill, New York, 1974.
3 1 Corinthians 12:12–21, Revised Standard Version of the Bible.
4 Charles Darwin, *The Origin of Species*, Dent, New York, 1967 (1859).
5 Weick, p. 51.

Chapter 24

1 Clifford Geertz, "Thick Description: Toward an Interpretive Theory of Culture," in *The Interpretation of Cultures*, Basic Books, New York, 1973, p. 5.
2 Michael Pacanowsky and Nick O'Donnell-Trujillo, "Organizational Communication as Cultural Performance," *Communication Monographs*, Vol. 50, 1983, p. 146.
3 Harrison Trice and Janice Beyer, "Studying Organizational Cultures Through Rites and Ceremonials," *Academy of Management Review*, Vol. 9, 1984, p. 654.

4 Clifford Geertz, "Deep Play: Notes on the Balinese Cockfight," in *Myth, Symbol, and Culture*, Norton, New York, 1971, p. 29.

5 Gareth Morgan, *Images of Organization*, Sage, Newbury Park, Calif., 1986, pp. 130–131.

6 Trice and Beyer, p. 655.

7 Michael Pacanowsky and Nick O'Donnell-Trujillo, "Communication and Organizational Cultures," *Western Journal of Speech Communication*, Vol. 46, 1982, p. 123.

8 John F. Love, *McDonald's: Behind the Arches*, Bantam, Toronto, 1986, pp. 143–144.

9 Geertz, "Deep Play," pp. 5, 26.

10 Trice and Beyer, p. 655.

11 Ibid., p. 658.

Public Rhetoric

1 Sonja K. Foss, Karen A. Foss, and Robert Trapp, *Contemporary Perspectives on Rhetoric*, 2d ed., Waveland, Prospect Heights, Ill., 1991, p. 14.

2 Plato, *Gorgias*, Lane Cooper (trans.), Oxford University, New York, 1948, p. 122.

3 Plato, *Praedrus*, 277, W. C. Helmbald and W. B. Rabinowitz (trans.), Bobbs-Merrill, Indianapolis, 1956, p. 72.

4 1 Corinthians 2:4, New Revised Standard Version of the Bible.

5 1 Corinthians 9:22, New Revised Standard Version of the Bible.

6 Hugh C. Dick (ed.), *Selected Writings of Francis Bacon*, Modern Library, New York, 1955, p. x.

Chapter 25

1 David J. Garrow, *Bearing the Cross*, William Morrow, New York, 1986, p. 284.

2 Lloyd Bitzer, "Aristotle's Enthymeme Revisited," *Quarterly Journal of Speech*, Vol. 45, 1959, p. 409.

3 Lane Cooper, *The Rhetoric of Aristotle*, Appleton-Century-Crofts, New York, 1932, pp. 187, 206.

4 Amos 5:24, Revised Standard Version of the Bible.

5 Attributed to Ralph Waldo Emerson by Dale Carnegie, *How to Win Friends and Influence People*, Pocket Books, New York, 1982, p. 29.

6 Cooper, "Introduction."

7 Ibid., p. 220.

8 Ibid., p. 2.

9 Voltaire, *Dictionnaire Philosophique*, "Aristotle," in Oeuvres Complètes de Voltaire Vol. 17, Librairie Garnier, Paris, p. 372.

Chapter 26

1 Marie Hochmuth Nichols, "Kenneth Burke and the New Rhetoric," *Quarterly Journal of Speech*, Vol. 38, 1952, pp. 133–144.

2 Kenneth Burke, "Rhetoric—Old and New," *The Journal of General Education*, Vol. 5, 1951, p. 203.

3 Ruth 1:16, Revised Standard Version of the Bible.

4 Kenneth Burke, *A Grammar of Motives*, Prentice-Hall, Englewood Cliffs, N.J., 1945, p. xv.

5 Kenneth Burke, "Definition of Man," in *Language as Symbolic Action*, University of California, Berkeley, 1966, p. 16.

6 Paul Dickson, *The Official Rules*, Dell, New York, 1978, p. 165.

7 Kenneth Burke, "On Human Behavior Considered 'Dramatistically,'" in *Permanence and Change*, Bobbs-Merrill, Indianapolis, 1965, p. 283.

8 Kenneth Burke, "The Rhetoric of Hitler's 'Battle,'" in *The Philosophy of Literary Form*, Louisiana State University, Baton Rouge, 1941, p. 191.

9 Ibid., p. 205.

10 Ibid., p. 203.

11 Ibid., p. 219.

12 Nichols, p. 144.

Chapter 27

1 Walter R. Fisher, *Human Communication as Narration: Toward a Philosophy of Reason, Value, and Action*, University of South Carolina, Columbia, 1987, p. 24.

2 Ibid., p. xi.

3 Walter R. Fisher, "Toward a Logic of Good Reasons," *Quarterly Journal of Speech*, Vol. 64, 1978, pp. 376–384.

4 See Hosea 1–3, 11 in the Old Testament.

5 Fredrick Buechner, *Peculiar Treasures*, Harper & Row, New York, 1979, pp. 45–46.

6 Fisher, *Human Communication as Narration*, p. 58.

7 Walter R. Fisher, "Clarifying the Narrative Paradigm," *Communication Monographs*, Vol. 56, 1989, pp. 55–58.

8 See Chapter 2, "The Hunt for a Universal Model (1970–1980), pp. 27–28.

9 Fisher, *Human Communication as Narration*, p. xi.

10 Ibid., p. 20.

11 Ibid., pp. 178–179.

12 William G. Kirkwood, "Narrative and the Rhetoric of Possibility," *Communication Monographs*, Vol. 59, 1992, pp. 30–47.

13 Fisher, *Human Communication as Narration*, p. 67.

Media and Culture

1 Elihu Katz and Paul Lazarsfeld, *Personal Influence*, The Free Press, Glencoe, Ill., 1955.

2 See J. G. Blumler and Elihu Katz, *The Uses of Mass Communication: Current Perspectives on Gratifications Research*, Sage, Beverly Hills, Calif., 1974; and Elihu Katz, "The Uses of Becker, Blumler, and Swanson," *Communication Research*, Vol. 6, 1979, pp. 74–83.

3 See "New Perspectives on Media and Culture," William Biernatzki and Robert White (eds.), *Communication Research Trends*, Vol. 8, No. 2, 1987, pp. 1–13; and Robert White, "Mass Communication and Culture: Transition to a New Paradigm," *Journal of Communication*, Vol. 33, No. 3, 1983, pp. 279–301.

Chapter 28

1 "Playboy Interview: Marshall McLuhan," *Playboy*, March 1969, p. 54.

2 Tom Wolfe, "Suppose He Is What He Sounds Like . . . ," in *McLuhan: Hot & Cool*, Gerald Stearn (ed.), Dial, New York, 1967, p. 19.

3 "Playboy Interview: Marshall McLuhan," p. 59.
4 Marshall McLuhan and Quentin Fiore, *The Medium Is the Massage*, Random House, New York, 1967, p. 50.
5 Jesus, John 8:32, New International Version of the Bible.
6 "Playboy Interview: Marshall McLuhan," p. 70.
7 Ibid., p. 62.
8 Ibid., p. 158.
9 Douglas Ehninger, "Marshall McLuhan: His Significance for the Field of Speech Communication," *Speech Journal*, Vol. 6, 1969, p. 19.
10 Alice Cooper, "School's Out Forever," Warner Bros., 1972.
11 Marshall McLuhan, *The Mechanical Bride*, Vanguard, New York, 1951. See *Journal of Communication*, Vol. 42, No. 4, 1992. The entire issue is devoted to state-of-the-art technology and applications of virtual reality.
12 "Playboy Interview: Marshall McLuhan," p. 66.
13 Dan M. Davin in *McLuhan: Hot & Cool*, p. 183.
14 Dwight Macdonald in *McLuhan: Hot & Cool*, p. 203.
15 Christopher Ricks in *McLuhan: Hot & Cool*, p. 25.
16 George N. Gordon, "An End to McLuhanacy," *Educational Technology*, January 1982, p. 42.
17 Tom Wolfe in *McLuhan: Hot & Cool*, p. 15.
18 Malcolm Muggeridge, *Christ and the Media*, Eerdmans, Grand Rapids, Mich., 1977.
19 Kenneth Boulding in *McLuhan: Hot & Cool*, p. 57.

Chapter 29

1 Jerome H. Skolnick, *The Politics of Protest*, Simon and Schuster, New York, 1969, pp. 3–24.
2 George Gerbner, Larry Gross, Michael Morgan, and Nancy Signorielli, "The 'Mainstreaming' of America: Violence Profile No. 11," *Journal of Communication*, Vol. 30, No. 3, 1980, p. 11.
3 George Gerbner, Larry Gross, Nancy Signorielli, Michael Morgan, and Marilyn Jackson-Beeck, "The Demonstration of Power: Violence Profile No. 10," *Journal of Communication*, Vol. 29, No. 2, 1979, p. 196.

Chapter 30

1 Stuart Hall, "Ideology and Communication Theory," in *Rethinking Communication Theory*, Vol. 1, *Paradigm Issues*, Brenda Dervin, Lawrence Grossberg, Barbara O'Keefe, and Ellen Wartella (eds.), Sage, Newbury Park, Calif., 1989, p. 52.
2 Ibid., p. 48.
3 Stuart Hall, "The Problem of Ideology—Marxism Without Guarantees," *Journal of Communication Inquiry*, Vol. 10, No. 2, 1986, p. 40.
4 Stuart Hall, Ian Connell, and Lidia Curti, "The 'Unity' of Current Affairs Television," *Working Papers in Cultural Studies No. 9*, Center for Contemporary Cultural Studies, University of Birmingham, Birmingham, England, 1976, p. 53.
5 Hall, "Problem of Ideology," p. 29.
6 Robert Frost, "Stopping by Woods on a Snowy Evening," *Poetry of Robert Frost*, Holt, Rinehart and Winston, New York, 1969, p. 224.
7 Clifford Christians, "Normativity as Catalyst," in *Re-*

thinking Communication Theory, Vol. 1, *Paradigm Issues*, Brenda Dervin, Lawrence Grossberg, Barbara O'Keefe, and Ellen Wartella (eds.), Sage, Newbury Park, Calif., 1989, p. 148.
8 Samuel Becker, "Communication Studies: Visions of the Future," in *Rethinking Communication Theory*, Vol. 1, *Paradigm Issues*, Brenda Dervin, Lawrence Grossberg, Barbara O'Keefe, and Ellen Wartella (eds.), Sage, Newbury Park, Calif., 1989, p. 126.

Media Effects

1 Paul Lazarsfeld, Bernard Berelson, and Hazel Gaudet, *The People's Choice*, Duell, Sloan and Pearce, New York, 1944.
2 A. W. van den Ban, "A Review of the Two-Step Flow of Communication Hypothesis," in *Speech Communication Behavior*, Larry L. Barker and Robert Kiebler (eds.), Prentice-Hall, Englewood Cliffs, N.J., 1971, pp. 193–205.
3 Fredric Wertham, *Seduction of the Innocent*, Rinehart, New York, 1954.
4 Dolf Zillmann, "Excitation Transfer in Communication-Mediated Aggressive Behavior," *Journal of Experimental Social Psychology*, Vol. 7, 1971, pp. 419–434.
5 Tony Schwartz, *The Responsive Chord*, Doubleday, New York, 1973.

Chapter 31

1 Albert Bandura, *Social Learning Theory*, Prentice-Hall, Englewood Cliffs, N.J., 1977, p. 27.
2 Ibid., p. 39.
3 Robert Liebert and Joyce Sprafkin, "The Surgeon General's Report," *The Early Window: Effects of Television on Children and Youth*, 3d ed., Pergamon, New York, 1988, pp. 79–107.
4 Bandura, p. 59.
5 Ibid., p. 27.
6 Ibid., p. 166.
7 "Batmania," *Newsweek*, June 26, 1989, p. 71.
8 Dolf Zillmann, J. L. Hoyt, and K. D. Day, "Strength and Duration of the Effect of Aggressive, Violent, and Erotic Communications on Subsequent Aggressive Behavior," *Communication Research*, Vol. 1, 1974, pp. 286–306.
9 Liebert and Sprafkin, pp. 75–77.
10 M. Lefkowitz, L. Eron, L. Walder, and L. Huesmann, *Growing Up to Be Violent: A Longitudinal Study of the Development of Aggression*, Pergamon, New York, 1977.
11 See Robert B. Cialdini, *Influence*, 2d ed., Scott, Foresman, Glenview, Ill., 1988, pp. 135–143.

Chapter 32

1 Maxwell McCombs and Donald Shaw, "A Progress Report on Agenda-Setting Research," a paper presented to the Association for Education in Journalism, Theory and Methodology Division, San Diego, Calif., on April 18–27, 1974, p. 28.
2 Walter Lippmann, *Public Opinion*, Macmillan, New York, 1922, p. 3.

3 Bernard C. Cohen, *The Press and Foreign Policy*, Princeton University, Princeton, N.J., 1963, p. 13.
4 Theodore White, *The Making of the President 1972*, Bantam, New York, 1973, p. 245.
5 Werner J. Severin and James Tankard, Jr., *Communication Theories*, 2d ed., Longman, New York, 1988, pp. 300–310.
6 Paul Lazarsfeld, Bernard Berelson, and Hazel Gaudet. *The People's Choice*, Duell, Sloan and Pearce, New York, 1944.
7 G. Ray Funkhouser, "The Issues of the 60's: An Exploratory Study in the Dynamics of Public Opinion," *Public Opinion Quarterly*, Vol. 37, 1973, p. 69.
8 John Carey, "How Media Shape Campaigns," *Journal of Communication*, Vol. 26, No. 2, 1976, pp. 52–53.

Chapter 33

1 Elisabeth Noelle-Neumann, *The Spiral of Silence*, University of Chicago, Chicago, 1984, pp. 70–71.
2 Ibid., pp. 62–63.
3 Ibid., p. 19.
4 Ibid., p. 41.
5 Solomon E. Asch, "Effects of Group Pressure Upon the Modification and Distortion of Judgments," in *Group Dynamics: Research and Theory*, Dorwin Cartwright and Alvin Zander (eds.), Row, Peterson, Evanston, Ill., 1953, pp. 151–162.
6 Noelle-Neumann, *The Spiral of Silence*, p. 182.
7 Elisabeth Noelle-Neumann, "Turbulences in the Climate of Opinion: Methodological Applications of the Spiral of Silence Theory," *Public Opinion Quarterly*, Vol. 41, 1977, p. 144.
8 Noelle-Neumann, *The Spiral of Silence*, pp. 17–18.
9 Elisabeth Noelle-Neumann, "Mass Media and Social Change in Developed Societies," in *Mass Media and Social Change*, Elihu Katz and Tamas Szecsko (eds.), Sage, London, 1981, p. 139.
10 Elisabeth Noelle-Neumann, "Return to the Concept of Powerful Mass Media," *Studies of Broadcasting*, Vol. 9, 1973, p. 77.
11 Elisabeth Noelle-Neumann, "The Theory of Public Opinion: The Concept of the Spiral of Silence" in *Communication Yearbook 14*, James A. Anderson (ed.), Sage, Newbury Park, Calif., p. 276.
12 Carroll Glynn and Jack McLeod, "Public Opinion du Jour: An Examination of the Spiral of Silence," *Public Opinion Quarterly*, Vol. 48, 1984, pp. 731–740.
13 Alexis de Tocqueville, *L'Ancien Régime et la Révolution*, Michel Levy Frères, Paris, 1856, p. 259.
14 Mihaly Csikszentmihaly, "Reflections on the 'Spiral of Silence,'" in *Communication Yearbook 14*, p. 297.
15 D. Garth Taylor, "Pluralistic Ignorance and the Spiral of Silence: A Formal Analysis," *Public Opinion Quarterly*, Vol. 46, 1982, pp. 311–335.
16 Csikszentmihaly, pp. 294–295.
17 Noelle-Neumann, "The Theory of Public Opinion," p. 274.
18 Elisabeth Noelle-Neumann, "Public Opinion and the Classical Tradition: A Re-Evaluation," *Public Opinion Quarterly*, Vol. 43, 1979, p. 155.
19 Noelle-Neumann, *The Spiral of Silence*, p. 184.

Intercultural Communication

1 Gerry Philipsen, *Speaking Culturally: Exploration in Social Communication*, State University of New York, Albany, 1992, p. 7.
2 Gerry Philipsen, "Speaking 'Like a Man' in Teamsterville: Cultural Patterns of Role Enactment in an Urban Neighborhood," *Quarterly Journal of Speech*, Vol. 61, 1975, pp. 13–22.
3 Philipsen, *Speaking Culturally*, p. 42.
4 Ibid., p. 3.
5 Donal Carbaugh, "Communication Rules in Donahue Discourse," in *Cultural Communication and Intercultural Contact*, Donal Carbaugh (ed.), Lawrence Erlbaum Associates, Hillsdale, N.J., 1990, pp. 119–149.
6 See chapter on cultural variability in William B. Gudykunst and Stella Ting-Toomey, *Culture and Interpersonal Communication*, Sage, Newbury Park, Calif., 1988, pp. 39–59.
7 Edward T. Hall, *Beyond Culture*, Anchor, New York, 1977, p. 91.

Chapter 34

1 Matthew 28:20, King James Version of the Bible.
2 William B. Gudykunst, "Uncertainty and Anxiety," in *Theories in Intercultural Communication*, Young Yun Kim and William B. Gudykunst (eds.), Sage, Newbury Park, Calif., 1988, pp. 125–128.
3 William B. Gudykunst, "Toward a Theory of Effective Interpersonal and Intergroup Communication: An Anxiety/Uncertainty Management (AUM) Perspective," in *Intercultural Communication Competence*, R. L. Wiseman and J. Koester (eds.), Sage, Newbury Park, Calif., 1993, p. 70 (note 4).
4 William S. Howell, *The Empathic Communicator*, Wadsworth, Belmont, Calif., 1982, pp. 29–33.
5 William B. Gudykunst, *Bridging Differences: Effective Intergroup Communication*, Sage, Newbury Park, Calif., 1991, p. 13.
6 William B. Gudykunst and Stella Ting-Toomey, *Culture and Interpersonal Communication*, Sage, Newbury Park, Calif., 1988, pp. 58–59.
7 Michael Sunnafrank, "Uncertainty in Interpersonal Relationships: A Predicted Outcome Value Interpretation of Gudykunst's Research Program," in *Communication Yearbook 12*, James A. Anderson (ed.), Sage, Newbury Park, Calif., 1989, p. 355.
8 William B. Gudykunst, "Uncertainty and Anxiety," in *Theories in Intercultural Communication*, Young Yun Kim and William B. Gudykunst (eds.), Sage, Newbury Park, Calif., 1988, p. 144.
9 Stella Ting-Toomey, "Cultural and Interpersonal Relationship Development: Some Conceptual Issues," in *Communication Yearbook 12*, James A. Anderson (ed.), Sage, Newbury Park, Calif., 1989, p. 379.
10 Brenda Dervin, "Comparative Theory Reconceptualized: From Entities and States to Processes and Dynamics," *Communication Theory*, Vol. 1, 1991, pp. 59–69.

Chapter 35

1 Penelope Brown and Stephen Levinson, "Universals in Language Usage: Politeness Phenomenon," in *Questions and Politeness: Strategies in Social Interaction*, Esther N. Goody (ed.), Cambridge University, Cambridge, Eng., 1978, p. 66.
2 L. Yutang, *My Country and My People*, John Day, Taipai, Republic of China, 1968, p. 199.
3 Stella Ting-Toomey, "Intercultural Conflict Styles: A Face-Negotiation Theory," in *Theories in Intercultural Communication*, Young Yun Kim and William Gudykunst (eds.), Sage, Newbury Park, Calif., 1988, p. 215.
4 Brown and Levinson, p. 66.
5 See, for example, Elizabeth G. Chua and William B. Gudykunst, "Conflict Resolution Styles in Low- and High-Context Cultures," *Communication Research Reports*, Vol. 4, 1987, pp. 32–37.

Gender and Communication

1 Robin Lakoff, *Language and Women's Place*, Harper & Row, New York, 1975.
2 Mary Steward Van Leeuwen, *Gender & Grace*, InterVarsity, Downers Grove, Ill., 1990, pp. 53–71.
3 Sandra L. Bem, "Androgyny vs. the Tight Little Lives of Fluffy Women and Chesty Men," *Psychology Today*, Vol. 9, 1975, pp. 58–62.
4 Cheris Kramarae, "Gender and Dominance," in *Communication Yearbook 15*, Stanley A. Deetz (ed.), Sage, Newbury Park, Calif., 1992, pp. 469–474.

Chapter 36

1 Deborah Tannen, *You Just Don't Understand*, Balantine, New York, 1990, p. 42.
2 Deborah Tannen, *Conversational Style: Analyzing Talk Among Friends*, Ablex, Norwood, N.J., 1984.
3 Ibid., p. vii.
4 Tannen, *You Just Don't Understand*, p. 259.
5 Ibid., p. 279.
6 Ibid., p. 16.
7 Ibid., p. 108.
8 Tannen, *Conversational Style*, p. 38.
9 Tannen, *You Just Don't Understand*, p. 48.
10 Ibid., p. 212.
11 Ibid., p. 62.
12 Ibid., p. 72.
13 Ibid., p. 150.
14 Ibid., pp. 120–121, 298.
15 Senta Troemel-Ploetz, "Review Essay: Selling the Apolitical," *Discourse & Society*, Vol. 2, 1991, p. 497.
16 Ibid., p. 491.
17 Ibid., p. 495.

Chapter 37

1 Cheris Kramarae, *Women and Men Speaking*, Newbury House Publishers, Rowley, Mass., 1981, p. 1.
2 Barrie Thorne, Cheris Kramarae, and Nancy Henley (eds.), *Language, Gender and Society*, Newbury House, Rowley, Mass., 1983, p. 9.
3 Cheris Kramar, "Folklinguistics," *Psychology Today*, Vol. 8, June 1974, pp. 82–85.

4 Edwin Ardener, "Belief and the Problem of Women," in *Perceiving Women*, Shirley Ardener (ed.), Malaby, London, 1975, p. 2.
5 Edwin Ardener, "The 'Problem' Revisited," in *Perceiving Women*, Shirley Ardener (ed.), Malaby, London, 1975, p. 22.
6 Ibid., p. 25.
7 Shirley Ardener, "The Nature of Women in Society," in *Defining Females*, Halsted, New York, 1978, p. 21.
8 Kramarae, *Women and Men Speaking*, p. 3.
9 Simone de Beauvoir, *The Second Sex*, H. M. Parshley (ed. and trans.), Bantam, New York, 1964, p. xv.
10 Kramarae, *Women and Men Speaking*, p. 3.
11 Julia P. Stanley, "Paradigmatic Women: The Prostitute," in *Papers in Language Variation*, David L. Shores and Carole P. Hines (eds.), University of Alabama, Tuscaloosa, 1977, p. 7.
12 Kramarae, *Women and Men Speaking*, p. 1.
13 Virginia Woolf, *A Room of One's Own*, Hogarth (Penguin edition), 1928, p. 45.
14 Dorothy Smith, "A Peculiar Eclipsing: Women's Exclusion from Man's Culture," *Women's Studies International Quarterly*, Vol. 1, 281–295.
15 Kramarae, *Women and Men Speaking*, p. 3.
16 Tillie Olsen, *Silences*, Delacorte/Seymour Lawrence, New York, 1978, p. 23.
17 Kramarae, *Women and Men Speaking*, p. 19.
18 Ibid., p. 12.
19 Ibid., p. 4.
20 Cheris Kramarae and Paula Treichler, *Amazons, Bluestockings, and Crones: A Feminist Dictionary*, 2d ed., Pandora, London, 1992, p. 17.
21 Ibid., p. 4.
22 Dale Spender, *Man Made Language*, Routledge & Kegan, London, 1980, p. 87.
23 Cheris Kramarae, "Punctuating the Dictionary," *International Journal of the Sociology of Language*, Vol. 94, 1992, p. 135.
24 Kramarae and Treichler, p. 4.
25 Cheris Kramarae, "Harassment and Everyday Life," in *Women Making Meaning: New Feminist Directions in Communication*, Lana Rakow (ed.), Routledge, New York, 1992, p. 102.
26 Julia T. Wood (ed.), "Special Section—'Telling Our Stories': Sexual Harassment in the Communication Discipline," *Journal of Applied Communication Research*, Vol. 20, 1992, pp. 383–384.
27 Karen A. Foss and Sonja K. Foss, "Incorporating the Feminist Perspective in Communication Scholarship: A Research Commentary," in *Doing Research on Women's Communication: Perspectives on Theory and Method*, K. Carter and C. Spitzack (eds.), Ablex, Norwood, N.J., 1989, p. 72.
28 Deborah Tannen, *Conversational Style: Analyzing Talk Among Friends*, Ablex, Norwood, N.J., 1984, p. 43.
29 Kramarae, "Punctuating the Dictionary," p. 146.

Ethical Theory

1 Sissela Bok, *Lying: Moral Choice in Public and Private Life*, Pantheon, New York, 1979, pp. xv–xxiii.

Chapter 38

1 J. M. Rist, *Epicurus: An Introduction*, Cambridge University, Cambridge, Eng., 1972, p. 124.
2 Epicurus, "Leading Doctrines, 8," cited in R. D. Hicks, *Stoic and Epicurean*, Charles Scribner's Sons, New York, 1910, p. 185.
3 Ayn Rand, *The Fountainhead*, Signet, New York, 1971, p. x.
4 John Stuart Mill, "Utilitarianism," in *Utilitarianism, Liberty, Representative Government*, H. B. Acton (ed.), E. P. Dutton, New York, 1972, p. 16.
5 Sissela Bok, *Lying: Moral Choice in Public and Private Life*, New York, 1979, p. 32.
6 Immanuel Kant, "On a Supposed Right to Lie from Altruistic Motives," in *Critique of Practical Reason and Other Writings in Moral Philosophy*, Lewis White Beck (trans. and ed.), University of Chicago, Chicago, 1964, p. 346.
7 Immanuel Kant, *Groundwork of the Metaphysic of Morals*, H. J. Paton (trans.), Harper Torchbooks, New York, 1964, p. 88.
8 Theodore White, *The Making of the President 1964*, Atheneum, New York, 1965, p. 228.
9 Aristotle, *Nicomachean Ethics*, H. Rackham (trans.), Harvard University, Cambridge, Mass. 1934, Bk. 4, Chap. 7.
10 "Enarrátiones in Psalmos LXIV.2," cited in *An Augustine Synthesis*, Erick Przywara (ed.), Shed and Ward, London, 1936, p. 267.
11 Richard of Chichester (c. 1200), in *The Hymnbook*, The United Presbyterian Church in the U.S.A., New York, 1955, p. 445.
12 Augustine, *Enchiridion, on Faith, Hope and Love*, Henry Paolucci (trans.), Henry Regnery, Chicago, 1961.
13 Augustine, "On Lying," in *Treatises on Various Subjects*, Vol. 14, R. J. Deferrari (ed.), Catholic University, New York, 1952, Chap. 14.
14 Micah 6:8, Revised Standard Version of the Bible.
15 Martin Buber, *Between Man and Man*, Macmillan, New York, 1965, p. 204.
16 Ronald C. Arnett, *Communication and Community*, Southern Illinois University, Carbondale, 1986, p. 37.

Communication Theory

1 Warren Thorngate, "'In General' vs. 'It Depends': Some Comments on the Gergen-Schlenker Debate," *Personality and Social Psychology Bulletin*, Vol. 2, 1976, p. 406.
2 Ibid.
3 C. David Mortensen, "Communication Postulates," in *Contexts*, Jean N. Civikly (ed.), Holt, Rinehart and Winston, New York, 1975, p. 21.
4 Karl Weick, *The Social Psychology of Organizing*, 2d ed., Addison-Wesley, Reading, Mass., 1979, p. 39.
5 Graham Chapman, John Cleese, Terry Gilliam, Eric Idle, Terry Jones, and Michael Palin, *The Complete Monty Python's Flying Circus: All the Words*, Volume Two, Pantheon, New York, 1989, p. 119.

Chapter 39

1 Stephen Littlejohn, "An Overview of Contributions to Human Communications Theory from Other Disciplines," in *Human Communication Theory*, Frank E. X. Dance (ed.), Harper & Row, New York, 1982, 243–285.
2 Robert Bostrom and Lewis Donahew, "The Case for Empiricism: Clarifying Fundamental Issues in Communication Theory," *Communication Monographs*, Vol. 59, 1992, pp. 126–127.
3 Ibid., pp. 109 and 127.
4 Stuart Hall, "Ideology and Communication Theory," in *Rethinking Communication*, Vol. 1, Brenda Dervin, Lawrence Grossberg, Barbara O'Keefe, and Ellen Wartella (eds.), Sage, Newbury Park, Calif., 1989, p. 52.
5 Ibid., p. 42.
6 Richard Rorty, *Consequences of Pragmatism*, University of Minnesota, Minneapolis, 1982, p. 197.
7 Isabel Briggs Myers, *Introduction to Type*, Consulting Psychologists, Palo Alto, Calif., 1987.
8 Ibid., p. 5.
9 George Gerbner, "The Importance of Being Critical—In One's Own Fashion," *Journal of Communication*, Vol. 33, No. 3, 1983, p. 361.
10 Gregory Bateson, *Mind and Nature: A Necessary Unity*, Bantam, New York, 1979, p. 242.
11 Marie Hochmuth Nichols, *Rhetoric and Criticism*, Louisiana State University, Baton Rouge, 1963, p. 18.
12 Celeste Michelle Condit, "The Birth of Understanding: Chaste Science and the Harlot of the Arts," *Communication Monographs*, Vol. 57, 1990, p. 323.
13 Ibid., p. 324. The term *hermeneutics* refers to principles of interpreting a text. In this context, the label designates a postmodern approach that has been influenced by European philosophers like Foucault, Heidegger, and Derrida. For an introductory discussion to postmodernism, see John Stewart, "A Postmodern Look at Traditional Communication Postulates," *Western Journal of Speech Communication*, Vol. 55, 1991, 354–379.

CREDITS AND ACKNOWLEDGMENTS

Part 1 Overview

Page 7 (Fig. 1.1): Two Boys and Cindy: Courtesy of Pepsi-Cola Company. Bob Garfield column reprinted by permission from the January 13, 1992, issue of *Advertising Age*. Contents copyright © 1992 by Crain Communication Inc.

Page 14 (Fig. 1.2): Twenty Questions to Guide Evaluation of Four Research Methods excerpted from Lawrence R. Frey, Carl H. Botan, Paul G. Friedman, and Gary L. Kreps, *Interpreting Communication Research: A Case Study Approach*, Prentice Hall, Englewood Cliffs, NJ, 1992, pp. 30–31, 89, 96, 130, 164, 171–172, 260–262, 292.

Page 32: Lyrics to "The Farmer and the Cowman" from the musical "Oklahoma" by Richard Rodgers and Oscar Hammerstein: Copyright © 1943 by Williamson Music Copyright Renewed International Copyright Secured Used by Permission All Rights Reserved

Part 2 Messages

Page 49 (Fig. 4.1): Shannon & Weaver Model adapted from Shannon and Weaver, *The Mathematical Theory of Communication*, p. 98. Copyright 1949 by the University of Illinois Press. Used with permission.

Page 54: Excerpt from Bob Goldsborough, *The Silver Spire*, Bantam Books, New York. Used by permission.

Page 61 (Fig. 5.1): The Semantic Triangle based on C. K. Ogden and I. A. Richards, *The Meaning of Meaning*, Harcourt Brace & World, New York, 1946, pp. 1–23.

Page 62 (Fig. 5.2): Utterances in Situations from Speculative Instruments by I. A. Richards, University of Chicago Press, 1955, pp. 17–38. Reprinted by permission of the publisher from Fogarty, Daniel, ROOTS FOR A NEW RHETORIC (Out of Print). (New York: Teachers College Press. © 1959 by Teachers College. Columbia University All Rights Reserved.)

Page 70 (Fig. 6.1): Characters of M*A*S*H in the Early Years: M*A*S*H © 1973 Twentieth Century Fox Film Corporation. All rights reserved.

Pages 71–75, 78: Dialogue from M*A*S*H from *The Complete Book of M*A*S*H* by Suzy Kalter, Abradale Press, Harry N. Abrams, Inc., New York, 1984. All Rights Reserved.

Page 71 (Fig. 6.2): A Model of Hierarchically Organized Meanings adapted from Cronen and Pearce, "The Coordinated Management of Meaning: A Theory of Communication," p. 71, in *Human Communication Theory*, Frank E. X. Dance (ed.), Harper & Row, New York, 1982, pp. 61–89.

Page 77 (Fig. 6.3): The Bulimic's Syndrome adapted from Robert Branham and W. Barnett Pearce, "Between Text and Context: Toward a Rhetoric of Contextual Reconstruction," p. 26, in *Quarterly Journal of Speech*, Vol. 71, 1985, pp. 19–36.

Page 82 (Fig. NV.1): Facial Expression of Emotion: Reprinted with the permission of Macmillan Publishing Company from SUCCESSFUL NONVERBAL COMMUNICATION: Principles and Applications by Dale G. Leathers. Copyright © 1986 by Dale G. Leathers.

Page 86: Excerpts from "Prologue: The Birth of Architecture" copyright 1965 by W H. Auden. Reprinted from W. H. AUDEN: COLLECTED POEMS, edited by Edward Mendelson, by permission of Faber and Faber Ltd.

Pages 90, 91 (Figs. 7.2 and 7.3): Based on Judee K. Burgoon and Stephen B. Jones, "Toward a Theory of Personal Space Expectations and Their Violations," *Human Communication Research*, Vol. 2, 1976, p. 142–143.

Pages 100–101: Excerpts from "The World of Wrestling" from MYTHOLOGIES by Roland Barth, translated by Annette Lavers. Translation copyright © 1972 by Jonathan Cape, Ltd. Reprinted by permission of Hill and Wang, a division of Farrar, Straus & Giroux, Inc.

Page 103 (Fig. 8.1): Adapted from Roland Barthes' "Myth Today" in *Mythologies*, Trans. Annette Lavers, Hill and Wang, New York, 1972, p. 115.

Part 3 Intrapersonal Communication

Page 125 (Fig.10.1): Maslow's Hierarchy of Needs adapted from Frank Goble, *The Third Force*, Grossman, N.Y., 1970, p. 50.

Page 125: Lyrics from "Gee, Officer Krupke" from WEST SIDE STORY by Leonard Bernstein and Stephen Sondheim. Copyright © 1957 (Renewed) by Leonard Berstein and Stephen Sondheim. Jalni Publications, Inc. U.S. & Canadian Publishers. G. Schirmer, Inc., (ASCAP) worldwide print rights and Publisher for the rest of the World International Copyright Secured All Rights Reserved Used by Permission

Page 138 (Fig. 11.1): Attribution Model from *An Introduction to Attribution Processes* (p. 32) by Kelly G. Shaver, 1983, Hillsdale, N.J.: Lawrence Erlbaum Associates, Inc., Publishers. Copyright 1983 by Lawrence Erlbaum Associates, Inc., Publishers. Reprinted by Permission.

Page 153 (Fig. 12.2): Based on Ruth Ann Clark and Jesse Delia "Cognitive Complexity, Social Perspective-Taking, and Functional Persuasive Skills in Second-to-Ninth-Grade Students," *Human Communication Research*, Vol. 3, 1977, pp. 128–134.

Part 4   Interpersonal Communication

Page 175 (Fig. 14.1): Theorems of Uncertainty Reduction Theory based on Charles Berger and Richard Calabrese, "Some Explorations in Initial Interaction and Beyond: Toward a Developmental Theory of Interpersonal Communication," *Human Communication Research*, Vol. 1, 1975, p. 100.

Pages 182–183 (Fig. RM.1): Fifty Strategies for Relational Maintenance in Marriage reprinted with permission from Leslie A. Baxter and Kathryn Dindia, "Marital Partners' Perceptions of Marital Maintenance Strategies," *Journal of Social and Personal Relationships*, Vol. 7, No. 2, Copyright 1990, by permission of Sage Publications Ltd.

Page 189: Excerpt from KNOTS by R. D. Laing. Copyright © 1970 by R. D. Laing. Reprinted by permission of Pantheon Books, a division of Random House, Inc.

Page 191 (Fig. 15.2): Matrix of Transactional Types adapted from Edna Rogers-Millar and Richard Farace, "Analysis of Relational Communication in Dyads: New Measurement Procedures," *Human Communication Research*, Vol. 4, p. 233. © 1975 Reprinted by permission of Sage Publications, Inc.

Pages 196, 203: Excerpts from Truman Capote, *In Cold Blood*, Random House, © 1965.

Page 200 (Fig. 16.2): Adapted from Michael E. Roloff, *Interpersonal Communication: The Social Exchange Approach*, Sage, Beverly Hills, 1981, p. 48.

Page 202 (Fig. 16.3): Based on Richard M. Emerson, "Social Exchange Theory," *American Sociological Review*, Vol. 35, 1976, pp. 335–362.

Page 203 (Fig. 16.4): Prisoner's Dilemma Transformation: Maximizing Joint Outcomes based on Paul Watzlawick, J. H. Weakland, and R. Fisch, *Change*, W. W. Norton, New York, 1974.

Page 208 (Fig. 17.1): A Typology of Relational Contradictions based on Leslie A. Baxter, "The Social Side of Personal Relationships: A Dialectical Perspective, in *Social Context and Relationship*, Vol. 3, Steve Duck (ed.), Sage, Newbury Park, Calif., 1993.

Pages 209–211, 214: Quotes from CHILDREN OF A LESSER GOD used by permission of Paramount Pictures. All Rights Reserved.

Page 222 (Fig. 18.1): Sample Cognitive Map Concerning Air Safety based on Carolyn Sherif, Muzafer Sherif, and Roger Nebergall, *Attitude and Attitude Change: The Social Judgment-Involvement Approach*, W. B. Saunders, Philadelphia, 1965.

Page 226 (Fig. 18.2): Sleep Study Results adapted from Bochner and Insko, "Communicator Discrepancy, Source Credibility and Opinion Change," *Journal of Personality and Social Psychology*, Vol. 4, 1966, pp. 614–622.

Page 240 (Fig. 20.1): Adapted and simplified from Petty and Cacioppo, "The Elaboration Likelihood Model of Persuasion," in *Advances in Experimental Social Psychology*, Vol. 19, Leonard Berkowitz (ed.), Academic Press, Orlando, 1986.

Part 5   Group and Public Communication

Page 250 (Fig. DM.1): Bales Interaction Categories from Robert Bales, *Personality and Interpersonal Behavior*, Holt, Rinehart and Winston, New York, 1970, p. 92. Used by permission of Robert Bales.

Page 256 (Fig. 21.1): Fisher's Categories of Verbal Interaction Applied to Hypothetical Task Group from Fisher, "Decision Emergence: Phases in Group Decision Making," p. 55, *Speech Monographs*, Vol. 37, 1970, pp. 53–66.

Page 257 (Fig. 21.2): Percentage of Interaction Response Coded for Each Category computed from data in Fisher, "Decision Emergence: Phases in Group Decision Making," p. 57, *Speech Monographs*, Vol. 37, 1970, pp. 53–66.

Page 268 (Fig. 22.1): Theoretical Analysis of Groupthink from Janis, Irving L., *Groupthink*, Second Edition. Copyright © 1982 by Houghton Mifflin Company. Used with permission. Reprinted with the permission of The Free Press, a Division of Macmillan, Inc., from DECISION MAKING: A Psychological Analysis of Conflict, Choice and Commitment by Irving L. Janis and Leon Mann. Copyright © 1977 by The Free Press.

Pages 319–320: Excerpt from PECULIAR TREASURES: A BIBLICAL WHO'S WHO by Frederick Buechner. Copyright © 1979 by Frederick Buechner. Reprinted by permission of HarperCollins Publishers Inc.

Part 6   Mass Communication

Page 361: Stanza from "Stopping by Woods on a Snowy Evening" from THE POETRY OF ROBERT FROST edited by Edward Connery Lathem. Copyright 1923, © 1969 by Henry Holt and Company, Inc. Copyright 1951 Robert Frost. Reprinted by permission of Henry Holt and Company, Inc.

Page 373 (Fig. 31.1): Child's Imitation of Adult Aggressive Behavior as Observed on Film: From Albert Bandura, Dorthea Ross, and Sheila Ross, "Imitations of Aggressive Film-Mediated Models," *Journal of Abnormal and Social Psychology*, Vol. 66, 1963, pp. 3–11. Used by permission of Albert Bandura.

Page 381 (Fig. 32.1): Adapted from Bruce Westley, "What Makes It Change," *Journal of Communication*, Vol. 26, No. 2, 1976, p. 46.

Part 7   Cultural Context

Page 405 (Fig. 34.1): "A Schematic Representation of the Basic Theory (Omitting Cultural Variability)" from William B. Gudykunst's "Toward a Theory of Effective Interpersonal and Intergroup Communication: An Anxiety/Uncertainty Management (AUM) Perspective," p. 38 in *Intercultural Communication Competence* by R. L. Wiseman and J. Koestler (eds.), Sage, Newbury Park, Calif., © 1993. Reprinted by permission of Sage Publications, Inc.

Page 420 (Fig. 35.2): Based on Stella Ting-Toomey, "Intercultural Conflict Styles: A Face-Negotiation Theory" in *Theories in Intercultural Communication*, Young Yun Kim and William Gudykunst (eds.), Sage, Newbury Park, 1988, pp. 213–235, and "Intergroup Diplomatic Communication: A Face-Negotiation Perspective," *Communicating for Peace: Diplomacy and Negotiation*, Felipe Korzenny and Stella Ting-Toomey (eds.), Sage, Newbury Park, 1990, pp. 77–95.

Page 423 (Fig. 35.3): Based on Stella Ting-Toomey, et al., "Culture, Face-Maintenance, and Styles of Handling Interpersonal Conflict: A Study in Five Cultures," in *Intercultural Journal of Conflict Management*, Vol. 2, 1991, pp. 275–296.

Pages 431–433, 435–437: Dialogue from *When Harry Met Sally* reprinted by permission of Nora Ephron. Copyright © 1990 by Castle Rock Entertainment.

Page 448 (Fig. 37.1): Excerpts from Kramarae and Treichler's Feminist Dictionary from Cheris Kramarae and Paula Treichler (eds.), *Amazons, Bluestockings and Crones*, Pandora (an imprint of HarperCollins Publishers Limited), London, 1992. Used by permission.

Part 8 Integration

Page 471 (Fig. CT.1): Classification of Theories Based on Weick's Model. Extension of Karl Weick, *The Psychology of Organizing*, 2d ed., Addison-Wesley, Reading, Mass., 1979, pp. 35–42.

Page 473 (Fig. CT.2): Anne Elk (John Cleese) Describes Her Brontosaurus Theory to Interviewer Graham Chapman on *Monty Python's Flying Circus*: Copyright © BBC.

Page 473: Monty Python Parody of Theorizing from *The Complete Monty Python's Flying Circus: All the Words, Volume Two*, Pantheon Books, New York, 1989, pp. 118–120.

INDEX